# THE NEW AMERICAN COMMENTARY

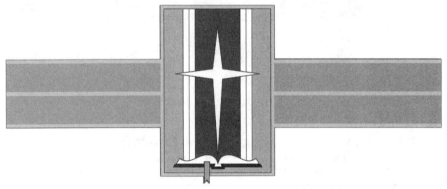

An Exegetical and Theological
Exposition of Holy Scripture

**General Editor**
E. RAY CLENDENEN

**Associate General Editor, OT**
KENNETH A. MATHEWS

**Associate General Editor, NT**
DAVID S. DOCKERY

Consulting Editors

**Old Testament**
L. RUSS BUSH
DUANE A. GARRETT
LARRY L. WALKER

**New Testament**
RICHARD R. MELICK, JR.
PAIGE PATTERSON
B. PAUL WOLFE

# THE NEW AMERICAN COMMENTARY

Volume
21B

## ZECHARIAH

George L. Klein

Nashville, Tennessee

© Copyright 2008 • B & H Publishing Group
All rights reserved.
ISBN 978-0-8054-9494-5
Dewey Decimal Classification: 224.1
Subject Heading: BIBLE. O.T. ZECHARIAH
Printed in the United States of America
12 11 10 09 08     8 7 6 5 4 3 2 1
LB

Unless otherwise stated all Scripture citations are from the *Holy Bible, New International Version®*. Copyright ©1973, 1978, 1984 by International Bible Society. Used by permission of Zondervan Publishing House. All rights reserved. Scripture quotations marked HCSB have been taken from the *Holman Christian Standard Bible®* Copyright 1999, 2000, 2002, 2003 by Holman Bible Publishers. Used by permission. Scripture citations marked TEV are from *Today's English Version, Second Edition* Copyright © 1966, 1971, 1976, 1992 American Bible Society. Used by permission. Scripture citations marked RSV are from the *Revised Standard Version of the Bible,* copyrighted 1946, 1952, © 1971, 1973 by the National Council of the Churches of Christ in the U.S.A. and used by permission. Scripture citations marked NASB are from the *New American Standard Bible.* © The Lockman Foundation, 1960, 1962, 1968, 1971, 1973, 1975, 1977. Used by permission. Scripture citations marked NRSV are from the *New Revised Standard Version of the Bible*, copyright © 1989 by the Division of Christian Education of the National Council of Churches of Christ in the United States of America. Used by permission. All rights reserved. Scripture citations marked NKJV are from the *New King James Version*, copyright © 1979, 1980, 1982, Thomas Nelson, Inc., Publishers. Scripture citations marked NLT are from the *Holy Bible, New Living Translation*, copyright ©1996. Used by permission of Tyndale House Publishers, Inc., Wheaton, Illinois 60189. All rights reserved. Scripture quotations marked ESV are from *The Holy Bible, English Standard Version*, copyright ©2001 by Crossway Bibles, a division of Good News Publishers. Used by permission. All rights reserved. Scripture citations marked NEB are from the *New English Bible*. Copyright © The Delegates of the Oxford University Press and the Syndics of the Cambridge University Press, 1961, 1970. Reprinted by permission. Scripture citations marked REB are from the *Revised English Bible*. Copyright © 1989 by Oxford University Press and Cambridge University Press. Reprinted by permission. Scripture citations marked LB are from *The Living Bible*. Copyright © Tyndale House Publishers, Wheaton, Illinois, 1971. Used by permission. Scripture quotations marked NJPS are from *TANAKH: A New Translation of THE HOLY SCRIPTURES According to the Traditional Hebrew Text*. Copyright © The Jewish Publication Society, 1985. Used by permission. Scripture quotations marked NET are from *The NET Bible: The Translation That Explains Itself*$^{TM}$ Copyright © 1996, 1997, 1998, 2000, 2001 by Biblical Studies Press, L.L.C. Used by permission. Scripture quotations marked NJB are from *The New Jerusalem Bible*. Copyright © 1990 by Darton, Longman & Todd, Ltd. and Doubleday, a division of Bantam Doubleday Dell Publishing Group. Used by permission.

*For*

My devoted wife, Denise Edwards Klein,

God's greatest earthly blessing in my life, and

"the apple of my eye"

(Zech 2:8b)

and

My daughters, Heather, Meghan, and Ashley,

extraordinary women in every respect, and

an undeserved "heritage from the Lord"

(Ps 127:3)

# Editors' Preface

God's Word does not change. God's world, however, changes in every generation. These changes, in addition to new findings by scholars and a new variety of challenges to the gospel message, call for the church in each generation to interpret and apply God's Word for God's people. Thus, THE NEW AMERICAN COMMENTARY is introduced to bridge the twentieth and twenty-first centuries. This new series has been designed primarily to enable pastors, teachers, and students to read the Bible with clarity and proclaim it with power.

In one sense THE NEW AMERICAN COMMENTARY is not new, for it represents the continuation of a heritage rich in biblical and theological exposition. The title of this forty-volume set points to the continuity of this series with an important commentary project published at the end of the nineteenth century called AN AMERICAN COMMENTARY, edited by Alvah Hovey. The older series included, among other significant contributions, the outstanding volume on Matthew by John A. Broadus, from whom the publisher of the new series, Broadman Press, partly derives its name. The former series was authored and edited by scholars committed to the infallibility of Scripture, making it a solid foundation for the present project. In line with this heritage, all NAC authors affirm the divine inspiration, inerrancy, complete truthfulness, and full authority of the Bible. The perspective of the NAC is unapologetically confessional and rooted in the evangelical tradition.

Since a commentary is a fundamental tool for the expositor or teacher who seeks to interpret and apply Scripture in the church or classroom, the NAC focuses on communicating the theological structure and content of each biblical book. The writers seek to illuminate both the historical meaning and contemporary significance of Holy Scripture.

In its attempt to make a unique contribution to the Christian community, the NAC focuses on two concerns. First, the commentary emphasizes how each section of a book fits together so that the reader becomes aware of the theological unity of each book and of Scripture as a whole. The writers, however, remain aware of the Bible's inherently rich variety. Second, the NAC is produced with the conviction that the Bible primarily belongs to the church. We believe that scholarship and the academy provide an indispensable foundation for biblical understanding and the service of Christ, but the editors and authors of this series have attempted to communicate the findings of their research in a manner that will build up the whole body of Christ. Thus, the commentary concentrates on theological exegesis while providing practical, applicable exposition.

THE NEW AMERICAN COMMENTARY's theological focus enable the reader to see the parts as well as the whole of Scripture. The biblical books vary in content, context, literary type, and style. In addition to this rich variety, the editors and authors recognize that the doctrinal emphasis and use of the biblical books differs in various places, contexts, and cultures among God's people. These factors, as well as other concerns, have led the editors to give freedom to the writers to wrestle with the issues raised by the scholarly community surrounding each book and to determine the appropriate shape and length of the introductory materials. Moreover, each writer has developed the structure of the commentary in a way best suited for expounding the basic structure and the meaning of the biblical books for our day. Generally, discussions relating to contemporary scholarship and technical points of grammar and syntax appear in the footnotes and not in the text of the commentary. This format allows pastors and interested laypersons, scholars and teachers, and serious college and seminary students to profit from the commentary at various levels. This approach has been employed because we believe that all Christians have the privilege and responsibility to read and seek to understand the Bible for themselves.

Consistent with the desire to produce a readable, up-to-date commentary, the editors selected the New International Version as the standard translation for the commentary series. The selection was made primarily because of the NIV's faithfulness to the original languages and its beautiful and readable style. The authors, however, have been given the liberty to differ at places from the NIV as they develop their own translations from the Greek and Hebrew texts.

The NAC reflects the vision and leadership of those who provide oversight for Broadman Press, who in 1987 called for a new commentary series that would evidence a commitment to the inerrancy of Scripture and a faithfulness to the classic Christian tradition. While the commentary adopts an "American" name, it should be noted some writers represent countries outside the United States, giving the commentary an international perspective. The diverse group of writers includes scholars, teachers, and administrators from almost twenty different colleges and seminaries, as well as pastors, missionaries, and a layperson.

The editors and writers hope that THE NEW AMERICAN COMMENTARY will be helpful and instructive for pastors and teachers, scholars and students, for men and women in the churches who study and teach God's Word in various settings. We trust that for editors, authors, and readers alike, the commentary will be used to build up the church, encourage obedience, and bring renewal to God's people. Above all, we pray that the NAC will bring glory and honor to our Lord who has graciously redeemed us and faithfully revealed himself to us in his Holy Word.

SOLI DEO GLORIA
The Editors

# Author's Preface

The book of Zechariah brims with enigma and paradox. The longest of the Minor Prophets, the New Testament writers quote from it more than almost any other Old Testament book. Unfortunately, readers today rarely examine its contents. It is a tragedy that a biblical book that influenced the Gospel writers so greatly, not to mention other portions of the New Testament, as much as any other Old Testament volume remains a closed book to so many in the Church today. As we will see in this commentary, Zechariah provides readers present and future unparalleled insights into the ways of God, with particular emphasis upon the work of the Messiah and the nature of the future Kingdom.

I wish to acknowledge a profound debt to the generations of biblical scholars who have pored over Zechariah, yielding insights upon which every successive generation depends. I stand on the shoulders of these giants, desiring to further the understanding of Zechariah and to elicit greater interest in this grand biblical book. I invite you to discover the broad horizons of Zechariah studies by also examining some of the works cited in this volume.

Further, I would be remiss if I failed to express appreciation to all those who have provided such important aid through the years in which I have prepared this commentary. My *Doktorvater*, Professor Stephen Geller, opened new doors to me in a doctoral seminar on apocalyptic that devoted significant attention to Zechariah. Numerous colleagues have extended countless insights and expressions of encouragement. Ray Clendenen, NAC General Editor and commentator, has lent suggestions for more years than either of us would care to acknowledge. Likewise, Ken Mathews, Associate General Editor and commentator, has provided equal measures of sage advice and friendship for a comparable length of time.

With the press of ministry assignments, it would have taken far longer to complete the wonderful task of preparing this commentary than it did without many tangible means of assistance offered by the trustees and administration of Southwestern Seminary. A special word of gratitude is due to Paige Patterson, NAC New Testament editor, commentator, and president of Southwestern for his support of the sabbatical I received. Craig Blaising, Provost, as well as David Allen, NAC commentator and Dean at Southwestern, could not have helped me more than they did. In the same vein, Paul Wolfe, NAC New Testament editor and Assistant Dean at Southwestern, has given me great assistance throughout the years.

Several others have given significant energy that provided me with helpful comments on the manuscript at varying stages of completion. My doctoral student, Perry Oakes, has read the manuscript and offered numerous recommendations. My assistants, Mike Belue and David Hutchison, have also demonstrated servanthood in countless ways. Mr. Dong Cho gave me significant assistance with the references to the Church Fathers. Notwithstanding the profound aid from many, the responsibility for every error and inadequacy of this volume rests solely with the author.

The greatest gratitude belongs to my family, however. My grandmother, Thelma Linam Webber, recently gone to be with the Lord, first instilled within me a deep love for the Old Testament and an appreciation for its application to my life. My mother, Faye Klein, similarly modeled a love for God's Word and has given encouragement throughout the years of preparing this study. My daughters, Heather, Meghan, and Ashley, gave great love, encouragement, and patience. Most importantly, my wife Denise offered love and support as only a godly wife can offer. Words could never adequately express my love and admiration for her and for our lives together, including the labor we share.

The writer of any commentary well understands how much he leaves out, not to mention how much remains to be understood. Furthermore, any commentator must resist the compulsion to say what there is not time to mention. Nonetheless, it is my prayer that the readers of this commentary will become enthralled with the book of Zechariah and will study it far more widely than this lone volume.

*George L. Klein*
Southwestern Baptist Theological Seminary
Ft. Worth, TX

# Abbreviations

## Bible Books

| | | |
|---|---|---|
| Gen | Isa | Luke |
| Exod | Jer | John |
| Lev | Lam | Acts |
| Num | Ezek | Rom |
| Deut | Dan | 1, 2 Cor |
| Josh | Hos | Gal |
| Judg | Joel | Eph |
| Ruth | Amos | Phil |
| 1, 2 Sam | Obad | Col |
| 1, 2 Kgs | Jonah | 1, 2 Thess |
| 1, 2 Chr | Mic | 1, 2 Tim |
| Ezra | Nah | Titus |
| Neh | Hab | Phlm |
| Esth | Zeph | Heb |
| Job | Hag | Jas |
| Ps (pl. Pss) | Zech | 1, 2 Pet |
| Prov | Mal | 1, 2, 3 John |
| Eccl | Matt | Jude |
| Song | Mark | Rev |

## Commonly Used Sources

| | |
|---|---|
| AB | Anchor Bible |
| *ABD* | *Anchor Bible Dictionary*, ed. D. N. Freedman |
| *AEL* | *Ancient Egyptian Literature*, M. Lichtheim |
| *Ag.Ap.* | *Against Apion*, Josephus |
| *AJSL* | *American Journal of Semitic Languages and Literatures* |
| Akk. | Akkadian |
| AnBib | Analecta Biblica |
| *ANEP* | *Ancient Near East in Pictures Relating to the Old Testament*, ed. J. B. Pritchard |
| *ANET* | *Ancient Near Eastern Texts*, ed. J. B. Pritchard |
| *Ant.* | *Antiquities of the Jews, Josephus* |
| AOAT | Alter Orient und Altes Testament |
| AOS | American Oriental Society |
| *AOTS* | *Archaeology and Old Testament Study*, ed. D. W. Thomas |
| AS | Assyriological Studies |
| ATD | Das Alte Testament Deutsch |
| *AUSS* | *Andrews University Seminary Studies* |

| | |
|---|---|
| AV | Authorized Version |
| *BA* | *Biblical Archaeologist* |
| BAGD | W. Bauer, W. F. Arndt, F. W. Gingrich, and F. W. Danker, *Greek-English Lexicon of the New Testament* |
| *BARev* | *Biblical Archaeology Review* |
| *BASOR* | *Bulletin of the American Schools of Oriental Research* |
| BDB | F. Brown, S. R. Driver, and C. A. Briggs, *Hebrew and English Lexicon of the Old Testament* |
| *BHK* | *Biblia Hebraica*, ed. R. Kittel |
| *BHS* | *Biblia Hebraica Stuttgartensia* |
| *Bib* | *Biblica* |
| BibOr | Biblica et orientalia |
| *BibRev* | *Bible Review* |
| *BJRL* | *Bulletin of the Johns Rylands University Library* |
| BJS | Brown Judaic Studies |
| BKAT | Biblischer Kommentar: Altes Testament |
| *BSac* | *Bibliotheca Sacra* |
| b. Sanh. | Babylonian Talmud, *Sanhedrin* |
| b. Hag. | Babylonian Talmud, *Hagiga* |
| BSC | Bible Study Commentary |
| BR | *Bible Review* |
| BST | Bible Speaks Today |
| BT | *Bible Translator* |
| BZ | *Biblische Zeitschrift* |
| BZAW | Beihefte zur ZAW |
| *CAH* | *Cambridge Ancient History* |
| CB | Cambridge Bible for Schools and Colleges |
| CBC | Cambridge Bible Commentary |
| *CBQ* | *Catholic Biblical Quarterly* |
| CBQMS | Catholic Biblical Quarterly Monograph Series |
| *CBR* | *Currents in Biblical Research* |
| CD | Cairo *Damascus Document* |
| CGTC | Cambridge Greek Testament Commentaries |
| *CHAL* | *Concise Hebrew and Aramaic Lexicon*, ed. William L. Holladay |
| Comm. | J. Calvin, *Commentary on the First Book of Moses Called Genesis*, trans., rev. J. King |
| *CSR* | *Christian Scholar's Review* |
| *CT* | *Christianity Today* |
| *CTR* | *Criswell Theological Review* |
| *CurTM* | *Currents in Theology and Mission* |
| *DOTT* | *Documents from Old Testament Times*, ed. D. W. Thomas |
| DSS | Dead Sea Scrolls |
| EBC | Expositor's Bible Commentary |
| *Ebib* | *Etudes bibliques* |
| *EE* | *Enuma Elish* |

| | |
|---|---|
| *EGT* | *The Expositor's Greek Testament* |
| EV(s) | English Version(s) |
| *EvQ* | *Evangelical Quarterly* |
| *EvT* | *Evangelishe Theologie* |
| *ExpTim* | *Expository Times* |
| FB | Forschung zur Bibel |
| FOTL | Forms of Old Testament Literature |
| *Gen.Rab.* | *Genesis Rabbah*, ed. J. Neusner |
| Gk. | Greek |
| GKC | Gesenius' Hebrew Grammar, ed. E. Kautzsch, tr. A. E. Cowley |
| GNB | Good News Bible |
| *GTJ* | *Grace Theological Journal* |
| HALOT | *The Hebrew and Aramaic Lexicon of the Old Testament*, ed. L. Koehler and W. Baumgartner, trans. M. E. J. Richardson |
| HAR | *Hebrew Annual Review* |
| HAT | Handbuch zum Alten Testament |
| HBD | *Harper's Bible Dictionary*, ed. P. Achtemeier |
| *HBT* | *Horizons in Biblical Theology* |
| HCSB | Holman Christian Standard Bible |
| HDR | Harvard Dissertations in Religion |
| Her | Hermeneia |
| HKAT | Handkommentar zum Alten Testament |
| *HS* | *Hebrew Studies* |
| HSM | Harvard Semitic Monographs |
| HT | Helps for Translators |
| *HTR* | *Harvard Theological Review* |
| *HUCA* | *Hebrew Union College Annual* |
| *IB* | *Interpreter's Bible* |
| IBC | Interpretation: A Bible Commentary for Teaching and Preaching |
| *IBS* | *Irish Biblical Studies* |
| ICC | International Critical Commentary |
| *IDB* | *Interpreter's Dictionary of the Bible*, ed. G. A. Buttrick et al. |
| *IDBSup* | Supplementary Volume to *IDB* |
| *IBHS* | B. K. Waltke and M. O'Connor, *Introduction to Biblical Hebrew Syntax* |
| *IEJ* | *Israel Exploration Journal* |
| IES | Israel Exploration Society |
| *Int* | *Interpretation* |
| *IOS* | *Israel Oriental Society* |
| *ISBE* | *International Standard Bible Encyclopedia*, rev., ed. G. W. Bromiley |
| ITC | International Theological Commentary |
| *ITQ* | *Irish Theological Quarterly* |
| *JAAR* | *Journal of the American Academy of Religion* |
| *JAARSup* | *Journal of the American Academy of Religion*, Supplement |

| | |
|---|---|
| JANES | *Journal of Ancient Near Eastern Society* |
| JAOS | *Journal of the American Oriental Society* |
| JBL | *Journal of Biblical Literature* |
| JBR | *Journal of Bible and Religion* |
| JCS | *Journal of Cuneiform Studies* |
| JEA | *Journal of Egyptian Archaeology* |
| JETS | *Journal of the Evangelical Theological Society* |
| JSS | *Journal of Jewish Studies* |
| JNES | *Journal of Near Eastern Studies* |
| JNSL | *Journal of Northwest Semitic Languages* |
| JPOS | *Journal of Palestine Oriental Society* |
| JRT | *Journal of Religious Thought* |
| JSOR | *Journal of the Society for Oriental Research* |
| JSOT | *Journal for the Study of the Old Testament* |
| JSOTSup | JSOT—Supplement Series |
| *JSS* | *Journal of Semitic Studies* |
| JTS | *Journal of Theological Studies* |
| JTSNS | *Journal of Theological Studies*, New Series |
| JOTT | *Journal of Translation and Textlinguistics* |
| Jub. | *Julilees* |
| KAT | Kommentar zum Alten Testament |
| KB | Koehler and W. Baumgartner, *Lexicon in Veteris Testamenti libros* |
| KD | *Kerygma und Dogma* |
| LCC | Library of Christian Classics |
| LSJ | Liddell-Scott-Jones, *Greek-English Lexicon* |
| LW | *Luther's Works. Lectures on Genesis*, ed. J. Pelikan and D. Poellot, trans. G. Schick |
| LXX | Septuagint |
| MT | Masoretic Text |
| NAB | New American Bible |
| NASB | New American Standard Bible |
| NAC | New American Commentary, ed. E. R. Clendenen |
| *NB* | *Nebuchadnezzar and Babylon*, D. J. Wiseman |
| *NBD* | *New Bible Dictionary*, ed. J. D. Douglas |
| NEB | New English Bible |
| NIB | The New Interpreter's Bible |
| NICNT | New International Commentary on the New Testament |
| NICOT | New International Commentary on the Old Testament |
| *NIDOTTE* | New International Dictionary of Old Testament Theology |
| NJB | New Jerusalem Bible |
| NJPS | Tanakh: The Holy Scriptures: The New JPS Translation according to the Traditional Hebrew Text |
| NRSV | New Revised Standard Version |
| *NRT* | *La nouvelle revue théologique* |
| *NT* | *Novum Testamentum* |

| | |
|---|---|
| *NTS* | *New Testament Studies* |
| NTT | Norsk Teologisk Tidsskrift |
| OBO | Orbis biblicus et orientalis |
| *Or* | *Orientalia* |
| OTL | Old Testament Library |
| *OTP* | *The Old Testament Pseudepigrapha*, ed. J. H. Charlesworth |
| OTS | *Oudtestamentische Studiën* |
| PCB | *Peake's Commentary on the Bible*, ed. M. Black and H. H. Rowley |
| *PEQ* | *Palestine Exploration Quarterly* |
| POTT | *Peoples of Old Testament Times*, ed. D. J. Wiseman |
| PTMS | Pittsburgh Theological Monograph Series |
| *PTR* | *Princeton Theological Review* |
| *Pss. Sol.* | *Psalms of Solomon* |
| RA | *Revue d'assyriologie et d'archéologie orientale* |
| *RB* | *Revue biblique* |
| REB | Revised English Bible |
| *ResQ* | *Restoration Quarterly* |
| *RSR* | *Recherches de science religieuse* |
| *RTR* | *Reformed Theological Review* |
| SANE | Sources from the Ancient Near East |
| SBLDS | Society of Biblical Literature Dissertation Series |
| SBLMS | Society of Biblical Literature Monograph Series |
| SBLSP | Society of Biblical Literature Seminar Papers |
| SBT | Studies in Biblical Theology |
| *Sib. Or.* | *Sibylline Oracles* |
| *SJT* | *Scottish Journal of Theology* |
| SJLA | Studies in Judaism in Late Antiquity |
| *SOTI* | *A Survey of Old Testament Introduction*, G. L. Archer |
| SP | Samaritan Pentateuch |
| SR | *Studies in Religion/Sciences religieuses* |
| *ST* | *Studia theologica* |
| Syr. | Syriac |
| TD | *Theology Digest* |
| TDNT | *Theological Dictionary of the New Testament,* ed. G. Kittel and G. Friedrich, trans. G. W. Bromiley |
| TDOT | *Theological Dictionary of the Old Testament*, ed. G. J. Botterweck and H. Ringgren, trans. J. T. Willis et al. |
| Tg(s). | Targum(s) |
| *Tg. Onq.* | *Targum Onkelos*, ed. B. Grossfield |
| *Tg. Neof* | *Targum Neofiti I*, ed. M. McNamara |
| *Tg. Ps.-J.* | *Targum Pseudo-Jonathan*, ed. M. Mahler |
| TJ | *Trinity Journal* |
| T.Levi | *Testament of Levi* |
| TLOT | *Theological Lexicon of the Old Testament*, ed. Ernst Jenni and Claus Westermann |

| | |
|---|---|
| TNTC | Tyndale New Testament Commentaries |
| TOTC | Tyndale Old Testament Commentaries |
| *T.Rub* | *Testament of Reuben* |
| *TS* | *Theological Studies* |
| *TWAT* | *Theologisches Wörterbuch zum Alten Testament*, ed. G. J. Botterweck and H. Ringgren |
| *TWOT* | *Theological Wordbook of the Old Testament*, ed. R. L. Harris, G. L. Archer Jr., B. K. Waltke |
| *TynBul* | *Tyndale Bulletin* |
| *UF* | *Ugarit-Forshungen* |
| Ug. | Ugaritic |
| *UT* | C. H. Gordon, *Ugaritic Textbook* |
| Vg | Vulgate |
| *VT* | *Vetus Testamentum* |
| VTSup | Vetus Testamentum, Supplements |
| WBC | Word Biblical Commentaries |
| WMANT | Wissenschaftliche Monographien zum Alten und Neuen Testament |
| *WTJ* | *Westminster Theological Journal* |
| YES | Yale Egyptian Studies |
| *ZAW* | *Zeitschrift für die alttestamentliche Wissenschaft* |
| *1 Clem.* | *1 Clement* |
| 1QapGen | Genesis Apocryphon from Qumran Cave 1 |
| 2 Apoc.Bar | Apocalypse of Baruch, Syriac |
| 4QDeutq | Deuteronomy text from fourth cave, Qumran |

## Apocrypha

| | |
|---|---|
| *Add Esth* | *The Additions to the Book of Esther* |
| *Bar* | *Baruch* |
| *Bel* | *Bel and the Dragon* |
| *1,2 Esdr* | *1, 2 Esdras* |
| *4 Ezra* | *4 Ezra* |
| *Jdt* | *Judith* |
| *Ep Jer* | *Epistl5e of Jeremiah* |
| *1,2,3,4 Mac* | *1, 2, 3, 4 Maccabees* |
| *Pr Azar* | *Prayer of Azariah and the Song of the Three Jews* |
| *Pr Man* | *Prayer of Manasseh* |
| *Sir* | *Sirach, Ecclesiasticus* |
| *Sus* | *Susanna* |
| *Tob* | *Tobit* |
| *Wis* | *The Wisdom of Solomon* |

# Contents

| | |
|---|---|
| Introduction to Book of Zechariah | 19 |
|    I. Introduction (1:1–6) | 79 |
|   II. Eight Night Visions and Oracles (1:7–6:8) | 89 |
|  III. Joshua's Crown (6:9–15) | 195 |
|  IV. Questions about Fasting and Future Blessings (7:1–8:23) | 207 |
|   V. Burdens from the Lord (9:1–14:21) | 253 |
| Selected Bibliography | 431 |
| Selected Subject Index | 443 |
| Person Index | 447 |
| Selected Scripture Index | 453 |

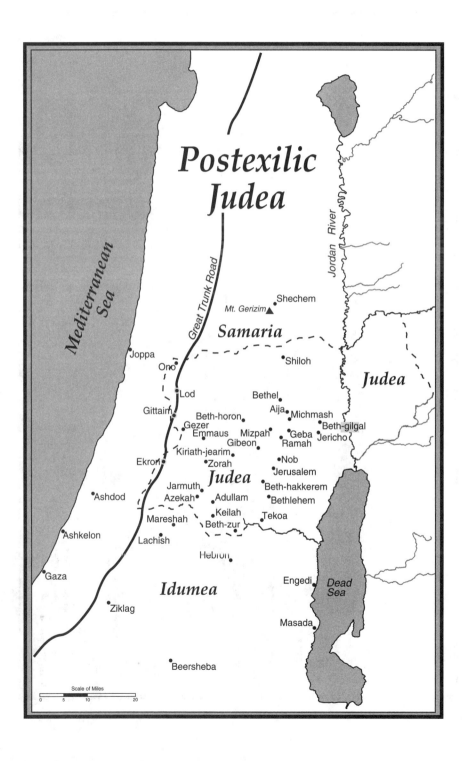

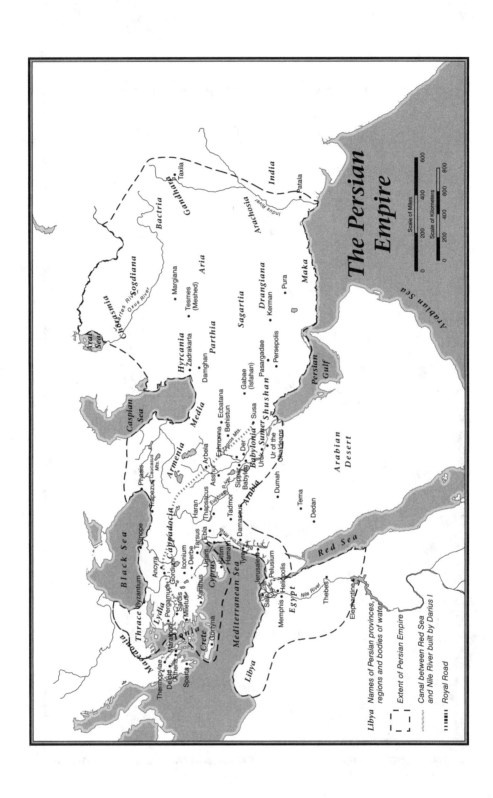

# Zechariah

---

## INTRODUCTION OUTLINE

1. Zechariah the Prophet
2. The Authorship of the Book
   (1) Historical Development of the Issue
   (2) Evidence for Dividing the Book of Zechariah
   (3) Factors Supporting Unified Authorship
   (4) Conclusion
3. Historical Era
4. Literary Style
   (1) Prose or Poetry
   (2) Apocalyptic
5. Structure of Zechariah
6. Text
7. Place of Zechariah Canonically
   (1) Zechariah and Intertextuality
   (2) Relation to Haggai
   (3) Relation to Malachi
   (4) Zechariah within the Old Testament
   (5) Influence on the New Testament
8. Theology of Zechariah
   (1) Israel/Jerusalem
   (2) Temple
   (3) Messiah
   (4) Kingdom
   (5) Judgment of God
   (6) Divine Faithfulness and Human Obedience
   (7) Cleansing from Sin
   (8) Leadership
9. Selected Bibliography

## INTRODUCTION

### 1. Zechariah the Prophet

With the exception of Zephaniah, we know more about Zechariah's lineage than any other Minor Prophet author. The book of Zechariah links the prophet to a priestly family, and particularly chaps. 1–8 also introduce the prophet personally, although without the psychological insight garnered from Hosea or Jonah.

The name Zechariah in Hebrew *(zĕkaryāh* or *zĕkaryāhû)* means "Yahweh remembers," a popular name belonging to some two dozen different individuals in the Old Testament alone. The name also appears in the New Testament as the name of John the Baptist's father (Luke 1:5; 3:2). Like many proper names in the Old Testament, Zechariah's name proclaims a theological message about God and his relationship with his people, Israel. While living in a day filled with political unrest and spiritual apathy, modern readers find it difficult to appreciate the bleak present (and future) that postexilic Israelites faced during the days of Zechariah the prophet's ministry. Every mention of Zechariah's name remonstrated against the people's lack of faith. The prophet's name, along with his message, consistently reminded the nation that the Lord had made a covenant with Israel, a binding commitment that God would assuredly keep. The people should respond to the reminder of the Lord's faithfulness with faith and obedience of their own. Israel's security and future hope will be as sure as the faithfulness of God himself, provided that the nation live obediently before the Lord.

The book of Zechariah also begins by introducing the prophet's ancestry, "the prophet Zechariah son of Berekiah, the son of Iddo." By listing multiple generations of ancestors who also enjoyed God's covenantal faithfulness, the genealogy links Zechariah with Israel's past, suggesting that the prophet embodies the assurances from the Lord himself that the people will enjoy a secure future full of the promises God had given to his people for generations.[1] Again, modern readers must remember that Zechariah's contemporaries had lost faith, and as a consequence, had lost hope in their future as well. The prophet aimed to spur Israel to expressions of faith and obedience that had been absent from the land for years.

The introductory genealogy does contain a puzzling statement. Why does Zech 1:1 identify Zechariah as "son of Berekiah, son of Iddo" when Ezra 5:1; 6:14 reads "Zechariah the prophet, the son of Iddo?" It would appear that Zech 1:1 contradicts Ezra 5:1 and 6:14. The simplest explanation is that Zechariah

---

[1] There is no basis for Conrad's claim that the genealogy "suggests distancing and separation from the past." See E. Conrad, *Zechariah* (Sheffield: Sheffield Academic Press, 1999), 46.

was the *son* of Berechiah and the *grandson* of Iddo. The Hebrew term *ben* often means "grandson" or "descendant" in other contexts (Exod 34:7; Prov 13:22).[2]

One implication of this conclusion is that Zechariah descended from priestly lineage, since Neh 12:4,16 identify Iddo as one of the priests who returned with Zerubbabel. For a fuller discussion of these questions, see the commentary on 1:1.

This opening verse portrays Zechariah as a *prophet*.[3] While the book does not focus on the prophet and his personal life in the way that the books of Hosea and Jonah do, the book of Zechariah presents its main character as a faithful servant of the Lord. The book of Zechariah focuses on the message God gives the prophet to deliver. Even though the book often does not rehearse the point that Zechariah explicitly fulfilled his divine mandate as other prophetic writings do, there is no question about the prophet's attention to discharging God's word to him. Mark Love correctly observes that "Zechariah is never depicted actually carrying out the tasks assigned to him."[4] However, Love misunderstands the perspective of the book of Zechariah when he complains that the prophet's character does not emerge in the book, calling Zechariah a "fragmented personae."[5] The literary development of Zechariah's character remains secondary to the message the Lord mandates the prophet to present to the people.

Developing an argument with some affinities to Love's, Conrad concludes that Zechariah is not even a prophet. Conrad maintains that Zech 1:1 declares that Iddo, not Zechariah, was a prophet.[6] Conrad believes that Zechariah functions solely as a "messenger," not as a prophet. For Conrad, Zechariah's phrase, the "former prophets" (1:4; 7:7,12), demonstrates that Zechariah sought to distance himself from the prophetic movement.[7]

Conrad's viewpoint hinges on his understanding that Iddo, not Zechariah, was the prophet. Admittedly, Zech 1:1 could be read as Conrad affirms, although this does not represent the most natural reading of the Hebrew syntax. On the other hand, Conrad does not address the message of Zech 1:7, which

---

[2] בֵּן. *HALOT*, 137–38. See Gen 31:28,55 (Hb. 32:1); 2 Sam 19:24 (Hb. 25); 2 Kgs 9:20 (also v. 14).

[3] For a review of scholarship on the subject of prophecy, see R. R. Wilson, *Prophecy and Society in Ancient Israel* (Philadelphia: Fortress, 1980), 1–19. K. Koch (*The Prophets. Vol. 2: The Babylonian and Persian Period*, trans. M. Kohl [Philadelphia: Fortress, 1984], 1–12) and D. L. Petersen (*The Roles of Israel's Prophets*, JSOTSup 17 [Sheffield: JSOT, 1981], 51–87) survey the function of the prophet in ancient Israel. J. Barton ("Prophecy [Postexilic Hebrew]" in *ABD*, 5:489–95) provides a valuable treatment of the prophet's role in postexilic Israel.

[4] M. C. Love, *The Evasive Text: Zechariah 1–8 and the Frustrated Reader* (Sheffield: Sheffield Academic Press, 1999), 87.

[5] Ibid., 91.

[6] Conrad, *Zechariah*, 31.

[7] Ibid., 34.

unequivocally asserts that Zechariah was a prophet. Furthermore, Zechariah's employment of the phrase "former prophets" emphasizes the divine message that men commonly understood to be "prophets," men of God, had delivered. Thus, "former prophets" cannot suggest that Zechariah failed to see himself as a prophet. Zechariah saw himself following in the glorious tradition of those prophets of renown to whom God had entrusted his word. Similarly, the prophet understood that the message he offered possessed the same divine authority as did the Scriptures recorded by the previous prophets.

Finally, references to Zechariah in the Gospel of Matthew and rabbinic tradition raise important questions about the end of Zechariah's life.[8] While condemning the unrighteousness of the Jewish leaders and predicting the coming judgment, Jesus said, "And so upon you will come all the righteous blood that has been shed on earth, from the blood of righteous Abel to the blood of Zechariah son of Berekiah, whom you murdered between the temple and the altar" (Matt 23:35). Some identify this Zechariah with "Zechariah son of Jehoiada the priest" (2 Chr 24:20–21). However, the major flaw in this understanding is the reference to Jehoiada as the father of Zechariah. The Chronicler emphatically noted that Zechariah's father was Jehoiada: "King Joash did not remember the kindness Zechariah's father Jehoiada had shown him but killed his son" (2 Chr 24:22a). This could not be the same individual as Zechariah the prophet since the Zechariah in Matthew is called the son of Berekiah. The Old Testament does not record anything about the martyrdom of Zechariah the prophet, but rabbinic literature from the early Christian period suggests that "Zechariah son of Berekiah" was murdered.[9] Coupled with the statement in the Gospel of Matthew, there is reasonable evidence to conclude that Zechariah the prophet was indeed martyred.

## 2. The Authorship of the Book

### (1) Historical Development of the Issue

After centuries of inquiry, the authorship of Zechariah stands as one of the most vexing and controversial questions of Old Testament introduction. Critical scholarship almost unanimously divides the book into at least two components, most frequently chaps. 1–8 and 9–14.[10] Many have also divided chaps.

---

[8] C. L. Blomberg, *Matthew* (Nashville: Broadman, 1992), 348–49. Also, C. L. Blomberg, *The Historical Reliability of the Gospels* (Downers Grove: InterVarsity, 1987), 193–95.

[9] S. H. Blank, "The Death of Zechariah in Rabbinic Literature," *HUCA* 12–13 (1937–38): 327–46. Although he acknowledged the existence of the rabbinic tradition concerning Zechariah's death, Blank did not accept this evidence as accurate.

[10] For a comprehensive survey of the discussion, see O. Eissfeldt, *The Old Testament: An Introduction*, trans. P. R. Ackroyd (New York: Harper & Row, 1965), 429–40.

9–14 into sections that supposedly arose from different sources.[11] Moreover, even some scholars within the broader evangelical camp have acquiesced to current scholarly preferences, attributing the book to two or more authors.[12] Nonetheless, it would be a mistake to suggest that dividing Zechariah has become an "evangelical" position.[13]

Joseph Mede, a seventeenth-century British scholar, emerged as one of the first to discuss the authorship of Zech 9–14 seriously. Mede focused on Matt 27:9–10 because the Gospel writer attributed a quote from Zechariah to Jeremiah. Mede maintained that the Holy Spirit led Matthew to correct what Mede believed was the erroneous Masoretic attribution of chaps. 9–14 to the prophet Zechariah.

Mede's handling of Matthew's quote from Zechariah moved Bishop Richard Kidder to conclude in 1699 that Zechariah arose from two distinct sources. After Kidder, the question of the unity of Zechariah became a widely debated issue throughout Europe and America. The discussion culminated in the publication of the landmark study by Bernhard Stade that articulated fully the classical critical position on the origins of the book.[14] Since Stade, a host of studies addressing the authorship of Zechariah have appeared, the vast majority of which fully support Stade's conclusions.[15] Some scholars have moved even further. Treves argued for a Maccabean date for chaps. 9–14, concluding that Judas Maccabeus wrote much, if not all, of those chapters.[16]

More recently, Zechariah studies devote significantly less attention to diachronic approaches. Literary methods direct many current works on Zechariah to view the book in a unified literary fashion without reverting to pre-critical positions regarding authorship.[17] These attempts to read Zechariah in a more holistic literary fashion have begun to appear with increasing frequency.

---

[11] E.g., B. Otzen, *Studien über Deuterosacharja* (Copenhagen: Prostand Apud Munksgaard, 1964), 170. It is far from the prevailing view; many critical scholars argue for the unity of chaps. 9–14; see A. F. Schellenberg, "One in the Bond of War: The Unity of Deutero-Zechariah," *Didaskalia* 12 (2001): 101–15.

[12] See W. S. LaSor, D. A. Hubbard, and F. W. Bush, *Old Testament Survey*, 2nd ed. (Grand Rapids: Eerdmans, 1996), 401–2.

[13] R. B. Dillard and T. Longman III, *An Introduction to the Old Testament* (Grand Rapids: Zondervan, 1994), 431–32.

[14] B. Stade, "Deuterozacharja," *ZAW* 1 (1881): 1–96; 2 (1882): 151–72, 275–309.

[15] For a more thorough review of the history of research on the unity of Zechariah, see B. Otzen, *Deuterosacharja*, 11–13 and P. D. Hanson, *The Dawn of Apocalyptic* (Philadelphia: Fortress, 1975), 287–90. J. Rogerson (*Old Testament Criticism in the Nineteenth Century: England and Germany* [Philadelphia: Fortress, 1984]) surveys the general landscape of biblical scholarship as these critical views developed.

[16] M. Treves, "Conjectures Concerning the Date and Authorship of Zechariah IX–XIV," *VT* 13 (1963): 196–207.

[17] For example, M. Butterworth, *Structure and the Book of Zechariah* (Sheffield: Sheffield Academic Press, 1992); Conrad, *Zechariah*; and J. E. Tollington, *Tradition and Innovation in Haggai and Zechariah 1–8* (Sheffield: Sheffield Academic Press, 1993). Also, R. David Moseman, "Reading the Two Zechariahs as One," *RevExp* 97 (2000): 487–98.

Floyd encourages literary studies to mature from their infancy. He writes, "It is odd that no recent commentaries have attempted to grasp either the ideational concept or the socio-historical context forming the matrix for the book as a whole."[18]

*(2) Evidence for Dividing the Book of Zechariah*

The reasons for ascribing different authorship to the two sections of Zechariah rest on the following arguments, which we will examine in turn.[19] First, many understand Matt 27:9–10 to indicate that Zechariah did not pen chaps. 9–14. It is apparent that this issue alone profoundly alters the way biblical scholars view the book of Zechariah.

Second, many believe that the two portions of Zechariah reveal very different historical viewpoints. For example, chaps. 1–8 portray history from a perspective that many scholars deem "prophetic eschatology," with marked similarities to the majority of the preceding prophetic material. Prophetic eschatology attempts to effect a correction of Israel's world by bringing it into conformity with God's will. In contrast, chaps. 9–14 reflect apocalyptic issues that presuppose an end to this world and the inauguration of a new world under God's dominion. Many scholars view the apocalyptic viewpoint as a significantly later development from the earlier prophetic eschatology, leading to the conclusion that the second half of Zechariah derives from a later period with different concerns than the first portion of the book.

Floyd builds on this common assumption with a distinctive conclusion. He follows critical scholarship in rejecting single authorship of Zechariah. However, Floyd criticizes most Zechariah scholarship for failing to treat the book as a literary unit. He writes, "For whatever reason, interpreters seem reluctant to confront the fact that the editors who put the prophetic corpus in its canonical form regarded all fourteen chapters of Zechariah as constituting a distinct prophetic book."[20] He continues, "The book's (Zechariah's) attainment of its canonical form is not only a literary phenomenon; it is also a historical event, and even a primarily historical approach must therefore deal at some point with the integration of 1–8 and 9–14 to form the book as a whole."[21]

Floyd suggests that chaps. 9–14 serve as a restatement or reinterpretation of chaps. 1–8, aiming to make Zechariah's message for an earlier age in the first half of the book meaningful for a later time. Floyd bases his conclusion largely on the Hebrew term *maśśā'*, commonly translated "burden."[22] He holds that

---

[18] M. H. Floyd, "Zechariah and the Changing Views of Second Temple Judaism in Recent Commentaries," *Religious Studies Review* 25 (1999): 262.

[19] Dillard and Longman (*Introduction*, 429–32) provide a helpful response to these arguments.

[20] Floyd, "Zechariah and the Changing Views," 262.

[21] Ibid.

[22] מַשָּׂא. See *HALOT*, 639–40.

this Hebrew term here "means something like 'a reinterpretation of a previous revelation.' "[23] While Floyd's understanding of the two sections of Zechariah should not be dismissed without reflection, his argument based on *maśśā'* does not bear scrutiny. The Hebrew word simply does not denote or connote what Floyd claims.[24]

Floyd's approach signals a renewed concern for the message of the entire book of Zechariah. For too long the literary and theological parallels between the respective portions of the book have suffered neglect. The latter portion of this commentary will consider carefully how chaps. 1–8 and 9–14 relate to each other.

Third, the literary features of the two sections of Zechariah's prophecy differ significantly. The book begins with Zechariah's night visions and sermons that place the prophet in the midst of the circumstances to which God commands him to speak. Alternatively, the final portion of the prophecy consists of two extended oracles dealing with differing epochs, presented without Zechariah playing a role in the oracles. Hence, scholars frequently conclude that the different genres provide clear evidence of separate authorship for the two sections.

Fourth, several additional factors converge, demonstrating to many that the traditional view of the unity of Zechariah requires correction. Prominent linguistic features in the two sections of Zechariah, such as vocabulary and syntax, change markedly between chaps. 1–8 and 9–14.

Fifth, chaps. 1–8 focus on the Persian period, while chaps. 9–14 appear to focus on different periods of Judah's history. Moreover, students of Zechariah's prophecy disagree strongly regarding the setting of chaps. 9–14. Some believe these chapters reflect the preexilic era, while others maintain that chaps. 9–14 describe the fourth century BC. Finally, many scholars identify the shepherds in 11:4–17 with a variety of figures in the Maccabean period. These diverse arguments will now receive further elaboration.

1. *Citation in Matt 27:9–10*. Eissfeldt maintains that the separation of chaps. 9–14 from the rest of the book expresses an ancient view, with the earliest testimony coming from the New Testament itself. Matthew quotes parts of Zech 11:12–13, which says that 30 pieces of silver will be paid out as the shepherd's reward (Matt 27:9–10), attributing the quote to the prophet Jeremiah.[25] According to Eissfeldt, Matthew anticipates the critical posture that chaps. 9–14 reflect the literary efforts of someone other than Zechariah, son of Iddo. In other words, Eissfeldt's approach suggests that an ancient tradition attributed chaps. 9–14 to someone other than Zechariah. Eissfeldt further posits that the Matthean reference proves that the tradition of dual authorship was more

---

[23] M. H. Floyd, *Minor Prophets. Part 2* (Grand Rapids: Eerdmans, 2000), 306.

[24] *HALOT*, 639–40 and BDB, 672.

[25] Eissfeldt, *Introduction*, 435.

compelling than the one that assigned all 14 chapters to Zechariah. Of course, if Eissfeldt's interpretation is correct, strong evidence exists for separating the authorship of the book between chaps. 1–8 and chaps. 9–14.

Predictably, a legion of interpretations of Matt 27:9 have emerged over the years. One of the most helpful suggests that the Matthean emphasis lies not with the payment of 30 silver coins, but with the field, a topic that Zech 11:12–13 does not mention at all. This understanding maintains that Matthew intentionally alluded to Jeremiah, probably to chap. 19. Jeremiah 19 speaks of "the blood of the innocent" (v. 4), "the potter" (vv. 1,11), the renaming of the valley (v. 6), the violence associated with the site (v. 11), as well as the judgment and burial of leaders (v. 11).[26] Thus, one may reasonably conclude that Matthew's "quote" alludes to texts from both Jeremiah and Zechariah. Apparently, Matthew gave precedence to the themes derived from Jeremiah because of the Gospel's explicit reference to the preexilic prophet. See the commentary on 11:13.

2. *Differing Views of History*. The next argument for dividing the book affirms that the two sections of Zechariah appear to have differing historiographic perspectives. These contrasting historical emphases lead many to deduce that Zechariah derives from at least two different authors. The apparent contrast between the "prophetic" vision in chaps. 1–8 and the "apocalyptic" material in chaps. 9–14 provides the primary support for this judgment. Scholarship generally assumes that prophetic historiography stresses "this worldly" concerns. According to this understanding, apocalyptic historiography considers "this world" beyond repair and dwells almost exclusively on "other worldly" eschatological matters.

While a fuller description of the differences between "prophetic eschatology" and "apocalyptic" literature follows later in this introduction, several remarks here will further the discussion. Anyone who embraces a unified authorship of Zechariah must not minimize the differences in the book. Real differences exist between the perspectives of prophetic eschatology and apocalyptic. The problem arises when one asserts that the two are incompatible with each other or that the two cannot come from the same pen or from proximate periods of time. The contention that apocalyptic did not arise in Israel until virtually the Maccabean period presents another difficulty, one we will study more thoroughly below.

---

[26] Blomberg, *Matthew*, 408–9. For similar arguments, see: R. H. Gundry, *Matthew* (Grand Rapids: Eerdmans, 1982), 555–58 and E. W. Hengstenberg, *Christology of the Old Testament*, reprint ed. (Grand Rapids: Kregel, 1970), 342–49. For comparable approaches from more of a New Testament perspective, see F. F. Bruce, "The Book of Zechariah and the Passion Narrative," *BJRL* 43 (1961): 336–53 and D. P. Senior, *The Passion Narrative According to Matthew* (Leuven: University Press, 1975), 347–52.

Isaiah presents clear indications that prophetic eschatology and apocalyptic can coexist and derive from the same source.[27] Certainly, most of Isaiah reflects the more common eschatological view of the future. The many Messianic texts in Isaiah illustrate the point well, for these passages generally envision a reshaping of Israel's future under the auspices of the Messianic King.

Even for those who posit multiple authorship of Isaiah, one can clearly discover both "prophetic" and "apocalyptic" literature within Isaiah 1–39, even though critical scholarship generally treats chaps. 1–39 as a literary unit from the hand of Isaiah son of Amoz. In the same section of the book, we discover the "Isaianic Apocalypse" (chaps. 24–27), which evidences an apocalyptic character. Suggestions that this apocalypse is "proto-apocalyptic" merely beg the question.[28] In the final analysis, no compelling evidence commends the contention that the prophetic eschatology and apocalyptic genres must unfold in a chronological sequence.[29]

Likewise, one cannot use a genre like apocalyptic to date a text with any precision.[30] Certainly as a genre, apocalyptic became progressively more common as the postexilic era developed into the Maccabean epoch. Nevertheless, it does not follow logically that a text comes from a late period merely because that genre became more popular in that latter day. One would not have to look far in literature to produce manifold examples to illustrate the point.

3. *Different Literary Shapes.* Zechariah 1–8 evidence a significantly different literary style from chaps. 9–14. The first half of the book comprises a series of night visions accompanied by interpretative sermons, while the second section contains two extended oracles. Further, the night visions have dates, but the two oracles that conclude the book do not. Again, chaps. 1–8 often speak of Zechariah personally, while the remainder of the book is relatively impersonal, describing cosmic events.

The differences between the two portions of Zechariah should not be underestimated. Nevertheless, one may challenge whether these differences represent adequate grounds for postulating divergent authorship as well. The book of Jeremiah, whose authorship has remained relatively unchallenged, illustrates that a single biblical author may fully employ significantly diverse genres.

4. *Different Linguistic Features.* Another important type of evidence for dividing the book derives from differences in vocabulary and other linguistic features that emerge when comparing Zech 1–8 with chaps. 9–14. Having already used a similar methodology to study the Pentateuch and the book of

---

[27] E. J. Tigchelaar, *Prophets of Old and the Day of the End: Zechariah, the Book of Watchers and Apocalyptic* (Leiden: E. J. Brill, 1996), 4; P. Hanson, "Apocalypse and Apocalyptic," in *ABD*, 281.

[28] R. K. Harrison, *Introduction to the Old Testament* (Grand Rapids: Eerdmans, 1969), 954–55.

[29] See Harrison, *Introduction*, 954–56.

[30] Tigchelaar, *Prophets of Old*, 4.

Isaiah, Yehuda Radday and Dieter Wickmann apply computer-aided linguistic analyses of Zech 1–8 compared with chaps. 9–14 in an attempt to discern any fundamental differences between the two sections of Zechariah.[31] Specifically, Radday and Wickmann establish the objective of their study:

> The purpose of the present study was to elucidate whether in the light of linguistics, the assumption of one or both of these breaks is justified; all other pros and cons such as thematic and historical reasons were intentionally disregarded. Its further purpose was to quantify, by means of statistics, the weight of the arguments for possible changes of authorship within the book and to express it in terms of probability values.[32]

Whereas some of Radday's conclusions about other sections of Scripture agree with the critical assessments of the text, his conclusions regarding Zechariah run counter to most understandings.[33] Basing his comments solely on linguistic grounds, Radday writes regarding the unity of Zechariah,

> Concerning the transition between ch. 8 and 9, it was found that from the point of view of language behaviour there is not sufficient evidence to postulate such a change or, statistically speaking, to reject the null hypothesis of a common origin of the two sections ch. 1–8 and ch. 9–11.[34]

In response, Stephen Portnoy and David Petersen argue that Radday and Wickmann's work proves to be invalid for studying Zechariah because they employ what Portnoy and Petersen deem an inappropriate methodology. Using their own analytical model, Portnoy and Petersen conclude that linguistic analysis discerns three separate units in Zechariah: chaps. 1–8, 9–11, and 12–14.[35]

In a more recent study, Butterworth incorporates linguistic inquiries as the preceding linguistic studies did. However, Butterworth includes far more literary and thematic questions than works like Radday's incorporate. Butterworth's findings discover more affinities between chaps. 1–8 and 9–14 than

---

[31] See especially Y. T. Radday and D. Wickmann, "The Unity of Zechariah in the Light of Statistical Linguistics," *ZAW* 87 (1975): 30–55, and Y. T. Radday and M. A. Pollatschek, "Vocabulary Richness in Post-Exilic Prophetic Books," *ZAW* 92 (1980): 333–46. Another very technical work, H. Van Dyke Parunak, *Linguistic Density Plots in Zechariah* (Wooster, Ohio: Biblical Research Associates, 1979), shows less concern with the critical implications of the study.

[32] Radday and Wickmann, "Unity of Zechariah," 54.

[33] For instance, in *An Analytical Linguistic Concordance to the Book of Isaiah* (Wooster, Ohio: Biblical Research Associates, 1971) and *The Unity of Isaiah in the Light of Statistical Linguistics* (Hildesheim: H. A. Gerstenberg, 1973), Radday argues that the differences between Isaiah 1–39 and chaps. 40–66 are too great for both sections to stem from the same author.

[34] Radday and Wickmann, "Unity of Zechariah," 54.

[35] S. L. Portnoy and D. L. Petersen, "Biblical Texts and Statistical Analysis: Zechariah and Beyond," *JBL* 103 (1984): 21.

even Radday and Wickmann detected. Butterworth states, "I conclude that we have found evidence of a connection between Zechariah 1–8 and 9–14, but not of an overall editing of the whole book."[36]

Using a somewhat different methodology, Andrew Hill studied the linguistic evidence as well. For centuries Hebrew scholars have noticed subtle differences in Hebrew syntax as one moves from Biblical Hebrew literature, written in the earliest eras, to the material coming from the latest books in the Old Testament. Robert Polzin produced an influential study that systematically presented the criteria on which numerous important studies rely.[37] Also relying on Polzin's organizational approach, Hill compared particular linguistic criteria in Zech 1–8 with those in chaps. 9–14.[38] After comparing widely accepted linguistic criteria in Haggai, Zech 1–8, Zech 9–14, and Malachi with Polzin's data from Chronicles and Ezra/Nehemiah, Hill concluded that Zech 1–8 and Zech 9–14 dated from the same historical era. Solely on linguistic grounds, Hill dated both "halves" of Zechariah to the era between c. 515 and 450 BC, most likely between c. 515 and 475 BC.[39]

No consensus has been achieved at this point regarding the implications of linguistics for the unity of the book. However, one may safely conclude that linguistics fails to provide a definitive argument for dividing Zechariah for at least two reasons. For one, linguists themselves have not reached general agreement about the method of undertaking a statistical study such as Radday and Wickmann attempted. Therefore at present, most conclusions reached by linguistic methodologies fail to convince the statistical practitioners themselves since the underlying methodology has yet to prove persuasive.

Relatedly, the common presupposition held by statistical linguists, namely that an individual author must use a consistent literary style, exemplifies the basic problem with using linguistic criteria to determine authorship. Without a doubt, any capable writer deliberately employs diverse linguistic and literary techniques as the mood, purpose, and recipients of the text changes.

5. *Focus on Disparate Periods of Judah's History.* Many scholars perceive that Zech 1–8 focus on the period of the restoration. Despite the virtual unanimity within critical scholarship that chaps. 9–14 do not concern themselves with the restoration, opinions concerning the emphasis of these chapters differ widely. Scholarly suggestions concerning the historical setting of chaps. 9–14 span a period from the preexilic epoch to several dates within the Maccabean times.

Throughout the majority of the nineteenth century the preexilic view of Zech 9–14 reigned. The reference to both Israel and Judah in 9:10,13; 10:6,

---

[36] Butterworth, *Structure and the Book of Zechariah*, 272.

[37] R. Polzin, *Late Biblical Hebrew: Toward an Historical Typology of Biblical Hebrew Prose* (Missoula, MT: Scholars Press, 1976).

[38] A. E. Hill, "Dating Second Zechariah: A Linguistic Reexamination," *HAR* 6 (1982): 105–34.

[39] Ibid., 105, 130–32.

read in highly literal terms, provides the primary evidence for this view. Moreover, the portrayal of Damascus and national Israel in chap. 9 might envision a preexilic setting. Additionally, the mention of the Assyrians and Egyptians appears to commend a date prior to the fall of Assyria in 612 BC.

However, Zechariah does not state that these principalities were free and independent at the time of writing, as some assume.[40] Moreover, "Israel" often occurs as a poetic word-pair with "Judah," or a similar synonym, even in texts written subsequent to the demise of national Israel.[41] For instance, Zech 8:13 well illustrates this point in a passage whose dating comes after the fall of Israel. One can therefore assert no claim regarding the existence of national Israel in these poetic passages. Regarding the mention of Assyria, Ezra 6:22 illustrates another reference to Assyria long after its demise as an empire.

Following Stade's analysis, the pendulum swung in favor of the postexilic understanding primarily on the basis of the reference to the Greeks in 9:13 and a different reading of chap. 9, one that notes its affinities with the invasions by Alexander the Great.[42] Presently, the postexilic view remains the most popular.[43] It would be misleading, though, to suggest that all critical scholars agree; witness Otzen's defense of the preexilic dating.[44]

Those espousing the unity of the book typically respond to the reference to the Greeks in one of the following ways. Some wish to reduce the question to whether the interpreter allows predictive prophecy. Such an argument is an *a priori* argument based on theological commitments rather than the exegetical and historical arguments that are the purview of this discussion. The argument begins with its own assumptions regarding the supernatural nature of Scripture and specifically the work of the Spirit in revealing and superintending the inspiration of the text. The reference to Greeks presents no difficulty to the reader who embraces the divine nature of the book of Zechariah.[45]

A different explanation, although not necessarily exclusive of the previous response, suggests that any reference to the Greeks does not speak definitively of Alexander or any of his successors. Rather, the Greeks, although not yet a preeminent world power, perhaps had already achieved enough political prom-

---

[40] G. L. Archer, Jr., *A Survey of Old Testament Introduction*, revised ed. (Chicago: Moody, 1974), 434–35.

[41] See Y. Avishur, *Stylistic Studies of Word-Pairs in Biblical and Ancient Semitic Literatures* (Neukirchen-Vluyn: Neukirchener, 1984), for an examination of the role of word pairs in Hebrew poetry.

[42] For a further treatment of these issues see B. S. Childs, *Introduction to the Old Testament as Scripture* (Philadelphia: Fortress, 1979), 475–76, and E. H. Merrill, *Haggai, Zechariah, Malachi* (Chicago: Moody, 1994), 75–77.

[43] See M. Treves, "Conjectures Concerning the Date and Authorship of Zechariah IX-XIV," *VT* 13 (1963): 196–207.

[44] Otzen, *Deuterosacharja*, 11–34.

[45] See Archer, *Survey*, 435–36.

inence to merit mention in 9:13.[46] Dillard and Longman defend their acceptance of this view by citing inscriptions from Sargon II and Sennacherib, dating as early as the eighth century BC, that describe the actions of Greek traders and mercenaries.[47] The references to Greece in Isa 66:19 and Ezek 27:13,19 also reflect the significance this people had attained by this point in history.

It is important not to minimize the complexity of the issues involved in dating Zech 9–14. Nonetheless, the vast differences in dating this section of Zechariah undermine the claim that these chapters could not come from the same epoch as the prophet Zechariah.

6. *Identification of the Shepherds with Maccabean Figures.* Although no consensus has emerged concerning the identity of the shepherds in Zech 11, many conclude that they refer to Maccabean figures. Some identify the good shepherd with the high priest Onias III who ministered during the years 187–175 BC. Onias IV, the high priest who was executed in the days of Judas Maccabeus, receives the recommendations of other scholars (see 2 Macc 13:1–8). Unfortunately, the suggested identification with Maccabean leaders numbers in the dozens, most of whom resided within the postexilic era. Some do uphold the preexilic understanding, though, such as the view cited by Otzen. He suggested that the shepherds referred to three real kings: Zechariah, Shallum, and Menahem.[48]

Moreover, the conjectures regarding the shepherds' identity prove to be highly subjective. In 1912, Mitchell reported that he had enumerated some 40 different individuals "covering the whole field of Hebrew history from the Exodus to the conquest of Palestine by the Romans, and including most of the men and institutions of any importance."[49] Baldwin says that this passage is "probably the most enigmatic in the whole Old Testament."[50] Consequently, we would do well not to draw inferences about the disunity of the book of Zechariah based on such tenuous evidence.[51]

### (3) Factors Supporting Unified Authorship

Up to this point in our discussion we have examined the major lines of argument for assigning the authorship of Zechariah to two or more individuals. We

---

[46] Dillard and Longman, *Introduction*, 431. For a similar perspective, see Harrison, *Introduction*, 952–53, and Edward J. Young, *An Introduction to the Old Testament* (Grand Rapids: Eerdmans, 1964), 280.

[47] Dillard and Longman, *Introduction*, 431.

[48] Otzen, *Deuterosacharia*, 24.

[49] H. G. Mitchell, J. M. P. Smith, and J. A. Bewer, *A Critical and Exegetical Commentary on Haggai, Zechariah, Malachi and Jonah*, ICC (Edinburgh: T. & T. Clark, 1912), 306.

[50] J. G. Baldwin, *Haggai, Zechariah, Malachi*, TOTC (Downers Grove, IL: InterVarsity, 1972), 181.

[51] For further discussion from divergent perspectives, see Harrison, *Introduction*, 953; C. L. Meyers and E. M. Meyers, *Zechariah 9–14*, AB (New York: Doubleday, 1993), 264–65; and R. L. Smith, *Micah-Malachi*, WBC (Waco: Word, 1984), 270.

have evaluated these reasons, concluding that they do not compel one to embrace the critical position. While the rationale behind most of these arguments emphasizes differences between the sections, one must note the substantive similarities between Zech 1–8 and 9–14. Thus, it is important to view the matter more positively and to provide reasons for accepting unified authorship.

As we have already noted, shifts in topics and purposes reasonably explain the differences that do occur between the two sections of the book. Nonetheless, in addition to the many significant differences within the book of Zechariah, there are also profound similarities among the motifs found in chaps. 1–8 as compared to chaps. 9–14. Interestingly, even scholars who assign chaps. 9–14 to Deutero-Zechariah acknowledge these parallels. For example, LaSor (et al.) states,

> There are connections, such as the covenant formula (8:8; 13:9), the divine protection of Jerusalem (2:5,8–10; 14:11), and the return of the exiles (8:7; 10:9–12). Most importantly, the climax of the second part of Zechariah is similar to that of the first: the inclusion of gentiles in the Jerusalem worship of the Lord (8:20–22; 14:16–19).[52]

Childs produces one of the most detailed treatments analyzing the similarities between the two "halves" of Zechariah. While he wholeheartedly accepts the critical understanding of the authorship of Zechariah, Childs emphasizes the "canonical shape" of the entire book. Even though Childs asserts that chaps. 9–14 "were not intentionally structured on the basis of 1–8," he does agree "that there is a surprising compatibility between the two books of material."[53]

In addition to the shared themes observed by LaSor above, Childs adds numerous others.[54] The theological points found in both sections of Zechariah follow. The notion of restored fertility occurs both in 8:12 and 14:6,8. A curse spreads over the entire land in 5:3 and is removed in 14:11. God pronounces judgment on the nations in 1:18–20 and 14:3–5. The nations turn to the Lord in 2:11; 8:20–22; and 14:6–9,16. Cultic rites are transformed in the future in 8:18–23 and 14:20–21. Both 4:6 and 12:10 describe an outpouring of the Spirit/spirit that would transform the people of God. God judges all who

---

[52] LaSor, Hubbard, and Bush, *Survey*, 408–9. See also, Ralph L. Smith, *Micah-Malachi*, 242, 248; and Raymond Person, *Second Zechariah and the Deuteronomic School* (Sheffield: JSOT, 1993), 140–42.

[53] Childs, *Introduction*, 482. In "The Relation of Zech 9–14 to Proto-Zechariah," ZAW 88 (1976): 227–39, R. A. Mason notes the following similarities: "the prominence of the Zion tradition; the divine cleansing of the community; universalism; the appeal to the earlier prophets; and the provision of leadership as a sign of the new age" (p. 227). Mason generally attributes these parallels to the deliberate efforts of Deutero-Zechariah to echo prominent themes from chaps. 1–8. For a more recent and similar perspective, note R. D. Moseman, "Reading the Two Zechariahs," 487–98.

[54] Childs, *Introduction*, 482–83.

swear falsely by his name in 5:4 and 13:3. The coming Messiah triumphs not by might, but in humility, as described in 3:8; 4:6; and 9:9–11.[55]

Perhaps the most encompassing similarity, according to Childs, is the uniform testimony of both "halves" of Zechariah that a new era will come for God's people, linked to the rebuilding of the temple in Jerusalem. Zechariah's eschatology did not concern the future exclusively, however, for it sought to give hope to the community's immediate needs.[56]

Furthermore, while one cannot claim that it was unusual for Old Testament prophets to rely on the work of their predecessors, Dillard and Longman note that both major sections of Zechariah demonstrate a heavy dependence on the earlier prophets. They observe the following thematic parallels: "1:4; Isa. 58 in 7:4–10; Amos 1:9–10; 5:27–62 in 9:1–8; Jer. 25:34–38 in 11:1–3; Ezek. 47:1–10 in 14:1–4."[57]

## (4) Conclusion

Students of the book of Zechariah would do well to heed Childs' caution before treating the two sections of Zechariah separately.[58] Childs declares that the testimony of the book is "in danger of being lost when the two parts of the book are separated."[59] He continues, "The function of developing a prophetic picture of the end time . . . is realized only in the combined process of theological reflection preserved in the whole book."[60] The differing emphases of chaps. 1–8 and 9–14 require what Childs deems "a holistic reading" to avoid the inevitable misinterpretation that ensues if the two sections of the book are not allowed to inform one another.

In the final analysis, strong arguments may be adduced in support of the multiple authorship of Zechariah. One can neither ignore the volume of literature on the subject nor the depth of research the question has engendered. Moreover, one should not suggest that those who divide the book are all controlled by broader agendas.

We have not found the arguments as set forth by critical scholars for dividing the book compelling. We have tried to arrive at our conclusion without

---

[55] Mitchell (*Zechariah*, 242–43) also cites the nineteenth-century commentator G. L. Robinson (*The Prophecies of Zechariah*, 1896) about the extensive list of affinities between the two sections of Zechariah.

[56] Childs, *Introduction*, 483. For further study of the thematic unity between the two sections in the book of Zechariah, see M. L. Ruffin, "Symbolism in Zechariah: A Study in Functional Unity" (Ph.D. diss., Southern Baptist Theological Seminary, 1986).

[57] Dillard and Longman, *Introduction*, 431.

[58] In fairness to Childs, we reiterate that he does not uphold the unified authorship of Zechariah. Moreover, Childs is not particularly concerned to relate either portion of Zechariah to a historical setting and the author who gave birth to the text. Rather, Childs seeks to emphasize the "canonical" significance of the text, reading the book as it came to be understood by the people of God.

[59] Childs, *Introduction*, 485.

[60] Ibid.

either diatribe or unfounded dogmatism. Baldwin's comments clearly express one of the fundamental problems with the critical approach: "Such a bewildering variety of views on both date and unity leaves the reader at a loss to know what to believe. The very fact that there is such diversity undermines confidence in the methodology used."[61] Thus, the sole point around which the critical approach can agree is the decision to divide the book after chap. 8, but there is no consensus in the evidence or explanation. Consequently, the critical view of the authorship of Zechariah merits rejection.

## 3. Historical Era

One cannot understand the sixth century BC in which the book of Zechariah falls without a deep appreciation for the lasting and devastating effects that the Babylonian exile held for Judah. The era immediately prior to the fall of Judah reflected an equally fragile peace and prosperity. Into the mix was added a cacophony of voices predicting a glorious future, in addition to the harbingers of doom. One major theological problem with social implications in the preexilic era was the doctrine of the inviolability of Zion. This was a false and pernicious doctrine, the "prosperity theology" of that day. This false teaching affirmed that Jerusalem could never fall as long as the Lord's temple remained in the city. Jeremiah mocked this false teaching, admonishing, "Do not trust in deceptive words and say, 'This is the temple of the LORD, the temple of the LORD, the temple of the LORD" (Jer 7:4). This heretical teaching rested on a false theology, certainly not on revelation from God.

The prophets castigated the false prophets and their deceptive teachings both for their profound misrepresentation of the Lord's message as well as the false hope it offered a desperate nation who turned in the wrong direction for aid. Many prophetic texts explicitly proclaimed the certainty and the imminence of the exile. The prophets rooted their teaching in the Torah where God ordained political defeat and exile for his people whenever they proved unfaithful. The momentous chapter on the blessings and curses destined for God's people when they chose either to obey or disobey the Lord's covenant, Deut 28, sets the stage for what God would do much later in biblical history. Among the manifold curses listed, this chapter mentions several of great significance for God's people, including: defeat before the nations (v. 25), flight from their enemies (v. 25), being displaced from their own homes and fields (vv. 30,33), loss of their prized property (vv. 30–31), and their children being taken exile with them to another nation (vv. 32,36,41,49–52,64–68). Deuteronomy 28:45–47 reiterates the message that these curses will only befall Israel if she chooses to spurn the Lord's commandments. Jeremiah continued the same themes, devoting most of his ministry to warning Judah to repent in order

---

[61] Baldwin, *Zechariah*, 68.

to forestall judgment. Jeremiah delivered one of his most significant messages on the theme of the exile, stating,

> Therefore the LORD Almighty says this: "Because you have not listened to my words, I will summon all the peoples of the north and my servant Nebuchadnezzar king of Babylon," declares the LORD, "and I will bring them against this land and its inhabitants and against all the surrounding nations. I will completely destroy them and make them an object of horror and scorn, and an everlasting ruin. I will banish from them the sounds of joy and gladness, the voices of bride and bridegroom, the sound of millstones, and the light of the lamp. This whole country will become a desolate wasteland, and these nations will serve the king of Babylon seventy years." (Jer 25:8–11)

When the Babylonians, led by Nebuchadnezzar II (605–562 BC), sacked Jerusalem in 587 BC, Judah ceased to exist as a sovereign nation. Baldwin summarizes all of Israelite history "in the sequence: chosen, privileged, presumptuous, rebellious."[62] The ensuing pathos, chaos, and despair was heightened by the illusory promises of the false prophets of the day. This resulted in an even deeper crisis of faith with a resulting loss of hope for the nation. Nothing would ever be the same again, and without the miraculous intervention of God, the people had no future. Ezekiel's vision of dry and defiled bones scattered throughout the land captured the spirit of the people as they struggled to see into their collective future.

The sacking of Jerusalem by the Babylonians devastated the city (Lam 2:2–12,20–22; 4:9–20; 5:1–18). Employing essentially a "scorched earth" military policy, the Babylonians leveled the city walls, razed the royal court, and utterly demolished the temple. According to Jer 52:28–30, Nebuchadnezzar deported 4,600 members of Judah to Babylon. The invaders pillaged the sacred items from the temple and sent them to Babylon (2 Kgs 25:8–15; Jer 39:8). Compounding the crisis, the Babylonians either exiled or executed the priests and other religious leaders (2 Kgs 25:18–21). After suffering these indignities, Judah lost not only its national identity, but more importantly the nation also no longer had the means to worship God through sacrifice to the Lord as commanded in the Torah. This unprecedented turn precipitated the single greatest crisis in the history of God's chosen people. But in the end, God did extend his blessings to his people, employing historical developments in the ancient Near East to restore the nation.

On the world stage, the sixth century saw equally momentous developments that influenced subsequent events for centuries to come. As the seventh century came to a close, some dominant regions began to lose sway, while others began their rise to ascendancy. For instance, the defeat of Pharaoh Neco at

---

[62] Ibid., 13.

Carchemish in 605 BC was one of a series of events signaling the diminishing of Egypt's hegemony. After the death of Nebuchadnezzar in 562 BC, political machinations and weak leadership diminished Babylon's political and military prowess, making the mighty conqueror of Judah and much of the rest of the ancient Near East vulnerable to defeat. To compound problems in their land, many Babylonians lost confidence in their ruler Nabonidus for his infelicity to their national gods and consequently did not contest the Persian intrusion strongly. Meanwhile, on the Hellenistic peninsula, the Greek peoples began to coalesce and to envision an empire of their own.

As the midpoint of the sixth century approached, the Persians held center stage, and no Persian received more notoriety than Cyrus (559–530 BC). After conquering the Medes in 550 BC, Cyrus turned his gaze toward Babylon whose weakened position resulted in her submission to Cyrus in 539 BC with a virtually bloodless victory. Thus ended the grand Babylonian empire and began the new Persian empire led by its Achaemenid Dynasty. Beyond Babylon's borders, by the end of 538 BC "all western Asia to the Egyptian frontier was his."[63]

Known not only for his political and military successes, Cyrus also left a lasting image as a wise, tolerant, and compassionate ruler. Cyrus ruled with a large measure of wisdom and foresight. Instead of ruling with an iron hand, Cyrus resolved to repatriate the peoples whom the Babylonians had exiled, including Judah, presenting himself as a liberator. He also extended financial support from the Persian treasury to underwrite their endeavors. In particular, Cyrus sought to promote the religious traditions of each nation, granting Persian funds and posturing himself as the most devoted follower of each and every deity. Cyrus wished that the conquered peoples would view him as a faithful worshipper of their national deities, reflecting only political philosophy, not religious conviction. The renowned Cyrus Cylinder discovered in 1879 overviews the great monarch's agenda, excerpts from which state,

> I am Cyrus, king of the world, great king, legitimate king, king of Babylon, king of Sumer and Akkad, king of the four rims (of the earth) . . . I (also) gathered all their (former) inhabitants and return (to them) their habitations. . . . May all the gods whom I have resettled in their sacred cities ask daily Bel and Nebo for a long life for me and may they recommend me (to him); to Marduk, my lord, they may say this: "Cyrus, the king who worships you, and Cambyses, his son."[64]

This policy thus allowed diverse peoples under Persian control to exercise a significant measure of self governance as well as to retain their cultural and religious identity.

---

[63] J. Bright, *A History of Israel*, third edition (Philadelphia: Westminster, 1981), 361.

[64] *ANET*, 316. See also A. Kuhrt, "The Cyrus Cylinder and the Achaemenid Imperial Policy," JSOT 25 (1983): 92–93.

Isaiah envisioned Cyrus in profound theological terms, quoting God's affirmation,

> who says of Cyrus, "He is my shepherd *[rōʿî]*[65]
> and will accomplish all that I please;
> he will say of Jerusalem, 'Let it be rebuilt,'
> and of the temple, 'Let its foundations be laid' " (Isa 44:28).

The clear royal imagery of "shepherd" attributed to Cyrus attests the Lord's desire to employ a pagan king for his sovereign purposes. Ezra 1:2 cites Cyrus's declaration that God had directed him to build the Lord a temple in Jerusalem. Accordingly, in the same year he vanquished the Babylonians, Cyrus issued a decree to rebuild the temple and to restore the worship of the Lord in Jerusalem (2 Chr 36:22–23; Ezra 1:1–4; 6:3–5).

Shortly thereafter the first wave of exiles braved the journey back to their promised land, following Sheshbazzar (Ezra 1:8,11; 5:14). Both Sheshbazzar (Ezra 5:16) and Zerubbabel (Ezra 3:1–8) played a role in laying the foundation for the temple. The temple foundation was completed in 536 BC (Ezra 3:8–13). Following this initial success, the rigors of daily life distracted the people and all work on the temple ceased (Ezra 4:1–5,24).[66] Further, those living in Jerusalem and its environs during the exile allied together to oppose the repatriates (Ezra 4:1–5).[67]

During the hiatus in temple reconstruction, the benevolent Cyrus died on the battlefield in 530 BC. Cyrus's successor was his son, Cambyses II, a lesser light to be sure. Always the despot, Cambyses routinely plundered the promised land, resulting in the daily struggles to provide a living (Hag 1:2–6,9). This deprivation clearly added to the people's inattention to the temple project. Cambyses's greatest accomplishment was defeating Egypt and adding it to the Persian empire. His tyrannical reign ended abruptly with his death in 522 BC under disputed circumstances. The tradition that Cambyses committed suicide must be weighed against Herodotus's assertion that he accidentally inflicted a wound on himself with his sword while dismounting his horse, an injury that proved fatal after an extended period.[68] Josephus's parting comment on Cambyses was that he was "bad by nature."[69]

Cambyses's unexpected death opened a path for one of the dead ruler's officers, Darius, to claim the throne of his deceased commander in 522 BC. Although only 28 years old when he assumed the throne, Darius aggressively

---

[65] רֹעִי. *HALOT*, 1260–62.

[66] Bright, *History of Israel*, 366.

[67] M. Smith, "Jewish Religious Life in the Persian Period," in *The Cambridge History of Judaism, vol. 1, Introduction: The Persian Period* (Cambridge: Cambridge University Press, 1984), 219–78.

[68] Herodotus, *Histories*, 3.64–66.

[69] Josephus, *Antiquities*, 11.26.

put down rebellion throughout the empire, which had erupted at the news of Cambyses's death. The dominion of Darius extended as far as modern-day Iran in the east and Asia Minor in the west. The famous Behistun Inscription carved into the side of an Iranian mountain chronicled these military exploits. In modern times the Behistun Inscription provided crucial linguistic information required initially to decipher cuneiform. This inscription is trilingual, stating the same royal message in three different languages, Babylonian cuneiform, Elamite, and Old Persian.[70]

After cementing the peace and establishing the legitimacy of his reign, Darius turned his attention to civic affairs such as roads, communication throughout the empire, the revision of tax codes, and standardizing the monetary system.[71] The importance of roads to facilitate traversing the empire emphasized the significance of Zechariah's horsemen traveling throughout the earth (1:10). In these pursuits Darius resembled Cyrus far more than his predecessor Cambyses. Darius reigned until 486 BC, one of the longer and more effective reigns in all of ancient Near Eastern history.

It appears that Darius took some two years to quell the final expressions of rebellion and bring calm to the empire. Darius achieved this objective around 520 BC, the year both Haggai and Zechariah began their public ministries. Zechariah's second dated prophecy (1:7–17) places the message in the second year of Darius's reign (v. 7). This oracle reaffirms the Lord's care for the nation, based on his covenant with them. Since their return, the years of hardship for the faithful, coupled with the seeming prosperity of the unrighteous, had taken their toll. Hope had dimmed, leading God to reaffirm to the people, "I am very jealous for Jerusalem and Zion" (v. 14b). The Lord added, "I will return to Jerusalem with mercy, and there my house will be rebuilt" (v. 16). Like Cyrus, Darius encouraged peoples under his reign to exercise freedom of religion according to their own ancient practices and preferences.

The lengthy period of inattention to the rubble-strewn temple precincts gave powerful testimony to the people's neglect of the Lord's "house." Both Haggai and Zechariah arose to confront and challenge the people to complete the temple (Ezra 4:24; 5:1–17; 6:14). When the reconstruction finally commenced in 520 BC, Darius would play a pivotal role. No sooner than the construction began, the Persian governor Tattenai and others challenged the Judahites's authority to rebuild the temple and sent a dispatch to Darius seeking clarification. Darius quickly replied, mandating work on the temple (Ezra 6:1–12; Hag 1:1–2) that was ultimately completed in 516 BC (Ezra 6:14–15).

As the leader in postexilic Judah, Zerubbabel played a crucial role as well in the reconstruction of the temple. The importance Zechariah ascribed to him

---

[70] *ANET*, 249, 250.

[71] E. Stern, "The Persian Empire and the Political and Social History of Palestine in the Persian Period," in *The Cambridge History of Judaism, vol. 1, Introduction: The Persian Period* (Cambridge: Cambridge University Press, 1984), 70–87.

(4:1–14) is noteworthy. The Old Testament is silent about the conclusion of Zerubbabel's life and ministry, and provides no information regarding his successor. Consequently, the scholarly conjecture has arisen that the Persians did not approve of the prophetic assertions on his behalf (Hag 2:21–23; Zech 4:6–9) and deposed him and demoted the Davidic House as well.[72] Joshua the High Priest also rallied the people to build God's house so that they could worship the Lord lawfully (Ezra 2:2; 3:8; 4:2; 5:2; Zech 3:1–10; 6:11). When finally completed, the people "celebrated the dedication of the house of God with joy" (Ezra 6:16), providing the means for renewed sacrifice. The biblical books from the postexilic era add very little concerning the temple activities in the years 518–458 BC.

One additional element of Darius's reign deserves comment. In addition to his promotion of a road system that fostered international relations, the Persian sovereign's ambitions looked toward Greece. Not only did Darius's policy toward the Greeks lead to the fateful day on the battlefield at Marathon, but it inaugurated years of brutal fighting between the Persians and the Greeks. This warfare culminated in the demise of the Persian empire at the hands of Alexander the Great in 332 BC. That Greece had already attained such power that she could hold the mighty Persian empire at bay by the beginning of the fifth century BC mitigates the critical argument that posits a late date to Zech 9–14 because of Zechariah's reference to the Greeks in 9:13. Biblical references to "Greece" from this period forward should neither surprise one nor suggest that biblical texts should be redated to later eras.[73]

After one of the more influential reigns in the ancient world, Darius was killed in Marathon in 486 BC. Xerxes I (486–465 BC) succeeded him, playing a prominent role in the Book of Esther. Xerxes carried the banner of war against Greece, but suffered decisive defeats on the battlefields at Salamis, Artemisium, and Thermopylae.

Into this milieu stepped Haggai and Zechariah in the latter portion of 520 BC. The precise nature of the relationship between Haggai and Zechariah remains obscure. One can safely assume that they labored together, presenting a similar unified message (Ezra 5:1; 6:14). Haggai exhorted his hearers to build the temple, encouraging them with the unexpected hope that "the glory of this present house will be greater than the glory of the former house" (Hag 2:9). Following Haggai's assurance by only a few weeks, Zechariah began with words of divine displeasure, "The Lord was very angry with your forefathers" (Zech 1:2), followed by a glorious hope for Judah, " 'return to me,' declares the LORD Almighty, 'and I will return to you,' says the Lord Almighty" (v. 3).

Haggai's public ministry began on the first day of the sixth month of the second year of Darius (Hag 1:1), which was 520 BC. Zechariah 1:1 dates the

---

[72] Baldwin, *Zechariah*, 17; Bryan E. Beyer, "Zerubbabel," *ABD*, 6:1084–87.
[73] Baldwin, *Zechariah*, 18.

inauguration of Zechariah's prophetic ministry to the eighth month of the same year, that is, approximately two months after Haggai's first public service for the Lord. Zechariah assigned his night visions (1:7–6:15) to the twenty-fourth day of the eleventh month of Darius's second year. The last specific date offered in the book of Zechariah appears in 7:1, the fourth day of the ninth month of the fourth year of Darius, some two years after the beginning of Zechariah's ministry. While ascribing the authorship of all 14 chapters to Zechariah the prophet, one cannot determine precisely the date when Zechariah presented chaps. 9–14. Possibly these chapters appeared shortly after the preceding prophecies.[74] Kenneth Barker suggests that Zechariah prepared chaps. 9–14 some years later and attempts to explain some of the differences between the two halves of the book.[75] In the final analysis, one cannot know the date for Zechariah's latter prophecies.

## A BRIEF LIST OF IMPORTANT DATES IN THE ANCIENT NEAR EAST AND JUDAH

| Year (BC) | Event |
| --- | --- |
| 587 | Fall of Judah |
| 550 | Cyrus defeats Midians |
| 539 | Cyrus conquerors Babylon |
| 538 | Edict of Cyrus, encouraging exiles to return to the Promised Land and rebuild the temple |
| 530–522 | Reign of Cambyses II, Darius's son, conqueror of Egypt |
| 522–486 | Reign of Darius I ("the Great") |
| 520 | Darius confirms Cyrus's decree to rebuild the temple; Haggai's sermons, Zechariah's eight night visions (1:7–6:8) |
| 518 | Zechariah's response to the delegation from Bethel (chaps. 7–8) |
| 516 | Completion and dedication of the temple |
| 490 | Defeat of Darius I at Marathon by Greeks |
| 486–465 | Xerxes I (Ahasuerus) reigns |
| 480 | Persians defeated at Thermopylae and Salamis by Greeks |
| 332 | Alexander the Great defeats Persians, ending the Persian hegemony and inaugurating the Hellenistic era |

---

[74] Merrill, *Zechariah*, 62.
[75] Barker, "Zechariah," 597.

## 4. Literary Style

### (1) Prose or Poetry

Over the years scholars have disagreed about the genre of Zechariah. A brief examination of the scholarly edition of the Hebrew Bible used a generation ago, *Biblia Hebraica Kittel* (*BHK*), reckons virtually all 14 chapters as prose.[76] In contrast, the current critical edition of the Hebrew Bible, *Biblia Hebraica Stuttgartensia* (*BHS*), treats most of the book as poetry.[77]

One does not have to read long to discover similar differences of opinion regarding many biblical texts, particularly prophetic passages.[78] Few would challenge the prosaic character of Zech 1–8. Chapters 9–14 do not evidence "high style" poetry as found in most of Isaiah or Amos. The final six chapters of Zechariah, however, unmistakably reflect a poetic style due to the quantity and sophistication of figurative language, including: parallelism, metaphors, metonymy, and other figures of speech. Much of the material in Zechariah, then, could be aptly designated "oracular prose."[79]

### (2) Apocalyptic

Apocalyptic derives its name from the Greek term *apocaluptō*, meaning "to disclose, reveal."[80] Apocalyptic literature seeks to reveal God's will for humanity to his own people, but through highly symbolic language it conceals that plan from the ungodly. Since apocalyptic focuses on the future when God will save his people and judge evildoers, the symbolic disclosures allow the chosen people to prepare for the great day of salvation.

Old Testament apocalyptic stands apart from other genres because of several distinctive emphases reflective of apocalyptic literature. Apocalyptic texts typically arose in times of great social unrest and include the following themes: the cosmic struggle between God and the forces of evil, the prominence of angels, a pessimistic view of history that sees humanity's only hope in the Lord's disruption of human history by establishing a new dominion, viewing history in several discrete sections, transcendentalism, and a tremendous amount of symbolism, especially symbolism involving animals and numbers.

---

[76] R. Kittel, ed., *Biblia Hebraica* (Stuttgart: Württembergische Bibelanstalt, 1937).

[77] Specifically, *BHS* considers the following passages in the book of Zechariah to be poetic: 1:3b,5–6,14b–17; 2:9–17; 3:7b–10; 4:6–10; 5:4; 6:12b–13; 7:4–5,8–10; 8:1–14,16b–17,20–22; 9:9–17; 10:1–12; 11:1–3,17; 14:1–16.

[78] For example, see the treatment of Malachi's literary style in G. L. Klein, "An Introduction to Malachi," *Criswell Theological Review* 2 (1987): 27–29.

[79] C. L. Meyers and E. M. Meyers, *Haggai, Zechariah 1–8* (Garden City, NY: Doubleday, 1987), lxiv.

[80] ἀποκάλυπτω. See the recent survey of the perspectives on apocalyptic literature in the Old Testament by T. R. Hobbs, "The Language of Warfare in Zechariah 9–14," in *After the Exile: Essays in Honour of Rex Mason,* ed. J. Barton and D. J. Reimer (Macon, GA: Mercer University Press, 1996), 125–28.

Apocalyptic reflects a wide diversity, however, defying efforts to classify it rigidly. One must also recognize that texts need not possess each of the foregoing elements in order to be apocalyptic.[81]

The following poem, originally published in the French Nazi newspaper *Paris-Soir*, and reprinted with explanation in *The Times* (London), illustrates the troubling social and political circumstances that produce apocalyptic literature as well as the concept of revelation to the chosen and concealment from those who must not know the full truth.[82] Written during the Nazi occupation of Paris, at first glance the poem appears to praise the German regime:

> We adore and admire Chancellor Hitler
> The eternal English land is unworthy of life.
> We curse, we crush the people beyond the sea;
> On earth, the Nazi alone will survive.
> Support, then, the German Führer,
> The youthful sailors will finish the odyssey.
> To them alone belongs a just punishment.
> The palm of the victor awaits the swastika.[83]

*The Times* article praises the clever poet who conceals his true feelings about the occupation and even dupes the Nazis into publishing a scathing denunciation of the Nazi movement. However, knowing how to decipher the poem properly leads one to the correct understanding. The article continues, demonstrating that if one divides each line into two, forming two distinct poems, the following results:

| | |
|---|---|
| We adore and admire | Chancellor Hitler |
| the eternal English land. | is unworthy of life. |
| We curse, we crush | The people beyond the sea |
| on earth the Nazi. | alone will survive. |
| | |
| Support, then, | The German Führer |
| the youthful sailors. | will finish the odyssey. |
| To them alone belongs | A just punishment |
| the palm of the victor. | awaits the swastika. |

To be sure, while Old Testament apocalyptic uses symbolism to reveal/conceal its message, it never requires its readers to rearrange texts in order to discern the true message! This modern example merely illustrates several important features of biblical apocalyptic. Nonetheless, this French poem shows how an author in tumultuous times can convey a message to the initiated with-

---

[81] R. L. Webb, "'Apocalyptic': Observations on a Slippery Term," *JNES* 49 (1990): 123.
[82] *The Times*, April 25, 1941, 3.
[83] Author's translation.

out compromising his true sentiments or warning those who are destined for judgment.

It is unclear how or when apocalyptic literature arose within the Old Testament epoch. One of the most common explanations from the scholarly community suggests that a crisis arose when some prophecy remained unfulfilled, giving rise to a new viewpoint, one that focused less on the imminent ramifications of the divine message and more on the distant future when the prophecies would see their completion.[84] Some conclude that apocalyptic envisions all of the Lord's prophecies for another world, abandoning hope in the present one.

The breadth of scholarly discussion about the origins of apocalyptic far surpasses what this treatment could even overview. Most scholars, however, claim that apocalyptic grew out of classical prophecy.[85] Cross believes that the classical prophets adapted diverse myths, particularly those dealing with creation and the divine warrior, in order to shift attention from the nation's historical disillusionment to a future cosmic kingdom where ancient promises would become reality. Cross sees a sharp break between classical prophecy and apocalyptic.[86] To Cross's conclusions Hanson adds his belief that the characteristic features of apocalyptic occurred late in Israel's history.[87] However, the book of Isaiah demonstrates that classical prophecy and apocalyptic can emerge from the same source and stand together in a common text.

Despite Hanson's claims that apocalyptic literature always reflects particularly late periods, the biblical text contains evidence of apocalyptic elements throughout its history. Some of the finest examples of this phenomenon occur in ancient Hebrew poetry. Besides, one cannot reliably date a text using genre-based criteria, even if a genre becomes frequent in a late era. The typical perspective holds that apocalyptic emerged from a visionary group that opposed the cult during the postexilic period. Oswalt correctly critiques this theory as having no merit due to the lack of evidence.[88] Similarly, von Rad's contention that apocalyptic arose out of wisdom's roots also suffers from an absence of biblical support.[89]

Youngblood injects numerous balanced perspectives on the relationship between prophecy and apocalyptic.[90] One of his most helpful observations

---

[84] E. W. Conrad, "The End of Prophecy and the Appearance of Angels/Messengers in the Book of the Twelve," JSOT 73 (1997): 65–79.

[85] S. L. Cook, *Prophecy and Apocalypticism: The Postexilic Social Setting* (Minneapolis: Fortress, 1995), *passim*.

[86] F. M. Cross, Jr., *Canaanite Myth and Hebrew Epic: Essays in the History of the Religion of Israel* (Cambridge, MA: Harvard University Press, 1973).

[87] P. D. Hanson, *The Dawn of Apocalyptic*.

[88] J. N. Oswalt, "Recent Studies in Old Testament Eschatology and Apocalyptic," *JETS* 24 (1981): 299.

[89] G. von Rad, *Wisdom in Israel*, trans. J. D. Martin, (Nashville: Abingdon, 1973).

[90] R. Youngblood, "A Holistic Typology of Prophecy and Apocalyptic," in *Israel's Apostasy and Restoration,* ed. A. Gileadi (Grand Rapids: Baker, 1988), 213–21.

counters the exaggerated differences postulated between the two genres, noting that significant similarities are often neglected. Moreover, Youngblood observes that the differences between apocalyptic texts in the Old Testament, coupled with important differences in scholarly analyses, make it difficult to stress lists of characteristics of apocalyptic passages. He reduces the *sine qua non* of apocalyptic to two features. First, apocalyptic has a more futuristic or eschatological emphasis than prophetic texts normally do. Second, apocalyptic passages rely heavily on the themes, if not the very words, of the earlier biblical prophets. While Youngblood's dual emphases may prove too simple to accommodate the biblical data, nonetheless he provides a needed balance to many scholarly excesses.

Much of the book of Zechariah mirrors apocalyptic concepts found elsewhere in the Old Testament, although the whole book does not equally reflect apocalyptic interests.[91] The first eight chapters of Zechariah lack most of the characteristic features of classic Old Testament apocalyptic. Reflecting an older perspective on the question, Mitchell goes so far as to deny that Zechariah as a whole should be considered apocalyptic.[92] However, a preponderance of apocalyptic motifs appear in chaps. 9–14. Zechariah describes the Lord in transcendent terms such as "God Almighty." The Lord eliminates all forces of evil on a cosmic scale (14:2, note also Ezek 38–39). The Messiah will reign from "sea to sea" (9:10). Chapter 14 also stresses the restoration of the temple, providing the site where all nations will gather to worship the Lord and celebrate his deliverance. This eschatological perspective in Zechariah does not preclude a concern with ethical life in the present, however. The moral imperative of chap. 8 powerfully demonstrates that Zechariah's concern with the "now" was as great as with the prophetic "then." Angels also figure prominently in Zechariah, especially in the earlier chapters of the book, and Zechariah employs symbolism extensively.

## 5. Structure of Zechariah

The past two hundred years of biblical scholarship has generally neglected literary considerations, viewing texts as heterogeneous while focusing on the historical settings that gave rise to the writings. From the Torah to Zechariah, most scholars have not examined the literary features that illustrate cohesion. While many have ultimately rejected Paul Lamarche's study of Zechariah, his literary analysis of Zech 9–14 has engaged students of the book for almost 50 years.[93] No modern commentary can fail to interact with the ground-breaking study of Lamarche who argued that the latter half of the book manifests a

---

[91] J. J. Collins, "Apocalyptic Themes in Biblical Literature," *Int* 53 (1999): 119.
[92] Mitchell, *Zechariah*, 105.
[93] P. Lamarche, *Zacharie IX–XIV: Structure Littéraire et Messianisme* (Paris: J. Gabalda, 1961).

chiastic arrangement. Subsequent to Lamarche, virtually every scholar has accepted the literary unity of chaps. 9–14, even those who fail to see the chiasm Lamarche observes. Lamarche's understanding of Zech 9–14 is as follows:

A Judgment and salvation of nations surrounding Judah (9:1–8)
  B Arrival of the messianic king (9:9–10)
    C Israel's battle and subsequent victory (9:11–10:1)
      D Idolatry and coming judgment (10:2–3a)
    C' Israel's battle and subsequent victory (10:3b–11:3)
  B' The nation rejects the shepherds (11:4–17)
    C" Israel's battle and subsequent victory (12:1–9)
  B" The Lord's representative pierced; mourning, purification of the people (12:10–13:1)
      D' Idols and false prophets purged from the land (13:2–6)
  B‴ Shepherd struck, testing, purification, return to God (13:7–9)
    C‴ Israel's battle and subsequent victory (14:1–15)
A' Judgment and salvation of all nations (14:16–21)[94]

Baldwin embraces Lamarche's analysis and contends that Zech 1–8 also reflects a chiastic arrangement.[95] She evaluates the night visions as below:

A Vision One (1:7–17)
  B Vision Two (1:18–21)
  B' Vision Three (2:1–13)
    C Vision Four (3:1–10)
    C' Vision Five (4:1–14)
  B" Vision Six (5:1–4)
  B‴ Vision Seven (5:5–11)
A' Vision Eight (6:1–8)[96]

Baldwin sees visions four and five as the theological apex of the night visions. She also notes that the book begins with an appeal for repentance and closes with the profound assertion that all nations will worship the Lord God.

Baldwin observes that this literary device is especially appropriate for Zechariah's message. She observes,

> Chiasmus is a stylistic device particularly well suited to the prophet's theme when he deals with the justice of retribution and the miracle of God's grace. It is capable of expressing exact equivalents or startling contrasts. Used as a pattern for the framework of the book it also welds together the prophet's own day and the end of time. The connecting links are the need of repentance, the certainty of judgment,

---

[94] Ibid., 112–13.
[95] Baldwin, *Haggai, Zechariah, Malachi*, 80–81.
[96] Ibid., 80.

the continuing mercy of God, and the Messianic figure who accomplishes His purposes.[97]

Baldwin acknowledged the uncertainty of several prospective correlations in the proposed chiasm.[98] Moreover, after some years of excess, scholarship has now begun to exercise greater caution before deeming a text chiastic.[99] Boda has given particular attention to the chiastic understanding of Zechariah, ultimately issuing a warning about the dangers of seeing chiasmus throughout the biblical text too freely.[100] Boda represents the cadre of scholars who see literary unity in the book, but fail to accept Lamarche's suggestion.

Lamarche fundamentally altered Zechariah studies for the better when he insisted on viewing the book more holistically. However, several problems with his analysis render the chiastic suggestion tenuous. Obviously, Lamarche's study does not actually represent a "chiasm," which reflects an A-B-B'-A' structure. The other prevailing problem is the somewhat strained thematic connection between various "paired" elements. For instance, Baldwin admits the problem with the B elements in Lamarche's interpretation.[101]

Although not as influential as Lamarche, Meredith Kline's analysis of the structure of Zechariah represents an important contribution to the discussion.[102] Kline understands the entire book as a literary whole from the hand of Zechariah son of Berekiah. Further, in studying all 14 chapters, the scope of Kline's study far exceeds Lamarche's examination of chaps. 9–14 in breadth as well as complexity.

Kline contends that Zechariah represents a diptych, which is a literary piece comprised of two equal parts. Unlike the overwhelming majority of studies that divide the book after chaps. 1–8, Kline argues that 6:9–15, Joshua's crown, functions as the hinge for the two halves of Zechariah. Kline views 6:9–15 as "the coronation investiture of a messianic prototype," highlighting the union between the royal and priestly offices occurring in this passage that typifies Christ.[103]

Kline next identifies 3:1–10, The Cleansing of the High Priest, and 11:1–17, The Judgment of the Shepherds, as the apogee of the two respective literary panels in which these texts appear. Kline observes that both passages contain prominent royal motifs and the main figure in each was a historical figure, un-

---

[97] Ibid., 81.
[98] Ibid., 79.
[99] See C. Blomberg, "The Structure of 2 Corinthians 1–7," *Criswell Theological Review* 4 (1989): 3–20, where Blomberg recommends several objective criteria for determining whether a passage truly manifests chiastic literary structure.
[100] Boda's effort, "Chiasmus in Ubiquity: Symmetrical Mirages in Nehemiah 9," JSOT 71 (1996): 55–70, is a gentle parody of the provocative work by J. W. Welch, *Chiasmus in Antiquity* (Hildesheim: Gerstenberg, 1981).
[101] Baldwin, *Zechariah*, 79.
[102] M. G. Kline, "The Structure of the Book of Zechariah," *JETS* 34 (1991): 179–93.
[103] Ibid., 179, 181–83.

like the other passages in the panels. He agrees with the majority of interpreters in assigning 1:1–6 the role of introduction to the night visions. However, he moves in a different direction in viewing the entirety of chaps. 7–8 as the introduction to chaps. 7–14.[104] Finally, Kline maintains that both 3:1–10 and 11:1–17 divide diptych structures of their own. For instance, 1:1–2:13 balances 4:1–6:8 symmetrically, while 7:1–10:12 and 12:1–14:21 mirror each other as well.[105]

Kline's important study is a welcome addition to the growing body of literature that aims to view Zechariah as a carefully fashioned literary whole. Nevertheless, many who appreciate Kline's holistic approach to the book have failed to see the formal correspondence between 3:1–10 and 11:1–17. Likewise, the complex themes located in Kline's postulated mini-diptychs revolving around 3:1–10 and 11:1–17 disclose such divergent themes that it is difficult to note the full extent of the symmetry that Kline defends.[106] This observation does not undermine the unity of the text, however, any more than claiming that a text does not reflect chiasmus somehow undermines its literary quality or unity.

Several structural studies posit a formal literary relationship between Haggai and Zech 1–8. Pierce even defends the view that Haggai/Zechariah/Malachi formed a literary whole.[107] The more widely adopted perspective views Haggai and Zech 1–8 as a single work produced in anticipation of the dedication of the restored temple. For instance, Meyers and Meyers conclude that Zech 7–8 form a conclusion to the Haggai-Zech 1–8 corpus.[108] They note the similar chronological heading at Hag 1:1 and Zech 7:1, making a frame around the intervening oracular material. A long series of scholars preceded Meyers and Meyers in contending that the same hand produced Haggai and Zech 1–8.[109]

Boda, however, views the relationship between Haggai and Zech 1–8 quite differently. He examines the heralded thematic unity between Haggai and Zech 1–8 that focuses on the rebuilding of the temple, contending that the similarities have suffered exaggeration while significant differences have been ignored. Most importantly, Boda observes that every sermon in Haggai focuses on the rebuilding of the temple. But Zech 1–8 examines a much broader array of topics than does Haggai, including the rebuilding of the city, political

---

[104] Ibid., 184–85.

[105] Ibid., 185–91.

[106] Floyd, *Minor Prophets*, 303; Merrill, *Zechariah*, 82–87.

[107] R. W. Pierce, "Literary Connectors and a Haggai/Zechariah/Malachi Corpus," *JETS* 27 (1984): 277–89.

[108] Meyers and Meyers, *Zechariah 1–8*, 381.

[109] For instance, P. R. Ackroyd, "The Book of Haggai and Zechariah I–VIII," *JSS* 3 (1952): 151–56; W. A. M. Beuken, *Haggai-Sacharja 1–8*, (Assen: Van Gorcum, 1967), 10–20; P. L. Redditt, "Zerubbabel, Joshua, and the Night Visions of Zechariah," *CBQ* 54 (1992): 249–59; R. A. Mason, "The Purpose of the 'Editorial Framework' of the Book of Haggai," *VT* 27 (1977): 413–21; and J. D. Nogalski, *Redactional Processes in the Book of the Twelve* (Berlin: De Gruyter, 1993).

leadership for the people of God, and standards for ethical conduct, among other themes.[110] While it is the case that Zech 1–8 addresses issues raised in Haggai, no convincing reason overturns the ancient understanding that Haggai and Zechariah have always stood as separate works. Consequently, the evidence points toward treating Haggai's sermons as distinct in literary terms from those of Zechariah.

The structure for the book of Zechariah followed in this volume is as follows:

## OUTLINE OF ZECHARIAH

I. Introduction (1:1–6)
II. Eight Night Visions and Oracles (1:7–6:8)
   1. The First Vision: The Man on a Red Horse (1:7–17)
   2. The Second Vision: Four Horns and Four Craftsmen (1:18–21 [Hb 2:1–4])
   3. The Third Vision: The Surveyor (2:1–13 [Hb 2:5–17])
   4. The Fourth Vision: The Cleansing of the High Priest (3:1–10)
   5. The Fifth Vision: The Gold Lampstand and Two Olive Trees (4:1–14)
   6. The Sixth Vision: The Flying Scroll (5:1–4)
   7. The Seventh Vision: The Woman in the Basket (5:5–11)
   8. The Eighth Vision: The Four Chariots (6:1–8)
III. Joshua's Crown (6:9–15)
IV. Questions about Fasting and Future Blessings (7:1–8:23)
   1. A Question about Fasting (7:1–7)
   2. A Call to Repentance (7:8–14)
   3. Future Blessings for Jerusalem (8:1–23)
V. Burdens from the Lord (9:1–14:21)
   1. Judgment and Salvation of Surrounding Nations (9:1–8)
   2. Introduction to the King (9:9–10)
   3. Israel's Battle and Ultimate Victory (9:11–10:1)
   4. Idolatry and Judgment (10:2–3)
   5. Israel's Battle and Victory (10:4–12)
   6. Judgment of the Shepherds (11:1–17)
   7. Israel's Battle and Victory (12:1–9)
   8. The Lord's Servant Pierced; Mourning and Purification (12:10–13:1)
   9. Idolatry and Judgment (13:2–6)
   10. Shepherd Struck; Judgment, Purification, and Return to God (13:7–9)

---

[110] M. J. Boda, "Zechariah: Master Mason or Penitential Prophet?" in *Yahwism after the Exile: Perspectives on Israelite Religion in the Persian Era,* ed. R. Albertz and B. Becking (Assen: Van Gorcum, 2003), 52–54.

11. Israel's Battle and Victory (14:1–15)
12. Judgment and Salvation of All Nations (14:16–21)[111]

## 6. Text

The Hebrew text of Zechariah comes down to us comparatively free of alternate readings, underscoring the reliability of the Masoretic textual tradition.[112] While the relatively pristine state of the Zechariah textual tradition does not mean that the Hebrew translates easily, it does signify that the Hebrew text available to us appears to reflect the earliest form of the text quite closely.[113] Mitchell provides a thorough catalog of textual variants based on alternate readings from ancient versions. Mitchell also enumerates a large number of emendations tantamount to scholarly "guesses" about how a passage might have read originally.[114] One should also consult the *Preliminary and Interim Report on the Hebrew Old Testament Text Project* for a discussion of the major textual variants in Zechariah, including assessments of the origin of the variant and the preferable reading.[115] While the ancient versions are generally excellent witnesses to the earliest form of Zechariah, the textual finds at Qumran also provide meaningful, but limited, evidence of the reliability of the textual tradition of Zechariah, as only fragmentary texts exist.[116]

One of the more notable alternate readings emerges in Zech 2:8 where the Hebrew text reads "his eye" but the versions read "my eye." Theological concerns about the stronger anthropomorphic reading, "my eye," prompted ancient scribes to alter the Hebrew text to "his eye." This well-known scribal alteration, known as the *tiqqune soferim* ("corrections of the scribes") occurs rarely in the Hebrew Bible—11 times according to one rabbinic tradition and 18 times according to another.[117]

---

[111] Ibid., 112–13.

[112] See the helpful discussions in: Baldwin, *Zechariah*, 81–84; Meyers and Meyers, *Zechariah 1–8*, lxviii; as well as Meyers and Meyers, *Zechariah 9–14* (New York: Doubleday, 1993), 50–51. See also A. van der Kooij, "The Septuagint of Zechariah as Witness to an Early Interpretation of the Book," in *The Book of Zechariah and Its Influence,* ed. C. Tuckett (Burlington: Ashgate, 2003), 53–64.

[113] Although he could not avail himself of the Qumran material, the monograph by T. Jansma ("Inquiry into the Hebrew Text and the Ancient Versions of Zechariah ix–xiv." OtSt [1950]: 1–142) contributes a helpful examination of the text critical data for the second section of the book. E. Lipinski ("Recherches sur le livre de Zacharie," *VT* 20 [1970]: 25–55) also discusses text critical issues at some length.

[114] Mitchell, *Zechariah*, 86–97, 222–31.

[115] D. Barthélemy et al., eds., *Preliminary and Interim Report on the Hebrew Old Testament Text Project*, 5 vols. (New York: United Bible Societies, 1979).

[116] D. Barthélemy, *Les Devanciers d'Aquila*, VTSup 10 (1963). Furthermore, several fragments of the Greek translation of Zechariah appeared at Qumran, including: 1:1,3–4,13–14; 2:2,7,16–17; 3:1,4–7; 8:19–21; 9:1–4 (cited by Barthélemy, *Les Devanciers*, 170–78).

[117] See E. Tov, *Textual Criticism of the Hebrew Bible*, 2nd revised ed. (Minneapolis: Fortress, 2001), 65–66.

The ancient versions appear to attest more alternate readings in Zech 9–14 than in chaps. 1–8. Scholars generally attribute these differences to the poetic character of chaps. 9–14, in contrast to the more prosaic character of chaps. 1–8. Thus, the more difficult poetic expressions seemed to challenge the ancient translators as they struggled to render the Hebrew text faithfully. Divergent readings in the versions typically appear to be attempts to simplify the more rigorous Masoretic Text. Consequently, most of these dissimilar readings in the versions probably do not merit consideration as credible variants worthy of supplanting the Masoretic Text. One finds a good illustration of this point in Zech 11:13 where the Hebrew reads "potter," the Septuagint suggests "furnace," the Syriac translates "treasury," and Jerome posits "sculptor."[118]

## 7. Place of Zechariah Canonically

### *(1) Zechariah and Intertextuality*

Few biblical authors approach Zechariah's sophistication, diversity, and quantity of intertextual citations.[119] The prophet drew widely from the biblical corpus available to him, employing manifold texts in varying fashions. Each case of intertextuality requires careful examination in order to determine how Zechariah employed earlier passages, since with rare exceptions, the book of Zechariah transforms earlier biblical genres or messages into distinctively different messages. For example, a blessing or curse from the Torah may become a statement in an oracle, and a legal text often morphs into an eschatological prediction. Zechariah's breadth of intertextual citations has virtually no Old Testament parallel.[120]

Zechariah seems primarily concerned to collect and reapply the messages from the prophets who preceded him in order to show his own audience how these oracles would see their fulfillment.[121] Meyers and Meyers add,

> They [the postexilic prophets] transformed existing authoritative predictive prophecies, without negating their sanctity or validity, into equally valid formulations that could erase the prevailing sense of

---

[118] Noted by Baldwin, *Zechariah*, 82.

[119] M. C. Love, *Evasive Text*. Note also the survey by M. A. Sweeney, "Zechariah's Debate with Isaiah," in *The Changing Face of Form Criticism for the Twenty-First Century*, ed. M. A. Sweeney and E. B. Zvi (Grand Rapids: Eerdmans, 2003), 344–48. See D. L. Petersen ("Zechariah 9–14: Methodological Reflections," in *Bringing out the Treasure: Inner Biblical Allusion in Zechariah 9–14*, ed. M. J. Boda and M. H. Floyd [Sheffield: Sheffield Academic Press, 2003], 210–24) for a discussion of problems of terminology and methodology in the study of Zechariah and intertextuality. See also R. Mason, "Why is Second Zechariah so Full of Quotations?" in *The Book of Zechariah and Its Influence*, ed. C. Tuckett (Burlington: Ashgate, 2003), 21–28.

[120] Meyers and Meyers, *Zechariah 9–14*, 44.

[121] R. North, *Prophecy to Apocalyptic via Zechariah* (Leiden: E. J. Brill, 1972), 51.

hopelessness and powerlessness while simultaneously sustaining traditional community values and beliefs.[122]

Zechariah's intertextuality comprises "quotation," "allusion," and "echo." Schaefer provides helpful definitions of these elusive concepts.

> Quotation occurs when an author reproduces the words or formulation of a literary source which is traceable from his choice of words or of turns of phrase. This involves the deliberate borrowing of significant and sufficient wording and phrasing in a form in which one would not have used them had it not been for a knowledge of their occurrence in this particular form in another source. . . . Allusions are limited to a word, a brief phrase, or an image that constitutes an indirect reference but can sometimes be traced to a source. Allusive reference may be intention, or it may be an 'echo.' The essence of the conscious allusion is the author's intention to recall previous oracles with their context; once the reader recognizes the reference, the horizons for comprehension are expanded. . . . A single word or phrase can be an echo, often unintentional, which results from the use of stock language in common circulation. The author reflects or replicates ideas that can be found in previous literature, but he may be unaware of the background source, and he does not wittingly advert to the original.[123]

The examples below exemplify the more prominent occurrences of intertextuality in Zechariah. These illustrative texts reflect quotation, allusion, and echo.

### EXAMPLES OF INTERTEXTUALITY IN ZECHARIAH[124]

| *Zechariah* | *Other Texts* | *Theme* |
|---|---|---|
| | *Genesis* | |
| 9:9 | 49:10–11 | Arrive on donkey |
| 9:11 | 37:24 | Waterless pit |
| 12:1 | chaps. 1–2 | Creation |
| 13:4 | 25:25 | Hairy cloak |

---

[122] Meyers and Meyers, *Zechariah 9–14*, 45.
[123] K. R. Schaefer, "Zechariah 14: A Study in Allusion," *CBQ* 57 (1995): 68–9.
[124] These examples reflect a collection drawn from these sources: A. Kunz, *Ablehnung des Krieges* (Freiburg: Herder, 1998), 61–74; A. M. Leske, "Context and Meaning of Zechariah 9:9," *CBQ* 62 (2000): 663–78; R. A. Mason, "The Relation of Zech 9–14 to Proto-Zechariah," 227–39; Meyers and Meyers, *Zechariah 9–14*, 40–45; Mitchell, *Zechariah*, 101–2; D. Rudman, "The Warhorse of the Lord," *Jewish Bible Quarterly* 28 (2000): 163–68; Schaefer, "Zechariah 14: A Study in Allusion," 66–91; and this author. Schaefer also lists numerous uncommon Hebrew phrases in Zech 14 that parallel other texts (p. 77).

| | | |
|---|---|---|
| 14:6–7 | 1:3–5 | New creation |
| 14:8 | 2:6,10–14 | Abundant, living waters |
| | ***Exodus*** | |
| 9:1–8 | 34:24 | I will cast out nations before you |
| 9:11 | 24:3ff | Blood of the covenant |
| 10:12; 13:3,9; 14:9 | 3:15; 6:3 | Name of God[125] |
| 12:8 | 13:21; 14:19 | Angel going before |
| 14:14 | 12:31–36 | Wealth of nation(s) plundered |
| 14:20 | 28:36; 39:30 | "HOLY TO THE LORD" |
| | ***Leviticus*** | |
| 13:9 | 26:12 | God's people, Israel's God |
| | ***Numbers*** | |
| 13:1 | 8:7; 19:9–31 | Fountain, cleansing sin |
| 13:9 | 31:23 | Purification by fire |
| | ***Deuteronomy*** | |
| 9:1–8 | 1:7–8; 11:24 | I will cast out nations before you |
| 10:2 | 18:10–11 | Deception of false prophets |
| 10:6 | passim | House of Joseph |
| 10:12; 13:3, 9; 14:9 | 12:5,11 | Name of God |
| 11:9,16 | passim | Curse describing devouring flesh |
| 11:10 | passim | Covenant breaking |
| 12:4 | 28:28 | Smite with madness, panic, blindness |
| 13:2 | 12:2–3 | Banish idols |
| 13:3 | 18:20–22 | Lying in the Lord's name |
| 13:3 | 13:6–10; 21:18–21 | Judgment by parents |
| 13:9 | 26:17–18 | God's people, Israel's God |
| 13:9 | passim | Covenantal relationship with God |
| 14:2 | 13:12–16 | Plunder |
| 14:4 | 5:4 | Theophany on mountain |
| 14:9 | 6:4 | The Lord is one |
| 14:11 | passim | Security of God's people |
| 14:13 | 7:23 | Panic of the Lord |
| 14:16 | 16:13–15; 31:9–13 | Booths |

---

[125] Only a few of the more important examples of this fundamental theological motif are included.

|  |  |  |
|---|---|---|
|  | *Joshua* |  |
| 10:10 | 17:16 | No room |
|  | *2 Samuel* |  |
| 14:9 | 7:13 | The Lord's kingdom extends over the whole earth |
|  | *1 Kings* |  |
| 11:17 | 13:4 | Withered arm |
| 13:4 | 19:13,19 | Hairy cloak |
|  | *2 Kings* |  |
| 9:9 | 19:21 | Daughter of Jerusalem |
| 10:2 | 17:17 | Deception of false prophets |
| 13:4 | 2:8,13,14 | Hairy cloak |
| 14:14 | 7:8 | Wealth of nation(s) plundered |
|  | *Job* |  |
| 10:3 | 39:19–25 | Mighty horse[126] |
|  | *Psalms* |  |
| 9:10 | 72:8 | Reign over all the earth |
| 9:17 | 133:1 | How attractive and beautiful |
| 10:2–3; 11:4 | 23:1; 80:1 | Shepherd motif |
| 10:4 | 118:22 | Cornerstone |
| 10:6 | 3:4; 4:1; 20:2; *passim* | The Lord answers |
| 10:11 | 74:13–17 | Sea of trouble |
| 10:12; 13:3,9; 14:9 | 75:2 | Name of God |
| 11:1 | 24:7 | Open (imperative) doors |
| 12:1 | 18:9; 104:2; *passim* | Creation |
| 12:2 | 75:8 | Cup motif |
| 14:4 | 29:6–8 | Earthquake, mountains move |
| 14:16 | 24:10; 98:6 | The Lord is king |
|  | *Ecclesiastes* |  |
| 10:2–3; 11:4 | 12:11 | Shepherd motif |

---

[126] See Rudman, "Warhorse," 166–68. K. A. Larkin observes an especially strong structural and lexical patterning between Zech 9–14 and Job. See Larkin, *The Eschatology of Second Zechariah: A Study of the Formation of a Mantological Wisdom Anthology* (Kampen: Kok Pharos, 1994), 241–47.

|  |  |  |
|---|---|---|
|  | *Song of Solomon* |  |
| 9:17 | 4:10; 7:1,6 | How attractive and beautiful |
|  | *Isaiah* |  |
| 1:17 | 51:3 | The Lord comforts Zion |
| 7:9–10 | 1:16–17,23 | Judge faithfully |
| 7:11–12 | 6:9–10 | Stubborn hearts |
| 7:13 | 1:15 | Judah called, God would not listen |
| 8:20–22 | 2:2–4 (Mic 4:2–3) | Nations come to the Lord's mountain and city[127] |
| 9:9 | 37:22 | Daughter of Jerusalem |
| 9:9 | 11:4 | Reign with righteousness |
| 9:10 | 43:17 | Cutting off chariots and horses |
| 9:11 | 42:7; 49:9; 61:1 | I will set captives free |
| 9:12 | 61:7 (see 40:2) | Restoration of double blessing |
| 9:13 | 49:2 | Judah and Ephraim are bows and arrows |
| 9:16 | 40:11; 62:3 | Flock of his people shine like jewels |
| 9:16 | 53:6 | People are like sheep |
| 9:17 | 62:2–3 | How attractive and beautiful |
| 10:4 | 22:23 | Peg |
| 10:6 | 41:17; 49:8 | The Lord answers |
| 12:1 | 40:22; 42:5; 43:1; 44:24; 45:12; 51:13,16 | Creation |
| 12:2 | 51:17,22 | Cup motif |
| 14:1–2 | 13:9,15–16 | Day of judgment coming |
| 14:2–3 | 30:32 | The Lord battles nations |
| 14:2 | 13:15–16 | Homes plundered, women ravished |
| 14:2 | 4:2–3 | Survivors in Jerusalem |
| 14:4–5 | 13:13–14 | Earthquake, upheaval, and flight of people |
| 14:4 | 3:13 | The Lord stands in judgment |
| 14:5 | 6:4 | Earthquake, mountains move |
| 14:6–7 | 2:5 | Light of the Lord |
| 14:8 | 2:3; 30:25 | Blessing flows from Zion |
| 14:10–21 | 2:2–22 | The Lord's house raised above mountains |
| 14:13 | 22:5 | Panic of the Lord |

---

[127] D. Rudman, "Zechariah 8:20–22 & Isaiah 2:2–4/Micah 4:2–3: A Study in Intertextuality," *Biblische Notizen* 107/108 (2001): 50–54.

| | | |
|---|---|---|
| 14:16–17 | 30:29 | Going up to worship the Lord on the mountain |
| 14:20 | chap. 4 | Holiness of restored Jerusalem |
| | **Jeremiah**[128] | |
| 1:4 | 25:5 | Return from evil ways |
| 1:12 | 25:11 | Seventy years |
| 8:14 | 4:28 | I determined to bring disaster on you |
| 9:5–6 | 25:20 | Wealth and sinfulness of Philistine cities |
| 9:9 | 23:5 | Reign with righteousness |
| 9:11 | 38:6 | Waterless pit |
| 10:2 | 14:14; 27:8–9 | Deception of false prophets |
| 10:2–3; 11:4; 13:7 | 17:16; 23:2; 31:10 | Shepherd motif [129] |
| 10:6 | 33:3 | The Lord answers |
| 10:7–8 | 23:3 | Israel multiplies |
| 10:12; 13:3, 9; 14:9 | 33:2 | Name of God |
| 11:3 | 25:36 | Wail of shepherds |
| 11:9 | 15:2 | Let the dying die |
| 12:1 | 10:12; 51:15 | Creation |
| 12:2 | 25:15–31; 49:12 | Cup motif |
| 12:10 | 6:26 | Mourning for only child |
| 13:9 | 7:23; 31:33 | God's people, Israel's God |
| 14:2 | 4:5–8; 25:1–21 | Nations against Jerusalem |
| 14:8 | 8:13 | Abundant, living waters |
| | **Lamentations** | |
| 1:6 | 2:17 | The Lord does as he purposes |
| 9:9 | 2:15 | Daughter of Jerusalem |
| 12:2 | 4:21 | Cup motif |
| | **Ezekiel**[130] | |
| 8:8 | 11:20; 36:28; 37:23 | They are my people; I am their God |
| 8:12 | 34:27 | The earth will yield its produce |
| 9:2–3 | chaps. 26–27 | Wealth and sinfulness of Philistine cities |

---

[128] Boda devotes significant attention to the relationship between Zechariah and Jeremiah ("Zechariah: Master Mason," 57–61).

[129] See Rudman, "Warhorse," 165–66.

[130] For a helpful discussion of Zechariah's use of Ezekiel's prophecy, see C. MacKay, "Zechariah in Relation to Ezekiel 40–48," *Evangelical Quarterly* 40 (1968): 197–210.

| | | |
|---|---|---|
| 9:4; 11:1 | 23:25 | Consumed by fire |
| 10:2–3; 11:4; 12:6; 13:7 | 34:8–9,23; 37:24 | Shepherd motif[131] |
| 10:9 | 5:10,12 | Israel scattered |
| 11:7 | 37:15–23 | Two staffs[132] |
| 13:2 | 14:1–8 | Banish idols |
| 13:3 | 14:9–10 | Lying in the Lord's name |
| 13:8 | 5:12 | Punishment by thirds |
| 13:9 | 37:23 | God's people, Israel's God |
| 14:1 | 38:12–13 | Spoil |
| 14:5 | 38:19–23 | Earthquake, mountains move |
| 14:8 | 17:5–8; 31:5,7; 47:1–12 | Abundant, living waters |
| 14:13 | 38:21 | Enemies kill one another |
| | *Hosea* | |
| 9:7 | 2:17 | Removal of Baals and other evidences of idolatry |
| 9:8; 10:6 | 2:20 | Safe dwelling of the people |
| 9:9–13 | 1:11 | Coming of eschatological Davidic king |
| 9:10 | 1:7; 2:18 | The Lord's destruction of armies |
| 9:10 | 1:7 | Deliverance from the Lord despite human action |
| 9:12 | 2:7 | Return of the people to the Lord |
| 9:15 | 2:21–23 | The Lord provides deliverance and abundance |
| 9:17 | 2:22 | The Lord gives grain and grape |
| 9:17 | 1:11 | Agricultural abundance makes Israel thrive |
| 10:6 | 2:21; 14:8 | The Lord answers |
| 10:6 | 9:6 | God's compassion or non-compassion on his people |
| 10:7 | 2:14 | Heart is seat of devotion to the Lord |
| 10:8 | 1:11 | Eschatological gathering of God's people |
| 10:9 | 2:23 | Israel scattered |

---

[131] Rudman, "Warhorse," 165–67.

[132] See the discussion in R. A. Mason, "Some Examples of Inner Biblical Exegesis in Zech. IX–XIV," in *Studia Evangelica, Vol. VII*, ed. E. A. Livingstone (Berlin: Akademie, 1982). See also M. H. Floyd, "Deutero-Zechariah and Types of Intertextuality," in *Bringing out the Treasure: Inner Biblical Allusion in Zechariah 9–14*, ed. M. J. Boda and M. H. Floyd (Sheffield: Sheffield Academic Press, 2003), 225–44.

| | | |
|---|---|---|
| 10:9 | 2:23 | The Lord sows Israel in the land |
| 10:10 | 2:15 | The exodus, a surety of future deliverance |
| 13:9 | 1:9; 2:20–23 | God's people, Israel's God[133] |
| | ***Joel*** | |
| 14:1 | 1:15; 2:1 | Day of the Lord coming |
| 14:2,12–17 | 4:11–16 | Nations gathered at Jerusalem |
| 14:4–7 | 2:10; 3:3–4; 4:15–16 | Cosmic reversals |
| 14:8 | 2:20; 3:18 | Abundant, living waters |
| 14:11,20–21 | 3:17,20–21 | Holiness of Jerusalem |
| 14:14 | 3:11–12 | Nations gathered |
| 14:19 | 3:19 | Desolation of Egypt |
| | ***Amos*** | |
| 3:2 | 4:11 | A burning stick snatched from fire |
| 9:4; 11:1; 12:6 | 1:4,7,10 | Consumed by fire |
| 9:5–6 | 1:7–8 | Wealth and sinfulness of Philistine cities |
| 10:12; 13:3,9; 14:9 | 5:8; 9:6 | Name of God |
| 12:10 | 8:10 | Mourning for only child |
| 13:5 | 7:14 | Denying being prophet |
| 14:5 | 1:1 | Earthquake, mountains move |
| | ***Micah*** | |
| 3:10 | 4:4 | Under a vine and a fig tree |
| 8:20–22 | 4:2–3 | Nations come to the Lord's mountain and city[134] |
| 9:9 | 4:8 | Daughter of Jerusalem |
| 10:2–3; 11:4 | 5:4 | Shepherd motif |
| 10:6 | 3:4 | The Lord answers |
| 13:4 | 3:5–8 | Shame of prophetic vision |
| | ***Zephaniah*** | |
| 2:14 | 3:14 | Coming of a king |
| 9:4; 11:1; 12:6 | 1:18; 3:8 | Consumed by fire |

---

[133] Ibid., 73–74.
[134] Rudman, "A Study in Intertextuality," 50–54.

| | | |
|---|---|---|
| 9:5–6 | 2:4 | Wealth and sinfulness of Philistine cities |
| 9:9 | 3:14 | Daughter of Jerusalem |
| 14:2 | 1:2–6,13 | The Lord's power directed toward Jerusalem |
| 14:21 | 1:11 | Merchants eliminated |

*(2) Relationship to Haggai*

*Literary Relationship.* The historical relationship of Zechariah's prophetic labors to those of Haggai is irrefutable.[135] Their respective prophetic activities overlapped, and they focused on similar issues. Beyond the parallels determined by ministering in the same historical setting, Meyers and Meyers defend the view that a common editor compiled the composite work they call "Haggai-Zechariah 1–8" between 520 and 515 BC.[136] They argue their position on several grounds. First, both prophets had similar themes and concerns. Second, Zech 8:9–12 seems especially aware of Haggai's teachings. Third, Meyers and Meyers maintain that the similarity of chronological headings in both books has an "interlocking" effect between the two books.[137] While Meyers and Meyers's observations concerning historical and theological correspondences between Haggai and Zechariah are correct, the evidence fails to demonstrate a literary unity forged by an unknown editor. Meyers and Meyers suggest the possibility that Zechariah himself served as the editor. It would be appropriate to conclude that the two canonical books of Haggai and Zechariah represent separate literary compositions and that the resemblance between the two prophetic ministries reflects their shared era and purpose.

*Theological Comparisons.* Of the many similarities shared by Haggai and Zechariah, one of the most important is the prophets' role in standing in the gap between an important past and an even more significant national future.[138] In the meantime, both lived in a day of small things, a time when the country, the city of Jerusalem, and even the temple lay in ruins.

God's attitude toward Israel reflects another major similarity between the two postexilic prophets and contrasts with the previous prophets. In the past, the Lord's ominous threats of judgment for Judah's sin hung heavily over the nation. All this changed with a resounding message of hope for a glorious

---

[135] For one of the most extensive surveys of literature on the subject, see Boda, "Zechariah: Master Mason," 51–54.

[136] Meyers and Meyers, *Zechariah 1–8*, lxix–lxx, 90.

[137] Meyers and Meyers suggest that the absence of the day of the month in Zech 1:1, the sole exception to the pattern of date formulas throughout the books of Haggai and Zechariah, unites Zechariah to the end of Haggai (*Zechariah 1–8*, 90). See their comment on 1:1.

[138] See the old but still helpful discussion by Fleming James, "Thoughts on Haggai and Zechariah," *JBL* 53 (1934): 229–35.

future after the exile. Nowhere is this hope more powerfully expressed than in Zech 1:16 where God proclaims, "I will return to Jerusalem with mercy."

Zechariah emphasized the sin of the people more than his contemporary Haggai. Granted, Haggai admonished his people about their faulty priorities in neglecting the temple, stating, "Is it a time for you yourselves to be living in your paneled houses, while this house remains a ruin?" (Hag 1:4). Likewise, Haggai led the people to acknowledge their uncleanness, which in turn polluted the whole land (Hag 2:11–14). Nonetheless, the hortatory theme, "be strong" (Hag 2:4), reflects the upbeat tone of Haggai's preaching.

Zechariah, however, began his prophecies with a somber warning that sin had been Judah's undoing, and it could be again (1:6). While Haggai focused on rebuilding the temple, Zechariah repeatedly stressed sin and its deleterious effects on the nation. Examples abound, such as the vision of Joshua clothed in filthy garments (chap. 3), the flying scroll inscribed with a curse (chap. 5), and the woman of wickedness (chap. 5). Thus, Zechariah shared Haggai's zeal to rebuild the temple, but Zechariah stressed the rebuilding of the people spiritually with even greater ardor.

James makes observations that speak to us still:

> Haggai and Zechariah were not towering figures in Israel's history. Compared with men like Amos or Isaiah they seem small indeed. So was every one else in their time. It was a day of small personalities, as well as of small things. But they had a greatness of their own. It lay in their faith and their practicality—their power to look beyond the insignificance of the present to a splendid future, and to take the first step towards it.[139]

James concludes that Zechariah assumed the same responsibilities that spiritual leaders to this day must shoulder, simultaneously calling the people of God both to repent and to build for a glorious future.

### (3) Relation to Malachi

Numerous suggestions have emerged regarding the relationship of Zechariah to Malachi. Eissfeldt, for one, thought it plausible that Malachi might well have been attached to Zechariah.[140] LaSor, Hubbard, and Bush offer a similar reconstruction of the book's history, arguing that "Malachi," which means "my messenger," was a title, not a proper name.[141] The primary underpinning of this argument is the repetition of the word *maśśāʾ* ("oracle") that begins pericopes in Zech 9:1; 12:1; and Mal 1:1.[142]

---

[139] James, "Zechariah," 235.

[140] Eissfeldt, *Introduction*, 440. More recently, P. Redditt promoted the same thesis in his "Zechariah 9–14, Malachi, and the Redaction of the Book of the Twelve," in *Forming Prophetic Literature*, ed. J. W. Watts and P. R. House (Sheffield: JSOT Press, 1996).

[141] LaSor, Hubbard, and Bush, *Survey*, 402, 408.

[142] מַשָּׂא. See *HALOT*, 639–40.

Childs does not dispute the observation about *maśśāʾ*, but he does challenge its significance. Childs continues by criticizing the effect that linking Malachi to Zechariah has on the canonical text of Zechariah, maintaining that this view both misleads and underestimates the similarities between the two sections of Zechariah.[143]

Harrison mentions another objection to the view that Malachi was once appended to "Deutero-Zechariah." He notes that other prophets such as Isaiah employed the term *maśśāʾ* analogously to the use in Zechariah and Malachi without even a remote possibility that the authorship of the Isaianic passages could be challenged.[144]

*(4) Zechariah within the Old Testament at Large*

*Relationship to Leviticus.* The night visions reveal strong affinities to themes associated with the Day of Atonement in Leviticus 16.[145] Zechariah's fourth vision, the Cleansing of the High Priest (3:1–10), describes the importance of the high priest having clean priestly vestments in order to serve the Lord. In this vision Joshua wears filthy priestly garments that God must change so that he could approach the Lord in his priestly role. These filthy garments symbolize the uncleanness of the priest.

The fourth vision mirrors Lev 16:6,11 where the priest had to make atonement for his own sin in order to serve the Lord in the Most Holy Place. The Flying Scroll (5:1–4) contains a curse on the people for their covenantal transgressions and focuses on the nation's collective iniquity. Likewise, the understanding that all of the people bear guilt for sinning against God functions as the underlying rationale for the Day of Atonement rituals, most notably the sacrifice for the people's sin (Lev 16:15).

Perhaps the most impressive parallels exist between the Azazel or "scapegoat" ritual (Lev 16:8,10,20–22,26) and the Woman in the Basket (5:5–11). In the well known "scapegoat" ritual, the priest laid hands on the goat, confessing the sins of the people and figuratively "placing them" on the goat.[146] After this ceremony, the priest expelled the goat from the camp with the people's sins upon the animal. The "woman" in the basket symbolizes the

---

[143] Childs, *Introduction*, 483.

[144] Harrison, *Introduction*, 954.

[145] S. Klouda provided helpful discussions about literary connections between Lev 16 and the night visions.

[146] For an intriguing glimpse into the specifics of the "scapegoat" ritual itself, see the Mishnaic discussions about how the priest should pray over the *azazel* and then expel him from the camp. Of the numerous discussions, see especially tractate *Yoma* 6. The rabbis reflected particular concern that the animal that bore the people's sin might come back home into the camp, returning their guilt with him. Since Lev 16 makes no provision for killing the scapegoat, the rabbis suggest taking the scapegoat to a precipice over a ravine and frightening the animal so that it would jump on its own accord to a certain death.

nation's sin, much like the "scapegoat" took the national sin with him into the wilderness.

*Relationship to Daniel.* Beyond Zechariah's obvious relationship to Haggai and Malachi, Zechariah shows strong affinities to Daniel. Childs writes: "Whereas Daniel portrays the period of Israel's 'indignation' before the coming of the new age from the perspective of the nations, and only deals with Israel's sufferings in conjunction with the agony of the end time, the reverse emphasis is found in Zechariah."[147] Apocalyptic language and interests also link Daniel and Zechariah. Further, Daniel and Zechariah witness powerfully to the hope Israel has for her God-ordained future.

*Relationship to Hosea (and other Minor Prophets).* Zechariah evidences various thematic similarities to those found in the Minor Prophets, particularly Hosea. Even noteworthy linguistic parallels exist.[148] Kunz focuses significant attention on the many parallel themes in both Hosea and Zechariah, listed above. These theological motifs address shared concerns of each prophet. The priority of a right relationship between the Lord and his people enjoys a place of great prominence (Hos 2:14; Zech 10:7). The concomitant rejection of every form of idolatry links both books (Hos 2:17; Zech 9:7). Further shared themes include: the Lord as the giver of every blessing, including agricultural abundance (Hos 2:22; Zech 9:17); deliverance (Hos 2:21–23; Zech 9:15); and safety while dwelling in the land (Hos 2:20; Zech 9:8; 10:6). Both prophets also stress the coming of a Messianic, Davidic king (Hos 1:11; Zech 9:9–13) who will usher in a great eschatological kingdom (Hos 1:11; Zech 10:8).

*(5) Influence on the New Testament*

One of the great ironies concerning the book of Zechariah is its relative obscurity to the modern church contrasted with its profound significance to the early church. Unfortunately, students of the Bible rarely study Zechariah today. However, strong reasons exist for suggesting that the book ascended to a place of paramount importance to the writers of the New Testament and to the early church at large.

The book of Zechariah exerted a profound influence over the New Testament, particularly in the realm of Messianic passages—a point long noted by New Testament scholars.[149] Several important themes from the book figure

---

[147] Childs, *Introduction*, 485.

[148] Kunz, *Ablehnung des Krieges*, 62, 73–74.

[149] A survey of many of the most important New Testament works includes: F. F. Bruce, "The Book of Zechariah and the Passion Narrative," *BJRL* 43 (1961): 336–53; Bruce, *New Testament Development of Old Testament Themes* (Grand Rapids: Eerdmans, 1968); I. M. Duguid, "Messianic Themes in Zechariah 9–14," in *The Lord's Anointed: Interpretation of Old Testament Messianic Texts,* ed. P. E. Satterthwaite, R. S. Hess, and G. J. Wenham (Grand Rapids: Baker, 1995), 265–80; C. A. Evans, "Jesus and Zechariah's Messianic Hope," in *Authenticating the Activities of Jesus*, ed. B. Chilton and C. A. Evans (Leiden: E. J. Brill, 1999), 373–88; R. T. France, *Jesus and the Old Testament: His Application of Old Testament Passages to Himself* (London: Tyndale, 1971); D. J.

prominently in the New Testament. One of the most important of these is the shepherd-king. From Zech 9:9 the King who rode into Jerusalem on a "donkey" reemerges in Matt 21:5 and John 12:15.[150] C. H. Dodd even suggests that Zechariah provided the Gospel writers with material of equal importance to the very *testimonia* of Christ's ministry.[151] Dodd isolates New Testament citations from Zechariah as follows:

| | |
|---|---|
| Zech 9:9 | Matt 21:5; John 12:15 |
| Zech 11:13 | Matt 27:9 |
| Zech 12:3 | Luke 21:24 |
| Zech 12:10 | John 19:37; Rev 1:7 |
| Zech 13:7 | Mark 14:27 |
| Zech 14:5 | 1 Thess 3:13 |
| Zech 14:8 | John 7:38 |
| Zech 14:21 | John 2:16[152] |

A new study by Ham outlines the important role the book of Zechariah played in the Gospel of Matthew.[153] Matthew relied quite heavily on Zechariah, alluding to the prophet at least eight times. Only Isaiah exerted a greater influence on the Gospel of Matthew than Zechariah. Two of the formula citations in Matthew (21:5; 27:9–10) owe their source to Zechariah. Another one of Matthew's explicit quotations comes from Zechariah as well (26:31).

Evans outlines numerous additional examples of Zechariah's influence on the Gospels.[154] He outlines the following illustrations:

| *Zechariah* | *Gospel* | *Content* |
|---|---|---|
| 11:11; 13:7 | Luke 12:32 | "Sheep that have no shepherd" |
| 14:4 | Matt 17:20 | Faith that can move mountains |
| 11:6 | Mark 9:31 | Jesus' anticipation of his arrest and martyrdom |
| 14:5 | Matt 25:31 | Coming of the Son of Man with angels |

---

Moo, *The Old Testament in the Gospel Passion Narratives* (Sheffield: Almond, 1983); P. Foster, "The Use of Zechariah in Matthew's Gospel," in *The Book of Zechariah and Its Influence,* ed. C. Tuckett (Burlington: Ashgate, 2003), 65–85.

[150] For a full discussion of the "shepherd-king" motif in the New Testament, see chap 8, "The Shepherd King" in Bruce, *New Testament Development,* 100–14.

[151] C. H. Dodd, *According to the Scriptures* (Digswell Place: James Nisbet, 1952), 64–65.

[152] Ibid., 64–67.

[153] See C. A. Ham, *The Coming King and the Rejected Shepherd: Matthew's Reading of Zechariah's Messianic Hope* (Sheffield: Sheffield Phoenix, 2005), which is a revision of Ham's dissertation, "Zechariah in Matthew's Gospel: Jesus as Coming King and Rejected Shepherd" (Ph.D. dissertation, Southwestern Baptist Theological Seminary, 2003).

[154] C. A. Evans, " 'The Two Sons of Oil': Early Evidence of Messianic Interpretation of Zechariah 4:14 in 4Q254 4 2," in *The Provo International Conference on the Dead Sea Scrolls,* ed. D. Perry and E. Ulrich (Leiden: E. J. Brill, 1999), 574–75.

Outside of the Gospels, the book of Zechariah exercised a significant influence on the book of Revelation.[155] Rogers identifies the following passages and themes from Zechariah that Revelation employed:[156]

| *Zechariah* | *Revelation* | *Content* |
| --- | --- | --- |
| 1:16; 2:5–9 | 11:1–2 | Measuring Jerusalem |
| Chaps. 1, 6 | Chaps. 6, 19 | Horses |
| 1:7–14; 6:1–8 | 6:1–8 | Four horsemen |
| 2:10–17 | 7:3–8:1 | Gathering nations |
| Chap. 3 | 3:4–5; 4:4; 6:11; 7:9,13–14; 14:14; 16:15; 19:13–15; 22:14 | Garments of the righteous |
| Chap. 4 | Chap. 11 | Lamp or Menorah |
| Chap. 4 | 11:3–4 | Two witnesses |
| Chap. 6 | 2:10; 3:11; 4:4; 6:2; 14:14; 19:12 | Crown |
| 12:10,12 (Dan 7:13) | 1:7 | Son of Man, pierced Shepherd |
| 14:4 | 11:13,15; 16:19 | Earthquake in Jerusalem |
| 14:6–22 | 21:23–22:5 | New Jerusalem |

## 8. Theology of Zechariah

One of the abiding problems of modern biblical scholarship is its disconnectedness from the theological implications of the text, including the value of the Bible for the church. For a book as difficult as Zechariah, this problem can easily become acute, leading to the necessity of treating particularly complex

---

[155] See R. R. Rogers's helpful treatment of the topic in "An Exegetical Analysis of John's Use of Zechariah in the Book of Revelation: The Impact and Transformation of Zechariah's Text and Themes in the Apocalypse" (Ph.D. diss., Southwestern Baptist Theological Seminary, 2002). See also D. Mathewson, *A New Heaven and a New Earth: The Meaning and Function of the Old Testament in Revelation 21.1–22.5* (Sheffield: Sheffield Academic Press, 2003), and A. Farrer, *A Rebirth of Images: The Making of St. John's Apocalypse* (Boston: Beacon, 1949).

[156] "John's Use of Zechariah." See also J. Day, "The Origin of Armageddon: Revelation 16:16 as an Interpretation of Zechariah 12:11," in *Crossing the Boundaries: Essays in Biblical Interpretation in Honour of Michael D. Goulder*, ed. S. E. Porter, P. Joyce, and D. E. Orton (Leiden: E. J. Brill, 1994 ), 315–26. Day argues that the term "Armageddon" in Revelation derives from Zech 12.

issues thoroughly.[157] The book of Zechariah deserves and demands a rigorous consideration of its theological significance.

For many of Zechariah's passages, the interpreter must struggle with the question of how and when the prophecies in the book will be fulfilled. For instance, it is difficult to determine whether God's word in chap. 8 has found its complete historical fulfillment. Even Cohen, the Jewish commentator, tacitly acknowledges that only a partial fulfillment occurs in the Maccabean period.[158] One cannot conclude that these oracles find their culmination in the restoration era, although the divine messages do provide hope for the postexilic community by reassuring them that the Lord has guaranteed their success and safety.

Regarding the fulfillment of this prophecy, the interpreter has three options. First, the oracles may refer only to the restoration era using hyperbolic language. According to this viewpoint, one cannot read the prophecies "closely" for the prophet never intended for them to be accepted point by point. However, this method should be rejected since it takes interpretative liberties that the text itself does not permit.

Second, the modern interpreter may treat the oracles in Zechariah as though they had a contemporary significance for Zechariah's day, as well as a future spiritual significance. According to this particular understanding, the ultimate fulfillment will occur in God's spiritual kingdom. Furthermore, this perspective limits the coming kingdom to a spiritual realm, precluding any physical character in the kingdom and reassigning every divine assurance that was extended to Israel in the Old Testament to the Church. This view often suggests that the Church functions as the "replacement" of Israel.

Third, another attempt to understand the fulfillment of Zechariah's prophecies suggests that the prophecies speak meaningfully, but incompletely, to the restoration period. Thus, Zechariah's oracles spoke directly to the spiritual needs of his audience, but the historical epoch of the prophet's day did not see the mature fruition of what God had decreed. The account of the Good Shepherd in chap. 11 serves as an example. While Zechariah personally embodied the symbolic action of shepherding the flock, receiving the people's scorn as thanks for his labors, and was paid the patronizing sum of thirty pieces of silver for his work, the depth of the passage saw its final scope fulfilled in the life of Jesus the Good Shepherd.

This final interpretative understanding concludes that the ultimate fulfillment of the Lord's promises in the book of Zechariah will occur in God's eschatological kingdom, a kingdom that will reflect both physical and spiritual dimensions. Thus, this interpretative understanding contends that the promises

---

[157] See the treatment of the problem in A. Wolters, "Confessional Criticism and the Night Visions of Zechariah," in *Renewing Biblical Criticism*, ed. C. Bartholomew, C. Greene, and K. Möller (Grand Rapids: Zondervan, 2000), 90–117.

[158] A. Cohen, *The Twelve Prophets* (New York: Soncino, 1948), 298.

of God to Zechariah far exceed in scope any historical "fulfillment" during Zechariah's era.

The book of Zechariah divides into three distinct movements, each with its own literary distinctives and theological contributions. Chapters 1–6 introduce the night visions, a series of eight visions with theological messages unique to each. An overview of the theological emphasis of each night vision is as follows:

| Vision | Image | Theological Message |
| --- | --- | --- |
| 1:7–17 | Man on a Red Horse | The Lord's Dominion over Israel's Rebuilding |
| 1:18–21 | Four Horns and Four Craftsmen | The Lord's Judgment on the Nations Persecuting Israel |
| 2:1–13 | Surveyor | The Lord's Bright Future for Jerusalem |
| 3:1–10 | Cleansing of the High Priest | The Lord Requires Holy Worship |
| 4:1–14 | Gold Lampstand and Two Olive Trees | The Lord's Provision Safeguards Israel's Future |
| 5:1–4 | Flying Scroll | The Lord Judges Israel for Breaking the Covenant |
| 5:5–11 | Woman in the Basket | The Lord Removes Sin from Israel's Midst |
| 6:1–8 | Four Chariots | The Lord's Sovereignty over All Creation |

Following these visions the discussion about Joshua's crown stresses the certainty of the high priest's leadership role in overseeing restored temple worship (6:9–15). Finally, Zech 9–14 stresses various eschatological themes such as the Lord's judgment of the nations, the Messiah's role in administering God's kingdom of peace and righteousness, the worship of the Lord by the nations that had formerly been God's enemies, purification from sin, and the central position that God's people Israel would enjoy in the kingdom. Since these theological messages usually occur in some measure in chap. 1–8 as well, the summary of Zechariah's theological message below encompasses the whole book.

### *(1) Israel/Jerusalem*

The topics of "Israel" and "Jerusalem" represent two of the most prevalent theological emphases in the book of Zechariah. Although the prophet speaks of "Israel," "Judah," and "Jerusalem" or "Zion" singly, this does not mean that one should always differentiate these terms sharply. For instance, Zechariah often uses "Israel" and "Judah" virtually interchangeably (8:13; 10:6). Moreover, the synonymous expressions "Jerusalem" and "Zion" frequently function as a metonymy, standing for the nation as a whole (1:14–17; 2:1–10). Alternatively, "Jerusalem" or "Zion" sometimes speaks of the city proper that served as the seat of worship of the Lord (14:16–21). Because of the prophet's commingling of the terms "Israel" and "Judah" with "Jerusalem" and "Zion," the theological significance of each of these terms should be discussed together.

With great frequency and force Zechariah declared that the Lord will remain true to his promises to his people. The earlier biblical assurances include both judgment for breaking the covenant and unimaginable blessing for obedience. Zechariah's treatment of these two themes is no different. The book contains numerous expressions of judgment on God's own people (1:2–6; 5:1–4; 10:11; 12:2), balanced with descriptions of great deliverance and blessing (2:8). The prophet rooted promises of weal and woe for Jerusalem and the nation at large in the description of covenantal blessings and curses outlined in Deut 28.

To begin, any theological discussion of divine judgment in the Old Testament must not fail to stress God's profound love for his people. For example, Zechariah described the Lord's relationship with Jerusalem in tender relational terms. In 1:14 he cites God saying, "I am very jealous for Jerusalem and Zion" (see 8:2). The result of God's covenant with Jerusalem (3:2), coupled with the obedience of her inhabitants, would be the dramatic restoration of the nation. For example, Zech 2:1–5 describes the Lord's personal role in protecting the city. All of chap. 8 overviews the eschatological changes Zion will see. These transformations include dramatic reversals from Jerusalem's conditions such as the Lord's dwelling again in the midst of Zion (8:3), safety for the young inhabitants and longevity for the aged (8:4–5), returning exiles from throughout the diaspora (8:7–8; see 10:6–12), prosperity (8:10–12), and serving as a conduit for God's blessings to all peoples (8:13,20–23; see 14:16–23).

The Lord promises that Zion will be called "the City of Truth" when the eschatological kingdom arrives (8:3). The Hebrew term for "truth" (*'emet*) actually signifies "faithfulness" to the covenant.[159] When the Lord comes to dwell within his holy city, the people will be transformed spiritually as promised in the new covenant (Jer 31:31–34) in just as dramatic a fashion as their physical circumstances. This faithfulness will manifest itself in the people's wholehearted compliance with divine law. Accordingly, interpersonal relationships will become unlike anything ever known since before the fall. Furthermore, several prophets taught that the last days would see the nations of the world streaming to Zion to the Lord's temple to worship God righteously (Isa 2:1–4; Mic 4:1–3). The faithful worship of God will transform the people's sinful culture into a society that demonstrates faithfulness to every member. The Lord's love for justice and righteousness manifests itself in his admonition to the

---

[159] אֱמֶת. *HALOT*, 68–69.

people to speak truthfully, to render justice to all in their society, and to avoid evil-doing against their neighbors in the interim while they await the onset of the glorious kingdom (8:16–17). Beyond the priority given to justice in Zech 8, chap. 7 expresses similar themes. The Lord Almighty declares, "Administer true justice; show mercy and compassion to one another. Do not oppress the widow or the fatherless, the alien or the poor. In your hearts do not think evil of one another" (7:9–10).

For the Christian interpreter, studying the references to "Israel" in the book of Zechariah in light of the broader use of the ethnic designation in both Testaments raises important hermeneutical and theological questions about the significance of the biblical prophecies regarding the term. In doing so, one must remain careful not to confuse the biblical entity of "Israel" in the Old Testament with either the modern day state of Israel or with any form of Judaism.

Blaising offers an excellent historical, hermeneutical, and theological survey of the role of Israel in God's eschatological kingdom.[160] Over the centuries, two predominant views regarding this issue have emerged. McComiskey, for example, epitomizes the first approach, which asserts a future hope for Israel. However, he redefines what is meant by "Israel" when he maintains that all of the Old Testament promises of God, including those found in Zechariah, would be fulfilled by the Church, a view known as "supersessionism."[161] According to this view, Israel as a national entity no longer holds a place in the kingdom of God. This perspective has enjoyed widespread adoption throughout the history of interpretation in the church, at least since the second century AD.

However, despite the prevalence of supersessionism, it remains preferable to view biblical references to "Israel" as applying to national Israel, not the Church.[162] According to this perspective, the Church and Israel both participate in God's eschatological promises, but neither will disappear in the end times. This interpretation rejects the figurative interpretation of Israel that applies biblical prophecies regarding Israel in the Old Testament to the Church. But this view of Israel does not embrace a two-covenant approach, which claims that national Israel enjoys a relationship with the Lord outside of Christ. Israel as a national entity, like the Church, will be united to God the Father through the work of Christ.

There are several reasons for embracing the national Israel interpretation. The importance of national Israel to the teachings of both Jesus and Paul serves as one important rationale for retaining a distinction between Israel and the Church. Moreover, the absence of compelling literary, theological, or historical reasons for treating "Israel" as a metaphor argues for hermeneutical

---

[160] C. A. Blaising, "The Future of Israel As A Theological Question," *JETS* 44 (2001): 435–50.

[161] T. E. McComiskey, "Zechariah," in *The Minor Prophets, Vol. 3*, ed. T. E. McComiskey (Grand Rapids: Baker, 1992), 1209.

[162] See H. K. LaRondelle, *The Israel of God in Prophecy: Principles of Prophetic Interpretation* (Berrien Springs, MI: Andrews University Press, 1983), 138.

consistency in the reading of the title. In summarizing his critique of supersessionism, Blaising writes, "However, supersessionism lives in Christian theology today purely on the momentum of its own tradition."[163]

## *(2) Temple*

Like the ministry of his contemporary Haggai, Zechariah's prophetic labor laid great stress on the priority of rebuilding the temple.[164] The people's reasons for turning their attention to other more mundane matters that they had deemed more pressing defied any reasonable defense in light of the priority of worshipping the Lord. The process of rebuilding the temple would demand "an act of dedication and of faith."[165] The theological basis for temple worship rests on a deep Old Testament foundation.

The election of Abraham's seed to the lofty position of God's chosen people, plus the avenue God provided for his sinful people to approach him in worship, both rested squarely on the foundation of the Lord's covenant. With God's mandate for sacrifice to be offered only in the temple, the connection between the covenant and the temple comes into clear focus. Ezekiel illustrated this connection in the vision of the dry bones, promising that the Lord would resurrect the "deceased" nation. Ezekiel quoted the Lord as stating, "I will make a covenant of peace with them; it will be an everlasting covenant. I will establish them and increase their numbers, and I will put my sanctuary among them forever" (37:26).

The temple served as the exclusive God-ordained site for the people to worship the Lord, although it possessed no intrinsic power that could deliver the people. Only God could offer protection for Judah. Despite the theological axiom that the Lord, not his temple, represented the source of Israel's strength, the people's inclination to forsake the God who had demonstrated his love for them led their hearts to wander from worshipping the Lord exclusively. This forsaking of God took many forms, but at its root it reflected the sinful desire to flee the Lord. One of the most nefarious examples of deserting God was clothed in theological garb. Jeremiah struggled against a notorious example of this rejection of God, a false teaching modern scholars refer to as the doctrine of the inviolability of Zion. This theological error declared that the temple itself would protect the nation from any foreign intruder because the Lord "dwelled" within (7:3–4).

No Old Testament passage provides greater insight into the importance of the temple than Deut 12. This foundational chapter enjoins Israel to remove every vestige of idolatry from the land at the explicit instruction of the Lord

---

[163] Blaising, "The Future of Israel," 436.

[164] W. O. McCready, "The 'Day of Small Things' vs. the Latter Days: Historical Fulfillment or Eschatological Hope?" in *Israel's Apostasy and Restoration,* ed. A. Gileadi (Grand Rapids: Baker, 1988), 228–31.

[165] Baldwin, *Zechariah,* 21.

and on the pain of severe judgment for disobedience. With equal emphasis, Deut 12:5 declares that the people must scrupulously restrict all formal worship of the Lord to "the place the LORD your God will choose from among all your tribes to put his Name there for his dwelling." The statement anticipates the "shekinah glory" on the temple, which indicates that the Lord "inhabits" the tabernacle—and later the temple. This place that the Lord "will choose" reflects both the "house of God" and the city in which it would reside.

In 2 Sam 6 David brought the ark to Jerusalem (cf. 1 Chr 13–15), preparing the way for his son Solomon to build the temple proper (1 Kings 5–8; 2 Chr 2–7). Once the work on the temple concluded and the house of God was properly dedicated, "the priests could not enter the temple of the Lord because the glory of the LORD filled it" (2 Chr 7:2; see 5:13–14; 1 Kgs 8:10).

Although the priority of temple worship underlies the entire book of Zechariah, "The Fifth Vision: The Gold Lampstand and Two Olive Trees" (4:1–14) holds particular prominence. This night vision paints a detailed picture of the intricate gilded light that represents the Lord's presence in the temple and the illuminating testimony of God's word to Israel and beyond. The symbolism of the flames that burned perpetually with oil drawn from the two surrounding olive trees gave powerful testimony to the majestic presence of God. Underscoring the supernatural character of the temple, v. 6 explains that the rebuilding of the temple will require the miraculous labors of God's "Spirit." Human initiative, however zealous, could never accomplish the rebuilding of a temple in which God would reside.

The New Testament assumed the truthfulness of the Old Testament understanding of the temple, adding much more individual dimensions to the theme. For instance, when Jesus sought to explain to the Sanhedrin that he was truly God and that he would provide the means for sinful humans to find spiritual restoration with the Lord, he described his body as the temple of God (Mark 14:58; John 2:19). The "temple" also appears metaphorically to believers in Jesus Christ who will serve as stones in the building of the Church. Paul described this construction thusly, "In him the whole building is joined together and rises to become a holy temple" (Eph 2:21; see 1 Pet 2:4–5).

*(3) Messiah*

The Gospel writers clearly understood that Zechariah devoted a great deal of attention to the theme of the coming Messiah. While the question of the messianic import of certain details in Zechariah's prophecies elicits debate, many passages predict diverse qualities of the person and the office of the

Messiah.[166] Zechariah employed numerous motifs found elsewhere in the Old Testament to communicate the Lord's messianic message.[167]

Although other messianic passages may enjoy more attention, one cannot ignore the prominent messianic contributions in chap. 3. In this chapter the prophet linked three messianic motifs that often punctuate Old Testament texts pointing to the ultimate High Priest: "servant," "branch," and "stone" (3:9). The priestly office of Joshua would find its fulfillment in the "Servant," also deemed "the Branch" *(ṣemaḥ)* in 3:8.[168] The "Branch" represents one of the Old Testament's most prominent messianic titles (see Isa 4:2; 11:1; Jer 23:5; 33:15; Ezek 17:22–24; Zech 3:8; 6:12). In this "Branch" metaphor as employed in chap. 3, the dual office of priest and king blend together into one unified person and office. Ultimately, the New Testament highlights the correlation of priestly and royal roles in the person of the Messiah, Jesus Christ.

One of the basic interpretative questions in Zech 3 is the meaning of the "stone." While the purely messianic view struggles with several details Zechariah incorporated in his prophecy, the "stone" holds typological significance. For instance, the prediction that "the stone the builders rejected has become the capstone; the LORD has done this, and it is marvelous in our eyes" (Ps 118:22–23) lays a christological foundation on which the New Testament built. Matthew 21:42 and 1 Pet 2:7–8 both apply this "stone" to Christ. Therefore, the "stone" metaphor also ultimately signifies the Messiah.

Joshua the high priest linked together two of the distinctive offices that the New Testament ascribes to Christ—king and priest (Zech 3:1–10; 6:9–14; cf. Melchizedek, the other individual in the Old Testament who was both king and priest, in Gen 14:18–20; Ps 110:4; Heb 7). The terminology of "servant," "branch," and "stone" all signify the royal office the Messiah will hold. Zechariah presented an unforgettable image of Joshua the high priest fouled with excrement, only to be later purified from his ceremonial and spiritual uncleanness and clothed with clean clothes. This miraculous transformation was effected by none other than God and indicates that the Lord will restore his relationship with all of his people by cleansing and forgiving them of their sin. In the vision of cleansing and clothing the high priest, Joshua represents the nation at large. Furthermore, Joshua's representation of the king draws from the Davidic covenant (2 Sam 7), promising that a Davidic king would indeed reign over the nation. These themes of cleansing and Davidic rule summarize fundamen-

---

[166] W. C. Kaiser, Jr., *The Messiah in the Old Testament* (Grand Rapids: Zondervan, 1995), 211–27; and Kaiser, *Toward an Old Testament Theology* (Grand Rapids: Zondervan, 1978), 207–10, 253–56.

[167] R. E. Clements, "The Messianic Hope in the Old Testament," JSOT 43 (1989): 3–19; and R. Mason, "The Messiah in the Postexilic Old Testament Literature," in *King and Messiah in Israel and the Ancient Near East,* ed. J. Day (Sheffield: Sheffield Press, 1998), 338–64.

[168] צֶמַח. See *HALOT,* 1034.

tal aspects of the Messiah, elements the New Testament applied forcefully to Christ.[169]

The messianic conception in the Old Testament, as well as in Zechariah, frequently focuses on kingship.[170] For instance, the tradition that the Messiah will descend from the line of David rests on the Davidic covenant in 2 Sam 7 where God promised his servant David that one of his descendants would sit on the throne forever. The importance of this covenant finds expression in the manifold affirmations that a Davidic king will reign over Zion, finding its final fulfillment in the person of "Jesus Christ the son of David" (Matt 1:1).

In Zech 9, however, the royal role of the Messiah appears in a unique form. In v. 9 the Messiah enters the scene riding a beast of burden, not a steed associated with military might. Riding on a lowly donkey, the Messiah will reign over a kingdom that he will administer peacefully through the strength of compelling righteousness, not brute force as other kings must exert. In addition to the peaceful connotation of the beast on which the coming King will ride, this Monarch will arrive "righteous and having salvation, gentle" (v. 9).

One of the most momentous messianic prophecies appears in 12:10, the Lord's Servant who was pierced through on behalf of the people. The messianic implications of this verse echo those of the Servant in Isa 53. Zechariah introduced this pierced Messiah as "an only child" and "a first born son." Both designations further strengthen the New Testament portrayal of Jesus Christ as "his firstborn" (Heb 1:6; see Rom 8:29; Col 1:15). Likewise, numerous New Testament passages teach that Jesus is the "Son of God" (Matt 3:17; John 1:34; Heb 1:5; passim). In chap. 12 Zechariah does not indicate why the Messiah is killed. However, the prophet does make it clear that the Messiah is murdered by and for the people whom he served. Zechariah 12 thus lays a precise biblical foundation for the crucifixion of Christ. Moreover, the prophet also describes how the people ultimately would lament their role in killing their faithful Servant, a theme that also anticipates the eschatological repentance of God's people in turning to Christ the Savior. Zechariah presents the Lord's promise that when the nation turns to him and to his "first born Son" in faith, God would pour out "a spirit of grace and supplication" on all of them. Consequently, "all Israel will be saved" (Rom 11:26).

## *(4) Kingdom*

The book of Zechariah makes a profound contribution to the biblical theology of the end times. While the symbolism the prophet employed does not allow one to see the future with complete clarity, nonetheless the imagery "like

---

[169] I. Duguid, "Messianic Themes," 265–80.
[170] Boda, *Zechariah*, 416.

pieces of stained glass diffusing the light of the sun, can only suggest 'what no eye has seen nor ear heard'" (1 Cor 2:9).[171]

Zechariah boldly surveyed the boundaries of God's coming Kingdom. While many might think it a remote possibility to envision a restored Judah, Zechariah proclaimed the message he had received from God. The Lord's declaration far exceeded mere restoration. Israel would become a place of blessing, security, and spirituality beyond anything she had ever experienced. Moreover, Zechariah announced that the whole creation would rest under the dominion of its sovereign Lord, renewed into the new creation that was free from the groaning caused by the blight of sin (cf. Rom 8). At several points in the book the prophet also spoke of God's dominion extending to the furthest corners of the world. For instance, 4:14 describes Judah's God as "the Lord of all the earth."

The coming kingdom will evidence several unique features. One of the most prominent characteristics of the eschatological kingdom will be peace. Several of the night visions stress the rest that God's people will enjoy (2:12; 3:10; 4:8–9; 8:1–15). Chapter 9 also strengthens the message of peace by presenting the coming messianic King arriving on a beast of burden, not a war horse (9:9). The Lord's kingdom will have no place for weaponry of war since God himself will maintain the peace. The Lord even promises to remove the chariots and war horses from the land, symbolizing the most advanced weapons of the day (9:10).

This well-being will not belong to Israel alone, however. The book of Zechariah emphatically extends God's blessings to all the nations of the earth who will finally turn to the Lord in repentance and true faith. For instance, Zech 6 broadens the scope of this miraculous tranquility to the entire world by developing the extent of God's dominion to the four corners of the globe. Chapter 8 promises that "many peoples and powerful nations will come to Jerusalem to seek the LORD Almighty and to entreat him" (v. 22). The same chapter declares that people from all nations, speaking every language, will come to worship with God's people (vv. 20–23).

The prophet made it clear on whom the ultimate agency for advancing God's kingdom rested. Zechariah balanced admonitions to the nation to work zealously with the reminder that the Lord ultimately was the one who held the power to bring his will into existence. No passage states this idea more clearly or beautifully than this one: "'Not by might nor by power, but by my Spirit,' says the Lord Almighty" (4:6b). Zechariah applied this truth to the almost insurmountable challenge of rebuilding the temple. However, the principle is timeless, just as applicable to modern readers as it was to Zechariah's hearers.

The image of the four chariots proceeding "throughout the earth" (6:1–8) expands on God's intervention in human affairs to inaugurate his kingdom. The Lord's emissaries will bring rest, that is, peace, to the most powerful opponents

---

[171] McComiskey, "Zechariah," 1234.

of God's kingdom. While the vision declares that the four chariots from the Lord proceed toward all four points of the compass subduing every enemy, v. 8 culminates in the affirmation that the gravest opponent of all, "the north country," will submit to the Lord's overwhelming might. When this fierce foe kneels before God, the remaining lesser powers surely will yield to the Lord as well (1:8–10; 2:11–12; 12:3).

Possibly the single most significant statement Zechariah made regarding the coming kingdom is its supernatural inception. Zechariah 14:3–9 outlines the coming of the Lord to the Mount of Olives and the ultimate deliverance and blessing that Zion will experience. The prophet wrote, "The LORD will be king over the whole earth. On that day, there will be one LORD, and his name the only name" (14:9).

The phrase "on that day" *(bayyôm–hahû')*[172] introduces the Day of the Lord in the book of Zechariah and throughout the prophetic literature. On this unique eschatological "day," the Lord will decimate every nation that had opposed God's people (Zech 12:3–9; 14:12–13). Although the Day of the Lord terminology does not actually appear in Zech 6:9–13 or 9:9–10, these two passages describe the same eschatological events. On this day, God's reign will become complete throughout his creation. In the New Testament "the day of the Lord" relates the coming of the kingdom often described in the Old Testament to the time when Jesus Christ will return to earth to inaugurate his reign over all creation (1 Thess 5:2,4; 2 Thess 2:2; 2 Pet 3:10; Rev 6:17; 16:14).[173] The final destruction of sinful nature in mankind on the day of the Lord is implied by Jeremiah in Jer 31:33–34 and by Paul in 1 Cor 5:5.

*(5) Judgment of God*

The judgment of God permeates the entire book of Zechariah, as it does the rest of the Old Testament. Often the concept is implicit, while frequently the divine anger boils to the surface and comprises a critical component of various texts. After only one verse in Zechariah, the prophet cautions all of his contemporaries that "the LORD was very angry with your forefathers" (1:2). In 1:15 the Lord declared that he was "very angry with nations that feel secure," casting a net broadly enough to encompass both Judah and the Gentile nations. Later, Zechariah reprised the message of 1:2, warning his contemporaries that just as "the LORD Almighty was very angry" with their forefathers, God's anger would also flame up once more if they refused to repent (7:12).

This wrath assumed a global perspective in 9:1–7 where the Lord foretold the fury he intended to pour out on every nation that had been an enemy of God and his people. This anger represented the appropriate divine response

---

[172] בַּיּוֹם הַהוּא.
[173] Kaiser, *Old Testament Theology*, 256; Duguid, "Messianic Themes," 277. See also T. F. Glasson, "Theophany and Parousia," *NTS* 34 (1988): 259–70.

to the sinfulness manifested by all mankind. From the expulsion of Adam and Eve from the garden (Gen 3), to the flood (Gen 6–8), to the judgments foretold in Zechariah, the Lord's anger burns against every expression of sin. These expressions of divine wrath are not dissimilar from numerous expressions throughout the New Testament. In particular, Paul stated that "the wrath of God is being revealed from heaven against all the godlessness and wickedness of men who suppress the truth by their wickedness" (Rom 1:18). Zechariah announced God's judgment on both Judah and the surrounding nations. As God's people, Judah received the greatest emphasis so that she might become righteous and testify concerning the God she served.

Zechariah also devoted significant attention to the judgment waiting for the Gentile nations, particularly in chaps. 9–14. Zechariah 9:1–8 presents one of the most thorough overviews of the judgment God will pour on the nations, mentioning peoples from Hadrach to Ashdod. Raabe offers several reasons for the extensive judgment oracles against the nations in a book that was not written for them.[174] First, a judgment against the nations gives Judah hope that the Lord will deliver her from her oppressors. Second, when judging the nations, God will displace them from their lands, making room for the promised booming population of Israel. Third, the judgment against the nations will remind Judah that she must place her trust in none other than God. Fourth, the defeat of the oppressors of God's people gives hope that they will finally experience peace (9:8). Fifth, judgment on the sinful nations will vindicate the righteousness of God. (See the Introduction to chaps. 9–14 below for further treatment of the topic.)

The appropriate human response to the prospect of divine wrath should be fear and repentance. The message Zechariah offers is timeless, equally appropriate for his forefathers, the community of his own day, and people living today. The prophet stated, "This is what the LORD Almighty says, 'Return to me,' declares the Lord Almighty, 'and I will return to you,' says the LORD Almighty" (1:3; see v. 6).

A major theological theme in the book of Zechariah, especially in chaps. 9–14, has the Lord marching across the pages of the text as the Divine Warrior. This warrior motif serves as an expression of the Lord's wrath against sinful mankind, Judah included. The Lord promises, "I will surely raise my hand against" anyone who "touches the apple of his [God's] eye" (2:8–9; see 14:12–15). As in Isaiah, the Lord's warrior role encompasses the extremes from waging war to waging peace. Zechariah 9:13 describes God's actions as a warrior who will bend Judah like a bow. In chap. 14 the Lord comes to fight

---

[174] P. R. Raabe, "Why Prophetic Oracles against the Nations?" in *Fortunate the Eyes That See: Essays in Honor of David Noel Freedman*, ed. A. B. Beck et al., (Grand Rapids: Eerdmans, 1995), 240–41.

and defeat the nations, and in Rev 19 the final Divine Warrior, Christ, will wage war against the forces of darkness (vv. 11–19).

In chap. 9 the Lord, the Divine Warrior, manifests his peaceful, humble ministry. As in the book of Isaiah, the contrasting characteristics of the Servant provide the pattern for interpreting the Divine Warrior's surprisingly different roles. Schellenberg comments,

> The servant is both exalted and despised (Isa 52:13–14), weak and strong (Isa 53:12), oppressed and prosperous (Isa 53:10). In the same way, the warrior brings peace (Zech 9:10) not only through acts of judgment (Zech 14:3) but also through his own pain (Zech 12:10; cf. Isa 53:5). Zechariah 9–14 is a single story of a shepherd who will risk his life to defend and save his sheep.[175]

Zechariah often shows how the Lord's faithful and righteous demeanor contrasts sharply with Judah's abusive leaders (10:3; 11:3–17).

### *(6) Divine Faithfulness and Human Obedience*

Throughout the book of Zechariah the prophet emphatically affirmed the Lord's resolve to fulfill his word, just as he had promised. Repeatedly the book states that the Lord will ensure that the temple is rebuilt and that his kingdom will come at last. The Lord often revisited prophecies he had made years before Zechariah's time in order to reassert his faithfulness to the covenant and to encourage the people to shoulder their own responsibility to serve him wholeheartedly through their obedience. Specifically, this obedience includes the completion of tasks God had assigned them such as the rebuilding of the temple.

At the heart of any discussion of God's faithfulness to his people one finds the prominence of the Lord's written revelation to them. This concept has its apex in the vision of the flying scroll (5:1–4). This flying scroll had enormous proportions, approaching 15 by 30 feet. Several features of this scroll underscore the importance of God's word. Certainly the size of the scroll stresses its significance. That it was "flying" indicates that the Lord had unrolled his message for easy reading, traveling throughout the land disclosing the message for all to read. The flying scroll also indicates that the message came from the Lord himself, not from human hands. The scroll conveyed a common prophetic sermon, pleading with the nation to repent of its sin and to embrace the law of the Lord. Thus, the scroll elevated the priority of God's word. Moreover, the scroll's message summoned all mankind to repent of its sin and to worship the Lord righteously. As the Lord proclaims elsewhere: "My word . . . goes out from my mouth: It will not return to me empty, but will accomplish what I desire and achieve the purpose for which I sent it" (Isa 55:11).

---

[175] Schellenberg, "One in the Bond of War," 115.

Zechariah 7 serves as something of a fulcrum for the balanced themes of God's faithfulness and the faithfulness he demands from his people. Echoing themes in Mic 6:6–8, Zechariah admonished, "Administer true justice; show mercy and compassion to one another. Do not oppress the widow or the fatherless, the alien or the poor" (7:9–10; see 8:16–17). These commands disclose the holy character of the God who gave the instruction, as well as the righteous quality of life that should also typify the Lord's children. Thus, Israel's faithful relationship with the Lord should exert a profound influence on the manner in which the people treat the individual members of their society.

Zechariah developed the theme of Judah's duty to obey the Lord with equal clarity.[176] The book begins with the painful reminder that the people's forefathers had failed to obey the Lord, with devastating results (1:2–6). After repeatedly enjoining the people to repent and seek cleansing from God, Zechariah concluded the first section of his book (chaps. 1–6) with the important conditional statement: "This [the rebuilding of the temple] will happen if you diligently obey the LORD your God" (6:15). In 7:8–10 the prophet adds the warning to the nation to complete faithfully the covenantal requirements placed on them by God. This list of duties includes such admonitions as "administer true justice" and "show mercy and compassion to one another." Zechariah 8:16–17 reiterates a comparable set of responsibilities.

Zechariah 9–14 stresses a different facet of the people's obligations to the Lord—seeking him wholeheartedly. The metaphorical statement, "return to your fortress, O prisoners of hope" (9:12), strongly encourages every reader to seek God as his ultimate goal (see 10:1). The judgment Judah receives in chap. 11 and the sentence the Lord hands down against the nations in chap. 12 both highlight God's desire for faithful service from his people by surveying the awful results of sin against their Creator. Finally, the cleansing from sin (13:1) and the universal worship of the Lord (13:2–6; 14:9,16,20–21) demonstrate the Lord's resolve to see faithful worship of the one true God.

In the midst of national circumstances so bleak that few moderns living in the western world can truly appreciate their despair, Zechariah reminded the community of faith about the sovereign rule their God exercises over his creation. Like many believers today, Judah tended to walk by sight, not by faith. Yet all of God's people must remember what a great God they serve. The psalmist Asaph understood the necessity of exercising faith in God in the midst of difficulties:

> But as for me, my feet had almost slipped;
>    I had nearly lost my foothold.
> For I envied the arrogant
>    when I saw the prosperity of the wicked.

---

[176] McComiskey, "Zechariah," 1016–19.

> Yet I am always with you;
>> you hold me by my right hand.
>
> You guide me with your counsel,
>> and afterward you will take me into glory.
>
> Whom have I in heaven but you?
>> And earth has nothing I desire besides you. (Ps 73:2–3,23–25)

The prayer, "I desire nothing besides you, O Lord," should reflect the attitude toward God both for Judah and for the Church in our own time.

### *(7) Cleansing from Sin*

Purification from the guilt that sin brought to individuals and the nation holds a prominent place in Zechariah's theological emphases. The first declaration in the book focuses on the importance of repentance from sin and the Lord's offer of restoration. Zechariah 1:3 affirms, "Therefore tell the people: This is what the LORD Almighty says: 'Return to me,' declares the LORD Almighty, 'and I will return to you,' says the LORD Almighty" (see v. 6). This promise reprises Jeremiah's reminder to the entire nation that the Lord would forgive them and restore them if they would only repent (Jer 18:7–10; see Ezek 33:11).

The metaphor of putting on clean clothes, washing, and refining also figure prominently in Zechariah. The book describes a remarkable scene in which Joshua the high priest was clothed in putrid garments, only to experience the cleansing that only the Lord could supernaturally provide. The implication of the vision goes well beyond that of the holy requirements for God's leaders, extending the promised cleansing to all of the people. Just as the priest must be ceremonially clean and holy in order to approach God in worship, the people must likewise be holy in order to serve their Lord. In one of the best known passages in the book, Zechariah described a fountain provided for all of the inhabitants of Jerusalem (that is, the whole nation—a metonymy). This fountain would flow "to cleanse them from sin and impurity" (13:1). Lastly, the prophet employs a very different metaphor, that of the refiner's fire. After bringing his people into the flame, God promises that he will "refine them like silver and test them like gold," all with the intent of purifying his people (13:9).

### *(8) Leadership*

Lastly, throughout the whole book of Zechariah one recognizes the gravity of leadership for God's people. The book presents a remarkable overview of the implications of both good and bad leadership on the community of faith. Zechariah also makes it painfully clear how harshly the Lord responds to bad leadership (2:3). Implicit in this topic is the caliber of Zechariah's role as prophetic guide for the nation. Zechariah's prominence does not rest with the prophet's charisma or any other natural quality. Rather, Zech 1:1 provides the explanation for the prophet's leadership: "The word of the LORD came to the prophet Zechariah."

Zechariah 3 offers significant insight into the topic of leadership. One notes again the episode in which Joshua the high priest stands before both God and the people utterly defiled in the most unspeakable terms. God's actions in purifying Joshua and clothing him with holy vestments emphasize the necessity of holiness and purity in the lives of the leaders for the Lord's people. Obedience to God's law also plays a crucial role in the leaders' preparation for divine service. The Lord declares to Joshua, "If you walk in my ways and keep my requirements, then you will govern my house and have charge of my courts, and I will give you a place among these standing here" (3:7; see 6:9–15). More than most biblical books, Zechariah comments on the immediate effects of leadership on the people. In an important commentary on the subject, the prophet stated that "the people wander like sheep oppressed for lack of a shepherd" (10:2).

Chapter 11 gives greater prominence to the importance of good leadership for God's people than any other portion of the book. The chapter shows the Lord's disgust for any leader who leads the flock astray (vv. 4–6). In this context the "worthless shepherd" (v. 17) represents every leader who takes advantage of God's people for personal gain. Verse 8 notes that for leadership to function as God intends, there must also be people who will follow godly leadership. When people reject God's guidance, sorrow follows for both the people and the leader as well (vv. 9–16). The apostle Peter provided the New Testament's perspective on this issue, echoing themes stressed in Zechariah (cf. Titus 1 and 1 Tim 3). Peter stated,

> Be shepherds of God's flock that is under your care, serving as overseers—not because you must, but because you are willing, as God wants you to be; not greedy for money, but eager to serve; not lording it over those entrusted to you, but being examples to the flock. And when the Chief Shepherd appears, you will receive the crown of glory that will never fade away. (1 Pet 5:2–4)

―――― SECTION OUTLINE ――――

I. INTRODUCTION (1:1–6)

―――― **I. INTRODUCTION (1:1–6)** ――――

¹In the eighth month of the second year of Darius, the word of the LORD came to the prophet Zechariah son of Berekiah, the son of Iddo:
²"The LORD was very angry with your forefathers. ³Therefore tell the people: This is what the LORD Almighty says: 'Return to me,' declares the Lord Almighty, 'and I will return to you,' says the LORD Almighty. ⁴Do not be like your forefathers, to whom the earlier prophets proclaimed: This is what the LORD Almighty says: 'Turn from your evil ways and your evil practices.' But they would not listen or pay attention to me, declares the LORD. ⁵Where are your forefathers now? And the prophets, do they live forever? ⁶But did not my words and my decrees, which I commanded my servants the prophets, overtake your forefathers?

"Then they repented and said, 'The LORD Almighty has done to us what our ways and practices deserve, just as he determined to do.'"

**1:1** Zechariah's first prophetic message came during the eighth month of Darius I's second year on the throne—October 520 BC,[1] only two months following the commencement of Haggai's preaching ministry.[2] Since Zechariah prophesied at the conclusion of the exile, there was no king in Judah to whose reign the prophet's ministry correlated. Thus, Zechariah dated his service to the rule of the Persian king, Darius I or Darius the Great.

Governing from 522–486 BC, Darius the Great was a well known king, particularly because of the famous Behistun Inscription that extols the Persian ruler's accomplishments. This massive cuneiform text carved on the side of a mountain largely enabled the decipherment of Akkadian, the language of Assyria and Babylonia,[3] and proclaimed many of the king's greatest accomplishments.

---

[1] Unlike the numerous other exact dates given in Haggai and Zechariah, only this one fails to mention the day of the month. Although the Syriac Peshitta contains a plausible variant, "the first day of the month," there is little basis for emending the Masoretic Text.

[2] J. G. Baldwin, *Haggai, Zechariah, Malachi*, TOTC (Downers Grove, IL: InterVarsity, 1972), 29; R. A. Parker and W. H. Dubberstein, *Babylonian Chronology 626 BC–AD 75* (Providence, RI: Brown University Press, 1956). See "The Historical Era" in the Introduction for a discussion of Darius I as well as a fuller correlation with the Julian-Gregorian calendar.

[3] The famous trilingual inscription written in Old Persian, Elamite, and Babylonian is chiseled on the side of one of the Zagros mountains in the Kermanshah region of present-day Iran, near Darius's ancient capital. Since this inscription incorporates parallel texts written in three different languages, the Behistun text played a pivotal role in the initial decipherment of cuneiform. See I. J. Gelb, *A Study of Writing*, 2nd ed., (Chicago: University of Chicago Press, 1963), 227.

According to ancient historical records as well as Zech 1:11, peace reigned over the Persian empire once Darius the Great had quelled the many rebellions throughout the kingdom. Nonetheless, despite the general serenity the empire experienced, the era also reflected tremendous political transition as the great Babylonian kingdom receded from view and Persia emerged to exert total dominance over the entire region. One constant amid all of the change, however, was Jerusalem's state of disrepair and the Israelite people's disenchantment with their future prospects. As he had done many times before, the Lord set apart a prophet and gave a word of revelation to him in order to guide and encourage the nation as they navigated uncharted territory.

After dating the prophecy that would follow, Zechariah affirmed that his message came directly from God himself. The phrase the prophet used, "the word of the LORD" *(dĕbar–YHWH)*, occurs frequently in the Old Testament, and especially in the writing prophets, to assert divine authority.[4] This expression typically functions as a technical term to claim divine revelation for a prophecy.[5] The same phrase opens the books of Hosea, Joel, Jonah, Micah, Zephaniah, and Malachi. Similar phrasing begins the book of Haggai also. Occurring dozens of times in the prophets alone, the phrase usually appears either at the beginning and/or ending of most prophetic oracles, not just at the beginning of prophetic books. For instance, the expression occurs repeatedly in the book of Zechariah.[6]

Verse 1 also introduces the prophet who received the divine message, "Zechariah son of Berekiah, son of Iddo" (see 1:7). This brief genealogy personalizes Zechariah, giving more information about the prophet himself than any of the other minor prophets except for Zephaniah. Amos, Obadiah, Micah, Nahum, Habakkuk, and Haggai offer no family information whatsoever. Hosea, Joel, and Jonah only mention the prophet's father. By providing this additional information, Zechariah emphasized his continuity with the past and served to distinguish him from others who bore this popular name.

The name "Zechariah," one of the most popular names in the Old Testament, attributed to some two dozen individuals history has recalled, means "Yahweh remembers."[7] Like so many other proper names in the Old Testament, Zechariah the prophet's name describes God's covenantal relationship with his people,

---

[4] The Hb. דְּבַר־יהוה emphasizes the Lord's role in communicating his word to his messenger (see 1:7; 4:8; 6:9; 7:1,4,8; 8:1,18). This term occurs over 150 times in the prophetic literature. For a thorough analysis of the phrase, see O. Grether, *Name und Wort Gottes im Alten Testament* (Giessen: Alfred Töpelmann, 1934), 62–65. This formula is similar in meaning to the equally common prophetic expressions נְאֻם־יהוה ("a saying of the LORD"), and כֹּה אָמַר יהוה ("thus says the LORD").

[5] *TDOT*, 3:111.

[6] Zech 1:1,7; 4:6,8; 6:9; 7:1,4,8; 8:1,18; 9:1; 11:11; 12:1.

[7] זְכַרְיָהוּ / זְכַרְיָה

assuring Israel that the Lord's relationship to his people continues, even during an era filled with discouragement and oppression.[8]

Although the theological significance of Zechariah's name could not be clearer, questions persist regarding the identity of Zechariah. These questions lead to several divergent interpretations concerning Zechariah the prophet, including the claim that several Zechariahs might have lived in the same era. The fundamental problem is that Zech 1:1 refers to "Zechariah son of Berekiah, the son of Iddo," while the genealogies in Ezra 5:1 and 6:14 fail to mention Berekiah. Hence, when Ezra mentions Zechariah, Ezra portrays the prophet solely as "son of Iddo." This omission of Berekiah in Ezra has long puzzled interpreters.

Numerous solutions to the question have emerged over the centuries. First, Jerome suggests that Zechariah was the son of Berekiah according to the flesh and son of Iddo according to the Spirit. Despite Jerome's storied role in the history of interpretation, his fanciful conclusion has influenced few because of its total lack of supporting evidence.

Second, others maintain that the reference to Berekiah represents nothing more than an unfortunate abbreviation of the name Jeberekiah in the brief genealogy of Isa 8:2 that mentions a Zechariah as the "son of Jeberekiah." However, the ancient manuscripts of the book of Zechariah support the reading "Berekiah," yielding absolutely no evidence for this view.

Third, some scholars who attribute the authorship of the canonical book of Zechariah to two "Zechariahs" consider chaps. 1–8 the work of Zechariah son of Iddo, while chaps. 9–14 reflect the efforts of the anonymous "Zechariah son of Berekiah." This suggestion remains unconvincing partly because the suggestion that multiple authors penned the book of Zechariah has its own difficulties and also due to the conjectural nature of the suggestion. The conclusion that there were two books of Zechariah that were awkwardly fashioned into one book by "Zechariah son of Berekiah, the son of Iddo" completely lacks evidence and suffers from the same tenuousness that any argument from silence endures. As stated above, the Hebrew textual tradition solidly supports the reading, "Zechariah son of Berekiah, the son of Iddo."

Fourth, Meyers and Meyers mention the possibility that there were two postexilic Zechariahs with the same immediate patronymic of Berekiah, requiring the grandfather's name to distinguish the two.[9] As with the previous suggestions, this view also lacks any external support.

---

[8] D. L. Petersen, *Haggai and Zechariah 1–8*, OTL (Philadelphia: Westminster, 1984), 128.

[9] C. L. Meyers and E. M. Meyers, *Haggai, Zechariah 1–8* (Garden City, NY: Doubleday, 1987), 92. See also the survey of the issues by M. A. Sweeney, "Zechariah's Debate with Isaiah," in *The Changing Face of Form Criticism for the Twenty-First Century*, ed. M. A. Sweeney and E. B. Zvi (Grand Rapids: Eerdmans, 2003), 340–43.

Fifth, some scholars have even conjectured that Berekiah may have died when Zechariah was young, making Zechariah the successor to Iddo. However, this unproven suggestion does not warrant serious consideration.

Sixth, another understanding identifies Berekiah as Zechariah's father, and Iddo as the prophet's grandfather.[10] This interpretation recognizes that the Hebrew word *bēn* ("son") can be readily translated "grandson of."[11] Understanding the word *bēn* ("son") both as "son" and "grandson" would parallel the case of Jehu where 2 Kgs 9:20 (also 1 Kgs 19:16) calls him "son of Nimshi," while 2 Kgs 9:2,14 call him "son of Jehoshaphat, the son of Nimshi." This interpretation lends itself to the passage quite well and accommodates the differences between the passages in Ezra and Zechariah.

Another passage, Neh 12, identifies Zechariah as a member of Iddo's family. When listing heads of priestly families during the time of Joiakim, Neh 12:16 presents Zechariah as one of Iddo's descendants. Nehemiah, however, does not explicitly state that the Zechariah he mentions is the same as the minor prophet.

The typical critical approach to the identity of Zechariah in Nehemiah discounts the historical reliability of the genealogy in 1:1 as well as the view that the book of Zechariah came from a single pen. Mitchell and Cross represent the critical position, concluding that Neh 12:16 probably refers to another Zechariah living during the postexilic era.[12] This negative stance toward the veracity of 1:1 and the likelihood that one person, the prophet Zechariah, produced the book bearing his name suffer from unwarranted biases.

Not all in the critical camp reach the same conclusion as Mitchell and Cross though. Blenkinsopp, for example, concludes that Zechariah in Nehemiah is the same as the minor prophet since both lived in the same era and both descended from someone named Iddo.[13] In the final analysis, the most plausible understanding identifies the Zechariah and Iddo in Neh 12:4,16 with those in the books of Zechariah and Ezra.[14]

The primary significance of Zechariah's genealogy reveals that Zechariah descended from a priestly line. Since the prophet Zechariah belonged to a

---

[10] So E. Achtemeier, *Nahum-Malachi* (Atlanta: John Knox, 1986), 111; Baldwin, *Zechariah*, 88–89; R. L. Smith, *Micah-Malachi*, WBC (Waco: Word, 1984), 183; M. F. Unger, *Commentary on Zechariah* (Grand Rapids: Zondervan, 1962), 19.

[11] See the case of Jehu who is introduced as "son of Nimshi" in 1 Kgs 19:16; 2 Kgs 9:20, but is presented as "son of Jehoshaphat the son of Nimshi" in 2 Kgs 9:2,14. The word בֶּן comfortably renders "grandson of." Among the numerous other examples, see Gen 31:28; 31:55 (Hb. 32:1); 2 Sam 19:24 (Hb. 19:25). See *TDOT*, 2:150; W. Rudolph, *Haggai, Sacharja 1–8* (Gütersloh: Gerd Mohn, 1976), 67.

[12] H. G. Mitchell, J. M. P. Smith, and J. A. Bewer, *A Critical and Exegetical Commentary on Haggai, Zechariah, Malachi and Jonah*, ICC (Edinburgh: T. & T. Clark, 1912), 83. For a critical discussion of the relationship of Neh 12 to Chronicles, Haggai, and Zechariah, see F. M. Cross, Jr., "A Reconstruction of the Judean Restoration," *JBL* 94 (1975): 11–14.

[13] J. Blenkinsopp, *Ezra-Nehemiah*, OTL (Philadelphia: Westminster, 1988), 339.

[14] Baldwin, *Zechariah*, 89.

priestly family (see Introduction), his personal connection to the priestly office and the manifold issues surrounding the worship of the Lord partially explains the great attention the prophet often gives to priestly matters.

Moreover, Nehemiah indicates that Zechariah and his family were among the faithful who had endured the exile. Not only did Zechariah receive a divine call to the prophetic office, he also knew personally what grievous circumstances his community had experienced. Zechariah's acquaintance with sorrow and uncertainty gave him credibility to speak to others who had suffered similarly.

When one turns to the New Testament, a further complication regarding Zechariah's lineage emerges after reading Jesus' pronouncement of judgment on the Pharisees for "the blood of Zechariah son of Berekiah, whom you murdered between the temple and the altar" (Matt 23:35; see Luke 11:51). The only reference to the martyrdom of any priest named Zechariah in the Old Testament occurs in 2 Chr 24:20–22, speaking of "Zechariah son of Jehoiada." Furthermore, the event narrated in 2 Chr 24 occurred c. 800 BC, precluding any identification with our prophet.[15] While a definitive solution to the question is unavailable, commentators tend either to suggest that our prophet was ultimately martyred or that Isaiah's associate, "Zechariah son of Jeberekiah" (Isa 8:2) is in view. The primary difficulty with both suggestions, however, is the absence of historical references to the martyrdom of either individual.

D. A. Carson addresses the problem from a New Testament perspective, summarizing the following possible solutions to the question of the identity of Zechariah in Matt 23:35:[16] (1) Zechariah, the father of John the Baptist could be the person in mind. However, there is no evidence that he was martyred. (2) Jewish zealots murdered Zechariah, son of Baris/Baruch/Bariscaeus, in the temple. Again, the evidence supporting this view is sketchy at best. (3) Matthew could have intended Zechariah, son of Berekiah (Zech 1:1), but once more, no reference to his martyrdom exists. (4) Jesus may have spoken of a Zechariah who is unknown to modern readers. (5) Matthew may have had Zechariah son of Jehoiada (2 Chr 24:20–22) in mind.

Verse 1 also identifies Zechariah as a prophet, establishing him as a member of the specially called ministers of God.[17] God inaugurated the prophetic

---

[15] See J. Bright, *A History of Israel*, 3rd ed. (Philadelphia: Westminster, 1981), 255.

[16] D. A. Carson, "Matthew" in *The Expositor's Bible Commentary* (Grand Rapids: Zondervan, 1984), 485–86.

[17] The Hb. word נָבִיא serves as the technical term for "prophet" in the Old Testament. *HALOT*, 661–62. The original meaning of the term cannot be ascertained, but W. F. Albright (*From the Stone Age to Christianity*, 2nd ed. [Garden City, NY: Anchor, 1957], 303) was the first to suggest that it derives from the Akkadian *nabû* "to call." See also W. von Soden, *Akkadisches Handwörterbuch* (Wiesbaden: Otto Harrassowitz, 1972), 2:699. For further study, see G. V. Smith, *The Prophets as Preachers: An Introduction to the Hebrew Prophets* (Nashville: Broadman and Holman, 1994); and J. Blenkinsopp, *History of Prophecy in Israel* (Philadelphia: Westminster, 1983); K. Koch, *The Prophets. Vol. 1: The Assyrian Period*, trans. M. Kohl (Philadelphia: Fortress, 1982); and Koch,

office in the Old Testament, although secular prophets emerged in ancient Near Eastern venues such as Mari. The call narratives in Isa 6, Jer 1, and Ezek 1 give insight into the gravity and spiritual character of the prophetic office. Biblical prophets were called by God to serve as spokesmen for the Lord himself. The power of their message was immeasurable, and von Rad noted that the prophets changed "the gears of history with a word of God."[18] The Old Testament prophet confronted rebellion against the Lawgiver wherever found, whether in royal courts, priestly circles, or among the common people throughout the land.

**1:2** The prophet's word from God came in the form of a sermon that resembles other sermons in which the preacher addresses the audience in the second person. Faithful to the homiletical genre, Zechariah repeatedly referred back to earlier teachings in the Torah as well as other divine commands, and he freely employed exhortation to enjoin his hearers to repent and return to God. (See the helpful parallels in Deut 20:1–9; Josh 1:1–11; 2 Chr 15:1–7; 19:6–7; 20:15–17; 30:6–9; Jer 7:1–26.)[19]

Zechariah began his first sermon with a painful reminder of Israel's current plight and the historical circumstances that led to their present difficulties. The prophet cautioned the people that the Lord is a God whose anger blazes at the sin of his people.[20] God's wrath in response to the nation's sin and his judgment on sinners characterize God's relationship with his people from the time of the fall (Gen 3) and the flood (Gen 6) to Zechariah's day and to today.[21] The Lord simply cannot tolerate sin among his people.

This oracle does not limit itself to reviewing the prior relationship between the Lord and the preexilic community, remembering why the nation finds itself in such difficult circumstances. Actually, the passage contains a rather thinly veiled threat that should the people of Judah continue in their sin, God might punish them again severely. Consequently, the people of God should fear God's holiness and respond accordingly. While often implicit, the theme of divine anger reappears forcefully in the book of Zechariah, especially in 1:15 and 7:12.

---

*The Prophets. Vol. 2: The Babylonian and Persian Period*, trans. M. Kohl (Philadelphia: Fortress, 1984); J. F. A. Sawyer, *Prophecy and the Biblical Prophets*, rev. ed. (Oxford: Oxford University Press, 1993); W. A. VanGemeren, *Interpreting the Prophetic Word* (Grand Rapids: Zondervan, 1990).

[18] von Rad, *Old Testament Theology*, 1:342.

[19] M. A. Sweeney, *The Twelve Prophets, Vol. 2*, Berit Olam (Collegeville, MN: Liturgical Press, 2000), 570.

[20] The Hb. construction, employing the cognate accusative of קֶצֶף, conveys particularly strong emotion; see *HALOT*, 1125 and BDB, 893.

[21] Three times in this section Zechariah refers to God as "Lord Almighty," *YHWH ṣĕbā'ōt*, often rendered "Lord of Hosts." This divine title portrays God as a warrior who brings both judgment and salvation to the penitent. See P. D. Miller, Jr., *The Divine Warrior in Early Israel* (Cambridge, MA: Harvard University Press, 1973), 170–75.

Zechariah warned his audience that the Babylonian exile ensued because their forefathers obstinately spurned the admonitions of the prophets who had pleaded with them to repent and be spared God's imminent judgment.[22] Lest there be any doubt about the accuracy of the former prophets' message, Zechariah reminded his readers that the historical events themselves vindicated the prophets and the truthfulness of their predictions. The people they denounced had long since passed from the scene (1:5). However, Zechariah relied on the abiding Word of God, in this case, a message of judgment, recalling Isaiah's similar confidence:

> So is my word that goes out from my mouth:
>   It will not return to me empty,
>   but will accomplish what I desire
>   and achieve the purpose for which I sent it (Isa 55:11).

Therefore, since the Lord's word of judgment continues to testify against lawlessness, Zechariah's hearers must take immediate action and repent in order to forestall judgment.

**1:3–6** Zechariah strongly evoked these past memories by quoting language used by the earlier prophets. In particular, Zechariah echoed the very expression most often associated with Jeremiah—return *[šûb]* to the Lord.[23] Zechariah's plea also reminded his audience of Isaiah's dual-pronged prophecy that "a remnant will return" (Isa 10:21), a message of both judgment and grace. Zechariah's use of *šûb* incorporates a pun on the meaning of the word. The initial occurrence of the term indicates repentance, a change of life. The latter usage conveys a change in the Lord's response to his people from judgment to favor.[24]

As judgment, the prophecy foretells the demise of the nation and the deportation of Judah. As an expression of grace, the "remnant" theme promises that God will remember his covenant with his people and ultimately will restore their fortunes.

The warning could not be clearer—the nation has the choice either of repenting from their sins or remaining stubborn and suffering a fate reminiscent of Judah of old. Zechariah, like Jeremiah, longed to see God's people spared the punishment their sins demanded. Although the threat to the well being of the postexilic community was real, Zechariah held out great hope for Israel's

---

[22] See 2 Chr 36:15–21 for a theological reflection on these tragic events. In Deut 28:15,45 Moses pronounces curses on those who break the Lord's covenant, using the same word הִשִּׂיגוּ found in Zech 1:6. See *HALOT*, 727.

[23] In Jer 18:11; 25:4–5; 35:15 the prophet exhorts the people to repent/return to God (שׁוּב); see the important study by W. L. Holladay, *The Root šûbh in the Old Testament* (Leiden: E. J. Brill, 1958). Other prophets preach the same message (see Isa 10:21; 45:22).

[24] A. Wolters, "Word Play in Zechariah," in *Puns and Pundits,* ed. S. Noegel (Bethesda: CDL Press, 2000), 223–24.

future, believing that the people would indeed turn from sin to God. Like their fathers who had faced their own mortality, each person must meet death as well (1:5). Judah must not procrastinate, counting on the long-suffering of God and the certainty of another day of life since God offers only a limited time for repentance.[25]

In his disputations with Pelagius, Augustine gave careful attention to v. 3, "Return to me . . . and I will return to You." Augustine strongly opposed the Pelagian view that God extended his grace based on the recipient's merits. In contrast, Augustine argued that God gives his grace freely, not on the basis of human worth to receive that grace. Commenting on v. 3, Augustine wrote, "One of these clauses—that which invites our return to God—evidently belongs to our will; while the other, which promises his return to us, belongs to his grace."[26]

It is important to recognize that Zechariah's message rests solidly upon covenantal language and concepts. To turn *from* the Lord means breaking covenant with him by turning toward "evil ways" and "evil practices" (1:4).[27] The covenantal terms "word" *(dābār)* and "statute" *(ḥōq)* in 1:6 further underscore the covenantal tone of the sermon.[28] Hence, for Israel to forsake the Lord represents treason. How could the people expect God to keep his covenant while they deliberately violate the covenant themselves?

The people's repentance *(šûb)* in 1:6b refers to the preexilic fathers who repented, albeit too late to avoid God's judgment. Verse 6 does not contradict 1:4, even though v. 6 indicates that Judah did repent, while v. 4 suggests that they did not.[29] Ezra 9:1–10:17 and Dan 9:1–19 describe the people's remorse for their sins after it was too late to avert the Babylonian exile. In typical Old Testament fashion, the prophet drew from history to make his theological point. Zechariah's contemporaries had an opportunity to learn from their forefathers' wayward paths, and in so doing, to insure God's future blessings on their lives.

The NIV properly translates the first particle *('ak)* in v. 6 with "but."[30] The particle serves to contrast the mortal generation of sinners and the prophets who confronted them with the eternal word of God that continues to testify against them.[31]

---

[25] D. Rudman, "A Note on Zechariah 1:5," *JNSL* 29 (2003): 33–39. Rudman suggests that Zechariah's statement ("And the prophets, do they live forever?") foretells the cessation of prophecy in general.

[26] Augustine, *De Gratia et libero arbitrio*, 5.10 (PL 44:888).

[27] See Holladay, *Root šûbh*, 141.

[28] These terms דָּבָר (*HALOT*, 211–12) and חֹק (*HALOT*, 346–47), respectively, occur in the following covenant texts: Deut 4:1–2; 17:19; 27:8–10. See E. H. Merrill, *Haggai, Zechariah, Malachi* (Chicago: Moody, 1994), 96.

[29] The emendation in BHS of אֶתְכֶם ("*you*") for אֲבֹתֵיכֶם ("*your fathers*") that is advocated in order to avoid the putative contradiction is unfounded and unnecessary.

[30] Hb. אַךְ. See *HALOT*, 45.

[31] See B. K. Waltke and M. O'Connor, *IBHS* (Winona Lake: Eisenbrauns, 1990), §39.3.5.d.

The overall purpose of the book of Zechariah aimed to encourage the people who found themselves in a state of profound discouragement that had clouded Judah's outlook. In light of this downcast outlook, it is surprising that Zechariah's first sermon began so darkly with a sharp call to repentance. Moreover, Zechariah moved beyond exhorting the people to repent to issuing a threat, a menacing announcement that matters could quickly go from bad to worse if the community failed to respond to the Lord.

Yet the warning was necessary as the nation could only realize the hope for the future that Zechariah held out for them if they remained in a right relationship to God. Judah must uphold the Lord's holiness, not trample it. Thus, any confidence must be contingent on God, his covenant, and his favor to the people. They certainly had no future without the Lord! Baldwin summarizes,

> If the hortatory tone, the reminder of judgment and reference to the anger of the Lord appear to be an inappropriate way to encourage a downcast people and spur them to action, the purpose is to provide solid ground for the promises to come.[32]

The future appears bright, but the prophet offers no unbridled optimism. A promising future rests on the people's willingness to humble themselves before the Lord in submission to his covenant and its holy demands. The profound promise of v. 3, "Return to me ... and I will return to you," takes on even greater significance in light of the Lord's holiness and his covenantal promises to Judah.

Zechariah's sermon found deep roots in Israel's historical experiences. The exile in 587 BC fulfilled the message of the prophets regarding the judgment and deportation of Judah. God remained faithful to his covenant, offering mercy on precisely the same grounds of divine grace and mercy that he had extended to their forefathers. Whether during the days of Jeremiah or Zechariah, restoration and security came hand in hand with repentance and holiness.

---

[32] Baldwin, *Zechariah*, 87.

─────────── SECTION OUTLINE ───────────

II. EIGHT NIGHT VISIONS AND ORACLES (1:7–6:8)
 1. The First Vision: The Man on a Red Horse (1:7–17)
 2. The Second Vision: Four Horns and Four Craftsmen (1:18–21)
 3. The Third Vision: The Surveyor (2:1–13 [Hb 2:5–17])
 4. The Fourth Vision: The Cleansing of the High Priest (3:1–10)
 5. The Fifth Vision: The Gold Lampstand and Two Olive Trees (4:1–14)
 6. The Sixth Vision: The Flying Scroll (5:1–4)
 8. The Eighth Vision: The Four Chariots (6:1–8)

─────────── **II. EIGHT NIGHT VISIONS AND ORACLES (1:7–6:8)** ───────────

While scholarship generally agrees that Zechariah's eight visions represent a literary unit, scholars diverge regarding the structure and overall message of the visions. Zechariah's visions focus initially on Judah's desperate need for encouragement and salvation. However, the message of the visions surpasses Judah's postexilic condition. The visions use sweeping language to introduce an eschatological day when the Messiah will reign over a kingdom in which all will have accepted God's offer of salvation.[1] Embracing a millennial interpretation, Unger suggests that "all of these visions have the same scope. They bridge the centuries and extend to the period of the restoration of the kingdom to Israel (Acts 1:6)."[2] Mitchell contends that the first three visions depict Judah's return from captivity, the fourth and fifth concern the anointed of the Lord, and the last three address the seat of wickedness and its removal.[3] Both Klaus Seybold[4] and Baruch Halpern[5] conclude that the primary emphasis of the visions was the reconstruction of the temple in Jerusalem. Specifically, Halpern argues that the prophet Zechariah stresses temple reconstruction because (1) Zech 1–6 explicitly discusses the temple, (2) the temple and other cultic imagery occur frequently in the visions, and (3) the divine warrior theme in this section of the book presupposes a cultic context.

---

[1] E. H. Merrill, *Haggai, Zechariah, Malachi* (Chicago: Moody, 1994), 93.
[2] M. F. Unger, *Commentary on Zechariah* (Grand Rapids: Zondervan, 1962), 25.
[3] H. G. Mitchell, J. M. P. Smith, and J. A. Bewer, *A Critical and Exegetical Commentary on Haggai, Zechariah, Malachi and Jonah*, ICC (Edinburgh: T. & T. Clark, 1912), 115.
[4] K. Seybold, *Bilder zum Tempelbau: Die Visionen des Propheten Sacharja* (Stuttgart: KBW, 1974), 100.
[5] B. Halpern, "The Ritual Background of Zechariah's Temple Song," *CBQ* 40 (1978): 189.

David Petersen forcefully challenges these widely embraced conclusions, maintaining that the visions do not concern temple renewal. Rather, Petersen believes the visions "stand somewhere between purely mundane concerns and an utopian vision of renewal."[6] Petersen attempts to critique the temple renewal view by suggesting that the references to the temple occur in the oracles, not in the visions themselves. Thus, Petersen attempts to drive a deep wedge between the visions and the oracles accompanying them, a methodology that is suspect, to say the very least, and does not enjoy wide scholarly support.

Moreover, Petersen correctly notes that not all of the visions expressly mention the temple or cult. In particular, the vision of the flying scroll (5:1–4) seems to concern itself with matters other than the temple. In a sense, Petersen's observation here has merit, but surely one should remain cautious in attempting to separate the temple and its restoration from the Torah and the righteousness it represented. To illustrate the problem with this approach, one can hardly imagine Ezra isolating the law of God from the temple and its restoration. In fact, Zechariah's visions emphasize building the people of God. Judah could not worship the Lord in an acceptable way unless the people's lives were moral and committed to uphold God's Word faithfully. One cannot claim that Zechariah was unconcerned with the temple or with Haggai's ministry. Rather, Zechariah stressed the more basic point—faithfulness to God's covenant.

Regarding the structure of Zechariah's visions, Petersen observes several shared themes among the night visions. He notes that each of the visions overflow with movement. One theme, the plan of God that progresses dramatically throughout the land, fulfills a major role in each of the visions. He also points out that the motif of "all the earth" *(kol–hā'āreṣ)*[7] occurs regularly in the visions, underscoring the universal scope of the Lord's activity.[8] In the final analysis, however, Petersen sees the visions as "heterogeneous," deriving from dissimilar historical settings and manifesting different perspectives.[9]

Contrastingly, the most helpful recent analyses note that the visions form a thematic unity. As noted in the Introduction, many have argued for a chiastic structure to this section of the book. For example, Baldwin maintains that the visions follow a pattern "a b b c c b b a" where the fourth and fifth visions convey the theological emphasis of the entire section.[10]

Meyers and Meyers refine the chiastic interpretation, concluding that the structure is "*a b c d c b a*," although they exclude the vision of the priest (3:1–10) from consideration because the formulaic introduction differs somewhat

---

[6] D. L. Petersen, "Zechariah's Visions: A Theological Perspective," *VT* 34 (1984): 196.
[7] כָּל־הָאָרֶץ.
[8] Petersen, "Zechariah's Visions," 198–202; D. L. Petersen, *Haggai and Zechariah 1–8*, OTL (Philadelphia: Westminster, 1984), 111–16.
[9] Petersen, *Zechariah 1–8*, 122.
[10] J. G. Baldwin, *Haggai, Zechariah, Malachi*, TOTC (Downers Grove, IL: InterVarsity, 1972), 80–81.

from the usual pattern of the other visions.[11] Meyers and Meyers's understanding contributes meaningfully, but their unwarranted omission of vision four (according to our numbering scheme), "The Cleansing of the Priest" (3:1–10), mars their argument. Despite significant and somewhat puzzling formulaic differences, there is little basis for removing the entire vision from this literary section. If one adopts Meyers and Meyers's general analysis and restores 3:1–10 to its rightful place, the following chiastic structure emerges:

A  Vision One: The Man on a Red Horse (1:7–17)
  B  Vision Two: Four Horns and Four Craftsmen (1:18–21)
    C  Vision Three: The Surveyor (2:1–13)
      D  Vision Four: The Cleansing of the High Priest (3:1–10)
      D′ Vision Five: The Lampstand and Two Olive Trees (4:1–14)
    C′ Vision Six: The Flying Scroll (5:1–4)
  B′ Vision Seven: The Woman in the Basket (5:5–11)
A′ Vision Eight: The Four Chariots (6:1–8)

Meyers and Meyers see a thematic unity in the visions, graphically illustrating the relationship between the visions as a series of concentric circles. Accordingly, the vision of "The Cleansing of the High Priest" complements "The Lampstand and Two Olive Trees." Retaining the fourth vision, we obtain the following analysis, based on Meyers and Meyers's observations.[12] The outermost circle, visions one and eight, manifests a universal perspective concerning the Lord's omniscience. The next circle, visions two and seven, treats international matters, emphasizing Judah's relationship to the empires. The third circle, visions three and six, stresses national issues, particularly those in Jerusalem. The innermost circle, visions four and five (according to our numbering), expresses the prophet's primary focus by emphasizing the temple and its leadership.[13]

---

[11] C. L. Meyers and E. M. Meyers, *Haggai, Zechariah 1–8* (Garden City, NY: Doubleday, 1987), lvii, 179–80.

[12]

| Our Numbering of Visions | Meyers and Meyers's Ordering of Visions |
|---|---|
| Vision 1 (1:7–17) | Vision 1 (1:7–17) |
| Vision 2 (1:18–21) | Vision 2 (1:18–21) |
| Vision 3 (2:1–13) | Vision 3 (2:1–13) |
| Vision 4 (3:1–10) | |
| Vision 5 (4:1–14) | Vision 4 (4:1–14) |
| Vision 6 (5:1–4) | Vision 5 (5:1–4) |
| Vision 7 (5:5–11) | Vision 6 (5:5–11) |
| Vision 8 (6:1–8) | Vision 7 (6:1–8) |

[13] Meyers and Meyers, *Zechariah 1–8*, lvi. Also, R. Lux, "Die doppelte Konditionierung des Heils: theologische Anmerkungen zum chronologischen und literarischen Ort des Sacharjaprologs (Sach 1, 1–6)," in *Gott und Mensch im Dialog*, BZAW 345, ed. M. Witte (Berlin: Walter de Gruyter, 2004), 571–73, 584–85.

The individual visions reveal a similar structure. Each begins with an introductory formula, followed by a brief description of what the prophet sees. Subsequently, the prophet sought an interpretation from the angel, which the angel ultimately provides. An oracle accompanies four of the visions (1:14–17; 2:6–13; 4:6–10; 6:9–15), further expanding the interpretation of the vision.

The manner in which the Lord communicated with Zechariah also draws significant attention. On the one hand we find Unger, who affirms that the prophet was not dreaming, but rather had full control of all of his faculties.[14] Concerned about the reliability of the revelation, Unger believes that the prophet should have been awake, although in a visionary state, in order to be "fully conscious" and cognizant of what was happening around him. Unger's presupposition is baseless, however. Elsewhere the Old Testament asserts that the Lord sometimes discloses his revelation through dreams. Surely one should not discount the dependability of Jacob's dream at Bethel merely because the revelation came through a dream.

Petersen, on the other hand, asserts again his conclusion that Zechariah was in fact asleep.[15] Petersen goes so far as investigating modern psychiatric studies of the dream state and the types and number of dreams *possible* in a single evening.[16] From these psychiatric studies Petersen determines that it was not possible for the prophet to experience all of these visions on the same evening as v. 7 seems to indicate.

Petersen's understanding misses the mark on several points. Can one actually determine that four to six dreams per evening are the maximum a person could experience? Much more pertinent is the special, spiritual nature of these visions. Since God gave these visions to Zechariah, one must recognize that their distinctive characteristics render them impossible to compare to ordinary dreams.

The text chooses not to give the reader precise details about the means that the Lord used to give the visions to the prophet. Zechariah merely affirmed that the Lord disclosed his message to him through visions. In the absence of additional information, the interpreter should not attempt to conclude more than the book itself provides.

Moreover, although the Lord communicates with his servants through diverse means, he gave visions to the prophets frequently in the Old Testament. Prominent examples occur in Isa 6; Jer 1:11–19; Ezek 1; 8; and Amos 7:1–9; 8:1–3; numerous additional examples occur also.

---

[14] Unger, *Zechariah*, 26.

[15] Petersen, *Zechariah 1–8*, 111–12.

[16] For example, A. Rechtschaffen, P. Verdone, J. Wheaton, "Reports of Mental Activity During Sleep," *Canadian Psychiatric Association Journal* 8 (1963): 409–14; and H. Roffwarg, et al., "The Effects of Long-Standing Perceptual Alteration on the Hallucinatory Content of Dreams," *Psychophysiology* 5 (1968): 219–25.

Confession and repentance hold a central place in the introduction to Zechariah. Ezra led the people in confession by "praying and confessing, weeping and throwing himself down before the house of God" (Ezra 10:1), proclaiming, "we have been unfaithful to our God" (10:2). Nehemiah prayed, "I confess the sins we Israelites, including myself and my father's house, have committed against you" (Neh 1:6b). Nehemiah 9 chronicles the nation's corporate confession of their sins. For Judah to receive God's blessings, they must acknowledge their continual rejection of God's law and petition him for his grace and forgiveness. As David understood:

> When I kept silent,
>   my bones wasted away
>   through my groaning all day long.
> For day and night
>   your hand was heavy upon me;
> my strength was sapped
>   as in the heat of summer.
> Then I acknowledge my sin to you
>   and did not cover up my iniquity.
> I said, 'I will confess
>   my transgressions to the LORD'—
> and you forgave
>   the guilt of my sin. (Ps 32:4–5)

## 1. The First Vision: The Man on a Red Horse (1:7–17)

⁷On the twenty-fourth day of the eleventh month, the month of Shebat, in the second year of Darius, the word of the LORD came to the prophet Zechariah son of Berekiah, the son of Iddo.

⁸During the night I had a vision—and there before me was a man riding a red horse! He was standing among the myrtle trees in a ravine. Behind him were red, brown and white horses.

⁹I asked, "What are these, my lord?"

The angel who was talking with me answered, "I will show you what they are."

¹⁰Then the man standing among the myrtle trees explained, "They are the ones the Lord has sent to go throughout the earth."

¹¹And they reported to the angel of the LORD, who was standing among the myrtle trees, "We have gone throughout the earth and found the whole world at rest and in peace."

¹²Then the angel of the LORD said, "LORD Almighty, how long will you withhold mercy from Jerusalem and from the towns of Judah, which you have been angry with these seventy years?" ¹³So the LORD spoke kind and comforting words to the angel who talked with me.

**¹⁴**Then the angel who was speaking to me said, "Proclaim this word: This is what the LORD Almighty says: 'I am very jealous for Jerusalem and Zion, **¹⁵**but I am very angry with the nations that feel secure. I was only a little angry, but they added to the calamity.'

**¹⁶**"Therefore, this is what the LORD says: 'I will return to Jerusalem with mercy, and there my house will be rebuilt. And the measuring line will be stretched out over Jerusalem,' declares the LORD Almighty.

**¹⁷**"Proclaim further: This is what the LORD Almighty says: 'My towns will again overflow with prosperity, and the LORD will again comfort Zion and choose Jerusalem.'"

Although the first of Zechariah's night visions presents enigmatic imagery, the primary thrust of vision one leaves little in doubt. The Lord desired to encourage and comfort his people with a reminder of his faithfulness and his presence. No matter how great their difficulties, the great "I AM" will surmount Judah's need. Hence, God's covenant love and mercy assure Judah of a secure future. Despite the sins and judgment of Judah's past, the poverty and persecution of their present, not to mention the uncertainty of their future, the Lord's presence provides comfort and security as the nation rebuilds and regains its place as a witness to the nations of the Lord's faithfulness. Vision one makes it clear that the Lord has decided to revitalize Jerusalem and rebuild the temple.[17]

**1:7** Verse 7 serves as a superscription for all eight visions (1:7–6:8). The date formula given here, "the twenty-fourth day of the eleventh month, the month of Shebat, in the second year of Darius," represents the fullest date formula found in the book of Zechariah. The date, February 15, 519 BC, was the evening in which God disclosed all of the night visions since the verse introduces the entire section.[18] This date falls three months after Zechariah's initial oracle (1:1). Furthermore, the date has special significance since it comes five months after the work to rebuild the temple had resumed (Hag 1:15). On this basis alone, the twenty-fourth day of the month had great significance for Zechariah and his audience, a fitting time to hear a word from the Lord.

Moreover, the month of Shebat is the eleventh month of the year. Thus, the twenty-fourth of Shebat falls only a few days prior to the New Year's festivities. H. G. May develops this observation, noting that New Year's was a time when ancient Near Eastern nations often coronated their kings. He suggests that the visions might function to prepare the nation spiritually for the coronation of Zerubbabel.[19] At the very least, however, we should note the powerful associa-

---

[17] M. A. Sweeney, *The Twelve Prophets, Vol. 2*, Berit Olam (Collegeville, MN: Liturgical Press, 2000), 575.
[18] Merrill, *Zechariah*, 61, 99–100.
[19] H. G. May, "A Key to the Interpretation of Zechariah's Visions," *JBL* 57 (1938): 173–84.

tion between New Year's and temple dedications. The emphasis on Jerusalem and the temple in the night visions fits particularly well in this setting.[20]

**1:8** Verse 8 begins the first of Zechariah's visions. While this vision occurred at night, the text states that Zechariah was awake, visualizing what God had revealed to him. While the typical word for "vision" *(ḥāzōn)*[21] does not occur in this passage, the idiom in v. 8 has a similar meaning, a point well captured by the NIV.[22] Thus, Zechariah was awake and conscious of events transpiring around him. Nonetheless, the ambience of the scene is rather dark and obscure, contrasting the Lord's omniscience and plans for his people with human ability to perceive fully what God is doing.[23]

Moreover, the reason for the description of "vision" coming to the prophet at night likely concerns the symbolism of night and day. While "night" frequently symbolizes sorrow or trouble (see Ps 18:28), the dawning of day portrays God's deliverance (see Pss 30:5; 46:5). If properly understood, Zechariah's symbolism portrayed a night watchman who guards the people under his care through a distressing night and waits for any sign of dawning hope of God's deliverance.[24]

Despite the lack of an objective description of Zechariah's experience, Mitchell's viewpoint that this event never happened is completely baseless. Without any warrant, Mitchell suggests that the visionary language functions as no more than "literary forms in which the prophet clothed his ideas, whatever their origin, for the purpose of securing for them prompter attention among those whom he sought to instruct and influence."[25]

Zechariah's vision focuses on the man and the horse he was riding. Much about this scene remains obscure. The "man" himself remains unidentified throughout the passage. In addition to the "man" in v. 8, an angel speaks in v. 9. Moreover, since the man in v. 10 standing among the myrtle trees does not have a horse, one cannot know if this is the same "man" as in v. 8. The angel of vv. 11–12 is the angel of the Lord. The referents for "these" and "they" in vv. 9–11 present additional challenges that we will examine shortly.

In this passage it is uncertain how many angels participate in Zechariah's vision.[26] Although some dissent exists, the majority of interpreters conclude

---

[20] The RSV and several commentators add the phrase "and Zechariah said" to the end of v. 7 to smooth the transition between the introductory heading of the verse and the first person narration in the verses to follow (see Baldwin, *Zechariah*, 94; Meyers and Meyers, *Zechariah*, 109). This suggestion is unnecessary since the passage presents no important difficulties in its current form.

[21] חָזוֹן. See *HALOT*, 301–2.

[22] The verb רָאִיתִי and its derivatives often signify a prophet or prophetic activities. For instance, the רֹאֶה stands frequently as a synonym for נָבִיא, "prophet," especially in the earlier prophetic writings (see 1 Sam 9:9, which clarifies this point).

[23] Meyers and Meyers, *Zechariah 1–8*, 111.

[24] R. L. Smith, *Micah-Malachi*, WBC (Waco: Word, 1984), 189.

[25] Mitchell, *Zechariah*, 117.

[26] Sweeney, *Twelve Prophets*, 576–77.

there are two.[27] Nevertheless, at points one cannot know precisely which of the two angels is speaking. Clark correctly observes that the repeated reference to "the angel who was talking with me" in vv. 9,13–14 all refer to the same angel.[28] Moreover, the individual addressed as "my lord" in v. 9 must also be one and the same as "the angel who was talking with me."

Whether the man standing among the trees also refers to "the angel who was talking with me" remains enigmatic. Most commentators agree that one should not identify the man among the myrtle trees with the angel speaking with the prophet.[29] Clark notes that "the angel who was talking with me" appears in 1:19; 2:3; 4:1,4; 5:5,10; 6:4—all designated with the same terminology. One should not be surprised if Zechariah did not use consistent terminology to refer to the angel over five separate night visions. Rather, he employed several different expressions referring to the angel in vision one.[30]

Unger, whose views represent many conservative and critical scholars, suggests that the "man" among the myrtle trees is none other than the angel of the Lord.[31] Unger reaches his conclusion based partially on the statement in v. 13 where the Lord himself spoke to the angel who accompanied Zechariah. Furthermore, v. 11 also supports this conclusion. Thus, we preserve the distinction between the "angel of the LORD" and the angel interpreting Zechariah's vision to him. Consequently, "the angel who was talking with me" in v. 9 represents Zechariah's angelic interpreter, not the angel of the Lord. Smith also concludes that the "man" portrays the angel of the Lord and sees the pronouns "these" and "they" in vv. 9–11 as referring to "the other angelic riders in the patrol."[32]

After such a discussion, a modern reader might chafe at the ambiguity in identifying characters in Zechariah's first vision, perhaps even charge Zechariah with poor writing. Nonetheless, these literary vagaries serve the prophet's theological point well, for the angels are heavenly, mysterious beings, incapable of precise description or understanding. What might seem like an important point to a modern reader was truly insignificant for Zechariah's purpose. The only point Zechariah needed to communicate was the heavenly origin of the messengers and the message they delivered.

Further, Unger maintains that this "man" is "emphatically presented while they (the other angels in the context) are presented only by implication."[33] Cu-

---

[27] For example, Baldwin, *Zechariah*, 93.
[28] D. J. Clark, "The Case of the Vanishing Angel," *BT* 33 (1982): 213–14.
[29] See Mitchell, *Zechariah*, 110; Sweeney, *Twelve Prophets*, 577.
[30] Clark, "Vanishing Angel," 214–15.
[31] Unger, *Zechariah*, 27. See also M. J. Boda, *The NIV Application Commentary: Haggai, Zechariah* (Grand Rapids: Zondervan, 2004), 196. S. R. Driver (*The Minor Prophets* [New York: Oxford University Press, 1904], 186–87) made this same identification in response to the critical dissection and emendation of this passage in his day.
[32] R. L. Smith, *Micah-Malachi*, 189. See the role of the angel of the Lord ("the LORD's messenger") in Hag 1:13.
[33] Ibid.

riously, however, the passage gives greater attention to the steed the man rode and where the horse and rider stationed themselves than to the man himself.

Zechariah envisioned a man astride a "red" horse, followed by three additional horses. Presumably, the angelic "men" mounted the three horses in the rear of the scene as the first horse carried a rider. The pronoun "they" in v. 11 surely refers to the riders on the latter three horses.

The primary significance of horses here, in contrast to other beasts such as donkeys or camels, evokes the memory of their use in military contexts.[34] Hence, the presence of horses in this vision connotes military supremacy and the prestige accompanying such power. The modern use of horses bears no relation to that of antiquity. For instance, little evidence survives of horseback riding in Zechariah's day. Instead, horses functioned as one of the most important military weapons in the ancient world, allowing armies to move quickly and to develop an offensive threat that would have been impossible without their use. Despite this unusual element of the story, the military overtones connote the angels' authoritative patrol throughout the whole earth (v. 10).[35] Sweeney suggests that the patrolling horses correspond to the widespread concept of horse mounted messengers used to deliver communication in the Persian empire.[36]

While the military significance of the horses is primary, we should also examine the horses' colors. A cursory survey of the way the ancient versions and modern translations handle the question points to significant ambiguity.[37] The term "red" (*ʾādōm*) seems relatively clear;[38] although the English translation is dubious since no horseman speaks of a "red horse." Whether the horse was sorrel, bay, chestnut, or roan, one cannot determine with certainty. Nonetheless, any of these options improve on the NIV's rendering, "red."

The second color label has been translated diversely.[39] The options range from "dappled" to "reddish brown." The Hebrew word in question is *śārōq*. "Reddish brown" enjoys the support of the lexicons,[40] whereas "dappled"

---

[34] S. v. "Horse," in *ABD*, 6:1136 and Clark, "Vanishing Angel," 216. For a discussion of the utilization of the horse in ancient warfare, see Y. Yadin, *The Art of Warfare in Biblical Lands* (New York: McGraw-Hill, 1963), 302.

[35] No objective reason exists to adopt H. Richter's ("Die Pferde in den Nachtgesichten des Sacharja," *ZAW* 98 [1986]: 96–100) thesis that the mention of horsemen in 1:7–17 as well as in 6:5–7 was artificially separated into different accounts by a redactor.

[36] Sweeney, *Twelve Prophets*, 578.

[37] For a survey of the versions' handling of this matter, see W. D. McHardy, "The Horses in Zechariah," *ZAW* 103 (1968): 174–79, who adds that he believes that the text should be revised to read "a red horse ... and behind him were yellow, black and white horses" (179). R. P. Gordon ("An Inner-Targum Corruption, [Zech. I 8]," *VT* 25 [1985]): 216–21 also surveys the problems the ancient versions had with the horses' colors.

[38] אָדֹם. See *HALOT*, 15–16.

[39] שָׂרֹק. See *HALOT*, 1357.

[40] See *HALOT* and BDB.

fails to have lexical support.[41] Zechariah portrayed the third color of horses as "white" (*lābān*), a rendering about which there is little doubt.[42]

Many have attempted to assign theological significance to these colors. Unger gives one of the more extreme examples when he writes,

> Does the color red speak of bloodshed and war and identify Him as the One who, as the result of the redemption He wrought at His first advent, will come to "judge and *to make war*" at His second advent (Rev. 19:11)?[43]

However, one must not invest the terms with too much importance—particularly from a canonical perspective. For such a typological interpretation to be attractive, all of the color terms should have theological significance, and their interpretation must be demonstrable, not left to the interpreter's whim. As a result, one should not invest the colors of Zechariah's horses with symbolic meaning.

The reference to the myrtle trees presents a similar difficulty. Just what symbolism, if any, does Zechariah intend regarding the myrtles? Sweeney's interpretation appears fanciful. He maintains that the myrtle leaves look like eyes, reinforcing the message of the horses patrolling the earth.[44] Unger again sees grand symbolism:

> The myrtle trees or shrubs beautifully symbolize Israel, the covenant people, in the role of an eternally elect nation, loved by the Lord, and the object of His unchanging purposes (Rom. 11:29).[45]

With greater restraint, one should note what the Old Testament does say about myrtles. The myrtle is an evergreen shrub growing seven to eight feet in height. This shrub is best known for its use in the construction of the booths used in the Feast of Tabernacles (Neh 8:15). The Feast of Tabernacles (or Booths) commemorated Israel's wilderness pilgrimage, recognized God's blessings at harvest time, and provided an opportunity for the people to renew or rededicate themselves to the Lord's covenant. Thus, the reference to myrtles connotes passages where God's faithful blessing and protection over his people was paramount. This association well suits Zechariah's purpose to encourage and motivate the disconsolate people.

**1:9–11** In these verses we continue to encounter two distinct angels. The angel talking with Zechariah offers to explain the meaning of the vision to the prophet, but it is the "man" among the myrtles who actually does the talk-

---

[41] The arguments produced by Gordon, "Corruption," 216–19, and adopted by Clark, "Vanishing Angel," 217, are not compelling.
[42] לָבָן. See *HALOT*, 517.
[43] Unger, *Zechariah*, 27.
[44] Sweeney, *Twelve Prophets*, 577.
[45] Unger, *Zechariah*, 27.

ing. Further, v. 11 states that the angel of the Lord stood among the myrtles. We conclude, along with most commentators, that the most natural reading in this text equates the angel of the Lord with the horseman standing among the myrtles in v. 8.

The subsequent question, the identity of the angel of the Lord *(mal'ak YHWH)*,[46] represents one of the more important questions regarding God's self-disclosure in the Old Testament.[47] These references to the angel of the Lord have long intrigued Old Testament students for several reasons. For one, the angel of the Lord always stands in the foreground in every scene in which he occurs, underscoring his importance. For another, he sometimes appears to be distinct from the Lord himself and at other times he seems to be one and the same with God.[48] Perhaps the most striking example of identification with God himself occurs in Gen 16:7–12 since the angel of the Lord speaks for God in the first person singular in v. 10. Furthermore, the Old Testament contains numerous other examples where the text seems to speak of God and the angel of the Lord interchangeably.

Over the years scholars have offered numerous identifications for the angel of the Lord. Traditionally, Christian interpreters have attempted to correlate the angel of the Lord with the Logos, the pre-incarnate Christ, a view Unger embraces. He writes,

> The Angel of the Presence, Jehovah-Christ, who had so wonderfully delivered their father Jacob is even now in the process of restoring His ancient people and preparing them for the revelation of His salvation at the end of the age.[49]

Unger's position is difficult to demonstrate biblically, however.

Others believe that the angel of the Lord was a mere angel, a created spiritual being.[50] The lesser angel view is untenable because God frequently identifies himself with the angel of the Lord.[51] In Old Testament contexts the angel of the Lord seems to represent a theophany of the Lord God himself. Not only have biblical scholars typically reached this conclusion, but theologians have frequently agreed.[52]

---

[46] מַלְאַךְ־יהוה.

[47] For a brief survey see R. L. Smith, *Old Testament Theology* (Nashville: Broadman and Holman, 1993), 107–14.

[48] See W. C. Kaiser, Jr., *Toward an Old Testament Theology* (Grand Rapids: Zondervan, 1978), 84–86. This is a conclusion also drawn by scholars approaching the matter from a more traditional, critical posture. For example, G. von Rad, *Old Testament Theology* (New York: Harper and Row, 1962), 1:285–89, and s.v. "Angels" in *ABD*, 1:250.

[49] Unger, *Zechariah*, 30.

[50] C. Westermann, *God's Angels Need No Wings* (Philadelphia: Fortress, 1979), 69.

[51] Note the following examples: Gen 16:11,13; 18:1–2,13,17; 22:11–12,15–18; 31:11,13; Exod 3:2,4.

[52] See J. L. Garrett, *Systematic Theology* (Grand Rapids: Eerdmans, 1990), 1:359–61; and

Nevertheless, we cannot equate the angel of the Lord with God himself in vv. 9–11 as is possible elsewhere in the Old Testament. The fundamental problem hinges on the conversation between God and the angel of the Lord in v. 12. Zechariah portrays two different beings conversing with one another. Therefore, it is necessary to identify two separate persons here.[53]

When reflecting on this passage, Augustine pondered the nature of angelic beings, wondering how angels could speak with humans in dreams (Matt 1:20), could have their feet washed by patriarchs (Gen 18:4; 19:2), or wrestle with Jacob (Gen 32:24). While Augustine did not disparage asking how angels could do such things, he wisely observed that the discussion must remain within reasonable limits "if those who take part avoid the error of thinking they know what they do not know. For what need is there of affirming or denying or making nice distinctions about these and similar matters, when ignorance of them imputes no blame?"[54]

As already noted, the horsemen signify the Lord's military might. God sent these angelic troops to patrol his earth, projecting his regal authority throughout the world. On their return, the angelic garrison delivered an astounding report of peace throughout the earth. Merrill notes with sensitivity to the Hebrew text that the verbal form translated by the NIV "we have gone" means "to assert dominion or sovereignty over."[55] A couple of well-known examples should suffice to illustrate this nuance. In Ezek 28:14 the king of Tyre in his arrogance seeks to assert his authority as he "walked around." The same verbal form describes Satan's "walking about" the earth in Job 1:7.

The image of horseback soldiers would be quite familiar to one living in the Persian era because such mounted troops were renowned in the Persian empire for the speed and power with which they could project the will of the Persian sovereign. The two primary questions we face here are: (1) Was the angels' report positive or negative? (2) To which time frame did their report refer?

Concerning the first question, the angels declare in v. 11, "We have gone throughout the earth and found the whole world at rest." One might merely assume that the message was positive. Barker, for instance, maintains that Persia was at rest around 520 BC with all of the empire's foes in submission. He cites the scenes of tranquility portrayed graphically on the renowned trilingual Behistun inscription as the king's enemies bowed in submission.[56] Unfortunately,

---

M. J. Erickson (*Christian Theology* [Grand Rapids: Baker, 1985], 443), who also reach a similar conclusion.

[53] Merrill, *Zechariah*, 103.

[54] Augustine, *Enchiridion de Fide, Spe et Charitate*, 59 (PL 40:260).

[55] Merrill, *Zechariah*, 104. The Hb. verb, הִתְהַלֵּךְ occurs in the *Hithpael*, which often expresses iterative or repeated action. See *HALOT*, 248.

[56] K. L. Barker, "Zechariah," EBC, 611–12. See also Meyers and Meyers, *Zechariah 1–8*, 115.

this scene is quite misleading, for Persia was not at peace during this era. Regarding the same inscription, Bright writes,

> Though Darius in his great trilingual inscription on the cliff at Behistun sought to belittle the extent of the opposition to him, it is clear that unrest exploded from one end of the realm to the other. Rebellions broke out in Media, Elam and Parsa, in Armenia, all across Iran to the farthest eastern frontier, while in the west both Egypt and Asia Minor were affected. . . . it must have seemed that the Persian Empire was literally flying to pieces.[57]

The idiom that the NIV renders "at rest and in peace" must connote oppression here because we know the political situation in Persia at this time was not altogether secure. Further, the peace that God's people "enjoyed" was the type of tranquility that emerges when a vanquished nation submits under the heavy hand of her oppressor.[58] The peace the angelic warriors observed was not the peace that would come in fulfillment of God's promise to restore Israel's well being in an idyllic fashion. Rather, the peace Zechariah described was the divinely imposed peace. In other words, this peace was tantamount to the people's resignation to endure the judgment God had foretold, completing the sentence the heavenly Judge had issued.

The second question focuses on the time frame this passage encompasses. Mitchell argues that the first vision refers retrospectively to the Babylonian era when their soldiers effectively quelled all insurrections.[59] However, no textual reason exists to make such a claim. The passage fits well with the historical context in Persia around 520 BC. The passage also seems to introduce the need for God's peace to dwell on the earth. Thus Baldwin writes, "It was sufficiently clear that the riots of 521 BC had not begun the eschatological battles which would usher in the Messianic age."[60] In conclusion, Petersen's remark fittingly summarizes this passage. He writes, "There is no disturbance, whether by earthly or divine agents. For most Israelites at most times in their history, this message would have been utterly welcome. Not so this time."[61] The postexilic community did not want this type of "peace." Instead, they longed for the Lord, their Divine Warrior, to do battle for them, liberating them so that they could enjoy the national sovereignty they had before the exile.

**1:12–13** The angel of the Lord finally delivered the message of divine intervention. One might normally anticipate a lament bemoaning the lack of peace in Israel (see Jer 47:6–7). In vv. 12–13 the lament resulted from the existence of peace—a peace that enslaved Israel and hindered what God intended

---

[57] J. Bright, *A History of Israel*, 3rd ed. (Philadelphia: Westminster, 1981), 369.
[58] See Baldwin, *Zechariah*, 96–97; Unger, *Zechariah*, 29.
[59] Mitchell, *Zechariah*, 121.
[60] Baldwin, *Zechariah*, 96.
[61] Petersen, *Zechariah 1–8*, 146.

to do through his people on a global scale. The news of peace on earth must have disheartened God's people, moving the angel of the Lord to intercede for a speedy resolution to the crisis and an end to the period of exile foretold by Jeremiah (25:11–12). Instead of the peace that the people expected and the angel of the Lord prayed for, the "shaking" from on high would usher in God's glory and his full favor to Zion. Similarly, Hag 2:6–7 states,

> This is what the LORD Almighty says: "In a little while I will once more shake the heavens and the earth, the sea and the dry land. I will shake all nations, and the desired of all nations will come, and I will fill this house with glory," says the LORD Almighty.

The angel of the Lord's intercessory prayer marks the beginning of the end of the Babylonian exile. The seventy-year exile Jeremiah prophesied would conclude shortly.[62]

Historians disagree over their understanding of the chronology of the exile. There are two different reckonings of the beginning and end of the seventy years of captivity.[63] One begins with 605 BC and the first deportation to Babylon and continues until 536/35 BC when the first contingent of returnees settled in Israel.[64] The other understanding calculates the beginning at 586 BC, commencing with the destruction of the temple, and marks the end of the exile with the completion of the temple in 516 BC.

Jeremiah's message seems ambiguous at this juncture. Jeremiah appears to predict that Judah would serve Babylon for seventy years (25:12). This view points toward the earlier dates, ending either in 536/35 BC as mentioned above, or 539 BC when Babylon actually fell. Alternatively, Jeremiah suggests that the exile would encompass the years of Judah's devastation (25:11), supporting the latter dating.[65] Baldwin argues that Jeremiah intended a double reference, influencing Zechariah's perspective on the dating.[66] Hence, interpreters both ancient and modern observe that while the seventy years can be calculated with remarkable precision, the beginning and ending points of the exile are flexible.[67] Besides, if Zechariah's community had believed that the seventy years rigidly applied to the fall of Babylon, they would not have felt apprehensive about the timing of the end of the exile.

---

[62] E. Lipinski ("Recherches sur le livre de Zacharie," *VT* 20 [1970]: 38) notes that the ancient Near Eastern world disclosed a pagan occurrence of divine wrath lasting seventy years. Esarhaddon's (681–669 BC) inscription indicates that Marduk was angry with his people and intended to punish Babylon for seventy years. In this inscription, Marduk relented and judgment lasted only eleven years.

[63] C. F. Whitley's suggestion ("The Term 'Seventy Years Captivity,' " *VT* 4 [1954]: 72) that "seventy years" here is the insertion of an editor subsequent to Zechariah lacks support.

[64] A. Orr, "The Seventy Years of Babylon," *VT* 6 (1956): 306.

[65] Baldwin, *Zechariah*, 97.

[66] Ibid.

[67] Merrill, *Zechariah*, 105; Baldwin, *Zechariah*, 97–98.

God's people wanted to know why their punishment had not ceased and why God had not yet restored their fortunes. The "angel" who was talking with Zechariah delivered the reply to Judah's question. The heavenly message would prove welcome indeed.

The angel recounted "kind and comforting words" from the Lord—assurances that God would soon begin restoring the temple, the cities, and indeed the people themselves. The word "comfort" *(niḥumîm)*[68] evokes strong parallels with Isa 40:1, where a comparable verbal form of the same word found in Zech 1:13 occurs.[69] Isa 40:1 proclaims the end of the exile and the beginning of God's restoration of his people. With as much pathos as in the Isaianic promise of deliverance, the angel declares to Zechariah that "the long night of waiting (seventy years)" was over.[70]

**1:14** After seeing the vision, Zechariah became responsible for proclaiming its content. The prophet's discovery about the Lord's attitude towards his people became a burden on Zechariah to instruct Judah regarding God's faithful response toward his people. "To proclaim" *(qěrāʾ)* strikes at the heart of what it meant to be a prophet.[71] The same Hebrew term occurs often in the prophets, but one of the most striking is in Isa 40:6: "A voice says, 'Cry out' *[qěrāʾ]*. And I said, 'What shall I cry? *[qěrāʾ]*. All men are like grass .... The grass withers and the flowers fail, but the word of our God stands forever."

Zechariah's interpreting angel declared that the Lord was utterly "jealous" for Jerusalem.[72] While jealousy strikes many moderns as a negative emotion, jealousy comprises a fundamental part of the vocabulary of love and often describes God's relationship to Israel. Jealousy describes the intensity of God's love toward his people. God's love is never passive. Rather, the Lord's love burns like a refiner's fire, consuming the dross and all impurities, as well as purifying the resulting precious relationship. The Lord's jealousy portrays his protective love for Israel, as well as his desire for faithful worship from his followers. Perhaps the most important observation about God's jealousy concerns the connection to the covenant that the term evokes. The first mention of God's jealousy occurs when the Lord made the covenant with Israel in Exod 20:5: "You shall not bow down to them or worship them (idols); for I, the LORD your God am a jealous God." Jealousy also occurs in Exod 34:14 and Deut 5:9, which are covenant contexts as well. Describing this special relationship between the Lord and Israel, Baldwin observes,

---

[68] נִחֻמִים. See *HALOT*, 688–89.

[69] In Isa 40:1 the prophet employed the Hebrew expression נַחֲמוּ נַחֲמוּ עַמִּי ("comfort, comfort my people").

[70] R. L. Smith, *Micah-Malachi*, 191.

[71] קָרָא. See *HALOT*, 1130.

[72] The Hb. verb קָנָא occurs with its cognate accusative, a strongly emphatic verbal construction. See the similar idiom in 8:2.

> Because they (Israel) are His, they can belong to no one else, hence the prohibition of idolatry and the sanctions against it in the third commandment; but these are followed by the assurance of "steadfast love to thousands of those who love me and keep my commandments" (Ex. 20:6). God's jealousy is a measure of the intensity of His love towards those with whom He has entered into covenant. So great is His love that He cannot be indifferent if they spurn Him by disobedience or sheer carelessness.[73]

God's jealousy burns like a fire (Deut 4:24) that not only burns against Israel for her infidelity toward the Lord (Deut 32:16,21), but it also enflames and consumes the nations for opposing God's beloved, Israel (Ezek 36:3–7; 38:19–23). The Lord's jealousy also plays an important role in Isaiah (9:7; 37:32; 42:13; 59:17). Ezekiel's teaching viewed God's jealousy prominently, containing one quarter of all references to divine jealousy in the entire Old Testament. Ezekiel pictured the Lord's jealousy for the faithful love of his people using the metaphor of a husband's jealousy for his adulterous wife (16:38,42; 23:35). Most frequently, God's jealousy burned against his people in wrath. Nahum 1:2 presents an exception in which the Lord's jealousy consumes his foes in defense of Israel.[74]

This same jealousy moved the Lord to restore Judah, to comfort her, and to protect her. Judah groaned for seventy years as God's fire scorched her for her sins. Now, the Lord's jealousy on behalf of Judah compelled him to renew his blessings to her. For God, the issue focuses on faithfulness to his covenant with Israel. Nowhere in the Old Testament is this commitment portrayed in more emotive terms than Hos 2:19–20:

> I will betroth you to me forever;
> > I will betroth you in righteousness and justice,
> > > in love and compassion.
> 
> I will betroth you in faithfulness,
> > and you will acknowledge the LORD.

While "Jerusalem" and "Zion" often serve as word pairs, functioning as synonymous terms in paired lines of Old Testament poetry,[75] Baldwin suggests that Zechariah intended a subtle distinction here.[76] Jerusalem routinely represents the epicenter of God's activity on earth. The name Zion connotes the most ancient history of the city, tying it directly to David who captured the city

---

[73] Baldwin, *Zechariah*, 102. For a more extensive development of these themes, see A. Petitjean, *Les oracles du Proto-Zacharie* (Paris: J. Gabalda, 1969), 79–81.

[74] *TWOT*, 3:1145–47.

[75] See Y. Avishur, *Stylistic Studies of Word-Pairs in Biblical and Ancient Semitic Literatures* (Neukirchen-Vluyn: Neukirchener, 1984) for an extensive treatment of the function and distribution of word pairs in ancient Semitic poetry.

[76] Baldwin, *Zechariah*, 99.

(2 Sam 5:7). Moreover, one frequently encounters references to Zion where the worship of the Lord functions as the explicit point of the passage (see 1 Kgs 8:1; Ps 84:7). The cultic significance of Zion evokes both God's responsibilities and Judah's duties. The Lord committed himself to assist Judah to reinstitute worship in the rebuilt temple. The people had the mandate to rebuild the cultic center and to remain faithful to the Lord in subsequent years.

**1:15** Here the Lord articulates the reason for his anger against the nations. God's anger burns because of the nations' rejection of the Lord, growing out of their sense of self-sufficiency, their feeling that they could "feel secure." The expression "feel secure" sometimes carries a positive connotation, for example when referring to the peace God would give to Jerusalem (Isa 32:18). The term functions negatively when speaking of those who have no need for the Lord (Amos 6:1). Although God intended to use Babylon as an instrument of his wrath against Judah for her sins, Babylon went beyond her divine mandate in oppressing Judah and desiring to usurp God's place among the people. Isaiah's prophecy of Babylon's fall clarifies the Lord's complaint:

> Sit in silence, go into darkness,
>   Daughter of the Babylonians;
> no more will you be called
>   queen of kingdoms.
> I was angry with my people
>   and desecrated my inheritance;
> I gave them into your hand,
>   and you showed them no mercy. . . .
> You said, "I will continue forever—
>   the eternal queen!" . . .
> Now then, listen, you wanton creature,
>   lounging in your security
> and saying to yourself,
>   "I am, and there is none besides me.
> I will never be a widow
>   or suffer the loss of children."
> Both of these will overtake you
>   in a moment, on a single day:
> loss of children and widowhood.
>   They will come upon you in full measure. (Isa 47:5–9)

Isaiah delivered a similar warning to Assyria in Isa 10:5–19, and perhaps a notice to Persia as well, by means of the example of Assyria and Babylon.[77]

---

[77] Merrill, *Zechariah*, 104–5.

Finally, the phrase translated in the NIV as "I was only a little angry" *(qāṣaptî měʿāṭ)* presents significant ambiguities.[78] The Hebrew phrase can have different meanings, as reflected in the different translations. Specifically, the term "a little" *(měʿāṭ)* leads to the primary interpretative problem. Does the expression mean that God was only "a little angry" as the KJV and NIV suggest? If so, what does Zechariah intend to say about God's anger? It is implausible to conclude that Zechariah meant that God was not very angry with Judah,[79] particularly in light of the dire circumstances the nation faced daily.

Another translation renders "a little" as a chronological term, not as an adjective qualifying "angry." According to this understanding, the passage states that the Lord was angry with Judah for "a little while," but that the nations added to the duration of God's judgment against Judah, the main point of the Lord's condemnation of the nations in v. 15.[80]

While the language of the passage could support either interpretation, it is preferable to conclude that God was only "a little angry" with Judah, meaning that he intended to discipline her as a parent would discipline a wayward child. He was not angry to the point that he sought to end his relationship with his people. The nations' crime would then add to the intensity of their judgment. The Lord would not seek to end Judah's identity as a political, social, and religious entity.

**1:16–17** These verses contain an oracle explaining the previous vision and convey the love and grace God would show to Israel—contrasted with his fierce anger and jealousy burning against the nations—by extending the "kind and comforting words" (v. 13). The promise of restoration Zechariah expresses echoes Ezekiel's assurance that the Lord's glory will return to the temple (Ezek 43:1–5; 48:35b). Nonetheless, the presence of God among his people was an assurance that all he promised would come to fruition. In prophesying Israel's restoration, Jer 30 made a similar point, arguing that God dwelling among his people ensured their restoration and well being.[81]

The NIV's "I will return to Jerusalem with mercy" suggests that the verb "return" is a future tense. The Hebrew form *(šabtî)* is a past tense, however. The use of a past tense verb underscores the certainty of what the Lord is about

---

[78] קָצַפְתִּי מְעָט. The frequently occurring term *měʿāṭ* ("a little") can refer to a limited amount of time or small number of most anything. See *HALOT*, 611 and BDB, 589–90 for surveys of the usage of this substantive.

[79] Another possibility suggests that God was "a little angry" with the nations because they provoked him with their rebellion.

[80] See Barker, "Zechariah," 613, and Petersen, *Zechariah 1–8*, 155, for two examples of interpreters who follow the chronological view.

[81] Unger's suggestion that Zechariah envisions a millennial temple here is not based on the data of the text *(Zechariah*, 33).

to do. The prophet saw the Lord's action as though God had already fulfilled it, using a verbal form that conveys completed action to stress the point.[82]

The "measuring line" the Lord brings to stretch out over Jerusalem represents the string line builders still use today in establishing the placement of foundations and the construction of straight walls. In several Old Testament texts God symbolically stretched out a line in the process of rebuilding (Job 38:5; Jer 31:39). Thus, the imagery reinforces the message that construction in Jerusalem the Lord will begin shortly.[83]

Verse 17 extends the promise of blessing to the towns surrounding Jerusalem and her temple. The other cities of the restoration will share the fortunes Jerusalem enjoys. This blessing will overflow the land, encompassing and uncontrollable like a flood.[84] As the exile began, Lam 1:2 intoned that the great city Jerusalem had "none to comfort her." Now the Lord himself assures his people that he will bring comfort to Zion (Isa 40:1).

Although not clear in the NIV, one encounters the Hebrew word 'ôd (often translated "again, further") four times in v. 17.[85] Meyers and Meyers summarize the importance of the repetition saying that the term expresses Zechariah's "understanding of continuity between the preexilic and postexilic communities, a continuity to be symbolized by the restored temple."[86]

The Lord commanded Zechariah to "proclaim further" the message of imminent restoration. This instruction linked the following promise to the former one, reiterating the message of hope and assurance. Even the pronoun "my" in the phrase "my cities" reinforces God's personal relationship with his people. (Similar themes occur in Hos 14:5–8; Joel 3:18–21; and Amos 9:11–15.)[87]

At the close of v. 17, Zechariah declares that the Lord chose Jerusalem. While the historical books make the point that God had elected Jerusalem (see 2 Chr 6:6, "I have chosen Jerusalem for my Name to be there"), no other prophet does so.[88]

In conclusion, Zechariah's first vision expresses God's grace, comfort, and blessing to Israel. This vision has several theological emphases. For one, the Lord himself loves his people, forgetting the past. Additionally, the presence of the angel of the Lord supernaturally benefits Israel. Because the Lord had elected and comforted his people, Israel could assure herself of a

---

[82] See G. L. Klein, "The Prophetic Perfect," *JNSL* 16 (1990): 45–60 for an analysis of how Old Testament writers, particularly the prophets, used the past tense of the Hb. verb to describe action as a *fait accompli*.
[83] Meyers and Meyers, *Zechariah 1–8*, 123.
[84] The Hb. term תְפוּצֶינָה means "to spread, scatter." In Prov 5:16 the term describes a gushing spring. See Petitjean, *Proto-Zacharie*, 67–69.
[85] עוֹד. See *HALOT*, 795–96.
[86] Meyers and Meyers, *Zechariah 1–8*, 124.
[87] Sweeney, *Twelve Prophets*, 580–81.
[88] Petitjean, *Proto-Zacharie*, 71–72.

bright future. God was no powerless deity, though. He reigned with complete sovereignty over every nation. Apart from this profound truth about the Lord, faith would represent little more than naïve, wishful thinking. The theological theme of creation stresses God's authority and dominion over his entire world. Despite any measure of circumstances that might seem to crush the hopes of the community of faith, the Lord's jealousy for his people demonstrates the faithful relationship God offers his people. As the psalmist instructs,

> Blessed is he whose help is the God of Jacob,
>   whose hope is in the LORD his God,
> the Maker of heaven and earth,
>   the sea, and everything in them—
>   the LORD, who remains faithful forever. (Ps 146:5–6)

Finally, for those nations who were not chosen and who had opposed God and his people, only a future of judgment awaits.[89]

## 2. The Second Vision: Four Horns and Four Craftsmen (1:18–21 [Hb 2:1–4])

**[18]Then I looked up—and there before me were four horns! [19]I asked the angel who was speaking to me, "What are these?"**

**He answered me, "These are the horns that scattered Judah, Israel and Jerusalem."**

**[20]Then the LORD showed me four craftsmen. [21]I asked, "What are these coming to do?"**

**He answered, "These are the horns that scattered Judah so that no one could raise his head, but the craftsmen have come to terrify them and throw down these horns of the nations who lifted up their horns against the land of Judah to scatter its people."**

Vision two consoles God's people by assuring them of God's control over all the players on the world political stage. Israel and Judah had suffered torment by nations who sought their destruction. This vision repeats the message of God's imminent judgment over those hostile powers, continuing the message of comfort in 1:13.

**1:18–19** Four of Zechariah's visions begin with the phrase, "Then I looked up" (see 2:1; 5:1; 6:1). The expression transitions from Zechariah's contemplation of the angelic message in the previous vision to the new revelation now given to him.

The four horns drew the prophet's attention, functioning as the initial focus of God's message. Throughout the Old Testament, as well as the ancient Near

---

[89] Charles Feinberg, *Minor Prophets* (Chicago: Moody, 1976), 38.

East, the horn represents strength and authority.[90] Though the bull symbolizes power, the bull's horn epitomizes everything the bull represented, much as horns represent the trophy of the hunt. For example, Deut 33:17 describes Joseph's power: "In majesty he is like a firstborn bull; his horns are the horns of a wild ox." In Ps 18:2 the psalmist praises the Lord declaring, "He is my shield and the horn of my salvation, my stronghold." Consequently, "to lift up the horn" means to assert one's power and prestige. Moreover, the Lord cuts off the horns of his foes in defeat (Ps 75:10).

Zechariah questioned "the angel who was speaking to me" (see v. 9) by asking, "What is the significance of *four* [emphasis mine] horns?" The angel replied that the horns represent those who have "scattered Judah, Israel and Jerusalem" (v. 19). The significance of the statement divides interpreters. Generally dating back at least as far as the Targumim, all agree that these horns refer to kingdoms. Do the four horns intend four *specific* empires or are they more general? If Zechariah envisioned particular empires, which are they?

Commentators who seek individual kingdoms in vision two cannot agree about which empires Zechariah envisioned. One ancient interpretation understood the empires to be Assyria, Babylon, Media, and Persia. Barker draws this same conclusion because he thinks that the verb "scattered" suggests that these "horns" have already persecuted God's people.[91] However, as we have observed previously, Old Testament authors sometimes employed the Hebrew past tense in future contexts, blunting the force of Barker's argument. Jerome, along with other church fathers, suggests a different identification, understanding the horns as Babylon, Medo-Persia, Greece, and Rome, paralleling Daniel's famous visions (chaps. 2 and 7).[92] Unger reaches a similar conclusion based on his conviction that the scope of the night visions "extends through the centuries and on to the establishment of the kingdom over Israel" inaugurated at the second advent of Christ.[93] Certainly, the identification of Babylon, Medo-Persia, Greece, and Rome has evidence to commend it. However, the text fails to demonstrate the certainty of this interpretation, so dogmatic confidence is not justified.

Alternatively, the difficulty of determining which kingdoms Zechariah intended could suggest that he may not have intended specific kingdoms at all.[94] Thus, the prophet's reference to four horns portrays the entirety of opposition to Judah, with foes attacking the nation from every side.[95] Zech 6:5 uses the

---

[90] O. Keel, *The Symbolism of the Biblical World* (New York: Crossroad, 1985), 86.
[91] Barker, "Zechariah," 615.
[92] Mitchell, *Zechariah*, 132.
[93] Unger, *Zechariah*, 37. See also Merrill, *Zechariah*, 110.
[94] Theodoret of Mopsuestia, cited approvingly by Mitchell, *Zechariah*, 133.
[95] Baldwin, *Zechariah*, 104; R. L. Smith, *Micah-Malachi*, 193.

expression "the four spirits of heaven" in a similar fashion. Unger's claim that "the four horns symbolizing Gentile persecution of the Jew were successive and not contemporaneous" lacks evidence as well.[96] Thus, the horns probably represent all those world powers that aggressively confront God's people. The anger that the Lord felt toward those opposed to his will and his people (v. 15) resurfaces in the following verses.

**1:20–21** Zechariah's vision continues with the appearance of "the four craftsmen." Significantly, Zechariah does not ask who these craftsmen are, a point modern interpreters should take to heart.[97] As was the case with the precise identification of the angelic interpreters in vision one, Zechariah's message takes precedence over the characters in the account. Moreover, one cannot determine why the prophet uses the imagery of a workman. While craftsmen typically use their strength and skill to build, they can also use those same abilities to destroy (Ezek 21:31). In response to Zechariah's question about what the craftsmen will do, the Lord first repeats what the four horns have done, then explains that the craftsmen have come to destroy the horns. Consequently, all who arrogantly seek to persecute God's people, and in so doing oppose the Lord himself, face ruin.

The second vision ends much as the first vision did. In both, Judah faces overwhelming opposition from all quarters. Nonetheless, God's people should receive encouragement from the knowledge that the Lord himself protects them and judges the unrighteous nations who spurn the Lord and persecute his people. The universal scope of persecution against Judah meets God's sure opposition.

Zechariah 1 alternates from calls for repentance to warnings about judgment for continued disobedience to the hope of a secure home that God offers those who put their faith in him. As Judah looked to her past to see the Lord's faithfulness to his word, so the nation had the confidence to await a blessed future in which God would build a secure, everlasting home for them. Isaac Watts built on similar themes when he wrote "O God, Our Help in Ages Past":

> O God, our help in ages past,
> Our hope for years to come,
> Our shelter from the stormy blast,
> And our eternal home!
>
> Under the shadow of Thy throne
> Thy saints have dwelt secure;
> Sufficient is Thine arm alone,
> And our defense is sure.

---

[96] Unger, *Zechariah*, 38.

[97] Unger (*Zechariah*, 39–41) argues at length that these craftsmen are based on the prophecies in Dan 2:31–45; 7:2–13 and find their fulfillment in the millennial kingdom.

Before the hills in order stood,
Or earth received her frame,
From everlasting Thou art God,
To endless years the same.

A thousand ages in Thy sight
Are like an evening gone;
Short as the watch that ends the night
Before the rising sun.

Time, like an ever rolling stream,
Bears all its sons away;
They, fly forgotten, as a dream
Dies at the op'ning day.

O God, our help in ages past,
Our hope for years to come,
Be Thou our guard while life shall last,
And our eternal home.[98]

### 3. The Third Vision: The Surveyor (2:1–13 [Hb 2:5–17])

¹Then I looked up—and there before me was a man with a measuring line in his hand! ²I asked, "Where are you going?"

He answered me, "To measure Jerusalem, to find out how wide and how long it is."

³Then the angel who was speaking to me left, and another angel came to meet him ⁴and said to him: "Run, tell that young man, 'Jerusalem will be a city without walls because of the great number of men and livestock in it. ⁵And I myself will be a wall of fire around it,' declares the LORD, 'and I will be its glory within.'

⁶"Come! Come! Flee from the land of the north," declares the LORD, "for I have scattered you to the four winds of heaven," declares the LORD.

⁷"Come, O Zion! Escape, you who live in the Daughter of Babylon!" ⁸For this is what the LORD Almighty says: "After he has honored me and has sent me against the nations that have plundered you—for whoever touches you touches the apple of his eye— ⁹I will surely raise my hand against them so that their slaves will plunder them. Then you will know that the LORD Almighty has sent me.

¹⁰"Shout and be glad, O Daughter of Zion. For I am coming, and I will live among you," declares the LORD. ¹¹"Many nations will be joined with the LORD in that day and will become my people. I will live among you and you will know that the LORD Almighty has sent me to you. ¹²The LORD will inherit Judah as his portion in the holy land and will again choose Jerusalem. ¹³Be still before the LORD, all mankind, because he has roused himself from his holy dwelling."

---

[98] Isaac Watts, *The Baptist Hymnal* (Nashville: Convention Press, 1991), # 74.

Vision three continues the themes of divine protection for God's people and the miraculous restoration of the land found in the previous two visions. The third vision emphatically declares that Israel should face her future with bold confidence, not because of her circumstances, but because of God's word. The Lord has given his absolute assurance of his presence and protection. Meyers and Meyers view vision three as a parallel to the sixth vision (5:1–4),[99] since both visions promote the significance of measurements as well as the importance of righteousness and the law among the people of God.[100]

**2:1–2** Verses 1–2 present the vision that Zechariah saw, followed by the interpretation of the vision. This vision opens with a continuation of the statement in 1:16 where the Lord proclaimed the message that the measuring line would be extended over Jerusalem, demonstrating the Lord's readiness to begin the rebuilding process. Zechariah and his visitor observed the initial stages of rebuilding where the divine surveyor officially plotted the city boundaries.

In Amos 7:7–9,17, the prophet from Tekoa also employed the metaphor of a measuring line much as Zechariah did at a later time. Amos 7:7–9 discloses the measuring line as the Lord's tool to quantify Israel's iniquity. As a profligate nation, Israel brought down the Lord's righteous indignation on herself. Amos 7:17 describes a surveyor's measuring line similar in function to the metaphor in Zech 2, but now the line is in the hands of foreigners who use it to partition the land of Samaria. Both uses of the measuring line in Amos 7 portray judgment. Some suggest that the metaphor of a measuring line carries negative connotations for other reasons. Since the measuring line defines the boundaries of the city, many conclude that the surveyor's intention focuses on limiting the growth of the city.[101] This negative interpretation is unnecessary, however, since any well-conceived building project requires careful planning, including a proper survey. The Lord's role in ordering a survey of the city suggests that God desires the rebuilt city to meet divine "code" in every way. The survey gives the nation greater confidence that their future belongs to God's greater building plan.

Zechariah's scene, in contrast to the picture in Amos, portrays God's blessing, representing the fulfillment of the restoration Jeremiah prophesied (32:1–15) when he bought the field at Anathoth at the inception of the Babylonian exile. Jeremiah's symbolic action demonstrated the certainty of God's plan to restore his people after their punishment was complete. Ezekiel also envisioned a resurveying as a prelude to rebuilding (40:3).[102] To be specific, Ezek 40–48 presents an additional striking parallel to Zechariah's third vision because both texts emphasize the necessity of rebuilding the city to exacting measurements, albeit on a scale different from those seen in preexilic days. Furthermore, many

---

[99] Vision five by Meyers and Meyers's count.
[100] Meyers and Meyers, *Zechariah 1–8*, 158.
[101] Boda, *Zechariah*, 222.
[102] For a helpful expansion of these themes, see Merrill, *Zechariah*, 114.

New Testament scholars see Zech 2:1, along with Ezek 40:3, as the primary Old Testament background for Rev 11:1, which reads, "I was given a reed like a measuring rod and was told, 'Go and measure the temple of God and the altar, and count the worshipers there.'" In Rev 11 the Lord pulls back the curtain to show John a glimpse of the rebuilt temple in the eschatological new Jerusalem.[103]

Interpreters disagree concerning the identity of the man speaking with Zechariah in vision three. Some scholars, such as the Jewish interpreter Rashi, contend that the man was the angelic interpreter who appears later in the vision.[104] This view is less than certain, however, due in part to the different terminology used in vv. 1 and 3. Verse 1 uses the term "man" (*'ādām*), whereas v. 3 refers to "the angel [*mal'āk*] who was speaking with me." It is possible that Zechariah saw the "man" in v. 1 and the "angel" in v. 3 as one and the same. On the other hand, it is equally plausible that the prophet intended different persons.

Jerome maintained that the "man" is the angel of the Lord. However, since the "man" is never identified in this narrative as the angel of the Lord and he does not play the prominent role in this passage that the angel of the Lord does in other texts where his presence can be identified with certainty, the position remains difficult to support.[105] Alternatively, Tigchelaar concludes that on a literary level, the surveyor symbolizes the exiles.[106] Curiously, when Tigchelaar rereads the passage theologically, he maintains that the surveyor is a heavenly being. Tigchelaar's conclusion that the literary and theological understandings must remain completely separate and dissimilar suffers from a fatal hermeneutical flaw. The wisest course follows the narrative's lead, choosing to leave the identity of the "man" unspecified and subordinate to the importance of the message itself.

Mitchell suggests that the unknown figure holding the measuring line further symbolizes those who desire to rebuild Jerusalem, but the figure questions whether their efforts should focus on the completion of the temple project before rebuilding the city wall.[107] Hence, this uncertainty echoes the conflict Haggai described in Hag 1:2: "This is what the LORD Almighty says: 'These people say, "The time has not yet come for the LORD's house to be built."'" These reasonably minded people did not necessarily oppose the temple project. They simply felt the walls should remain the priority.

---

[103] Although he agrees with this assertion, K. A. Strand argues that Lev 16 also lies behind Rev 11:1. See Strand, "An Overlooked Old-Testament Background to Revelation 11:1," *AUSS* 22 (1984): 317–25.

[104] Cited by Mitchell, *Zechariah*, 136.

[105] Ibid. See also Barker, "Zechariah," 616.

[106] E. J. Tigchelaar, *Prophets of Old and the Day of the End: Zechariah, the Book of Watchers and Apocalyptic* (Leiden: E. J. Brill, 1996), 65.

[107] Mitchell, *Zechariah*, 137.

Throughout much of Israel's history the people focused far more attention on their own efforts to secure their safety than on devotion to worshipping the Lord. Little wonder, then, that God's people turned in many different directions other than the Lord for their security. Inevitably, the postexilic community faced the pressing question of whether they could safely begin to rebuild the temple when Jerusalem had no city walls and stood defenseless. Thus, Ezra 4:1–5 describes the historical basis for the legitimate concern postexilic Judah encountered:

> When the enemies of Judah and Benjamin heard that the exiles were building a temple for the LORD, the God of Israel. . . . The peoples around them set out to discourage the people of Judah and make them afraid to go on building. They hired counselors to work against them and frustrate their plans during the entire reign of Cyrus king of Persia and down to the reign of Darius king of Persia.

Without doubt, the account in Ezra reflects only one of the threats confronting those attempting to rebuild Jerusalem. The postexilic community's concern about safety was real, irrespective of whether they pursued their security from the Lord.

In contrast, Sweeney reaches a diametrically different understanding of Zechariah's imagery and rationale for building the temple without first completing the city wall. Sweeney suggests that the restored city would include too many inhabitants and such great numbers of livestock that a city completely enclosed with a wall could not contain them all.[108] Sweeney views these circumstances in the most positive light of all, a sign of the Lord's miraculous blessings on the people. Petersen shares Sweeney's optimistic interpretation, endorsing the view that no city wall could encircle such a robust population. To illustrate his point, Petersen produces the example of the Persian city Pasargadae. This city had no defensive walls due to the practical impossibility of constructing a wall around a city of its scale. Pasargadae was also well-known for its numerous altars to its inhabitants' gods.[109]

**2:3–5** The angelic interpretation of the vision in vv. 3–5 argues against the apprehensive attitude of the people, naturally worried about their well-being and prospects for success. The people's confidence should lay solely with God's attention to his people's every need.

Surely it must have been difficult for Zechariah's contemporaries to envision the city of Jerusalem on the scale described in vv. 4–5. The land lay relatively desolate. To speak of Jerusalem filled with people and livestock did not accurately depict what the postexilic community saw with their own eyes. God promised to bless his people and to expand their fortunes beyond their most

---

[108] Sweeney, *Zechariah 1–8*, 586.
[109] Petersen, *Zechariah 1–8*, 171.

idealistic dreams. Once more the prophet related the divine word to his people in another attempt to bolster the disheartened remnant with the truth of God's presence and the blessings that would follow.

Another question arises regarding when this prophecy found its fulfillment. Nehemiah's generation certainly never saw the fulfillment of this prophecy, for he had to cast lots in order to compel the people to move into Jerusalem (Neh 11:1–2). Jerusalem came closer to holding an expansive population during the life of Christ, but few suggest that the book of Zechariah ultimately points to a first century AD fulfillment. Beyond these conclusions, alternate interpretations differ markedly.

As a result of the problem of identifying the timing of the grand scale of Zechariah's promised repopulation of Jerusalem, some see this prophecy's consummation in the Church.[110] While a popular interpretation for centuries in some circles, one should not simply identify the Church with Israel. Of course, such an assertion involves a great hermeneutical divide. In spite of opposing views, Israel and the Church cannot be one and the same. Neither should one affirm that the Lord's unfulfilled promises to Israel in the Old Testament will be automatically transferred from Israel to the Church with the coming of Christ and the Jewish community's rejection of Christ as their Messiah.

Others suggest that the passage points to a future, earthly kingdom.[111] Unger offers the clearest exposition of this perspective. He writes:

> The purpose of this third night vision (in the series of eight) is to set forth prophetically the restoration of Jerusalem with reference to Zechariah's time, but also in larger scope, to describe the yet future *fulfillment* in the kingdom age, when the city will become the capital of the millennial earth. Particularly emphasized is the great increase in size, population, wealth, spirituality, and security of the city.[112]

The primary reason for this conclusion lies with the expansive language of vv. 3–5, which many premillennial interpreters argue has never had a historical fulfillment.[113]

The scope of God's promises does not adequately correspond to any historical epoch. The massive repopulation of Jerusalem, the Lord as "a wall of fire" around Zion, the Lord's glorious reign from within his holy city, and the many nations who "will be joined with the LORD in that day" all prefigure an eschatological fulfillment.

It is problematic hermeneutically, however, to posit an interpretation whose fulfillment was so remote historically from Zechariah and his disconsolate

---

[110] Baldwin, *Zechariah*, 106–7.
[111] Barker, "Zechariah," 617; Feinberg, *Minor Prophets*, 45; Merrill, *Zechariah*, 116–18; and Unger, *Zechariah*, 43.
[112] Unger, *Zechariah*, 43.
[113] See Barker, "Zechariah," 616.

audience as to lack any measure of encouragement or relevance to their historical situation. Consequently, the prophecies signify a limited fulfillment in which postexilic Judah saw a repopulation of Jerusalem, divine protection, and a renewed commitment to worship the Lord. No one living in the darkest days of the exile or the years immediately thereafter could have envisioned anything short of God's wondrous work on their behalf. This partial fulfillment prefigures what God would accomplish on the eschatological Day of the Lord. Consequently, Merrill appropriately concludes that the passage possesses a dual referent: the initial and partial fulfillment occurred in Zechariah's day, while the ultimate focus of his prophecy will come to full fruition in the millennium.[114]

Yet the anticipation of a populous Judah characterizes texts describing the postexilic era. Isaiah 49:19 speaks of the land when it states, "Though you were ruined . . . now you will be too small for your people." Jer 31:27 declares that "days are coming . . . when I will plant the house of Israel and the house of Judah with the offspring of men and of animals." Ezek 36:11 prophesies, "I will increase the number of men and animals upon you, and they will be fruitful and become numerous. I will settle people on you as in the past and will make you prosper more than before." Many additional passages illustrate the same point.

It would appear from this brief survey that the language of Zech 2:3–5 does not differ markedly in scope from the language used in other prophetic materials. Granted, Zechariah focused more on the city of Jerusalem and less on the nation as a whole when compared to his fellow prophets.[115] Nonetheless, the broad language of Zech 3 does not allow an interpretation that applied to Jerusalem alone. Zechariah's pericope addressed grand issues, such as the hope for a glorious land after the Lord renewed his blessings to his people. This divine promise held significance both for postexilic Judah and for God's people in the eschatological age.

Jerusalem's walls figure prominently in vision three as an additional motif. Initially, Zechariah favorably described the absence of walls as a practical reality for a city that outgrew its capability to contain its inhabitants, and the prophet did not portray Zion as vulnerable to her enemies simply because she had no city walls. Nonetheless, the people needed protection in their undefended circumstances. To meet this need the Lord promised personally to serve as a "wall of fire" providing a sure defense for his city, a theme mentioned later in 9:8.[116] Perhaps the most surprising feature of the "wall of fire" theme is the

---

[114] Merrill, *Zechariah*, 116.

[115] Petersen, *Zechariah 1–8*, 171.

[116] For an intriguing survey of the rabbinic treatment of the wall of fire motif, see I. Chernus, " 'A Wall of Fire Round About': The Development of a Theme in Rabbinic Midrash," *Journal of Jewish Studies* 30 (1979): 68–84. See also Petersen, *Zechariah 1–8*, 171.

use of fire as a future reward for Israel's faithfulness, since fire often represents judgment in both Testaments, as well as in the rabbinic literature.[117]

Throughout Scripture, fire represents God's powerful presence. In Exod 3:2–4:14 God appears to Moses in a burning bush, and in 13:21 he guides his people through a pillar of fire. Even the New Testament continues the fire theme in Heb 12:29 that describes God as "a consuming fire." Although Isa 26:1 does not mention fire, the verse portrays the Lord as the wall that protects Israel. In addition to serving as the fire around the perimeter of the city, the Lord's glory within the city ensures the strength of Judah's covenant with her God.

Reinforcing the Lord's covenant relationship with his people, the Hebrew expression translated "I myself will be" (*'ehyeh*) powerfully echoes Exod 3:14, "I AM WHO I AM. This is what you are to say to the Israelites: 'I AM' has sent me to you."[118] Both Zech 2:5 and Exod 3:14 use the same verbal form, signifying the Lord's covenant and his personal, strengthening presence with his people as he guides them through the vicissitudes the future would bring. Baldwin summarizes, "God is both dealing with potential enemies and protecting His people, in the same way and on the same covenant basis as He did at the Exodus."[119] Even the combination of fire and glory recalls the exodus (Exod 13:22; 14:20). The pair of themes also figures together prominently when the Lord's presence occupies the tabernacle (Exod 40:34).

Elsewhere, the term "glory" describes God's magnificent presence in the temple (see Hag 2:3,7,9).[120] In Zechariah, the Lord's glory reassures the remnant that God will aid the rebuilding of the temple. The Hebrew word for "glory" (*kābôd*) functions similarly throughout the Old Testament by describing the presence of the Lord.[121] Despite this reference to the rebuilding of the temple, vision three highlights the rebuilding of Jerusalem as a whole.

**2:6–7** Verses 6–13 summarize the message of the first three visions, applying them forcefully to the postexilic community. Verse 6 begins a new oracle that elicits a response to the Lord's word given in the previous section.[122] The foregoing visions all proclaim that the Lord honors his covenant with his people. With the Lord on the verge of acting on Judah's behalf in an unprecedented fashion, God's people should have faith in him and take immediate action to put feet to their faith. Nothing should stand in the way of the people as they face the challenges of rebuilding the temple.

---

[117] Chernus, "Wall of Fire," 68.

[118] The Hebrew אֶהְיֶה echoes throughout the Old Testament in the name "the Lord" (Yahweh) and in the New Testament in numerous ways, including the "I am" passages in the Gospels.

[119] Baldwin, *Zechariah*, 107.

[120] כָּבוֹד. See *HALOT*, 457–58; BDB, 458–59.

[121] See Exod 24:16,17; 40:34, 35; 1 Kgs 8:12; 2 Chr 5:14; Ezek 1:28; 8:4; 9:3; 10:19; 11:22; 43:2,4,5; 44:4; Isa 6:3.

[122] Baldwin, *Zechariah*, 107–8; Merrill, *Zechariah*, 119.

In v. 6 the word that the NIV translates "come" *(hōy)* actually means "ho!" or "woe!"[123] The Hebrew word *hōy* signifies particularly strong emotion and usually introduces a solemn warning (cf. Isa 55:1). The exhortation addresses the exiles who have yet to leave Babylon. Zechariah attempts to persuade these skeptics to return to Jerusalem to assist in the rebuilding process, particularly in light of the Lord's strong assurances of protection and blessing in the previous verses. Even more important than their construction efforts on the temple, Zechariah wanted the people to exercise genuine faith in the Lord again.

Zechariah's vigorous encouragement to his fellow exiles might seem superfluous when God himself had emphatically promised that the restoration would prove glorious. However, to most of the exiles, Zechariah's prophecy was little more than empty talk. They had lost faith in God, feeling that he had turned his back on them. Judah had lost sight of the theological significance of the exile, failing to see it as the divine punishment foretold by the preexilic prophets. Consequently, the social and political upheaval of the exile further eroded their faith in the Lord and in the reliability of his word.

In the preexilic epoch, the false doctrine of the inviolability of Zion had held out the baseless hope that Jerusalem could not be defeated by any human foe simply because of the Lord's presence in the temple in the midst of Jerusalem. This false doctrine ignored biblical warnings concerning imminent judgment on the nation in passages from Deut 28 to the book of Jeremiah. Not surprisingly, the doctrine of the inviolability of Zion enjoyed the devotion and optimistic hopes of the people. Who would not want to eschew Jeremiah's harsh words in favor of the boundless optimism of the false prophets who "tickled the ears" of their hearers. So when the exile finally arrived, the terrible distortion of God's word kept many people from seeing their circumstances as the fulfillment of divine promises of judgment for sin. Instead, they erroneously concluded that God had rejected his people, further eroding their faith in the Lord. Thus, many understood the exile as God's breach of covenant, a divine act abandoning his people forever. Moreover, on a socio-political level, life in Babylon for Judah's descendants was often better economically than the exiles had ever experienced before. The lure of materialism proved too strong for many who went into exile, just as it does today.

The Lord's word to the people required faith, not sight, for what they could see with their eyes in Jerusalem was little more than ruin and decay, followed by an unending rebuilding process to be endured under the harshest and most threatening of conditions. No wonder Zechariah was compelled to exhort his contemporaries emphatically and repeatedly "to return" to the land of promise. In the end, though, only a small minority chose to do so.

"The land of the north" recalls Jeremiah's warnings that Judah's oppressor would come "from the north" (Jer 6:22; 10:22). The expression also clearly

---

[123] הוֹי. See *HALOT*, 242; BDB, 222–23.

delineates Babylon as the human antagonists of God's people. Now with the judgment complete, Judah must retrace her steps both physically and spiritually in order to rediscover God's blessings. Zechariah recognized that some in the diaspora never found their way to Babylon, hence the appeal to those scattered to "the four winds of heaven" (see Isa 43:5–6). God did not want to lose any of his lost sheep, wherever they might have wandered. For instance, Jer 40:11 indicates that some fled to Moab, Ammon, and Edom. Even Jeremiah himself, coerced by a contingent of officials, fled to Egypt (Jer 43:4–7) in pursuit of a secure land in which to dwell. Thus, all Judahites, wherever their personal exile had led them, should exercise faith in the Lord and experience the blessings of God's glorious future for his people.

In the former days, the house of Judah sought to avoid judgment, the punishment God sent to discipline his wayward people through the Babylonian empire. Verse 7 declares a dramatic polarity. The Lord exhorts his people to escape from Babylon's hegemony by fleeing to Zion, their God-ordained refuge. This pronouncement also predicts God's judgment on the Babylonians for their hubris and disdain for the Lord. The warning of v. 7 suggests that those from Zion who dawdled or deliberately chose to remain among "the Daughter of Babylon" would suffer the same fate. The Lord's declaration also evokes memories of the exodus when the people had to act in faith in obedience to the astounding promises God had delivered through Moses. The commands to flee and to escape precede the Lord's reason for the commands. God's instruction comes "for their good and His glory."[124]

**2:8** This verse possibly presents as many interpretative dilemmas as any other passage in the book of Zechariah. A brief survey of the text-critical issues that arise in v. 8 confirms this observation, acknowledging that the interpretative problems that gave rise to scribal efforts to clarify the text have existed since ancient times.

One of the more vexing issues focuses on *'aḥar kābôd šĕlāḥanî*, which strictly translated reads, "after glory he sent me."[125] The interpretative questions tend to focus on "after glory." Translators frequently have not been content to render *'aḥar kābôd* as "after glory," despite the fact that this is precisely what the Hebrew phrase means. Consequently, the phrase has been translated in several different ways with differing meanings, many of which go well beyond what the Hebrew text actually says.

The fundamental problems in v. 8a are threefold. The first issue focuses on the meaning of the preposition *'aḥar*, normally translated "after."[126] Second, what is the significance of the word *kābôd* ("glory")? Third, what did

---

[124] Merrill, *Zechariah*, 120.
[125] The Hebrew אַחַר כָּבוֹד שְׁלָחַנִי (*'aḥar kābôd šĕlāḥanî*) is "the most puzzling clause in the book" according to R. L. Smith (*Micah–Malachi*, 196).
[126] See *HALOT*, 35–36; BDB, 29–30.

Zechariah intend when he employed the two words joined together in a phrase that literally reads "after glory?"

Chary ventures that the phrase should read, "with insistence he sent me."[127] More recently, Baldwin adopts Chary's suggestion.[128] Chary relies on Scott's argument, which assigns a non-typical translation value for the Hebrew preposition, understanding the word that is regularly translated "after" to mean "with."[129] Further, this interpretation also renders the word *kābôd*, commonly translated "glory," as "insistence," based on Chary's claim that the noun *kābôd* fundamentally carries the notion of "weight" or "heaviness." Kloos has examined Chary's examples supporting his translation of both *'aḥar* and *kābôd*, showing that none is above suspicion.[130]

The NIV handles the issues differently by supplying the pronoun "me" and understanding the pronoun as the object of "glory." This treatment yields: "after he has honored me and has sent me." Like the previous attempt, the Hebrew text does not support this translation at all. The word "glory" in the Masoretic Text is a noun, not a verb. Further, the addition of the pronoun "me" is an interpolation since the pronoun does not occur in the verse, nor does the passage imply its addition.

Yet another solution takes the preposition to mean "after" but believes the word "glory" *(kābôd)* speaks directly of the Messiah. Unger represents this position.[131] He writes,

> This statement anticipates the New Testament revelation of the Father sending the Son to glorify Him, both in His first advent . . . and in His second advent. . . . The phrase "after glory" accordingly describes the ministry of Messiah in which He *vindicates* and *demonstrates* the glory of God, particularly as He will punish Israel's enemies and deliver and establish His own people in kingdom blessing.[132]

Again, neither the plain meaning of the Hebrew text nor the literary context in general indicate that Zechariah intended a Messianic interpretation with the phrase "after glory."

Tiemeyer offers a more recent suggestion: "Afterwards, honor will send me against the nations who are spoiling you." She then views the entire passage metaphorically. For her, the Lord's own honor compelled him to punish the nations. She reinterprets "send" to mean "to commission." However, Tiemeyer does not imply a messianic interpretation.[133] Unlike many explanations, Tie-

---

[127] Théophane Chary, *Aggée-Zacharie-Malachie* (Paris: Librairie Lecoffre, 1969), 70.
[128] Baldwin, *Zechariah*, 109–110.
[129] See R. B. Y. Scott, "Secondary Meanings of '*aḥar*'," *JTS* 50 (1949): 178–79. This preposition means "with" in a few Old Testament passages, including Exod 11:5; Ps 73:24; Eccl 12:2.
[130] C. J. L. Kloos, "Zech. II 12: Really a Crux Interpretum?" *VT* 25 (1975): 729–36.
[131] Unger, *Zechariah*, 49.
[132] Ibid.
[133] L. Tiemeyer, "Compelled by Honour—A New Interpretation of Zechariah II 12A (8A),"

meyer attempts a thorough analysis of the text without resorting to emendations or strained translations of expressions in the context. Although her approach has merit, it is not entirely convincing.

Cohen offers still another suggestion, arguing that Zechariah's "mission would bring honor and glory to Israel when God executes judgment upon the nations for their treatment of Israel."[134] This concept appears unlikely as well, however, totally lacking linguistic or literary support.

Kloos maintains that the preposition *'aḥar*, normally rendered "after," introduces a purpose clause. This approach concludes that the Lord's purpose in sending Zechariah was to bring glory to God himself.[135] The HCSB supports this view with the translation, "He has sent me for His glory."[136] Unfortunately for this proposal, understanding *'aḥar* as the introduction to a purpose clause is tenuous indeed. Like so many of the "solutions" to this question, the Hebrew syntax of v. 8 does not indicate a purpose clause.

Other methods for dealing with the meaning of *'aḥar kābôd* aim to emend the actual words of the Hebrew text. Scholars have long suggested a wide variety of emendations of the phrase, believing that the interpretive solution to the phrase lies with rearranging the text.[137] Most of the scholarly suggestions are quite implausible since they do not have any support to commend them for consideration. An exception to the far-fetched proposals, BHK and BHS both recommend emending the word *aḥar* ("after") with the relative pronoun *'ăšer*.[138] This clever emendation changes the translation from "after glory" to "according to his glory." This suggestion also lacks textual support.

Another view associates "glory" with God's coming judgment.[139] In Ezek 39:21–29 the Lord's "glory" inflicts punishment on the nations for their refusal to obey divine law. While the association between Zech 2:8 and Ezek 39:21–29 is quite loose, this interpretation does make sense of the context.

A final approach offers the most satisfactory solution to this perplexing phrase. This interpretation suggests that the phrase functions as a temporal clause with the translation, "*after* the glory [that is, the vision], the Lord sent me." Accordingly, this view believes that Zechariah referred back to his prophetic call, affirming that his prophetic ministry, as well as the night vision from the Lord that he was about to relate, both occurred subsequent to receiving his prophetic call.[140]

---

*VT* 54 (2004): 370–72.

[134] A. Cohen, *The Twelve Prophets* (New York: Soncino, 1948), 278.

[135] Kloos, "Zech. II 12," 729–36. See also Merrill (*Zechariah*, 122) who adopts Kloos's interpretation.

[136] See R. L. Smith, *Micah–Malachi*, 196.

[137] T. C. Vriezen ("Two Old Cruces," OtSt 5 [1948]: 88–91) believes the work of a glossator confused the passage. He proposes that rearranging the text provides the solution to what Vriezen calls "this tortured text."

[138] אֲשֶׁר. See *HALOT*, 98–99.

[139] Boda, *Zechariah*, 236.

[140] The NRSV follows this understanding, as do Meyers and Meyers, *Zechariah*, 164–65;

Before adopting this temporal understanding, the meaning of "glory" presents challenges that must be addressed. On what specific grounds can one conclude that "glory" refers to Zechariah's vision from God? Admittedly, the "*kābôd* = prophetic call" view makes sense in the context, but it lacks overwhelming evidence. Relatedly, could the Hebrew word *kābôd* correspond to the heaviness or insistence with which the Lord compelled Zechariah to accept the divine assignment?[141] This understanding correlates *kābôd* with *maśśā'* ("burden") that ensued from the Lord's prophetic call to Zechariah. No concrete evidence validates this conclusion either.

The term "glory" often represents the presence of God in the Old Testament.[142] There are striking similarities between the Lord's glory manifested during his theophany to the prophet Zechariah and to God's glorious appearances to earlier prophets such as Ezekiel when he received his prophetic call (Ezek 1). Mitchell claims that Zechariah most likely employed some of his language and imagery from Ezek 1:28.[143] With an interesting turn, Sweeney argues that the phrase *'aḥar kābôd* refers to the "back of glory," that is, the "back" of the Lord as he allowed himself to be "seen" in the theophany found in Exod 33–34.[144] Proponents of this view point to another noteworthy parallel in Isa 6—one of the most famous prophetic call passages in the Old Testament—where Isaiah saw God's "glory" filling the whole earth. In Isa 6:3 the preexilic prophet similarly employed *kābôd* to visualize the Lord's presence.

Although several of the suggestions appear quite attractive at first glance, ultimately most prove untenable. In the final analysis, one should translate the prepositional phrase "after glory" and then struggle to determine what Zechariah intended. The phrase most likely affirms that Zechariah only began his preaching ministry after God gloriously appeared to Zechariah to call him as a prophet.

In contrast to the enigmatic first half of v. 8, the second half of the verse stands out as one of the most famous texts in the book.[145] The Lord declares that "whoever touches you [Judah] touches the apple of his eye." Petersen discusses this particularly strong response from God:

> Anyone who acts injuriously toward Israel is, at the same time, acting injuriously toward Yahweh, toward one of the most sensitive and important parts of Yahweh's being. It is no accident that the eye is

---

Mitchell, *Zechariah*, 142; and Petitjean, *Proto-Zacharie*, 113–14.

[141] R. L. Smith, *Micah–Malachi*, 196.

[142] Meyers and Meyers, *Zechariah 1–8*, 165.

[143] Mitchell, *Zechariah*, 141–42; Ralph L. Smith, *Micah–Malachi*, 196.

[144] Sweeney, *Twelve Prophets*, 589.

[145] T. J. Finley argues that Zechariah selected the Hebrew term בָּבֶה (*bābeh*, "gate" or "pupil"), a *hapax legomenon*, in order to make an ironic pun on the pride of Babylon (" 'The Apple of His Eye' [BABA 'EGO] in Zechariah II 12," *VT* 38 [1988]: 337–38). This pun rests on the similarity between *bābeh* ("gate") and "Babylon" בָּבֶל (*bābel*) in Hebrew See *HALOT*, 107–8; BDB, 93.

referred to here. It is a supremely sensitive part of the human organism.¹⁴⁶

Zechariah drew from Deut 32:10b, "He shielded him and cared for him; he guarded him as the apple of his eye," which alludes to the exodus.¹⁴⁷ The "apple" or "pupil" of the eye represents the most vulnerable portion of the eye, that which must be guarded most carefully. Thus, Zechariah's anthropomorphism eloquently portrayed the Lord's most tender protective response toward his people. Zechariah's comment about the Lord's affectionate response to his people moved Augustine to develop the Christological implications of the statement.

Augustine commented that God sent his Son, Jesus Christ, to the lost sheep of the house of Israel. These lost sheep are the "apple of God's eye." Augustine added: "The comparison of these lost sheep to the apple of God's eye is explained by the perfection of God's love. And, of course, it was to this flock of sheep that the apostles belonged."¹⁴⁸

Verse 8b contains one of the 18 places in the Old Testament where ancient scribes deliberately altered the Masoretic Text, clearly for theological reasons.¹⁴⁹ Although our Hebrew text reads "*his* eye" (*ʿēnô*), this was not the earliest reading. Originally, the text read "*my* eye" (*ʿênî*).¹⁵⁰ The anthropomorphism suggested by "my eye" must have proven too strong for some ancient scribe, compelling him to change the text in order to preserve his understanding of God's transcendence.¹⁵¹

**2:9** Verse 9 begins describing how God will protect the apple of his eye. Continuing the anthropomorphic representation of the Lord's eye, Zechariah describes God's defeat of Judah's oppressors with a mere motion of the hand (see Isa 11:15; 19:16 for comparable gesturing). The prophet, as the Lord's personal messenger, so represented God's very presence that Zechariah's gesture symbolically portrayed the Lord's as well.¹⁵² Moreover, the raising of the hand may symbolize the initiation of military action against the Lord's opponents.¹⁵³

---

¹⁴⁶ Petersen, *Zechariah 1–8*, 177.

¹⁴⁷ See also Ps 17:8, "Keep me as the apple of your eye: hide me in the shadow of your wings."

¹⁴⁸ Augustine, *De Civitate Dei contra Paganos*, 20.30 (CCSL 48:755).

¹⁴⁹ E. Tov, *Textual Criticism of the Hebrew Bible*, 2nd revised ed. (Minneapolis: Fortress, 2001), 64–67.

¹⁵⁰ עֵינִי/עֵינוֹ. See *HALOT*, 818.

¹⁵¹ See Russell Fuller, "Early Emendations of the Scribes: The *Tiqqun Sopherim* in Zechariah 2:12," in *Of Scribes and Scrolls*, ed. H. Attridge, J. J. Collins, T. H. Tobin (Lanham, MD: University Press of America, 1990), 21–28.

¹⁵² E. Conrad, *Zechariah* (Sheffield: Sheffield Academic Press, 1999), 83.

¹⁵³ J. E. Tollington, *Tradition and Innovation in Haggai and Zechariah 1–8* (Sheffield: Sheffield Academic Press, 1993), 228–29.

Zechariah predicted another dramatic prophetic reversal. The prophet already declared that the enslaved exiles would be freed. Zechariah now proclaimed that those who had been impoverished would be enriched by plundering their very oppressor, an allusion to the Israelites' plundering of the Egyptians at the time of the exodus (Exod 12:36). Thus, Zechariah announced a total reversal of Judah's fortunes. Both Isaiah (14:2) and Ezekiel made similar pronouncements. Ezekiel 39:10b declares, "And they [Israel] will plunder those who plundered them and loot those who looted them, declares the Sovereign LORD." Hence, a time would come when the enemies of God's people would be unable to harm Judah. At least those enemies would prove powerless against them because of the Lord's supreme care for his own. Verse 9 evokes Hag 2:6–9, which says that God will "shake the nations" and cause the "present house" to have greater glory than the "former house." The dramatic change in the circumstances of God's people is comparable to when Haman was hanged on the gallows he had prepared for Mordecai (Esth 7:10). The purpose of Zechariah's oracle goes beyond encouragement of the people. The "LORD Almighty" also desires to validate the fact of Zechariah's divine mandate to be prophet through the confirming might of God's words and deeds.

**2:10** Rooted in the Davidic covenant, the Lord promises to come and dwell among his people in Zion. The imperatives "shout" *(rānnî)* and "rejoice" *(wĕśimḥî)* command God's people to rejoice at the Lord's imminent arrival. This particular word pair also occurs together in Isa 35:10.[154] Typically, one encounters such exhortations (with similar, but not identical expressions) in songs of praise to God. Among the many examples one could cite, Pss 96 and 98 best illustrate the exultant praise that exists in contexts portraying the Lord as Israel's enthroned king. Similar themes occur in Zeph 3:14–15.

The reason for exultation lies in God's arrival to dwell among his people in the day of restoration.[155] The Lord declares, "I am coming" *(bāʾ)*.[156] The verbal form is a participle and indicates imminent action.[157] The Lord would soon make his presence manifest to Judah. Thus, Zechariah spoke of events that would begin to happen in his own day.[158]

Furthermore, the term translated "to dwell" *(šākan)*, as we have seen elsewhere in Zechariah, evokes strong memories of expressions found in Exodus

---

[154] Baldwin (*Zechariah*, 110) incorrectly states that this pair does not exist together elsewhere in the Old Testament. For a fuller discussion of poetic word pairs in general and this pair in particular, see Y. Avishur, *Stylistic Studies in Word Pairs*.

[155] Unger (*Zechariah*, 51) sees Zechariah's statement, "I am coming," as an exclusively messianic prophecy, predicting not the Messiah's first coming but his second advent in preparation for what he calls "full millennial blessing."

[156] בָּא. *HALOT*, 112–14.

[157] The *futur instans* use of the Hebrew participle conveys imminent action; see GKC, § 115 p.

[158] Conrad, *Zechariah*, 84–85.

and Ezekiel.[159] The same Hebrew term describes God's coming to dwell in the midst of the tabernacle (Exod 29:42–46) and later in the temple (1 Kgs 6:13). Comparable but not identical language occurs in Ezek 43:1–9 where the exilic prophet foretold how the Lord's glory will reside within the restored, eschatological temple. The well-known text in John 1:14, "The Word became flesh and made his dwelling among us," also builds on the Old Testament concept of the Lord's dwelling in his temple and transforms the idea into his indwelling believers.[160] The God who faithfully keeps his covenant promises with Israel to provide and to protect reminds the people what his faithful presence will mean for their lives. While these words soothed the Judahites' fears, the divine message also served as a veiled threat to all who did not find themselves in a faithful relationship with the Lord, a theme that also fits well in the context.

This biblical concept of God dwelling among his people probably seemed unremarkable to the ancients. To the modern mind, though, the concept appears truly foreign. The people of Judah did not take the affirmation about the Lord dwelling in Zion literally. The notion that God created the whole universe and was therefore totally distinct from his creation in any physical sense represents one of the Old Testament's major theological contributions. The understanding that no tree or mountain or even the earth itself could contain the Lord God or represent him—hence the strict prohibition of all idol worship—stands as a fundamental difference between paganism and Old Testament teaching. Unlike the pagan deities in the ancient Near East, the Lord does not require a physical place where he could dwell. Balancing this assertion about God's separateness from his creation, however, was his nearness or presence among his covenant people. God's immanence stands as an equally radical theological teaching to his separateness. Nonetheless, biblical writers often emphasize the Lord's nearness to those he loves. Indeed, no position holds more blessing for God's people than to be near him.[161]

**2:11** When God returns to take his throne in Jerusalem, the nations will join with Judah in serving the Lord.[162] While v. 10 presupposes both the Abrahamic and Mosaic covenants, v. 11 draws exclusively on the Abrahamic covenant, showing how this covenant will be fulfilled when the nations are joined with the Lord. In Gen 12:3 God proclaims, "All peoples on earth will be blessed

---

[159] The Hebrew verb found in Zech 2:10, שָׁכַן, means "to inhabit" and relates linguistically to the word for tabernacle, מִשְׁכָּן. See *HALOT*, 646–47, 1496–1500; BDB, 1015–16.

[160] See also 1 Cor 3:16; 6:19; 2 Cor 6:16.

[161] For a very helpful discussion of these themes, see Merrill, *Zechariah*, 125–28. Also, see the theological treatment of the motif of the Lord's presence in S. Terrien, *The Elusive Presence* (San Francisco: Harper & Row, 1978).

[162] As in Gen 12, the *niphal* verb may be translated either as a passive, "be joined," or as a reflexive, "join themselves." In Gen 12 and Zech 2:11 the passive is preferable. See G. L. Klein, "The Meaning of the *Niphal* in the Hebrew Bible" (Ph.D. diss., Dropsie College for Hebrew and Cognate Learning/Annenberg Research Institute, 1992).

through you." In that day the peoples of the earth will share with Israel the distinction of being "the people of God." No longer will these nations be Gentiles, *gōyîm*.[163] Instead, they will become the people of God, *ʿām*,[164] a Hebrew word that the Old Testament uses for Israel. Throughout the Old Testament, the word *ʿām* evokes the memory of the covenant the Lord made with Israel.

Throughout the Old Testament the Lord expresses his desire to make the nations his own.[165] A particularly important passage for this issue, Isa 56:6–7 speaks clearly about the nations participating in a covenant with the Lord,

> And foreigners who bind themselves to the LORD to serve him,
>   to love the name of the LORD, and to worship him,
> all who keep the Sabbath without desecrating it
>   and who hold fast to my covenant—
> these I will bring to my holy mountain
>   and give them joy in my house of prayer.
> Their burnt offerings and sacrifices
>   will be accepted on my altar;
> for my house will be called
>   a house of prayer for all nations.

In particular, one should note the message of Jonah where God forgave the repentant inhabitants of Nineveh, as well as the story of Ruth where a Moabitess became the ancestor of King David. Micah 4:2 echoes the theme of foreigners joining Judah in the worship of the Lord: "Many nations will come and say, 'Come, let us go up to the mountain of the LORD . . . He will teach us his ways.'" Isaiah depicted foreign nations' pilgrimage to Zion in order to worship the Lord (2:2–4; 25:6–10; 56:1–8; 66:18–24).[166]

Zechariah did not promote universalism, however. While the prophet predicted that the nations will become God's people *(ʿām)*, they must do so on the Lord's terms. Throughout the earth, those who desire to worship God must come to the temple in Jerusalem and worship God alone and according to the righteous law that he had disclosed. Those who rejected the Lord's righteous law would have no part in his kingdom.

Beyond God's intention to include the nations in his blessings, Israel had a responsibility to fulfill a "missionary mandate." Although the word "missionary" is anachronistic in an Old Testament context, many passages in the first Testament indicate the responsibility that God's people had to other peoples to teach them God's word. Although a frequently ignored issue, a formidable corpus of scholarly literature focuses on the question of whether Israel had

---

[163] Hebrew גּוֹיִם. *TDOT*, 2:426–29.
[164] Hebrew עַם. *TDOT*, 2:426–27; 9:174–77; *TLOT*, 897–919.
[165] To illustrate, see Pss 47:9; 96:1; 97:1; 98:4; Isa 42:6; 49:6; Hag 2:7.
[166] See Tollington, *Tradition and Innovation*, 233–35.

any divine mandate to witness about God's glory to the nations.[167] In the final analysis, it seems clear that Israel did bear a responsibility for being a witness to its pagan neighbors. Of course, this does not mean that they were to fulfill a missionary charge that paralleled in every way the commands in the New Testament. Nor does this suggest that Israel seriously attempted to discharge her duties.

Thus, the Lord's eschatological plans include the Gentiles joining Judah in worshipping him. For Judah, however, the emphasis lies on her special role in the future. God does not address the nations in v. 11; he continues addressing Judah. For her, the inclusion of the Gentiles in the worship at the rebuilt temple affirms to Judah that her role in the future would be significant indeed. The text provides substantive encouragement for Judah to redouble her efforts to complete the rebuilding of the temple so that it could serve the glorious purpose for which the Lord intends it.

The passage does not attempt to pinpoint when this spiritual ingathering would take place. Zechariah used the temporal marker most often found in prophetic oracles expressing an eschatological orientation: "in that day." The prophets regularly employed this phrase when they wished to indicate that a prophecy speaks of the future without being more specific. The most Zechariah could clearly envision was an unprecedented spiritual reformation of the nations. On this unique day the Lord will initiate a kingdom centered in Zion.

In v. 11 the speakers change abruptly. The beginning of the verse, "Many nations will be joined with the LORD," most likely comes from the angelic interpreter. The next phrase, "will become my people," apparently restates the word of God, particularly in light of the covenant tone of the phrase "my people." However, like v. 9, v. 11 ends with the assertion, "You will know that the LORD Almighty has sent me."[168] Clearly, this statement cannot be attributed to the Lord himself. The speaker must have shifted once more. Thus, the angelic interpreter is probably the one affirming that the fulfillment of the Lord's prophecy will ultimately demonstrate the authenticity of the message that Zechariah had delivered.[169]

---

[167] Perhaps one of the strongest defenses of the view that Israel had a missions mandate, although not identical to that issued in the New Testament, can be found in H. H. Rowley, *The Missionary Message of the Old Testament* (London: Carey, 1945). For an opposing perspective, see R. Martin-Achard, *Israël et les nations: La perspective missionnaire de l'Ancien Testament* (Neuchâtel: Delachaux, 1959). The following works address the question from a missiological perspective: M. Daniel Carroll R., "Blessing the Nations: Toward a Biblical Theology of Mission from Genesis," *Bulletin for Biblical Research* 10 (2000): 17–34; D. Filbeck, *Yes, God of the Gentiles Too: The Missionary Message of the Old Testament* (Wheaton: Billy Graham Center, 1994); and J. H. Kane, "Missions in the Old Testament," in *Christian Missions in Biblical Perspective* (Grand Rapids: Baker, 1976).

[168] Verse 9 does not include the phrase "to you" that v. 11 adds, because v. 9 addresses the nations, whereas v. 11 speaks to Israel.

[169] See T. E. McComiskey, "Zechariah," in *The Minor Prophets, Vol. 3*, ed. T. E. McComiskey (Grand Rapids: Baker, 1992), 1064.

**2:12** We have seen that v. 11 carefully avoids embracing universalism. Verse 12 shuns the impression that Judah would lose her identity or her special position before God when the nations come together to worship the Lord. Israel would continue to enjoy her honored place as God's own chosen people. The focus of v. 12 shifts somewhat abruptly from a global conversion toward God in the previous verse, to the return of a small people dwelling in a humble land, a "holy land," a phrase that does not occur elsewhere in Scripture. Once again, Zechariah's language and imagery evoked the memory of the exodus account, where a similar expression describes the ground on which Moses stood before the Lord's theophany near the burning bush (Exod 3:5).

The "slight" or "humble" condition of the people turns to glory and to prominence because Israel is the Lord's own inheritance. The covenant inseparably binds God to Israel and Israel to God. Accordingly, the Lord will "take possession" of Judah and will "choose" Jerusalem once more, employing the language of election found in covenant contexts.[170] Through Zechariah the Lord desires to underscore that his act of inheriting and choosing Judah was not the first time the relationship had been reaffirmed. Likely, it would not be the last. Even though the Gentile nations would someday worship the Lord alongside Judah—much as Isa 14:1; 19:22–25; 60:1–6; 62:1–5 portray—Judah would retain her distinctness and her special relationship with the Lord.[171] Therefore, if the Lord has such grand plans for the temple, Zechariah's contemporaries must labor tirelessly to complete the rebuilding process.

**2:13** In keeping with the majesty of the Lord's astounding pronouncements, all humanity will stand before God in mute awe. NIV's "mankind" translates a common Hebrew word that more literally means "flesh" *(bāśār)*.[172] Thus, Zechariah exhorted all humanity to worship God. Zechariah echoed Habakkuk's famous words, "The LORD is in his holy temple; let all the earth be silent before him" (2:20).[173] Just as Ezekiel saw the Lord's glory return to the temple and fell prostrate before God in worship (see Ezek 43), Zechariah and his audience must do likewise after glimpsing a future that was almost too bright to behold.

Somewhat redundantly, Zechariah reminded his readers why God deserves such adulation: "he has roused himself from his holy dwelling." "To rouse" *(nē'ôr)* represents another anthropomorphic portrayal of God.[174] Ps 121:3–4

---

[170] See Isa 41:8, "But you, O Israel, my servant, Jacob, whom I have chosen."

[171] See Isa 60:3, "Nations will come to your light, and kings to the brightness of your dawn."

[172] בָּשָׂר. See *HALOT*, 164. N. P. Bratsiotis emphasizes that this word frequently contrasts the Lord with his human creation by underscoring the distance that exists between God and humanity (*TDOT*, 2:327). This meaning appropriately reminds the readers that the Lord is like none other and should receive commensurate worship.

[173] See also Zeph 1:7 where the prophet admonishes his hearers, "be silent before the Sovereign LORD," in light of the impending Day of the Lord.

[174] נֵעוֹר. In Zech 4:1 the same verb describes an angel awakening the prophet from his sleep. See *HALOT*, 802–3; BDB, 734–35.

reminds us: "Indeed he who watches over Israel will neither slumber nor sleep. The LORD watches over you."

Although the language of "holy dwelling" occurs several times in the Old Testament, two instances stand out. In the first, Deut 26:15, the Lord looks down on his people from his holy dwelling place in heaven in order to bless his people Israel. In the other, Ps 26:8, the temple represents God's abode. Zechariah intended the heavenly venue, signifying that what has begun in the heavenly realm will transfer to the earthly one.[175]

In conclusion, Barker notes that each of the visions Zechariah has now disclosed alternate between themes of blessing and judgment. Barker writes,

> The first vision introduced the judgment (or curse) and blessing motif (1:15–17). That motif is then developed in the second and third visions in an alternating cycle: judgment for the nations (1:18–21) but blessing and glory for Israel (2:1–5); judgment for the nations (2:6–9) but blessing for Israel—and the nations (2:10–13).[176]

The hope of future blessing for all who worship the Lord far surpasses anything Zechariah's contemporaries might have anticipated. Probably their greatest aspiration was to see a restoration that approximated what they had known before the exile. The Lord astounded his people, not only by granting them a more glorious hope than they had known, but also by extending a measure of grace to the nations beyond what the Gentiles had ever realized (or even knew enough spiritually to desire).

Furthermore, the temple figured prominently in Zechariah's understanding of how and where blessing would come to the postexilic community. Failure to acknowledge the Lord's sovereignty and to worship him in his temple in Zion would precipitate judgment. Although some might think Zechariah's emphasis on the temple was secondary, Zechariah's visions do not support such an interpretation of his aims. Zechariah consistently encouraged the rebuilding of the temple and instructed the nation about its future prominence. Mitchell exaggerates his claim at this point when he states,

> It is therefore probable that it was the preaching of Zechariah, rather than that of Haggai, which, after the first enthusiasm had subsided, held the Jews to their sacred but laborious task, during the four years that elapsed before the temple was completed.[177]

The vision concludes with key theological concepts held in tension, concepts that figure prominently in subsequent biblical revelation. The poles of God's transcendence and his immanence represent one such tension Zechariah

---

[175] Petersen (*Zechariah 1–8*, 185) disagrees, maintaining that the emphasis in this passage rests solely on the temple in Jerusalem.

[176] Barker, "Zechariah," 621.

[177] Mitchell, *Zechariah*, 145.

upheld. Two distinct, but not conflicting, portraits of the Lord emerge from the first visions. The Lord stands near his people, indeed dwelling in their very midst. Yet God also resides far above the mundane world of his creation.

The tension between universality and particularity also becomes apparent in Zechariah's visions. This tension is more apparent than real, but deserves comment. In vision three the Lord suggests that all the nations will taste the Lord's salvation. However, in the earlier visions Zechariah portrayed the nations receiving judgment, while in each of the first three visions Judah enjoys an exalted, exclusive relationship with God. In both Zech 1:17 and 2:12 we read that "the LORD . . . will choose Jerusalem."

Like v. 13, Ps 46:10 challenges believers of all ages to

> Be still, and know that I am God;
> I will be exalted among the nations,
> I will be exalted in the earth.

The life of genuine faith in the Lord and obedience to his will daily demands the profound acknowledgement that the Lord is indeed God. The beautiful message of v. 13 may have inspired the fourth century writer of the *Liturgy of St. James*, from which we get the hymn "Let All Mortal Flesh Keep Silence":

> Let all mortal flesh keep silence,
> And with fear and trembling stand;
> Ponder nothing earthly minded,
> For with blessing in His hand,
> Christ our God to earth descendeth,
> Our full homage to demand.
>
> Rank on rank the host of heaven
> Spreads its vanguard on the way,
> As the Light of light descendeth
> From the realms of endless day,
> That the powers of hell may vanish
> As the darkness clears away.
>
> At His feet the six-winged seraph;
> Cherubim with sleepless eye,
> Veil their faces to the Presence,
> As with ceaseless voice they cry,
> Alleluia! Alleluia!
> Alleluia! Lord Most High. Amen.[178]

---

[178] From *The Liturgy of St. James*, trans. G. Moultrie, in *Baptist Hymnal*, # 80.

## 4. The Fourth Vision: The Cleansing of the High Priest (3:1–10)

¹Then he showed me Joshua the high priest standing before the angel of the LORD, and Satan standing at his right side to accuse him. ²The LORD said to Satan, "The LORD rebuke you, Satan! The LORD, who has chosen Jerusalem, rebuke you! Is not this man a burning stick snatched from the fire?"

³Now Joshua was dressed in filthy clothes as he stood before the angel. ⁴The angel said to those who were standing before him, "Take off his filthy clothes."

Then he said to Joshua, "See, I have taken away your sin, and I will put rich garments on you."

⁵Then I said, "Put a clean turban on his head." So they put a clean turban on his head and clothed him, while the angel of the LORD stood by.

⁶The angel of the LORD gave this charge to Joshua: ⁷"This is what the LORD Almighty says: 'If you will walk in my ways and keep my requirements, then you will govern my house and have charge of my courts, and I will give you a place among these standing here.

⁸"'Listen, O high priest Joshua and your associates seated before you, who are men symbolic of things to come: I am going to bring my servant, the Branch. ⁹See, the stone I have set in front of Joshua! There are seven eyes on that one stone, and I will engrave an inscription on it,' says the LORD Almighty, 'and I will remove the sin of this land in a single day.

¹⁰"'In that day each of you will invite his neighbor to sit under his vine and fig tree,' declares the LORD Almighty."

The fourth and fifth visions differ significantly from visions one to three in several distinctive respects. The introductory formula, "I looked up and saw" does not appear in the fourth or fifth visions, and no angelic interpreter emerges to explain the meaning of the fourth vision, unlike previous visions. Further, Zechariah himself functions as an active participant in visions four and five, whereas the prophet remains in the background in chaps. 1–2. Moreover, the content of the fourth and fifth visions is relatively simple when compared to the earlier visions, describing real people and objects, unlike the other-worldly figures portrayed in visions one to three.

The common scholarly view that these differences require positing divergent authorship and historical setting is unwarranted and places the biblical author in a literary straightjacket.[179] Moreover, no biblical evidence supports such a conclusion. It is impossible to demonstrate that the prophet Zechariah did not pen these next two night visions as well, modifying his literary presentation on the basis of what God disclosed and the tenor of the message. Scholarship should grant the biblical author the freedom to modify his presentation of the Lord's revelation to him. Notwithstanding genuine differences between

---

[179] For a discussion of the arguments for separating visions four and five from the other night visions, see R L. Smith, *Micah–Malachi*, 199–200. Note also A. S. van der Woude, "Zion as Primeval Stone in Zechariah 3 and 4," in W. T. Claassen, ed., *Text and Context: Old Testament and Semitic Studies for F. C. Fensham* (Sheffield: JSOT Press, 1988), 237–48; N. L. A. Tidwell, "*Wā'ōmar* (Zech 3:5) and the Genre of Zechariah's Fourth Vision," *JBL* 94 (1975): 343–55.

the visions, a more sensitive literary approach to visions four and five observes that the distinctive character and message of the fourth vision leads to the differences noted above. Moreover, both visions four and five deserve to be read in the broader literary setting of the whole corpus of the night visions.

In the preceding three visions Zechariah surveyed the rebuilt city of Jerusalem.[180] In visions four and five the prophet envisioned the temple and its courts. The previous visions sketch the Lord's grand designs for his city, his people, and how the nations would finally turn to him. Visions one, two, and three assure the wavering people that God will keep the promises of a restored vibrant temple that he had made to Ezekiel (chaps. 40–48), ultimately fulfilling that grand prophecy. The fourth vision, The Cleansing of the High Priest, addresses the problem of a holy God who desires to accomplish great things through his sinful people. Zechariah 3:1–5 reveals the vision proper that Zechariah saw, while verses 6–10 disclose the vision's explanation.

Both the fourth and the fifth visions stress the importance of true faith in the lives of Judah's spiritual and political leaders in order for the Lord's kingdom to advance. In the fourth vision, the high priest Joshua, symbolizing the people as a whole (as vv. 8–9 make plain), receives cleansing, forgiveness, and righteousness in preparation for assuming his role in the future kingdom. This vision also reverberates with the common Isaianic title for the coming Messiah, the "Branch." With an unexpected turn of several themes found in Zech 3:1–7, Malachi proclaimed that both priests and people would have offal smeared on them to show the Lord's disdain for their false piety (Mal 2:1–3). In Malachi the Lord spread the filth on the impious, unlike Zechariah where God removed such impurities to symbolize the cleansing from sin he gave to Joshua the high priest. Both prophets wrote of the Lord's promise to rebuke sin (see Zech 3:2 and Mal 2:3).

Butterworth's monograph gives special attention to the integrity and literary structure of chap. 3. He maintains that the chapter follows a chiastic pattern as follows:

"Thus says Yahweh of hosts,

  A  If you will walk *(hālak)* in my ways
    B  and if you will keep my charge *(šāmar mišmartî)*
      C  then also you will judge my house
    B′  and you will also keep *(šamar)* my courts
  A′  and I will also give you access *(mahlĕkîm)*"[181]

---

[180] For a fuller discussion of differences between visions four and five compared to the others, see Meyers and Meyers, *Zechariah 1–8*, 213–16.

[181] M. Butterworth, *Structure and the Book of Zechariah* (Sheffield: Sheffield Academic Press, 1992), 116. See also W. H. Rose, *Zemah and Zerubbabel: Messianic Expectations in the Early Postexilic Period*, JSOTSup 304 (Sheffield: Sheffield Academic Press, 2000), 142–51; T. Pola, "Form and Meaning in Zechariah 3," in R. Albertz and B. Becking, eds., *Yahwism after the Exile: Perspectives on Israelite Religion in the Persian Era* (Assen: Van Gorcum, 2003), 158–62. Both

**3:1** The text does not specify who disclosed the vision of Joshua the high priest to Zechariah. Perhaps the interpreting angel made the disclosure. It seems more likely, though, that the Lord himself made the revelation since the fourth vision, unlike the former visions, does not identify an angelic interpreter. Some commentators raise concerns about the different introductory formula in vision four, concluding that the variance points to a different author or literary origin.[182] However, the phrase "he showed me" (3:1) complements the phrases, "then I looked up" (1:18) and "then the LORD showed me" (1:20).

The heavenly court provides the scene for the vision Zechariah saw, underscoring the gravity of the issues the accuser raised against Joshua. Although the setting occurs in heaven, not a courtroom, the text has a judicial flavor. Joshua, the defendant, whose fouled vestments portray his own defilement, also epitomizes sinful Judah. If the high priest is so filthy, how much more the nation as a whole. The angel of the Lord represents God's interests in the case. Satan functions as the prosecutor in the trial. Satan's presence in vv. 3–4 serves as an accusation of Joshua's guilt in committing crimes against the Lord. These transgressions disqualified the priest from divine service. The setting in Zech 3 bears a striking resemblance to the heavenly courtroom in Job 1 where Satan accused Job before God. However, the overwhelming guilt of Joshua, contrasted with Job's innocence, highlights the most distinctive differences between Zech 3 and Job 1.

Joshua the high priest appears also in Ezra 2:2 and Neh 7:7 as "Jeshua."[183] The name means "Yahweh saves." Joshua also figures prominently in Hag 1:1,12,14; 2:2,4, as well as in Zech 6:11. We know that Joshua was the son of Jehozadak (2 Kgs 25:18; 1 Chr 6:40–41; Jer 52:24), who was the son of Seraiah, the chief priest when the exile began in 587 BC. The Babylonians executed Seraiah, and presumably Jehozadak fathered and raised Joshua in Babylon. Joshua was probably an old man by the time of Zechariah's vision.[184]

Joshua's significance in the Book of Haggai clearly indicates the crucial role he played in the restoration community, along with his co-laborer for the Lord, Zerubbabel. As illustrated throughout prophetic literature, the prophets routinely addressed the king as an individual who represented the nation as a whole. Quite infrequently does a prophetic oracle speak to the king as well as to an individual priest. However, Hag 1:1 provides an example where both leaders are in view. The fact that the only political leader Haggai could address was a governor, not a king, does not diminish Joshua's importance as a leader for the community.

---

Rose and Pola argue for the literary unity of chap. 3.

[182] For example, Meyers and Meyers, *Zechariah 1–8*, 179.

[183] For a helpful survey concerning Joshua's role in the fourth vision, see Meyers and Meyers, *Zechariah 1–8*, 16–17.

[184] Merrill, *Zechariah*, 131.

Zechariah, along with Haggai, calls Joshua the "high priest" *(hakkōhēn haggādôl)*.[185] In preexilic biblical texts, the title was "chief priest" *(hakkōhēn hārōʾš)*.[186] Likely the high priest designation marks more than a new title. It appears that high priest here points to an expanded administrative role for this priestly office.[187] These broadened duties probably focused on fiscal matters such as fundraising for the temple restoration and the oversight of expenditures for this mammoth construction project. Joshua certainly faced a monumental financial task. Raising offerings presented tremendous difficulties since the people were relatively few in number, and those present were either comparatively poor or did not solidly back the temple construction. The scope of the rebuilding endeavor was overwhelming since essentially nothing from the previous temple remained. Everything either needed repair or complete replacement. Even without a shortage of funding, the scope of the reconstruction effort would humble any administrator.

The identity of Satan has engendered a great deal of discussion over the centuries. Many Christian interpreters have simply concluded that Satan in Zech 3:1–2 is none other than Satan of the New Testament (e.g., Luke 22:31), the fallen angel devoted to opposing God and persecuting the Lord's saints. This interpretation, while plausible, is anything but certain.[188]

To illustrate the complex and controversial character of this question, a survey of prominent, conservative Old Testament scholars' views illustrates the diversity of responses to this question, setting the stage for further discussion. All of these scholars affirm the reality of the fallen angelic being Satan in the New Testament. Merrill Unger dogmatically declares, "It would be highly arbitrary to take Satan in any other sense than the great personal spiritual adversary, so well known in Scripture in general."[189] Eugene Merrill states a similar conclusion, though less dogmatically.[190] Merrill's colleague, Kenneth Barker, comes to a much more tentative position: "One cannot be dogmatic, as it is sometimes difficult to determine when (or if) a common noun also began to function as a personal name."[191]

More cautious still, both McComiskey and Baldwin demur before identifying "Satan" in Zech 3 with the fallen angel who figures so prominently in the New Testament. McComiskey comments, "The description of this figure in the text is too vague for us to draw any other conclusions, and thus the use of this

---

[185] הַכֹּהֵן הַגָּדוֹל. See Lev 21:10; Num 35:25,28; Josh 20:6.

[186] הַכֹּהֵן הָרֹאשׁ. *HALOT*, 462; *TDOT*, 7:71–72. See also J. Bailey, "The Usage of the Post Restoration Period Terms Descriptive of the Priest and High Priest," *JBL* 70 (1951): 217–25.

[187] Meyers and Meyers, *Zechariah 1–8*, 17,180–82.

[188] For a survey of the question, see M. E. Tate, "Satan in the Old Testament," *RevExp* 89 (1992): 461–74.

[189] Unger, *Zechariah*, 57–58.

[190] Merrill, *Zechariah*, 133.

[191] Barker, "Zechariah," 623.

datum in any theological description of Satanology is tenuous."[192] Baldwin adds, "The Hebrew has the definite article, and is not using the word (Satan) as a name, but as a common noun in the sense of 'the accuser'."[193] A survey of the etymology of the word and its usage in the Old Testament offers grounds for making a determination concerning the meaning in Zech 3.

The Hebrew word *śāṭān* fundamentally means "adversary" or "accuser."[194] The Hebrew term frequently applies to a human adversary. For example, when describing Solomon's opponents the text reads, "Then the LORD raised up against Solomon an adversary *[śāṭān]*, Hadad the Edomite" (1 Kgs 11:14). The primary Hebrew lexicon, *HALOT*, lists numerous other examples that signify an "accuser" or an "opposing party." The lexicon also surveys uses that apply to an angelic being, but the mere presence of the Hebrew term in an Old Testament text does not in and of itself determine how the word functions.

With the definite article "the" *(ha-)*, neither *śāṭān* nor any other noun in biblical Hebrew serves as a proper name in the Old Testament except on rare occasions.[195]

In surveying the grammatical issue, Joüon and Muraoka restate the consensus among grammarians that proper nouns in Hebrew do not normally accept the definite article.[196] Two of the rare occurrences Joüon and Muraoka note are Ai, *hā'ay* ("The Ruin"),[197] and Gibeah, *haggib'āh* ("The Hill").[198] Joüon and Muraoka cite rare exceptions where proper nouns that continue to have their "appellative" meaning (that is, their meaning as a common noun) do occur with the definite article.[199] Few additional uncontested examples of a proper noun with the definite article occur in the Old Testament.

The term *śāṭān* in Zech 3:1–2, however, occurs with the definite article. Most likely, *śāṭān* in Zech 3, as well as in Job 1:6–12; 2:1–7, does not function as a proper name in the sense that the word appears in the New Testament.[200] Accordingly, the word serves as a common noun or a title, a description of the figure's role in the biblical story.[201] We can say, though, that the posture of

---

[192] McComiskey, "Zechariah," 1069.

[193] Baldwin, *Zechariah*, 113.

[194] שָׂטָן. See *HALOT*, 1317 and BDB, 966.

[195] In 1 Chr 21:1, "Satan" (used as a proper noun without the definite article) "incited David to take a census of Israel."

[196] P. Joüon and T. Muraoka, *A Grammar of Biblical Hebrew. Part Three: Syntax* (Roma: Pontificio Istituto Biblico, 1991), § 137b.

[197] הָעַי. See *HALOT*, 815–16.

[198] הַגִּבְעָה. See *HALOT*, 174–75. In addition to Ai and Gibeah, the Jordan (הַיַּרְדֵּן) and the Lebanon (הַלְּבָנוֹן) also occur with the article. In 12 cases out of 31 of "the half-tribe of Manasseh" the tribal name takes the article.

[199] Ibid, § 137d. "God" (הָאֱלֹהִים) and "Baal" (הַבַּעַל) often take the article.

[200] For an overview of connections between Zech 3 and Job 1, see M. C. Love, *The Evasive Text: Zechariah 1–8 and the Frustrated Reader* (Sheffield: Sheffield Academic Press, 1999), 197–98.

[201] Conrad, *Zechariah*, 89.

*śāṭān* at "his [Joshua's?] right hand" signifies courtroom imagery.[202] A similar usage to the one found in Zech 3:1 occurs in Ps 109:6: "Appoint an evil man to oppose him; let an accuser [Hb. *śāṭān*] stand at his right hand."

Verse 1 makes absolutely no attempt to identify *śāṭān*. Interpreters should take their cue from the text itself; since the identity of *śāṭān* is secondary to the purpose of the fourth vision, Zechariah subordinated the person of *śāṭān* to the message of the vision. The key interpretative issue does not rest on the identity of *śāṭān* but on his role. The person *śāṭān* functions as the heavenly antagonist who seeks to discredit God's servant by accusing him of his sinfulness and ceremonial defilement. Conrad points out that *śāṭān* does not speak in vision four, unlike the angelic messengers whose speeches play such a prominent place in the foregoing visions. Conrad also observes that the non-speaking role of *śāṭān* underscores his inferior status to the other angelic messengers.[203]

Baldwin properly notes, "The fuller development of the doctrine of a personal and devilish opponent of God is a feature of the New Testament."[204] While "Satan" in v. 1 probably is not Satan in the New Testament, nonetheless he opposes God in a malicious way, as v. 2 clearly indicates.[205]

**3:2** Whatever *śāṭān*'s grounds for the accusation in v. 1 were, v. 2 plainly indicates that the Lord did not agree with the accuser's assessment. God responded to *śāṭān* by accusing him and rebuking him for the evil he planned against Judah. The Lord's rebuff of *śāṭān* implicitly reaffirms Judah's covenantal relationship with God (see 1:17; 2:12). The repetition of the phrase "rebuke you" underscores the Lord's resolve to reprove *śāṭān*. The Hebrew term for "rebuke" (*gā'ar*) represents the Lord's particularly strong invective against his opponents.[206] Caquot notes that the word has "a strong anthropopathic thrust, and almost always denotes a threatening manifestation of the anger of God."[207] The word "rebuke" communicates such strong divine cursing that the expression became a curse formula widely attested in the postexilic period, including the documents of the Qumran community.[208] Jude reflects this malediction when it expresses the prayer that the Lord would rebuke the devil (v. 9). Jude, however, admonishes believers not to revile the devil themselves, for this is God's task.

The statement that "the LORD has chosen Jerusalem" occurs in 3:2 but also in 1:17 and 2:12. God's election of his people serves as the reason for the

---

[202] Tidwell, "*Wā'ōmar* [Zech 3:5]," 347.
[203] Ibid., 92.
[204] Baldwin, *Zechariah*, 113.
[205] R. K. Harrison (*Introduction to the Old Testament* [Grand Rapids: Eerdmans, 1969], 1036–41) and Merrill (*Zechariah*, 132–34) provide excellent surveys of the issue.
[206] גָּעַר ("to cry out"). See *HALOT*, 199–200.
[207] *TDOT*, 3:51.
[208] *TDOT*, 3:52.

Lord's indignant response to *śāṭān*, who accuses Joshua in v. 1. But the Lord rebukes *śāṭān* in v. 2 because of God's relationship to Jerusalem. God's response to *śāṭān* also shows his tenderness toward his suffering people.

The phrase "a burning stick snatched from the fire" echoes Amos 4:11, which states, "I overthrew some of you as I overthrew Sodom and Gomorrah. You were like a burning stick snatched from the fire." Just as the Lord plucked Lot from the burning brimstone falling on Sodom and Gomorrah, so had the Lord delivered Joshua and the people of God he represented from the burning judgment of the exile. The same theme appears in Isa 7:4 where Isaiah sarcastically spoke of Rezin and Pekah as "these two smoldering stubs of firewood." These passages highlight God's grace in rescuing his people before judgment crushed them, offering them salvation so they could serve him in peace and security (see also 1 Cor 3:15). Possibly, the exodus also served as a backdrop for v. 2. Deuteronomy 4:20 and Jer 11:4 describe the Lord's delivering Israel from Egyptian bondage by using the metaphor of pulling the nation out of an iron-smelting furnace.[209] This figure of speech must have held particular significance for Joshua since his grandfather Seraiah was assassinated by Judah's foes (2 Kgs 25:22–26). Surely, to be "snatched from the fire" also alluded to the nation's recent deliverance from the Babylonian exile.

**3:3** Few verses in the Old Testament portray a more graphic or repugnant scene than v. 3. Throughout the Old Testament, clothing symbolizes a person's office. Royal robes rest upon kings (1 Kgs 22:10). Prophets cloak themselves in their mantles (1 Kgs 19:19). Priests wear their cultic vestments (Exod 28–29). Who could fathom a priest preparing to lead in worship while wearing filthy, desecrated garments?

Furthermore, the Old Testament gives significant attention to the manner in which priests conducted their duties. For instance, biblical law mandated that Aaron and his descendants serve the Lord while ceremonially clean and clothed according to divine decree (Lev 8:5–9). Likewise, Joshua had to don the required priestly vestments in order to lead worship in a manner that would be acceptable to the Lord. (For a fuller description of the priestly vestments, see Exod 28.)

Nevertheless, Joshua stands humiliated before the angel, and presumably the Lord as well, wearing excrement-covered priestly raiment. The NIV translates the Hebrew *ṣôʾîm* in a diplomatic fashion, although the term in question certainly refers to excrement.[210] Second Kings 18:27 (= Isa 36:12) presents one of the clearest and most shocking uses of the term: "men sitting on the wall—who, like you, will have to eat their own filth and drink their own

---

[209] For a helpful survey of the nuances of Zechariah's imagery, see Petersen, *Zechariah 1–8*, 192–93.

[210] The Hebrew צוֹאִים refers to human excrement or vomit. See *HALOT*, 992; BDB, 844.

urine?" While this scene utterly appalls the reader at the levels of hygiene and social stigma, the theological significance goes still deeper.

Baldwin suggests that the word "filthy" might refer either to the soot soiling his clothing after being plucked out of the furnace (v. 2) or to dust that he had deliberately spread upon himself as a sign of mourning for guilt against the Lord.[211] While either suggestion fits the context adequately, neither interpretation harmonizes with the meaning of the Hebrew term. The Hebrew word translated "filthy" simply does not refer routinely to something that had been dirtied and should be washed as soon as possible. Alternatively, Ibn Ezra suggested that Joshua wore polluted vestments because the people's poverty precluded their ability to provide their high priest with suitable attire.[212] But again, the language occurring in this passage does not signify poverty. Instead, something inexcusable and far more revolting is in sight.

Lev 22 legislates the manner in which priests conducted their duties, and v. 3 cautions: "If any of your descendants is ceremonially unclean and yet comes near the sacred offerings that the Israelites consecrate to the LORD, that person must be cut off from my presence. I am the LORD." Zechariah 3:3 presents Joshua as utterly defiled, standing in the Lord's court in an official capacity, a transgressor who came before the Lord unworthily by violating Lev 22:3. Joshua's defiled condition contrasts sharply with the holy splendor of the Lord and his heavenly court. Repugnance characterized Joshua's sin, and Judah's as well.

Tiemeyer links Joshua's defilement to that of the nation as a whole. Specifically, she contends that Zech 3 addresses the theological problem raised, but left unresolved, in Hag 2.[213] Hag 2:10–14 introduces a national crisis in which Judah's sin separates her from the Lord, and as God's people, scandalizes his holy reputation among the nations. After discussing a test case that illustrates the point of defilement with the priests, Haggai wrote, "'So it is with this people and this nation in my sight,' declares the LORD. 'Whatever they do and whatever they offer there is defiled'" (2:14). Haggai clearly indicates that the nation remains powerless to rectify her situation. Judah's past actions utterly desecrated the nation, and anything further she attempts only serves to exacerbate her problem. Moreover, Haggai portrays the problem starkly, refraining from offering any indication of how the problem might be addressed. Joshua, the unclean high priest, represented the defilement of the entire priesthood and the nation. Zechariah 3 teaches Judah how cleanness and a relationship with God could be restored.

Their defiled state before God represented the basic problem that Joshua and his people faced. Put differently, how can a righteous God countenance, let

---

[211] Baldwin, *Zechariah*, 114.
[212] Cited by Cohen, *Twelve Prophets*, 280.
[213] L. Tiemeyer, "The Guilty Priesthood (Zech 3)," in *The Book of Zechariah and Its Influence*, ed. C. Tuckett (Burlington: Ashgate, 2003), 1.

alone bless, Joshua (and Judah whom the priest represents) when human efforts to attain "righteousness" caused divine revulsion? This fundamental question permeating the Bible asks how the righteous Lord can have a relationship with sinful people. The final biblical answer resides in the Messiah, Jesus Christ, "who takes away the sin of the world" (John 1:29).

Since Joshua represents Judah, evidently the Lord continued to see both Joshua and Judah as guilty sinners before him, even though they had completed their punishment during the exile. Mitchell adds that Judah was "so evidently guilty that, as the high priest's silence would suggest, an express accusation was unnecessary and a successful defense impossible."[214] Despite their abject guilt before the Lord, God's rebuke of "Satan" highlights the mercy the Lord intended to extend to his people. Of the abundant number of Old Testament texts portraying the Lord's merciful character, Hos 11:9 is one of the most blessed: "I will not carry out my fierce anger, nor will I turn and devastate Ephraim. For I am God, and not man—the Holy One among you. I will not come in wrath."[215]

**3:4** Lev 22:6–7 offers the remedy for priestly uncleanness: a ceremonial bath and presumably a change of priestly vestments also. Accordingly, the angel orders the unnamed angels in Joshua's presence to assist the high priest in removing his filthy clothes. Immediately following the symbolic act, the angel of the Lord explains the significance of putting ceremonially clean vestments on the high priest. In replacing his filthy clothes, the Lord removed Joshua's iniquity, forgiving the sin that made the high priest so odious before God. In v. 9 the Lord takes away the sin of the land, underscoring the point that Joshua symbolizes the people as a whole. Zechariah portrayed the sin the Lord forgives by using the term "iniquity" *('āwōn)*, one of the more distinctive words for sin in the Old Testament, which can be defined as "perversion or deliberate sin against the Lord."[216] Exod 28:36–38 employs the same word for sin, explaining how the priest received on himself the sin of the people:

> Make a plate of pure gold and engrave on it as on a seal: HOLY TO THE LORD. Fasten a blue cord to it to attach it to the turban; it is to be on the front of the turban. It will be on Aaron's forehead, and he will bear the guilt *['āwōn]* involved in the sacred gifts the Israelites consecrate, whatever their gifts may be. It will be on Aaron's forehead continually so that they will be acceptable to the LORD.

The portrait of cleansing from sin reappears frequently throughout the Bible. Hebrews 10:22 well illustrates the multitude of texts that describe the Lord's

---

[214] Mitchell, *Zechariah*, 150–51.
[215] See also Isa 4:3–4 where the motifs of restored Zion, inhabitants soiled with filth, and fire also occur in the same passage. See Petersen, *Zechariah 1–8*, 193–94, for a discussion of parallels between Zech 3:3 and Isa 4:3–4.
[216] עָוֹן. See *HALOT*, 800 and BDB, 730–31.

purifying those who trust in him: "Let us draw near to God with a sincere heart in full assurance of faith, having our hearts sprinkled to cleanse us from a guilty conscience and having our bodies washed with pure water."

The latter part of v. 4 is rich with symbolism. After removing Joshua's vile raiment, the angel declares that the high priest would receive "rich garments" so that he could wear proper attire in the Lord's presence. The word translated "rich" only occurs here and in Isa 3:22. The Hebrew word *maḥălāṣôt* describes "especially fine, white garments."[217] Typically, the Old Testament describes priestly clothing as "holy" garments, not the "rich" garments of v. 4. Exodus 28:2 illustrates this message: "Make holy garments for your brother Aaron."

On a more theological plane, the Bible employs the metaphor of clothing to picture the Lord spiritually transforming those who believe in him with salvation and imputed righteousness. Isaiah 61:10 declares,

> I delight greatly in the LORD;
>   my soul rejoices in my God.
> For he has clothed me with garments of salvation
>   and arrayed me in a robe of righteousness,
> as a bridegroom adorns his head like a priest,
>   and as a bride adorns herself with her jewels.

Just as Joshua formerly bore the collective iniquity of the people, now he carries the grace and forgiveness the Lord had just imparted both to Joshua and to Judah. Not only had the people fully paid the debt for their crimes against God in the exile, but now they experience total forgiveness for their sins and cleansing from their ceremonial impurity that resulted from dwelling in a foreign unclean land.

**3:5** Somewhat surprisingly, v. 5 begins "Then I said," apparently introducing Zechariah as the subject of the verb. Several ancient versions, along with many modern commentators, alter the text to read "then he said" in order that the Lord might continue as the subject of the verb.[218] This ancient attempt to simplify the Hebrew text should be rejected on two grounds. First, simpler readings usually represent inferior readings, reflecting artificial attempts to standardize texts according to the reader's preferences. Second, biblical narrative in general, and prophetic literature in particular, routinely shifts speakers more abruptly than readers typically encounter in modern texts. The Old Testament is replete with similar examples.

The filthy clothes removed from Joshua must have included a dirty hat or mitre. The priestly mitre normally worn by priests bore the inscription, "HOLY

---

[217] מַחֲלָצוֹת. *HALOT*, 569.
[218] Tidwell ("*Wā'ōmar* [Zech 3:5]," 352) argues that the MT reflects the original text. Petersen (*Zechariah 1–8*, 197) strongly maintains that the text should read "then he said," not primarily on text-critical grounds, but on the supposition that the prophet could not have participated in such a stately heavenly ceremony.

TO THE LORD" (Exod 28:36; 39:30). Accordingly, Zechariah instructed that the high priest receive "a clean turban."[219] Thus, with Joshua's priestly clothing completely changed, he could minister before the Lord with ceremonial cleanness and righteousness.[220] Joshua's clothing symbolized his new spiritual condition (see Matt 22:11–13). Although vv. 1–5 do emphasize the point that the high priest's vestments are now ceremonially clean, the focus does not rest on the official character of the attire that Joshua now wears. Significantly, the Lord changed Joshua's clothing, cleansing the high priest from the guilt of his sin; Joshua did not, and could not cleanse himself. It was the Lord who expiated his sins and those of the people.

Baldwin argues that Zechariah's fourth vision completes the thought first introduced in 1:1–6 where the Lord pronounces his anger with the people for their sins.[221] Zech 1:1–5 assures that those who repent from their sins (1:4–6) would indeed obtain forgiveness and restoration from the Lord. The phrase "the angel of the LORD stood by" adds solemnity to the vision, emphasizing the importance to the Lord of the actions by sending his personal emissary to oversee their completion.

**3:6–7** In recommissioning Joshua as high priest, the angel of the Lord makes a profound promise to Joshua, contingent on the high priest's fulfillment of two requirements. The angel of the Lord authoritatively pronounces the Lord's own decree that gives the two conditions for granting Joshua expanded authority as a priest. The phrase, "if you will walk in my ways and keep my requirements," conveys the dual duties. These two criteria, "walk in my ways" and "keep my requirements," might first appear to be a hendiadys, a figure of speech using two terms to express a single idea. Yet, however similar the two terms seem, the Hebrew words do have different connotations.

The first verb is "walk" *(hālak)*, which occurs frequently in the Old Testament with the metaphorical sense of living one's life.[222] "To walk" means to live life in a moral and spiritual fashion, abiding by the Lord's decrees (see Pss 1:1; 23:4. 101:6 says, "My eyes will be on the faithful in the land, that they may dwell with me; he whose walk is blameless will minister to me").[223] This expression characterizes Joshua's personal spirituality. Before the high priest can minister, his own integrity of life must be unimpeachable.

The second phrase, "keep my requirements" *(mišmartî tišmōr)*, serves as a technical expression for the faithful completion of the priest's official duties

---

[219] Sweeney claims that the Hebrew word for turban, צָנִיף, in 3:5 refers to a royal turban, not a priestly one *(Twelve Prophets*, 597). *HALOT* (1038) disputes Sweeney's suggestion.

[220] Petersen *(Zechariah 1–8*, 199–202) carefully details similarities between Zech 3 and other Old Testament occasions when the priest officially changes his attire, including investiture ceremonies (Exod 29 and Lev 8) and the Day of the Atonement (Lev 16).

[221] Baldwin, *Zechariah*, 115.

[222] הָלַךְ. See *HALOT*, 246–48 and BDB, 234.

[223] Deut 8:6 expresses the similar concept, establishing a standard of godly living for all of the Deuteronomic material.

elsewhere in the Old Testament.[224] Particularly in Num 3 where levitical responsibilities are outlined, this phrase repeatedly describes priests who dutifully fulfill their divine mandate. For instance, Num 3:7 introduces the priests' responsibilities to Aaron and Israel: "They are to perform duties for him *[šāmrû 'et-mišmartô]* and for the whole community at the Tent of Meeting by doing the work of the tabernacle." Moreover, these cultic responsibilities expanded to include civil administration and other legal responsibilities in the postexilic era when the people had no king.[225]

Together, the two concepts of walking and keeping God's law signify obedience to the Lord and living a righteous personal life that scrupulously upholds the additional priestly mandates (Deut 8:6; 10:12–13). Moreover, v. 7 explicitly demonstrates that the angel's charge addresses Joshua both as an individual and as Judah's representative.

The second half of v. 7 contains the apodosis to the protasis found in the first half of the verse. The first privilege faithfulness bestows is that Joshua will receive sole authority over the temple (see Deut 17:8–13).[226] As we have already discussed, in the postexilic era changing political and religious circumstances attributed far greater authority to the high priest, which became an elevated position also reflected in the Gospels. The phrase, "have charge of my courts," parallels the earlier statement "govern my house." Thus, "courts" refers to the temple precincts. In other words, these two phrases, "my house" and "my courts," do not express distinctly different concepts. Joshua, and presumably his successors as well, will emerge as religious autocrats to an extent never before seen in Jerusalem.

The angel of the Lord makes a second promise to the high priest, contingent on Joshua's spirituality and devotion to his priestly tasks. The angel assures Joshua that he will have "a place among these standing here." Verse 4 indicates that "these standing here" are the cadre of angels in their midst (see Jer 23:18). Joshua, the high priest whom the Lord exalts still higher, will have direct access to the throne of God. Only the high priest could enter the holy of holies, and only once a year (Lev 16), but the declaration made to Joshua far surpasses this privilege by granting Joshua entry into the Lord's heavenly throne room.

One can easily see how Joshua's new judicial responsibilities and his unprecedented access to the Lord's holy courts mark a significant development in the Old Testament priesthood. Reading Joshua's expanded role from a canonical, New Testament perspective enhances his transitional role further. Ultimately, Joshua's high priestly position points to Jesus Christ, the faithful High Priest who mediates and intercedes for the people of God with perfection and

---

[224] מִשְׁמַרְתִּי תִּשְׁמֹר. *HALOT*, 649–50, 1581–84.
[225] Meyers and Meyers, *Zechariah 1–8*, 194–95.
[226] See R. Mason, "The Prophets of the Restoration," in *Israel's Prophetic Tradition*, ed. R. Coggins, A. Phillips, and M. Knibb (Cambridge: Cambridge University Press, 1982), 147.

finality. The biblical teaching on Christ's superior priesthood finds its consummate expression in Heb 4:14–16:

> Therefore, since we have a great high priest who has gone through the heavens, Jesus the Son of God, let us hold firmly to the faith we profess. For we do not have a high priest who is unable to sympathize with our weaknesses, but we have one who has been tempted in every way, just as we are—yet was without sin. Let us then approach the throne of grace with confidence, so that we may receive mercy and find grace to help us in time of need.

**3:8** The injunction to Joshua begins with the imperative, "listen."[227] The verbal form mirrors that found in the Shema in Deut 6:4, emphasizing the importance of the message to follow. Fellow priests, Joshua's "associates," seat themselves with the high priest. The scene would be familiar to Ezekiel who often appeared in the midst of numerous fellow servants of the Lord (Ezek 8:1; 14:1; 20:1; 33:31). These men portend future expressions of the Lord's blessing.

While Zechariah's associates probably refer to priests, Petersen correctly observes that the identification of these men lacks definitive proof.[228] Nevertheless, Petersen offers the conjectural suggestion that Joshua's associates held prominent positions in the emerging society being redefined in and around Jerusalem, albeit not the priesthood. Petersen maintains that these socialites might include some of those whom Ezra 2 and Neh 7 listed as returnees from Babylon.[229] Joshua's fellow priests, however, symbolize good things the future will bring (see Isa 8:18 where Isaiah's children have a similar significance). Consequently, Joshua's associates most likely served as priests.[230] In the end, Petersen's view is not as convincing as the traditional interpretation.

The future blessings the priests embody find fulfillment in the one the Lord calls "my servant," who is also "the Branch" *(ṣemaḥ)*.[231] "Branch" is one of the Old Testament's most prominent messianic titles, an appellation also found in the ancient Near East.[232] A third-century BC Phoenician inscription uses

---

[227] שָׁמַע. See *HALOT*, 1571–72.
[228] Petersen, *Zechariah 1–8*, 209.
[229] Ibid.
[230] Mitchell, *Zechariah*, 156.
[231] צֶמַח. See *HALOT*, 1034.
[232] For a general survey of the development of messianic themes in the Old Testament, see the following: J. H. Charlesworth, ed., *The Messiah: Developments in Earliest Judaism and Christianity* (Minneapolis: Fortress, 1992); E. W. Hengstenberg, *Christology of the Old Testament,* reprint ed. (Grand Rapids: Kregel, 1956); W. C. Kaiser, Jr., *The Messiah in the Old Testament* (Grand Rapids: Zondervan, 1994); C. R. North, *The Suffering Servant in Deutero-Isaiah,* 2nd ed. (Oxford: Oxford University Press, 1948); and P. E. Satterthwaite, R. S. Hess, G. J. Wenham, eds., *The Lord's Anointed: Interpretation of Old Testament Messianic Texts* (Grand Rapids: Baker, 1995). R. E. Clements's study ("The Messianic Hope in the Old Testament," JSOT 43 [1989]: 3–19) should receive special attention since it takes a more positive, canonical approach to the fulfillment of Old

the word "branch" to denote the legitimate king.[233] In the Old Testament, the prophets often used the term "branch" (see Isa 4:2; 11:1; Jer 23:5; 33:15; Ezek 17:22–24; Zech 3:8; 6:12).[234] Paralleling Isaiah's message concerning the Davidic "Branch," Jeremiah wrote,

> "The days are coming," declares the LORD,
>    "when I will raise up to David a righteous Branch,
> a King who will reign wisely
>    and do what is just and right in the land.
> In his days Judah will be saved
>    and Israel will live in safety.
> This is the name by which he will be called:
>    The LORD Our Righteousness" (Jer 23:5–6; see 33:15–16).

Thus, Jeremiah anticipated the twin themes of a Davidic ruler and the safety the Messiah will bring to Judah at last.

Zechariah's use of "Branch" evokes the rich connotations introduced by previous texts. In his own day, Zechariah had witnessed an extended period of decline for the Davidic dynasty. In that milieu, Zechariah chose a messianic title that had great significance biblically, which also employed the imagery of a sprout or shoot coming up out of a stump to portray renewed vitality and hope.[235] The Branch as a metaphor represents a large verdant plant yielding bounty for Judah.[236] More importantly, the metaphor portrays the whole Davidic line of kings, culminating in Christ.[237]

While Isaiah, among others, uses the title "Branch" to refer to the coming Messiah, Isaiah refers to Messiah with greater frequency as the "Servant" (ʿebed).[238] The Hebrew term ʿebed functions in many different ways in the Old Testament.[239] When ascribed to humans, the "servant of the Lord" stands as

---

Testament Messianic expectations in the New Testament than do most Old Testament scholars.

[233] W. Beyerlin, ed., *Near Eastern Religious Texts Relating to the Old Testament* (Philadelphia: Westminster, 1978), 232–34.

[234] Boda, *Zechariah*, 256–57.

[235] W. H. Rose, *Zemah and Zerubbabel*, 106, 108. Also, W. H. Rose, "Messianic Expectations in the Early Post-Exilic Period," *TynBul* 49 (1998): 373–76.

[236] Kaiser, *Messiah*, 156–58, 164–67, 187–89, 211–15.

[237] W. H. Rose ("Messianic Expectations in the Early Postexilic Period," in *Yahwism after the Exile: Perspectives on Israelite Religion in the Persian Era*, ed. R. Albertz and B. Becking [Assen: Van Gorcum, 2003], 174–81) argues at length that the appellation "Branch" cannot have messianic significance. Rose desires to interpret "Branch" as "growth." To illustrate his point, Rose renders Jer 23:5, "Days are coming . . . when I will raise up to David a righteous Branch" as "I will raise up for David righteous growth." Too lengthy to treat in this volume, Rose's linguistic and literary arguments prove unconvincing, failing to overthrow centuries of semantic understanding and biblical interpretation.

[238] עֶבֶד. See *HALOT*, 774–75.

[239] Interpretations of the "servant" are so numerous and controversial that the famous Old Testament scholar, S. R. Driver, abandoned his commentary on Isaiah because he felt overwhelmed by the scope of the material (North, *Suffering Servant*, 1).

the highest title that the Old Testament bestows on humans. Accordingly, few individuals achieve the honor. Those so described in the biblical text include Abraham, Isaac, and Jacob (Deut 9:27); Moses (Num 12:7); Job (Job 1:8); David (2 Sam 3:18); Hezekiah (2 Chr 32:16); Israel (Isa 41:8); and the coming Suffering Servant (Isa 52:13; 53:11). A rare application of "servant" applies to one who, although not a believer in the Lord, functions at a critical juncture in history to fulfill the Lord's plan, as did Nebuchadnezzar (Jer 25:9; 27:6) and Cyrus (Is 44:26–45:1). The New Testament picks up the older usage, portraying Christ as a "servant" (Matt 12:18; Acts 2:13,26; 4:27,30; Rom 15:8; Phil 2:5–8).

Zechariah envisioned a single Davidic successor who would execute justice and righteousness throughout the land as Jeremiah had foretold (Jer 23:5). However, Zechariah did not reveal the successor's identity. Haggai 2:23 describes Zerubbabel as the Lord's servant, the one who would usher in the new righteous reign. As a result, some conclude that Zechariah referred to Zerubbabel here as well.[240] On the other hand, at the time Zechariah prophesied, Zerubbabel had led in the restoration of the temple for some time. While the precise date of Zerubbabel's arrival in Jerusalem to begin the temple reconstruction defies precise determination, Bright asserts that the two termini cannot exceed 538 to 522 BC.[241] Since we date the night visions to 520 BC, one can safely assert Zerubbabel's presence in Jerusalem at the time of this prophecy. Consequently, Zerubbabel could not be the Branch the Lord was about to bring to Jerusalem.[242]

**3:9** Once more, Zechariah abruptly shifted metaphors. The prophet moved from "branch" to "servant" to "stone." An amazing array of distinctively different interpretations attempt to explain the significance of the stone set before the prophet in the fourth vision. A brief list of suggestions for the stone's meaning in this context includes a capstone, a jewel in a priestly breastplate, a gem set in a crown, building materials for the temple, a metaphor referring to the temple itself, a rock in the holy of holies, an altar, the holy mountain, the Messiah, the kingdom of God, and the nation of Israel—and these are only a few of the more prominent interpretations.[243] In the search for a solution, one must ask several initial questions. Is the stone a metaphor for a historical person, and if so, who is he? If the stone represents an actual stone, did Zechariah intend a cornerstone used in a construction project? Did the stone have some ritual

---

[240] See Petersen, *Zechariah 1–8*, 210–11; Conrad, *Zechariah*, 95. For an overview of the arguments for and against identifying the Branch as Zerubbabel, see Rose, *Zemah and Zerubbabel*, 130–41.

[241] Bright, *History of Israel*, 367; Merrill, *Zechariah*, 152.

[242] Meyers and Meyers, *Zechariah 1–8*, 203; Mitchell, *Zechariah*, 156.

[243] Cited by E. E. Le Bas, "Zechariah's Enigmatic Contribution to the Corner-Stone," *PEQ* 82 (1950): 107. See also Le Bas, "Zechariah's Climax to the Career of the Corner-Stone," *PEQ* 82 (1950): 139–55.

significance? After determining the significance of the stone proper, interpreters must next attempt to determine the meaning of the "eyes" on the stone and the significance of the inscriptions written on it. While the attempts to answer these questions are quite diverse and complex,[244] three dominant interpretations emerge.

The first general approach to the interpretive questions accepts that Zechariah continued the common motif of rebuilding the temple that appears throughout his visions as well as that of the other postexilic biblical prophets. Hence, this view understands the stone either as a cornerstone or a capstone employed in the construction of the temple (see Isa 28:16; also 1 Cor 3:11; 1 Pet 2:4–7).[245] This building-materials view finds support in the ready association between the stone and materials used for construction. Although Zechariah's night visions manifest significant diversity in themes, they all stress the importance of rebuilding the temple so that Judah and the gathered nations can worship the Lord. Thus, the building-materials view harmonizes readily with one of the prophet's major theological themes, the gathering of all mankind to worship God at his temple.

Many, but certainly not all, who accept the building-materials interpretation maintain that the passage does not fit within its immediate context because 3:10 does not concern the rebuilding of the temple. Rather, these scholars often move v. 9 to the end of chap. 4, accompanying 4:6–10, a passage making reference to the capstone of the temple.[246] This unwarranted move fails to recognize that 3:9 envisions the day when the foundation of the temple was already laid. Further, most who embrace this interpretation understand the inscriptions on the stone as royal annals intended to preserve the king's memory, much as Mesopotamians inscribed on the cornerstones of their temples to capture the exploits of their monarchs for posterity.[247]

Even though the building-materials interpretation enjoys the support of many leading exegetes and the benefit of plausible historical comparisons with the ancient Near East, the view faces substantial challenges. The suggestion that the multiple inscriptions engraved on the stone are royal annals rests on purely conjectural grounds with little positive evidence to support the conclusion that the engravings represented royal inscriptions.[248] The practice of inscribing the king's annals on political and religious monuments, although widespread in Mesopotamia, was very rare in Israel. The concept of royal

---

[244] Petitjean, *Proto-Zacharie*, 161–206.

[245] Ibid., 179; see also B. Halpern, "Ritual Background," 167–90.

[246] J. C. VanderKam, "Joshua the High Priest and the Interpretation of Zechariah 3," *CBQ* 53 (1991): 564–65.

[247] Ibid.

[248] Cohen (*Twelve Prophets*, 282) quotes Kimchi's fanciful suggestion that the inscriptions refer to the seven greatest leaders during this period: Joshua, Zerubbabel, Ezra, Nehemiah, Haggai, Zechariah, and Malachi.

inscriptions lauding the king's exploits does not fit the character of the Old Testament's understanding of the king, who served as the Lord's representative on earth and ruled solely to glorify God, never himself.[249] Mitchell mentions an even greater problem—the temple's cornerstone was already laid when the angel of the Lord delivered this message.[250] Furthermore, according to Zech 4:7–9, Zerubbabel, not Joshua, oversaw the completion of the temple. Finally, the building-materials view does not fit the context of chap. 3 particularly well. Consequently, in addition to the difficulties with the details of v. 9, the interpretation falls short of producing the necessary burden of proof since 3:1–10 does not concern the temple as such.

A second interpretation concludes that the stone portrayed the Messiah. Many of those who accept the messianic view maintain that Zechariah's prophecy predicts Christ's first advent. This position draws its strength primarily from the context. One cannot deny that the fourth vision has strong messianic overtones. The titles "Branch" and "Servant" both have messianic significance throughout the Old Testament. The "stone" motif also has messianic nuances within the larger Old Testament context.[251] For instance, the messianic stone was an occasion for stumbling to all who did not believe in him. Psalm 118:22–23 says, "The stone the builders rejected has become the capstone; the LORD has done this, and it is marvelous in our eyes" (cf. Isa 8:13–15; 28:16). The motif in this verse reappears in Matt 21:42 and 1 Pet 2:7–8, showing that a canonical reading that fully takes the New Testament into account may point toward a messianic interpretation of Zech 3:9.[252] For the one who believes in the Lord, the stone provides help that never leads to dismay (Isa 28:16; 1 Pet 2:6). Moreover, Eph 2:19–22 portrays Christ as the chief cornerstone on which his Church rises.

The messianic understanding held by Christian scholars from the time of the early church to the present often identifies the engraving on the stone as the wounds Christ suffered when atoning for the sins of humanity.[253] Alternatively, Unger believes the engravings portray "eyes" on the faces of the stone that mark the stone with a supernatural authentication that he is indeed the Messiah.[254] Merrill's view is that the "eyes" actually refer to the Lord's eyes "which

---

[249] There are exceptions: Saul erected a monument for himself (1 Sam 15:12), and archaeologists have found the famous Siloam inscription, lauding one of Hezekiah's achievements.

[250] Mitchell, *Zechariah*, 157.

[251] Barker, "Zechariah," 626.

[252] For example, S. Kim suggests that the Parable of the Wicked Husbandmen in Mark 12 draws from several Old Testament passages: Ps 118:22–23; 2 Sam 7:12–16; and especially Zech 3:8–9; 4:7–10; 6:12–13. See Kim, "Jesus—The Son of God, the Stone, the Son of Man, and the Servant: The Role of Zechariah in the Self-Identification of Jesus," in *Tradition and Interpretation in the New Testament: Essays in Honor of E. Earle Ellis*, ed. G. F. Hawthorne and O. Betz (Grand Rapids: Eerdmans, 1987), 134–45.

[253] Barker, "Zechariah," 626.

[254] Unger, *Zechariah*, 67.

range throughout the earth" (4:10) "to strengthen those whose hearts are fully committed to him" (2 Chr 16:9).[255] The messianic perspective believes that the stone's removal of sin "in a single day" predicts the redemptive suffering of Christ on the cross.

The messianic interpretation provides a strong tie to more general messianic motifs in Zechariah's fourth vision, as well as canonical connections between the stone imagery and clear messianic prophecies. Although this view has strong support, several significant questions remain. For instance, one cannot simply surmise that "stone" serves as a messianic title, along with "branch" and "servant," as some interpreters do.[256] While the "stone" imagery can refer to the Messiah as the passages listed above demonstrate, the term does not speak of the Messiah in the Old Testament in the majority of passages where the term occurs. Consequently, it does not necessarily follow that the stone in v. 9 speaks of the Messiah either. At best, vv. 1–10 yield mixed evidence. The context of chap. 3 both supports and undermines the messianic interpretation of "stone," as we will shortly see. Only the references to "servant" and "branch" in v. 8b lend meaningful support to the messianic approach. Nevertheless, the majority of the passage (vv. 1–8a) points away from the messianic view.

The inscriptions on the stone present an even greater challenge for the messianic view. If the stone speaks of the coming Messiah, what do the engravings on the stone represent? Even though the interpretations of these inscriptions vary widely, most agree that *something* was written on the stone. The citation from the early Church Fathers claiming that the engravings speak of the wounds Christ bore on the cross borders on allegory and has no support from the text itself.[257] Merrill's recommendation that actual eyes inscribed on the stone represent God's eyes moving to and fro looking for those faithful ones whom he might bless equally lacks clear biblical support. The text of Zech 3 does not plainly state that eyes are inscribed on the stone. The opinion that the eyes represent God's eyes roving the earth finds no support from Zech 3 or any text alluding to chap. 3. Again, Unger's understanding that the engravings reproduce "eyes" on the stone that identify the stone as the long-awaited Mes-

---

[255] Merrill, *Zechariah*, 142–43; Sweeney, *Twelve Prophets*, 603.
[256] Ibid.
[257] Barker, "Zechariah," 626. The Church Fathers embracing a Christological view of Zech 3 include Augustine, Gregory of Nyssa, Cyprian, Ambrose, Jerome, Theodoret of Cyr, Justin Martyr, Lactantius, and Origen. See Gregory of Nyssa, *Contra Eunomium*, 3.4.19 (Gregorii Nysseni Opera 2:140); Cyprian, *Treatise, Ad Qvirinvm*, 2.13 (CCSL 3:46–47); Ambrose, *De interpellatione Job et David*, 3.10.27 (PL 14:888); idem., *Epistolarum*, 45.987.C (PL 16:1198); Jerome, *Contra Fufinum*, 2.18.510.D (PL 23:461); idem., *Tractatvs de Psalmo* 109 (CCSL 78:226); Augustine, *De Nuptiis et Concupiscentia*, 2.50 (PL 44); Theodoret of Cyr, *Commentary on Zechariah*, 3.1–6 (Patrologia graeca 81:1892); Justin Martyr, *Iustini Martyris Dialogus Cum Tryphone*, 116 (Patristische Texte und Studien 47:269–70); Lactantius, *Institutions Divines*, 4.14.9–13 (SC 377:126); Origen, *Homélies Sur S. Luc*, 14.4–5 (SC 87:220).

siah remains unconvincing. Hence, the messianic view experiences difficulties handling the exegetical detail of inscriptions written on the stone.

In sum, only if the interpreter closely connects v. 9 to v. 8b alone—excluding the remainder of the passage—could one find it attractive to view the stone as the Messiah. However, when one stresses the relationship between v. 9 to the entire passage (vv. 1–10), the messianic position becomes less convincing.

The third major approach understands the stone to represent a large gem like the stones inscribed with the names of Israel's tribes in the high priest's breastplate (Exod 28). Several factors commend this view. To begin, a gem placed within the high priest's vestments fits well within the vision Zechariah received in vv. 1–5. Joshua's unclean vestments and the Lord clothing the high priest with clean clothing functions as the major motif in the first half of the fourth vision. Thus, in the initial portion of the chapter the vision emphasizes the change of raiment given to the high priest and the cleansing from personal guilt that the new vestments represent. The last interpretation of the significance of Joshua's stone sees the engraved stone completing the priestly vestments since the stone functioned as an important feature of the high priest's official accoutrements in the preexilic era.

Exod 28:15–21 and 39:2–21 provide the ancient description of the high priest's official clothing and may also serve as background for understanding Zechariah's "stone."[258] Exod 28:9 describes the ephod containing inscribed stones using the same word for "engraving" that occurs in Zech 3:9, "Take two onyx stones and engrave on them the names of the sons of Israel."[259] Further, in Exod 28:15–21 the Lord instructed Aaron to have artisans fashion a breastpiece that would contain twelve stones, one representing each of the twelve tribes. This third understanding believes that Zechariah drew explicitly from Exod 28 when describing Joshua's investiture as a cleansed high priest by using both themes and actual wording from the Mosaic text.

Furthermore, v. 9 indicates that the stone will remove the people's iniquity (*'āwōn*) in a single day.[260] While the emphasis on cleansing from sin in a single day represents one of Zechariah's distinctive contributions, the idea of cleansing from sin for God's people in their great eschatological future occurs with some frequency in the Old Testament (Isa 1:26; 4:3–4; 32:1–8; Jer 31:33–34; Dan 9:24).[261] Zechariah also addresses purification and forgiveness from sin elsewhere in the book (12:10; 13:1).

The significance of God's removing the people's sin in a single day depends primarily on the meaning of "stone" the interpreter adopts. For the messianic view, as we have already mentioned, the single day speaks of the day Christ died on the cross, bearing the world's sins. For the gemstone and vestment

---

[258] Similar information, with slightly less specificity, occurs in Exod 29 as well as Lev 8; 16.
[259] מְפֻתַּח פִּתֻּחַ. *HALOT*, 988.
[260] The word for iniquity (עָוֹן) occurs also in v. 4.
[261] R. L. Smith, *Micah–Malachi*, 202.

approach, the single day refers to the time when the priest officially stood before the Lord offering an expiatory sacrifice. However, on a canonical level, the day of expiation also points toward that day when Christ suffered on the cross. Thus, when one considers the New Testament perspective, God's promise to "remove the sin of this land in a single day" has an ultimate fulfillment in the personal work of Christ, but one interpretation is messianic *per se* and the other is typological.

Perhaps this divine cleansing from sin also lends a clue to understanding the enigmatic phrase "seven eyes" inscribed on the stone. The Hebrew word translated "eyes" (*ʿēnāyim*) occurs in the dual, a nominal form typically reserved for pairs of things.[262] Thus, the term should be rendered "pairs of eyes."[263] Zechariah may envision seven pairs of "eyes," that is, 14 "eyes."[264] These 14 "eyes" may allude to Exod 28 where the priestly vestment contained 14 stones, 12 stones representing the Twelve Tribes of Israel, plus the Urim and Thummim. The 14 "eyes" inscribed on Zechariah's stones recall all of the stones in the high priestly vestment from Aaronic times. The major change in Zech 3, however, is the presence of only one stone. This stone represents the tribe of Judah, the only tribe remaining after the exile.[265] Sweeney counts only "the seven eyes" though, ignoring the dual number of the noun. He further correlates the seven eyes, the Lord's "eyes," to the seven-branched lampstand in Zech 4:2,10.[266]

One should also note that a few scholars attempt to translate the word "eyes" differently. The term *ʿēnāyim* may be translated "eyes" (Gen 3:7), "fountains" (Neh 2:14), or "springs" (Gen 16:7). Some have objected that the translation "eyes" does not harmonize well with the cleansing motif so prominent in chap. 3. Lipinski suggests that the idea of "springs" readily relates to the purification that Zechariah describes.[267] Lipinski sees a thematic unity between the springs in Zech 3 and 14, along with Ezek 47. He also notes that all three passages encompass eschatological events in which a great fountain symbolizes the Lord's blessings, and especially the cleansing God offers. Lipinski further believes that the rock struck by Moses in the wilderness stands in the background to Zechariah's "springs" in chap. 3 (see Exod 17:6; Num 20:8). According to this view, the New Testament may have chap. 3 in mind when it takes the concept of refreshing water and applies it to Christ as the Rock who provides spiritual drink for his believers (1 Cor 10:4). On the other hand, Lipinski argues that

---

[262] עֵינָיִם. See *HALOT*, 818–19.
[263] Meyers and Meyers, *Zechariah 1–8*, 208; VanderKam, "Joshua the High Priest," 568.
[264] On the other hand, Waltke-O'Connor states that words that generally occur in the dual often use the dual form when a plural sense is intended (B. K. Waltke and M. O'Connor, *An Introduction to Biblical Hebrew Syntax* [Winona Lake: Eisenbrauns, 1990], §7.3b). See Zech 4:10.
[265] VanderKam, "Joshua the High Priest," 568.
[266] Sweeney, *Twelve Prophets*, 603.
[267] Lipinski, "Reserches sur le livre de Zacharie," 26–28. See also R. L. Smith, *Micah–Malachi*, 201–2.

Zechariah has cleansing in mind, not a motif of refreshing. In the final analysis, the merits of the vestment approach to Zechariah's stone do not depend on the correctness of Lipinski's suggestion. If the stone signifies the gemstones in the high priestly vestments, the prophecy may be summarized this way:

> Joshua is invested with his splendid garments as a sign that a new age is dawning. That new age is characterized by two facts: a Davidic heir is coming, but more importantly in this context the temple cult will once more serve its function of removing guilt and atoning for sin. . . . As removal of his filthy garments represented the erasure of his guilt, so donning splendid high-priestly vestments meant that the cult, headed by the high priest, would once more effect its ancient goal of restoring the damaged relations between God and his people.[268]

Ultimately, the question of the stone's significance defies certain resolution. The messianic position does not harmonize with the themes in vv. 1–10 particularly well. On the other hand, a stronger case exists for both the building-materials and the gemstone interpretations. The gemstone view, however, presents the least number of challenges, while best complementing the overall thrust of vv. 1–10.[269]

Whatever interpretation of the stone one adopts, the passage clearly establishes a direct connection to the priestly office.[270] We have already noted that the "Branch" emphasizes the royal office the Messiah will hold. Thus, Zechariah combines two of the Old Testament's most powerful offices into one, jointly held by the same individual.[271] Of course, the only other individual in the Old Testament holding both the offices of king and priest was Melchizedek (Gen 14:18–20; Ps 110:4), the mysterious, typological figure who foreshadowed Christ and the royal-priestly offices he held (Heb 5:6; 7:1–17).

It is important to recognize that adopting the vestments interpretation does not preclude a messianic implication. While the directly messianic interpretation possesses attractive elements, it ultimately remains unconvincing. However, one may properly envision Joshua the high priest prefiguring Jesus Christ as typology. Christ functions as the ultimate High Priest whose intercessory ministry fulfills creation's need for an intermediary with the Lord.

**3:10** Verse 10 begins with the expression "in that day." The meaning of this familiar prophetic formula depends on one's interpretation of the oracle as a whole. One rendering suggests "in that *distant* day" and the other view, "on

---

[268] VanderKam, "Joshua the High Priest," 569.
[269] For a more detailed analysis of the different interpretations of v. 9, see VanderKam, "Joshua the High Priest," 553–70.
[270] Mitchell, *Zechariah*, 157–59.
[271] R. L. Smith, *Micah–Malachi*, 201.

the *same* day," as used in v. 9b.[272] The futuristic tone of Zech 3 supports the former understanding.

The phrase "under his vine and fig tree" existed in antiquity and conveyed the ultimate joy and satisfaction that God's people had so longed to experience (see 1 Kgs 4:25; 2 Kgs 18:31; cf. John 1:48). Micah 4:4 uses similar language to describe the messianic age: "Every man will sit under his own vine and under his own fig tree, and no one will make them afraid, for the LORD Almighty has spoken."

Petersen assigns an additional meaning to the metaphor of "vine and fig tree." He believes that the botanical imagery of v. 8 continues in v. 10, where the Branch appears. He contends that Zechariah linked the idea of a Davidic king with a prosperous age to come.[273] Zechariah made it quite clear, though, that the coming messianic age will reflect peace unlike anything Israel had ever known. The invitation to enjoy God's blessings extended to Israel's neighbors and reflected a new spirit of harmony and fellowship among the Lord's people, not to mention with her neighboring nations.

Baldwin summarizes the message of vv. 8–10 as follows: "The 'living water' of the fountains causes the Branch to shoot up (verse 8), washes away guilt (9) and ensures prosperity (10)."[274] Rom 11:26–27 continues a similar message: "And so all Israel will be saved, as it is written: 'The deliverer will come from Zion; he will turn godlessness away from Jacob. And this is my covenant with them when I take away their sins.'"

Zechariah 3 dramatically underscores the utter sinfulness of all, including Judah's religious leaders. As the account of the Lord's cleansing Joshua and providing him with suitable clothing graphically portrays, only God can cleanse the sinful human heart and prepare it for worship. The beloved hymn "Grace Greater Than Our Sin" echoes the same theme:

> Marvelous grace of our loving Lord,
> Grace that exceeds our sin and our guilt,
> Yonder on Calvary's mount outpoured,
> There where the blood of the Lamb was spilt.
>
> Dark is the stain that we cannot hide,
> What can avail to wash it away?
> Look! There is flowing a crimson tide;
> Whiter than snow you may be today.
>
> Marvelous, infinite, matchless grace,
> Freely bestowed on all who believe;
> All who are longing to see His face,

---

[272] Meyers and Meyers, *Zechariah 1–8*, 212.
[273] Petersen, *Zechariah 1–8*, 212–13.
[274] Baldwin, *Zechariah*, 117–18.

Will you this moment His grace receive?

Grace, grace, God's grace,
Grace that will pardon and cleanse within,
Grace, grace, God's grace,
Grace that is greater than all our sin.[275]

## 4. The Fifth Vision: The Gold Lampstand and Two Olive Trees (4:1–14)

¹Then the angel who talked with me returned and wakened me, as a man is wakened from his sleep. ²He asked me, "What do you see?"

I answered, "I see a solid gold lampstand with a bowl at the top and seven lights on it, with seven channels to the lights. ³Also there are two olive trees by it, one on the right of the bowl and the other on its left."

⁴I asked the angel who talked with me, "What are these, my lord?"

⁵He answered, "Do you not know what these are?"

"No, my lord," I replied.

⁶So he said to me, "This is the word of the LORD to Zerubbabel: 'Not by might nor by power, but by my Spirit,' says the LORD Almighty.

⁷"What are you, O mighty mountain? Before Zerubbabel you will become level ground. Then he will bring out the capstone to shouts of 'God bless it! God bless it!'"

⁸Then the word of the LORD came to me: ⁹"The hands of Zerubbabel have laid the foundation of this temple; his hands will also complete it. Then you will know that the LORD Almighty has sent me to you.

¹⁰"Who despises the day of small things? Men will rejoice when they see the plumb line in the hand of Zerubbabel.

"(These seven are the eyes of the LORD, which range throughout the earth.)"

¹¹Then I asked the angel, "What are these two olive trees on the right and the left of the lampstand?"

¹²Again I asked him, "What are these two olive branches beside the two gold pipes that pour out golden oil?"

¹³He replied, "Do you not know what these are?"

"No, my lord," I said.

¹⁴So he said, "These are the two who are anointed to serve the LORD of all the earth."

When properly functioning as the seat of worship, the Lord's house always had a lampstand providing light within. The tabernacle contained a single golden lampstand lighting the holy place (Exod 25:31–40). Later, the temple possessed ten lampstands made of pure gold, five on each side of the front of the inner sanctuary (1 Kgs 7:49). However, not until Zech 4 does the issue of the lampstand within the Lord's temple arise again. In each instance, the light produced by the lampstands represents God's glory and his presence among his people. Moreover, the lampstands may also symbolize the people of God and the role

---

[275] J. H. Johnston, *Baptist Hymnal*, #329.

they should play reflecting the Lord's light to the nations. We will return to the question of the lampstand's significance at the end of the discussion on v. 14.

The fifth vision (4:1–14) aims to encourage Zerubbabel, Joshua, and Zechariah by announcing that Zerubbabel will complete the temple. The fifth vision complements the fourth in several significant ways. Merrill summarizes several of these similarities: "Both deal with cultic persons or objects (the high priest and the menorah respectively), both mention historical persons contemporary to the prophet (Joshua and Zerubbabel), both refer to temple building, and both reach their climax on a strong messianic note."[276] Additionally, both visions underscore the Lord's presence with his people and the temple. The ceremony in the fourth vision involves the priest, while the fifth vision gives the corresponding ceremony for the governor.[277]

Old Testament scholarship often suggests that Zechariah's fifth vision does not reflect a unified literary text in its current shape, typically concluding that 4:6b–10 do not belong to the same oracle.[278] Many scholars believe the solution to the irregular contours of vision five lies with significantly rearranging chap. 4.[279] For example, commentators frequently excise vv. 6b–10 and move them elsewhere, treating the remaining pericope as a discrete literary unit. However, several contemporary scholars appear less adamant about rearranging this vision.[280] In fact, many believe that the pericope coheres quite closely.[281]

Merrill offers a convincing interpretation of the whole of chap. 4 as a unit.[282] He concludes that vv. 1–3 introduce the vision Zechariah witnessed. Verses 7–10 include a prophetic oracle that vv. 4–6 and vv. 11–14 frame, providing an interpretation of what the prophet had just seen and heard.

A variety of additional literary affinities further substantiate that the chapter represents a unified whole. For instance, vv. 5 and 13 both contain identical questions directed to the interpreting angel, followed by negative replies. The olive trees in v. 3 foreshadow the two figures in v. 14 who receive the Lord's anointing to serve him. Moreover, the whole passage builds progressively to its climax in v. 14.[283] Meyers and Meyers add,

> However, from a literary viewpoint, the intrusive nature of the Zerubbabel oracles in chapter 4 does not by virtue of that fact demand their

---

[276] Merrill, *Zechariah*, 145.

[277] Conrad, *Zechariah*, 106.

[278] D. L. Petersen, "Zerubbabel and Jerusalem Temple Reconstruction," *CBQ* 36 (1974): 367; B. B. Bruehler, "Seeing through the עינים of Zechariah: Understanding Zechariah 4," *CBQ* 63 (2001): 431; R. L. Smith, *Micah–Malachi*, 203–4.

[279] Petersen, *Zechariah 1–8*, 237–44.

[280] For example, both Meyers and Meyers (*Zechariah 1–8*, 266–68) and R. L. Smith (*Micah–Malachi*, 206) maintain that vv. 6b–10, although interrupting the flow of the vision, belong where they occur in chap. 4.

[281] Van der Woude, "Zion as Primeval Stone," 239; Tigchelaar, *Prophets of Old*, 24.

[282] Merrill, *Zechariah*, 149–52.

[283] Ibid., 150.

excision or rearrangement. On the contrary, chapter 4 in its present form is a classic envelope construction. The opening and closing units correspond with each other. . . . The material in Zechariah 4 appears in this way because of purposeful arrangement and not through later careless or thoughtless handling of prophetic materials. Chapter 4 as a whole should be seen as a single literary construct.[284]

**4:1–2** For reasons the text does not explain, the fifth vision gives details about the angel's awakening the prophet in order to show him the vision—details that do not appear in the other visions. Possibly, Zechariah awoke from the previous vision only to experience another.

After awakening, Zechariah immediately recognized a golden lampstand (*měnôrat zāhāb*).[285] While some transliterate *měnôrat* as "menorah" in v. 2 (NIV "lampstand"), this translation seems ill advised in this context.[286] Zechariah's lampstand probably did not resemble the shape of the menorah used in modern Jewish iconography. The style of menorah familiar today was rare in the postexilic era and does not correspond well with the complex description of lights and bowls pictured here. Although Baldwin states that the "modern" style of menorah is unknown prior to the first century BC,[287] Keel pictures an isolated example of a lamp from Zechariah's era that closely resembles the menorah known today.[288]

The Hebrew text's description of the specific design of the lamps presents lexical difficulties that, in turn, engender text-critical variances. The phrase in question reads literally, "seven and seven pipes to the lamps." The ambiguity of the expression allows several different interpretations. Influenced by the Septuagint, which omits the first "seven," as well as the discovery of a seven-spouted lamp at Tel Dan, many maintain that Zechariah's lampstand had only seven lights.[289] According to this view, the lampstand's notoriety derives solely from its construction out of pure gold. Another possibility suggests that the phrase might refer to a single bowl supplying oil to seven lamps on either side of the bowl, yielding a total of fourteen lamps.[290] This approach reads the *waw* conjunction in its simplest conjunctive sense, "A 'and' (plus) B."

A third interpretation concludes that the two nouns "seven" in the phrase "seven and seven" function as multipliers, producing a total of forty-nine

---

[284] Meyers and Meyers, *Zechariah 1–8*, 267–68.
[285] See R. North ("Zechariah's Seven-Spout Lampstand," *Bib* 51 [1970]: 183–206) for discussion, drawings, and photographs that relate to Zechariah's lampstand. For detailed literary treatments of the lampstand, see Meyers and Meyers, *Zechariah 1–8*, 229–40; and Petersen, *Zechariah 1–8*, 217–24.
[286] מְנוֹרַת זָהָב. *HALOT*, 600.
[287] Baldwin, *Zechariah*, 119.
[288] O. Keel, *Symbolism*, 165–66.
[289] Meyers and Meyers, *Zechariah 1–8*, 231–33; Mitchell, *Zechariah*, 161–62; Petersen, *Zechariah 1–8*, 220–22.
[290] Merrill, *Zechariah*, 147–48.

individual lights on the same lampstand.[291] Hence, each of the seven lamps has seven pipes and each of the seven pipes has a wick or lip. The Hebrew conjunction *waw* functions distributively according to this understanding, much as it does in 2 Sam 21:20 where the expression "six and six" clearly indicates that each of the Philistine hero's hands and feet had an extra digit, totaling 24 digits. Some confusion exists between the translations, "pipes" and "lips."[292] The rendering, "pipe," represents a modern conception. The Hebrew term *mûṣ āqôt* simply refers to a "narrowing," resulting in a conduit through which the oil could flow to the flame.[293]

In the final analysis, v. 2 presents issues one cannot resolve. The prophet does not attempt to describe what he saw with any measure of detail. The first "seven" might be a dittography, a textual corruption where a scribe inadvertently writes a word (or phrase) twice. However a dittography appears highly unlikely since the Septuagint's omission of the first "seven" appears to be a simplification of the Masoretic Text or an accidental omission of the word.[294]

It seems more likely that the lampstand Zechariah saw comprised a cylindrical base with a bowl resting on top. Around the perimeter of the bowl the potter pinched together the rim to form a small trough in which the wicks could lay. However, one cannot know whether the lampstand has 14 or 49 lights. The Hebrew text accommodates either possibility. Even though Merrill objects that 49 is virtually impossible because of the undue complexity of such a lampstand, North's rendering demonstrates the feasibility of the design.[295]

Irrespective of the number of lamps, the unique design of Zechariah's lampstand made it highly unusual, unlike any other lampstand portrayed in the Old Testament. In addition to the spectacle of light such an unusual configuration produced, the solid gold lampstand made it dazzling to behold. Even more important than its unique appearance, the lampstand possessed important theological significance that we will examine shortly.

**4:3** Next, Zechariah saw two olive trees, one on either side of the lampstand.[296] Since lamps normally burned olive oil in ancient Israel, the presence of the two olive trees probably symbolizes a continual supply of oil to keep the lamps burning. Verse 12 reveals that these trees produce oil that flows unaided into the golden lampstand. Thus, the lampstand did not require human effort to ensure a continual supply of oil. One cannot make more detailed claims about

---

[291] Baldwin, *Zechariah*, 120; Unger, *Zechariah*, 71. For an artist's rendering, see *IDB*, 3:66; and North, "Lampstand," 192, 195, 201.

[292] Sweeney, *Zechariah*, 604.

[293] מוּצָקוֹת. See *HALOT*, 559.

[294] D. Barthélemy et al., eds., *Preliminary and Interim Report on the Hebrew Old Testament Text Project*, 5 vols. (New York: United Bible Societies, 1979), 5:399.

[295] Merrill, *Zechariah*, 147–48; North, "Lampstand," 192, 195, 201.

[296] For a discussion of the influence (albeit minimal in Strand's view) of Zech 4 on Rev 11, see K. A. Strand, "The Two Olive Trees of Zechariah 4 and Revelation 11," *AUSS* 20 (1982): 257–61.

the symbolism of the olive trees until the interpreting angel answers Zechariah's upcoming question. As Mitchell notes, Zechariah's olive trees represented "diminutive images of the things they were intended to represent."[297]

**4:4–5** Although olive trees grew widely in ancient Israel, Zechariah asked the interpreting angel, "What are these, my lord?"[298] The angel's response makes it clear that the discussion focused on the olive trees' symbolism, not their identification. The angel's reply suggests, "Don't you know?" Moreover, the angel's retort serves as a literary device to focus greater attention on the importance of the items Zechariah observed in the vision.[299]

Even though Zechariah knew what he saw, he did not know what the vision signified. Furthermore, the interpreting angel declined to answer Zechariah's question, something he had not done previously in the book. The effect of delaying his answer to the prophet heightens the importance of the questions Zechariah originally posed. Zechariah would not receive the angel's response until the final verse of the vision.[300]

To what does the demonstrative pronoun "these" refer in Zechariah's question ("What are *these*?")? Several suggest that Zechariah asks only about the meaning of the olive trees,[301] but the text does not clearly indicate that Zechariah's question was just about the trees. More likely, the prophet wondered what the entire vision connoted, including the particular features in the vision such as the lampstand and olive trees.[302]

**4:6** Verse 6 is one of the more famous verses in the Old Testament and contains the angel's response to the prophet's inquiry in v. 5. Nonetheless, the reply does not focus on the olive trees, for they will receive attention later in the chapter. The angel proceeded to explain the meaning of the lampstand that Zechariah saw.

For several decades, scholars have realized that Zech 4:6b–10 shows striking parallels to inscriptions discovered on Mesopotamian royal buildings.[303] Laato revisits the material from Akkadian building inscriptions and notes numerous similarities. The following parallels, plus several others that are omitted, occur in both Mesopotamian sources and Zech 4:

---

[297] Mitchell, *Zechariah*, 162.

[298] Conrad offers a contrasting perspective suggesting that Zechariah did not recognize the restored temple since he had never seen the former one (*Zechariah*, 112).

[299] Love, *The Evasive Text*, 124.

[300] Meyers and Meyers (*Zechariah 1–8*, 240–41) understand the angel's question as a taunt to Zechariah, asking aloud how a prophet who has access to the Lord's throne room does not know the significance of what he observes. While this interpretation is possible, the angel's response does not make it clear that Zechariah receives a rebuke. Rather, a preferable explanation is that the angel's question stresses the point the angel desires to underscore.

[301] Baldwin, *Zechariah*, 120; Meyers and Meyers, *Zechariah 1–8*, 240.

[302] C. F. Keil and F. Delitzsch, *Minor Prophets,* reprint ed. (Grand Rapids: Eerdmans, 1980), 265; Mitchell, *Zechariah*, 162.

[303] R. Ellis (*Foundation Deposits in Ancient Mesopotamia* [New Haven: Yale University Press, 1968]) has produced one of the most recent and exhaustive studies of these parallels.

1. God gives a command to rebuild the temple.
2. The king or divine representative assists in the (re)building.
3. The ruins of the old temple were razed in preparation for the new construction.
4. The inscriptions recount in great detail the rebuilding process.
5. The king placed his own deposits in the foundation.
6. Religious ceremonies accompany the rebuilding of the temple.
7. Priests or kings pronounce divine blessings on the newly constructed temple.
8. The king re-inaugurates the cult at the new temple.[304]

To be sure, some of these similarities appear stronger than others.

Verse 6 suggests that the oil in vv. 2–3 symbolizes the Spirit of the Lord and continues the theme of the Lord's provision for the ongoing reconstruction of the temple: "Zechariah's work on the temple and in the lives of the people was to be completed, not by human might or power, but by divine power—constant and sufficient."[305] Merrill paraphrases Amsler in stating that "all the resources of Persia were at Zerubbabel's disposal, but even these could not overcome the sense of discouragement felt by the struggling community."[306]

This vision given to Zerubbabel accompanies the preceding vision (3:1–10) the Lord offered to Joshua. The two visions stand together to encourage the two most important leaders in the postexilic community, one political and the other religious, affirming that as a result of God's blessings, their efforts would succeed.[307] This welcome expression of hope strengthened the resolve of Judah's leaders and thereby the nation as a whole.

The angel expressed the Lord's promise to Zerubbabel in an unusual manner since the truncated sentence lacks both subject and predicate. The passage declares that only the Lord's power can attain any lasting accomplishment. No one but the Lord can guarantee that Zerubbabel and his people will prevail over their insurmountable hurdles, whether rebuilding the temple or overcoming other pressing difficulties. The repeated negative statements about human sufficiency underscore the utter dependency of all humanity on God.[308]

The first negative, "not by might," signifies the image of the military might the people would likely attempt to muster to protect themselves from their foes (see 1 Sam 17:20; 1 Kgs 5:13–18).[309] The Hebrew term, *běḥayil*, basically re-

---

[304] A. Laato, "Zachariah 4,6b–10a and the Akkadian Royal Building Inscriptions," *ZAW* 106 (1994): 56–62.

[305] Barker, "Zechariah," 629.

[306] S. Amsler, *Aggée Zacharie 1–8* (Neuchatel: Delachaux & Niestlé, 1981), 93, cited by Merrill, *Zechariah*, 152–53.

[307] Baldwin, *Zechariah*, 121.

[308] Unger, *Zechariah*, 75.

[309] בְּחַיִל.

fers to "strength."[310] The word also indicates "faculty, power," that is, the ability to effect something. The Lord's blunt reminder declares that human agency is always insufficient to bring the Lord's plans to fruition. The next negative, "nor by power" *(bĕkōaḥ)* indicates human resources in a more general sense (see Neh 4:10 where the same term describes the laborers' strength).[311] The preposition *bĕ* (NIV "by") indicates agency or means.[312]

Together, the terms "might" and "power" form a hendiadys encompassing the panoply of human resources that one might marshal in order to effect God's will.[313] The theological message repeats that of the tower of Babel episode (Gen 11:1–9), when combined human effort and hubris was negligible in God's eyes. Little wonder that v. 6 enjoys its status as one of the best known and most quoted passages from the book of Zechariah. Irrespective of the audience, whether Zechariah, Zerubbabel, or the believer today, salvation and blessing come not through human effort but from the gracious hand of God.

The final phrase of the triad expresses its point positively, declaring the means by which Zerubbabel and the rest of the nation can accomplish God's will for his people. The third phrase, "by my Spirit," introduces the one who will carry out the Lord's mandate, again intimating the scope of what the Lord can do for his people (cf. Hag 2:5; Zech 6:8). Perhaps the best indication of Zechariah's intention in employing the terms "might" and "power" emerges in v. 7a. The rebuilding of the temple will succeed if, and only if, the Lord stands behind their efforts. Laato maintains that the phrase likely originates in a traditional royal ideology that admonished Israel's kings never to put their trust in anyone other than the Lord.[314] Ps 33:16 articulates this same concept: "No king is saved by the size of his army; no warrior escapes by his great strength." Furthermore, Ps 33:20 presents the proper corrective: "We wait in hope for the LORD; he is our help and our shield."

The interpreting angel attributed the divine quote to "the LORD Almighty."[315] The Hebrew term *(ṣĕbā'ôt)* is usually translated "Almighty" or "Hosts" and also connotes a military image, emphasizing the compelling power and authority that the Lord uses to accomplish whatever he wills.[316] This unfathomable power belonging to the Lord awaits the people of God through his agent, the Spirit of the Lord.

The Spirit of the Lord occurs with some frequency in the Old Testament. Baldwin surveys the roles the Spirit of the Lord fills in the Old Testament, which

---

[310] *HALOT*, 311–12.

[311] בְּכֹחַ. *HALOT*, 468–69.

[312] בְּ. GKC, § 119 o.

[313] There is little basis for Meyers and Meyers's (*Zechariah 1–8*, 244) suggestion that Zechariah here warned Zerubbabel not to instigate insurrection against Persia.

[314] Laato, "Zachariah 4,6b–10a," 66.

[315] יְהוָה צְבָאוֹת. *HALOT*, 995–97.

[316] F. M. Cross, Jr., *Canaanite Myth and Hebrew Epic* (Cambridge, MA: Harvard University Press, 1973), 65, 68–70; J. E. Hartley, "צְבָאוֹת," *TWOT*, 2:750–51.

includes completing creation (Gen 1:2), parting the Red Sea (Exod 15:8), and reviving the dead bones in Ezekiel's vision (37:1). Not only must the Spirit participate in order for any God-given task to reach completion, the Spirit must also work so that human service may bring suitable glory to the Lord.[317]

**4:7** Verse 7 continues the interpreting angel's explanation to the prophet (and Zerubbabel) begun in the previous verse. While v. 6 emphasizes that the temple's completion depends on the Lord's power, v. 7 simply reaffirms that the temple will see its reestablishment, without particular attention to the means. The exuberant tone of v. 7 raises the eyes of the disconsolate postexilic community toward a horizon filled with worship and exultation.

In v. 7 the angel boldly turned away momentarily from the subject at hand to address the "mighty mountain" using apostrophe, a figure of speech where the author intentionally turns away from the one he addresses in order to speak to an imaginary hearer.[318] The expression "mighty mountain" also functions as a metaphor, but to what or whom does it refer? Laato and Tollington believe the "mountain" here represents the ruins of the former temple that need to be cleared from the site in order to rebuild the new temple.[319] Petersen offers a creative interpretation, maintaining that the "mighty mountain" refers to Zerubbabel as the most important figure during this epoch.[320] Accordingly, the person of Zerubbabel must contrast with "you," the unnamed adversary hindering Zerubbabel. Petersen concludes that Joshua must serve as the referent of "you," a view one should categorically dismiss due to its utterly conjectural character.[321]

Another view attempts to link the common Old Testament usage of the mountain motif as the site of the Lord's temple with the meaning of "mountain" in v. 7.[322] This same nuance of "mountain" occurs elsewhere (Pss 24:3; 48:1–2; Isa 2:2–3; Jer 31:23).[323] Thus, this view sees the mountain as the temple, while the leveling refers to the foundation work prior to the actual construction.

Barker suggests a much broader metaphorical view. He claims that the mountain signifies anything that hinders the rebuilding of the temple, such as active opposition to the building project (Ezra 4:1–5,24) or the people's lack of drive to see the task to its completion (Hag 1:14; 2:1–9).[324] This interpretation

---

[317] Baldwin, *Zechariah*, 121.

[318] E. W. Bullinger, *Figures of Speech Used in the Bible*, reprint ed. (Grand Rapids: Baker, 1968), 901.

[319] Laato, "Zacharia 4,6b–10a," 66; Tollington, *Tradition and Innovation*, 149. See Tigchelaar, *Prophets of Old*, 37. For an English translation of an Akkadian ritual text outlining the procedure for repairing a temple, see *ANET*, 339–42.

[320] Petersen, *Zechariah 1–8*, 239–40.

[321] Petersen (*Zechariah 1–8*, 240) believes that Zechariah plays on the Hebrew words "mighty mountain" (*har–haggādôl*) and "chief priest" (*hakkōhēn haggādôl*).

[322] Meyers and Meyers, *Zechariah 1–8*, 244–45.

[323] For an extensive treatment of the mountain theme, see R. J. Clifford, *The Cosmic Mountain in Canaan and the Old Testament* (Cambridge, MA: Harvard University Press, 1972).

[324] Barker, "Zechariah," 630.

best fits the tenor of v. 7a, which declares that God will level the great mountain, obliterating all opposition to God's plan.

Furthermore, Smith observes that Zech 4:7 echoes Isa 40:4 and 42:16, using eschatological language.[325] Isa 40:4 reads,

> Every valley shall be raised up,
>   every mountain and hill made low;
> the rough ground shall become level,
>   the rugged places a plain.

Thus, Zechariah's purview extends beyond the reconstruction of the temple to encompass God's kingdom.[326]

The capstone ceremonially laid at the conclusion of the temple's rebuilding expresses the Lord's reassurance that no obstacle would hinder the divine plan. The Hebrew term rendered "capstone" *(hā'eben hārō'šāh)*[327] has fueled extensive discussions for years.[328] The current emphasis on Mesopotamian parallels with v. 7 focuses on determining points of comparison between Judah's temple and Mesopotamian ones.[329] While this approach yields limited benefits, the main point of the passage is not the details of architecture but the fact that the temple has been completed. Hence, the translation "capstone" fits the sense well. Tollington maintains that the capstone refers to one of the original foundation stones recovered from the ruins of the Solomonic temple.[330] However, such a conclusion goes beyond the evidence.

During the dedication ceremony the people all declare "God bless it! God bless it!" A closer translation might read, "Grace, grace to it!" The Hebrew word *ḥēn* (NIV "bless") serves as one of the Old Testament's most commonly used terms in the semantic field of words for "grace."[331] The word sometimes describes the beauty of a woman (Prov 31:30), a deer (Prov 5:19), a stone (Prov 17:8), or ornaments (Prov 1:9). In the overwhelming number of occurrences in the Old Testament, the word *ḥēn* typically refers to divine favor that its human recipients have not earned.[332] Thus, the primary emphasis of v. 7b rests with the prayer for divine favor on the rebuilt temple and an acknowledgement of God's grace manifested through the successful completion of the project. Baldwin's suggestion that the term *ḥēn* also envisions the temple's beauty is

---

[325] R. L. Smith, *Micah-Malachi*, 206.

[326] In Matt 17:20 the word "mountain" is again symbolic of challenges to God's kingdom on earth (cf. Matt 21:21 and 1 Cor 13:2).

[327] הָאֶבֶן הָרֹאשָׁה. *HALOT*, 8.

[328] For a helpful survey of approaches see Meyers and Meyers, *Zechariah 1–8*, 246–48.

[329] Note the general approach modeled by Ellis, *Foundation Deposits*, 12–14; and Halpern, "Ritual Background," 167–90.

[330] Tollington, *Tradition and Innovation*, 150.

[331] חֵן. *TDOT*, 5:22–36 and *TLOT*, 439–47.

[332] *HALOT*, 332.

possible but doubtful.[333] The gracious provision of the Spirit of God to accomplish the task at hand is a key emphasis not only in vv. 6–7 but throughout the night visions.

**4:8–9** The second oracle to Zechariah concerning Zerubbabel asserts the certainty of the completion of the temple once more, disregarding how remote that possibility appeared to Zechariah's audience whose eyes could see little beyond the rubble that once was their temple. Furthermore, the mention of Zerubbabel laying the capstone stresses the imminent conclusion of the rebuilding project. The laying of the foundation refers to the events of 538–537 BC (Ezra 3:8–11; 5:16) when the temple foundation was first laid. After the completion of the temple in 516 BC (Ezra 6:14–16), all would know of God's faithfulness.

The final phrase, "Then you will know that the LORD Almighty has sent me to you," presents difficulties since the verse does not identify the antecedent of the pronoun "me." The angel of the Lord and the prophet Zechariah serve as the two primary candidates. Unger argues that because the Word of the Lord came to the prophet, the pronoun must refer to the angel of the Lord.[334] With equal confidence, Merrill asserts that "me" refers to Zechariah, reaffirming the legitimacy of Zechariah's prophetic office.[335] Since vv. 8–9 appear to represent another oracle delivered to Zechariah, the pronoun "me" probably refers to the prophet.

**4:10** This verse echoes Hag 2:3–4, "Who of you is left who saw this house in its former glory? How does it look to you now? Does it not seem to you like nothing? But now be strong . . . for I am with you." Evidently, many of Zechariah's contemporaries expressed dissatisfaction with the end result of the temple, not to mention many other rebuilding projects, feeling that these construction projects did not compare favorably with what existed prior to the exile. The Hebrew word *baz* (NIV "despises") means "to scorn, reject, or treat with contempt" (see Gen 25:34 where Esau scorned his birthright).[336]

The second half of v. 10 presents two problematic interpretative issues. First, the Hebrew expression *hāʾeben habbĕdîl* (NIV "plumb line") yields interpretive ambiguities.[337] The expression occurs nowhere else in the Old Testament

---

[333] Baldwin, *Zechariah*, 122.
[334] Unger, *Zechariah*, 77.
[335] Merrill, *Zechariah*, 161.
[336] בָּז. *HALOT*, 114–15.
[337] הָאֶבֶן הַבְּדִיל. While אֶבֶן means "stone," the second word's meaning is uncertain. *HALOT* (110) suggests that the primary significance of the term is "tin." BDB (95) understands the term to mean "plummet," an alternate meaning of the term that normally means "alloy, tin, dross." Sweeney (*Twelve Prophets*, 611–12) contends that Zech 9–14 develops many themes in chap. 4. Among these, Sweeney claims that the "tin" stone in v. 10 signifies the smelting of Jerusalem to remover her impurities. According to BDB, this word derives from the Hebrew root בָּדַל meaning "to separate, divide," hence the origin of the suggestion that our word means "chosen" or "select."

and could mean "chosen stone," referring to the capstone in v. 7.[338] Many modern interpreters suggest that the phrase refers again to the ceremonial rebuilding of the foundation of the temple. The work by Ellis mentioned above follows this approach.[339] Traditionally, most believe that the term speaks of a bob at the end of a plumb line used in construction to make walls vertical.[340] Consequently, when the people saw Zerubbabel holding the plumb line as the temple construction drew to a close, all would know that the Lord had done a great thing in their midst.

The parenthetical expression concluding v. 10 also presents difficulties. The words "these seven" likely refers back to the seven lamps of v. 2.[341] The lamps symbolizing God's continual presence and protection reminded Zerubbabel that the Lord's power far exceeded whatever problem he might face as the people undertook the great project.

Barker believes the "eyes" refer anthropomorphically to the Lord, reminding Zerubbabel of God's transcendence and sovereignty.[342] The phrase "range throughout the earth" also suggests the Lord's omniscience, recalling the themes of 2 Chr 16:9. The message of the fifth vision bears strong similarities to the first vision where the horses walking throughout the earth signify God's ultimate dominion over his creation. While some attempt to identify the "seven eyes" in 4:10 with those in 3:9,[343] the context suggests otherwise, particularly since the "eyes" in 3:9 were inscribed on a stone.

**4:11–12** Following the intervening oracle in vv. 6–10, the question and answer session of vv. 4–5 resumes. In v. 11 the prophet asks a general question, followed by a specific one in v. 12. Both questions sought clarification regarding the vision Zechariah saw in vv. 2–3. Zechariah's prior question focused on the lampstand; now he asks about the olive trees. In particular, Zechariah asked the angel about the "branches" of the olive trees. Several scholars regard v. 12 as totally spurious, a comment added later by a glossator.[344] No external evidence to the passage exists to make such a claim. Furthermore, internal evidence does not support the claim that v. 12 intrudes into the overall vision. Rather, the second question in v. 12 focuses Zechariah's point in this vision much like concentric circles draw the eye toward the inner circle.

---

[338] Baldwin, *Zechariah*, 122–23.

[339] Meyers and Meyers, *Zechariah 1–8*, 253. Tigchelaar takes the point a step further, suggesting that the stone used to rebuild the temple identified the temple with God's creation. He adds that the temple rested in the midst of Zion, the center around which creation revolved (*Prophets of Old*, 32–36). See also Ellis, *Foundation Deposits*, 20–21.

[340] Mitchell, *Zechariah*, 191.

[341] Mitchell, *Zechariah*, 163. Tigchelaar's claim that the eyes belong to members of the divine assembly lacks supporting evidence (*Prophets of Old*, 31).

[342] Barker, "Zechariah," 630.

[343] So Merrill, *Zechariah*, 161–62.

[344] Mitchell, *Zechariah*, 164–65; Petersen, *Zechariah 1–8*, 229.

Unlike anything occurring in nature, the boughs of the olive trees have extensions near the "gold pipes."[345] The NIV and many other modern translations accept "branches" as the meaning of the Hebrew term šibbălē.[346] The *Tanakh*, the new JPS translation of the Old Testament, struggles with the term in v. 12, yielding the following translation: "And I further asked him, 'What are the two *tops* [italics added] of the olive trees that feed their gold through those two golden tubes?'" While the meaning of the Hebrew term this translation renders "tops" appears doubtful, the word seems to refer to some type of extension protruding from the branches, allowing the oil to flow unaided by human hands directly into the perpetually burning lampstand.

Alternatively, one may also render the Hebrew šibbălē as "ears of corn."[347] This view sees the "ear of corn" as the fruit cluster on the olive tree, stressing fertility and the restoration of prosperity throughout the land once the temple resumes its role as the place for worshipping the Lord. While the idea of renewal and fertility of the land certainly resides in God's promise, "ear of grain" does not fit the context of "extensions" on an olive tree well.

Further, whatever the precise nature of the "extensions," Zechariah informs us that through these conduits flowed *(hamrîqîm)* the golden oil to the lampstand.[348] These extensions somehow join the two golden pipes that drain the golden oil into the lamp's reservoir. The picture the prophet gave us remains obscure, and Zechariah appears unconcerned about bringing the image into sharper focus. The Hebrew word translated "pipes" here occurs nowhere else in the Old Testament.

The continuous flow of golden oil continues the motif of gold introduced by the golden lampstand. Golden oil refers to the purest and finest oil possible. Moreover, the never-ending supply of oil symbolizes God's continuous provision for the people's many needs in the midst of daunting challenges. (See Hos 2:8; Joel 2:19,24 where an abundant supply of oil reflects God's blessings on his people.) Throughout the Old Testament, oil symbolizes honor (Judg 9:9), joy (Ps 45:8), and favor (Deut 33:24; Ps 23:5).[349]

**4:13–14** When Zechariah asked the interpreting angel to explain the significance of the vision once more, the angel responded by asking Zechariah if he perceived the meaning of what he saw. The trees, like the lamps and the oil previously mentioned, exhibited symbolism beyond the plain meaning of the text. The interpreting angel finally clarified this deeper meaning.

After leading Zechariah to acknowledge a second time that he did not understand the vision's import, the interpreting angel identified the two trees as *šĕnê*

---

[345] Merrill (*Zechariah*, 154) suggests the rendering "extension."
[346] שִׁבֲּלֵי. *HALOT*, 1393–94.
[347] *HALOT*, 1394; BDB, 987. See also Conrad, *Zechariah*, 101; and Rose, *Zemah and Zerubbabel*, 184.
[348] הַמְרִיקִים. *HALOT*, 1228.
[349] *Encyclopedia Judaica*, 12:1349.

*běnê–hayyiṣhār*, "the two sons of oil" (NIV "the two who are anointed").[350] This unusual expression evokes several distinct connotations. The term "oil" in v. 14 differs from the customary Hebrew word for oil *(šemen)* used in anointing services.[351] The word "fresh oil" signifies unmanufactured oil (see Hag 1:11), representing the new crops' yield.[352] The Old Testament also associates "fresh oil" with agricultural blessing (see Deut 7:13), giving hope of prosperity to the struggling postexilic community. Theologically, the fresh oil's unrefined state further deemphasizes human agency in God's supernatural provision for Israel. The oil flows directly from the trees into the lampstand without human hands to refill their oil reservoirs. Throughout vision five Zechariah emphasized the theme of God's protection and provision, contrasting them with the frailty of human activity.

Many translate the phrase *běnê–hayyiṣhār* as "anointed." Some rabbinic interpretation viewed Zech 4:14 as messianic.[353] One common rabbinic view sees the "two" as Aaron and the Messiah; another has Aaron and David. However, both the translation and the subsequent understanding remains clouded.

The rendering "anointed" raises further questions. While the olive trees picture Joshua and Zerubbabel, one would not expect the angel to refer to these two leaders as "anointed."[354] In the Old Testament only those holding two offices, the priesthood and the monarchy, required anointing in order to perform their sacred duties. Presumably, Joshua had already received anointing as a priest. On the other hand, Zerubbabel did not actually serve as king, but rather functioned as a Persian vassal.[355] Likely, the Persian satrapy would have frowned on their appointee receiving official anointing. Apparently, the vision idealized Zerubbabel's role and predicted for him a greater place than he had held in the past. Moreover, Zerubbabel could rightly lay claim to the Davidic throne as a legitimate heir of David, a grandson of Judah's exiled king Jehoiachin (1 Chr 3:17–19).

For Israel, Zerubbabel's fortunes as a political leader portend the nation's own well-being. Thus, as surely as Zerubbabel's responsibilities and autonomy increase, Israel's fortunes would as well. The fifth vision aims to bolster the nation's confidence in the future. Petersen wrongly suggests that this vision exists to alter the political landscape in postexilic Judah. The vision does not attempt to replace the established monarchy with a diarchy.[356] Instead, the fifth vision

---

[350] שְׁנֵי בְנֵי הַיִּצְהָר.

[351] שֶׁמֶן. *HALOT*, 1567–69.

[352] *HALOT*, 427.

[353] C. A. Evans, "'The Two Sons of Oil': Early Evidence of Messianic Interpretation of Zechariah 4:14 in 4Q254 4 2," in *The Provo International Conference on the Dead Sea Scrolls*, ed. D. Perry and E. Ulrich (Leiden: E. J. Brill, 1999), 566.

[354] For a helpful discussion of anointing, see R. de Vaux, *Ancient Israel* (New York: McGraw-Hill, 1965), 102–7.

[355] Baldwin, *Zechariah*, 124; de Vaux, *Ancient Israel*, 399.

[356] Petersen maintains that the vision seeks to establish a diarchic form of leadership for the

predicts that the political and religious life of the community will be strong and will enjoy vibrant, God-ordained leadership. Floyd notes that the role of these temple leaders involved the supervision of temple activities. The welfare of the postexilic community depended on the faithfulness of her leaders.[357] Cohen nicely summarizes the point of the olive trees' symbolism:

> The allusion is clearly to Joshua and Zerubbabel, the representative of the priestly and regal offices. They are the channels by which Israel (symbolized by the lamps) is kept supplied with the Divine spirit (symbolized by the oil).[358]

Verse 14 concludes with the phrase "the Lord of all the earth." Thus, the fifth vision ends with an emphasis on the Lord's sovereign rule over the whole creation, not just Israel. We should note again Mic 4:1–13, which bears several striking parallels to Zech 4. The theme of "the mountain of the LORD's temple," the prominence of Zion for God's reign, and the Lord's universal dominion represent a few of the more important similarities (see Rev 19:15–16). Moreover, the angel's reply also clarifies the purpose of all God-ordained leadership from biblical times until the present—"to serve the Lord of all the earth."

After surveying the scope of chap. 4, neither Zechariah nor the angel who talked with the prophet interpreted the central element in the vision, the lampstand. Consequently, many suggestions about its meaning have arisen. Baldwin believes that the lampstand "represents not the Lord but the witness of the temple and the Jewish community to Him."[359] This interpretation draws largely from the broader biblical context since the motif of the Lord's believers bearing light and witnessing for him occurs often in Scripture. (See Matt 5:14–15; John 8:12; Eph 5:8–9; Phil 2:15; Rev 1:20 for New Testament perspectives on believers' light-bearing responsibilities.)[360]

Various interpretations associate the lampstand with God. Petersen suggests that the lampstand symbolizes "divine presence."[361] Floyd concludes that the central position of the lampstand in the temple underscores the Lord's sover-

---

postexilic community (*Zechariah 1–8*, 234).

[357] M. H. Floyd, *Minor Prophets. Part 2* (Grand Rapids: Eerdmans, 2000), 382.

[358] Cohen, *Twelve Prophets*, 286. Tigchelaar argues against identifying the olive trees with Joshua and Zerubbabel, concluding that doing so makes the Lord dependent on human leaders in order to effect his divine purposes (*Prophets of Old*, 21–22). Tigchelaar's perspective does not adequately acknowledge the role God grants his servants in the administration of the heavenly kingdom.

[359] Baldwin, *Zechariah*, 124. See E. Achtemeier, *Nahum-Malachi* (Atlanta: John Knox, 1986), 124; Clements, *God and Temple*, 133; Rose, *Zemah and Zerubbabel*, 182.

[360] See Rowley, *The Missionary Message*; Filbeck, *Yes, God of the Gentiles Too*; Kane, "Missions in the Old Testament."

[361] Petersen, *Zechariah 1–8*, 234. See also Meyers and Meyers, *Zechariah 1–8*, 274; Floyd, *Minor Prophets*, 382.

eignty over the entire earth.[362] Unger argues that "the golden lampstand thus portrays Messiah as both Light and Lord of the whole earth in the kingdom age revealed to and through His restored nation Israel."[363] In the final analysis, chap. 4 does not provide sufficient detail to determine the precise meaning of the lampstand. That the prophet did not clarify the question suggests that the question was not primary for him. However, the association of the lampstand with the Lord himself probably best suits the overall message of the centrality of the Lord, illumining all from the midst of his temple. The Lord's presence in the temple provides the unending source of light to all nations, drawing all to Jerusalem to worship. Isaiah 60:1–3 offers a similar theme:

> Arise, shine, for your light has come,
>     and the glory of the LORD rises upon you.
> See, darkness covers the earth
>     and thick darkness is over the peoples,
> but the LORD rises upon you
>     and his glory appears over you.
> Nations will come to your light,
>     and kings to the brightness of your dawn.

Zechariah's fifth vision had a lasting influence over the broader biblical message. For instance, in Rev 11:1–13 John drew from Zech 2, and especially chap. 4, in foretelling the ministry of the "two witnesses." The measuring line in the hand of John the prophet (Rev 11:1) evokes Zech 2 since both passages portray a biblical prophet envisioning the restoration of worship in the temple. For Zechariah, references to the temple referred to the house of worship rebuilt by the postexilic community. For John, the temple, the site of worship in God's future kingdom, represented God's presence and his people's access to him in the kingdom. Many modern interpreters relate this temple to Ezekiel's temple (chaps. 40–47). Whether Ezekiel intended a real physical temple or a symbolic one remains a point of controversy.[364]

Merrill summarizes several additional points of connection between Zech 4 and Rev 11. Both passages emphasize the temple, as well as describing its measurements and rebuilding (Zech 2:1–5; 4:9–10; Rev 11:1–2). Also, both texts picture the two olive trees witnessing before the whole earth (Zech 4:9–10; Rev 11:4).[365] John comments on Zech 4, in that the olive trees witness to the Lord's righteousness and his mighty acts of salvation for his people.

Finally, both chaps. 3 and 4 present important Messianic teachings. The themes of "the servant" (3:8), "the branch" (3:8), "the rock" (3:9), "the stone"

---

[362] Floyd, *Minor Prophets*, 384.
[363] Unger, *Zechariah*, 82.
[364] For a survey of different interpretations of Ezekiel's temple, see L. E. Cooper, Sr., *Ezekiel* (Nashville: Broadman & Holman, 1994), 351–53, 376–81.
[365] Merrill, *Zechariah*, 157.

(4:7), and the temple all have significance for the restoration era and beyond. This messianic significance includes Joshua and Zerubbabel as well. Baldwin summarizes,

> Joshua and Zerubbabel, priest and Davidic prince, who together are the means of bringing new hope to the community. Through the high priest acquittal is pronounced and access to God's presence made possible; through the prince the Temple is completed and the lampstand allowed to shine out to the world. Two 'messiahs' or anointed ones have their roles co-ordinated; neither is adequate without the other . . . but the two functions were to be brought together in the person and work of Christ.[366]

One of the primary theological emphases for Zech 4 resides in the declaration, "not by might nor by power, but by my Spirit" (4:6). This grand biblical truth assures believers that God provides for his people supernaturally. Deliverance comes then from God, not through human ingenuity. Wolters explains that "the whole mountain of seemingly insuperable problems which [the church] faces today, from persecution to consumerism, from modernism to postmodernism, will ultimately become a plain before the Davidic king."[367]

Zechariah 4 extends the unending promise of God's grace to those who place faith in him. The restoration of every soul and the national restoration proceed "not by might nor by power, but by my Spirit." Just as chap. 4 addresses rebuilding of the individuals' hearts as well as the reconstruction of the temple, readers today must remember the same divine promise. The words of "How Firm a Foundation" make the point well:

> How firm a foundation, ye saints of the Lord,
> Is laid for your faith in His excellent Word!
> What more can He say than to you He hath said,
> To you who for refuge to Jesus have fled?
> To you who for refuge to Jesus have fled?
>
> Fear not, I am with Thee; O be not dismayed,
> For I am thy God, and will still give thee aid;
> I'll strengthen thee, help thee; and cause thee to stand,
> Upheld by My righteous, omnipotent hand,
> Upheld by My righteous, omnipotent hand.[368]

---

[366] Baldwin, *Zechariah*, 125.

[367] A. Wolters, "Confessional Criticism and the Night Visions of Zechariah," in *Renewing Biblical Criticism*, ed. C. Bartholomew, C. Greene, and K. Möller (Grand Rapids: Zondervan, 2000), 114.

[368] John Rippon, *Baptist Hymnal*, # 338.

## 6. The Sixth Vision: The Flying Scroll (5:1–4)

¹I looked again—and there before me was a flying scroll! ²He asked me, "What do you see?"
I answered, "I see a flying scroll, thirty feet long and fifteen feet wide."
³And he said to me, "This is the curse that is going out over the whole land; for according to what it says on one side, every thief will be banished, and according to what it says on the other, everyone who swears falsely will be banished. ⁴The LORD Almighty declares, 'I will send it out, and it will enter the house of the thief and the house of him who swears falsely by my name. It will remain in his house and destroy it, both its timbers and its stones.'"

While the fifth vision stresses the religious and political leadership the Lord ordains to guide his people, the sixth vision focuses on the community's desperate need for spiritual repentance in order for God to bless the people with a restoration of the land. The vision of the flying scroll places conditions on the assurances of restoration in the previous visions—as in the vision of the surveyor (2:1–13)—cautioning the people that God's blessing remains contingent on their own obedience to his law. The warning of the sixth vision reinforces the message previously delivered to Israel by the preexilic prophets, including Jeremiah. Thus, the tone of chap. 5 shifts somewhat in the sixth and seventh visions from strong assurances of deliverance to veiled threats of judgment for all who fail to heed the warnings to trust the Lord and to obey him. The Old Testament consistently offers the hope of salvation, abundance of blessings, and a faithful relationship with the Lord for all who keep his statutes with both obedience and faith. With equivalent forcefulness, numerous texts such as Deut 28 threaten all who disobey God with judgment, including famine, military and political defeat, plagues, disasters, and exile from the land of promise.

**5:1–2** Unlike previous visions where an introduction to the message occurs (see 4:1), the sixth vision begins abruptly with the startling appearance of a flying scroll *(mĕgillāh)*.[369] Other visions introduce the characters in the vision, such as the horses in vision one or the interpreting angel, prior to disclosing the Lord's message. The sixth vision begins with the Hebrew word *wāʾāšûb* (NIV "again"). It remains unclear, though, what Zechariah repeated.[370] Zechariah's reply seems to repeat his prior response to the vision of the lampstand in chap. 4.[371] In contrast to several of the previous visions, the interpreter questioning Zechariah remains unidentified (cf. 2:3). In all probability, however, the interpreting angel continued his role in previous passages, so he is the one explaining the vision to Zechariah.[372]

---

[369] The Hebrew word for scroll is מְגִלָּה and refers to a rolled and continuous volume, not to a book or codex. *HALOT*, 545.
[370] וָאָשׁוּב. *HALOT*, 1430.
[371] Meyers and Meyers, *Zechariah 1–8*, 277.
[372] Conrad (*Zechariah*, 113–14) suggests that since Zechariah never saw Solomon's temple, the prophet received thorough instructions and descriptions explaining the details of the new temple.

The "scroll" Zechariah noticed possessed gigantic proportions, twenty cubits in length and ten cubits in height. On the widely held assumption that the biblical cubit approximates eighteen inches, this scroll measured some 30 feet long and 15 feet high.[373] It bears more resemblance to a modern billboard than to an ancient scroll. The suggestion that the scroll reached 15 feet thick strains the meaning of the text beyond what it can support.[374]

Some commentators attempt to correlate the significance of these dimensions with the porch of the temple (1 Kgs 6:3), which had the same dimensions.[375] Despite attempts to associate the measurements of the flying scroll with other prominent sites in the Old Testament, all efforts fail to demonstrate any literary or theological connection to the temple. Based on the dimensions of biblical scrolls found at Qumran, David Noel Freedman notes that the dimensions of the flying scroll exceeded the known size of extant manuscripts by 40 times. Freedman emphasizes the heavenly origin of the flying scroll, inferring that the size of the heavenly scroll implies that the heavenly temple was itself forty times larger than the earthly temple in Zion.[376]

Obviously, the proportions of the scroll indicate that Zechariah saw no ordinary scroll. Typically, scrolls in postexilic Judah measured eight to ten inches in height and up to 20 feet in length. Even the great Isaiah scroll discovered at Qumran (1QIsa$^a$), although produced a few centuries later, measured just 24 feet in length.[377] Although the Isaiah scroll from Qumran was large enough to prove cumbersome to one attempting to handle it, the flying scroll in Zech 5 dwarfed it.

Despite uncertainty concerning the dimensions of the scroll, the symbolism of a scroll before Zechariah clearly communicated several points. Most important of all, the presence of the scroll in the sixth vision elevated the prominence of the written message as well as authenticating the prophet Zechariah as the authoritative spokesman from God to the people. The word "scroll" evoked strong biblical connotations as a frequent vehicle for communicating the divine message, while the size of the scroll emphasized its importance. The angel revealed the content of the divine message in the final verses of the vision as Zechariah gazed at the vision in bewilderment.

Zechariah's depiction of the scroll as "flying" also has great significance. For instance, "flying" suggests that someone had unrolled the scroll. As a result, the scroll lay open for all to read. God chose neither to conceal his message nor to disclose it only to a select few. The scroll publicly proclaims the

---

[373] *ABD*, 6:899–901.

[374] Merrill, *Zechariah*, 166–67.

[375] See Halpern, "Ritual Background," 178–79; Mitchell, *Zechariah*, 168–69; among many others.

[376] D. N. Freedman, "The Flying Scroll in Zechariah 5:1–4," in *Studies in Near Eastern Culture and History*, ed. J. A. Bellamy (Ann Arbor, MI: University of Michigan Press, 1990), 42–48.

[377] E. Würthwein, *The Text of the Old Testament* (Grand Rapids: Eerdmans, 1979), 8.

Lord's condemnation of the people's sin and his call for them to repent. The ruinous exile, whose residual effects the people still endured, provided persuasive proof that the Lord treats the matter of sin among his people severely.

Smith maintains that a *flying* scroll indicates that the message comes from God himself, not from any mere person.[378] He also believes that the description reflects the speed with which the Lord's message will arrive. Further, human hands never touch a "flying scroll." God retains sole responsibility for sending this message to his people. Like the fifth vision, vv. 1–4 diminish human agency in order to highlight the supernatural nature of what God is doing. The flying scroll may also signify God's omniscience and omnipresence, representing "a law in effect everywhere (see 'over all the land')."[379] Ultimately, however, the sight of a flying scroll of unprecedented proportions demonstrates that the scroll functions in the prophecy as a symbol of divine authority. Zechariah's vision remains unparalleled within its biblical and ancient Near Eastern context.

**5:3–4** The interpreting angel quickly disclosed that the flying scroll contains a curse on Judah for her disobedience in breaking the covenant with the Lord. Inherent in the Mosaic covenant, God's moral stipulations resulting in either blessing or cursing depended on the people's faithfulness in obeying the Lord's law (see Deut 28). Thus, the flying scroll symbolizes the Lord's law.[380] This curse written on the flying scroll spreads out over "the whole land," probably a reference to the whole land of Judah since the covenant the Lord made with his people lies behind this vision. This initial application of God's word to Judah does not preclude its ultimate application to the remainder of the earth. However, the sixth vision primarily addresses Israel, not all of creation.[381]

The word "curse" *(ʾālāh)* occurs infrequently in the Old Testament, usually in the context of covenantal passages.[382] For instance, Deut 29:10–21 establishes a clear link between covenant and cursing. Moreover, the word *ʾālāh* (v. 3) has several uses in the Hebrew Bible. It may refer to an unknown perpetrator of a crime (Judg 17:2). The term may speak of the accused whose guilt cannot be proven (Num 5:21–28). Lastly, it may describe the terms of a covenantal arrangement between parties (Gen 26:28). The latter two uses come into view in Zech 5:1–4 where the people bear guilt for breaking the covenant the Lord made with them.[383]

The angel pronounced the sentence of "guilty" for the two crimes of stealing and swearing falsely. While Judah bore guilt for many other sins that the

---

[378] R. L. Smith, *Micah–Malachi*, 208.
[379] Meyers and Meyers, *Zechariah 1–8*, 279.
[380] Floyd, *Minor Prophets*, 389.
[381] Contra Conrad (*Zechariah*), 114).
[382] אָלָה. *HALOT*, 51 and *TDOT*, 1:261–66.
[383] Petersen, *Zechariah 1–8*, 247–49.

angel could have identified, most commentators believe that these two crimes represent a whole collection of sins. The restoration of justice in the land assured the community of faith that those who had temporarily escaped judgment would now receive their rightful recompense.

The sins mentioned in the vision also clearly evoke the Decalogue. The thief breaks the eighth Commandment (Exod 20:15), while the false witness (in the name of the Lord) transgresses the third (Exod 20:7,16). Meyers and Meyers state, "Zechariah, like Jeremiah (chap 7) and Hosea (chap 4) before him, is citing the Decalogue in his plea for legal stability and social justice."[384]

Any suggestion that these two crimes against God's law represent two of the most frequent sins of Zechariah's era misses the point.[385] The two crimes Zechariah mentioned represent all of the commandments in each of the two tables of the Ten Commandments. The first table focuses on commandments that have special reference to the Israelites' relationship with God. The second table governs the people's relationships with one another. Hence, the angel's decree in vv. 3–4 pronounces judgment on the people because they had broken every commandment about faithfulness to the Lord as well as every commandment about relationships with their neighbors. Baldwin summarizes, "*Every one who steals* is a pithy way of saying 'every one who wrongs his neighbour,' and *every one who swears falsely* (invoking the divine name) sums up blatant disregard for God's holiness."[386]

Moreover, the New Testament continues and develops the foregoing observations about transgressing divine law. For instance, Jas 2:10 states, "For whoever keeps the whole law and yet stumbles at just one point is guilty of breaking all of it." James's emphasis accurately reflects the Old Testament viewpoint and does not function as a New Testament corrective to the perspective of the Old Covenant. Since all mankind broke God's law, guilt was collective, not merely individual. Consequently, the interpreting angel in Zech 5 pronounced guilt on the whole land of Israel, not merely on selected lawbreakers.

The oath of innocence that tested the guilt of the accused furnishes the background for the sixth vision. When a person sinned by failing to give testimony (Lev 5:1) or took someone's property without being discovered (Judg 17:2), the one injured by the actions of the anonymous party pronounced a curse on the unknown transgressor. Thus, this legal action declares the sinner "guilty" because of his sin alone, not because he was caught and formally declared guilty. Biblical examples include the test for the unfaithful wife (Num 5:11–31) and heaven's judging of those who fail to discharge an oath made before the Lord's altar (1 Kgs 8:31–32).[387]

---

[384] Meyers and Meyers, *Zechariah 1–8*, 284–85.
[385] Sweeney, *Twelve Prophets*, 617; Conrad, *Zechariah*, 113.
[386] Baldwin, *Zechariah*, 127.
[387] R. L. Smith, *Micah–Malachi*, 208.

In conclusion, Zechariah saw the Lord's curse flying throughout the land, entering the homes of those who bear guilt against God. Elsewhere the Old Testament personifies the word of God going forth to do the Lord's bidding. Isaiah 55:11 declares, "My word that goes out from my mouth: It will not return to me empty, but will accomplish what I desire and achieve the purpose for which I sent it" (cf. Ps 147:15). This step of divine judgment and cleansing stands as a prerequisite to the restoration and other blessings the Lord holds for his people. Verse 4 ends with the declaration that the houses of the guilty will be torn down (Ezra 6:11; Dan 2:5; 3:29). In the phrase "to destroy the house," "house" functions as a metonymy for the inhabitants of the house (cf. Ps 127:1). All who spurn God's righteousness will taste his judgment.

### 7. The Seventh Vision: The Woman in the Basket (5:5–11)

⁵Then the angel who was speaking to me came forward and said to me, "Look up and see what this is that is appearing."

⁶I asked, "What is it?"

He replied, "It is a measuring basket." And he added, "This is the iniquity of the people throughout the land."

⁷Then the cover of lead was raised, and there in the basket sat a woman! ⁸He said, "This is wickedness," and he pushed her back into the basket and pushed the lead cover down over its mouth.

⁹Then I looked up—and there before me were two women, with the wind in their wings! They had wings like those of a stork, and they lifted up the basket between heaven and earth.

¹⁰"Where are they taking the basket?" I asked the angel who was speaking to me.

¹¹He replied, "To the country of Babylonia to build a house for it. When it is ready, the basket will be set there in its place."

Although the seventh vision bears subtle structural dissimilarities to the other night visions, its message continues the thematic development of the previous ones. The motif of holiness that the Lord desired to characterize Judah shapes the vision of the woman in the basket as well the message of judgment written on the flying scroll. God described the land as "the holy land" (2:12), but the land remained polluted. Zechariah envisioned a day when the Lord would take away the people's sin (3:9). The sixth vision focuses on the Lord's removal of sin from the land, revisiting the promise of cleansing from sin that God extended to Joshua the high priest (3:1–15). Furthermore, the seventh vision continues the theme of forgiveness from sin, portraying the banishment of the people's transgressions to Babylon, the seat of wickedness on earth.[388] Zechariah recognized that the whole nation bore the guilt of sin against God. The thief and the false witness in the sixth vision represent every member of

---

[388] Barker, "Zechariah," 634.

the nation. Hence, all of God's people stand in need of repentance and forgiveness (1:2–6).[389]

Michael Floyd notes a number of thematic contrasts and correlations between the fifth, sixth, and seventh visions.[390] In one important contrast, the golden vessels in the fifth vision overflow with oil, while the measuring basket in 5:5–11 stands empty, except for the "wickedness" it contains. The golden lampstand portrays the abundance that living in accord with the Lord's covenant provides, standing in stark contrast to the empty measuring basket that results from sinning against God.

The sixth and seventh visions also show marked similarities. In both visions, the object of the vision flies. The flying scroll and the measuring basket both have dimensions far surpassing the measurements of such everyday objects. Further, the key element in both visions, the flying scroll and the measuring basket, "command the respect" or devotion of those who receive the divine vision.[391] Lastly, Floyd notes that the measuring basket that goes forth from the sanctuary bears some resemblance to the rays of the lampstand in chap. 4 proceeding outward from the temple.[392] Despite the aforementioned similarities, the significance of the rays of light from the lampstand stand in stark contrast to the import of the basket. The rays of light emanating from the temple represent the Lord's presence and the blessings that he grants, whereas the measuring basket containing "wickedness" symbolizes the very opposite.

**5:5–6**   As in previous visions, the interpreting angel appears in order to ask Zechariah what he sees. Comparable to the opening of vision six, Zechariah responded to the angel by asking for the angel's help to understand what the prophet had seen. The interpreting angel named the image an "ephah," a measuring basket used for dry measure (see Lev 5:11; 1 Sam 17:17; Ruth 2:17). Most estimate the ephah to contain approximately 4.5 to 10 gallons. Put in contemporary terms, the ephah closely approximates the capacity of the modern bushel.[393] Moreover, like the scroll in vision six, the focal point in vision seven possessed exaggerated proportions since an ephah with a ten gallon capacity could not contain a woman crouched within.

Since the oversized ephah or measuring basket in chap. 5 diverged so radically from the norm, the ephah may also evoke the practice of using shortened measuring baskets in the earlier days of Israel's history. These smaller than standard measures represented the injustice during Joel's day (8:5). Many passages, including Deut 25:14–15, admonish the Israelites to ensure that all

---

[389] Baldwin, *Zechariah*, 128.
[390] M. H. Floyd, "The Evil in the Ephah: Reading Zechariah 5:5–11 in Its Literary Context," *CBQ* 58 (1996): 51–68.
[391] Ibid., 53–54.
[392] Ibid., 57.
[393] *ABD*, 6:903–4.

measures represent just measures in deference to the holy and just character of their God. Like the scroll in the previous vision, the ephah in the seventh vision also flies.

Several scholars view both the basket and the woman differently, following imagery discovered by archaeology. Instead of envisioning an enormous basket, numerous scholars believe the woman in chap. 5 represented a female idol that could fit in an ephah.[394] The numerous extant examples of Canaanite goddesses used in idolatrous rites provide the background for this interpretation.[395]

The interpreting angel expands his explanation, adding the Hebrew phrase *zō't ʿênām bĕkol–hā'āreṣ* (NIV "This is the iniquity of the people").[396] However, the Masoretic Text actually reads the Hebrew word *ʿênām*, which means "their eye," a problematic word indeed for the sense of the context.[397] Little wonder that the versions struggled with the meaning of the word, resulting in variant readings. This difficulty has engendered a variety of suggested solutions.

Many interpreters contend that the reading, "their eye," faithfully represents the original text. Commentators from Kimchi to Calvin adopt this view, arguing that the pronominal suffix expresses an objective genitive, "the eye [of God] *on* them [the evildoers]." According to the objective genitive viewpoint, the eye of the Lord sees people everywhere, emphasizing God's omniscience.[398]

The famous Jewish commentator Rashi approached the problem differently, focusing on the antecedent of the pronominal suffix. Rashi affirmed the integrity of the Masoretic Text, maintaining that the "eyes" referred to the eyes of all the evildoers in the land who constantly scout for opportunities to do more evil.[399]

Merrill also argues for retaining the Masoretic reading ("their eye") on text-critical grounds. He suggests that "their eye" represents the *lectio difficilior*, the difficult reading. This text-critical principle argues for adopting the more difficult reading on the assumption that the easier reading probably reflects a scribal correction or simplification. However, Merrill's understanding may misread Zechariah's intention and apply the basic text-critical procedure too rigidly.[400] Tov cautions that if one applies the *lectio difficilior* principle strictly,

---

[394] See Tigchelaar, *Prophets of Old*, 61; Sweeney, *Twelve Prophets*, 620–21; and Conrad, *Zechariah*, 119.

[395] *ANEP*, 128, 129, 131, 132, 133, 135.

[396] זֹאת עֵינָם בְּכָל־הָאָרֶץ.

[397] עֵינָם. *HALOT*, 817–20.

[398] See J. Calvin, *Commentaries on the Twelve Minor Prophets: Volume 5, Zechariah and Malachi* (Grand Rapids: Eerdmans, 1950), 134; D. Kimchi, *Commentary upon the Prophecies of Zechariah* (London: James Duncan, 1837), 49; Floyd, "Evil in the Ephah," 56; and Merrill, *Zechariah*, 172–73.

[399] Cited by Cohen, *Twelve Prophets*, 288.

[400] Merrill, *Zechariah*, 172.

the truly unintelligible reading always presents the most difficult reading. Thus, any text-critical guideline serves as a general guideline, and no more.[401]

The NIV rejects the Masoretic reading *ênām*, adopting the rendering "iniquity" attested in one Hebrew manuscript, the Septuagint, and the Syriac Peshitta, a Septuagintal daughter text, all of which read *ăwōnām* ("their iniquity").[402] The majority of Old Testament scholars also conclude that *ăwōnām* preserves the original textual reading. This variant reading commends itself as a misreading of one Hebrew letter.[403] Moreover, when evaluating the internal or literary evidence to the question of the proper reading, the reference to "wickedness" in v. 7 establishes an internal literary parallel that some maintain bolsters confidence in the translation "iniquity."

In summary, the NIV adoption of the Septuagint reading stands on marginal, yet defensible, grounds. Nevertheless, any conclusion precludes dogmatism. Both external evidence (manuscript) and internal evidence (thematic and literary) could point toward either "their eye" or "their iniquity." However, the scholarly and circumspect approach evidenced by Barthélemy and others ultimately chooses to retain the reading, "their eye." Barthélemy acknowledges that the decision to select either variant suffers from "significant doubt."[404] In the final analysis, the received reading "their eye" should be retained.

Irrespective of the reading chosen, one anticipates a third person singular feminine suffix, "her," on the word "eye," referring to the woman in the basket. Instead, a third person plural pronominal suffix occurs: *"their* eye." Floyd observes that the plural suffix refers back to the thief and the one who swears falsely in 5:3–4.[405] As noted above, the thief and the false witness symbolize the crimes of the entire nation. With the unfolding vision, the angel clearly began to identify the people as the iniquitous ones. The High Priest received cleansing from his sin (chap. 3), and now the people stand in need of a similar cleansing from God, the only one capable of forgiving sins.

**5:7–8** The curious character of the seventh vision becomes more bizarre when a leaden lid rises to reveal a woman concealed within the basket. The angel elected not to identify the one who lifted the lid on the basket. Neither did Zechariah clarify the significance that the lid was made of lead.[406] The only observation one can make with reasonable confidence is that such a

---

[401] E. Tov, "Criteria for Evaluating Textual Readings: The Limitations of Textual Rules," *HTR* 75 (1982): 432–35.

[402] עֲוֹנָם. *HALOT*, 800.

[403] This textual problem likely arose from the misreading of either the *yod* or the *waw* in the pre-vocalized Hebrew text. Other examples occur in the Old Testament since these two letters resemble one another in the square Hebrew script (Isa 5:29; 11:6; 33:13). Würthwein, *Text of the Old Testament*, 106.

[404] Barthélemy, et al., *Preliminary and Interim Report*, 5:viii, 403.

[405] Floyd, *Minor Prophets*, 393.

[406] Early Christian interpreters such as Gregory of Nyssa, Ambrose, and Origen identified the leaden lid with sin. See Gregory of Nyssa, *De Virginitate*, 18.395 (Gregorii Nysseni Opera

heavy lid indicates that the contents of the basket must remain securely within the basket.[407] Sin and its resulting uncleanness must be separated from God's people.

The angel explained that this woman symbolizes wickedness *(hāriš'āh)*.[408] The scene is reminiscent of Rev 17:3–5, which pictures an evil woman with "Babylon the Great" written on her forehead. Students of chap. 5 have long asked why the passage personifies wickedness with a woman. The question becomes more acute today in light of heightened gender-related issues. The silence of chap. 5 has not diminished the number of solutions offered.

Jeremias suggests that Zechariah's choice of a woman to epitomize wickedness relates to the role of the Babylonian goddess Inanna, the "Queen of Heaven."[409] This view sees the symbolism of the woman in the seventh vision as a polemic against Mesopotamian idolatry, interpreting the woman as the Babylonian deity whom God will forcibly remove from Judah and return to Shinar. Alternatively, Mason attempts to relate the woman with the unclean menstruating woman in Ezek 36:17, although Zech 5 fails to provide any literary or linguistic support for this conclusion.[410] Another inadequate notion maintains that ever since the fall of man and woman (Gen 3) the woman bore responsibility for the introduction of evil.[411] This view, however, does not do justice to the high view in which the Old Testament holds women[412] or of the responsibility all bear for sinning against the Lord.[413]

Mitchell presents the most plausible view by pointing out that Zechariah simply followed the lead of the prophets preceding him who associate idolatry and wickedness, using the metaphor of prostitution to convey the ugliness of sin.[414] No prophet relied more heavily on this association than Hosea (see 2:2; see also Ezek 16). Meyers and Meyers maintain that Zechariah envisioned idolatry, but they further suggest that the visions caution all readers about the danger of false religion entering into Israelite culture through intermarriage with foreign wives.[415] While the woman may well represent idolatry,

---

8/1:322); Ambrose, *Epistolarum*, 2.758.D (PL 16:921); and Origen, *Homélies sur l'Exode*, 6.4 (SC 321:180).

[407] Meyers and Meyers, *Zechariah 1–8*, 299.

[408] הָרִשְׁעָה. *HALOT*, 1295–96.

[409] Sweeney, *Twelve Prop*hets, 620–23; *ABD*, 5:586–88.

[410] R. Mason, *Haggai, Zechariah, and Malachi* (Cambridge: Cambridge University Press, 1984), 58.

[411] Petersen, *Zechariah 1–8*, 257–58.

[412] Love contends that the subjugation of the woman by imprisoning her and forcibly returning her to the basket amounts to little more than misogyny and violence against women (*The Evasive Text*, 209–10). However, Love's reader-response hermeneutic misrepresents both the significance of the seventh vision and the Old Testament's view of women.

[413] Nor does it accord with Paul's theology of Adam's sin in Rom 5:14 and 1 Cor 15:22.

[414] Mitchell, *Zechariah*, 173.

[415] Meyers and Meyers, *Zechariah 1–8*, 301–2.

particularly in light of 5:11, any reference to intermarriage lacks support from the context.

Yet another approach observes the abundance of figurines portraying Canaanite goddesses that archaeologists have discovered. Conrad develops the association of a female Canaanite idol with the woman in chap. 5 and the imagery of a cultic figurine.[416] He suggests that the image of an idol, particularly one with fertility connotations, fits the context well. It certainly was the case that idolatry represented a fundamental spiritual problem for Judah. What could be more appropriate than to banish all idolatry to Babylon, infamous for her own idolatries, as well as the site of Judah's punishment for her own idolatry?

In this vein, one must not neglect the point that the ephah, a container normally used to hold the abundance of the harvest, stood empty. A basket that should brim with the harvest's bounty remains empty since no fertility goddess could fill the ephah. The empty ephah bears mute testimony to the infertility resulting from Judah's abandonment of the Lord's covenant. In its litany of curses for covenantal disobedience, Deut 28:17 states, "Your basket and your kneading trough will be cursed." Verse 18 proclaims a curse on both the crops and the young of the herds and flocks (see also vv. 22–24,29,33,38–42,48,51).

However, Baldwin offers perhaps the simplest solution to the gender issue.[417] Since the Hebrew word for "wickedness" *('ăwōnām)* is feminine, the prophet personifies wickedness as a woman. Perhaps the most notable example of a similar usage, although positive in tone, occurs in Prov 8 (and other passages) where the author personifies the feminine noun *ḥokmāh* ("wisdom") as "Lady Wisdom" who calls out for the foolish to seek her benefits.[418] In conclusion, the portrayal of wickedness as a woman does not reveal misogyny, but rather a personification that has nothing specifically to do with gender.

The woman's wickedness symbolizes the iniquity of Judah as a whole. Mitchell develops this theme, arguing at some length that the wickedness of the woman specifically refers to idolatry in the land.[419] Without doubt, Judah did practice idolatry to an extensive degree during this period (Ezra 9; Mal 2:11). While this passage offers no indication that the woman's wickedness speaks solely of idolatry, v. 11 gives reason to conclude that idolatry represents a portion of the sin the woman represents. However, the reference to theft and bearing false witness in 5:3 mitigates against merely equating "wickedness" with idolatry. The people's sin included not only idolatry, as Ezra and Malachi attested, but also theft, false witness, and the remainder of sins addressed in the Decalogue.

---

[416] Conrad, *Zechariah*, 116–17.
[417] Baldwin, *Zechariah*, 129.
[418] חָכְמָה. *HALOT*, 314–15.
[419] Mitchell, *Zechariah*, 173–74.

As soon as the lid of the basket rose, the woman hiding within attempted to escape. Dramatically, the angel forced the woman back into the basket giving her no additional opportunity to escape and spread her evil about the land.[420] The verb *wayyašlēk* (NIV "he pushed") suggests that the woman struggled with the angel, even though he prevailed.[421] The woman appears so threatening in this vision that she must remain in strict confinement under the powerful guard of the Lord's angels.

**5:9** The woman in the basket appeared suddenly. Likewise, the two winged "women" appeared before the prophet. The angel gives no indication of the identity of these two "women" who now appear in the vision, only offering a few cursory remarks. Curiously, the text describes the women as having the wings of a stork. Although the stork is an unclean animal (Lev 11:19), the comparison between the women's wings and those of the stork seems to focus on the size and strength of their wings, not on any notion of uncleanness.[422] Consequently, the winged women flew with strength and grace as did their animal counterparts. In the vision, the two women carried the basket with the woman inside from Jerusalem back to Babylon.

The angel may also intend an additional meaning for "stork." Even though the stork ranks among the unclean animals, it also had the reputation for caring tenderly for its own young.[423] This observation lies behind the pun in the Old Testament between the Hebrew word for "stork" *(ḥăsîdāh)*[424] and the word rendered "loyal" or "faithful" *(ḥāsîd)*.[425] This same tender care for the helpless young marks the Lord's treatment of his "young," the Israelites.[426]

The women's mission focuses on removing sin from the land. In light of this objective, most conclude that the women function as the Lord's emissaries, although the text does not explicitly say so.[427] Furthermore, in previous visions, most notably the fifth vision (chap. 3), these passages emphasize divine action to the exclusion of human intervention. In the seventh vision, and in v. 9 in particular, only the Lord himself can remove the people's sins from the land. The people are powerless and cannot remove their own sins.

Moreover, the angelic women have the "wind in their wings." This expression may only indicate the ease with which they carry out their divine mandate.

---

[420] Barker, "Zechariah," 634.

[421] וַיַּשְׁלֵךְ. *HALOT*, 1527–29. The verb often has forceful or violent connotations.

[422] Contra Conrad (*Zechariah*, 120) who believes that the winged women are detestable.

[423] Note the example of the eagle. Although this raptor was ceremonially unclean, nonetheless the Old Testament portrays the bird as a noble animal (Prov 23:5).

[424] חֲסִידָה. *HALOT*, 337.

[425] חָסִיד. *HALOT*, 337.

[426] Sweeney, *Twelve Prophets*, 622; Love, *The Evasive Text*, 206.

[427] The Talmudic view (cited by Cohen, *Twelve Prophets*, 289) that the two women return to Babylon and represent the twin vices of "hypocrisy" and "pride" (*Sanh.* 24a) has no biblical support.

On the other hand, the word for "wind" *(rûaḥ)* can also mean "spirit."[428] If Zechariah intended the translation "spirit," the prophet further underscored the notion that only divine initiative can remove sin since the Lord's might empowered the women's movements. Just as the Lord acted graciously to give Joshua clean vestments (chap. 3), so God will act to cleanse his people.

Zechariah noted that the basket and its wicked contents hang "between heaven and earth." The suspension of the measuring basket, together with divine agents carrying the basket filled with wickedness, appears to make the theological point that Israel's holy God cannot come into contact with sin, reinforcing the importance of an intermediary such as Joshua or Zerubbabel.

**5:10–11** The two flying women took the basket to Babylon, although the Hebrew text designates the country as "Shinar," an ancient name for Babylon (Gen 10:10). Zechariah's use of the name Shinar evokes the memory of the tower of Babel episode that was also set in the plain of Shinar (Gen 11:1–9). The tower of Babel story epitomizes the hubris of mankind and its desire to worship itself, not the Creator of heaven and earth. Further, those who recently returned to Jerusalem had seen great evil in Babylon. Now, the former exiles saw some of the evil that they brought back with them to Judah purged from their land and returned to Babylon. The ignoble Babylon would be an appropriate place to send the basket full of wickedness because of its association with evil and its indelible identification as the place where God sent his sinful people into exile.

The angel declared that the basket would return to Babylon so that it may reside in the "house" that would be built for it. Sin, in the form of idolatry, would remain in confinement in Babylon, in the "house" built to imprison it. In vv. 4 and 11 the "house" serves as the site for the judgment of sin. In v. 11 the winged woman fled to Babylon to construct a house to incarcerate evil. In 5:4 the word of God destroys every house in which evil resides. The judgment in v. 4 foreshadows the sentence the righteous Judge will mete out against every form of idolatry.

The "house" *(bēt)* in v. 11 may refer to a temple. The word "house" in Babylonian writings speaks of a temple. Of the diverse examples one could cite, note *E-KUR*, "house of the mountain" (the name of a temple in Nippur), and *E-GAL*, the "big house" or "temple."[429] Babylonian temples often assumed the form of man-made "mountains" called "ziggurats" that generally resembled Egyptian pyramids.

The same usage of the word "house" occurs in the Hebrew Bible. For instance, in the Davidic covenant (2 Sam 7:5–7), the word "house" *(bēt)* refers to the temple David intended to build for the Lord.[430] Furthermore, the usual

---

[428] רוּחַ. *HALOT*, 1195–1201.

[429] Mitchell, *Zechariah*, 175. See Wolfram von Soden, *Akkadisches Handwörterbuch* (Wiesbaden: Otto Harrassowitz, 1985), 1:196.

[430] בַּיִת. *HALOT*, 124–29.

word for "temple" in the Hebrew Old Testament probably originated from that same Sumerian word *E-GAL*, "big house," that is, "the important house."[431] The newly built temple in Babylon provided a residence for the idolatry taken from Judah. The removal of idolatry from Judah had long been an ideal in the Old Testament. Deuteronomy teaches that idolatry could find no place among God's people (see 4:15–31; 29:25–26; cf. Rev 14:8). This purification of the whole land parallels the cleansing of the high priest Joshua in chap. 3.

One must not misunderstand the significance of the symbolism of the women carrying evil back to Babylon. The Lord most assuredly did not sanction idolatry by sending his angels to establish idolatrous worship in a pagan temple in Babylon. Rather, the passage indicates that the Lord expunges sin, including all forms of idolatry, sending it back to its symbolic home.[432] Summarizing the point of the passage, Floyd observes,

> (1) In a couple of poetic and highly figurative passages Yahweh's forgiveness of sin is described in terms of his sending it far away (Ps 103:2; Mic 7:19b). (2) In biblical and other ancient Near Eastern texts there are rituals of purification and atonement that are based on the concept of sin's spatial displacement (e.g., the rituals for purification from leprous infection in Lev 14:2–9,33–53 and for the Day of Atonement in Leviticus 16). (3) There are ancient Near Eastern texts that describe a god's deportation of evil from the land of his people to the land of their enemies; among them are some Hittite texts that also feature the motif of evil's confinement in containers to *[sic]* lead lids.[433]

The transport of the woman in the basket to Babylon, symbolically removing Israel's sin from the land, bears striking parallels to the Azazel rite in Lev 16. Better known as the "scapegoat," the Azazel also bore the nation's impurities, figuratively taking them outside the camp.

From Genesis through Revelation, Babylon represented the epitome of a high-handed, rebellious people (Gen 11:1–9). The Old Testament often prophesied against Babylon. For instance, Isaiah's oracle against her represents one of the more prominent curses against ancient Shinar (see Isa 13:1–14:23). Babylon opposed God consistently, just as she regularly opposed the Lord's people with equal fervor. This opposition comes to its biblical and eschatological culmination in the book of Revelation, where John pronounces this curse against her: "Fallen! Fallen is Babylon the Great, which made all the nations drink the maddening wine of her adulteries" (Rev 14:8). Revelation 17:5 continues the

---

[431] Hebrew הֵיכָל (*hêkāl*); see *TDOT*, 3:382–83.

[432] For a discussion of similar acts, see D. P. Wright, *The Disposal of Impurity: Elimination Rites in the Bible and Hittite and Mesopotamian Literature* (Atlanta: Scholars Press, 1987).

[433] Floyd, "Evil in the Ephah," 64. See also the "Daily Prayer of the King," *ANET*, 397. For further lists of pertinent ancient Near Eastern texts, see Floyd, "Evil in the Ephah," 64, n. 24.

thought: "MYSTERY—BABYLON THE GREAT—THE MOTHER OF PROSTITUTES—AND OF THE ABOMINATIONS OF THE EARTH." Finally, John foretells Babylon's ultimate doom: "Woe! Woe, O great city, O Babylon, city of power! In one hour your doom has come!" (18:10).

Zechariah 5 gives particular attention to the prevalence of sin and its sordid effects on the rebellious nations, both in the lives of every individual as well as in the corporate life of God's people. This chapter also stresses God's coming judgment on sin. The only proper human response to the Lord's holiness and his invitation to serve him is repentance, obedience, and worship. James Lowell's lyrics pointedly admonish the same theme in "Once to Every Man and Nation":

> Once to ev'ry man and nation comes the moment to decide,
> In the strife of truth with falsehood, for the good or evil side;
> Some great cause, some great decision, off'ring each the bloom or blight,
> And the choice goes by forever 'twixt that darkness and that light.
>
> Then to side with truth is noble, when we share her wretched crust,
> Ere her cause bring fame and profit, and 'tis prosperous to be just;
> Then it is the brave man chooses while the coward stands aside,
> Till the multitude make virtue of the faith they had denied.
>
> By the light of burning martyrs, Christ, Thy bleeding feet we track,
> Toiling up new Calv'ries ever with the cross that turns not back;
> New occasions teach new duties, ancient values test our youth;
> They must upward still and onward, who would keep abreast of truth.
>
> Tho' the cause of evil prosper, yet the truth alone is strong;
> Tho' her portion be the scaffold, and upon the throne be wrong;
> Yet that scaffold sways the future, and behind the dim unknown,
> Standeth God within the shadow, keeping watch above His own.[434]

## 8. The Eighth Vision: The Four Chariots (6:1–8)

**¹I looked up again—and there before me were four chariots coming out from between two mountains—mountains of bronze! ²The first chariot had red horses, the second black, ³the third white, and the fourth dappled—all of them powerful. ⁴I asked the angel who was speaking to me, "What are these, my lord?"**

**⁵The angel answered me, "These are the four spirits of heaven, going out from standing in the presence of the Lord of the whole world. ⁶The one with the black horses is going toward the north country, the one with the white horses toward the west, and the one with the dappled horses toward the south."**

---

[434] *Baptist Hymnal*, # 470.

**⁷When the powerful horses went out, they were straining to go throughout the earth. And he said, "Go throughout the earth!" So they went throughout the earth.
⁸Then he called to me, "Look, those going toward the north country have given my Spirit rest in the land of the north."**

The eighth vision shares several striking elements with the first vision (1:7–17).⁴³⁵ Conrad believes the similarities are so striking that the first and eighth visions form an inclusio.⁴³⁶ Whether an inclusio actually exists, the prophet certainly intended for his readers to recognize the strong affinities between these visions.⁴³⁷ Both visions describe different colored horses going throughout the earth, although the colors of the horses in the two visions differ. Both visions focus on four elements. Four horses figure prominently in the first vision. The eighth vision presents four chariots with horses pulling them.

On the other hand, the eighth vision does not mention the riders who figure prominently in the first vision, although most interpreters assume their presence in chap. 6. In both visions one and eight the Lord dispatches the key figures of the vision to fulfill his divine assignment (1:10; 6:7). Furthermore, the theme of "rest" plays a significant role in the first (1:11) and eighth (6:8) visions, signifying the angelic messengers' completion of their heavenly mandate.⁴³⁸ The messengers finished their task of completing Judah's restoration and introducing the accompanying peace the nation would enjoy.

Further, both visions reflect a cosmic scope, focusing not just on Israel and her neighbors, but on all of the Lord's created order. The horses in vision one stood in a ravine, while the chariots of the latter vision emerged through a valley between the two bronze mountains. Many scholars believe that the first vision occurs at dusk and the eighth vision appears to Zechariah at dawn on the same evening. Some even explain the "mountains of *bronze*" as the color of the mountains when the dawning rays of the sun strike them.⁴³⁹ The suggestion that vision one commenced at dusk and vision eight began at dawn may seem attractive at first glimpse. However, the text does not confirm it.⁴⁴⁰ While acknowledging these similarities between visions one and eight, numerous important differences occur between the two visions. Among these many differences, the mountain motif represents one of the most significant distinctives, a point that will receive attention later.⁴⁴¹

---

⁴³⁵ Meyers and Meyers, *Zechariah 1–8*, 332–33; Merrill, *Zechariah*, 181–82.
⁴³⁶ Conrad, *Zechariah*, 121.
⁴³⁷ Butterworth offers a detailed analysis of the relationship between visions one and eight (*Structure and the Book of Zechariah*, 137–49).
⁴³⁸ Tigchelaar, *Prophets of Old*, 62.
⁴³⁹ Boda, *Zechariah*, 319.
⁴⁴⁰ G. von Rad, *Old Testament Theology,* trans. D. M. G. Stalker (New York: Harper and Row, 1965), 2:287.
⁴⁴¹ R. L. Smith, *Micah–Malachi*, 213. Mitchell comments that emending the word "myrtles" (הַהֲדַסִּים) in 1:8,11 to "mountains" (הֶהָרִים) further enhances the symmetry between the visions

**6:1** After looking up, Zechariah saw another vision, adding to the revelation disclosed in prior visions; hence the insertion of the word "again." The prophet observed four chariots coming from between two bronze mountains. In the Old Testament, chariots not only served as the mode of transportation for the military, but they occasionally carried individuals of high social standing (see Absalom in 2 Sam 15:1).[442] Even the Lord himself appeared in the theophany to Ezekiel in a chariot (Ezek 1:15–21). However, in most instances the Old Testament refers to chariots as the ultimate military weapon during Zechariah's time. Frequently, Egypt built and exported the war chariots of the day, while the horses to pull these war machines may have come from Cilicia, otherwise known as Kue (see 1 Kgs 10:28–29).[443] Zechariah predicted that a time would come when the Lord would "take away the chariots" (9:10), instead of commissioning them.[444]

Conrad concludes that references to chariots recall the temple furnishings.[445] He bases his claim on other Old Testament passages that describe chariots as a part of the design of the ark of the covenant or other cultic furnishings. First Kings 7:30–33 describes the stand for the ephah that had wheels like those on chariots fashioned into its base. Similarly, 1 Chr 28:18 portrays the representations of chariot wheels that the Lord included in the symbolism of the ark. Lampstands also figure prominently in 1 Chr 28 as they also do in the book of Zechariah.

Isaiah 66:15–16 echoes themes found in Zech 6:

> See, the LORD is coming with fire,
>   and his chariots are like a whirlwind;
> he will bring down his anger with fury,
>   and his rebuke with flames of fire.
> For with fire and with his sword
>   the LORD will execute judgment upon all men,
>   and many will be those slain by the LORD.

Likewise, Ps 68:17 introduces several motifs that Zech 6:1 makes explicit:

> The chariots of God are tens of thousands
>   and thousands of thousands;
> the LORD has come from Sinai into his sanctuary.

---

(*Zechariah*, 178). No evidence exists to justify such an emendation. The Masoretic Text reads well in its received form.

[442] See 2 Sam 15:1; 2 Kgs 5:21; 9:27; 10:15. *ABD* (1:888–92) provides a helpful survey of chariots in the ancient Near East. See Keel for representations of ancient chariots and a brief discussion of the "worship" of weaponry in Israel (*Symbolism of the Biblical World*, 235–36).

[443] Bright, *History of Israel*, 216–17.

[444] Mitchell, *Zechariah*, 177.

[445] Conrad, *Zechariah*, 123.

Ps 68:17 pictures the Lord as a military commander with a myriad of chariots at his command, as does Zech 6:1. Also, Ps 68 describes God abiding in his residence on Mount Sinai. Thus, the Lord's military might depicts the more profound theological message that God reigns with sovereignty over his entire creation. No empire or geographic expanse can hinder the Lord's rule. Moreover, the four chariots further emphasize the Lord's total dominion over the four corners of the earth. God's word (5:1–4) and his authority extend everywhere. Thus, the theological significance of the Lord's chariots emerging from between the bronze mountains expresses the absolute sovereignty God holds over his entire creation.

Nowhere else in the Old Testament does the expression "mountains of bronze" appear. The mountain motif, however, occurs with some frequency in the Hebrew Bible. Mountains sometimes represent hindrances to the people of God (see the discussion on 4:7).[446] Mountains may symbolize kingdoms as well (Dan 2:35). In 6:1, "mountains" likely refers to the Lord's abode, a metaphor well suited to the context of this passage.[447]

Worshippers of other deities in the ancient Near East portrayed their gods as living on various mountains. The Bible describes God living on Mount Zion (Pss 48:1,3; 132:13–14), on Mount Zaphon (Ps 48:2), and on Mount Sinai (Judg 5:4–5).[448] However, the Israelites did not believe that the Lord literally resided on Mount Zion or any other mountain, although they often employed figurative language to speak of God "dwelling" on Zion. In Zech 6:1, the angel chose not to identify from which two mountains the chariots departed. One view suggests Mount Zion and the Mount of Olives as the identity of the two mountains, although another significant interpretation deserves brief examination.[449]

Commentators have long puzzled over the idiom "mountains of *bronze*." Many suggest that the reference to "bronze" evokes the imagery of the two bronze pillars standing before the temple (1 Kgs 7:15–22).[450] Keel concludes that the bronze mountains represent the doors of the temple.[451] Still others link the bronze material comprising the mountains to the bronze serpent raised on a standard during the wilderness experience (Num 21:9). One cannot show that Zechariah's reference to "bronze" in v. 1 recalls the bronze serpent simply because the word "bronze" occurs in both texts. Additionally, the prominence

---

[446] Merrill provides a helpful survey of mountain symbolism (*Zechariah*, 182–83).

[447] Again, in Zech 14:1–8 the prophet introduces a great "mountain." In chap. 6 the chariots come out from between two mountains, but in chap. 14 the Day of the Lord will see the Lord's anointed Messiah splitting the Mount of Olives in two.

[448] For a discussion of the theme of the mountain of God in the Old Testament and in ancient Near Eastern literature, see Clifford, *The Cosmic Mountain*. See also Keel, *Symbolism of the Biblical World*, 113–20.

[449] Barker, "Zechariah," 636.

[450] Sweeney, *Twelve Prophets*, 624.

[451] Keel, *Symbolism of the Biblical World*, 22–24; see also *ANEP*, 683–85.

of bronze in ancient metalworking renders any association with the bronze serpent highly unlikely.[452]

Although it might sound curious in light of modern metallurgy, bronze symbolized strength in the ancient world, a point Rashi noted.[453] For instance, the great statue in Nebuchadnezzar's dream comprised a belly and thighs made of bronze (Dan 2:32). In a later vision Daniel saw an eschatological vision of a man with "legs like the gleam of burnished bronze" (Dan 10:6). The emblem of strength fits the unusual phrase "mountains of bronze" well. The whole passage underscores the Lord's mighty reign over his creation, hegemony that no effort from rebellious humanity could thwart. Petersen summarizes the point of the vision well: "Zechariah sees the edge of the human domain, the gates of heaven at the boundary of the perceptible world."[454]

Floyd recognizes the theme of the Lord's dominion over the world, but he focuses on the polemical force of God's spreading reign.[455] Floyd suggests that the Lord departed from Mount Zaphon (literally meaning, "the north," see Exod 14:2) and moved southward toward Mount Teman. Mount Zaphon had a long association with Baal worship and functioned as the sacred mountain of Baal-Hadad in Canaanite mythology.[456] The word "Teman" means "south" (see Jer 49:20; Amos 1:12; and especially Zech 9:14).[457] If Floyd's suggestion stands that the two mountains in v. 1 represent Mt. Zaphon and Mt. Teman, the symbolism stresses the Lord's victory over the most incipient paganism. The whole passage, then, would function as a polemic against every form of idolatry, particularly Baalism. Thus, the triumphant procession of the chariots of the Lord from between the mountains pictures the Lord's victory over the false claims made in the name of empty idols, most notably Baal. The ultimate theological message of the passage is clear. Beginning in the northern regions where much ancient Near Eastern idolatry originated, God's kingdom would spread southward without hindrance over the whole world. This long awaited victory foreshadows themes Zechariah will develop in chap. 9.

**6:2–3** Zechariah never explained the symbolism of the colored horses. Consequently, any conclusion one might reach concerning the horses' colors

---

[452] Unger, *Zechariah*, 101.

[453] Cited by Cohen, *Twelve Prophets*, 290. While bronze probably represents strength, Rashi's view that the mountains represents kingdoms does not fit the sense of the passage as well as the suggestion that the mountains portray God's heavenly realm.

[454] Petersen, *Zechariah 1–8*, 268. Much of Petersen's discussion proves unacceptable because of his over-reliance on ancient Near Eastern mythology for determining the meaning of the biblical text. Also, see Baldwin, *Zechariah*, 130.

[455] Floyd, *Minor Prophets*, 400.

[456] J. de Savignac, "Le sens du terme *Ṣâphōn*," *UF* 16 (1984): 273. Canaanite mythology viewed Mount Zaphon as the place where the gods feasted (*CTA* 4.5.106–17) and the site from which Baal made his pronouncements (*CTA* 3.3.10–28).

[457] *HALOT*, 1754–55.

remains tentative. One approach holds that the colors function solely to distinguish the horses, having no further importance.[458] Alternatively, others attempt to determine precisely what the colors might signify. A particularly popular view associates the horses' colors in Zech 6 with the colors of the horses in Rev 6:1–8. Following this approach, Unger suggests that white indicates victory (Rev 6:2; also 19:11,14), red stands for bloodshed (Rev 6:4), black represents judgment (Rev 6:5–6), and the dappled color signifies death (Rev 6:8).[459] Unger fails to demonstrate the accuracy of his association with the diverse colors of horses and concepts such as judgment. Neither does Unger prove that the colors of the horses in Rev 6 rest on that of the horses in Zech 6.

The interpretation that the colors signify geographical regions might have merit, but it also lacks certainty.[460] Much like the symbolism in the prophecy in Dan 7, the ancient rabbis believed that the colors of the horses symbolized world kingdoms. Babylon, Medo-Persia, Greece, and Rome represented probable candidates. However, any association between the colors and world kingdoms must remain tentative at best.[461]

The ambiguity of the color terminology applied to the fourth horse (6:3b) raises additional questions. Many translations render the Hebrew idiom (*běruddîm 'ămuṣṣîm*) used to describe the fourth horse as "dappled."[462] The phrase literally means "dappled strong."[463] The concluding adjective "strong" best applies to all four horses though, not merely the final one.

Conrad develops the theme of strength in vv. 1–3, linking the strong one in Zech 6:7 to the mounted horsemen in 1:10–11 whose job it was to patrol "throughout the earth" on the Lord's behalf.[464] Floyd pursues a similar identification of the horsemen in chap. 1 with the chariots in chap. 6.[465] Presumably, the chariots had drivers, perhaps even angelic reinsmen. Irrespective of the color symbolism Zechariah intended, however, the presence of war horses symbolizes the Lord's omnipotence and dominion over all creation.

**6:4–5** As in previous visions (see 4:4,11), Zechariah asked the interpreting angel to explain the significance of the vision before him. In response, the angel confirmed that the chariots represented "the four spirits of heaven." The antecedent of "these" in v. 4 is the chariots. The Hebrew word *ruḥôt* (NIV "spirits") in v. 5 is the plural of the same word that the NIV renders "wind" in

---

[458] Smith, *Micah-Malachi*, 214.

[459] Unger, *Zechariah*, 102–3.

[460] Smith, *Micah-Malachi*, 214. Meyers and Meyers believe the colors of the horses represent the four points of the compass (*Zechariah 1–8*, 320).

[461] Cohen, *Twelve Prophets*, 290.

[462] בְּרֻדִּים אֲמֻצִּים. *HALOT*, 65, 154. The word בְּרֻדִּים means "dappled."

[463] Merrill provides a good overview of the interpretive options (*Zechariah*, 183–87).

[464] Conrad, *Zechariah*, 121–22.

[465] Floyd, *Minor Prophets*, 399.

5:9.⁴⁶⁶ The word legitimately conveys both ideas.⁴⁶⁷ Contextual factors come into play when deciding which meaning of the Hebrew best fits the passage, although the literary and theological milieu in chap. 6 does not give sufficient information to answer the question definitively.

Consequently, commentators split equally over which meaning of *rûaḥ* Zechariah employed in v. 5. Many cite Ps 104:4 to support the view that the proper rendering of *ruḥôt* in v. 5 should be "winds." Ps 104:4 reads, "He makes *winds* his messengers, flames of fire his servants." Likewise, in Zech 5:9 the same word *rûaḥ* describes angels flying through the air, lending additional support for the meaning "wind" in 6:5, although not all agree with the translation "wind" in 5:9. Moreover, Baldwin believes that "winds" best fits the eighth vision since wind, like horses, can travel at will over the face of the entire earth, and v. 5b implies that the Lord's "spirits" encompass the world.⁴⁶⁸ Additionally, other prophets correlated the two motifs many find in v. 5—the four winds from God in conjunction with the four directions. For instance, Jer 49:36 states,

> I will bring against Elam the four winds
>   from the four quarters of the heavens;
> I will scatter them to the four winds,
>   and there will not be a nation
>   where Elam's exiles do not go.

Dan 11:4 and Zech 2:6 convey similar uses of the word "wind," and Zech 7:14 refers to the mighty scattering whirlwind.

Mitchell argues for a variation of the "winds from heaven" interpretation. Following Kimchi, Mitchell contends that v. 5 speaks neither of "winds" nor of "spirits," but rather of the *directions* the four winds blow.⁴⁶⁹ He suggests that this is the reason the text does not specify which directions God sends his "four spirits of heaven." This view maintains that the Lord's angels travel in the direction of the four "winds," that is, the four points of the compass.⁴⁷⁰ Relatedly, Tigchelaar sees the winds describing the direction to which the chariots head, thus rendering the passage, "These are going out to the four winds of heaven."⁴⁷¹ Feinberg also commends the translation "winds."⁴⁷²

However, others conclude that the meaning "spirits" best suits the eighth vision. They argue that in 6:5 the context focuses on angelic beings. For ex-

---

⁴⁶⁶ רוּחַ. *HALOT*, 1195–1201.
⁴⁶⁷ Ibid.; BDB, 924–26. See *TLOT*, 1202–20, especially 1204–7, 1212–18; see also D. I. Block, "The Prophet of the Spirit: The Use of *RWH* in the Book of Ezekiel," *JETS* 32 (1989): 27–49.
⁴⁶⁸ Baldwin, *Zechariah*, 131.
⁴⁶⁹ Mitchell, *Zechariah*, 179.
⁴⁷⁰ See *NIDOTTE*, 3:1074.
⁴⁷¹ Tigchelaar, *Prophets of Old*, 63.
⁴⁷² Feinberg, *Minor Prophets*, 92.

ample, Merrill concludes that "spirits" is the proper translation based on "the superhuman, militaristic work the spirits must perform (see 4:6) and because the spirits have just come from the presence of the Lord of the earth."[473] Hence, Merrill believes that v. 5 introduces the Lord's ministering "spirits" who serve as God's personal agents. Furthermore, the noun translated "winds/ spirits" is plural. The Spirit (singular) of God, that is, the Holy Spirit, cannot be the focus in this verse. The singular form of the word *rûaḥ* in v. 8 does refer to the Spirit of God. The plural *ruḥôt* (NIV "spirits") in v. 5 designates the Lord's emissaries.[474]

In conclusion, both views present legitimate interpretative options. However, Zech 6:5 appears to focus on the role the four divine emissaries serve in extending God's authority on earth. Accordingly, the translation "spirits" offers the preferable understanding. These angelic beings function as God's ambassadors on earth.[475] Kaiser, Block, et al. write, "Frequently the Spirit of God represents the agent/agency by which God exercises his sovereign control over individuals. Occasionally the effects are calamitous. . . . But usually God's Spirit operates on behalf of his people by energizing them (Ezek 2:2)."[476]

The interpreting angel did not tell Zechariah where the four spirits would go. The prophet merely knew that the four spirits left the very presence of the Lord in his heavenly court as his agents to project his dominion. Floyd adds that the chariots functioned as invisible forces doing God's bidding throughout creation, demonstrating the Lord's power and effecting the changes God desires on earth.[477]

Theologically, the words "four spirits of heaven . . . of the whole world" declare the sovereign character of God. Merrill contributes a helpful theological insight into v. 5: "The four chariots are sent forth to reclaim all the earth for the suzerainty of YHWH, a result that also follows the splitting of the mountain in the day of YHWH (Zech. 14:9). Once this is brought to pass, there will be peace in Jerusalem (14:11) and in the whole earth (6:7–8)."[478] Moreover, the spirits' free movement may indicate the autonomy and power with which the Lord's agents go out from Jerusalem throughout the cosmos.[479]

**6:6** This verse presents significant textual difficulties. Among the challenges, v. 6 begins rather unnaturally with the relative pronoun "which" in the

---

[473] Merrill, *Zechariah*, 187; see E. B. Pusey, *The Minor Prophets: A Commentary,* reprint ed. (Grand Rapids: Eerdmans, 1995), 2:370.
[474] רֻחוֹת.
[475] Merrill, *Zechariah*, 188.
[476] *NIDOTTE*, 3:1075.
[477] Floyd, *Minor Prophets*, 399.
[478] Merrill, *Zechariah*, 183.
[479] Meyers and Meyers, *Zechariah 1–8*, 322–23.

Hebrew text without an expressed antecedent. Translated literally, the phrase yields "which with it the black horses." Scholars attempt to posit reasonable solutions to the awkward reading. Baldwin follows the editorial suggestion in *BHS*, which adds the following phrase to the beginning of v. 6, "The red horses went towards the east country."[480] Nevertheless, this phrase has no ancient textual witnesses to support the conclusion.[481]

Smith (among others) believes that Zechariah referred to "the chariot," yielding the following translation: "Whereupon (the chariot) with the black horses are *[sic]* going to the land of the north."[482] The demonstrative pronoun "these" found in vv. 4 and 5 supports the "chariot" interpretation. In v. 4 Zechariah asks the angel, "What are *these*?" referring back to the chariots in vv. 1–3. The angel responds in v. 5 saying, "*These* are," which has the same antecedent as the word "these" in the previous verses.

Another textual problem emerges in v. 6. The Hebrew word ʾaḥărêhem literally means "after them" and follows the phrase "the white horses."[483] Thus, the Masoretic Text indicates that the chariot drawn by the black horses goes northward, followed by the chariot with the white horses. Despite the absence of textual evidence supporting a change of the Hebrew text, many scholars adopt an emendation of the text. For instance, the NIV follows most commentators in accepting a slight emendation of the Hebrew text so that it reads "toward the west" (ʾaḥărê hayyām).[484] The expectation that this verse should portray the horses proceeding in all four directions provides the chief reason scholars frequently emend the text. In the final analysis, however, the emendation, clever as it is, remains unnecessary to produce a meaningful reading.[485] Moreover, no external textual evidence of any type exists to substantiate the alteration. Accordingly, one should follow the Masoretic Text. The resulting translation of v. 6a should read as does the NIV footnote: "The one with the black horses is going toward the north country, the one with the white horses after them."

Verse 6 shifts attention from the chariots in the previous section to the horses themselves, an emphasis that will continue throughout the remainder of the passage. Verse 6 also contains other unexpected descriptions of the horses.[486] For instance, the order in which v. 6 mentions the horses varies slightly from their introduction in vv. 2–3. Also, v. 6 fails to mention the red horses.

---

[480] Baldwin, *Zechariah*, 131.

[481] Sweeney, *Twelve Prophets*, 626–27.

[482] R. L. Smith, *Micah-Malachi*, 212. See Meyers and Meyers, *Zechariah 1–8*, 324.

[483] אַחֲרֵיהֶם. *HALOT*, 34–36.

[484] אַחֲרֵי הַיָּם. Baldwin (*Zechariah*, 131–32), Barker ("Zechariah," 637–38), and Meyers and Meyers (*Zechariah 1–8*, 325)—among many others—accept this emendation. Others such as Merrill (*Zechariah*, 185–86) reject the notion of altering the Masoretic Text.

[485] Mason, *Zechariah*, 60.

[486] Although I differ with many of her conclusions in this section, Baldwin offers a helpful summary of these emphases (*Zechariah*, 138–40).

Further, the Masoretic Text in its present form does not send a horse eastward in the direction of the Arabian desert, but this observation only concerns those interpreters who anticipate the Lord's sending his chariots to the four points of the compass. We have already examined and rejected the textual emendation that would send a chariot westward. Excepting preconceived notions of what the text *ought* to say, it ultimately does not matter whether or not God sent his angels in four different directions.

Following the Masoretic Text's reading closely, three chariots "go out." A chariot pulled by "dappled horses" goes south in the direction of Egypt. The black horses and their chariot head north to assault Babylon.[487] Following the black horses, the white horses head in a northerly direction also.[488] Note that no chariot travels to the east. The temple faced east because the Old Testament figuratively viewed the east as the direction from which the Lord would approach when he comes to establish his kingdom. One may then surmise that Zechariah understands that the Lord will come from an eastward direction.

Baldwin reconstructs the text so that chariots proceed in all four directions, a conclusion without substantiation from manuscript evidence. Nonetheless, she offers a helpful summary of the passage's main emphasis:

> So far as the prophet's message is concerned the only group of importance is that which goes to the north (north and east, understood), where the struggle for world domination had for centuries been concentrated. Egypt was still an important power, hence the mention of the south also, but to the west there was nothing of importance going on to warrant special mention. From a stylistic point of view the prophet gains by leaving the other two directions vague. It is enough to know that the Lord is triumphant over the dominant world powers. The lesser are included with the greater.[489]

**6:7–8** Although Zechariah did not refer to the chariots in these verses, the war machines remained in view. The horses described in v. 7 function as a metonymy, a figure of speech in which one thing, the horses, represents something else, the chariots. All of the divine emissaries anxiously desired to fulfill their mission. However, the Lord's messengers may not initiate their mission until they receive authorization from their Commander. The Lord has absolute autonomy to issue such decrees over every nation and over all history.

---

[487] Mitchell suggests that the color black aptly symbolizes the "north" (צָפוֹן) since the northern region, particularly Babylon, connoted "a dark and gloomy region" (*Zechariah*, 179). No linguistic association exists, however. See HALOT, 1046–47; and BDB, 860–61. Figuratively, Babylon epitomized the dark and evil empire in the minds of Israelites.

[488] Merrill overviews the issues well (*Zechariah*, 186–87).

[489] Baldwin, *Zechariah*, 140.

The Hebrew phrase the NIV renders as "go/went throughout the earth" occurs three times in v. 7. The repetition underscores the emphatic character of the expression. Moreover, the phrase echoes the language found in 1:10, signifying patrolling the earth in a military sense.

As v. 8 continues, the angel proclaimed victory and rest in the "north country." Although Babylon did not lie to the north of Israel geographically, the desert terrain to the immediate east and northeast of Israel required Mesopotamian foes to enter Israel from the north. So the north represents Babylon, the seat of all political unrest and evil in the minds of the Israelite community. Thus, by extension, the metonymy indicates that if peace comes to the north where the most powerful empire of the day resided, then peace would arrive throughout the world.

Of course, Zechariah was not the first prophet to announce divine judgment on Babylon for her sins against the Lord. Many oracles proclaimed Babylon's impending doom. In particular, note the following Isaianic oracles: In Isa 13 God declares that "Babylon, the jewel of kingdoms, the glory of the Babylonians' pride, will be overthrown by God like Sodom and Gomorrah" (v. 19). Similarly, the prophecy naming Cyrus as the Lord's "shepherd who will accomplish all that I please . . . to subdue nations before him and to strip kings of their armor" (Isa 44:28–45:1) prophesied the defeat of Babylon.

The book of Isaiah gives great prominence to the paradise motif, prophecies that focus on worldwide peace and the restoration of the entire creation. These eschatological passages occur with some frequency in other prophetic books, but Isaiah predicted the character of the kingdom with greater clarity and frequency than any other.[490] Isaiah foretold everlasting peace, an unending reign by the Davidic Messiah, plus righteousness and justice on earth such as had not existed after the fall. These prophecies found a partial fulfillment in the security and blessings that the Lord would grant to his people during the restoration in the postexilic epoch. However, one cannot maintain that the peace described in any of the paradise passages reached its complete fulfillment in the days of the writing prophets. Thus, Baldwin summarizes the eschatological importance of vv. 7–8 nicely when she writes, "The sequel is in v. 15, but the climax of history is to be a person, not a building, and the inclusion of vv. 9–15 with the last of the visions points to the One for whom the temple was intended (Mal. 3:1)."[491]

Verse 8 contains the interpreting angel's recitation of the Lord's quote to his divine messenger. "My Spirit" speaks of the Lord's Spirit. The Lord's "spirits" *(ruḥôt)* in v. 5 are plural, suggesting a group of personal emissaries of the Lord. In contrast, *rûaḥ* in v. 8 refers to a singular servant of the Lord, different from the "spirits" in v. 5.

---

[490] For instance, see Isa 9:1–7; 11:1–16; Zech 1:11.
[491] Baldwin, *Zechariah*, 132.

While previous visions emphasize tranquility in Israel (2:12; 3:10; 4:8–9), chap. 6 stresses the peace the world will experience because the Lord has exerted the dominion he enjoyed all along. The Lord and his servants can finally rest because the creation now experiences the peace for which God originally created it.[492] Ever since the fall of man, creation has groaned and longed for its restoration (Rom 8:22). The eighth vision draws to a close with a sense of finality: "God's in his Heaven – All's right with the world"[493]—not just in word alone, but in reality.

---

[492] Tigchelaar notes that the resting of the Spirit corresponds to the Lord's rest on the seventh day of creation (*Prophets of Old*, 66).

[493] Robert Browning, "Song," *Pippa Passes*.

---
SECTION OUTLINE
---

III. JOSHUA'S CROWN (6:9–15)

---
## III. JOSHUA'S CROWN (6:9–15)
---

⁹The word of the LORD came to me: ¹⁰"Take [silver and gold] from the exiles Heldai, Tobijah and Jedaiah, who have arrived from Babylon. Go the same day to the house of Josiah son of Zephaniah. ¹¹Take the silver and gold and make a crown, and set it on the head of the high priest, Joshua son of Jehozadak. ¹²Tell him this is what the LORD Almighty says: 'Here is the man whose name is the Branch, and he will branch out from his place and build the temple of the LORD. ¹³It is he who will build the temple of the LORD, and he will be clothed with majesty and will sit and rule on his throne. And he will be a priest on his throne. And there will be harmony between the two.' ¹⁴The crown will be given to Heldai, Tobijah, Jedaiah and Hen son of Zephaniah as a memorial in the temple of the LORD. ¹⁵Those who are far away will come and help to build the temple of the LORD, and you will know that the LORD Almighty has sent me to you. This will happen if you diligently obey the LORD your God."

Few scholars agree about how this oracle relates to the previous context. Sweeney connects vv. 1–8 and vv. 9–15, suggesting that the patrol of the horses relates to the inauguration of worship in the new temple.[1] Sweeney also views the temple as the visible manifestation of the Lord's sovereignty on earth. Accordingly, the patrol of the chariots throughout the earth further underscores the theme of God's dominion. Baldwin views vv. 9–15 as a continuation of 6:1–8, although she does not think vv. 9–15 belong to the original vision.[2]

Verses 9–15 share several important motifs with the night visions. These parallels suggest that this pericope comments on the night visions. In particular, the prominence of Joshua the high priest in chap. 3 and 6:9–15 links these two visions. Moreover, the theme of the "branch" in 3:8 reemerges in 6:12. Likewise, the twin emphases of priest and king found in chaps. 3–4 occur together in vv. 9–15. Thus, the whole coronation scene in chap. 6 presupposes that the temple will be completed and Jerusalem will be restored, prevalent themes throughout the night visions.[3]

---
[1] M. A. Sweeney, *The Twelve Prophets, Vol. 2*, Berit Olam (Collegeville, MN: Liturgical Press, 2000), 628.
[2] J. G. Baldwin, *Haggai, Zechariah, Malachi*, TOTC (Downers Grove, IL: InterVarsity, 1972), 130.
[3] For a development of these themes, see E. H. Merrill, *Haggai, Zechariah, Malachi* (Chicago:

However, the themes in the eighth vision differ significantly enough from 6:9–15 that it becomes difficult to posit a direct connection between the two halves of chap. 6. Therefore, 6:9–15 was probably written at a later time in Zechariah's ministry. Yet, moving beyond chap. 6, the oracles beginning in 7:1 date almost two years after Zechariah's night visions. Thus, one can hardly assign 6:9–15 to these latter oracles. So, the oracle focusing on Joshua's crown cannot be tied too closely to either the preceding or following sections of the book of Zechariah. Instead, the section on Joshua's crown serves as a structural hinge for Zechariah, linking two major sections of the book.

**6:9–10** Zechariah's next oracle begins with the familiar prophetic assertion of divine inspiration: "The word of the LORD came to me" (see also 4:8; 7:4; 8:1,18). Unlike many of the preceding oracles, no interpreting angel appears to guide the prophet's understanding.

Verse 10 introduces several newly returned exiles from Babylon who play a significant role in the next stage of reordering Jerusalem. Two questions surface immediately in v. 10: "Who are the exiles?" and "What was taken from these exiles?"

One must first ask if "Heldai, Tobijah, and Jedaiah" even function as proper names. The Septuagint translates these names as appellatives—descriptive or classifying names—as "from the rulers, from the useful men, and from those who have understood it." Despite the antiquity of the Septuagint, few scholars accept the Septuagintal understanding; most view the Hebrew as three proper names.

Irrespective of how one understands the names, many of the faithful probably accompanied those mentioned by name in their pilgrimage back to Jerusalem.[4] Zechariah likely mentioned these exiles in v. 10 because of their importance. If the nouns do serve as proper names, the identity of Heldai, Tobijah, and Jedaiah remains a mystery. Even though the same names appear elsewhere in the Hebrew Bible, most of the other occurrences cannot refer to the figures in v. 10.

The only other Heldai in the Old Testament is in a list of David's warriors (1 Chr 27:15).

Tobijah represents a relatively common yet important name in the era. Ezra 2:60 mentions a Tobijah, but Ezra also indicates that since Tobijah could not trace his genealogy, he could not serve as a priest (2:59,62). The Tobijahs in

---

Moody, 1994), 193–94, 196–200; C. L. Meyers and E. M. Meyers, *Haggai, Zechariah 1–8* (Garden City, NY: Doubleday, 1987), 366–68; and A. Petitjean, *Les oracles du Proto-Zacharie* (Paris: J. Gabalda, 1969), 268–70.

[4] Meyers and Meyers conclude that Heldai represents a delegation of exiles. They argue on the grounds that "Heldai" immediately follows the word גּוֹלָה ("exiles") and is not preceded by the preposition מֵאֵת ("from"), which occurs before each of the other names (*Zechariah 1–8*, 340). Likely, Heldai and his companions also represent other exiles in this episode. Meyers and Meyers's argument remains tenuous, however.

Ezra 2 and Zech 6 are probably different individuals.[5] Another Tobijah appears in Neh 2:10,19.[6]

Significantly, an influential family descended from one named Tobijah who lived during the Hasmonean period.[7] A rock hewn cave in the Transjordan region preserved Aramaic inscriptions bearing the name Tobijah. Mazar dates these inscriptions to the era of Zechariah the prophet and identifies this Tobijah as the one in Zech 6:10.[8] However, Frank Cross challenges Mazar's dating of the Aramaic inscription and its identification with Tobijah in v. 10.[9]

Likewise, the name Jedaiah occurs elsewhere in the Old Testament (Ezra 2:36; Neh 7:39; 11:10; 12:6–7,19,21; 1 Chr 9:10). While the Jedaiah in v. 10 may not be the same individual as mentioned in other passages, the practice of naming individuals after one of their male ancestors suggests that the figure mentioned in v. 10 may be related to the other Jedaiahs. Mazar concludes that the absence of lineage with the names of Tobijah and Jedaiah indicates that they belonged to such well known families that listing lineages was superfluous.[10] Since Mazar's understanding lacks evidence, it is basically an argument from silence.

Zechariah's selection of truly renowned individuals to contribute to the restoration effort and to witness the solemn ceremony underscores the political and religious importance of the prophet's action.[11] The involvement of such conspicuous people must have exerted great influence over the community and left a lasting impression.

Verse 10 continues with Zechariah's command to the assemblage of exiles to proceed to the house of Josiah son of Zephaniah. The identity of Josiah remains uncertain. Although Josiah is a widely attested name from the postexilic period, one cannot know with certainty if the Josiah in v. 10 appears in the other texts. A priest named Zephaniah functioned as a leader among the priests at the time of the exile (2 Kgs 25:18). However, insufficient evidence survives to determine if the Josiah in v. 10 is related to the Zephaniah in 2 Kgs 25:18. Although the evidence is inconclusive, Josiah might be the great-grandson of Zephaniah in 2 Kgs 25:18 based on papponymy, the practice of naming a child after his grandfather.[12]

---

[5] Meyers and Meyers, *Zechariah 1–8*, 341; see J. Bright, *A History of Israel*, 3rd ed. (Philadelphia: Westminster, 1981), 382–85.

[6] One of the Lachish letters also mentions a Tobijah (letter 3, line 19), but nothing more is known of his identity.

[7] B. Porten, *Archives from Elephantine* (Berkeley: University of California Press, 1968), 117.

[8] B. Mazar, "The 'Tobiads'," *IEJ* 7 (1957): 137–41.

[9] F. M. Cross, Jr., "The Development of the Jewish Scripts," in *The Bible and the Ancient Near East*, ed. G. E. Wright, reprint ed. (Winona Lake, IN: Eisenbrauns, 1979), 195, n. 75.

[10] Mazar, "Tobiads," 229.

[11] Meyers and Meyers, *Zechariah 1–8*, 342.

[12] Ibid., 345.

Three out of four of the personal names listed in v. 10—Tobijah, Jedaiah, and Josiah—contain the theophoric element *Yah* in their name, an abbreviation for Yahweh. This theophoric component in these proper names suggests a measure of genuine faith in the Lord among the general populace of those returning from Babylon. One must use caution not to attribute too much significance to these theophoric elements when seeking to discern more information about a specific individual, however. While the divine elements indicated faith in the Lord among the community at large, the names do not prove that the individual men themselves evidenced exemplary measures of faith.[13] The fact that these individuals returned to the land of promise offers the best indication of their faith in the Lord and their confidence in the covenant that their God had made with their forefathers and with them.

The Hebrew text of v. 10 fails to mention what Zechariah must take from the exiles—NIV supplies "silver and gold."[14] The Hebrew has the preposition "from" before the names of Heldai, Tobijah, and Jedaiah, indicating that each should contribute something. Cohen translates the Hebrew quite closely: "Take of them of the captivity, even of Heldai."[15] Most translators feel constrained to add an object to the verb "take," however conjectural their efforts might be. The ambiguity of the verse has led to several suggestions that attempt to resolve the dilemma.

Some recommend that the word "offering" should be added following the word "take," yielding "take the *offering*."[16] NIV probably adds the words "silver and gold" after the verb "take" because "silver and gold" function as the object of the verb "take" in v. 11a.[17] Additionally, since several passages refer to the extensive contributions of silver and gold made by the postexilic community to the temple reconstruction project (Ezra 2:68–69; 6:5; Hag 2:8), these texts add further credence to the "silver and gold" interpretation in v. 10.

Alternatively, Mitchell maintains that God commanded Zechariah to take certain persons to Josiah's house.[18] Mitchell argues that if Zechariah intended "silver and gold" to be the object of the verb "take," he would have stated as much.[19] Mitchell's interpretation, "take from the captives Heldai, and Tobijah, and Jedaiah," requires that one emend the text. The Hebrew is literally, "take from the captives—from Heldai, and from Tobijah, and from Jedaiah."

---

[13] Contra M. F. Unger, *Commentary on Zechariah* (Grand Rapids: Zondervan, 1962), 110–11.

[14] לָקוֹחַ. GKC, § 113.4 discusses the infinitive absolute when functioning as an imperative. See Exod 20:8 for a similar usage of the infinitive absolute.

[15] A. Cohen, *The Twelve Prophets* (New York: Soncino, 1948), 292.

[16] For example, see Unger, *Zechariah*, 110.

[17] The NEB also adds "silver and gold," but the JB inserts "offering."

[18] H. G. Mitchell, J. M. P. Smith, and J. A. Bewer, *A Critical and Exegetical Commentary on Haggai, Zechariah, Malachi and Jonah*, ICC (Edinburgh: T. & T. Clark, 1912), 183.

[19] Ibid., 184.

However, the Hebrew text does not require an emendation since the passage is not unintelligible. Equally inappropriate, one must not claim that the prophet could not use ellipsis, the omission of words for literary effect. Consequently, since v. 11 indicates that the object of the verb "take" is "silver and gold," one can supply the words "silver and gold" in v. 10.

Assuming the correctness of the "silver and gold" view, differing opinions emerge concerning the symbolism associated with the precious metals. Conrad believes that silver and gold represent plunder from Babylon, the evil empire, taken by the exiles for the reconstruction of the temple.[20] Others contend that the silver and gold anticipate the crown that would ultimately rest in the temple as a memorial to the Lord's faithfulness.[21] However, nothing about either view excludes the possibility of the other understanding. In the end, both interpretations capture important observations about the significance of the silver and gold. To be sure, Judah's impoverished state suggests that any silver or gold in her possession had come from her former captor, Babylon. Moreover, the crown holds great significance in the remainder of chap. 6. Verse 11a states that Zechariah must collect silver and gold for the purpose of making the crown. Zechariah 6:14 also places prominence on the crown that would rest on Heldai, Tobijah, Jedaiah, and Hen—understood as four different names for the same individual.[22]

Tollington notes parallels between the return from the Babylonian exile and Israel's departure from Egypt during the exodus.[23] Moses accepted offerings of silver and gold that the Israelites received as plunder from their Egyptian captors for use in the construction of the tabernacle (Exod 25:1–3; 30:11–16; Num 7). Likewise, Zechariah accepted offerings for the construction of the new temple. In this way, God identifies Zechariah with none other than Moses. Zechariah's dual roles parallel the multiple roles or offices held by Samuel (1 Sam 9:1–10:16), Zadok (1 Kgs 1:38–40), and Jehoiada (2 Kgs 11:12).[24]

**6:11** Verse 11 expresses the objective of the preceding action, fashioning a crown for Joshua the high priest. The text uses a rare word in the plural for "crown" *('ăṭārôt)*, one that normally occurs in royal passages.[25] The plural form raises the question of how many crowns Zechariah fashioned.

Some feel that v. 13 suggests that two crowns are fashioned, one for Joshua and the other for Zerubbabel.[26] Kimchi followed this view, maintaining that

---

[20] E. W. Conrad, *Zechariah* (Sheffield: Sheffield Academic Press, 1999), 125.

[21] J. E. Tollington, *Tradition and Innovation in Haggai and Zechariah 1–8* (Sheffield: Sheffield Academic Press, 1993), 122; M. H. Floyd, *Minor Prophets. Part 2* (Grand Rapids: Eerdmans, 2000), 405.

[22] See discussion of the question on v. 14 below.

[23] Tollington, *Tradition and Innovation*, 123.

[24] Sweeney, *Twelve Prophets*, 630.

[25] עֲטָרוֹת. Although BDB (742) translates the form as a singular, *HALOT* (815) views the form as plural.

[26] Merrill, *Zechariah*, 196–98; R. L. Smith, *Micah-Malachi*, WBC (Waco: Word, 1984), 218.

the text omits mentioning the crowning of Zerubbabel for fear of offending the Persian authorities.[27] However, this view rests wholly on an argument from silence regarding Zerubbabel's crowning and a misunderstanding of the word "crown."

A variation of the two crown interpretation suggests that Zechariah had two crowns made, one of gold for Zerubbabel and the other of silver for Joshua the high priest.[28] This understanding, although theoretically possible, reads into the text an interpretation that the passage itself does not substantiate. Still another perspective claims that multiple crowns existed, one for Joshua and one for each of the four figures in v. 10.[29]

Alternatively, many conclude that the Lord instructed Zechariah to prepare only one crown. The word "crown" is plural in v. 14 also, although the adjoining verbal form that the NIV translates "will be given" is singular.[30] The phenomenon of plural nouns with singular meaning and accompanied by singular verbs (see Prov 1:20) occurs elsewhere, a usage that Zechariah seems to employ here.

Thus, there is no need to revocalize the Hebrew word ʿăṭārôt as a singular.[31] Since the Masoretic Text offers a reading that is clear (though difficult), one should retain the received Hebrew reading.[32] The plural noun "crowns" may refer to the majesty or excellence of the crown, a well known use of plural nouns in the Old Testament.[33] Floyd focuses on the discussion about the number of crowns, noting that the actual number of crowns remains uncertain. He draws attention to the main point of the passage, which is that Zechariah received divine instructions to crown only one individual, Joshua the high priest (v. 11).[34]

Mitchell, following a long line of critical reinterpretations of Zech 6, concludes that the text originally read "Zerubbabel" where "Joshua" now stands in v. 11.[35] This critical reconstruction argues that after Zerubbabel died, his influence waned to such an extent that a zealous scribe replaced his name with "Joshua" in order to enhance the latter's social standing. Mitchell's view runs

---

[27] Cited by Cohen, *Twelve Prophets*, 292.

[28] Meyers and Meyers, *Zechariah 1–8*, 350. See also J. J. Collins, "The Eschatology of Zechariah," in *Knowing the End from the Beginning: The Prophetic, the Apocalyptic and Their Relationships*, ed. L. L. Grabbe and R. D. Haak (London: T. & T. Clark, 2003), 77–81.

[29] Sweeney, *Twelve Prophets*, 630.

[30] תִּהְיֶה.

[31] Unger, *Zechariah*, 112.

[32] Tollington, *Tradition and Innovation*, 166.

[33] Baldwin, *Zechariah*, 133. See J. C. L. Gibson, *Davidson's Introductory Hebrew Grammar-Syntax* (Edinburgh: T. & T. Clark, 1994), § 20 (c). While this usage normally refers to animate ideas, the plural does apply to inanimate ones occasionally, such as תְּרָפִים ("idols").

[34] M. H. Floyd, *Minor Prophets*, 405.

[35] Mitchell, *Zechariah*, 185–86.

counter to the historical assessment of Zerubbabel's prominence, not to mention the highly conservative scribal attitudes toward revising the sacred text.

The crowning of Joshua in v. 11 does not represent his investiture as a high priest since he had already been serving in that office.[36] Placing a crown upon Joshua conferred honor on him for the pivotal role he played in the inauguration of worship during the restoration.[37] While Zech 4:6–10 stresses the heightened role Zerubbabel had in the postexilic community, the crowning of Joshua also emphasized the momentous role the high priest had played in fulfilling the Lord's promises to his people. Beyond the honor accorded to Joshua, the crowning served as a sign of God's resolve to fulfill his promise to send a future leader to his people. Hence, Joshua's crowning prefigured the elevated status of the coming "Branch" who would usher in the Lord's eschatological kingdom.[38]

Furthermore, Joshua's crowning does not signify that he began filling the dual roles of king and priest. Zerubbabel continued to serve his people in the political realm. Consequently, Unger's attempt to style Joshua as a newly appointed priest-king who functioned as a type of Christ, the ultimate priest-king, contradicts the historical situation.[39]

**6:12** Verse 12 prophesies that the "Branch" will come and rebuild the temple (cf. 3:8).[40] From at least the time of the Jewish Targums, Zechariah's "Branch" has been interpreted as a messianic appellation, even though the passage initially addresses Zerubbabel. Since 4:9–10 explicitly states that Zerubbabel will begin and complete the temple of the restoration era, the prophet appears to envision a much broader application than Zerubbabel's labors alone could fulfill.

The temple serves as a place where the Lord meets his people to atone for their sins. Providing the possible background to v. 12, Isaiah associates the ministry of the Lord's "Branch" with the fruitfulness of the land, survivors of a calamity (probably the exile), and cleansing from sin: "In that day the Branch of the LORD will be beautiful and glorious, and the fruit of the land will be the pride and glory of the survivors in Israel. . . . The Lord will wash away the filth of the women of Zion; he will cleanse the bloodstains from Jerusalem" (Isa 4:2,4).

---

[36] Floyd, *Minor Prophets*, 407.

[37] Petitjean mentions the possibility that the crowning of Joshua might signal a political break between Joshua and Zerubbabel (*Proto-Zacharie*, 282–86). The further implication, that the crowning ceremony represents an attempt to mend a rift between the prophetic office represented by Zechariah and the priestly one Joshua fills, proves baseless (see Cohen, *Twelve Prophets*, 293).

[38] Tollington, *Tradition and Innovation*, 168; see W. H. Rose, *Zemah and Zerubbabel: Messianic Expectations in the Early Postexilic Period*, JSOTSup 304 (Sheffield: Sheffield Academic Press, 2000), 159.

[39] Unger, *Zechariah*, 112.

[40] The NIV rendering, "Here is the man," should read more literally, "Behold the man" (הִנֵּה־אִישׁ), and Pilate's similar statement in John 19:5 is an allusion, albeit unwitting.

Jeremiah 23:5–6 also echoes the Isaianic theme of the Lord's Branch:

"The days are coming," declares the LORD,
"when I will raise up to David a righteous Branch,
a King who will reign wisely
  and do what is just and right in the land.
In his days Judah will be saved
  and Israel will live in safety.
This is the name by which he will be called:
  The LORD Our Righteousness" (cf. 33:15–16).

The various passages from Isaiah and Jeremiah merge both royal and priestly offices into the messianism of the Branch.[41] In Zech 3 the Branch's priestly service receives emphasis. Nonetheless, while giving significant prominence to priestly matters (6:11,13–15), chap. 6 also underscores the royal responsibilities. Baldwin summarizes the point of the passage: "His [Zechariah's] hearers had been prepared for the Branch to fulfill priestly and kingly functions and therefore would realize that both Joshua and Zerubbabel contributed to the work of the coming Branch, while neither alone adequately represented him."[42]

Consequently, no contemporary of Zechariah could fully satisfy the sweeping prophecies about the Branch's ministry. On the one hand, the phrase in context does speak of the ministry of Zerubbabel and Joshua. Consequently, it is wrong for Unger to view this text as though it were exclusively messianic, with no application in Zechariah's time.[43] However, in light of the broader messianic application of the Branch concept, it would seem reasonable to claim that the imagery ultimately points to the person of Christ. A typological understanding fits both the immediate and broader canonical contexts well.

Although Meyers and Meyers do not see Zech 6:12 as a prediction about Christ's ministry, they contend that the Branch does not speak of Zerubbabel or any other contemporary of Zechariah.[44] Likewise, they believe that the temple that the Branch will build does not represent the temple built during the restoration.[45] Meyers and Meyers argue that Zechariah's prophecy bears no relation to the events of the prophet's own day, but their view is unconvincing. The prophet's message of encouragement expressed through the affirmation of the ministries of both Zerubbabel and Joshua bore direct application to Zechariah's audience while they embarked on rebuilding the nation. However,

---

[41] See Rose, *Zemah and Zerubbabel*; and Rose, "Messianic Expectations in the Early Post-Exilic Period," *TynBul* 49 (1998): 373–76.

[42] Baldwin, *Zechariah*, 135. See also Joyce G. Baldwin, "Ṣemaḥ as a Technical Term in the Prophets," *VT* 14 (1964): 93–97.

[43] Unger, *Zechariah*, 112.

[44] Meyers and Meyers, *Zechariah 1–8*, 356.

[45] Ibid., 357.

it is noteworthy that Meyers and Meyers conclude that no contemporary of Zechariah fulfilled the scope of the prophecy about the Branch in Zech 6 or in any other passages.

The next phrase in v. 12, *ûmittaḥtāyw yiṣmāḥ* (NIV "he will branch out from his place")[46] is a pun on the name *ṣemaḥ* ("Branch").[47] Using figurative language to express the emergence of the Messiah, Isaiah writes: "He grew up before him like a tender shoot, and like a root out of dry ground" (53:2). The precise significance of the expression "from his place" remains obscure though.

The final phrase in 6:12, *ûbānāh 'et–hêkal YHWH* (NIV "and build the temple of the LORD"),[48] should not be excised from the text on the preconceived notion that it does not fit the passage or that it is a scribal error (cf. v. 13a).[49] Rather, the *waw* consecutive on the verbal form translated "will build" links this verb to the previous verb "he will branch out," demonstrating that the notion of "branching" leads to "building."

**6:13** Verse 13 begins almost precisely the way v. 12 concludes, with the phrase "he will build the temple of the LORD." Many seek to delete the repeated phrase, just as others desire to remove the comparable phrase in v. 12, concluding that dittography (a scribal error in which a text is inadvertently copied twice) explains the reason for the repeated phrase.[50] Others conclude that an editor joined two totally separate oracles, each oracle containing the repeated phrase, with the literary seam falling between v. 12 and v. 13.[51] Such clumsy editing does not accord with the high literary quality of the chapter or of the book as a whole. Rather, the repetition was intentional and functions to emphasize the certainty of the temple's construction and the crucial role the Branch will fill in the rebuilding project.[52]

Moreover, v. 13 begins with the emphatic pronoun "he," indicating that the Branch, not Joshua or Zerubbabel, will ultimately rebuild the temple. The preceding visions lay great emphasis on the role Zerubbabel played in the reconstruction of the temple. Verse 13 dramatically begins by pointing to another figure whose significance would surpass even that of Zerubbabel.

Some suggest that this verse, as well as chap. 3, introduces a diarchy into the political situation in ancient Judah.[53] Verse 13 appears to address Joshua

---

[46] וּמִתַּחְתָּיו יִצְמָח. *HALOT*, 1033–34.

[47] צֶמַח. *HALOT*, 1034.

[48] וּבָנָה אֶת־הֵיכַל יהוה.

[49] Mitchell, *Zechariah*, 189.

[50] See Barthélemy et al., eds., *Preliminary and Interim Report on the Hebrew Old Testament Text Project*, 5 vols. (New York: United Bible Societies, 1979), 5:406.

[51] Petitjean, *Proto-Zacharie*, 289.

[52] B. A. Mastin's study of several of the text critical problems in v. 13 argues that the Masoretic Text is superior to that of the Septuagint ("A Note on Zechariah VI 13," *VT* 26 [1976]: 113–15).

[53] Tollington, *Tradition and Innovation*, 175; Conrad, *Zechariah*, 126. Tollington adds that the diarchic ruler served a short-term objective, enabling the people to cohere as a community and to

the high priest, but it also includes royal motifs not associated with the priesthood. To lessen this tension, several commentators suggest that v. 13 speaks to Joshua and Zerubbabel together. This interpretation yields the following:

> And he (Zerubbabel) shall build the temple,
> and he (Joshua) shall put on splendor,
> and he (Zerubbabel) shall sit and rule upon his throne;
> and he (Joshua) shall be priest upon his throne;
> and a counsel of peace shall be between them.[54]

This innovative approach attempts to solve a pressing problem in the passage: How can a priest and king both sit on the throne? One must take liberties with the text to defend the notion of a diarchy, a concept that neither biblical nor historical sources support. Further, v. 13 does not give any basis for concluding that both Joshua and Zerubbabel are present, with Zechariah addressing each sequentially in v. 13. While the Old Testament does not merge the offices of priest and king, with the exception of Melchizedek (Gen 14:18–20; Ps 110:4), the coalescence of both becomes a prominent theme in the New Testament, fulfilled in the Messiah, Jesus Christ (Heb 4:14–16; 7; 8:1; cf. Rev 20:4–6).

The phrase, "he will be clothed with majesty *[hôd]*," yields questions also.[55] Baldwin suggests that the term *hôd* means "royal honor" as in Ps 45:4 and Dan 11:21.[56] However, the subsequent phrase literally reads, "he will be a priest upon his throne." Hence, Zechariah described a priest sitting in regal splendor on his royal seat. More than any other Old Testament passage, with the exception of Ps 110, Zech 6:13 declares that the coming Davidic Messiah will also fill the role of priest.

Those who conclude that Zechariah spoke to both Joshua and Zerubbabel maintain that the "harmony between the two" here refers to the cooperation of Joshua and Zerubbabel as they fulfill their respective duties. The problem, of course, rests with identifying the antecedent of "the two of *them*" in the Hebrew text. We have already seen that one cannot defend the view that both Zerubbabel and Joshua are present and are both addressed by v. 12. Zechariah predicted a concord between the priestly and royal offices, and both are offices that the Branch will hold.[57]

---

ready themselves for a new age when the Branch would take the reins of the Lord's kingdom. Rose offers compelling arguments against the diarchy view (*Zemah and Zerubbabel*, 169–70). Rose's more important arguments include the absence of evidence supporting an equal position of authority for the royal figure and priest, the lack of mention of either Zerubbabel or Joshua in Ezra 6, and the lack of reference to the high priest in the covenant renewal ceremony in Neh 10.

[54] P. R. Ackroyd, *Zechariah* (London: Nelson, 1962), 649.
[55] הוֹד ("majesty"). *HALOT*, 241.
[56] Baldwin, *Zechariah*, 136.
[57] Unger, *Zechariah*, 114.

**6:14** Once placed in the temple, the crown in v. 11 assumes new significance as a "memorial." The crown commemorated the sacrificial giving of those who contributed silver and gold to fashion it. The crown identified the temple as the seat of royal authority.[58] The diadem also encourages all who see it to remember the Lord's faithfulness in ensuring that all he promised his people had come to fruition.

The identity of those who received the crown evokes questions since the names do not accord with those in v. 10. Tobijah and Jedaiah appear in both lists. However, we find "Heldai" in v. 10, but "Helem" in v. 11. Moreover, v. 10 mentions "Josiah son of Zephaniah" while "Hen son of Zephaniah" emerges in v. 14. One of the simplest solutions suggests that the different names constitute alternate names for the same individual, a practice not unknown in the Old Testament. Thus, Hen, which means "grace" or "gracious one," serves as another name for Josiah, which means "Yahweh heals" or "may Yahweh give."[59] Along the same lines of argument, Helem signifies another form of the name Heldai.[60]

**6:15** "Those who are far away" refers not just to those who still have not returned from the exile but also to the foreign nations. The concept of people who have taken themselves far from God spiritually develops the theme of the Gentiles turning to the Lord, first introduced in 2:11 and continued in 8:22.[61] Moreover, the motif occurs in numerous other passages, including Isa 2:2–4; 56:6–7; and 60:1–7.

The prediction that the nations would submit to the Lord's universal dominion occurs throughout the Old Testament.[62] No passage encompasses the themes in v. 15 more thoroughly than Ps 110:1–2:

> The LORD says to my Lord:
>  "Sit at my right hand
> until I make your enemies
>  a footstool for your feet."
> The LORD will extend your mighty scepter from Zion;
>  you will rule in the midst of your enemies.

---

[58] Floyd, *Minor Prophets*, 407.

[59] Alternatively, A. Demsky argues that the Hebrew לחן refers to the temple official responsible for overseeing the assets of the temple ("The Temple Steward Josiah ben Zephaniah," *IEJ* 31 [1981]: 100–2).

[60] Merrill differs from most in concluding that Heldai and Helem are different individuals (*Zechariah*, 202). On the other hand, Merrill concludes that Josiah and Hen refer to the same person.

[61] Meyers and Meyers note that the meaning of the phrase is subject to alternate interpretations (*Zechariah 1–8*, 364–65). While the beginning of the verse has a universalistic tone, the statement about the Lord's sending the prophet to the people suggests that "those who are far away" speaks of Israelites who remain in exile. The final phrase warning the people to be obedient to the Lord can support either interpretation.

[62] See Merrill, *Zechariah*, 200–1.

The ending of v. 15, "if you diligently obey the LORD your God," appears to quote Deut 28:1, the influential Deuteronomic chapter outlining the blessings and curses awaiting Israelites who choose either to obey or to disobey the Lord. Using emphatic language, Zechariah evokes the memory of everything Deut 28 represents. The passage also echoes the eschatological theme of Hag 2:7 (see also Mic 4:1–2). Further, the prophet's words recall the new covenant in Jer 31:33–34 where the people of God obey their Lord from their hearts.

Thus ends Zechariah's initial prophecies, which began in 1:7, concerning the restoration of worship in the rebuilt temple. Sweeney observes that Zech 6:1–15 "concludes the prophet's vision reports in 1:7–6:15 by pointing to the crowning of the Branch and the building of the Temple as signs of the ultimate restoration of Zion."[63] For millennia, biblical writers and theologians alike have understood the central role Zion will enjoy as the seat of God's eschatological reign. The prospect of the Messiah's rule in Zion moved Isaac Watts to write,

> Come, we that love the Lord, and let our joys be known;
> Join in a song with sweet accord, join in a song with sweet accord,
> And thus surround the throne, and thus surround the throne.
>
> The hill of Zion yields, a thousand sacred sweets,
> Before we reach the heav'nly fields, before we reach the heav'nly fields,
> Or walk the golden streets, or walk the golden streets.
>
> We're marching to Zion, beautiful, beautiful Zion;
> We're marching upward to Zion, the beautiful city of God.[64]

---

[63] Sweeney, *Twelve Prophets*, 623. See M. J. Boda, "Oil, Crowns and Thrones: Prophet, Priest and King in Zechariah 1:7–6:15," *Journal of Hebrew Scriptures* 3 (2001), journal on-line (accessed 29 November 2005; available from http://purl.org/jhs; Internet). Boda discusses the purpose of Zech 1–6, with special attention to the question of Zechariah's agenda in correcting leadership problems in his day and looking forward to the coming Messiah. Boda views Zech 1–6 as an indictment of the priestly tradition, assuring the readers that the Branch will correct priestly excesses.

[64] *The Baptist Hymnal*, # 524.

―――――――― SECTION OUTLINE ――――――――

IV. QUESTIONS ABOUT FASTING AND FUTURE BLESSINGS
(7:1–8:23)
1. A Question about Fasting (7:1–7)
2. A Call to Repentance (7:8–14)
3. Future Blessings for Jerusalem (8:1–23)

## IV. QUESTIONS ABOUT FASTING AND FUTURE BLESSINGS (7:1–8:23)

**Introduction**

Approximately two years had elapsed since Zechariah received the night visions. The construction of the temple proceeded apace. Now, the postexilic community began to face new concerns regarding religious observances. The arrival of a group of exiles returning from Babylon with questions about how to make their own religious preferences harmonize with the expectations of the believers in Jerusalem served as the immediate issue that precipitated the divine oracle. However, the pressing question regarding the observance of fasting in Jerusalem presents only one of the theological uncertainties faced by the newcomers.

**Structure of Zechariah 7–8**

Zechariah 7–8 function as a literary bridge between the night visions and sermons of chaps. 1–6 with their focus on problems facing Zechariah's audience and chaps. 9–14 with their eschatological perspectives.[1] The dating formula in 7:1 differentiates chaps. 7–8 from the night visions in 1:7–6:15. Likewise, the introduction of the significant term *maśśā'* ("burden" or "oracle" but untranslated in NIV) in 9:1 sets chap. 9 apart from the preceding sections of the book. Further, striking literary features within Zech 7–8 delineate these chapters as a separate unit.

First, Zech 7:1–3 and 8:18–23 form an inclusio, binding chaps. 7 and 8 together.[2] Chapter 7 begins with a question posed to the Lord and his prophets.

―――――

[1] M. Boda, "From Fasts to Feasts: The Literary Function of Zechariah 7–8." *CBQ* 65 (2003): 393.

[2] M. Butterworth, *Structure and the Book of Zechariah* (Sheffield: Sheffield Academic Press, 1992), 151.

The reply does not appear until the conclusion of chap. 8 (vv. 18–23).³ Moreover, the distinctive Hebrew expression *lĕḥallôt ʾet–pĕnē YHWH* ("to entreat the LORD") occurs in both Zech 7:2 and 8:21, linking the chapters into a single unit.⁴ The phrase occurs in the Old Testament to convey a petitioner's earnest plea for relief from trying circumstances.

Several have also argued that Zech 7–8 forms a chiastic structure.⁵ Ollenberger delineates the proposed chiastic analysis as follows:

A  Embassy with question about fasting (7:1–3)
  B  God's answer concerning fasting (7:4–6)
    C  Ancestors' misconduct (7:7–12a)
      D  Judgment against the ancestors (7:12b–14)
        E  Exhortation (8:9–13)
      D'  Salvation in the present and future (8:1–8, 14–15)
    C'  The community's conduct (8:16–17)
  B'  God's edict concerning fasting (8:18–19)
A'  Embassy to seek the Lord (8:20–23)⁶

This chiastic analysis has not gained wide acceptance, though. Many have concluded that chaps. 7–8 do not manifest a clear chiastic structure, viewing the analysis as somewhat contrived.⁷ To give but two examples of strained pairings, the relationship between C and C', as well as that between D and D', does not offer particularly compelling reasons for accepting the chiastic interpretation. A more beneficial interpretation eschews chiasm in favor of a more rigorous approach that reads the text more closely.

Clark and Butterworth have devoted significant effort into clarifying the literary organization of chaps. 7 and 8.⁸ Clark produced a refined three-tiered structure for chaps. 7–8, although the most detailed portions of his analysis may prove too ambitious since evidence undergirding the third tier becomes rather tenuous.⁹ Still, Clark's basic structural observations concerning chaps. 7–8 are helpful:

---

³ Ibid., 394.

⁴ לַחֲלוֹת אֶת־פְּנֵי יהוה. *HALOT*, 317; BDB, 318.

⁵ R. B. Chisholm, *Interpreting the Minor Prophets* (Grand Rapids: Eerdmans, 1989), 255; P. J. Scalise, "An Exegesis of Zechariah 7:4–14 In Its Canonical Context," *Faith and Mission* 3 (1986): 60.

⁶ B. C. Ollenberger, "Zechariah," in *The New Interpreters Bible*, ed. L. Keck (Nashville: Abingdon, 1996), 7:790.

⁷ Butterworth, *Structure and the Book of Zechariah*, 163; Boda, "From Fasts to Feasts," 396. The excesses of chiastic interpretations led Boda to pen "Chiasmus in Ubiquity: Symmetrical Mirages in Nehemiah 9," JSOT 71 (1996): 55–70.

⁸ Butterworth, *Structure and the Book of Zechariah*, 151; David J. Clark, "Discourse Structure in Zechariah 7:1–8:23," *BT* 36 (1985): 328–35.

⁹ D. Clark, "Discourse Structure," 329–35.

| Major Divisions | Sub-Divisions | *hyh* *dbr*–YHWH[10] | *kh ʾmr* YHWH ṣbʾwt[11] |
|---|---|---|---|
| Zech 7:1–3 | 7:1–3 | 7:1 | |
| Zech 7:4–7 | 7:4–7 | 7:4 | |
| Zech 7:8–14 | | 7:8 | 7:9 |
| Zech 8:1–17 | 8:1–6 | 8:1 | 8:2, 3, 4, 6 |
| | 8:7–11 | | 8:7, 9 |
| | 8:12–17 | | |
| Zech 8:18–23 | 8:18–23 | 8:18 | 8:19, 20, 23[12] |

As a bridge, Zech 7–8 serves as a conclusion to chaps. 1–6 and an introduction to chaps. 9–14. Chapters 7–8 reflect similar vocabulary and literary style to the previous six chapters of the book. Boda outlines several noteworthy parallels.[13] Zech 1:2–3 and 7:5–6 both begin with sermons addressed to Zechariah's generation before reminding the audience of the experiences faced by prior generations (1:4–6a and 7:7–14).[14] Both sections lay great emphasis on the role of the Lord's prophets, including citations from the works of these prophets (1:4b; 7:9–10). Boda adds the following details that reveal the symmetry between chaps. 1 and 7 and illustrate the concluding role played by chap. 7:

| | | |
|---|---|---|
| Speech to present generation | 1:2–3 | 7:5–6 |
| Description of past generation | 1:4–6a | 7:7–14 |
|    Proclaim (קרא), earlier prophets (הנבאים) הראשנים) messenger formula (כה אמר יהוה צבאות) | 1:4a | 7:7, 9a |
|       Quotation from earlier prophets | 1:4b | 7:7b–10 |
|       Description of former generation's response | 1:4c | 7:11–12 |
|       Description of discipline of God (כה אמר יהוה צבאות) | 1:5–6a | 7:13–14 |
| Focus returns to present generation | 1:6b | 8:14–23[15] |

Zechariah 7–8 also reflects several prominent themes introduced in the preceding chapters of the book. The tidings of all the nations coming to Jerusalem to worship the Lord appear in 2:11; 6:15; 8:3,7–8,21–23. Further, assurances that the temple will be rebuilt figure prominently in both chaps. 1–6 and 7–8 (6:12; 8:3,9). In addition, the prophet exhorted the people to obey the Lord as a prerequisite for blessing (6:15; 7:8–14; 8:16). The Lord's requirement that the nation live righteously in his sight, fully cognizant of their past judgment

---

[10] "The word of the LORD came," היה דבר־יהוה.
[11] "Thus says the LORD of Hosts," כה אמר יהוה צבאות.
[12] Clark, "Discourse Structure," 329–32, 335.
[13] Boda, "From Fasts to Feasts," 402–5.
[14] W. A. M. Beuken, *Haggai-Sacharja 1–8*, (Assen: Van Gorcum, 1967), 88–103.
[15] Boda, "From Fasts to Feasts," 403.

and looking forward to future blessings, represented the people's greatest need in chaps. 7–8. As a glimmer of prosperity appeared before the struggling community, their natural inclination focused on their own daily necessities to the exclusion of more lasting and significant spiritual concerns (Hag 1:4). Zechariah cautioned the nation that she must devote herself completely to the Lord again.

The occasion for the prophetic revelation presents the most noteworthy difference between the night visions and the oracular material in chaps. 7–8. In chaps. 1–6 Zechariah received a message from the Lord, often through God's intermediary, the interpreting angel. However, chaps. 7–8 treat responses to specific questions that the returning exiles faced in their endeavor to live faithfully before the Lord.

The shift between the first person narration in chaps. 1–6 and the third person found in chaps. 7–8 represents another noticeable difference between the two sections of the book. In addition, while previous chapters of Zechariah dwell on the conspicuous roles played by Zerubbabel and Joshua, neither character appears again in chap. 7 or chap. 8 or later in the book. While much of Old Testament scholarship attributes these changes (among others) to the hand of an editor shaping chaps. 7–8 and chaps. 9–14 some time after the prophet Zechariah received the revelation, concrete evidence to corroborate this viewpoint does not exist. Instead, the different genres and the differing aims of the respective sections better explain the differences between chaps. 1–6 and chaps. 7–8.[16]

Looking forward to the latter six chapters of the book of Zechariah, Boda surveys the literary themes in chaps. 7–8 that establish a foundation for Zech 9–14. These motifs include the "Zion tradition, communal cleansing, universalism, and the former prophets."[17] Chapters 7–8 also stress the message of leadership for the nation, a point Zech 9–14 develops much further. Boda concludes, "Zechariah 7–8 balances woe with weal, warning with promise, judgment with salvation, fasts with feasts."[18]

## 1. A Question about Fasting (7:1–7)

**¹In the fourth year of King Darius, the word of the LORD came to Zechariah on the fourth day of the ninth month, the month of Kislev. ²The people of Bethel had sent Sharezer and Regem-Melech, together with their men, to entreat the LORD ³by asking the priests of the house of the LORD Almighty and the prophets, "Should I mourn and fast in the fifth month, as I have done for so many years?"**

---

[16] J. G. Baldwin, *Haggai, Zechariah, Malachi*, TOTC (Downers Grove, IL: InterVarsity, 1972), 141; Rex Mason, *Preaching the Tradition: Homily and Hermeneutics after the Exile* (Cambridge: Cambridge University Press, 1990), 198–205.

[17] Boda, "From Fasts to Feasts," 406.

[18] Ibid.

⁴Then the word of the LORD Almighty came to me: ⁵"Ask all the people of the land and the priests, 'When you fasted and mourned in the fifth and seventh months for the past seventy years, was it really for me that you fasted? ⁶And when you were eating and drinking, were you not just feasting for yourselves? ⁷Are these not the words the LORD proclaimed through the earlier prophets when Jerusalem and its surrounding towns were at rest and prosperous, and the Negev and the western foothills were settled?'"

**7:1** One can date Zechariah's prophecy in v. 1 with remarkable precision. The "fourth day of the ninth month of Kislev" in King Darius' fourth year fell on December 518 BC. Thus, the oracles in chaps. 7 and 8 arrived about two years after Zechariah received the night visions. Further, the oracles in Zech 7–8 preceded the rededication of the temple by two or three years, an event that occurred on March 516 BC, although some place the event a year later.[19] The date in v. 1 plainly marks the time when the Lord delivered the first oracle to Zechariah. The text contradicts the suggestion that the stated date refers to the date when the exiles returned, not to the time of the oracle.[20]

The month Kislev reflects the Babylonian name for the month. Only after Nehemiah introduced the Babylonian names of the months to Israel for official use in about 444 BC did the foreign designations see widespread use. Consequently, many believe that the presence of this supposedly late name reveals an editor's work.[21] However, Zechariah's use of Kislev provides insufficient grounds to attribute the appearance of the term to editorial activity. It is impossible to ascertain when variant names began to emerge in the postexilic era. The prophet had already employed a Persian chronological reference when he dated his prophecy to the "fourth year of *King Darius*." Moreover, the strong Babylonian cultural influences on the entire region undermine any argument that deems Babylonian terms like Kislev as late additions to the text.

Petersen concludes that Zechariah's reference to Darius as "King" specifically indicates that the prophet saw Darius as the legitimate king of Judah, in addition to Persia.[22] Petersen believes that calling Darius "King" demonstrates dissatisfaction with Zerubbabel, emphasizing that the great leader of Judah did not fulfill the prophecies concerning the Branch. Petersen further attributes the phrase "King Darius" to a later redactor who wished to stress to his readers that the historical situation had changed and that the glorious kingdom of which Zechariah had spoken remained unfulfilled. Granted, one would not expect the Old Testament to designate a pagan king ruler over God's chosen people. Yet Petersen's perspective fails to give objective evidence for redactional activity. More telling still, Zech 7:1 never states that Darius was king *over* Judah

---

[19] *ABD*, 6:363.
[20] R. L. Smith, *Micah-Malachi*, WBC (Waco: Word, 1984), 219.
[21] H. G. Mitchell, J. M. P. Smith, and J. A. Bewer, *A Critical and Exegetical Commentary on Haggai, Zechariah, Malachi and Jonah*, ICC (Edinburgh: T. & T. Clark, 1912), 195.
[22] D. L. Petersen, *Haggai and Zechariah 1–8*, OTL (Philadelphia: Westminster, 1984), 282.

in any sense. Quite simply, Zechariah's reference to "King Darius" provides a chronological reference point in a fashion seen often in the Old Testament. The absence of a generally agreed upon calendar as exists in the modern world left little option other than to employ key events in contemporary history as benchmarks of time.

**7:2–3** A cursory survey of translations of v. 2 discloses a surprising variety of renderings. Although the language of the verse appears relatively straightforward, the difficulty revolves around identifying the subject and the object of the verb "sent." The Hebrew word order translated in a literal, sequential fashion reads, "He sent Bethel Sharezer and Regem-Melech and his men." From these words derive three distinctly different translations, each of which results in a significantly different interpretation.

The least plausible understanding involves an emendation in v. 1. Lipinski argues that "Darius" in v. 1 serves as the subject of "sent" in v. 2.[23] In order to make his interpretation viable, however, Lipinski must delete an entire phrase, the formulaic introduction, "the word of the LORD came to Zechariah." Lipinski's deletion thus yields the statement, "King Darius . . . sent Sharezer." He suggests that Darius sent his emissaries to safeguard the responsible stewardship of his contributions toward the reconstruction of the temple. In the end, Lipinski's view fails because he must resort to emending the Hebrew text without any external or internal biblical support for the decision.

A second approach maintains that "Bethel Sharezer" serves as a proper name of a person and functions as the subject of the verb "sent."[24] Hence, this interpretation results in the translation, "Bethel Sharezer sent." Biblical and extra biblical evidence indicates the plausibility of this translation. For instance, Jer 39:3 lists a similar compound personal name, "Nergal Sharezer." Moreover, non-biblical texts reveal several examples of "Bethel" used in compound names.[25] Also, several Aramaic texts from Elephantine include "Bethel" in a compound name.[26]

Importantly, Hyatt cites an Akkadian text from the time of Nabonidus (556–539 BC), the well known Babylonian king who reigned slightly before the time of Zechariah, which reads the Akkadian equivalent of "Bethel Sharezer."[27] Hyatt concludes that the individual mentioned in the Akkadian text might refer to the same individual in Zech 7:2. The cuneiform parallel demonstrates that "Bethel Sharezer" functioned as a proper name in the era. Nonetheless, in the final analysis one cannot prove conclusively that the figure in v. 2 represented

---

[23] E. Lipinski, "Recherches sur le livre de Zacharie," *VT* 20 (1970): 37.

[24] See Baldwin who adopts this view (*Zechariah*, 142).

[25] For an introduction to this evidence, see J. P. Hyatt, "A Neo-Babylonian Parallel to *Bethel-Sar-Eser*, Zech 7.2," *JBL* 56 (1937): 387–94.

[26] See B. Porten, *Archives from Elephantine* (Berkeley: University of California Press, 1968), 169–70, 176 n. 110.

[27] Hyatt, "Neo-Babylonian Parallel," 388–90.

an individual, let alone a prominent individual mentioned in an extra-biblical text.[28]

To buttress her acceptance of the personal name approach, Baldwin adds a further point. The Babylonians razed the temple in Jerusalem on the seventeenth day of the fifth month (2 Kgs 25:8). This was the event commemorated by the fasting in the fifth month. Transposed to the Gregorian calendar, the cataclysmic destruction occurred on August 14, 586 BC.[29] Baldwin suggests that the entourage of religious inquirers must have come from Babylon since they would have arrived some three and a half months after the fast should occur.[30] According to Ezra 7:7–9, it took approximately four months to make the journey from Babylon to Israel. This allowed ample time for a trip to Judah to obtain a response and for the return to Babylon with instructions about how the community should proceed before the next year's fast. Baldwin claims that the timing of the question seems puzzling if the group came from Bethel. However, Baldwin fails to address a telling question. If the religious leaders needed to send a delegation on such a lengthy journey from Babylon to Jerusalem in order to discern whether they should perpetuate a fast, why would the trip begin at the time the fast was scheduled to occur?[31]

The NIV rendering of v. 2, "The *people of* Bethel had sent Sharezer," illustrates a third approach to the question. Although the Hebrew text does not include the word "people,"[32] this interpretation concludes that the inhabitants of Bethel sent a delegation consisting of "Sharezer and Regem-Melech" for clarification of a matter of religious practice.[33]

Located slightly more than ten miles north of Jerusalem, Bethel had long served as a center of worship.[34] For most of these years, Bethel functioned as a center for pagan worship. For instance, 1 Kgs 12:29 discloses that Jeroboam I established a calf worshipping cult in Bethel. Despite her nefarious past, Bethel emerged after the exile as home to 223 faithful worshippers of the Lord (Ezra 2:28). Thus, the second suggestion believes that these faithful ones in Bethel desired a clarification about religious observance that only the

---

[28] E. W. Conrad adopts the view that Bethel Sharezer was an individual (*Zechariah* [Sheffield: Sheffield Academic Press, 1999], 135). Conrad also contends that Zechariah's reference to a person whose name does not include the theophoric element, that is, does not contain the element *Yah* from *Yahweh*, foreshadows the coming of foreign nations to worship the Lord in the rebuilt temple.

[29] E. H. Merrill, *Haggai, Zechariah, Malachi* (Chicago: Moody, 1994), 208.

[30] Baldwin, *Zechariah*, 142.

[31] See Mitchell, *Zechariah*, 196.

[32] "People" in the Old Testament normally translates the Hebrew עַם, which refers to the chosen people, Israel. *HALOT*, 837–39.

[33] M. F. Unger, *Commentary on Zechariah* (Grand Rapids: Zondervan, 1962), 120–21; see M. H. Floyd, *Minor Prophets. Part 2* (Grand Rapids: Eerdmans, 2000), 412; M. A. Sweeney, *The Twelve Prophets, Vol. 2*, Berit Olam (Collegeville, MN: Liturgical Press, 2000), 637.

[34] Floyd's claim that Bethel "refers not to the city, but rather to a god of the same name" (*Minor Prophets*, 421) lacks corroborating evidence.

leadership in the temple could provide.[35] Barker adopts this view and contends that these proper names that evidence strong Babylonian influences reflect the Babylonian birthplace of these individuals.[36]

Of the three approaches, the first suggestion warrants summary dismissal in the face of overwhelming evidence to the contrary. The second view, which takes Bethel Sharezer as the name of an individual, presents certain strengths. The attestation of the cognate word for Bethel Sharezer in Akkadian (a language related to Biblical Hebrew), used as a personal name, supports the personal name interpretation. Nevertheless, the third view, the Bethel view adopted by the NIV, offers the most credible understanding. The existence of Bethel Sharezer in a foreign language, albeit a cognate one, results in a rather weak argument for a similar usage in Zech 7. The simpler and more likely view sees Bethel as the common Old Testament toponym functioning as metonymy for the inhabitants of the city. Similar modern usages illustrate the point. For example, one may hear that "Wall Street remains skeptical," where "Wall Street" is metonymy for the financiers who work in the Wall Street business district.

Verse 2a indicates that "Bethel sent" two parties to entreat the Lord. "Sharezer" serves as one object of the verb "sent" in the sentence. Most assume that "Regem-Melech" represents another proper noun, just as "Sharezer" seems to function. Several names similar to Regem-Melech occur in the Old Testament, such as Nathan Melech (2 Kgs 23:11), Regem (1 Chr 2:47), and Ebed-Melech (Jer 38:7). Further, Gordon lists a Ugaritic parallel in which the bearer of the name served as the king's spokesman.[37] Possibly, Regem-Melech functioned as a royal emissary who came to Jerusalem on official business.[38]

Second Kings 25:8 recounts the Babylonian destruction of the temple on the seventeenth day of the fifth month. This momentous event moved the community to commemorate the tragedy with a season of fasting. After almost 70 years of observance, the people wanted to know if the practice should be continued. Biblical law did not mandate this day of fasting, heightening the need for clarification. The singular verb translated "Should I mourn" represents the question the people voiced collectively.

The pilgrims sought resolution to their question from both priest and prophet. One expects the priest to provide the definitive reply. On the other hand, questioning the prophet appears unusual since the priesthood holds autonomy over religious matters. Presumably, the "prophets" refer to Haggai and Zecha-

---

[35] See F. S. North, "Aaron's Rise in Prestige," *ZAW* 66 (1954): 191–99. North believes that the Septuagint and a Targum reverse the order of the nouns, making Bethel the destination of the inquirers. The text-critical evidence does not support North's conclusion.

[36] K. L. Barker, "Zechariah," EBC, 643.

[37] Baldwin, *Zechariah*, 142–43; C. H. Gordon, *Ugaritic Textbook* (Rome: Pontifical Biblical Press, 1965), 1010, lines 1–2.

[38] See the treatment by Sweeney, *Twelve Prophets*, 638–39.

riah, although 8:9 intimates that other prophets may also have ministered before the Lord during this period.

In conclusion, a group of the Lord's worshippers from Babylon sought an authoritative statement from the religious leadership in Jerusalem regarding the propriety of holding the fast that commemorated the fall of Jerusalem. The question focused on whether the Lord's covenantal people should continue a fast of mourning or whether their perspective should look forward to the promised restoration.[39] The community of the faithful required Jerusalem's blessing before any change in religious practices could take place.[40]

"To entreat the LORD" *(lĕḥallôt 'et–pĕnê YHWH)* means to approach God through prayer or sacrifices seeking rescue from difficult circumstances. The phrase always signifies imploring help from the Lord in times of great need (1 Kgs 13:6). The expression sometimes involves confession of sin (Dan 9:13). One meaning focuses on mollifying the Lord's wrath by offering sacrifice (1 Sam 13:12). The fact that the pilgrims sought an answer to their religious question in Jerusalem indicates that the worship of the Lord and the religious hierarchy serving the temple were both well established by Zechariah's time and were clearly understood to emanate from Jerusalem. The idiom "to entreat the Lord" occurs throughout the Old Testament where various "official representatives" of the Lord and his people entreat God's favor, including Moses (Exod 32:11), the man of God (1 Kgs 13:6), priests (Mal 1:9), kings (1 Sam 13:12; 2 Kgs 13:4; Jer 26:19; 2 Chr 33:12), and the "we" of the community of faith (Dan 9:13). In Ps 119:58 an individual worshipper entreats the Lord.[41]

**7:4–5** In this section the Lord did not reply to the specific question about fasting posed by the entourage from Bethel; a response to this query does not appear until 8:18–23. Rather, God shifted the focus by questioning the sincerity of the people's fasting and responding with a series of rhetorical questions.[42] What had begun as a time of genuine contrition for sin and the suffering that ensues had deteriorated into a mere ritual performed legalistically. As commanded in numerous other passages, God enjoined the people to focus again on the heart-felt repentance that should mark any such commemoration. Barker adds, "They had turned it [the fast] into a time of self-pity for their

---

[39] Y. Hoffman, "The Fasts in the Book of Zechariah and the Fashioning of National Remembrance," in *Judah and the Judeans in the Neo-Babylonian Period*, O. Lipschits and J. Blenkinsopp, ed. (Winona Lake, IN: Eisenbrauns, 2003), 169–218.

[40] A. Cohen, *The Twelve Prophets* (New York: Soncino, 1948), 294.

[41] *TDOT*, 4:408.

[42] The Hebrew term for "people" (עַם הָאָרֶץ, literally, "people of the land") occurs frequently in the Old Testament. While many scholars suggest that the expression refers to the male social and political leaders in Israel, the usage in Zech 7 applies generically to the whole nation. See R. de Vaux, *Ancient Israel* (New York: McGraw-Hill, 1965), 70–72; E. W. Nicholson, "The Meaning of the Expression *'am hā'ārez* in the Old Testament," *JSS* 10 (1965): 59–66; and S. Zeitlin, "The AM HAAREZ: A Study in the Social and Economic Life of the Jews before and after the Destruction of the Second Temple," *JQR* 23 (1933): 45–61.

physical condition, devoid of genuine repentance and moral implications."[43] Verse 5 raises the pointed question of whether the worshippers had truly kept the religious observance for the Lord's sake in light of God's inquiry, "was it really for me?" In contrast, v. 6 offers the real motivation, "was it not really for *yourselves*?" The repetition of the pronoun "yourselves" makes the contrast still stronger. A practice that began in mourning and self denial had degenerated into a religious activity performed merely out of self interest.[44]

In v. 5, the Lord shifted the focus from the specific question about fasting posed by the delegation of religious leaders to the weightier matter of the entire nation's commitment to God. He states, "Ask all the people of the land and the priests." By addressing the priests Zechariah acknowledged the sway that the priests held over the nation. The exhortation to the priests to submit to prophetic authority indicates that Zechariah, along with other prophets, did not see priestly authority as unassailable. God had ordained the Old Testament priesthood to fulfill the established divine law. The prophetic office functioned as a complement to the priests, serving as conduits through whom the Lord instructed his people regarding new circumstances and the sanctioned means of appropriating sacred law.

Verse 5 also expands the scope of the original question. In v. 3 the inquirers asked about a fast observed annually during the fifth month. Verse 5 includes this day of observance and introduces another fast observed in the seventh month. Possibly, the fast in the seventh month marks the assassination of Gedaliah (2 Kgs 25:25; Jer 41:1–3).[45] However, this suggestion remains purely conjectural. Thus, the oracle begins by broadening its circle of concern as the sermon begins to expose the people's deepest motivations for their religious activities.

The phrase "the past seventy years" suggests that the period of the exile had drawn to a close. For a full discussion of the duration of the exile, see the comments on 1:12 above. To summarize those conclusions, one may view the period of 70 years in two distinct, yet compatible, ways. One approach considers the first deportation to Babylon in 605 BC as the *terminus a quo* for the exile, concluding seven decades later in 536/35 BC when the first contingent returned. The second understanding begins the exile at 586 BC and culminates with the reconstruction of the temple in 516 BC. We conclude that Zechariah retains both interpretations, used interchangeably here in chap. 7, as did Jeremiah and other prophets. In other words, the biblical text seems to introduce a deliberate ambiguity in the reckoning of the 70 years. Following the biblical lead, the interpreter should accept both modes of reckoning.[46]

---

[43] Barker, "Zechariah," 644.
[44] Ibid.
[45] Merrill, *Zechariah*, 209; Petersen, *Zechariah 1–8*, 285.
[46] Baldwin, *Zechariah*, 97; Orr, "The Seventy Years of Babylon," *VT* 6 (1956): 306.

**7:6** The Old Testament contains numerous statements affirming the Lord's desire to receive sacrifices that his people offered from a worshipful heart.[47] Zechariah neither supported nor condemned the practice of fasting.[48] The people obtained no simple response to their original question about fasting. The reply the Lord gave them required profound spiritual introspection to obtain the appropriate answer.

At the point of God's desires regarding his people's fasting, Zechariah relied heavily on Isaiah's earlier prophecies. The prophet Isaiah explicitly stated that fasting without righteousness and justice brings no pleasure to the Lord (Isa 1:10–17; 58:1–7). These Isaianic passages parallel the themes in Zech 7 very closely, serving as a theological foundation for Zechariah's teaching. In Isa 1 the Lord states,

> "The multitudes of your sacrifices—
>     what are they to me?" says the LORD. . . .
> "I have no pleasure
>     in the blood of bulls and lambs and goats. . . .
> Stop bringing meaningless offerings!
>     Your incense is detestable to me. . . .
> When you spread out your hands in prayer,
>     I will hide my eyes from you;
> even if you offer many prayers,
>     I will not listen.
> Your hands are full of blood;
>     wash and make yourselves clean. . . .
> Seek justice,
>     encourage the oppressed.
> Defend the cause of the fatherless,
>     plead the case of the widow." (Isa 1:11,13,15–17)

Much later in the book, God states,

> " 'Why have we fasted," they say,
>     "and you have not seen it?
> Why have we humbled ourselves,
>     and you have not noticed?'
> Yet on the day of your fasting, you do as you please
>     and exploit all your workers.
> Your fasting ends in quarreling and strife,
>     and in striking each other with wicked fists.
> You cannot fast as you do today

---

[47] See 1 Sam 15:22–23; Isa 1:11–17; Hos 6:6; Mic 6:6–8; cf. 1 Cor 10:31 for a similar thought.
[48] Scalise, "Exegesis of Zechariah," 61–62.

> and expect your voice to be heard on high.
> Is this the kind of fast I have chosen,
> only a day for a man to humble himself?
> Is it only for bowing one's head like a reed
> and for lying on sackcloth and ashes?
> Is that what you call a fast,
> a day acceptable to the LORD?
> Is not this the kind of fasting I have chosen:
> to loose the chains of injustice
> and untie the cords of the yoke,
> to set the oppressed free
> and break every yoke?" (Isa 58:3–6)

As in Isaiah, also in Zech 7 hypocritical ritual and fasting are juxtaposed with social justice, proving the emptiness of the people's faith. To apply Isaiah's language to the question posed by Zechariah, had fasting enabled the people's "voice to be heard on high"? The emphatic answer to the Lord's rhetorical question was a resounding, No!

Zechariah's companions found themselves accused of false worship before the Lord. This represented a very serious charge in any epoch. However, for a people who had recently emerged from the long exile, which was God's judgment that resulted from the hypocrisy and idolatry of their forefathers, the accusation shocked and frightened the people. The nation recoiled from the prospect of another punishment on the scale of the Babylonian exile.

Verse 6 completes the thought of vv. 4–5 where the Lord asked, "When you fasted . . . was it really for me?" Fasting displeased God when practiced out of a legalistic heart. Moreover, the opposite—feasting—offended God equally when not practiced with genuine spirituality.

In conclusion, the Lord did not condemn fasting. Fasting and other forms of contrition pleased him when they developed the people's spirituality. Consequently, God did not look favorably upon their fasting because it "showed no promise of betterment, being an expression, not of godly sorrow for past offences, but of selfish regret for the loss of their country and their liberty. They pitied themselves, but they had not learned to fear the Lord."[49]

**7:7** Zechariah did not proclaim a new message. Manifesting clear continuity with the earlier prophetic themes, v. 7 declares that what the Lord now reveals simply reiterates the message from God disclosed by the "earlier prophets."[50] As in 1:4, Zechariah assumed that the people possessed a full awareness

---

[49] Mitchell, *Zechariah*, 200.
[50] The "direct object marker" את at the beginning of v. 7 presents syntactical difficulties. The Septuagint resolves the problem by replacing the Hebrew particle with אלה ("these"). Jean Hoftizer ("The Particle את in Classical Hebrew," OtSt 14 [1965]:76–77) concludes that v. 7 continues the thought of v. 6, yielding the translation, "Are you then not these who did eat and drink the words which God has spoken?"

of the former prophets' teachings. The people also understood that if their forefathers had heeded the message of the "earlier prophets" they would now be looking out on a scene of prosperity and habitation, not utter destruction.

Perhaps no portion of the geography of Israel painted a more desolate picture than the "Negev," the southernmost part of the nation. Although utterly desolate today, the Negev once saw a landscape dotted with a significant population during the biblical era. The "western foot lands" provided homes to orchards, producing olives and many other valuable crops. These "foot lands" lay between the Judean hills and the plains of Philistia. The reference to rest and prosperity establishes a foundation on which the Lord will correlate true worship, divine blessing, and social justice in 7:8–14.

Some interpreters debate whether the statement "these words" in v. 7 refers back to the previous context in chap. 7 or to the pericope that follows. Mitchell declares dogmatically that only "careless" exegesis concludes that v. 7 accompanies the preceding section, but he fails to substantiate his claim.[51] The solution lies in understanding the verse's role in the argument of the chapter.

Verse 7 serves as a literary bridge connecting the previous section to the next, and like any effective transition, shares strong affinities with both paragraphs it links. In vv. 1–6 Zechariah declared that the people stood guilty of legalism, failing to worship the Lord with a sincere heart. This same fault marked all of preexilic Judah's sins. Zechariah looked at the despoiled countryside as vindication of the message of the "earlier prophets." The "earlier prophets" wedded sin and judgment, and history had proven them to be true prophets.

Likewise, Zechariah tied postexilic Judah's rebellion against God with the possibility of further judgment should she fail to repent before the Lord. The prophet built on the painful memories of former judgments to admonish the nation that God's wrath would surely fall again if the people chose to ignore God's word. Certainly, chap. 7 does not present Zechariah's first warning to his contemporaries to repent. Chapter 3 also taught that the people shared Joshua's uncleanness. However, the strongest exhortation in the book occurs in 1:2–3 when Zechariah proclaimed, "The LORD was very angry with your forefathers. Therefore tell the people: 'Return to me,' declares the LORD Almighty, 'and I will return to you.'"

Thus, v. 7 concludes vv. 1–6 and also introduces the remainder of the chapter that pointedly instructs the nation to repent. Jeremiah 22:21 declares, "I warned you when you felt secure, but you said, 'I will not listen.'" Zechariah inverted Jeremiah's message. Now that the people experienced overwhelming insecurity, he pled with his flock to heed God's word and turn again to their Lord with a whole heart.

---

[51] Mitchell, *Zechariah*, 200.

## 2. A Call to Repentance (7:8–14)

⁸And the word of the LORD came again to Zechariah: ⁹"This is what the LORD Almighty says: 'Administer true justice; show mercy and compassion to one another. ¹⁰Do not oppress the widow or the fatherless, the alien or the poor. In your hearts do not think evil of each other.'
¹¹"But they refused to pay attention; stubbornly they turned their backs and stopped up their ears. ¹²They made their hearts as hard as flint and would not listen to the law or to the words that the LORD Almighty had sent by his Spirit through the earlier prophets. So the LORD Almighty was very angry.
¹³"'When I called, they did not listen; so when they called, I would not listen,' says the LORD Almighty. ¹⁴'I scattered them with a whirlwind among all the nations, where they were strangers. The land was left so desolate behind them that no one could come or go. This is how they made the pleasant land desolate.'"

**7:8** Baldwin objects to the placement of v. 8, contending that the verse breaks the flow of the passage and must rest in its present location due to an editorial insertion. The problem for Baldwin is the location of the phrase, "the word of the LORD came again to Zechariah," in the middle of the oracle.[52] However, Baldwin's concern fails to account for the frequency with which prophetic oracles repeat the Hebrew expression, "the word of the LORD came to" *(wayĕhî dĕbar–YHWH ʾel–),* one of the common prophetic affirmations that their message came from the Lord himself.[53] While numerous prophetic texts illustrate the same point, a cursory review of Amos 1 with the oft-mentioned statements, "This is what the LORD says" and "says the LORD," refutes the notion that the placement of the phrase in the middle of an oracle indicates editorial activity.

**7:9–10** These verses directly quote the Lord's prescription for true righteousness. Echoing themes that occur frequently in the prophets, God commanded the people to focus less on fasting and more on "justice, mercy, compassion, and not oppressing" the downtrodden. Verse 9 presents two positive commands, balanced by two negative instructions in v. 10. The Lord draws from some of the richest theological vocabulary when delivering his instructions.

Eichrodt states that the Old Testament never views "justice" *(mišpāṭ)* as an abstract or impersonal notion. Instead, justice denotes the rights and duties each party possesses. These privileges arise from the shared covenant the Lord made with his people. Accordingly, everyone has his own special *mišpāṭ*.[54] The task of righteousness requires all to render consistently this justice and the ethical claims that *mišpāṭ* demands. Thus, the Lord intended for his righteous-

---

[52] Baldwin, *Zechariah*, 145. See also Meyers and Meyers, *Haggai, Zechariah 1–8* (Garden City, NY: Doubleday, 1987), 398.
[53] וַיְהִי דְּבַר־יהוה אֶל־.
[54] מִשְׁפָּט. *HALOT*, 651–52.

ness to extend to all in order to safeguard the wellbeing of those united into one community under divine law.[55]

The first positive command, "administer true justice" *(mišpaṭ ʾemet šĕpōṭû)*,[56] evokes a typical prophetic message concerning the Lord's profound concern with justice for all of his people.[57] This theme receives its first exposition in Exod 18:19–23 where God ordered Moses to render true decisions, and in so doing, to "show them the way to live." On a deeper level, the Lord himself models what godly ethics are among his people. No passage states this more plainly than Lev 19:2, "Be holy because I, the LORD your God, am holy." Thus, the people bear the responsibility to live justly as their God epitomizes justice. Amos 5:24 teaches, "But let *justice* roll on like a river, righteousness like a never-failing stream!"

Likewise, Jer 22:3 states, "This is what the LORD says: Do what is just and right." Jer 7:5–7 also illustrates Zechariah's point well:

> If you really change your ways and your actions and deal with each other justly, if you do not oppress the alien, the fatherless or the widow and do not shed innocent blood in this place, and if you do not follow other gods to your own harm, then I will let you live in this place, in the land I gave your forefathers for ever and ever.

Somewhat surprisingly, Zechariah described the justice God requires as *"true* justice."[58] Zechariah placed the phrase "true justice" in an emphatic position, preceding the verb, in order to stress its importance. While all justice is "true"—that is, there could not exist such a thing as "untrue justice"—the word for "true" *(ʾemet)* occurs often in the Old Testament to describe the character of the Lord (Exod 34:5–7; Ps 86:15; 2 Tim 2:13).[59] However, "true" does not reflect the proper sense of the word in v. 8.

The word *ʾemet* can express the ideas of "reliability," "permanence," "truth," and "faithfulness"; the notion of faithfulness best captures the sense in this passage.[60] God's faithfulness reflects his consistent nature on which humanity may confidently rely (Ps 146:6). Furthermore, the inclusion of the word "faithfulness" evokes all that the covenant with the Lord represents, enjoining Judah to treat her neighbor as she has been treated by God (cf. Col 3:13). Faithfulness sometimes appears to function as a technical term characterizing the legal obligations each party has to the covenant.

---

[55] W. Eichrodt, *Theology of the Old Testament,* trans. J. A. Baker (Philadelphia: Westminster, 1961), 1:241.
[56] מִשְׁפַּט אֱמֶת שְׁפֹטוּ.
[57] *TDOT*, 1:310–15.
[58] אֱמֶת. *HALOT*, 68–69.
[59] *Theological Dictionary of Old Testament Theology and Exegesis*, 1:428–29.
[60] *HALOT*, 68–69.

On the human level, the Lord demands that Judah must always show faithfulness to her neighbor because doing so reflects the nature of God himself (Zech 8:16). Furthermore, the Lord requires faithfulness or consistency in the administration of justice (Ezek 18:8), in giving witness (Prov 14:25), and in the king's reign (Prov 29:14). Proverbs 23:23 encourages the faithful to pursue faithfulness as one would the most prized of possessions. A failure to practice faithfulness represents one of the Lord's most frequent complaints against his people. Jeremiah decried the people saying, "Friend deceives friend, and no one speaks the *truth*" (4:5). Hosea continued, "There is no *faithfulness,* no love, no acknowledgement of God in the land" (4:1).

The word that the NIV translates "administer" means "to judge." In v. 9, however, the term does not mean to hand down judicial decisions, for God gives the command to those who do not have the authority to issue legal determinations. Rather, the exhortation requires every inhabitant of Judah to promote social harmony, respect, and judgment throughout society.

Verse 9 also contains the second positive mandate, "show mercy," conveying another obligation the Lord's people must fulfill.[61] Without doubt, the first Hebrew term *(ḥesed)*, which the NIV translates "show mercy," stands as one of the most important theological words meaning "grace" in the Old Testament.[62] Notoriously difficult to translate, no English translation can capture the breadth of the word's connotations and denotations. The word communicates the idea of "loyalty" or "faithfulness" to fulfill an obligation to someone with whom one has a relationship. These relationships include marriage (Gen 20:13), friends (1 Sam 20:15), and associates (2 Sam 10:2).[63] Hence, the Bible ascribes "loyalty" to a person, never to a concept. Theologically, the word *ḥesed* conveys the very "essence of the covenant relationship."[64] The Hebrew Bible uses the term *ḥesed* frequently to characterize the ideal both in human relationships as well as the relationship between the pious and the Lord.

God emphasized the covenant he made with his people by first demonstrating his *ḥesed* to his people (Ruth 2:20; 2 Sam 7:15). While many modern translations render the word "mercy," the result of God's faithfulness yields much more than mercy toward his loved ones. Forgiveness (Exod 34:6–7), blessing (Ps 107:8), protection (Ps 44:26), and general kindness (Gen 24:12) represent an abbreviated list of the favors God's faithfulness bestows on Judah.

Like their God who redeems them, loyalty represents the proper way individuals sharing a relationship should treat one another, although *ḥesed* does not establish the relationship itself. Loyalty demands mutuality, like that also

---

[61] חֶסֶד. *HALOT*, 336–37.
[62] *TDOT*, 2:44–64.
[63] Baldwin, *Zechariah*, 146.
[64] N. Glueck, *Ḥesed in the Bible*, trans. A. Gottschalk (New York: KTAV, 1975), 55. See also the helpful study by C. F. Whitley, "The Semantic Range of *Ḥesed*," *Bib* 62 (1981): 519–26.

implied in the notion of "relationship" itself, in order that loyalty may continue.[65]

God requires his people to manifest loyalty to each other. In answer to the question in Mic 6:6 about what the Lord desires his servants to bring to him in worship, God gave the following reply in v. 8:

> He has showed you, O man, what is good.
> And what does the LORD require of you?
> To act justly and to love mercy *(ḥesed)*
> and to walk humbly with your God.

Thus, Mic 6:6–8, like Hos 12:6–7 and Zech 7:9, requires humble and faithful conduct from an Israelite toward his neighbor.[66]

The command for mercy is half of a two-part obligation, "show mercy *and compassion*." Like the Hebrew word for "mercy," the word for "compassion" *(reḥem)* also evokes strong connotations.[67] Related etymologically to the Hebrew word for "womb," *reḥem* expresses tenderness toward another like a mother manifests gentle, devoted feelings toward the fruit of her womb. Theologically, *reḥem* signifies "something that goes beyond what ought to be given."[68] In this spirit, Jacob sent Benjamin and his other sons back to Joseph with the prayer that "God Almighty will grant you mercy before the man" (Gen 43:14). Speaking of the Lord, Exod 34:6–7 portrays God as, "The LORD, the LORD, the *compassionate* and gracious God, slow to anger, abounding in love and faithfulness, maintaining love to thousands, and forgiving wickedness, rebellion and sin." Thus, the Lord charges the community to treat each other with this same spirit of compassion.

Verse 10 mirrors the two positive admonitions in v. 9 with two requirements stated in the negative. As the first requirement, Zechariah warned his audience never to "oppress" a fellow Israelite who might not enjoy equal social protection, such as a widow or an orphan.[69] This was not intended to limit God's admonition to widows and orphans. Rather, these groups represent everyone who does not have a defender. The Mosaic law governs the way these constituencies should be treated (Exod 22:22; 23:6–9; Lev 19:15–18; Deut 10:18–19; 24:14). The theme of protecting the vulnerable in society occurs often in the prophets as well (see Isa 1:17; Jer 7:6; Amos 2:6–7; 4:1; 5:11–12; 8:4).

The prophets had good reason to focus so often on the oppression of the downcast in their communities. When a society faces caring for those who are

---

[65] K. D. Sakenfeld, *Faithfulness in Action: Loyalty in Biblical Perspective* (Philadelphia: Fortress, 1985), 16–17. This helpful study includes a revision of Sakenfeld's Harvard dissertation.

[66] *TDOT*, 5:61.

[67] רַחֲמִים. *HALOT*, 1218–19.

[68] *Theological Dictionary of Old Testament Theology and Exegesis*, 3:1094.

[69] F. C. Fensham, "Widow, Orphan and the Poor in Ancient Near Eastern Legal and Wisdom Literature," *JNES* 21 (1962): 129–39.

perceived to be unable to contribute to their economic well being, that culture's spirituality quickly manifests itself. As the old political maxim states, "A true measure of any society is the way it treats those who cannot protect themselves."[70] Sadly, Judah's sinfulness and her faithlessness to the Lord's covenant with her resulted in scandalous oppression of the needy throughout the nation's history. This insensitivity grieved the Lord and deteriorated Judah's society from within. Irenaeus expressed a similar concern, worried about the church's inclination to follow Judah's negative example. Irenaeus cited Zech 7, admonishing every Christian to "shun evil and do good" (Ps 34:12–14) by caring for the needy.[71] Gowan continues the point: "Then it is up to 'the righteous' in that society to find ways, institutional or otherwise, to correct that which does not measure up to the Old Testament vision of a people where the widow, orphan, immigrant, and their counterparts do not have to cry out to the Lord because of those who afflict them."[72]

Verse 10 concludes with the sweeping admonition, "do not think evil of one another," the second negative mandate Zechariah delivered. This phrase encompasses each of the preceding commands, much like Matt 22:36–39 offers an insightful commentary on the instructions God had given in the Old Testament:

> "Teacher, which is the greatest commandment in the Law?"
>
> Jesus replied: " 'Love the Lord your God with all your heart and with all your soul and with all your mind.' This is the first and greatest commandment. And the second is like it: 'Love your neighbor as yourself.' All the Law and the Prophets hang on these two commandments."[73]

**7:11–12** This portion of chap. 7 employs the spiritual failures of preexilic Israel as an example that cautioned Zechariah's contemporaries about their own spiritual condition. Specifically, the same fate might happen to them if they chose the path of rebellion their fathers followed. The familiar cycle of disregarding God's message, rebellion, warning, and judgment characterized both the preexilic and postexilic communities. Consequently, Judah in the sixth century BC manifested the same sins as her fathers. The unsettling reminders given in vv. 11–12 applied to Zechariah's community as well as to their ancestors.

Despite receiving a command from the Most High and enjoying his faithfulness for generations, the nation consistently chose to rebel against God. A mere glance at their surroundings would confirm to Judah that the Lord treats

---

[70] D. E. Gowan, "Wealth and Poverty in the Old Testament," *Int* 41 (1987): 341–53; W. C. Kaiser, Jr., *Toward Old Testament Ethics* (Grand Rapids: Zondervan, 1983), 108–9, 161–62.

[71] Irenaeus, *Contre les Hérésies*, 4.17.3 (SC 100:586–89).

[72] Gowan, "Wealth and Poverty," 353.

[73] See Conrad, *Zechariah*, 139.

sin seriously. Clearly, Zechariah's generation would suffer the same fate if they continued in their transgressions.

Zechariah employed three metaphors to illustrate the nation's iniquitous response to their God. The first figure of speech, "they turned their backs" *(wayyittĕnû kātēp sōrāret)*, appears also in Neh 9:29.[74] Literally, "they presented a stubborn shoulder." Nehemiah pairs this phrase with "they stiffened their necks" *(ʿorpām hiqšû)*, recalling Deut 9:6 where Moses rebuked Israel for being "a stiff-necked people" *(ʿam–qĕšēh–ʿōrep*; see also Ezek 3:8–9).[75] For an agrarian society, few images more effectively communicate uselessness than the picture of an obdurate ox refusing to submit to the yoke. Likewise, God deemed sinful Israel profitless to himself and to her neighbors when she resisted the purpose for which the Lord had created her.

The second figure, "stopped up their ears" *(wĕʾoznêhem hikbîdû miššĕmōaʿ)*, graphically describes Judah's recalcitrance.[76] Isa 6:10 expresses a similar idiom, although in Isaiah the dulled ears result from divine judgment: "Make the heart of this people calloused; make their ears dull and close their eyes."[77] Although some day his law will be written on the hearts of his people (Jer 31:33), Zechariah's audience would not even let God's word get past their ears.

The final figure of speech Zechariah employed pictures tempered hearts whose hardness approaches that of flint *(wĕlibbām śāmû šāmîr)*.[78] Ezek 3:9 describes a similar state of spiritual intransigence using a similar metaphor: "I will make your forehead like the hardest stone, harder than flint." Since the Old Testament routinely focuses on the group, not the individual, the word "heart" *(lēb)* often focuses on the collective heart of the group (see Gen 42:28). The Old Testament contains three opposing idioms that clearly contrast with the hard heart or the heart of flint.[79] First, Pss 34:19; 51:19 speak of the "broken of heart" *(lēb nišbār)*.[80] Second, numerous passages (see Deut 10:16; 30:6) describe the obedient heart as the "circumcised heart" *(ʿorlat lēb)*.[81] Third, Ezek 36:26 declares, "I will give you a new heart *[lēb ḥādāš]* and put a new spirit in you; I will remove from you your heart of stone *[lēb hāʾeben]* and give you a heart of flesh *[lēb bāśār]*."[82]

The nation had rebelled against every expression of divine authority. Judah rejected God's law, the Mosaic legislation given to mold the nation into a testimony of God's righteousness to the watching world. The people spurned the

---

[74] וַיִּתְּנוּ כָתֵף סֹרָרֶת.

[75] עַם־קְשֵׁה־עֹרֶף.

[76] וְאָזְנֵיהֶם הִכְבִּידוּ מִשְּׁמוֹעַ.

[77] See the discussion of intertextuality in the Introduction; see also Sweeney, *Twelve Prophets*, 644.

[78] וְלִבָּם שָׂמוּ שָׁמִיר. *HALOT*, 1562–63.

[79] *TWOT*, 2:640–41. *TDOT*, 7:399–437, especially 421–30.

[80] לֵב נִשְׁבָּר. *HALOT*, 513–15, 1403–4.

[81] עָרְלַת לֵב. *HALOT*, 886.

[82] לֵב חָדָשׁ/לֵב הָאֶבֶן/לֵב בָּשָׂר. *HALOT*, 294, 7–8, 164, respectively.

Lord's word personally delivered by the earlier prophets. Israel also rebuffed the Spirit of the Lord as he spoke through the prophets. God's Spirit "instructed" (Neh 9:20) and "admonished" the people through the prophets (Neh 9:30). Second Peter 1:21 continues this theme: "For prophecy never had its origin in the will of man, but men spoke from God as they were carried along by the Holy Spirit."

Predictably, the Lord's response to Judah's insolence reflected intense anger, just as 1:7 describes. Sadly, the Old Testament tells the repeated story of Israel's sin and the consequent judgment she suffered. From Horeb, to Kadesh, to Jerusalem, Israel rebelled, always with the same outcome of divine judgment. The reader might consider disparaging Israel for her waywardness, until realizing that her behavior mirrored all humanity's consistent attitude toward God.

**7:13–14** Verse 13 parallels 1:3, which states, "'Return to me,' declares the LORD Almighty, 'and I will return to you.'" In 7:13a the NIV reads "I called," following only the Syriac version, striving to harmonize this verb with "I would not listen" in 13b. Both the weak textual support for "I called" and the frequent shifts of person in Old Testament narrative mitigate against accepting the variant. The Masoretic Text's "he called" should be retained. Baldwin explains the shift in person in the Hebrew text: "The prophet has been using the third person in the previous verses, and he continues to do so until suddenly he finds himself using the very words of the Lord, so vivid is the message in his mind."[83]

The verb "scatter" describes the Lord's judgment on Israel elsewhere in the Old Testament (Deut 28:45–52; Prov 1:27; Isa 40:24; Hos 4:19).[84] God would scatter Judah to Babylon, to Egypt, and beyond if his people rejected the Lord's instruction. Zechariah drew on the metaphor of a blowing wind or a whirlwind that would scatter God's people far from the home God intended for her to inhabit.

Verse 14 ends on a melancholy note. The people's sin resulted in the scattering of the people and the desolation that befell "the pleasant land" promised to Abraham and all of his descendants. Jeremiah 3:19 employs the same idiom when referring to the land of Israel. The land that God created "flowing with milk and honey" (Exod 3:8,17; 13:5; Num 13:27; Deut 6:3; Josh 5:6) lay ruined because of Judah's sin.

Zechariah has yet to respond to the initial query about fasting, a reply that will come at the end of chap. 8. Instead of dealing with a superficial question, the prophet turned to the heart of the nation's spiritual condition. Clearly, Judah found it easier to mourn her losses stemming from the exile and the

---

[83] Baldwin, *Zechariah*, 148.
[84] וָאֲסָעֲרֵם. *HALOT*, 762.

ensuing deprivations than to repent and express sorrow over their sinful hearts before the Lord.

The chapter concludes far from where it began. The pilgrims came from a distance seeking clarification on a relatively minor religious matter. To their surprise, they did not initially receive an answer to the question they posed. Instead, the leaders and the nation they represented suffered a brutally frank accusation concerning their legalistic, sinful attitudes toward the Lord and his requirements for their hearts and lives. Implicit in God's indictment was the threat that what had happened to the preexilic community would occur again in the postexilic epoch if the people of the covenant refused to repent.[85] In Zech 1–6 God offered repeated promises of blessing, encouraging the nation while they struggled to rebuild. However, the prophet cautioned that God's assurances of blessing ultimately rested solely on their obedience. The Lord's encouragement in the night visions, as in the vision of the surveyor in chap. 2, does not stand alone. Blessing resulted from obedience as the full light of the warning texts illumines. Baldwin summarizes the chapter's emphasis:

> No mention of the fast-days is made in the sermon, but Zechariah has gone to the heart of the problem. It was easy to spend fast-days mourning their losses, but harder to face up to God's continuing demands. Were they any more prepared than their fathers to work out in everyday life the spirit of God's law? The purpose of fast-days was to give them renewed incentive to do so through renewed experience of confession, forgiveness and future hope.[86]

Deut 8:7–10 reminds us of how the Lord desires his nation's land to appear:

> For the LORD your God is bringing you into a good land—a land with streams and pools of water, with springs flowing in the valleys and hills; a land with wheat and barley, vines and fig trees, pomegranates, olive oil and honey; a land where bread will not be scarce and you will lack nothing; a land where the rocks are iron and you can dig copper out of the hills. When you have eaten and are satisfied, praise the LORD your God for the good land he has given you.

The desolation lying before Zechariah and his contemporaries resulted from the disobedience of postexilic Judah's forefathers. Should the present generation fail to repent from their sins and turn to the Lord with a whole heart, they

---

[85] This interpretation obviously understands chap. 7 both as a reminder of past events as well as a pointed warning of what the future might hold for the nation if they did not live righteously. Petersen's suggestion that this passage of woe stands here solely as a transition for the prophecy of weal in chap. 8 fails to recognize the conditional nature of God's promises or the depths of the Lord's anger over Judah's sin (*Zechariah 1–8*, 296).

[86] Baldwin, *Zechariah*, 148.

too would effect devastation on the land. The pleasant land described in Deut 8 would be nothing more than a fleeting memory.

In the end, Zech 7 addresses true worship and the natural consequences that result when God's people worship the Lord. Chapter 7 also portrays the painful effects for Judah when spurning God's word. Sounding much like Hosea or Amos, Zechariah linked true worship with justice and mercy that every genuine believer in the Lord should faithfully extend to others, particularly the downtrodden (7:8–10). Christian Witt captured these themes in his hymn, "O My Soul, Bless God the Father":

> O my soul, bless God the Father;
> All within me bless His name;
> Bless the Father, and forget not
> All His mercies to proclaim.
>
> As it was without beginning,
> So it lasts without an end;
> To the children's children ever
> Shall His righteousness extend.
>
> Unto such as keep His cov'nant
> And are steadfast in His way;
> Unto those who still remember
> His commandments, and obey.[87]

### 3. Future Blessings for Jerusalem (8:1–23)

¹Again the word of the LORD Almighty came to me. ²This is what the LORD Almighty says: "I am very jealous for Zion; I am burning with jealousy for her."

³This is what the LORD says: "I will return to Zion and dwell in Jerusalem. Then Jerusalem will be called the City of Truth, and the mountain of the LORD Almighty will be called the Holy Mountain."

⁴This is what the LORD Almighty says: "Once again men and women of ripe old age will sit in the streets of Jerusalem, each with cane in hand because of his age. ⁵The city streets will be filled with boys and girls playing there."

⁶This is what the LORD Almighty says: "It may seem marvelous to the remnant of this people at that time, but will it seem marvelous to me?" declares the LORD Almighty.

⁷This is what the LORD Almighty says: "I will save my people from the countries of the east and the west. ⁸I will bring them back to live in Jerusalem; they will be my people, and I will be faithful and righteous to them as their God."

⁹This is what the LORD Almighty says: "You who now hear these words spoken by the prophets who were there when the foundation was laid for the house of the LORD Almighty, let your hands be strong so that the temple may be built. ¹⁰Before

---

[87] *The Baptist Hymnal*, # 21.

that time there were no wages for man or beast. No one could go about his business safely because of his enemy, for I had turned every man against his neighbor. ¹¹But now I will not deal with the remnant of this people as I did in the past," declares the LORD Almighty.

¹²"The seed will grow well, the vine will yield its fruit, the ground will produce its crops, and the heavens will drop their dew. I will give all these things as an inheritance to the remnant of this people. ¹³As you have been an object of cursing among the nations, O Judah and Israel, so will I save you, and you will be a blessing. Do not be afraid, but let your hands be strong."

¹⁴This is what the LORD Almighty says: "Just as I had determined to bring disaster upon you and showed no pity when your fathers angered me," says the LORD Almighty, ¹⁵"so now I have determined to do good again to Jerusalem and Judah. Do not be afraid. ¹⁶These are the things you are to do: Speak the truth to each other, and render true and sound judgment in your courts; ¹⁷do not plot evil against your neighbor, and do not love to swear falsely. I hate all this," declares the Lord.

¹⁸Again the word of the LORD Almighty came to me. ¹⁹This is what the LORD Almighty says: "The fasts of the fourth, fifth, seventh and tenth months will become joyful and glad occasions and happy festivals for Judah. Therefore love truth and peace."

²⁰This is what the LORD Almighty says: "Many peoples and the inhabitants of many cities will yet come, ²¹and the inhabitants of one city will go to another and say, 'Let us go at once to entreat the LORD and seek the LORD Almighty. I myself am going.' ²²And many peoples and powerful nations will come to Jerusalem to seek the LORD Almighty and to entreat him."

²³This is what the LORD Almighty says: "In those days ten men from all languages and nations will take firm hold of one Jew by the hem of his robe and say, 'Let us go with you, because we have heard that God is with you.'"

## Introduction

Zechariah 7–8 forms a literary unit in which chap. 7 offers a negative response to the question about fasting and an even more pessimistic view of Judah's present spirituality than Zechariah had offered up to this point in the book. Chapter 8 balances the harsh tone of chap. 7 with emphatic assurances about God's certain blessings for Zion's future. Zechariah intended for his audience to balance the message of both chapters in order to achieve a proper theological balance between the poles of judgment and promise.[88]

The tension between sin and blessing pervades the entire Old Testament, dating back at least as far as the differing emphases of the Abrahamic covenant

---

[88] Petersen declares that the relationship between chaps. 7 and 8 simply amounts to that of the past to the future (*Zechariah 1–8*, 297–98). In other words, chap. 7 simply describes what happened in the past, whereas chap. 8 envisions the future. But this view fails to reckon with the exhortations to obey God in chap. 7 that Zechariah gave directly to his community, surely looking forward to the future.

and the Mosaic covenant. The Old Testament gives frequent assurances both of the Lord's unchanging faithfulness to his covenant and to Israel with whom he first forged the covenant (Deut 28:1–14). These pledges of God's blessing permeate the book of Zechariah as well (see 1:7–21; 2:1–13; 3:1–5,8–10; 4:1–14; 6:1–15; 8:1–23; 9:1–11:3; 12:1–9; 13:1–14:21). In contrast, the Old Testament often warns Judah that God's judgment necessarily follows the people's unrepentant sin (Deut 28:15–68). This theme of judgment for habitual sin also appears prominently in Zechariah's prophecy (see 1:2–6; 3:7; 5:1–11; 7:1–14).

Like other theological antinomies such as divine sovereignty and human freedom or election and free will, Old Testament theology demands that the preservation of the tension between judgment and blessing must be maintained to preserve a balance. Emphases that stress one theological maxim to the exclusion of the other fail to account for the theological balance Zechariah maintained.[89] The Lord's "burning jealousy" (8:2b) for Zion[90] not only constrains him to chastise Judah for her disobedience, but also compels him to protect her and to provide her a glorious future.

## Literary Structure

Meyers and Meyers suggest that chap. 8 comprises seven completely separate oracles that an editor has woven together, yielding the following analysis:

| | |
|---|---|
| 8:2 | Oracle 1 |
| 8:3 | Oracle 2 |
| 8:4–5 | Oracle 3 |
| 8:6 | Oracle 4 |
| 8:7–8 | Oracle 5 |
| 8:9–13 | Oracle 6 |
| 8:14–15 | Oracle 7 |
| 8:16–17 | Coda[91] |

Meyers and Meyers's approach isolates oracles primarily based on the occurrence of the phrase, "This is what the LORD Almighty says" *(kōh ʾāmar YHWH ṣĕbāʾôt)*.[92] However, this criterion proves unconvincing because the

---

[89] For instance, R. L. Smith stresses blessing, noting that most prophetic books conclude with a message of hope (*Micah–Malachi*, 229). Smith suggests that chap. 8 likely ended Zechariah's prophecy on a hopeful note, seeing Zech 9–14 as a separate work from a different author.

[90] קִנֵּאתִי לְצִיּוֹן קִנְאָה גְדוֹלָה וְחֵמָה גְדוֹלָה קִנֵּאתִי לָהּ. *HALOT*, 1109–10, 326. See also Zech 1:14 for the similar expression, "I am very jealous for Jerusalem." The cognate accusative construction functions to emphasize the Lord's jealousy.

[91] Meyers and Meyers, *Zechariah 1–8*, 428–29. Beuken views chap. 8 somewhat similarly (*Sacharja 1–8*, 156–83). Beuken sees vv. 1–6 as a separate oracle, vv. 7–8 as a late editorial addition, and vv. 9–13 as a Levitical sermon. Moreover, Beuken understands vv. 9–13 and vv. 14–15 to be separate oracles with different origins.

[92] כֹּה אָמַר יְהוָה צְבָאוֹת.

Old Testament prophets so frequently punctuated their writings with multiple expressions of divine inspiration for their oracles. For example, Jeremiah employs the same idiom 157 times and Ezekiel 125 times.[93] The prophets adopted several idioms to convey the point of divine authority for their sermons, including the phrase *kōh ʾāmar YHWH* ("thus says the LORD"). Like his fellow prophets, Zechariah frequently employed the phrase *kōh ʾāmar YHWH* in this chapter, repeatedly affirming the divine origin and authority of his messages for Judah.

Methodologically speaking, form criticism fails to provide adequate evidence for assigning each occurrence of the phrase to a separate oracle. For instance, v. 19 begins with the same introductory formula, *kōh ʾāmar YHWH*. However, v. 19 immediately follows the similar phrase in v. 18 that introduces the larger section of chap. 8. It would seem that the presence of the second formula within a section of the chapter mitigates against using this prophetic formula to distinguish separate oracles. Moreover, chap. 8 stands as a carefully shaped literary whole, not an anthology of seven or more discrete oracles, most of which do not exceed one or two verses in length, woven together by an undetermined editor. Hence, the repetition of the phrase *kōh ʾāmar YHWH* in vv. 18–19 demonstrates that the expression has rhetorical and theological value, but does not always isolate literary units. Surely then, one cannot use the formulaic expression alone to isolate separate sermons in the broader context.[94]

Furthermore, one wonders how meaningful or appropriate it is to designate one or two verses as a sermon like Meyers and Meyers do. Although still somewhat tenuous, Baldwin's suggestion that chap. 8 preserves numerous "texts" from Zechariah's sermons fits the evidence better.[95] The literary cohesion of chap. 8 mitigates against analyses that tend to atomize the passage.

Finally, the divine epithet "LORD Almighty" *(YHWH ṣĕbāʾôt)* occurs 17 times in chap. 8, certainly one of the most notable features of Zechariah 8.[96] This divine name, sometimes translated "LORD of hosts" or "LORD of Hosts," conveys the might and authority God possesses on earth. Consequently, it proclaims that God accomplishes all that he promises to do. Judah's overwhelming needs surpassed all human abilities to satisfy. Indeed, only the efforts of the LORD Almighty could prove adequate to aid Judah's plight.

Instead of a fragmented chapter, Zech 8, together with chap. 7, presents a unified literary whole. Zechariah 8 addresses two questions. Verses 1–17 develop the first issue, temple reconstruction, exhorting the people to redouble

---

[93] *HALOT*, 461.
[94] For a brief survey of different analyses of the literary structure of chap. 8, see Petersen, *Zechariah 1–8*, 297. See also the helpful treatment in D. J. Clark and H. A. Hatton, *Haggai, Zechariah, and Malachi* (New York: United Bible Societies, 2002), 196–98.
[95] Baldwin, *Zechariah*, 148; see also Cohen, *Twelve Prophets*, 297.
[96] יְהוָה צְבָאוֹת. *HALOT*, 995–97.

their efforts in order to see the project to its completion.[97] As an incentive, Zechariah built on the theme of faithfulness to the covenant that God enjoined his people to discharge completely. Further, the prophet held out the promise of unimaginable restoration and prosperity. The last unit, vv. 18–23, concludes both chap. 8 and the larger structure made up of chaps. 7–8. Moreover, vv. 18–23 resolve the unanswered question in 7:1–7 concerning the propriety of fasting to commemorate the fall of Jerusalem at the beginning of the exile.[98]

**8:1–2** Abruptly, the tone of rebuke in chap. 7 modulates into a description of Zion's glorious future.[99] Yet the diverse messages in the two chapters bear more similarities than many scholars acknowledge. Barker observes: "In the preceding section [chap. 7] Israel was to repent and live righteously after the punishment of her captivity; here [chap. 8] she is to repent and live righteously because of the promise of her future restoration."[100]

Verse 2 states, "I am very jealous for Zion" (*qinnēʾtî lĕṣîyôn qinʾāh gĕdôlāh*), which is an echo of 1:14.[101] To summarize the previous discussion, "jealousy" grows out of the covenant relationship, describing the Lord's protective love for Israel, his beloved.[102] While the term often portrays God's desire for exclusive worship from his children (Exod 20:5–6; 34:14), the expression also explains God's burning anger against the nations who oppose Israel (Ezek 36:3–7; 38:19–23).[103] Jealousy describes God's strong emotion on Israel's behalf that shows "an intolerance for rivals," whether the interloper emerges in the guise of a false god competing with the Lord for the nation's worship, or represents one of the nations that were challenging Israel's physical well being. Isaiah 42:13 summarizes many of the themes of divine jealousy from v. 2:

> The LORD will march out like a mighty man,
>   like a warrior he will stir up his zeal [jealousy];
> with a shout he will raise the battle cry
>   and will triumph over his enemies.

---

[97] W. Rudolph divides the Zech 7–8 unit into three components: 7:4–17; 8:1–17; and 8:18–23 (*Haggai, Sacharja 1–8* [Gütersloh: Gerd Mohn, 1976], 142–52).

[98] Floyd, *Minor Prophets*, 411–12.

[99] Although the chapter begins with a typical prophetic formula, v. 1 does not identify its intended audience. The NIV adds the interpretative phrase "to me." Even though the prepositional phrase does not appear in the Hebrew text, the NIV translators added the phrase to clarify the identity of the prophecy's original audience.

[100] Barker, "Zechariah," 649–50.

[101] קִנֵּאתִי לְצִיּוֹן קִנְאָה גְדוֹלָה. As in 1:14, Zechariah employed a cognate accusative to emphasize the point of burning divine jealousy.

[102] "Jealousy" does not convey fertility or sexual connotations, contra Petersen (*Zechariah 1–8*, 297). Beuken concurs that Zechariah did not suggest sexual connotations in the jealousy metaphor (*Sacharja 1–8*, 175–77).

[103] *TWOT*, 3:1145–47.

Similarly, Isa 59:17 declares:

> He put on righteousness as his breastplate,
> and the helmet of salvation on his head;
> he put on the garments of vengeance
> and wrapped himself in zeal [jealousy] as in a cloak.

Elsewhere, the Lord's jealousy opposed Israel. In Zech 8, God's jealousy moved the Lord to provide for his people's needs.[104]

Zechariah 8:2 so clearly parallels 1:14 that one wonders why Zechariah chose to repeat the theme of divine jealousy so closely. While any biblical writer may emphasize themes deemed sufficiently significant, in this case it seems that the prophet addressed the nation's disbelief that the Lord could remain committed to his covenant with them. Additionally, Judah remained deeply troubled that the nations enjoyed rest and prosperity despite the fact that Judah, the people of the covenant, had yet to see such benefits herself. As a result of this disparity, the people feared that the Lord had ceased to uphold his covenant with the chosen seed and had begun to show favor to the nations instead. Further, the progress on the temple had not resulted in improved circumstances for the people's everyday existence. The spiritual malaise, if not outright discouragement, moved the prophet to reiterate the theme of God's jealous love for his people. This burning love resulted in an exclusive relationship between the Lord and Judah and would ultimately result in a glorious future.[105]

**8:3** The initial section of chap. 8, vv. 1–17, focuses on the changes that God's presence in Jerusalem will produce.[106] The renaming of the great city demonstrates that the character of Zion will change. Further, only the Lord has the power or authority to alter Jerusalem's designation (Isa 62:2–4).

Verse 3 also reintroduces the theme of God's return to Zion. This motif previously appeared in 1:16, "I will return to Jerusalem with mercy, and there my house will be rebuilt." One encounters the same message in 2:10, "I am coming, and I will live among you." The promise that God would reside in Zion within the very heart of the nation offers the strongest possible encouragement that Judah's future rests on a secure foundation (Ezek 43:1–5; Hag 1:8). The perfect tenses in the Hebrew text are prophetic perfects, using verbs that normally convey completed action, that is, past tense verbs. Biblical authors employed the prophetic perfect to describe a future action as certain to occur—in other words, as though the action was as good as already done.[107]

---

[104] Baldwin, *Zechariah*, 149.
[105] T. E. McComiskey, "Zechariah," in *The Minor Prophets, Vol. 3*, ed. T. E. McComiskey (Grand Rapids: Baker, 1992), 1137.
[106] R. L. Smith, *Micah-Malachi*, 232.
[107] See G. Klein, "The Prophetic Perfect," *JNSL* 16 (1990): 45–60.

Furthermore, Zechariah selected the Hebrew word translated "dwell" *(šākan)* as a metaphor for the Lord's new relationship to Jerusalem.[108] This word often occurs in passages where the Lord (or his glory) meets his people.[109] A noun related to the Hebrew word for "dwell" serves as a primary term for the Lord's tabernacle *(miškān;* see Zech 2:10–11).[110]

Zechariah described the results of God's return to Zion using a combination of old and new motifs. As the first consequence of God's presence, Jerusalem would become the "City of Truth," a unique phrase in the Old Testament. The Hebrew term for "truth" *('emet)* is rendered "*true* justice" in 7:9. The English translation "truth" suggests a meaning somewhat different from that which the Hebrew term connotes.[111] In English, "truth" connotes an abstract, philosophical concept. Zechariah intended a quite different meaning in this passage.

The word "faithfulness" far better captures the original meaning of the Hebrew term *'emet* in this context. The Lord's presence in Zion would result in the city becoming known as the "City of Faithfulness." The concept of faithfulness signifies the obligations both parties, the Lord and his people, have to the covenant. The Lord intended for Jerusalem's newly established faithfulness to witness both human faithfulness and divine faithfulness. In terms of human faithfulness, the people of Zion will live lives of obedience to covenantal obligations when the kingdom finally arrives. On the divine level, the miraculous transformation of faithless and adulterous Jerusalem into a city of obedience and worship to the Lord will proclaim to the nations God's greatness and his wondrous deeds.

Jerusalem's future faithfulness will mark the righteous treatment every Israelite should give to his neighbor. The prophet made this point plainly when he admonished them to "Speak the truth to each other" using the term *'emet* (v. 16). Isaiah announced a similar expectation when he wrote, "Afterward you will be called the City of Righteousness, the Faithful City" (1:26), equating the themes of righteousness and faithfulness. Both Isaiah's and Zechariah's prophecies explained that changing Jerusalem's name, and therefore her character, necessitated God's intervention. Like other texts in Zechariah (see Zech 3–4), the prophet downplayed human agency in the arduous tasks of rebuilding the land and restoring righteousness. Only God possesses the power to work such miracles in the individual or corporate lives of his people.

Zion's faithfulness will also characterize the city's relationship with God. When describing God, faithfulness delineates the Lord's execution of his judgment on behalf of Israel (Ps 146:6). Thus, "City of Faithfulness" assures Judah

---

[108] שָׁכַן. *HALOT*, 1496–1500.

[109] In Exod 24:16 God's glory "settled" on Mount Sinai, and in Exod 40:35 the cloud "settled" on the tent of meeting.

[110] מִשְׁכָּן. *HALOT*, 646–47. For a fuller discussion of the Lord's return to Jerusalem, see comments at 1:16.

[111] אֱמֶת. *HALOT*, 68–69.

that God will protect her from all external threats. Judah need no longer fear that the Lord will lose patience and will ultimately terminate his covenantal relationship with the nation, God's chosen ones.

In other words, the moniker "City of Faithfulness" portrays the quality of the nation's spiritual relationship with their God in the coming kingdom. Although not a present reality, the Lord promised to do a wondrous thing in the future. In previous discussions we developed the covenantal character of the word "faithfulness." Consequently, faithfulness will characterize the people's response to the covenant the Lord had made with them. Put simply, Zion will become obedient to God's word as never before. In sum, Jerusalem's faithfulness describes the Lord's rule in several ways. God wishes that human relationships should evidence a high degree of mutual respect and concern. Faithfulness also promises that God will manifest his covenantal loyalty, which will protect and provide for Jerusalem's needs.

Not only will the new name and altered character of Jerusalem transform into the model of faithfulness, Zechariah also drew on a familiar theme to picture the Lord's special relationship to his people. The prophet portrayed "the Holy Mountain" as the Lord's personal abode. The mountain motif, like the jealousy and faithfulness themes, occurs with some frequency in the Old Testament and also serves a significant role in the book of Zechariah.[112] The designation "*Holy* Mountain" represents a new emphasis on the mountain imagery. Zechariah describes the mountain as holy because the Lord will dwell on it and because it belongs to God (Zech 14:20–21). Furthermore, the mountain metaphor in v. 3 probably refers to the Jerusalem temple. Ezekiel 20:40 specifically equates the mountain of the Lord to the temple: "For on my holy mountain, the high mountain of Israel, declares the Sovereign LORD, there in the land the entire house of Israel will serve me, and there I will accept them. There I will require your offerings and your choice gifts, along with all your holy sacrifices."[113] In a similar vein, Zion would become holy because the Lord's gracious presence imputed his holiness to his people. Joel 3:17 draws together the various themes from Zech 8:3, declaring,

> Then you will know that I, the LORD your God,
>   dwell in Zion, my holy hill.
> Jerusalem will be holy;
>   never again will foreigners invade her.

The desolation of Jerusalem testified to the world that the Lord's promises of a populated Zion remained unfulfilled (Isa 54:1). The Lord had declared to

---

[112] The biblical significance of the Lord's dwelling on the mountain originates in the Sinai narratives.

[113] Mitchell demurs, considering the possibility that "mountain" may refer to Jerusalem (*Zechariah*, 207; see Isa 11:9; Jer 37:13). Mitchell does not deny the viability of the temple interpretation.

Abraham long ago that his descendants would be innumerable and that these offspring would become the source of immeasurable blessing to the nations (Gen 15:5; 17:2,6; 22:18). Abraham's seed eagerly awaited the fulfillment of God's promises to them.

**8:4–5** Verse 3 emphasizes the spiritual benefits Judah will reap when the Lord comes to inhabit the city. The next two verses shift the perspective from Zion's spiritual state to the material benefits God's blessings will provide, including growing families, long life, political security, and peace (Isa 65:20–25; Jer 30:19–20). Such an idyllic scene exceeded Judah's fondest hopes during Zechariah's day and remains a promise that the Lord has not completely fulfilled. Only a miraculous act by God could bring this picture of tranquility to reality.

The references to the very old (v. 4) and to young children (v. 5) in the passage function as a merism: the mention of the extremes of the human lifespan suggest that the entire population will enjoy an atmosphere of renewal and blessing. All inhabitants, even the most defenseless in society, can live securely.[114] The very young will have the freedom to enjoy the carefree play that rightly belongs to childhood. Those in their middle years will divide their time equally between their work and the leisure their labors have earned them. The aged will rest peacefully after a lifetime of toil, celebrating the riches of God's blessings.[115]

The Old Testament describes children as a blessing from God (Ps 127). But children also represent the future for any society. Further, the themes of play and rest stand in sharp contrast to the endless labor necessary to rebuild the land. Zechariah promised that Jerusalem will see her children play again, and Zion will hear the laughter of her children once more.

Speers concludes,

> Too often men are apt to measure a city's significance by its business, professions, and industry, its buildings, its wealth, its art and culture. Zechariah suggests that we measure the significance of our cities by their effect upon two groups easily overlooked—the old and the young.[116]

**8:6** Following grand predictions about spiritual blessing and the repopulation of Jerusalem, the people naturally raised concerns about the fulfillment of the Lord's word. Could prophecies that appear as far-fetched as those proclaimed in vv. 1–5 actually come to pass? After years of deferred hope and devastating circumstances in their everyday world, Judah struggled to accept the

---

[114] Barker, "Zechariah," 650.
[115] Mitchell, *Zechariah*, 208.
[116] T. C. Speers, *Zechariah* (Nashville: Abingdon, 1956), 1085.

word from God with faith. The Lord responded with a pointed rebuke, echoing the chastisements he had given at other critical junctures in Israel's history.

God began by asking if what seemed "marvelous" in human eyes would actually prove "marvelous" in his own sight? In other words, should an action be too difficult for the Lord to accomplish merely because the deed exceeds human reach? Here Zechariah used the Hebrew term *pālēʾ*, which is common in the Old Testament for portraying "wondrous, awe inspiring" deeds.[117] In Ps 139:14 the psalmist employed the same word to describe how wonderfully God had fashioned his human frame.

In two other Old Testament passages individuals questioned God's ability to accomplish what he had promised he would do, also using the Hebrew word *pālēʾ*. In Gen 18:14 the angel asked Sarah if it was too difficult for the Lord to open her womb. Jeremiah posed a similar question when considering whether the devastation caused by the Babylonians could ever be reversed after the exile drew to a close (32:17,27).

Thus, the point of Zechariah's rhetorical question could not be clearer: how can any human being judge God's ability to fulfill his own word? Baldwin properly notes, "It is as difficult to believe the promises as it is to take seriously the threats of judgment."[118] The solution to Judah's crisis of faith in the Lord's ability to give life to his words depends on the nation's comprehension of the character of God. Thus, to doubt God is to fail to see the Lord for who he truly is. Judah must remember the theological point mentioned later in Scripture: "What is impossible with men is possible with God" (Luke 18:27). Hence, faith in God represents the most difficult challenge for God's people in any age. From the Lord's perspective, faith remains the ultimate test of spirituality, since "without faith it is impossible to please God" (Heb 11:6).

To complicate matters further, Judah's dispirited condition made the Lord's assurances appear all the more unlikely. Petersen explains that "a weak people is likely to have difficulty in thinking of a powerful God, the more so if this deity is the god of a defeated people."[119]

Zechariah addressed this oracle to "the remnant of this people." The word "remnant" *(šěʾērît)* occurs three times in Zechariah (8:6,11,12) and numerous additional times in the prophets, functioning as a technical term for those who had survived the exile.[120] Haggai used the same term (1:12,14; 2:2), as did Isaiah (46:3), to refer to those who had lived through the Babylonian exile to return to the land of promise. A related nominal form serves as the basis for the name of Isaiah's son Shear-Jashub (meaning "a remnant will return"), a name that portends the future of both judgment and restoration God plans for his people (7:3).

---

[117] פָּלֵא. *HALOT*, 927–28.
[118] Baldwin, *Zechariah*, 150.
[119] Petersen, *Zechariah 1–8*, 301.
[120] שְׁאֵרִית. *HALOT*, 1380–81.

**8:7–8** Zechariah's next unit begins with the Lord's promise to "save" his people (see Jer 30:7–11). The Hebrew word for "save" occurs in a variety of contexts. "To liberate from captivity" represents one of the most frequent uses of the word for salvation in the Old Testament and seems to provide the most appropriate nuance in this context.[121] Furthermore, the Hebrew word found in v. 8 *(môšîaʿ)* often serves as a title for the Messiah.[122]

The Lord's promise to save "my people" from the east and the west indicates that Zechariah predicted more than the end to the exile when the chosen people would return from Babylon in the east.[123] The combination of east and west speaks not only of geographical locales, but also serves as another merism, encompassing Abraham's seed everywhere. These far-flung people God would bring back to Zion. Similar themes occur in Isa 11:1–11; 43:5–6; Jer 31:8.

Verse 8 stresses the unique relationship Israel will enjoy with her God: "they will be my people, and I will be . . . their God." Few phrases evoke stronger covenantal memories than this expression. In the Abrahamic covenant, accompanying the circumcision rite, God promised to Abraham and his descendants, "I will be their God" (Gen 17:8). God reaffirmed this word during the times of crisis during the Egyptian bondage (Exod 6:7). The concept reemerges, linked to the Mosaic covenant, which adds the motif of the Lord's dwelling among his people. Anticipating the covenantal theme so important in Zech 8, Exodus proclaims, "Then I will dwell among the Israelites and be their God. They will know that I am the LORD their God, who brought them out of Egypt so that I might dwell among them. I am the LORD their God" (Exod 29:45–46; see also 19:5–6).

Another major covenant in the Old Testament, the new covenant, also uses the same language to communicate the bonds of faithfulness linking God and Israel. Jeremiah 31:33 proclaims, "'This is the covenant I will make with the house of Israel after that time,' declares the LORD. 'I will put my law in their minds and write it on their hearts. I will be their God, and they will be my people.'" Thus, Zechariah chose this phrase that employed some of the strongest possible terms to recall the covenant the Lord had forged with Judah.

God's adoption of Israel provides the people confidence that the rubble now covering Judah will disappear so that the nation can experience restoration, both in terms of their material culture and especially with reference to the people's own spiritual well being. The exilic prophet Ezekiel predicted a similar national resurrection, visualizing Judah as the scattered bones of scores of decomposed corpses. Like Zechariah, Ezekiel promised that God would reattach and vivify the bleached, scattered human bones in the valley to fulfill his com-

---

[121] For a discussion of words built from the root ישׁע, see *HALOT*, 448–49.
[122] מוֹשִׁיעַ. *HALOT*, 562.
[123] Unger, *Zechariah*, 138.

mitments to the covenant and bring glory to his name (Ezek 37). The bygone days when God declared Israel "Not My People" (*lōʾ ʿammî*; Hos 1:8–11)[124] will transform into a new glorious day. In this wonderful day Judah will return to her former status as "My People" (*ʿammî*; Hos 2:23)[125] in the estimation of the Lord.

Ultimately these themes, particularly the ones from Hosea, assume eschatological proportions in the New Testament. Paul understood that the notion of "My People" predicted more than Judah's spiritual renewal. "My people" includes Gentiles, with the bold promise that they too will receive the salvation their Israelite brothers have enjoyed for years. Romans 9:24–26 and 1 Pet 2:10 give significant emphasis to the inclusion of the Gentiles within God's ancient promise to Judah. Commenting on this theological development, Wolff adds,

> Since the people outside Israel—who are Not-My-People and Without-Pity—are to become a part of the blessed people of God (Rom 9:24f; 1 Pt 2:10), these words are becoming fulfilled. But this is not yet completed with respect to Israel (Rom 10:1; 11:26) or the nations (Rev 7:9ff).[126]

Rather, the Lord himself ensures that salvation comes to all who will call on God's name.

Verse 8 concludes with two added attributes characterizing the Lord's relationship to his people. He shows himself to be "faithful and righteous."[127] In Isa 1:26 the same two terms also describe the future Jerusalem: "afterward you will be called the City of Righteousness, the Faithful City."[128]

**8:9** Verses 9–17 begin the second oracle in chap. 8, again using illustrations from the past (see v. 14) to challenge the community to immediate action.[129] For the moment, Zechariah left the grand eschatological promises for Judah's future, and he returned to the perennial topic of rebuilding the temple. With the LORD Almighty himself giving the admonition to work, the people received the divine mandate to redouble their efforts in order to complete their house of worship. All that God would do in Zion's future would be predicated on the presence of the restored temple and Judah's faithfulness to the covenant their Lord graciously made with them.

---

[124] לֹא עַמִּי. The word עַמִּי ("my people") functions as a legal, covenantal term for Israel's betrothal to the Lord.

[125] עַמִּי.

[126] H. W. Wolff, *Hosea* (Philadelphia: Fortress, 1974), 29.

[127] We have already examined the word translated "faithful" in 7:9; 8:3. The word "righteous" (צְדָקָה) describes the fundamental nature of the Lord's holiness that he desires his people to embody. *HALOT*, 1006–7.

[128] R. L. Smith, *Micah-Malachi*, 234.

[129] For further discussion of the structure of vv. 9–17, see R. L. Smith, *Micah-Malachi*, 235.

To "let your hands be strong" means to work with diligence and encouragement (Judg 7:11; 2 Sam 2:7). The same phrase also occurs in v. 13, forming an inclusio or literary bracket for this subsection of chap. 8.

Zechariah did not specify which prophets he referred to when he said, "the prophets who were there when the foundation was laid for the house of the LORD Almighty." The exhortation to begin the rebuilding project under Zerubbabel's command (Ezra 3:7–13) apparently did not involve prophetic activity, thus excluding this event as a possible referent for Zech 8:9.[130] Most likely, Zechariah related his own prophecy to the one declared by Haggai when he issued his own instruction to the people to begin construction on the temple (Hag 1:7–11; 2:15–19). This work commenced in December 520 BC.

**8:10–11** Zechariah explained why the nation must "let her hands be strong" in order to fulfill her divine mandate. The harsh conditions made even survival challenging. To do anything beyond meeting life's basic necessities would require sacrifices of time and financial resources reaching almost heroic levels.

"Before that time" refers to the period before the laying of the temple foundation, between 530 and 520 BC, when the Babylonian exile and the years immediately following resulted in privation for "man and beast" alike (Hag 1:6–11). In Jer 7:20 the prophet foretold the harsh conditions that would fall "on man and beast" during the exile (see Ezek 14:13 for a similar expression). The absence of wages for everyone in the land illustrates utter economic ruin for Judah.

To compound these hardships, Judah also faced the "enemy" *(ṣar)* who threatened her national security.[131] But Zechariah did not specify the identity of the *ṣar*. Ezra 4:1–5 describes how these enemies, including the Samaritans, sought to discourage God's people and to hinder them from completing the temple. Petitjean concludes that *ṣar* specifically relates to those nations who oppose Israel (see Jer 30:16).[132]

The emphasis in v. 10 lies on economic hardship. Judah's enemies hindered agricultural work and trade. Thus, as long as her foes thwarted her economic recovery, Judah could not experience the security or wholeness the term "peace" *(šālôm)* connotes. Accordingly, the theme of peace occurs prominently in this section (see vv. 10,16,19).

Merrill stands virtually alone in interpreting *ṣar* as the impersonal concept "adversities."[133] The term can be translated either as "enemy" or "distress."[134]

---

[130] Baldwin, *Zechariah*, 151; Mitchell, *Zechariah*, 210.

[131] The same expression occurs in Deut 28:7 to describe one significant blessing the Lord provides to those who keep his covenant: "the LORD will grant that the enemies who rise up against you will be defeated before you."

[132] A. Petitjean, *Les oracles du Proto-Zacharie* (Paris: J. Gabalda, 1969), 392–93.

[133] Merrill, *Zechariah*, 224–26.

[134] צָר. *HALOT*, 1052–53.

To be more precise, two separate Hebrew words called homonyms are involved. While both words appear and sound identical, both primary Hebrew lexicons, the superior *HALOT* and the older BDB, treat the two words separately, relating them to different Hebrew roots with disparate meanings as well.[135] Merrill appears to reject the lexicons' understanding of homonyms, concluding that either meaning fits v. 10 well. Even so, Merrill maintains that "distress" fits the context better stylistically.[136] However, the next clause in v. 10b suggests that the enmity experienced in Judah between neighbors is an extension of the antipathy Judah faces from surrounding peoples. Consequently, the context focuses on Judah's enemies.

Finally, God declared that he "had turned every man against his neighbor." Meyers and Meyers suggest that this statement reveals fundamental problems of law and order in a society that compounds their economic and political woes.[137] This fits the overall picture of social breakdown the postexilic writers lament. Baldwin abstracts the social and political situation: "Misunderstandings, resentments, animosity, characterized even Jewish society, according to the last clause of this verse. When God withholds His blessing the symptoms are poverty, insecurity, and broken relationships."[138]

Verse 11 promises that times have changed, and that the Lord will provide his nation with a different future than their present circumstances could reasonably lead them to expect. Because of Judah's commitment to see the temple reconstruction to its conclusion (Hag 2:18–19), the Lord will bring blessing to his people again.

**8:12** Verse 12 demonstrates the strong literary and theological ties between Zechariah and Haggai, his prophetic contemporary. As judgment for the people's laggardly approach to rebuilding the temple, Hag 1:10–11 proclaims, "Therefore, because of you the heavens have withheld their dew and the earth its crops. I called for a drought on the fields and the mountains, on the grain, the new wine, the oil and whatever the ground produces, on men and cattle, and on the labor of your hands." However, after the nation's repentance and recommitment to their divine task, Haggai (2:19) reversed the curse on the land: "Is there yet any seed left in the barn? Until now, the vine and the fig tree, the pomegranate and the olive tree have not borne fruit. 'From this day on I will bless you.'" This reversal of fortunes Haggai outlined serves as the backdrop for Zechariah's prophecy. Looking into the future, the exilic prophet Ezekiel reaffirmed a comparable promise (34:25–29).

---

[135] *HALOT* distinguishes the two words as the homonyms צַר I "restraint, anxiety" and צַר II "enemy" (1052, see 1058–59). Likewise, BDB (864–65) associates צַר "distress" with צרר II "suffer distress," while it derives צַר "enemy" from the separate word צרר III "vex."

[136] Merrill, *Zechariah*, 225.

[137] Meyers and Meyers, *Zechariah 1–8*, 421.

[138] Baldwin, *Zechariah*, 152.

Actually, this fertility motif has roots deep within the Torah itself. Leviticus 26:3–10 assures that God grants rain and abundant grapes, both themes found in Zech 8:12, for those who obey the Lord's commands. Deuteronomy 28:11–12 makes similar promises of the blessing of agricultural bounty as God's response to the faithfulness of his people.

Significant parallels exist between the challenges Israel faced during the conquest and those the postexilic community encountered.[139] In both situations Israel had to take possession of the land and to harvest its bounty in order to fulfill the promises God had made to them. Although they continually attempted to achieve the objectives through human means, only the nation's faith could grasp these divine promises. Safe possession of the land that God had first promised to Abraham, and the abundance that the land should yield, could come only through obedience to their Lord's commands. Baldwin notes that "the prophet's needy contemporaries were the spiritual descendants of Joshua, who was repeatedly told to 'be strong' (Jos. 1:6,7,9,18; cf. Zc. 8:13b), and who triumphed."[140]

In another sense, Zechariah faced a situation that contrasts markedly with Joshua's circumstances. Formerly, the land of Canaan yielded great abundance, but the nation could not yet receive her possession because the promised territory remained in the hands of others. In the postexilic epoch, the people dwelled in the land, but the fields were not productive. Nevertheless, in both eras, faith in God provided the means to obtain and to accomplish what God intended for his loved ones.

"The seed will grow well" presents interpreters with additional challenges. The Hebrew text, *kî zera' haššālôm*, reads literally, "for the seed of peace."[141] The Septuagint attempts to smooth out and interpret the Masoretic Text by taking the noun "seed" as a verb "sow"—"I will sow peace"—but this is merely an ancient attempt to revise the Hebrew and should be rejected. Petersen concludes that the seed metaphor indicates that the sowing process will proceed slowly and will necessitate patience.[142] Meyers and Meyers, along with Mitchell, suggest that the phrase means "prosperous sowing."[143] But neither of these suggestions fits the typical meaning of the word "peace" *(šālôm)*. A preferable interpretation takes the genitive ("of peace") adjectivally. This interpretation concludes that the meaning "the seed will be peaceful" reverses the lack of security lamented in v. 10. In this way, Zechariah declares that sowing will occur during a period of security, during an absence of war.[144]

---

[139] Petersen, *Zechariah 1–8*, 307.
[140] Baldwin, *Zechariah*, 152.
[141] כִּי־זֶרַע הַשָּׁלוֹם.
[142] Petersen, *Zechariah 1–8*, 307.
[143] Meyers and Meyers, *Zechariah 1–8*, 422–23; Mitchell, *Zechariah*, 214.
[144] Unger, *Zechariah*, 142.

**8:13** The language of blessing and cursing in this verse reflects covenantal phraseology common in the Old Testament (Deut 28; Jer 24:9; 25:18). The Lord alone has the authority and the power to remove curses and to extend blessing. After briefly alluding to their former accursed state, 8:13 develops the theme in v. 7, "I will save my people." Additionally, the declaration "you will be a blessing" is reminiscent of God's commitment to Abraham in Gen 12:3. The divine promise to Abraham's descendants that their foes would face the Lord's curse assured the patriarch's descendants that salvation would be theirs because of God's faithfulness to his chosen people.

Moreover, the Lord describes Judah's former condition as "an object of cursing among the nations." This portrayal does not merely mean that the nations cursed Judah. Rather, Israel's abject state was so bereft of life's necessities that even the pagan nations concluded that God had scorned his people.

Three times in this chapter Zechariah spoke of the "remnant" who would taste God's blessings (vv. 6,11,12). Verse 13 shifts this emphasis on the remnant by referring to "Judah and Israel." This word pair reinforces the longevity of God's promised blessing to the people of the covenant. Like the allusion to the patriarch Abraham, Zechariah envisioned the whole history of God's people stretching back centuries before the Second Temple epoch. Zechariah understood that the postexilic remnant corporately represented the generations of ancestors who had also held claim to the Lord's promises.[145]

Verse 13 concludes with the same admonition with which v. 9 begins. The Lord enjoined everyone in the nation to "let your hands be strong." God's renewed blessing provides reason for encouragement. Moreover, the command "do not be afraid" finds its power in the character of God and in his decree (see Phil 2:12–13; 4:6). The question of faith turns on human ability to recognize the Lord's true glory and the willingness to act on that knowledge.

**8:14–15** Verses 14–17 form a literary sub-unit of the larger section, out of which vv. 1–17 focus on the rebuilding of the temple. Verses 14–15 outline what God will do to bless his people, while vv. 16–17 describe what Judah is responsible for accomplishing in order to satisfy the Lord's demands.

Zechariah used an "as . . . so" literary device to show the certainty of the Lord's resolve. Once, God determined to force the Babylonian yoke upon Judah's back (Jer 4:28). With equal certitude, the Lord decreed that he would bestow favor on his people. Since this promise has not reached its culmination, the people cannot yet experience the reality of God's proclamation in their daily lives. Zechariah understood that the faith of the nation was wavering. Judah's decision to trust God rested solely on the character of the Lord himself (Jer 32:40–41; Ezek 36:11). Using a clever, unexpected argument, God's judgment on the nation in the past argues as a pledge for her future fortunes from the Lord.

---

[145] T. McComiskey, "Zechariah," 1148.

Perhaps the strongest theological theme in these verses is the Lord's determination to bring his will to fruition.[146] The Hebrew verb translated "determined" *(zāmamtî)*, when God is the subject of the sentence, always introduces God's intention to bring judgment (see Jer 4:28; 51:12).[147] The sole exception occurs in v. 15 where Zechariah employed *zāmamtî* to express God's intention to do good. Hence, Zechariah's selection of a word for resolve with such a negative connotation underscores the dramatic reversal of fortune Israel will experience. Significantly, God gives the reason for the former judgment but does not reiterate here why he resolves to bless the nation. This silence emphasizes divine sovereignty and the wonder of God's extension of grace to his people.[148]

**8:16–17** Old Testament covenants, as well as secular ancient Near Eastern ones, consistently begin with a recitation of God's (or the king's) marvelous acts on behalf of the people before explaining the legal obligations to the recipients. For instance, Exod 20:2–3 outlines the Lord's deliverance of Israel from Egypt prior to handing down the law. Similarly, Zech 8:11–15 enunciates God's blessings as a prelude to discussing the Lord's expectations for his chosen people.

Thus, vv. 16–17 do not focus on divine assurances but on the nation's responsibilities for righteous living as God's representatives on earth (see Mic 6:8). Moreover, these prophetic passages reinforce the strong moral admonitions in 7:9–10. The introductory statement, "These are the things you are to do," recalls the instruction in Jas 1:22, "Do not merely listen to the word. . . . Do what it says."

The first exhortation, "speak the truth to each other," does not appear in chap. 7, but the spirit of the command fits the tone of the previous chapter well (cf. Ps 15:2–3). Moreover, the instruction to render "true judgment" resembles several exhortations in chap. 7 (see v. 9). Deuteronomy 21:19 and Ruth 4:1–11 describe similar practices as well. The notion of truth/faithfulness functions as a sub-theme throughout this section of Zechariah (vv. 3,8,19).

Concerning v. 17 Petersen remarks, "A change in Yahweh's intentions for Zion signals a call for proper intentions in the house of Israel."[149] The two negative commands in v. 17 balance the positive exhortations found in the previous verse. In the list of "the six things the LORD hates" (Prov 6:16–19), God detests "a lying tongue" and "a false witness who pours out lies."

Verse 17 reiterates the most prominent theme from 7:10, "do not plot evil." The second injunction forbidding "swearing falsely" attempts to protect God's

---

[146] For a fuller discussion of Zechariah's use of the theme of divine sovereignty, see Merrill (*Zechariah*, 228–29) and Petersen (*Zechariah 1–8*, 309–10).

[147] זָמַמְתִּי. *HALOT*, 273; *TDOT*, 4:88.

[148] For a helpful discussion of the Old Testament perspective on God's will, see H. Van Dyke Parunak, "A Semantic Survey of *NḤM*," *Bib* 56 (1975): 512–32.

[149] Petersen, *Zechariah 1–8*, 311.

holy reputation for truthfulness. Zechariah's command not to swear falsely also safeguards the integrity of Judah's entire judicial system as well as enhancing the quality of personal relationships in the postexilic community.

To spurn the Lord's commands is tantamount to embracing that which God "hates." Loving that which the Lord hates is equivalent to hating God himself. Exodus 20:5-6 cautions that the Lord's jealousy burns, punishing those who hate him for several generations. In the final analysis, however, God's people from every age must shun all manner of evil and false witness. Baldwin summarizes the point:

> Equally vindictiveness, hatred, falsified evidence lead to a breakdown of mutual trust. The Lord says not only that they are wrong but that He hates them (cf. Mal. 2:16). It is for this reason that God's law is to be kept. It is an expression of His character and of His wish, and His people fulfill it to please Him (Jn. 8:29). Here is the theological basis of ethics.[150]

**8:18–19** Chapter 8 draws to a compelling close by returning to the subject of fasting, first broached in 7:3. After several excursuses addressing pointed concerns about spiritual motivation and covenantal faithfulness, the Lord returns to the doleful topic of fasting. God desired to transform the festivals into occasions for rejoicing because they celebrated the Lord's renewed blessing for his people. Judah no longer served as "an object of cursing among the nations" (v. 13). Neither will Israel bear the brunt of God's judgment for their idolatry. Instead, "many peoples . . . will come to Jerusalem to seek the LORD Almighty" (v. 22).

After a repeated, emphatic assertion that his sermon was of divine origin, Zechariah quoted God as saying that all of the former fasts would become times for rejoicing in Israel's relationship with the Lord (see Jer 31:10–14). Zion's great joy will cause episodes of judgment and deprivation to recede into a faded memory. Up to this point in Zechariah's revelation, the prophet had declared that the Lord will "restore the nation" (1:16–17; 2:10; 3:9; 4:9; 8:3–8,11–13), appoint his messianic leaders (3:5,7–8; 4:7–8,14; 6:12–13), and rule as sovereign over the nation of Judah as well as govern all the other nations of the world (1:10–11; 2:5,10–11; 6:7–8; 8:8).[151]

In 7:3,5 the envoy asked whether the Lord was pleased with the fasts being observed in the fifth and seventh months. However, 8:19 includes these two fasts and adds the two other fasts being held in the fourth and tenth months. At first, it appears that God might intend to stress the observance of these four fasts, or even desire to add to them as an expression of genuine repentance. To

---

[150] Baldwin, *Zechariah*, 154.
[151] Merrill, *Zechariah*, 231.

the contrary, the prophet mentioned all four to dramatize the metamorphosis from fasting to feasting.[152]

Each of the four fasts that Zechariah mentioned recalled various events surrounding the fall of Jerusalem. But no records precisely indicate what specific events the fasts portrayed. The fast held during the tenth month probably recalls the initial siege on the city (Jer 39:1; 2 Kgs 25:1–2).[153] Petersen suggests that the fast in the fourth month remembers the successful attack on Jerusalem (Jer 39:2).[154] Merrill disagrees, maintaining that the fast in the fourth month honors the memory of the beginning of the siege against Jerusalem.[155] Ultimately, insufficient evidence survives to resolve this question. The fast in the fifth month mourns the actual fall of the city and the razing of the temple (2 Kgs 25:8–21; Jer 52:12–30; Zech 7:3). Lastly, the fast in the seventh month probably recalls the murder of the ruler Gedaliah whom Nebuchadnezzar had appointed over the people (2 Kgs 25:25; Jer 41:1–3; Zech 7:5).

Zechariah strongly conveyed the rejoicing that the future will bring by using three synonyms for joyfulness. The term "joyful" *(śāśôn)* means "exultation or rejoicing," especially in light of the Lord's favor (see Ps 51:8).[156] Likewise, the Hebrew term for "glad occasions" *(śimḥāh)* signifies "mirth."[157] This latter expression, when describing gladness in a social setting, may refer to the fellowship that family and friends share around a meal (see Gen 31:27). If this is the case, it presents a particularly pregnant connotation in light of Zechariah's transformation from fast to feast. Last, the Hebrew phrase for "happy festivals" *(mōʿădîm)* does not occur elsewhere in the Old Testament, but the expression speaks of good or pleasant assemblies. Whereas past memories of Jerusalem brought lament and pain, future memories of Zion will focus on the feasting within the city: "Look upon Zion, the city of our festivals" (Isa 33:20).

Verse 19 concludes with the imperative, "love truth and peace." Although the injunction to love occurs in many truly significant theological texts, the command does not appear frequently in the Old Testament. In Lev 19:18,34 (see also Matt 22:39; Mark 12:31; Luke 10:27; Rom 13:9; Gal 5:14; Jas 2:8) God commands his faithful to "love your neighbor as yourself." Further, Deut 6:5, the *Shema*, requires believers to "love the LORD your God with all your heart and with all your soul and with all your strength." Neither admonition refers to an "emotional" response that God expected Israel to direct either to one another or to himself. Rather, the faithfulness or obedience to the covenant God

---

[152] Hoffman contends that the differences in the months of fasting mentioned in the question (7:3), the prophet's first reply (7:5–6), and his second answer (8:19) simply reflects the widely differing practices of fasting among the people during the postexilic era ("The Fasts in the Book of Zechariah," 195).

[153] Meyers and Meyers, *Zechariah 1–8*, 388.

[154] Petersen, *Zechariah 1–8*, 313.

[155] Merrill, *Zechariah*, 231.

[156] שָׂשׂוֹן. *HALOT*, 1363.

[157] שִׂמְחָה. *HALOT*, 1336–37.

had made with his people represents the essential idea of "love." Furthermore, the biblical use harmonizes nicely with the ancient Near Eastern covenants that use similar vocabulary to require obedience to the covenant.[158] Thus, v. 19 concludes with the command for every Judahite to show covenantal faithfulness both to God and man.

A final Old Testament passage requiring Israelites to demonstrate love deserves mention. Amos 5:15 states, "Hate evil, love good; maintain justice in the courts." In a like vein, Zechariah wrote, "love truth and peace." It is this love for the Lord and for one's neighbor that undergirds all spirituality and ethics.

**8:20–22** In 2:11 Zechariah declared that "many nations will be joined with the LORD in that day and will become my people. I will live among you." The prophet concluded this major section of his book by reprising the theme of the Gentiles' worshipping the Lord, developing the point with further detail. Ultimately, the theological notion of the nations coming to Jerusalem to worship the Lord refers back to the Abrahamic covenant when God promised the patriarch that "all peoples on earth will be blessed through you" (Gen 12:3). A host of other Old Testament passages teach the same message (see Isa 2:1–5; 23:23–25; 45:14; 49:2–3; 60:1–3; 66:18; Mic 4:2–5).[159] Of these renowned texts, Isa 2:2–3 stands out:

> In the last days
>   the mountain of the LORD's temple will be established
>     as chief among the mountains;
>   it will be raised above the hills,
>     and all nations will stream to it.
>
> Many peoples will come and say,
>   "Come, let us go up to the mountain of the LORD,
>     to the house of the God of Jacob.
>   He will teach us his ways,
>     so that we may walk in his paths."
>   The law will go out from Zion,
>     the word of the LORD from Jerusalem.

The Abrahamic covenant assured Israel that she will become the channel of blessing between the Lord and the nations of the world. Further, Gen 1–11 develops the theme of "*why* all the families of the earth need the blessing" the Lord offers.[160] Wolff asserts that beginning in Gen 12, the nations increasingly

---

[158] W. L. Moran, "The Ancient Near Eastern Background of the Love of God in Deuteronomy," *CBQ* 25 (1963): 77–87. Also, D. J. McCarthy, *Treaty and Covenant* (Rome: Pontifical Biblical Institute, 1963).

[159] D. Rudman, "Zechariah 8:20–22 & Isaiah 2:2–4/Micah 4:2–3: A Study in Intertextuality," *Biblische Notizen* 107/108 (2001): 50–54.

[160] Wolff, "The Kerygma of the Yahwist," *Int* 20 (1966): 145.

experienced what it meant to enjoy the Lord's blessing.[161] Thus, Ps 47, a royal psalm, offers a mature expression of the eschatological promise that the nations will turn to the Lord in faith:

> Clap your hands all you nations;
>  shout to God with cries of joy. . . .
> For God is the King of all the earth;
>  sing to him a psalm of praise.
> God reigns over the nations;
>  God is seated on his holy throne.
> The nobles of the nations assemble
>  as the people of the God of Abraham
> for the kings of the earth belong to God;
>  he is greatly exalted. (Ps 47:1,7-9)

With the responsibility of the nations' spiritual state resting on Judah's shoulders, "Israel can only fulfill her commission of redemption . . . in the world, which has gone before her ever since Genesis 12:3b, when she herself confesses her God with undivided loyalty and uprightness of life."[162]

Moreover, Zech 8:23 declares that ten foreigners speaking the different languages of the world will stand with every Judahite. Accordingly, Zechariah's prophecy represented a reversal of the divine decree in the tower of Babel passage (Gen 11:1–9).[163] The apostle Paul continued this theme in Gal 3:8: "The Scripture foresaw that God would justify the Gentiles by faith, and announced the gospel in advance to Abraham: 'All nations will be blessed through you.'"

Verse 20 describes those who travel to Jerusalem as "inhabitants of cities." This prediction surely stood beyond the comprehension of Zechariah's audience. For one thing, Judah lay in ruins. What existed in the land for the pilgrims to visit during Zechariah's day? What more would the future offer for Abraham's seed or for the Gentiles who would join in the celebration of worship? Moreover, those journeying to Zion came from cities, not from the pastoral life where they might migrate more easily.[164] Thus, the pilgrims must risk their security and way of life for the spiritual blessings awaiting them in Jerusalem. The "City of David," once known only as the seat of Israelite worship, now becomes the center for the worship of the Lord by Judah and Gentile alike. The bond tying together all those who worship the Lord erases all nationalistic lines, including those that had circumscribed the community of Judah for generations.

---

[161] Ibid., 150.
[162] Ibid., 157.
[163] Smith, *Micah-Malachi*, 241.
[164] Petersen, *Zechariah 1–8*, 317–18.

The phrase "to entreat the LORD" *(lĕbaqqēš ʾet–YHWH*; vv. 21 and 22) occurs also in 7:2.[165] When used in secular contexts, the expression describes appeasement, seeking mercy or favor. In the spiritual domain, the phrase portrays the preparation of the worshipper's heart for prayer to the Lord. Typically, sacrifice also plays an important role in passages where people "entreat the LORD."[166]

Finally, Meyers and Meyers offer a significantly different interpretation of vv. 20–22 that merits brief mention.[167] They suggest that the "nations" coming to worship the Lord in Jerusalem were not foreigners, but different political factions within Judah. Meyers and Meyers base their conviction on an interpretation of the Hebrew word for "peoples" *(ʿammîm)* in this passage.[168] Although they note that the singular of this noun *(ʿām)* regularly refers exclusively to Israel,[169] they are incorrect in suggesting that the plural of the Hebrew noun in the same way always speaks of Israel. Rather, the plural typically refers to the nations generally, much like the usual word for "Gentiles" *(gôyim)*.[170] Consequently, since the Hebrew word for nations signifies foreign nations, the interpretation Meyers and Meyers offer cannot be correct.[171]

**8:23** Zechariah dates the fulfillment of this grand prophecy to the time he designates "in those days" *(bayyāmîm hāhēmmāh)*.[172] Like the use in 2:11, the prophets employed this phrase frequently to describe a future event when the writer did not desire to state specifically the time of the fulfillment.[173] The "day" to which Zechariah referred is the "Day of the LORD," the day in which God will bring his eschatological promises to fruition.[174]

Zechariah prophesied that the Day of the LORD will see ten Gentiles in Zion worshipping the Lord for every Judahite. The number ten is not literal, but rather symbolizes the totality of humanity. The symbolic use of the number ten occurs in other Old Testament passages (see Gen 31:7; Lev 26:26).

The confession on the lips of the nations will demonstrate that they have completed their spiritual pilgrimage (Isa 45:14; 49:18). Mitchell writes, "The speech is a confession by the gentiles that they have finally found the Power after whom they have hitherto been blindly and vainly groping, the only Saviour,

---

[165] לְבַקֵּשׁ אֶת־יהוה. *HALOT*, 152.

[166] *TDOT*, 4:409. Merrill illustrates the religious use of the term with Moses' mediatorial actions in Exod 32:11–13 when he "sought the favor of the LORD" in asking God to spare the idolatrous people *(Zechariah*, 233–34).

[167] Meyers and Meyers, *Zechariah 1–8*, 436–37. Perowne defends the same interpretation *(Zechariah*, 106).

[168] עַמִּים. *HALOT*, 838.

[169] עַם. *HALOT*, 837–39.

[170] גּוֹיִם. *HALOT*, 182–83.

[171] See BDB, 766–67; and Jenni-Westermann, *Theologisches Handwörterbuch*, 2:318–21.

[172] בַּיָּמִים הָהֵמָּה.

[173] Unger *(Zechariah*, 150) cannot argue successfully that the phrase "in those days" is so precise that it "means in millennial times."

[174] *TDOT*, 6:30–31.

in the God of the Hebrews."[175] The theme of seeking the Lord that stands so prominently in vv. 20–22 transforms into "grasping" him in v. 23, a topic mentioned twice in a single verse. Thus, Rom 14:11 (see also Phil 2:11) portends, "'As surely as I live,' says the Lord, 'every knee will bow before me; every tongue will confess to God.'"

The Hebrew word translated "Jew" *(yĕhûdî)* actually means "Judahite" (see Jer 34:9; the plural is in Esth 2:5; 3:4; Jer 52:28,30).[176] This does not signify Rabbinic Judaism, which developed subsequent to the postexilic era and is therefore out of place in the context of Zech 8. Some scholars opt for the expression "Yehud" to capture the idea of the word and to avoid anachronism.

The gesture, "to take firm hold of . . . the hem of his robe," occurs only here and in 1 Sam 15:27. Numerous other occasions of this gesture appear in the ancient Near Eastern literature. This important nonverbal communication indicated supplication and submission.[177]

The Gentiles' statement to the Judahites, "Let us go with you, because we have heard that God is with you," presumes that the nations will recognize Judah's unique relationship with the Lord as well as the righteousness that God's people manifest. Thus, in the great eschatological day, the pagan nations will be able to observe and to participate in Israel's righteousness at last. The testimony of the Gentiles concerning Abraham's descendants will demonstrate the transformation of Judah's spiritual state from unrighteousness to righteousness. Moreover, the nation's newly found understanding of righteousness also indicates that the pagan nations' spiritual blindness will become sight. Theodore of Mopsuestia observes,

> God will make the return of the remainder so conspicuous that many people who are from different nations and have shared that calamity will perceive God's care for the people. They will lay hold of any one of them and use him as a guide for a return to Jerusalem, since everyone is sufficiently stirred up to that end from the clear realization that God is with them on the basis of the incredible deeds done for them.[178]

As chap. 8 concludes, the prophet completes the first part of the book, leaving Judah with ample reason to have confidence in the future. The Lord's own assurances, indeed his very presence dwelling among the people in Zion, give

---

[175] Mitchell, *Zechariah*, 216.

[176] יְהוּדִי. *HALOT*, 394.

[177] P. A. Kruger, "Grasping the Hem in Zech 8:23: The Contextual Analysis of a Gesture," in *"Feet on Level Ground:" A South African Tribute of Old Testament Essays in Honor of Gerhard Hasel*, ed. K. Van Wyle (Berrien Center, MI: Louis Hester, 1996), 188–89.

[178] Theodore of Mopsuestia, *Commentary on Zechariah*, 8.23 [Patrologia graeca 66:552]. See R. Hanhart, *Sacharja 1–8* (Neukirchener-Vluyn: Neukirchener, 1998), 556–61, for a helpful overview of Calvin and Luther's approach to this passage. Both Reformers viewed the Church as the successor to God's promise to Israel in Zech 8.

all the faithful great optimism for their destiny. Psalm 126 captures the nation's changing fortunes well:

> When the LORD brought back the captives to Zion,
>     we were like men who dreamed.
> Our mouths were filled with laughter,
>     our tongues with songs of joy.
> Then it was said among the nations,
>     "The LORD has done great things for them."
> The LORD has done great things for us,
>     and we are filled with joy.
> Restore our fortunes, O LORD,
>     like streams in the Negev.
> Those who sow in tears
>     will reap with songs of joy.
> He who goes out weeping,
>     carrying seed to sow,
> will return with songs of joy,
>     carrying sheaves with him.

―――――――――――― SECTION OUTLINE ――――――――――――

V. BURDENS FROM THE LORD (9:1–14:21)
   1. Judgment and Salvation of Surrounding Nations (9:1–8)
   2. Introduction to the King (9:9–10)
   3. Israel's Battle and Ultimate Victory (9:11–10:1)
   4. Idolatry and Judgment (10:2–3)
   5. Israel's Battle and Victory (10:4–12)
   6. Judgment of the Shepherds (11:1–17)
   7. Israel's Battle and Victory (12:1–9)
   8. The Lord's Servant Pierced; Mourning and Purification (12:10–13:1)
   9. Idolatry and Judgment (13:2–6)
   10. Shepherd Struck; Judgment, Purification, and Return to God (13:7–9)
   11. Israel's Battle and Victory (14:1–15)
   12. Judgment and Salvation of All Nations (14:16–21)

―――――――― V. BURDENS FROM THE LORD (9:1–14:21) ――――――――

**Introduction**

Many have long agreed with the claim that "Chapters 9–14 are perhaps the most problematic six chapters in the Bible."[1] Every conclusion about authorship, unity with Zech 1–8, historical setting, literary structure, purpose, and interpretation of individual texts faces great dissent among commentators. Nonetheless, the final section of the book of Zechariah offers some of the richest theological insights the Old Testament has to offer.

In many respects the book of Zechariah stands as a capstone or culmination to prior biblical revelation. Chapters 1–8 develop themes of covenant, blessing and judgment, holiness, acceptable worship to the Lord, the restoration of Judah, and the ultimate restoration when God establishes the eschatological kingdom. The Introduction develops the point that few biblical authors attained the quantity or sophistication of intertextual relationships as did Zechariah, especially in chaps. 9–14. Consequently, the book of Zechariah, particularly the final six chapters, functions much like a lens, both focusing and refracting theological concepts from the remainder of the Old Testament. Zechariah reiterates the great theological themes of the Old Testament, bringing them into sharp focus for his contemporaries and ours. Just as Zechariah brought distant

―――――――――――――――――――――――

[1] D. J. Clark, "Discourse Structure in Zechariah 9–14: Skeleton or Phantom?" in *Issues in Bible Translation*, ed. P. C. Stine (New York: United Bible Societies, 1988), 64.

biblical teachings into view, likewise the prophet made it possible for his readers to observe forthcoming biblical and eschatological developments that lay beyond human ability to perceive.

As already noted in the Introsduction, Zech 9–14 probably had a more direct influence on the writers of the Gospels than any other Old Testament passages. C. H. Dodd observed that Zech 9–14 provided the New Testament writers with material of equal importance to the very testimony of Christ's ministry.[2]

Chapters 9–14 develop both Messianic and eschatological truths that became primary emphases in each of the Gospel accounts of Jesus Christ's earthly ministry. Because of the tremendous impact that Zech 9–14 had on the New Testament, not to mention on the Church's understanding of the Savior's work and his future kingdom, students of Zechariah should pursue this challenging portion of the book enthusiastically.

**Structure of Zechariah 9–14**

Despite diverse questions about chaps. 9–14, it is unnecessary to resort to the common approaches that relegate this section of Zechariah to another author who lived and ministered during a different time from Zechariah son of Berekiah, son of Iddo (1:1). As was argued in the Introduction, strong historical, literary, and theological reasons exist for maintaining the long-held view that chaps. 9–14 came from the same pen as did chaps. 1–8. Moreover, the traditional approach to the unity of the book of Zechariah best handles the biblical material contained in chaps. 9–14. Douglas Jones comments, "The well-established critical view that Zech. ix–xiv is quite separate in date and content from Zech. i–viii has not yet led to a satisfactory interpretation of the later chapters."[3]

Relatedly, one should not approach chaps. 9–14 as merely a disparate collection of sayings that have no organic connection with each other. At the most basic level, chaps. 9–11 and 12–14 each stand as unified sections with numerous organic affinities with one another. The most obvious connection between chaps. 9–11 and chaps. 12–14 is the presence of the introductory formula found in 9:1 and 12:1. In both introductory verses Zechariah employed the frequently used prophetic word *maśśāʾ*, a common word whose translation scholars dispute.[4] The word *maśśāʾ* may be translated either "burden" or "oracle." In either case, the presence of this expression both delineates the two sub-sections of Zech 9–14 and functions as an obvious literary link that unites the two sections into a cohesive unit. In addition to the symmetry introduced by the two *maśśāʾ* units, Zechariah wove together numerous thematic threads, fashioning chaps.

---

[2] C. H. Dodd, *According to the Scriptures* (Digswell Place: James Nisbet, 1952), 64–65.

[3] D. R. Jones, "A Fresh Interpretation of Zechariah IX–XI," *Vetus Testamentum* 12 (1962): 241.

[4] מַשָּׂא. See *HALOT*, 639–40; and BDB, 672.

9–11 and chaps. 12–14 into a single literary fabric. These motifs will receive attention in the introduction to Zech 12.

Further, several influential studies of the overall literary structure of chaps. 9–14 have recently emerged, beginning with the ground-breaking study by Paul Lamarche, which argues for the internal literary and theological cohesion of Zech 9–14.[5] Not only did Lamarche note unity within chaps. 9–14 without resorting to special pleading, he also suggested that the final six chapters of Zechariah have been arranged in a chiastic pattern. Lamarche presents the following structure of Zech 9–14:

A Judgment and salvation of surrounding nations (9:1–8)
  B Introduction to the king (9:9–10)
    C Israel's battle and ultimate victory (9:11–10:1)
      D Idolatry and judgment (10:2–3a)
    C' Israel's battle and victory (10:3b–11:3)
  B' The people reject the shepherds (11:4–17)
    C" Israel's battle and victory (12:1–9)
  B" Yahweh's Servant pierced; mourning and purification (12:10–13:1)
      D' Idolatry and judgment (13:2–6)
  B'" Shepherd struck; judgment, purification, and return to God (13:7–9)
    C'" Israel's battle and victory (14:1–15)
A' Judgment and salvation of all nations (14:16–21)[6]

While those scholars who are already committed to the view that Zech 9–14 cannot have a structural unity generally discount Lamarche's work, a large contingent of scholars have embraced Lamarche's insights. For instance, David Clark has reached strikingly similar conclusions to Lamarche while using quite different literary tools.[7] A linguist employing discourse strategies, Clark identifies repeated Hebrew expressions that introduce new subsections in chaps. 9–14. While this is not an appropriate setting to survey the repeated Hebrew terms Clark finds, it will suffice to say that his observation of the placement of terms such as "on that day" seem to introduce new sections or thought units within chaps. 9–14. More importantly, Clark's analysis independently reproduces many of the results presented in the older study by Lamarche.

The chiastic interpretation offered by Lamarche and generally affirmed by Clark had a mixed reception. Many scholars have accepted his analysis outright.[8] Others, such as Boda, express reluctance to accept every "chiastic"

---

[5] P. Lamarche, *Zacharie IX–XIV: Structure Littéraire et Messianisme* (Paris: J. Gabalda, 1961).
[6] Ibid., 112–13.
[7] Clark, "Discourse Structure in Zechariah 9–14," 64–80. See also R. D. Moseman, "Reading the Two Zechariah's as One," *RevExp* 97 (2000): 487–98.
[8] J. G. Baldwin, *Haggai, Zechariah, Malachi*, TOTC (Downers Grove, IL: InterVarsity, 1972), 79–81.

pairing suggested by Lamarche.[9] As discussed in the Introduction, not all of Lamarche's paired terms rise above suspicion. Further, his chiastic treatment does not follow the typical A-B-C-C'-B'-A' pattern. However, enough symmetry exists in chaps. 9–14 that scholarship has returned in large measure to the view that the final six chapters of the book of Zechariah hold numerous literary and theological relationships.

These results lead to the conclusion that the soundest interpretive methodology rejects any treatment of Zech 9–14 that atomizes these chapters into fragmented sections having no discernible structure or purpose. Instead, it appears that chaps. 9–14 form a unified sub-unit of the book as a whole. Further, the various paragraphs comprising chaps. 9–14 relate to each other with discernible logical, literary, and theological symmetry.

The first paragraph in Zech 9–14 declares the Lord's judgment and subsequent salvation of the surrounding nations. Among the Old Testament prophets, messages of judgment against the nations as a whole include passages such as Isa 13–23, Jer 46–51, Ezek 25–32, Obadiah, and Nahum, as well as Amos 1:3–2:3 and Zeph 2:4–15. Surveying this list reinforces the point that the prophets devoted a significant portion of their space and energies condemning peoples for whom the prophetic books were not primarily intended. Why then did the prophets give so much attention to pagan nations?

In a very helpful survey of this question, Paul Raabe outlines several important theological and rhetorical observations that should guide the interpreter.[10] To begin, Raabe cautions against forcing any prophetic oracle into a single mold, recognizing that the biblical authors often communicated several messages on different levels to diverse audiences in the same text.[11]

As relates to Israel, judgments against the nations serve four distinct roles, according to Raabe. First, every judgment pronounced against any dominant power or against those nations who had persecuted Israel effectively promised God's people that the Lord would deliver them and give them victory over their foes. This theme occurs commonly throughout the prophets, and ultimately rests on God's design that Israel would be a blessing to the nations (see Gen 12:2–3; Jer 50–51). Second, as the Lord judged the unbelieving nations who oppressed Israel, he would displace these unfaithful nations from their lands, yielding territory for Israel that God had originally promised to his people. The biblical promise does not point toward world domination by Israel, which would be the ultimate expression of imperialism. Rather, God intends for Israel

---

[9] M. Boda, "Zechariah: Master Mason or Penitential Prophet?" in *Yahwism after the Exile: Perspectives on Israelite Religion in the Persian Era,* ed. R. Albertz and B. Becking (Assen: Van Gorcum, 2003), 52–54.

[10] P R. Raabe, "Why Prophetic Oracles against the Nations?" In *Fortunate the Eyes That See: Essays in Honor of David Noel Freedman,* ed. A. B. Beck, et al. (Grand Rapids: Eerdmans, 1995), 236–57.

[11] Ibid., 240.

to possess the land he had originally promised to Abraham and his descendants (see Gen 12:1; 15:18). Third, when the nations in whom Israel had foolishly and sinfully trusted for safety fell under divine judgment, all Israel would then appreciate the futility of trusting in anyone or anything other than the Lord himself (see Isa 20). Israel must always remember that her hope rested in the Lord alone. Fourth, the Lord's judgment against all nations that demonstrated hostility to God and his people prepares the way for a future time of restoration in which Israel will finally experience peace (see Zech 9:8).[12] This eschatological emphasis enjoys particular prominence in Zech 9–14. Finally, the Lord's judgment on every expression of sinfulness, often epitomized by the nations' insolence toward the Lord, upholds God's righteous character.

Regarding the pagan peoples, Raabe adds that oracles against the nations convey numerous messages from the Lord. To begin, God's judgment demonstrates the impotence of the nations' gods, thus revealing the Lord as the only true God. Consequently, only the Lord merits worship (see Zech 9:5). Moreover, after judgment the vanquished nations will flee to Zion either for safety (see Isa 16:1–5) or to honor the Lord with offerings (see Hag 2:6–9). Third, the defeat of oppressing nations will result in great joy and relief for the world (see Jer 51:48). Fourth, judgment against the nations will end the arrogant self-sufficiency of those nations who had rejected God and persecuted his people (see Zech 9:8), making way for the righteous kingdom the Lord will establish.[13]

In conclusion, Raabe outlines the basic rhetorical message of the oracles against the nations. These divine reports fall into three distinct categories: those intended for every person, those that applied only to Israelites, and the declarations only for non-Israelites. For every hearer, these oracles argue that no one can escape God's judgment. The Lord controls the future and judges sin wherever he finds it. Why then should anyone resist? Should not every person repent and cast himself on God's mercy?

For the Israelites, judgments against the nations comforted the despairing and brokenhearted nation (see Zech 9:8). Also, they taught Israel to shun foreign alliances that reflected a lack of faith in God and a willingness to compromise God's holiness. Further, oracles against the nations sometimes functioned as a backdrop for prophetic judgments against Israel in which the prophet argued that Israel's faith and moral living failed to rise above the levels of the pagan nations (see Amos 1–2).

For the non-Israelite audience, these sermons held out the promise of avoiding judgment if the nation would repent (see the book of Jonah). Alternatively, when God had determined that he would judge a people, the prophets may have announced this fact in advance so that once the judgment came, those who

---

[12] Ibid., 241.
[13] Ibid.

survived might understand what had happened to them. This gave the survivors an opportunity to turn their hearts to God in faith (see Isa 19:16–18).[14]

**Genre of Zechariah 9–14**

Finally, one must note the distinctively different literary genre found in Zech 9–14. Chapters 1–8 reveal a highly literate example of Hebrew prose, but chaps. 9–14 are predominantly poetry. Although the Introduction addresses fundamental distinctions between prose and poetry, several points deserve emphasis here. One cannot identify figurative language as the sole distinguishing feature of Zechariah's poetic section. Chapters 1–8 repeatedly employ metaphor, symbolism, personification, and metonymy. Other elements, both objective and subjective, distinguish the poetic material.

Semantic parallelism rests upon the creative interplay of word pairs.[15] When the meaning of one line of poetry intersects the meaning of its paired line, the semantic interplay rests on the foundation of either stock word pairs such as "rejoice greatly"//"shout" or unexpected choices of complementary terms.[16] This semantic parallelism represents the most prominent difference between the literary style of Zech 1–8 and chaps. 9–14.

In addition, numerous examples of figurative language and distinctive grammatical features of poetry (seen in poetic texts elsewhere in the Old Testament) further contrasts Zechariah's poetry from his prose material. Finally, terseness of style and more emotional language mark the poetic passages in Zechariah, most notably chaps. 9–14.

**1. Judgment and Salvation of Surrounding Nations (9:1–8)**

<sup>1</sup>**An Oracle**

**The word of the LORD is against the land of Hadrach**
 **and will rest upon Damascus—**
 **for the eyes of men and all the tribes of Israel**
 **are on the LORD—**
**<sup>2</sup>and upon Hamath too, which borders on it,**
 **and upon Tyre and Sidon, though they are very skillful.**
**<sup>3</sup>Tyre has built herself a stronghold;**
 **she has heaped up silver like dust,**
 **and gold like the dirt of the streets.**
**<sup>4</sup>But the LORD will take away her possessions**

---

[14] Ibid., 250–51.

[15] See the well regarded introductory treatments of Hebrew poetry by L. Alonso-Schökel, *A Manual of Hebrew Poetics* (Roma: Pontifical Instituto Biblico, 1988); A. Berlin, *Dynamics of Biblical Parallelism* (Bloomington: Indiana University Press, 1985); and W. G. E. Watson, *Classical Hebrew Poetry: A Guide to Its Techniques* (Sheffield: JSOT Press, 1984).

[16] Y. Avishur, *Stylistic Studies of Word-Pairs in Biblical and Ancient Semitic Literatures* (Neukirchen-Vluyn: Neukirchener, 1984).

and destroy her power on the sea,
and she will be consumed by fire.
⁵Ashkelon will see it and fear;
Gaza will writhe in agony,
and Ekron too, for her hope will wither.
Gaza will lose her king
and Ashkelon will be deserted.
⁶Foreigners will occupy Ashdod,
and I will cut off the pride of the Philistines.
⁷I will take the blood from their mouths,
the forbidden food from between their teeth.
Those who are left will belong to our God
and become leaders in Judah,
and Ekron will be like the Jebusites.
⁸But I will defend my house
against marauding forces.
Never again will an oppressor overrun my people,
for now I am keeping watch.

**9:1** Verses 1–8 focus on God's judgment and salvation of the surrounding nations, as does the mirror paragraph in 14:16–21. God's holiness demands that he judge sin and expel it from his kingdom. Only after dealing with sin will the Lord offer salvation to the peoples.

Verse 1 begins with the Hebrew word *maśśāʾ*, a common word whose translation scholars dispute.[17] The word *maśśāʾ* may be translated either "burden" or "oracle."[18] The rendering "burden" rests upon a generally accepted etymology of the word that apparently derives from the meaning "to take up or carry." Passages such as Exod 23:5; Isa 22:25; Jer 17:1 support this meaning.

While either translation ("burden" or "oracle") has merit, the Hebrew word probably functions as a formal title that introduces prophetic declarations.[19] The NIV translates *maśśāʾ* as "An Oracle" but moves the phrase to the level of a sectional heading, and unfortunately this formatting makes it appear to the English reader that "An Oracle" represents a translator's addition, much like paragraph headings. Instead, *maśśāʾ* serves as an integral component of the Hebrew text. The accents inserted into the Hebrew text by the Masoretic scribes suggest that the word *maśśāʾ* accompanies the phrase that follows, which lends further support to the rendering "oracle of."

The word *maśśāʾ* occurs prominently in Zech 9:1; 12:1; and Mal 1:1, in each case introducing a major section of the book. The repetition of this distinctive term solidifies the literary and thematic relationship in Zech 9–14. The

---

[17] מַשָּׂא. See *HALOT*, 639–40; and BDB, 672.

[18] P. A. H. de Boer, *An Inquiry into the Meaning of the Term maśśāʾ* (Leiden: E. J. Brill, 1948).

[19] T. McComiskey, "Zechariah," in *The Minor Prophets, Vol. 3*, ed. T. E. McComiskey (Grand Rapids: Baker, 1992), 1159.

identical use of *maśśā'* in Mal 1:1 also forges a relationship between Zech 9–14 and the book of Malachi. But this does not mean that one should adopt the view that Zech 9–14 and Malachi together comprise a separate biblical book.[20]

The Hebrew term *maśśā'* also conveys an authoritative saying in 2 Kgs 9:25–26. Of particular importance for Zech 9–14, the term introduces a divine judgment in 1 Kgs 21:19; Jer 23:33; and other passages. In Zechariah, *maśśā'* introduces the collection of prophecies in chaps. 9–14 that pronounce judgment on the unbelieving nations. The same word *maśśā'* in these prophecies also offers hope for salvation and restoration for Judah. As an authoritative word from the Lord, the word *maśśā'* also emphasizes the prophet's obligation to communicate God's word, despite the fact that the prophet would most likely prefer not to do so were it not for his divine mandate. The *maśśā'* signified the sacred duty that the prophet carried to fulfill the mandate placed on him by God.[21]

Merrill also notes that *maśśā'* frequently introduces eschatological contexts. In particular, Isaiah used the term in this fashion (Isa 13:1; 14:28; 15:1; 17:1; 19:1; 21:1,11,13; 22:1; 23:1). Consequently, with the numerous eschatological emphases in Zech 9–14, Zech 9 appropriately begins with *maśśā'* as well.[22]

Zechariah declared that the word of the Lord would come against a series of peoples. Theologically, the Old Testament portrays God's word as an active force accomplishing the Lord's will in history, among both the nations and his people Israel. The effects of God's word on earth include doing good (Mic 2:7), healing (Ps 107:20), falling on a nation in judgment (such as Israel in Isa 9:8 [Hb. 9:7]), coming as a destructive fire (Jer 5:14), and transforming future events into the shape the Lord desires (Ezek 12:28).[23]

Zechariah 9 begins with an oracle against Hadrach, a geographic designation that does not occur elsewhere in the Old Testament. Long unknown historically, the city has been identified in Assyrian texts, including those of Tiglath-Pileser III.[24] The reference to Hadrach as the first city to experience the power of the word of the Lord serves at least two purposes. First, Hadrach lies to the north of the other sites listed by Zechariah. Just as the Lord's judgment on Judah came from the north commencing the exile, so would God's word overrun the northern nations with a dramatic reversal. Second, Hadrach apparently lay beyond the greatest extent of either the Solomonic or Davidic kingdom.[25] Thus, Zechariah predicted that the Lord's authority would extend beyond the

---

[20] See M. H. Floyd, "The מַשָּׂא as a Type of Prophetic Book," *JBL* 121 (2002): 401–22; E. R. Clendenen, "Malachi," in R. A. Taylor and E. R. Clendenen, *Haggai, Malachi*, NAC (Nashville: Broadman & Holman, 2004), 241–43.

[21] de Boer, *Inquiry*, 214.

[22] E. H. Merrill, *Haggai, Zechariah, Malachi* (Chicago: Moody, 1994), 241.

[23] McComiskey, "Zechariah," 1031.

[24] *ANET*, 282–83.

[25] C. L. Meyers and P. Meyers, *Zechariah 9–14* (New York: Doubleday, 1993), 92.

most expansive boundaries ever known during Old Testament times. God's dominion would also overshadow pagan peoples.

As Zechariah's gaze turned southward, he viewed Damascus, the capital of Aram (Syria), a center of commerce, and a major city during the Persian era. Damascus also opposed Judah bitterly during most of her history (Amos 1:3). A few commentators question precisely what Zechariah meant when he stated that "the word of the LORD . . . will rest upon Damascus." While some claim that the phrase might express encouragement for Damascus,[26] no evidence in the text supports this view. More likely the prophet intended that the Syrian city will submit to the Lord totally because of the power of God's word. The march of God's word, like a mighty army, will conquer city after city toward its southern goal of Jerusalem. The Lord declares that his kingdom will extend beyond the borders of Judah, having a universal scope encompassing even long-time foes of God and his people.[27]

Verse 1b begins with "for" *(kî)*.[28] The particle *kî* functions in diverse ways in different Old Testament contexts. For instance, *kî* can introduce either direct or indirect discourse, purpose clauses, and result clauses, to name the most common uses.[29] McComiskey argues that *kî* here shows purpose, introducing "proximate causation, giving the broad reason for the divine activity."[30] McComiskey's explanation yields the following understanding of v. 1, "The word of the Lord is against the land of Hadrach . . . *because* the eyes of men and all the tribes of Israel are on the Lord." However, McComiskey's interpretation does not adequately treat the meaning of the passage.

Rather than a purpose clause, the *kî* functions more appropriately to introduce a result clause.[31] In other words, the final half of v. 1 gives the outcome of the action introduced in the first half of the verse. In light of the discussion above concerning the theology of the power of God's word, v. 1 suggests that the mighty word of God results in various peoples, including Israel, turning to the Lord in obedience and worship. Viewing v. 1b as a result clause leads to the following understanding, "The word of the Lord is against the land of Hadrach . . . *with the result that* the eyes of men and all the tribes of Israel are on the Lord." The power of God's word Zechariah described reminds one of Heb 4:12a, "For the word of God is living and active, sharper than any double-edged sword."

The second half of v. 1 has long drawn extensive scholarly attention. To put the question plainly, many believe that the Hebrew idiom *ʿên ʾādām* (NIV "the eyes of men," though *ʾādām*, "man," is singular) produces an "awkward"

---

[26] Baldwin, *Zechariah*, 159.
[27] Meyers and Meyers, *Zechariah 9–14*, 92.
[28] כִּי. See *HALOT*, 470–71; and BDB, 471–75.
[29] *IBHS*, § 38.4 a, 38.7 a.
[30] McComiskey, "Zechariah," 1159.
[31] *IBHS*, § 38.3.

reading.³² Despite the fact that the Masoretic Text makes good sense in its context, scholars often emend or alter one or both of the Hebrew words in the phrase ʿên ʾādām, although no manuscript evidence supports these conclusions.³³ Scholars routinely emend the word ʾādām to the morphologically similar term ʾărām³⁴ ("Aram").³⁵ Paul Hanson changes ʿên ("eyes of") to ʿam³⁶ ("people of"),³⁷ resulting in the translation "the people of Aram are on the Lord." Mitchell changes ʿên to ʿārê³⁸ ("the cities of"),³⁹ resulting in the translation "the cities of Aram are on the Lord."

Scholars who emend v. 1 as do Hanson and Mitchell argue that their suggestions better fit the context of Zech 9:1–8. However, even Meyers and Meyers concede that "the need to emend the Hebrew is questionable."⁴⁰ The *Preliminary and Interim Report on the Hebrew Old Testament Text Project* reaches a similar conclusion and views the Masoretic Text as certainly correct and deserving acceptance.⁴¹

So the decision to retain the traditional Hebrew reading rests on several arguments. First, the Masoretic Text reads well as it stands and should not be considered "awkward" because of a preconceived notion of what the verse should say. Second, no manuscript evidence supports the emendations. Finally, Meyers and Meyers make two additional literary points for rejecting the emendations in favor of the Masoretic Text. Altering the reading "eyes of" destroys the motif of the eyes of the Lord keeping watch over his people, an important theme for Zechariah. The nouns "eye" and "eyes" occur over ten times in Zech 1–8. The repetition of the word "eye" in 9:1 adds a literary and theological link between this paragraph and the first half of the book. Moreover, ʾādām ("men") also appears in 12:1,⁴² connecting chap. 9 with chap. 12.

---

³² Meyers and Meyers, *Zechariah 9–14*, 92. See J. J. O'Rourke, "Zechariah 9,1, *ʿÊN ʾĀDĀM*," *CBQ* 25 (1963): 123–28; and E. Zolli, "*ʿEYN ʾĀDĀM* (ZACH. IX 1)," *VT* 5 (1955): 90–92.

³³ M. Dahood, "Zacharia 9,1, *ʿÊN ʾĀDĀM*," *CBQ* 25 (1963): 123–24; E. Zolli, ibid.; P. J. van Zijl, "A Possible Interpretation of Zech. 9:1 and the Function of 'The Eye' (*ʿAYIN*) in Zechariah," *JNSL* 1 (1971): 59–67. All three survey the issues on these suggested emendations.

³⁴ אֲרָם. See *HALOT*, 89. The Hebrew consonants *resh* and *dalet* look similar and have been confused for one another.

³⁵ van Zijl, "Possible Interpretation," 59–67.

³⁶ עַם. See *HALOT*, 837–38.

³⁷ P. D. Hanson, "Zechariah 9 and the Recapitulation of an Ancient Ritual Pattern," *JBL* 92 (1973): 42.

³⁸ עָרֵי. See *HALOT*, 821–22.

³⁹ H. G. Mitchell, J. M. P. Smith, and J. A. Bewer, *A Critical and Exegetical Commentary on Haggai, Zechariah, Malachi and Jonah*, ICC (Edinburgh: T. & T. Clark, 1912), 263. See also the NRSV which follows this reading.

⁴⁰ Meyers and Meyers, *Zechariah 9–14*, 94.

⁴¹ D. Barthélemy et al., eds., *Preliminary and Interim Report on the Hebrew Old Testament Text Project*, 5 vols. (New York: United Bible Societies, 1979), 5:410–11. This report is a collection of opinions on textual criticism from several renowned scholars.

⁴² Meyers and Meyers, *Zechariah 9–14*, 94.

What then does it mean to say that "the eyes of men ... are on the Lord?"[43] Ps 123:1–2 presents a parallel usage:

> I lift up my eyes to you,
> > to you whose throne is in heaven.
> As the eyes of slaves look to the hand of their master,
> > as the eyes of a maid look to the hand of her mistress,
> so our eyes look to the LORD our God,
> > till he shows us his mercy.

When Judah's foes—the Lord's avowed enemies—look to God in submission and worship, God's new kingdom will be a universal one, characterized by faith, obedience, and peace.

The point that even "the tribes of Israel" will turn to the Lord reinforces the same message that "the eyes of men ... on the Lord" communicates. Zechariah was written centuries after the fall of Israel to the Assyrians in 722 BC, and the state of Israel was nothing more than a memory. For Zechariah to prophesy that Israel's tribes will worship God again envisions a glorious eschatological time in which Israel, lost and dispersed among the nations, would turn to the Lord along with her formerly idolatrous neighbors. Zechariah's vision evokes the prophecy of Ezekiel, who also foretold the restoration of the land of Israel (47:13,21–22; 48:19,29,31).

**9:2–3** Verse 2 continues the thought of v. 1a, describing the regions over which the word of the Lord would prevail. Not only was Hamath a prominent Syrian city situated on the Orontes river, it also served as a province in the Persian empire. The city featured prominently in the campaigns of Tiglath-Pileser III and Sargon II. The hated Greek monarch Antiochus IV (Epiphanes) renamed Hamath after himself, Epiphania.[44] Several biblical accounts list Hamath within the limits of the promised land (Num 13:21; Josh 13:5; Judg 3:3).[45] This observation holds particular importance since Zech 9:1–8 focuses on the recovery of the land of promise.

It is noteworthy that Zechariah included Hamath among those sites whose occupants would turn to the Lord in the future kingdom. Amos 6:1 includes Hamath among the complacent ones in Zion on whom God's judgment would fall. Jeremiah made a similar pronouncement against Hamath (49:23). Zechariah forcefully affirmed the Lord's astounding promise; even the enemies of Judah would someday turn to God in worship.

The Old Testament often pairs the cities Tyre and Sidon (Jer 27:3; Ezek 27:8; Joel 3:4). Tyre was famous for her mighty fortifications built for her defense during the reign of King Hiram, associate of King David of Israel. Tyre

---

[43] McComiskey's suggestion that the phrase should be translated "the Lord's eye is on humankind" poorly renders the *lamed* on the phrase ליהוה ("Zechariah," 1160).

[44] Mitchell, *Zechariah*, 264.

[45] Baldwin, *Zechariah*, 159.

withstood a five-year siege by the Assyrians. Later she endured a thirteen-year siege by the Babylonian king Nebuchadnezzar shortly after he successfully captured Jerusalem.[46]

Zechariah's statement "Tyre has built herself a stronghold," functions as a word play. The Hebrew word *ṣōr* ("Tyre")[47] sounds like the Hebrew root of the term *māṣôr* ("stronghold").[48] The expression scorns Tyre's self-sufficient actions. The arrogant and self-reliant attitude exhibited by Tyre throughout her history led other prophets to declare her doom (Isa 23:8–9). The classical prophetic condemnation of Tyre occurs in the book of Ezekiel who saw Tyre as the epitome of hubris and rejection of the Lord (see Ezek 28:2–10).

Ultimately, Alexander the Great fulfilled the Lord's promise of abasement for Tyre, devastating the city to such an extent that she never regained her former prominence.[49]

Verse 3 describes Tyre's wealth with a startling simile. Zechariah noted that Tyre had gathered tremendous riches as readily as one might sweep dust from a house or collect dirt from the city streets. The Hebrew word translated "heaped up," *wattiṣbār*, occurs rarely in the Old Testament.[50] The most illuminating other occurrence is in Exod 8:14 (Hb. 8:10) where the putrid frogs that infested Egypt were piled into fetid stacks.

Tyre's profane wealth presented Judah with a profound theological tension. How could a city that intentionally spurned the Lord attain such a profligate lifestyle? In stark contrast, how could God's own people face such an endless series of calamities? God's ultimate judgment on Tyre awaited a future resolution.[51] Similarly, the vindication of God's exalted people loomed in the distance.

**9:4** The Hebrew text of v. 4 begins with the common particle *hinnēh*,[52] often translated "behold," though the NIV does not translate it at all. However antiquated the English rendering "behold" may sound to modern ears, the particle serves an important function, emphasizing either the imminence of an action or underscoring the content of a verse. Both ideas exist in v. 4. The Lord is on the verge of bringing the inhabitants of Tyre under submission, a judgment the inhabitants of Tyre long merited. Vetter adds that "the indicative function of the particle in prophetic announcements of salvation . . . (e.g., 1 Kgs 11:31; 13:3; Isa 38:8; cf. Josh 3:11) may be explained in terms of a

---

[46] Meyers and Meyers, *Zechariah 9–14*, 97.

[47] צֹר. (*ṣōr*) See *HALOT*, 1053.

[48] מָצוֹר. See *HALOT*, 623. See also A. Wolters, "Word Play in Zechariah," in *Puns and Pundits* (S. Noegel, ed., Bethesda: CDL Press, 2000), 224.

[49] For a discussion of Alexander's fulfillment of the Lord's prophecy against Tyre, as well as the view that Zech 9:1–8 was written as a response to the Greek general's striking victory, see M. Delcor, "Les allusions à Alexandre le Grand dans Zach IX 1–8." *VT* 1 (1951): 110–24.

[50] וַתִּצְבָּר. See *HALOT*, 999; and BDB, 840.

[51] M. F. Unger, *Commentary on Zechariah* (Grand Rapids: Zondervan, 1962), 154.

[52] הִנֵּה. See *HALOT*, 252.

divine decision pronounced in response to an inquiry (e.g., in holy war: Judg 1:2; 1 Sam 24:5)."[53]

For the first time in the book, Zechariah employed the divine title *ădōnāy* ("Lord") instead of the Tetragrammaton (YHWH or "the LORD") or some other divine epithet. The word *ădōnāy* emphasizes God's sovereignty.[54] The epithet also frequently portrays God as victor over his foes in battle (Deut 3:23; Pss 37:13; 55:10; Isa 22:5; 40:10; Amos 8:9; Zech 9:14).[55]

The phrase "and destroy her power on the sea" presents several questions. The first question focuses on the significance of the Hebrew word *ḥayil* ("power"), but the term may also be translated "wealth."[56] The NIV's "power" reinforces the point of v. 3a that describes the mighty "stronghold" Tyre built to provide security. Alternatively, v. 3b stresses Tyre's unfathomable riches. Accordingly, the other nuance of *ḥayil* comes into view.[57] Some might wrestle with which nuance Zechariah intended.[58] Attempting to choose one of these two meanings leads to the wrong solution, however. Instead, the prophet most likely chose *ḥayil* because this word carries both meanings. Tyre was renowned both for her defensive might as well as her riches, but neither could save her in the onslaught of divine judgment. Everything that symbolizes Tyre's lofty position among the nations would be destroyed so that only a memory of her prominence would remain.

Despite the strength of Tyre's fortifications and her resolve in resisting her foes, the city fell to Alexander the Great in 332 BC. After seven months Alexander subdued the city, dramatically fulfilling Zechariah's prophecy. Once Alexander breached Tyre's walls, he destroyed the city, executed many civic leaders, and enslaved large numbers of the populace. Tyre survived as a city, but never regained its former splendor or prominence.[59] As Ezek 28 had predicted, Tyre and her surrounding cities would be cast down from their vaunted position, down to the pit full of shame and weakness.

Alexander's momentous conquest of Tyre, at least 150 years following Zechariah's prophecies, leads some scholars to argue that Zech 9–14 must be dated much later, to the time of Alexander.[60] This attempt to redate Zechariah and divide chaps. 1–8 from chaps. 9–14 reveals an unwillingness to consider the divine character of Zechariah's message in which the prophet consistently declared that his message came from the Lord himself. Zechariah's Lord was

---

[53] *TLOT*, 380.
[54] אֲדֹנָי. See *HALOT*, 12–13.
[55] Merrill, *Zechariah*, 243.
[56] חַיִל BDB, 298.
[57] See Zech 14:14 where חַיִל also means "wealth."
[58] McComiskey, "Zechariah," 1161.
[59] Baldwin, *Zechariah*, 160.
[60] Meyers and Meyers, *Zechariah*, 102–3.

not only capable of foretelling future events, but also of directing history as he prepared the way for his eschatological kingdom.

**9:5–7** In vv. 5–7 Zechariah listed four of the five capital cities of Philistia, called the Pentapolis.[61] Zechariah omitted only Gath, as also do Jer 25:20; Amos 1:6–8; and Zeph 2:4–6. Perhaps Zechariah overlooked Gath either because the city had already fallen to Uzziah's military campaigns in the Philistine plains (2 Chr 26:6) or because Ashdod had overshadowed Gath's former importance.

Amos had already prophesied the destruction of Gaza and Ashdod:

> "I will send fire upon the walls of Gaza
>   that will consume her fortresses.
> I will destroy the king of Ashdod
>   and the one who holds the scepter in Ashkelon.
> I will turn my hand against Ekron,
>   till the last of the Philistines is dead,"
> says the Sovereign LORD. (Amos 1:7–8)

The Lord told Zechariah that his judgment of Gaza and Ashdod would so devastate the region that foreigners would come to repopulate the desolate cities.

In 332 BC, ignoring the painful example of the sack of Tyre at the hands of Alexander, Gaza chose to resist the Greek conqueror. It only required five months for Alexander to bring Gaza to her knees. Once Gaza was defeated, Alexander ordered the king of Gaza, Batis, seized. After putting thousands of the citizens to death, Alexander sold the remnant into slavery. Alexander bound Batis to a chariot and dragged him through the streets of the city until dead.[62]

In the middle of v. 6, the narration shifts abruptly from the third person to the first. Speaking in the first person, the Lord proclaimed to Zechariah, to Philistia, and to the watching world what he intended to do. God would take the Philistines, whose arrogance had become proverbial, and transform them into a people for himself. Before the Lord could incorporate any of the Philistines into the remnant of Judah, however, first he had to judge their sin and cleanse them from the profane things in their midst.

Using the figure of speech synecdoche in v. 7, Zechariah referred to "blood" and "forbidden food" to picture the odious idolatrous practices of the Philistines. Although limited knowledge about Philistine religion survives, their detestable religious rites included worshipping idols, improper sacrifice, and eating unclean food. The Hebrew term *šiqqûṣ*, meaning "forbidden food" or "abominable things," typically occurs in Old Testament contexts that describe

---

[61] For a treatment of the archaeological evidence for Philistia, see Trude Dothan, *The Philistines and Their Material Culture* (New Haven: Yale University Press, 1982), especially pp. 219ff.

[62] Unger, *Zechariah*, 156.

paganism.⁶³ Deut 29:17 employs the same term to describe Egyptian idolatries, and Hos 9:10 uses the term to picture the shameful activities of Israel at Baal-Peor.⁶⁴ Isaiah condemned similar practices, castigating those who ate unclean meat and sacrificed in a forbidden fashion (Isa 65:4; 66:3,17).

In 2 Sam 24:16 (1 Chr 21:18), which outlines David's conquest of Jerusalem, the king chose not to destroy the Jebusites. Instead, the Jebusite people became a part of Judah. Likewise, Zechariah foretold that Judah would absorb the Philistine population into her own. Zechariah saw this eventuality in a positive light. The Philistines would be delivered from their idolatry and sin into the light and liberty of worshipping the Lord. Ekron, Ashdod, and Gaza—cities belonging to Judah at the time of the conquest (Josh 15:45–47)—once again would become a part of the people of promise and the land of promise after generations of rebellion against the Lord.

Verse 7 begins with the repulsive imagery of a man with blood dripping from his mouth. If not repugnant enough, the man had unclean food stuck between his teeth. This disgusting scene transforms into a picture of encouragement when one remembers that this scene predicted the ultimate defeat of all ungodliness and idolatry. The debasement of the false pride of the nations opens the way for the worship of the Lord in righteousness.⁶⁵ Unger adds, "Judgment will not only fall on the neighboring nations who have been Israel's ancient enemies, and a remnant of them be converted, but the Lord will carefully protect and preserve His own people for the coming of Messiah their Savior and eventual World Conqueror."⁶⁶ A partial fulfillment of Zechariah's prophecy occurs in Acts 8:40 where Philip brought the gospel not only to the Ethiopian, but also to Azotus. Azotus is the Roman name for the old Philistine city Ashdod.⁶⁷

**9:8** Verse 8 culminates in the Lord's climactic triumph over the nations, with the victory of the Lord finally reaching Jerusalem. There the Lord ultimately camps at "my house" *(lĕbêtî).*⁶⁸ The word "house" may refer to the temple,⁶⁹ but more likely the term has a broader application in v. 8, signifying the land of promise. This is how the word functions in Jer 12:7 as well as Hos 8:1; 9:15.⁷⁰ However, by metonymy "house" specifies not just the land, but more importantly, the people who occupy the promised land. Of the numerous New Testament passages that portray the people of God as the Lord's house, none relates more closely to Zech 9:8 than Heb 3:6: "But Christ is faithful as a

---

⁶³ שִׁקּוּץ. See *HALOT*, 1640–41.
⁶⁴ Merrill, *Zechariah*, 245.
⁶⁵ McComiskey, "Zechariah," 1162–63.
⁶⁶ Unger, *Zechariah*, 157.
⁶⁷ Baldwin, *Zechariah*, 161.
⁶⁸ לְבֵיתִי. For a survey of the use of בַּיִת ("house") in the Old Testament, see *TDOT*, 2:111–16.
⁶⁹ Meyers and Meyers, *Zechariah 9–14*, 119.
⁷⁰ K. L. Barker, "Zechariah," EBC, 659.

son over God's house. And we are his house, if we hold on to our courage and the hope of which we boast."

The day in which alien armies defiled the promised land with their unclean feet would end because the Lord promises to keep close watch over his possession. This assurance resumes a theme introduced in Zech 2:5 where the Lord says, "I myself will be a wall of fire around it [Jerusalem]." Zechariah 1:16 expresses a similar idea.

The Hebrew word for "defend" *(miṣṣābāh)* occurs nowhere else in the Old Testament as it is spelled in v. 8.[71] Over the past century, many commentators have attempted to replace the Masoretic reading with one that reads "sacred pillar." As a textual emendation, this suggestion does not rest on the witness of ancient manuscripts and should be rejected.

Verse 8 links the initial paragraph in chap. 9 to other themes throughout chaps. 1–8. First, the Lord's declaration that he keeps watch over his land recalls 4:10 where "the eyes of the LORD range through the earth," seeing all and controlling all. In both passages, "the Lord's all-seeing eye purposes to defend and provide for His people."[72] Verse 1 also speaks of the eye, but the eye belongs to men who look to the Lord for protection and guidance. Zechariah 9:9 serves as the cause—because the Lord's eye is always on his kingdom ("for now I am keeping watch"); v. 1 functions as the effect—that the inhabitants' eyes will look to their God ("the eyes of men are on the LORD"). The initial section of the second half of the book of Zechariah presents two basic truths: the Lord will reign victoriously, and he will gather the remnant of alienated peoples to himself in his eschatological reign.

Second, both Zech 9:8 and 7:14 include the same Hebrew idiom, *mēʿōbēr ûmiššāb*, an unusual expression meaning "to march back and forth."[73] The phrase occurs quite infrequently, here connecting chap. 9 to chap. 7. The NIV does not communicate the identical Hebrew idiom in both passages with like English idioms. But the Hebrew text plainly links God's message of salvation in v. 8 with a similar message in 7:14 that foretells the Lord's judgment on all who choose not to listen to God's call to obedience and repentance.

While the English word "oppressor" communicates adequately enough, the Hebrew term *nōgēś* makes the point more vividly.[74] The word *nōgēś* occurs in numerous places in the Old Testament to convey a "tyrant" (Isa 9:3), a "donkey driver" (Job 39:7), and "one who exacts tribute" (Dan 11:20). Zechariah used the term in an unusual positive sense to describe leadership during the

---

[71] מִצָּבָה. *HALOT* translates the word "garrison" (620). Many scholars such as Mitchell (*Zechariah*, 272) seek to change the text to מַצֵּבָה ("sacred pillar"). See HALOT, 620–21. No reliable reason exists for making this change. See Barthélemy, *Preliminary and Interim Report*, 5:412. The Masoretic Text reads quite satisfactorily as it now stands.

[72] Baldwin, *Zechariah*, 162.

[73] מֵעֹבֵר וּמִשָּׁב.

[74] נֹגֵשׂ. See *HALOT*, 670; and BDB, 620.

Messianic kingdom (10:4). But no use of the word was more vivid for Zechariah and his audience than "slave driver," evoking their enslavement in Egypt (Exod 3:7). Anyone belonging to Judah would immediately associate a powerful negative connotation with this term.

Verses 1–8 continue the holy war tradition found throughout the Old Testament. From Exod 15 through Hab 3 to the book of Zechariah, the Lord appears as a mighty warrior, victorious over evil forces that oppose his righteous kingdom. The Lord's reign will emanate from Jerusalem where the Lord's throne will rest.[75]

Zechariah declared that "never again" would an oppressor come and go over the land of promise, the Lord's territory, as one would trample one's own backyard. It is certainly the case that Alexander the Great did just that, repeatedly entering and leaving Israel from Egypt during his brief reign. But the focus of v. 8 certainly looks beyond Alexander. The universal and eschatological tone of the text suggests a fulfillment on a scale that the nation has never experienced. Days will come when no oppressor—whether Alexander, Caesar, or any other of the Lord's foes—will transgress God's holy place. The "never again" in v. 8 foreshadows the introduction of the divine King in v. 9 and finds its ultimate fulfillment in the end-times victory of Christ at his Second Advent. The scope of God's glorious reign surpasses anything that transpired in subsequent centuries following Zechariah's ministry,[76] so the passage clearly points to an eschatological fulfillment.

## 2. Introduction to the King (9:9–10)

> **⁹Rejoice greatly, O Daughter of Zion!**
>   **Shout, Daughter of Jerusalem!**
> **See, your king comes to you,**
>   **righteous and having salvation,**
>   **gentle and riding on a donkey,**
>   **on a colt, the foal of a donkey.**
> **¹⁰I will take away the chariots from Ephraim**
>   **and the war-horses from Jerusalem,**
>   **and the battle bow will be broken.**
> **He will proclaim peace to the nations.**
>   **His rule will extend from sea to sea**
>   **and from the River to the ends of the earth.**

---

[75] Many of the psalms capture the message of the Lord's victory over all of his foes (see Pss 2; 9; 24; 29; 46; 47; 48; 68; 76; 97; 98; 104; 110).

[76] For a survey of approaches to this section, see B. Otzen, *Deuterosacharja*, 10–34; and T. Collins, "The Literary Contexts of Zechariah 9:9," in *The Book of Zechariah and Its Influence*, ed. C. Tuckett (Burlington: Ashgate, 2003), 29–40.

Only after the Lord establishes his kingdom in the regions to the north of Judah will the Messiah come to reign. In introducing Judah's long-awaited King, v. 9 describes the King's character and v. 10 portrays his accomplishments.

**9:9** In vv. 9–10 the Lord speaks, promising to bring peace to all of the nations, as v. 10 makes clear. That the Lord speaks distinguishes God from the Messiah. One cannot identify the messianic King with the Lord himself.[77]

Verse 9 juxtaposes two distinct concepts, the nation's response to the arrival of the King whom generations of God's people had longed to see, with a treatment of the demeanor of the King himself. Zechariah could not see the details of Alexander the Great's fulfillment of the prophecies in vv. 1–8. Nor could the prophet envision the hubris for which Alexander was renowned. However, Zechariah certainly must have appreciated the arrogance of the world's most influential kings, much like Ezekiel condemned the king of Tyre (28:11–19). The contrast between the pride of the panoply of the secular kings and the humility of the messianic King prophesied in v. 9 could not be starker.

This messianic prophecy begins with the Lord's exhortation addressed to the "Daughter of Zion," also called the "Daughter of Jerusalem." Both appellations focus on the personal relationship between the Lord and his people. The poetic parallelism between the word pairs employs a synecdoche, an additional figure of speech in which the name of the city, Zion/Jerusalem, stands for all of her inhabitants, thus summoning all people to "rejoice greatly." The verbal form *gîlî mĕʾōd* ("to rejoice") is an imperative, commanding every hearer to obey.[78] Verse 9 parallels a similar command in Zeph 3:14–15:

> Sing, O Daughter of Zion;
> > shout aloud, O Israel!
> Be glad and rejoice with all your heart,
> > O Daughter of Jerusalem.
> The LORD has taken away your punishment,
> > he has turned back your enemy.
> The LORD, the King of Israel, is with you;
> > never again will you fear any harm.

The second half of Zech 9:9 gives the reason for Judah's jubilation. After they had waited until their hope had expired, the appearance of Judah's King finally seemed imminent. The NIV translates the Hebrew word *lāk* as "to you."[79] While the NIV rendering is accurate, the word can also mean "for your benefit."[80] The Hebrew idiom allows one to accept both options. Zechariah

---

[77] Merrill, *Zechariah*, 252; Meyers and Meyers, *Zechariah 9–14*, 132.
[78] גִּילִי מְאֹד. *HALOT*, 189–90.
[79] לָךְ.
[80] This use is a dative of interest or ethical dative. See GKC, § 119s, and *IBHS*, § 11.2.10d; T. Muraoka, "On the So-Called *Dativus Ethicus* in Hebrew," *JTS* 29 (1978): 495–98.

declared that the Messiah would soon emerge in the midst of Judah, "to you." More than mere appearance, this messianic King would come for the express purpose of saving his people. In his first advent, Jesus Christ fulfilled both nuances of *lāk*, coming to the people and for their personal benefit.

In this important prophecy, Zechariah disclosed the character (v. 9) and the accomplishments (v. 10) of the coming Messiah. Before focusing on his deeds, Zechariah called attention to the Messiah's four distinct characteristics. First, the Messiah will be "righteous." The Hebrew term *ṣaddîq* is one of the most important theological terms in the entire Old Testament.[81]

To understand the word "righteous" precisely presents challenges that interpreters have long faced. A brief survey of uses clarifies what lay behind Zechariah's use.[82] In its most basic sense, righteousness reflects conformity to an established standard. For instance, the Bible calls for weights and measures to show "righteousness," that is, to be honest in all business dealings (Lev 19:36). In its theological sense, righteousness reflects moral standards that rest on the character of God himself. The Bible presents the concept of "righteous" as the opposite notion of *rāšā'* ("evil").[83] These divine norms govern the life and work of the king (2 Sam 8:15), protect and complete the life of the righteous individual (Prov 13:6), and represent the Lord's hope for his people collectively (Deut 6:25). Righteousness surpasses an abstract divine attribute; God intends for his righteous standard to flood over the faithful like a rushing torrent (Isa 48:18). In an eschatological sense, "righteous" describes the godliness and truth that will characterize the coming eschatological kingdom (Jer 23:5; Isa 59:14). The term also describes salvation in an eschatological sense (Dan 9:24). In the future kingdom, "righteousness" will also come to the pagan nations (Isa 51:5). Perhaps most significant of all for understanding Zech 9:9, the coming Messiah will be readily identified by his righteousness (Isa 9:6–7; 11:4–6; 16:5; 32:1). In describing the righteousness of the coming Messiah, Zech 9 simply builds upon a solid Old Testament foundation of messianic prophecies.

The biblical story of the coming messianic King likely begins with Gen 49:10–11: "The scepter will not depart from Judah. . . . He will tether his donkey to a vine." The Judaic commentary, *Genesis Rabbah*, also connects the donkey tied to the vine in Gen 49 to a messianic interpretation.[84] Zechariah's Messiah represents the culmination of the Lord's promise to David of a Davidic King who would reign perpetually: "Your house and your kingdom will endure forever before me; your throne will be established forever" (2 Sam 7:16).[85] The Old Testament often reminds its readers that the Messiah must

---

[81] צַדִּיק. See *HALOT*, 1001–3.

[82] *TLOT*, 1049–61; *TDOT*, 12:243–62.

[83] רָשָׁע. *HALOT*, 1295–96.

[84] *Gen. Rab.*, 98.9, 99.8.

[85] The theme of the coming Davidic Messiah fills the Old Testament. See Hos 3:4–5; Amos

descend from David, fulfilling the pivotal promises in the Davidic covenant (2 Sam 7:11–16). Isaiah's numerous messianic prophecies build on the theme of the Messiah's righteousness. Isaiah 9:7 reads in part,

> He will reign on David's throne
>   and over his kingdom,
> establishing and upholding it
>   with justice and righteousness
>   from that time on and forever.

In his important prophecy of the Branch, Isaiah declared: "with righteousness he will judge the needy, with justice he will give decisions for the poor" (11:4). Isaiah also stresses the righteous character of the Branch, announcing that "Righteousness will be his belt" (11:5), "See, a king will reign in righteousness" (32:1), and "By his knowledge my righteous servant will justify many, and bear their iniquities" (53:11). Isaiah made it clear that the Messiah's righteousness manifested itself in his deeds as he administered the Lord's purposes for his kingdom. Psalm 2:6 says, "I have installed my King on Zion, my holy hill."[86]

Second, the Messiah comes "having salvation," that is, bringing salvation to his people. One can translate the Hebrew term *nôšāʿ* either as a passive verb, "having salvation," or as a reflexive, "manifesting himself as a savior." The passive view makes the Messiah the recipient of salvation, deliverance granted to him by another. The reflexive idea maintains that the Messiah, by virtue of his own might, saved himself.[87]

Some scholars wish to exclude the reflexive idea, arguing that the passive understanding, "saved," teaches that the Messiah had been saved from some terrible ordeal by the Lord.[88] Mitchell agrees, claiming that the Messiah will reign victoriously "in the might of the God of Israel . . . His triumph, therefore, stands as the triumph of the faith of the Servant of Yahweh."[89] Barker recommends translating this verb "saving" in order to capture both passive and

---

9:11–12; Mic 5:2–4. See A. M. Leske, "Context and Meaning of Zechariah 9:9," *CBQ* 62 (2000): 663–78, for a recent overview of scholarly approaches to v. 9.

[86] For a helpful treatment of messianic viewpoints in ancient Israel, see J. Klausner, *The Messianic Idea in Israel: From Its Beginning to the Completion of the Mishnah* (London: Allen and Unwin, 1956).

[87] נוֹשָׁע. See *HALOT*, 448–49; Joüon-Muraoka, *Grammar*, § 51, has additional information about the reflexive and passive uses of the *Niphal* stem. See also George L. Klein, "The Meaning of the *Niphal* in the Hebrew Bible" (Ph.D. diss., Dropsie College for Hebrew and Cognate Learning/Annenberg Research Institute, 1992).

[88] R. L. Smith, *Micah-Malachi*, WBC (Waco: Word, 1984), 256. Smith adds, "He [the messianic king] will be saved by Yahweh." Smith's view suggests that the king will receive divine help and favor so that whatever he does will prosper: "He will keep his covenant and rule righteously." See also Baldwin, *Zechariah*, 165.

[89] Mitchell, *Zechariah*, 273.

reflexive nuances.[90] Barker's approach acknowledges both the Lord's role in placing the Messiah in his royal office as well as the Messiah's fundamental role as Savior.

One can hardly read Zechariah's vision about the future king without appreciating the hope that a Messiah bearing salvation offered to Judah. More importantly, the Messiah, Jesus Christ, would ultimately fulfill this prophecy beyond any measure the postexilic community could appreciate. In several passages Isaiah paired the twin ideas of "righteousness" and "salvation" (45:8; 46:13; 51:4–5), both distinctives of Christ's ministry (1 Pet 3:18; 2 Pet 1:1).

Third, the Messiah Zechariah described would show himself to be "humble" or "lowly." The NIV translates the Hebrew word ʿānî as "gentle."[91] The same term describes the humility of Moses in Num 12:3. The word can also mean "poor" (Zech 7:10; 11:7,11) or "afflicted" (Isa 14:32; 51:21; 54:11). The humility of the messianic King also echoes themes in Isaiah. Messianic prophecies in Isaiah prominently state both the Messiah's righteousness and his humility. The Messiah's lowly state figured prominently in Isa 53, especially vv. 2b–3:

> He had no beauty or majesty to attract us to him,
> He was despised and rejected by men,
>  a man of sorrows, and familiar with suffering.
> Like one from whom men hide their faces
>  he was despised, and we esteemed him not.

In demonstrating to a Jewish community that Jesus was the Christ, Matthew cited the Lord's words: "Come to me, all you who are weary and burdened, and I will give you rest. Take my yoke upon you and learn from me, for I am gentle and humble in heart, and you will find rest for your souls. For my yoke is easy and my burden is light" (Matt 11:28–30). Matthew connected Isaiah's description of the Messiah with the words and character of Jesus Christ in a compelling fashion no reader could easily misunderstand.

Fourth and last, Zechariah foretold a Messiah who would come to his people "riding on a donkey, on a colt, the foal of a donkey." Of the four qualifications introducing the Messiah, this last feature presents the most questions. Initially, one must ask, why would the Messiah arrive on a donkey? What significance does the donkey have?

It was not unusual for kings in the biblical era to mount donkeys (Judg 5:10; 10:4; 12:14). David himself rode a donkey when fleeing from one of Saul's onslaughts (2 Sam 16:2). Lipinski argues that donkeys served as the royal mount of choice in the ancient Near East, particularly as illustrated in the Mari texts.[92] One must temper Lipinski's conclusion with the realization that he describes

---

[90] Barker, "Zechariah," 662.
[91] עָנִי. See *HALOT*, 856; *TDOT*, 11:239–52; F. du T. Laubscher, "The King's Humbleness in Zachariah 9:9. A Paradox?" *JNSL* 18 (1992): 125–34.
[92] E. Lipinski, "Recherches sur le livre de Zacharie," *VT* 20 (1970): 51.

practices well over one millennium prior to Zechariah's day. Without a doubt, though, the ancients did not view donkeys as ignoble animals, particularly when compared to horses, as some might think today.[93]

The most important conclusion about the significance of the donkey in Zech 9 is the very different connotation the donkey had compared to the horse. Horses represented one of the most advanced military weapons of the day. The constant threat of military action continually tempted Israel to trust in her weaponry, or that of her allies, rather than placing her faith in the Lord. Several passages pointedly remind Israel that trusting in horses for salvation will always proves useless (Isa 2:7; 31:1; Mic 5:10; Hag 2:22). The Lord's "pleasure is not in the strength of the horse" (Ps 147:10). Verse 10 alludes to the fact that God's ways are not man's ways when it comes to bringing peace to the kingdom. The Messiah would remove these war horses from Jerusalem, and other weapons of warfare, when his kingdom reign began. Symbolically, the new Messiah riding a beast of burden, not an animal known for its military value, powerfully underscores the peaceable kingdom over which the Messiah will rule. Thus, the symbolism of riding a donkey emphasizes the peaceable mission of the Messiah.

The parallelism of "his donkey" and "his colt" in Gen 49:11 anticipates the parallelism in Zech 9:9 between "a donkey" and "a colt, the foal of a donkey." Zechariah portrayed a single animal described with word pairs in poetic parallelism. Genesis 49 uses the same poetic technique and describes the donkey as tied up, awaiting its opportunity to serve.

The Gospel accounts draw from Zech 9:9 to show Jesus' fulfillment of this messianic prophecy. Matthew mentions two beasts of burden, not just one (Matt 21:2,7). Matthew surely did not portray a "circus trick" in which the Lord rode two animals simultaneously.[94] Rather, the Gospel writer emphasized to a Jewish audience that the Lord totally fulfilled the most minute detail of the prophecy that Zechariah had foretold.[95]

When the Lord Jesus entered Jerusalem during his triumphal entry, he was hailed as "King of the Jews."[96] Tragically, not only did the Jews reject Jesus

---

[93] *ANET*, 238; and Keel, *The Symbolism of the Biblical World* (New York: Crossroad, 1985), 280. Using rather curious logic, T. R. Hobbs argues that the king riding on a donkey represents "an image of domination" ("The Language of Warfare in Zechariah 9–14," in *After the Exile: Essays in Honour of Rex Mason*, ed. J. Barton and D. J. Reimer [Macon, GA: Mercer University Press, 1996], 125). The typology of the early church fathers such as Justin Martyr viewed the donkey as a prefigurement of the salvation of the Gentiles. See Justin Martyr, *Iustini Martyris Dialogus Cum Tryphone*, 53 (Patristische Texte und Studien 47:157); Clement of Alexandria, *Le Pédagogue*, 1.5.15.1–3 (SC 70:138); Chrysostom, *In Joannem homiliae*, 66.1.395.C–D (COO 8:453–54); and Caesarius of Arles, *Sermo*, 113 (CCSL 103/1:472).

[94] Barker, "Zechariah," 664.

[95] See also D Instone-Brewer, "The Two Asses of Zechariah 9:9 in Matthew 21," *TynBul* 54 (2003): 87–98.

[96] Matt 21:1–11; Mark 11:1–11; Luke 19:28–40; John 12:12–15.

as their Messiah, they also spurned the peace that he had offered them (Luke 19:39–44). Irenaeus lamented that they did not "understand that all the prophets announced his two advents: the one, indeed, in which he became a man subject to stripes . . . and sat upon the foal of an ass . . . but the second in which he will come on the clouds . . . slaying the impious with the breath of his lips."[97]

**9:10** Verse 10 furthers the theme of the Messiah's accomplishments, focusing on the epoch of peace he will introduce. His dominion will result in peace for all creation. Zechariah continued the similar prophecies in earlier prophets. For instance, Isaiah had declared that swords would become plowshares (2:4), bloody warriors' boots would burn in the fire (9:5), and the wolf would live peaceably with the lamb (11:6).

God promised to eliminate the chariot, the war horse, and the battle bow, the three primary assets in any ancient armory (Mic 5:10). The Lord had once created a peaceable, orderly universe, but it was shattered by disobedience to his command (Gen 1–3). In the coming day of eschatological renewal and recreation, the Lord will restore his creation to what he had originally intended when he first fashioned it.

The verb *wĕhikrattî* ("I will take away," literally "I will cut off") is applied to both Ephraim and Jerusalem, linking them together.[98] Zechariah saw the capital of Judah in the south, Jerusalem, united again with Ephraim, the most significant tribe of Israel in the north. The prophets frequently portrayed Israel and Judah reunited to symbolize the unimaginable extent of the Lord's restoration of his creation. Ezekiel joined two sticks together, symbolizing Ephraim and Judah (37:16–20). Jeremiah extended the new covenant to Israel and Judah (31:31). Moreover, Isaiah prophesied that all jealousy between Judah and Israel would cease (11:13) when the Root of Jesse reigned.

The extent of the Messiah's rule, described as "from sea to sea," could mean from the Nile to the Euphrates (Gen 15:18), from the Mediterranean to the Red Sea, or from the Mediterranean to the Dead Sea.[99] Instead of one of these interpretative options, the geographic expression serves as a merism, describing two extremes with the intent of portraying all lands. Thus, the Messiah will reign over every nation. His reign will emanate from Zion, Jerusalem. The word "Jerusalem" means "city of peace," a fitting site for the Messiah's peaceful, righteous rule.

The one hope for world peace rests in the person of the Messiah and his righteous reign. Quite appropriately, none of the Gospel writers cite v. 10 when explaining how Jesus Christ's triumphant entry fulfilled the prophecy of Zech 9:9. Only after Christ's second coming will creation see v. 10 fulfilled.

---

[97] Irenaeus, *Contre les Hérésies*, 4.33.1 (SC 100:802–804).
[98] וְהִכְרַתִּי. *HALOT*, 501.
[99] Barker, "Zechariah," 663. Magne Saebø ("Vom Grossreich zum Weltreich," *VT* 28 [1978]:83–91) compares the eschatological perspectives of Pss 72:8; 89:25; and Zech 9:10b as each text prophesies the Lord's universal dominion.

## 3. Israel's Battle and Ultimate Victory (9:11–10:1)

> ¹¹As for you, because of the blood of my covenant with you,
> I will free your prisoners from the waterless pit.
> ¹²Return to your fortress, O prisoners of hope;
> even now I announce that I will restore twice as much to you.
> ¹³I will bend Judah as I bend my bow
> and fill it with Ephraim.
> I will rouse your sons, O Zion,
> against your sons, O Greece,
> and make you like a warrior's sword.
>
> ¹⁴Then the LORD will appear over them;
> his arrow will flash like lightning.
> The Sovereign LORD will sound the trumpet;
> he will march in the storms of the south,
> ¹⁵ and the LORD Almighty will shield them.
> They will destroy
> and overcome with slingstones.
> They will drink and roar as with wine;
> they will be full like a bowl
> used for sprinkling the corners of the altar.
> ¹⁶The LORD their God will save them on that day
> as the flock of his people.
> They will sparkle in his land
> like jewels in a crown.
> ¹⁷How attractive and beautiful they will be!
> Grain will make the young men thrive,
> and new wine the young women.
>
> ¹Ask the LORD for rain in the springtime;
> it is the LORD who makes the storm clouds.
> He gives showers of rain to men,
> and plants of the field to everyone.

**9:11–12** Two distinct elements in v. 11a link the following passage with the preceding one. First, the verse begins with the particle *gam* (meaning "also" but not translated in the NIV).[100] Verses 1–10 describe the unstoppable onslaught of the Lord's victory over every enemy of righteousness and peace. Zechariah 9:11–17 continues the theme of God's kingdom, overviewing the process by which the Lord would establish his promised kingdom of peace by conquering his foes and saving his people. Second, the pronoun "you" beginning v. 11 is a feminine singular form. The parallel phrases, "Daughter of Zion" and "Daughter of Jerusalem," in v. 9 serve as the grammatical antecedent of "you" since the word for daughter *(bat)* is also feminine sin-

---

[100] גַּם. See *HALOT*, 195–96.

gular.[101] Verses 11–12 also contain extensive battle imagery: "prisoners" (v. 11), "fortress" (v. 12), "bow" (v. 13), "sword" (v. 13), "trumpet" (v. 14), and "slingstones" (v. 15). This imagery reinforces the theme of the Lord's might as he compels the insubordinate nations to cease warring and worship him in truth and peace.

Zechariah begins by exhorting his hearers to "return." The Hebrew word *šûbû* has a long history in the Old Testament demanding repentance and spiritual restoration.[102] Nowhere does the imperative *šûbû* occur with more frequency or pathos than in Jeremiah.[103] For instance, Jeremiah pleaded "Return, faithless Israel" (3:12); " 'Return, faithless people,' declares the LORD, 'for I am your husband' " (3:14); and " 'If you will return, O Israel . . .' then the nations will be blessed by him" (4:1–2). Zechariah's use of the word *šûb* thus evokes the memory of Jeremiah's life-long ministry preaching a message of repentance and revival. Judah ignored "the weeping prophet" and reaped the consequences. Now she had the opportunity once again to turn to her Lord for guidance and protection.

"The blood of the covenant" provides the basis on which the Lord would deliver his people. Zechariah did not clarify which Old Testament covenant he viewed as the foundation for the Lord's deliverance of Judah. Many commentators conclude that the prophet referred to the Mosaic covenant.[104] Since the Mosaic covenant was the one covenant that the Lord consummated with the shedding of an animal's blood (Exod 24:1–8), Zechariah likely had this covenant in mind. Mitchell observes: "It was their [Judah's] neglect of this covenant that moved Yahweh to drive them from the country, and it is his faithfulness to it that explains the promise of a restoration."[105]

Only in Exod 24:8 does the exact expression, "blood of the covenant" *(dam–habběrît)*, occur.[106] Throughout the Old Testament blood functions as a sign of the covenant itself.[107] Not until the New Testament would the complete phrase "blood of the covenant" reappear. When the Savior introduced the Lord's Supper, he stated, "This is the blood of the covenant, which is poured out for many" (Mark 14:24). Only in Christ would the Lord's faithfulness to his people find its ultimate fulfillment.

The Lord promises to free the prisoners. The NIV translation, "I will free," renders a perfect tense verb, a verbal form that normally portrays completed action. The perfect tense routinely occurs in Old Testament narrative to describe past events. However, Zechariah's use of a perfect tense verb for action

---

[101] בַּת. *HALOT*, 165–66.
[102] שׁוּבוּ. *HALOT*, 1427–34, esp. 1429–30.
[103] See W. L. Holladay, *The Root Šûbh in the Old Testament* (Leiden: E. J. Brill, 1958).
[104] See Barker, "Zechariah," 666; and Unger, *Zechariah*, 165.
[105] Mitchell, *Zechariah*, 278.
[106] דַּם־הַבְּרִית. *HALOT*, 224–25, 157–59; *TDOT*, 3:248–49.
[107] Merrill, *Zechariah*, 258–59.

that obviously would occur in the future indicates that, from the Lord's perspective, the action was as good as done.[108]

God also declares that he will liberate the prisoners from "the waterless pit." The metaphor recalls the waterless pit in which Joseph's brothers threw him (Gen 37:24). Similarly, Jeremiah's foes sought to rid themselves of God's faithful, weeping prophet by casting him into a pit without water (Jer 38:6). In a more figurative vein, Isaiah described the ministry of the Servant of the Lord, including his work "to free captives from prison and to release from the dungeon those who sit in darkness" (42:7). For Zechariah, the metaphor "waterless pit" refers to the Babylonian exile, and the "prisoners" symbolized, at least in part, those Judahites remaining in exile.[109] Zechariah may have also intended an additional figurative sense to the concept of "prisoners" that describes the nation's enslavement to sin, difficult circumstances, and political oppression. Moreover, insofar as the Lord postponed the ultimate fulfillment of this prophecy to the eschatological kingdom, the metaphor of the "waterless pit" refers to those prisoners of sin who longed for the release that only the righteous Judge could decree.

Verse 12 exhorts the Judahites to return to their "fortress," which translates a Hebrew word that rarely occurs in the Old Testament; in fact, the precise form used here does not appear elsewhere in the Bible. For this reason, many scholars have sought to excise the term from the verse, although the ancient manuscript evidence unambiguously supports retaining the word. A similarly spelled word describes a "sheepfold" in Mic 2:12. Judah's newly found fortress represents a total reversal of her earlier circumstances in the waterless pit.

Zechariah probably intends the word "fortress" to refer to Jerusalem, at least in part. For the Judahites remaining in exile, Jerusalem functioned as the hope of a fortress, albeit in a limited sense. Most of the people who intended to return to the promised land had long since departed Babylon and arrived in Jerusalem and her environs. For them, Zion offered significant sanctuary from life's hardships. Ultimately though, only the Lord himself could provide Judah with lasting security. The Old Testament often pictures the Lord as a fortress or stronghold, using a variety of terms. For instance, Ps 9:9 (Hb. 9:10) reads, "The Lord is a refuge for the oppressed, a stronghold in times of trouble."[110]

The Lord promised to "restore twice as much" to Judah as she possessed before. The concept of "double" in Zech 9 may function as it does in Job 42:10 where "double" actually means twice as much as the original amount. Alternatively, "double" may speak of an equivalent amount to what the Lord had granted previously, thus signifying a copy or a mirror portion, not twice as much. Irrespective of the nuance intended by Zechariah, the Lord clearly

---

[108] Klein, "The Prophetic Perfect," *JNSL* 16 (1990): 45–60.
[109] Barker, "Zechariah," 666.
[110] For a sampling of similar themes, see Pss 18:2; 31:3; 59:9,19; 71:3; 91:2; 94:22; 144:2; Jer 16:19; Nah 1:7.

promises great blessings and restoration of long-lost possessions beyond what any Judahite could expect.

**9:13** Verse 13 employs the language of divine warfare to express the Lord's eschatological message, showing how the promise of a twofold restoration in v. 12b will come to fruition. Using metaphor, God speaks of Judah as a bow, a weapon of war that will subjugate the nations when used as a tool in the Lord's hands.[111] On her own, Zion can do nothing to protect herself, let alone vanquish the peoples who have long opposed both Abraham's seed and the Lord himself. When his people are used solely for the Lord's purposes, no one can halt God's kingdom.

Zechariah's passing mention of Greece ("Javan," Hb. *yāwān*[112]) has drawn tremendous attention for centuries. Verse 13 plainly declares that in the future day of divine victory, God will use Judah as an instrument to defeat Greece. Two questions come into sharp focus. First, how should one understand a reference to Greece in a sixth-century BC book? More specifically, was the reference to Greece anachronistic since the Hellenistic nation truly became a world power two centuries later? Second, how should the interpreter understand the fulfillment of the prophecy that Judah would defeat Greece?

Not surprisingly, many scholars argue that the reference to Greece in v. 13 supports the conclusion that the book of Zechariah dates to the third century BC.[113] Others opt to treat "Greece" as a gloss that was added to the text long after Zechariah penned the book.[114] The historical evidence does not warrant either conclusion, but rather agrees well with the perspective of Zech 9.

While Greece did not become prominent enough to vie for world domination until the time of Alexander the Great, the historical record supports the claim that the Hellenistic nation had begun to flex her political will centuries before the time of Alexander.[115] No more than 20 years elapsed between

---

[111] S. M. Paul, "A Technical Expression from Archery in Zechariah IX 31a," *VT* 39 (1989): 495–96.

[112] יָוָן. *HALOT*, 402. M. J. Boda (*The NIV Application Commentary: Haggai, Zechariah* [Grand Rapids: Zondervan, 2004], 421) claims that Zechariah's mention of "your sons, O Javan" may have alluded to Javan, the ancient descendant of Japheth in the table of nations (Gen 10:2). However, in the context of the reference to the nations Judah, Ephraim, and Zion, Zechariah was probably referring to a nation called Javan, that is, Greece.

[113] Otto Eissfeldt, *The Old Testament: An Introduction*, trans. P. R. Ackroyd (New York: Harper & Row, 1965), 437; Mitchell, *Zechariah*, 279. See Paul Redditt, "Nehemiah's First Mission and the Date of Zechariah 9–14," *CBQ* 56 (1994): 666. Redditt argues that the reference to the Greeks proves inconclusive for dating the final chapters of Zechariah.

[114] Hanson, *The Dawn of Apocalyptic* (Philadelphia: Fortress, 1975), 298. Others wish to alter the reference to Greece on the grounds that the word disrupts the meter of the passage (Rudolph, *Haggai, Sacharja 9–14* [Gütersloh: Gerd Mohn, 1976], 184).

[115] M. Delcor, "Les allusions à Alexandre," 110–24. Delcor stresses the interpretation that Zechariah focused on Alexander in this passage. In contrast, Paul Hanson argues that one must not confuse mundane war with cosmic war, concluding that the apocalyptic genre of Zech 9 mitigates against any historicizing method. See Hanson, "Zechariah 9 and the Recapitulation," 37–59.

Zechariah's prophecy and the time when Greece possessed sufficient military might to rebel openly against Persia. Greece had become so formidable that after hostilities broke out with Persia, the preeminent world power of the day, the Persian army could not quell the Greek uprising for generations.[116] Greece attained such strength by Zechariah's time that Merrill observes, "It did not even require divine revelation to see that this [Greece's military ascendancy] was imminent."[117] One should not infer, however, that the political landscape in the late sixth or early fifth centuries BC suggested that a direct conflict between Greece and Judah was imminent.

The second question is, When would God fulfill his prophecy regarding Greece? While Zion successfully encountered the Hellenists in battle in 165 BC, the universal and eschatological tone of chap. 5 suggests much more than a regional conflict.[118] The events foretold in v. 13 would only see their culmination when the Lord ultimately establishes his kingdom on earth.

**9:14–16** This subsection of Zech 9 begins with Israel's struggle, picturing Judah as "prisoners" in a "waterless pit." The passage concludes with a banquet in which God's people have ample food to "devour." Unlike previous texts where God sent an intermediary to speak for him, the Lord himself appears here to fulfill his promises.[119] This passage uses the language of a storm, often employed to describe theophany in the Old Testament. God's appearance gave Judah the security and provisions she needed to survive.[120] No Old Testament passage provides a more compelling background to Zech 9:14–16 than Exod 19:16–19 where the Lord himself came down on the mountain with awesome majesty to deliver the law to Moses. Just as the Sinai event demonstrated the Lord's unspeakable power and validated his special relationship with his people, so the theophany in Zech 9 reminded the postexilic community that God would do no less for them than he had done for Israel in days past when she suffered under the heavy Egyptian hand.

The scene of a raging rain storm portrays lightning as arrows from the Lord himself. Numerous passages describe God's hurling lightning to earth like arrows (Pss 18:13–14; 144:5; Hab 3:4). Deuteronomy 32:41 portrays lightning as the Lord's sword. Lightning represents a primary visual component of a theophany (Exod 19:16–20; Ps 18:7–15; Hab 3:3–15). Now, the audible portion of the scene resounds.

---

[116] Meyers and Meyers, *Zechariah 9–14*, 19, 21–22.

[117] Merrill, *Zechariah*, 261. Meyers and Meyers (*Zechariah 9–14*, 147–48) reach similar conclusions.

[118] McComiskey, "Zechariah," 1171.

[119] The word "appear" translates יֵרָאֶה. *HALOT*, 1160. Although translated as a passive *Niphal*, the form is actually a classic example of a tolerative *Niphal* in which the Lord allowed himself to be seen by human eyes (Klein, "*Niphal*").

[120] See 2 Sam 22:8–18; Pss 18:7–15; 29; and Hab 3:3–15 for similar examples of theophany.

Surprisingly, Zechariah did not mention the crack of thunder in response to the lightning. Normally, thunder accompanies lightning in the biblical texts, passages that often describe thunder as the Lord's voice (Deut 5:22; Ps 29:3–9). Instead, blasts from the "trumpet" *(šôpār)* replace the sound of thunder in the tumultuous theophany.[121] The resounding call of the *šôpār* signaled the beginning of various rituals, including the beginning of the Sabbath. The *šôpār* also blew to celebrate momentous events (1 Kgs 1:34; 2 Kgs 9:13), seasonal festivities (Ps 81:3), and particularly to call the nation to war (Judg 3:27; 1 Sam 13:3). In apocalyptic passages like Zech 9, the *šôpār* called the Lord's people to worship (see Isa 27:13). However, this is the only passage in the Old Testament where the text employs an anthropomorphism in which the Lord himself blows the *šôpār*.

One must also consider the possibility that Zechariah's reference to lightning had polemical significance. Baal, the fertility god whose worship often enticed the Israelites into idolatry, was a rain god. In the Ugaritic epics, Baal rode the storm cloud with a bolt of lightning in his right hand, ready to hurl to earth. Many biblical passages repudiate Baal worship by portraying the Lord as the only God who can do the wonders the Baal worshippers falsely attributed to their idol.[122]

Verse 14 concludes by stating that the Lord will arrive in the storms coming from the south. The reference to the south powerfully counters the normal Old Testament connotation to the word "north," a geographic term that always carried negative overtones. For example, the prophets often described judgment coming from the north. The preexilic prophets threatened Israel, and later Judah, with the prospect of marauding armies coming down out of the north to invade the land of promise. This danger first came from Assyria and then later Babylon (Jer 1:13–16; 4:5–31; 6:22–26). Moreover, Judah viewed the north as the land of the exile (Jer 3:12; 16:15; 31:8; Zech 2:6). In contrast, God's blessings often came from the south (Judg 5:4–5; Nah 1:3; Hab 3:3), a dramatic reversal of the norm.

Zechariah introduced God with the divine title "the LORD Almighty" *(YHWH ṣĕbā'ôt)* in v. 15, a familiar designation for God in the book of Zechariah.[123] Frequently translated "Lord of Hosts," this divine epithet underscores the Lord's power, especially his military might. The Lord of Hosts will arrive not only to subdue Judah's enemies, but also to shield his people from their foes. The divine title emphasizes the primary theological point of the paragraph: the day will come when the Lord will ultimately vanquish every foe.

---

[121] שׁוֹפָר. *HALOT*, 1447–48

[122] The book of Hosea and the Elijah and Elisha stories contain excellent accounts of polemics against Baalism. See L. Bronner, *The Stories of Elijah and Elisha as Polemics Against Baal Worship* (Leiden: E. J. Brill, 1968).

[123] יהוה צְבָאוֹת.

God's holy war against those who oppose his kingdom will come to a decisive and final end.

Verse 15 presents the outcome of the Lord's theophany. The declaration that "the LORD Almighty will *shield* them" promises divine protection from enemies who would otherwise easily overrun Judah. The term *yāgēn* ("will shield")[124] echoes the use of verbal forms derived from the same verbal root promising God's protection of Jerusalem from the onslaught of the Assyrians in the eighth century BC (see Isa 37:35; 38:6; 2 Kgs 19:34). Zechariah's readers must have appreciated the verbal link with earlier texts that foretold one of the Lord's miracles on behalf of their forefathers and the assurance that God offered for their future deliverance. God's promise of protection rested on the power and glory of the Lord himself. The linguistic connection drew attention to the fact that the Lord had performed miracles for his people before.

Smith notes that v. 15 presents more difficulties than any other verse in this passage, as a survey of different English translations illustrates.[125] The first major question concerns the phrase *wĕ'ākĕlû* (literally "they will devour"), which the NIV renders "they will destroy."[126] The Hebrew term often signifies judgment and overwhelming devastation (Deut 4:24; Jer 2:30; Ezek 7:15). This nuance fits Zechariah's prophecy well, describing the consuming victory God will grant his people over the nations. Quite apart from the judgmental overtones of "devour," the word also routinely means "to eat." The "waterless pit" of the exile, the want of material goods, and not least, the spiritual hunger of the people, had emaciated the nation. Using the metaphor of a feast, Zechariah described bounty that will satisfy Judah's appetite when they "roar as with wine" and are "full like a bowl." In God's coming kingdom the Lord's children will enjoy an abundance of both material and spiritual blessings. Further, the verse continues the paradise motif of lasting peace on earth often pictured in Old Testament texts (cf. Isa 9; 11).

The next clause illustrates the prevailing theme of security: "they will destroy and overcome with slingstones" *('abnê–qela')*.[127] Slingstones represented one of the most important weapons of warfare in the ancient Near East. Used in comparatively long distance battles, a skilled army wielding slingstones could wreak havoc on opposing forces.[128] However, interpreters can read Zechariah's reference to slingstones in distinctly different ways. Many scholars desire to emend the Masoretic Text to read "slingers" *(bĕnê qōlēa')*.[129] Despite the

---

[124] יָגֵן. *HALOT*, 199.

[125] R. L. Smith, *Micah-Malachi*, 260.

[126] וְאָכְלוּ. *HALOT*, 46–47.

[127] אַבְנֵי־קֶלַע. *HALOT*, 7–8, 1105–6. Merrill (*Zechariah*, 261–62) offers a helpful survey of the various understandings of "slingstones."

[128] See Y. Yadin, *The Art of Warfare in Biblical Lands* (New York: McGraw-Hill, 1963), 296–97; and R. de Vaux, *Ancient Israel* (New York: McGraw-Hill, 1965), 2:53–54.

[129] בְּנֵי קֹלֵעַ. Meyers and Meyers (*Zechariah 9–14*, 153–54) survey a variety of additional proposed emendations.

variety of clever suggestions about this reading, the received Hebrew text reads well and should be retained. "Slingstones" functions as a metonymy for the warriors who wielded the weaponry. The text then focuses not on the destruction of the weapons, but rather on the warriors whose evil impulses the Lord would blunt.

Zechariah compared the coming fullness of Israel's blessing to that of the "bowl used for sprinkling the corners of the altar." The metaphor of a full bowl communicates the point of abundant blessings effectively, although v. 15 portrays no ordinary bowl. Leviticus 4:3–7 describes the use of the bowl to which Zechariah refers, the sacred receptacle that held the bull's blood. From this bowl the priest sprinkled blood on the corners of the altar to honor the Lord (cf. Exod 24:6–8). A similar use of the bowl occurs in Zech 14:20, which describes sacrificial bowls placed before the altar inscribed with the sacred message "Holy to the LORD."

Verse 16 shifts metaphors twice, initially introducing the pastoral imagery of shepherd and flock. "Sheep" often serve as a metaphor for God's people in the Old Testament (see Jer 23:1; Ezek 36:37; Zech 10:2; 11:4,7,11,17; 13:7). With comparable frequency, the Lord appears in the text as the Shepherd (Gen 48:15; Pss 23:1; 80:1; 95:7; Isa 40:11; Hos 4:16; Mic 7:14). The appearance of God results in the salvation and security of Judah. As a shepherd defends his sheep at all costs, so the Lord ensures Judah's well-being, as he does for his people of every age.

The second metaphor in v. 16 compares the magnificence of God's goodness to the dazzling display of light reflected by jewels in a crown. Further, Zechariah developed a wordplay on "stone," contrasting slingstones (v. 15) with precious stones. Both types of stones conveyed the effects of the Lord's covenant with Judah, protection from enemies and abundant blessing. In chap. 9 Zechariah reprised the theme of a stone that he first introduced in 3:9. As in Exod 28:17–21 and Zech 3:9, the gem stones in 9:16 each represent the people of God gleaming with the Lord's light.

The word "crown" *(nēzer)* distinguished the individual set apart by God for special service in his kingdom.[130] In the Old Testament the term designates a king's crown (2 Sam 1:10; 2 Kgs 11:12) as well as the crown worn by the high priest (Exod 29:6; Lev 8:9). While the reference to the crown in chap. 9 does not exclude royal connotations, the priestly significance seems primary in light of the priestly emphasis of the book of Zechariah (especially chap. 3). Judah will soon serve the Lord in full, righteous array. Exodus 19 lies behind the theophany of chap. 9, as already noted. Exodus 19:6 speaks to the issue of Israel's priesthood to the Lord: "You will be for me a kingdom of priests and a holy nation." Similarly, Isa 61:6 says, "You will be called priests of the LORD, you will be named ministers of our God."

---

[130] נֵזֶר. *HALOT*, 684.

The phrase "on that day" *(bayyôm hahû')* typically introduces prophecies with an eschatological focus in the prophetic books.[131] As noted in the comments about Greece in v. 13 above, Zechariah offers hope of the Lord's salvation of his people. The prophet saw a future assurance that far surpassed anything those experiencing the postexilic era could imagine.

Verse 16 concludes by giving the Lord's rationale for his blessings extended to Judah. She is precious to God, more valuable than precious stones in a sovereign's crown. Isaiah 62:3 states a similar notion: "You will be a crown of splendor in the LORD's hand, a royal diadem in the hand of your God." The Lord's commitment to his people defies human understanding. McComiskey develops the theological point of comparing Judah to gems in a crown: "The powerful forces opposing Christ's kingdom may have periodic successes, but they will never vanquish that kingdom because it is the royal insignia of God's sovereign rule in the world."[132]

**9:17–10:1** The theme of God's promised salvation in v. 16 continues with a significant shift to the agricultural metaphor of rain. Few meteorological events remind humans of their powerlessness over creation more than a protracted drought. Using real life circumstances close to the everyday lives of his audience, Zechariah employed metaphors of crops, sheep, and especially rainfall to remind the people that no help exists for them other than God himself. Indeed Zechariah, like many biblical authors preceding him, viewed rain as an emblem of the Lord's salvation.[133] Deut 11:13–14 assured Israel that "if you faithfully obey the commands I am giving you today—to love the LORD your God and to serve him with all your heart and with all your soul—then I will send rain on your land."

"Grain" and "new wine" function as symbols of prosperity, standing in contrast to the image of the haggard people in v. 11. Frequently, the Old Testament pairs grain and wine to represent the Lord's bountiful blessings (Gen 27:28; Num 18:12; Deut 33:28; Isa 36:17). Since "new wine" *(tîrôš)* refers to the first pressings of the grapes, the term probably does not refer to an intoxicant.[134] The prophets often promised an eschatological day when creation would no longer suffer under the pain of sin, yielding harvests humans will not have known since the garden of Eden. Several prophetic passages illustrate the point of agricultural blessing in the end times when Israel finally experiences the restoration (see Isa 4:2; 30:23; Ezek 34:26; Amos 9:13).

---

[131] בַּיּוֹם הַהוּא. Merrill, *Zechariah*, 263. Also, Simon J. De Vries, "Futurism in the Preexilic Minor Prophets Compared with That of the Postexilic Minor Prophets," *BZAW* 325 (2003): 267–70.

[132] McComiskey, "Zechariah," 1174.

[133] K. Elliger, ed., *Das Buch der zwölf kleinen Propheten II: Die Propheten Nahum, Habakuk, Zephanja, Haggai, Zacharja, Maleachi* (Göttingen: Vandenhoeckt & Ruprecht, 1975), 154.

[134] תִּירוֹשׁ. Some view the question of whether this was fermented wine differently. *HALOT*, 1727–28.

The NIV's "How attractive and beautiful they will be" suggests that the pronoun "they" refers back to the jewels in v. 16. Although this is plausible, many translations and interpreters differ. The RSV has "it," which is similar to the NKJV's "its." The KJV reads "his" as does the NRSV. While the NIV, and the majority of other translations, interpret the Hebrew to refer to the gemstones, and by extension to the people of God, the KJV and NRSV view the antecedent of the pronoun either as the Lord or the Messiah.

Both pronominal suffixes in question are third person masculine *singular*. Unger strongly advocates the messianic interpretation, viewing the pronominal antecedent as the Messiah himself. Unger believes that v. 17 breaks out in an expression of praise to the Messiah for his "goodness" (NIV "attractive") and his "beauty."[135] Merrill adds a similar possibility—that v. 17 may extoll the Lord—but he acknowledges that the ambiguity of the Hebrew text precludes certainty.[136] In the final analysis the text allows for either view: that the pronoun refers back to the gemstones in v. 16, or either to the Messiah or the Lord. But the antecedent of Hebrew pronouns typically occurs in the immediately preceding context. Lacking certainty, the best approach to the question locates the antecedents in v. 16, the gemstones. Further, it is not unusual for a third person masculine singular pronoun to represent a plural antecedent. The NIV translation reproduces this approach well.

Zechariah 10:1 follows the themes in the preceding verses so closely that scholars have long argued that one should not separate it from chap. 9. Zechariah 10:1 continues the theme of bounty and joy that God's people will receive when the Lord's kingdom comes. God promised Zechariah and the rest of the nation that great blessing would replace the judgment they had endured if only they would remain obedient to the Lord. The promise of God and its fulfillment loomed right before Judah. Like many other texts in the book of Zechariah, the scope of the prophecy projected into the distant future. For example, the drought was "right here right now," just as the Old Testament had often predicted as a judgment from God (Deut 28:21–22). Now the rain which only the Lord had the power to shower on the nation would come in response to obedience (Deut 28:12). The word for "rain" *(malqôš)* in the prayer in v. 1a ("Ask the LORD for rain in the springtime") differs from the other terms for rain, which signify "latter rain."[137] In the parallel eschatological passage in Joel, *malqôš* (2:23) symbolizes eschatological blessing, not merely rainfall. The rain God promised will drop showers of blessing on the people just as the Lord declared that he will "pour out my Spirit on all people" (2:28).

As in Zech 9:14, 10:1 likely inveighs against Baalism. Idolatry led Judah to generations of judgment and misery. The Lord desired that his people never

---

[135] Unger, *Zechariah*, 171.
[136] Merrill, *Zechariah*, 264.
[137] מַלְקוֹשׁ. *HALOT*, 594.

forget that only he could send the rain and the resulting prosperity. Jeremiah put the matter plainly, "Do any of the worthless idols of the nations bring rain?" (14:22) The non-existent god Baal falsely claimed to ride the storm cloud even though the Lord himself had created that cloud (10:1).

When the prophet exhorted his readers to "return to your fortress" (9:12), he reminded them all that only the Lord can serve as a true fortress for his people. Chapter 9 both warns and promises that God can and will preserve and protect his people. Why should anyone vainly seek elsewhere for blessing? Augustine developed the point further, stating that the fortress in v. 12 referred to Jesus.[138] Accordingly, Luther's famous hymn leads the faithful to remember the God who serves as their true Protector and Benefactor:

> A mighty fortress is our God,
> A bulwark never failing;
> Our helper He, amid the flood
> of mortal ills prevailing:
> For still our ancient foe
> Doth seek to work us woe:
> His craft and pow'r are great,
> And, armed with cruel hate,
> On earth is not his equal.
>
> Did we in our own strength confide,
> Our striving would be losing;
> Were not the right Man on our side,
> The Man of God's own choosing:
> Dost ask who that may be?
> Christ Jesus, it is He;
> Lord Sabaoth, His name,
> From age to age the same,
> And He must win the battle.
>
> And tho' this world, with devils filled,
> Should threaten to undo us,
> We will not fear, for God hath willed
> His truth to triumph thro' us:
> The Prince of Darkness grim,
> We tremble not for him;
> His rage we can endure,
> For lo his doom is sure,
> One little word shall fell him.

---

[138] Augustine, *Enarrationes in Psalmos*, 60.5 [61:4; CCSL 39:768].

That word above all earthly pow'rs,
No thanks to them abideth;
The Spirit and the gifts are ours
Thro' Him who with us sideth:
Let goods and kindred go,
This mortal life also;
The body they may kill:
God's truth abideth still,
His kingdom is forever.[139]

## 4. Idolatry and Judgment (10:2–3)

> ²The idols speak deceit,
>     diviners see visions that lie;
> they tell dreams that are false,
>     they give comfort in vain.
> Therefore the people wander like sheep
>     oppressed for lack of a shepherd.
> ³"My anger burns against the shepherds,
>     and I will punish the leaders;
> for the LORD Almighty will care
>     for his flock, the house of Judah,
>     and make them like a proud horse in battle.

**10:2** Zechariah 10:1 admonishes the nation to pray to the Lord, realizing that all blessings come from him. Verse 2 contrasts sharply with v. 1, lamenting that trusting in idols results in nothing but judgment and sorrow. With the following section Zechariah shifted his focus from the ideals of the restoration the Lord would effect to the present spiritual state of the nation. Themes of future blessing, righteousness, and deliverance abruptly turn to idolatry, falsehood, and aimlessness. Zechariah 9 focuses on the nation's struggle with their foes. Both chapters engage the theme of peace and well being that the Lord resolves to bring to his forlorn flock.[140]

Chapter 10 addresses the internal threat posed by corrupt rulers.[141] Verse 2 begins with a causal clause that articulates the reason God's judgment will rain on the spiritual leaders in the land, in contrast to the showers of blessings promised in 10:1. Zechariah 10:2 condemns the idolatry that has pervaded Judah. Astonishingly, the doleful punishment of the exile had not taught the next generation of God's people the folly of turning to idols for guidance or protection. One should expect Judah to remember how zealously the Lord opposed

---

[139] "A Mighty Fortress Is Our God," *The Baptist Hymnal*, # 8.

[140] M. A. Sweeney, *The Twelve Prophets, Vol. 2*, Berit Olam (Collegeville, MN: Liturgical Press, 2000), 668.

[141] M. H. Floyd, *Minor Prophets. Part 2* (Grand Rapids: Eerdmans, 2000), 472.

every manifestation of idolatry. The Lord Almighty had declared, "I am very jealous for Jerusalem and Zion" (1:14; 8:2).

Zechariah employed a term for "idols" *(tĕrāpîm)* that occurs several times in the Old Testament.[142] The word first appears in Gen 31:19 to describe the household gods Rachel stole from her father Laban. In Judg 17:5; 18:5, *tĕrāpîm* functioned in rituals for the divination of future events.[143] Samuel condemned the use of *tĕrāpîm* by God's people, comparing Saul's blatant act of disobedience in offering illegal sacrifices to the Lord (1 Sam 13:1–11) to the odious sin of idolatry (1 Sam 15:23). Hosea 3:4 acknowledges the sinful practice of worshipping *tĕrāpîm* in the eighth century BC. Although it does not specifically mention the worship of *tĕrāpîm*, Deut 18:10–12 is a key passage that condemns such practices, including all divination to predict the future, portraying these shameful acts as "detestable" to the Lord.

Using personification, Zechariah portrayed the inanimate *tĕrāpîm* as though they were talking, speaking "deceit" *('āwen)* to the nation.[144] Basically connoting disastrous circumstances, *'āwen* describes the misfortune that always follows evil actions in the lives of the people of Israel. As a natural consequence of evil behavior, *'āwen* never describes the specific acts of God in the Old Testament. Zechariah's usage fits the meaning of the word well, picturing the calamitous outcome of listening to a non-god for direction.

Word pairs in biblical Hebrew poetry yield helpful insights into the way the author paralleled the meanings of the words. The term *'āwen* precedes *šeqer* ("falsehood"), its paired word, in Zech 10:2 as well as in Job 11:11; Ps 41:6 (Hb. 7); and Isa 59:4. The word *šeqer* signifies a lie (Mal 3:5) or a breach of faith.[145] Of particular relevance to Zech 10:2, the Old Testament applies *šeqer* to "delusive dreams" (Jer 23:32); a "deceptive vision" (Jer 14:14); and "the prophet and the one who teaches lies" (Isa 9:14; Mic 2:11).[146]

"Diviners" attempted to foretell the future, undaunted by the Lord's absolute prohibition of their activities in Deut 18.[147] Jeremiah also struggled against theological falsehood, including the doctrine of the inviolability of Zion, and railed against the false prophets, diviners, interpreters of dreams, and mediums who prophesied lies to the nation (Jer 27:9–10; also 23:32). Since the diviners and dreamers conveyed messages that the Lord did not sanction, any comfort these misleaders offered the people would assuredly prove to be in "vain." The Hebrew term Zechariah chose to communicate the notion of "vain" is *hebel*;

---

[142] תְּרָפִים. *HALOT*, 1794–96; *TLOT*, 1433–34.

[143] K. van der Toorn, "The Nature of the Biblical Teraphim in the Light of the Cuneiform Evidence," *CBQ* 52 (1990): 203–22.

[144] אָוֶן. *HALOT*, 22; *TLOT*, 60–62. See *TDOT* (1:140–47) for a helpful survey of the use of the term in the Old Testament.

[145] שֶׁקֶר. *HALOT*, 1648–49.

[146] Ibid., 1649. See *TLOT*, 1399–1405.

[147] See F. H. Cryer, *Divination in Ancient Israel and its Near Eastern Environment* (Sheffield: JSOT Press), 1994, for a helpful and thorough treatment of divination in Israel and beyond.

the same word in Ecclesiastes expresses the utter futility of any endeavor that does not rest solely on serving the Lord.[148] Moreover, numerous other passages use *hebel* in polemics against worshipping idols (see Ps 31:6 [Hb. 7]; Isa 57:13; Jer 8:19; 10:14–15; 51:18; Jon 2:8). Seemingly, Judah and her leaders preferred to listen to anyone other than the Lord.

The prophet likened the result of false prophecy on the welfare of the nation to the wandering of a flock of sheep. Verse 2b closely parallels Ezekiel's statement:

> My sheep wandered over all the mountains.... They were scattered over the whole earth, and no one searched or looked for them. Therefore, you shepherds, hear the word of the LORD: As surely as I live, declares the Sovereign LORD, because my flock lacks a shepherd and so has been plundered and has become food for all the wild animals, and because my shepherd did not search for my flock but cared for themselves rather than my flock, ... I am against the shepherds. (Ezek 34:6–8,10)

The oppression suffered by Judah resulted from the lack of a righteous shepherd to guide the people in the Lord's path. The "shepherd" represented a widely known metaphor for a ruler in the ancient Near East as well as in the Old Testament. In the prologue to his renowned code of laws, Hammurabi identified himself as "the shepherd, called by Enlil."[149]

In the Old Testament, "shepherd" functions as a royal metaphor that applies to human kings, the Lord himself, and the messianic King. When praying to the Lord for his successor, Moses asked that Joshua would be a shepherd for the sheep (Num 27:17). Jeremiah complained about the shepherds in his day: "The shepherds are senseless and do not inquire of the LORD" (Jer 10:21). Ezekiel devoted all of chap. 34 to the theme of the ruthless shepherds of Israel who plundered and abandoned their flock, God's people, contrasting the faithlessness of these shepherds with the coming Davidic monarch who would serve as the ultimate faithful Shepherd for God's flock (Ezek 34:23–24). On a divine level, the beloved metaphor to generations of believers, "The LORD is my shepherd" (Ps. 23:1), extols God's faithful rule over the life of his faithful people (see Ps 100:3; Isa 40:11). Additionally, Ezek 34:23–24 employs the shepherd motif to introduce the messianic King.

The New Testament further develops the Old Testament's teaching about the coming messianic Shepherd. Matthew explained that the birth of Jesus fulfilled the prophecy, stating that "out of you [Bethlehem] will come a ruler who will be the shepherd of my people Israel" (Matt 2:6). After the onset of his

---

[148] הֶבֶל. See Eccl 1:2,14; 2:1,15,21,23,26; 3:19; 4:4,7,8,16; 5:9; 6:2,9,11; 7:6; 8:14; 11:8,10; 12:8. *HALOT*, 236–37; *TDOT*, 3:313–20.

[149] *ANET*, 164.

earthly ministry, Jesus echoed the message of Zech 10:2b and compassionately observed the people around him as "harassed and helpless, like sheep without a shepherd" (Matt 9:36). In John 10:14 Jesus asserted himself to be "the good Shepherd" who knows his sheep and whose sheep know him. The New Testament shows that the early church recognized Jesus as the "great Shepherd of the sheep" (Heb 13:20; see 1 Pet 5:4). Finally, Rev 7:17 announces the eschatological hope for the Shepherd to reign over the kingdom: "For the Lamb at the center of the throne will be their shepherd."

Many tragic episodes of judges and kings who turned to illegitimate sources of revelation punctuate the Old Testament story. These ancient means of divination included casting arrows like lots (Ezek 21:21), the examination of animal fetuses, scrutinizing livers for anomalies that people throughout the ancient Near East thought could predict future events, consideration of dreams, and attempts to conjure the dead. For example, Saul sought the medium at Endor (1 Sam 28); Ahab pursued Baal (1 Kgs 16:31); Ahaziah asked Baal-Zebub for information about the future (2 Kgs 1:2); Ahaz desired the protection of the Assyrian deities and offered sacrifices in an idolatrous fashion (2 Kgs 16:10–18); and Manasseh sacrificed his own son in his futile pursuit of direction and protection from Baal and Asherah (2 Kgs 21:1–9).[150] Whatever the empty conduit of revelation Israel's leaders pursued, the essence of their sin was rejecting God's genuine revelation and looking to avenues that could neither reliably guide nor ultimately satisfy.

The early church did not fail to appreciate the implications of Zech 10:2 for the leadership of the church. The Apostolic Constitution refers to Paul's instructions about the spiritually minded restoring those who were caught in sin in a gentle manner (see Gal 6:1), and then continues:

> God by Isaiah says to the bishops, "Comfort you, comfort you my people . . ." It therefore behooves you, upon hearing those words of his, to encourage those who have offended, and lead them to repentance, and afford them hope, and not vainly to suppose that you shall be partakers of their offenses on account of such your love to them. Receive the penitent with alacrity and rejoice over them, and with mercy and bowels of compassion judge the sinners. . . . It is your duty, O bishop, neither to overlook the sins of the people nor to reject those who are penitent, that you may not unskillfully destroy the Lord's flock or dishonour his new name which is stamped upon his people, and you yourself be reproached as those ancient pastors were.[151]

---

[150] Merrill, *Zechariah*, 270–71.
[151] A. Ferreiro, ed., *The Twelve Prophets*, Ancient Christian Commentary on Scripture (Downers Grove, IL: InterVarsity, 2003), 264–65.

**10:3** Verse 3 begins with the Lord's anger burning against the "shepherds," the leaders of Judah. The precise reference Zechariah intended when describing Judah's leaders as shepherds remains an important question. Many have understood the shepherds to be Davidic rulers or governors during Zechariah's day. Paul Hanson has been widely associated with this Davidic interpretation of the shepherds.[152] However, Meyers and Meyers provide evidence for a non-Davidic understanding of "shepherds" in v. 3.[153] Their first observation recognizes that the action in the ensuing verses does not appear to deal with Davidic rulers. Secondly, Meyers and Meyers note that the preceding context harshly judges false prophets for their harmful leadership among God's people. It is quite likely that this critique continues in v. 3.

Zechariah next chose an unusual and highly unflattering term for "leaders" *(hā'attûdîm)*, which normally refers to a male goat or sheep in the Old Testament (Gen 31:10–12; Deut 32:14; Jer 51:40).[154] The same word applies to political leaders in Isa 14:9 when Isaiah metaphorically described the grave's excitement to receive the departed spirits of leaders who had once held sway in their earthly realms, but now death had reduced them to the level of those whom the leaders had once ruled. These same rulers that the grave would swallow thought it unnecessary to submit to the Lord in life. In death, though, they would experience the unending judgment their disobedience warranted.

The second half of v. 3 transitions from the problems of past and present leadership in Judah to the good news of a future reign that would reflect God's righteousness. Zechariah's stern warning to Judah's idolatrous leaders contrasts sharply with the prophet's tidings of reassurance in vv. 4–12.

A significant pun in v. 3 mirrors the themes of Judah's faithless leaders in Zechariah's day (v. 3a), as well as the assurance of a blessed future reign (v. 3b).[155] But the pun on the verbs *'epqôd* and *pāqad*, where the prophet employed different tenses of the same verbal root,[156] does not come through in English. The NIV phrases in question are "I will *punish ['epqôd]* the leaders" and "the LORD Almighty *will care for [pāqad]* his flock, the house of Judah."

The verb *pāqad* often signifies judgment and punishment (Isa 24:21; Jer 11:22) as it does in Zech 10:3a. However, the verb *pāqad* can also communicate tenderness and pathos, as expressed in Exod 3:16 when God observed the great plight of the Israelites in Egyptian bondage. Similarly, the same verb introduces God's blessing on Sarah by healing her barrenness and allowing her

---

[152] Hanson, *Dawn of Apocalyptic*, 329–31.

[153] Meyers and Meyers, "The Future Fortunes of the House of David: The Evidence of Second Zechariah," in *Fortunate the Eyes That See: Essays in Honor of David Noel Freedman in Celebration of His Seventieth Birthday*, ed. A. B. Beck, et al. (Grand Rapids: Eerdmans, 1995), 213–14.

[154] הָעַתּוּדִים. *HALOT*, 902–3.

[155] Wolters, "Word Play in Zechariah," 224.

[156] אֶפְקוֹד/פָּקַד. *HALOT*, 955–58, especially 956. This is the word often translated as "visit" in the King James Version.

to conceive (Gen 21:1). This is the meaning of *pāqad* in Zech 10:3b—so great was the Lord's love for his people that the failure of the shepherds to discharge their duties honorably moved God to come personally to care for his flock and to rescue them from their duplicitous leaders.

In the end, the Lord's tender care for his flock would transform her into an unrecognizable image. With a surprising twist, Zechariah portrays Judah after her metamorphosis as a battle horse. Up to this point horses have represented military imagery in a negative light, but Baldwin comments, "Those who in their submission to the Lord are like sheep become invincible as war-horses in His service."[157]

### 5. Israel's Battle and Victory (10:4–12)

> ⁴**From Judah will come the cornerstone,**
>     **from him the tent peg,**
>     **from him the battle bow,**
>     **from him every ruler.**
> ⁵**Together they will be like mighty men**
>     **trampling the muddy streets in battle.**
> **Because the LORD is with them,**
>     **they will fight and overthrow the horsemen.**
>
> ⁶**"I will strengthen the house of Judah**
>     **and save the house of Joseph.**
> **I will restore them**
>     **because I have compassion on them.**
> **They will be as though**
>     **I had not rejected them,**
> **for I am the LORD their God**
>     **and I will answer them.**
> ⁷**The Ephraimites will become like mighty men,**
>     **and their hearts will be glad as with wine.**
> **Their children will see it and be joyful;**
>     **their hearts will rejoice in the LORD.**
> ⁸**I will signal for them**
>     **and gather them in.**
> **Surely I will redeem them;**
>     **they will be as numerous as before.**
> ⁹**Though I scatter them among the peoples,**
>     **yet in distant lands they will remember me.**
> **They and their children will survive,**
>     **and they will return.**
> ¹⁰**I will bring them back from Egypt**
>     **and gather them from Assyria.**
> **I will bring them to Gilead and Lebanon,**

---

[157] Baldwin, *Zechariah*, 174.

and there will not be room enough for them.
¹¹They will pass through the sea of trouble;
   the surging sea will be subdued
   and all the depths of the Nile will dry up.
Assyria's pride will be brought down
   and Egypt's scepter will pass away.
¹²I will strengthen them in the Lord
   and in his name they will walk,"
                              declares the LORD.

**10:4** Verse 4 focuses on the primary outcome of the Lord's visitation of his flock, the introduction of the Messiah described as the cornerstone, the tent peg, and the bow of war. Each of these three metaphors emphasizes different aspects of the Messiah's character and role. The metaphors stress the Messiah's strong leadership, victorious reign, and the position of paramount importance he will play in Judah's grand future.

Zechariah began by reminding his hearers that the Messiah would arise from Judah. Genesis 49:10 first proclaims the relationship between the tribe of Judah and the Messiah:

"The scepter will not depart from Judah,
   nor the ruler's staff from between his feet,
until he comes to whom it belongs
   and the obedience of the nations is his."

The first metaphor Zechariah ascribed to the Messiah is the "cornerstone" *(pinnāh)*.[158] Not surprisingly, this is often a construction or architectural term in both Testaments. Some of the better Old Testament examples occur in Exod 27:2; 43:20, which portray the corners of the altar. In 2 Chr 28:24 *pinnāh* stands for the corners of buildings in Jerusalem. In 2 Kgs 14:13; 2 Chr 25:23; 26:15 the term refers to the wall around Jerusalem. Although Zechariah used a different term in chap. 4, his mention of the cornerstone in chap. 10 evokes the memory of the "capstone" in 4:7, literally, the "premier stone."[159] Depending on the interpretation adopted, this stone in chap. 4 refers either to the cornerstone that formed the most important portion of the temple foundation or the capstone that symbolized the completion of the house of God.

More significantly, *pinnāh* functions metaphorically, often referring to the people themselves as a cornerstone (Job 38:6; Ps 118:22; Isa 28:16; Jer 51:26). The Old Testament also employs the word *pinnāh* to describe leaders or chiefs who played a crucial role in the protection of Israel, such as the chiefs of the people who had gathered at Mizpah (Judg 20:2). First Samuel 14:38 also illustrates this usage, describing the men who had gathered to speak to the king.

---

[158] פִּנָּה. *HALOT*, 944–45.
[159] Meyers and Meyers, "Future Fortunes of the House of David," 214.

Most important of all, Ps 118:22 has received significant attention for its employment of *pinnāh*, not just for any individual but for the Messiah. It states, "The stone the builders rejected has become the capstone."[160] This highly significant messianic prophecy plays a crucial role in New Testament teaching about Jesus Christ's messianic ministry. In all three Synoptic Gospels, Jesus applied this teaching to himself: "Have you never read in the Scriptures: 'The stone the builders rejected has become the capstone; the Lord has done this, and it is marvelous in our eyes?'" (Matt 21:42; see Mark 12:10–11; Luke 20:17). The same passage played an important role in Peter's sermon before the Sanhedrin (Acts 4:11). Paul described Christ Jesus as the cornerstone in the building that is the Church (Eph 2:20), and 1 Pet 2:6–7 makes a similar point.

The cornerstone metaphor aptly sketches the Leader among all of the leaders in the Old Testament, the Messiah. The cornerstone metaphor is an appropriate portrayal of the essential role the Messiah will play in building up the household of God, that is, the people of God. Baldwin eloquently summarizes the concept of the cornerstone: "[it] symbolizes the steadfast strength on which a whole edifice can depend."[161] Hence, the weight of God's house, his people, will rest squarely on the Messiah.

Zechariah's second metaphor is the "tent peg" *(yātēd)*.[162] This Hebrew term receives several distinct uses in the Old Testament, and the tent peg is prominent (Exod 27:19; 35:18). It could be a peg for hanging valuables on a wall (Ezek 15:3). The "firm place" found in the NIV of Ezra 9:8 renders the same Hebrew word. In this prayer Ezra praised God for his graciousness in allowing a remnant to survive and for "giving us a *firm place* in his sanctuary." Isaiah introduces a different use of the metaphor where the peg represents the son of David, Eliakim, who will remain as firmly as the peg driven deep into a "firm place" (Isa 22:23–24). The comparison of Eliakim to a peg closely parallels Zechariah's picture of the Messiah as a peg. Unlike Eliakim who ultimately "will give way; it will be sheared off and will fall" (Isa 22:25), the Messiah of whom Zechariah spoke would never fail nor would his reign ever cease. In v. 4 the peg thus symbolizes the support for the people, the one on whom the weight of the nation's needs rests.[163]

The final metaphor for Messiah is the "battle bow" *(qešet milḥāmāh)*.[164] The introduction of the battle bow portrays the conquest that the new God-ordained leader would achieve. The victory will result in great benefit for Judah, and more importantly, the glory of God. In 2 Kgs 13:17 the bow symbolized

---

[160] Mason, "Some Examples of Inner Biblical Exegesis in Zech. IX–XIV." In *Studia Evangelica, Vol. VII*, ed. E. A. Livingstone (Berlin: Akademie, 1982), 114–15.

[161] Baldwin, *Zechariah*, 174.

[162] יָתֵד. *HALOT*, 450–51.

[163] In Gal 2:9 James, Peter and John are called "pillars," a similar notion with regard to the church.

[164] קֶשֶׁת מִלְחָמָה. *HALOT*, 1155–56, 589.

bold commitment to fulfill the Lord's will. The arrow shot by Elisha received the name, "The LORD's arrow of victory, the arrow of victory over Aram!" For Judah to possess a battle bow in her arsenal suggests something important concerning her future power and autonomy. The themes elaborate the prediction in Zech 10:3 that the Lord Almighty will make Judah "like a proud horse in battle." With God's help, she will someday hold the might to dwell safely again in the land promised so long ago to Abraham. Even more dramatic, all of those who have been dispersed can return to their homeland in Judah.[165] In subsequent biblical material, the bow in the hand of the rider on the white horse demonstrates the overwhelming power of the Lord's emissary, the one who "rode out as a conqueror bent on conquest" (Rev 6:2).

These three metaphors represent the great responsibilities that accompany the leadership of God's people, responsibilities that only the Messiah could perfectly fulfill.

The phrase "from him every ruler" first restates the point that future leaders will come from Judah. Then these rulers who will lead the nation will come from the people themselves, not the foreign tyrants whose boot the nation had felt for so many generations. The Hebrew term Zechariah chose for ruler is *nōgēś*, an unusual choice.[166] The prophet employs the term in a wholly positive sense in v. 4. However, this same expression refers to the Egyptian taskmasters in Exod 3:7. Zechariah used the word in its usual negative sense in 9:8. In order to capture the positive use of *nōgēś* in 10:4, Meyers and Meyers recommend translating the word as "overseer."[167]

Many scholars have suggested that v. 4 employs the formal use of holy war language. For instance, Merrill says that this passage "should be interpreted in the context of holy war."[168] Those who disagree maintain that the Lord does not wage war in this passage. While it is the case that Zechariah does not portray God as a warrior in this passage, the holy war motif does emerge as the Lord grants ultimate victory for his people over their foes.

**10:5** Verse 5 continues the thought of the preceding verse, stating that Judah "will be like mighty men." The Hebrew term for "mighty men" *(gibbōrîm)* in the plural always refers to warriors, military men.[169] The word describes David's elite army (2 Sam 23:8), and Ps 103:20 expands the use of the term significantly by ascribing it to all of the Lord's servants, including angels "who do his bidding." This angelic connotation broadens Zechariah's perspective beyond human agency, including even the heavenly host who participate in the Lord's victories.

---

[165] Meyers and Meyers, *Zechariah 9–14*, 202.
[166] נֹגֵשׂ See *HALOT*, 670; and BDB, 620.
[167] Meyers and Meyers, *Zechariah 9–14*, 203.
[168] Merrill, *Zechariah*, 272; see Mason, *Haggai, Zechariah, and Malachi* (Cambridge: Cambridge University Press, 1977), 99.
[169] גִּבּוֹרִים. *HALOT*, 172.

The phrase "trampling the muddy streets in battle" is difficult to understand. Some add the word "foe" (see RSV), yielding, "trampling the foe in the mud." Mic 7:10 presents similar imagery:

> Then my enemy will see it
>   and will be covered with shame,
> she who said to me,
>   "Where is the Lord your God?"
> My eyes will see her downfall;
>   even now she will be trampled underfoot
>   like mire in the streets.

Verse 5 concludes with a causal clause, "because the LORD is with them." Herein lies the secret to Judah's victory; God will fight for her and empower her to vanquish her enemies again in the future as he had in the past. This theme of incomparable eschatological victory occurs in numerous other predictive passages (see Ps 2; Isa 9:4–7; 11:4; 63:1–6; Jer 30:7–8; Mic 4:13). The great coming victory recalls one of the greatest victories in Israel's history—the conquest. Joshua 1:5b states, "As I was with Moses, so I will be with you; I will never leave you nor forsake you." Jeremiah proclaims the same principle: " 'Do not be afraid of them, for I am with you and will rescue you,' declares the LORD" (Jer 1:8).

Even with superior manpower, any greater advantage for Judah's opponents becomes meaningless, futile before the devastating onslaught from the Lord's army. Throughout the ancient Near East the horse served as the epitome of a military weapon.[170] As in the first vision (The Man on a Red Horse; 1:7–17) and the eighth vision (The Four Chariots; 6:1–8), Zechariah rehearsed the military significance of the horse. The infantry treading in the mud will vanquish the cavalry, the horsemen of v. 5b, an outcome no military tactician could anticipate. The same theme is found in Hag 2:22: "I will overturn royal thrones and shatter the power of the foreign kingdoms. I will overthrow chariots and their drivers; horses and their riders will fall, each by the sword of his brother." But in Zech 10:5 the Hebrew word behind NIV "overthrown" means "put to shame" (wĕhōbîšû).[171]

**10:6** Verse 6 transitions from Zechariah's proclamation outlining God's future plans for Judah to the Lord's first person narrative of what he intends to do. Much like 9:6, here God begins with a statement of divine resolve: "I will." In v. 6 the Lord guarantees that he will strengthen Judah and Joseph, and the two proper names serve as a poetic word pair, reflecting one another and forming the building blocks upon which Zechariah's poetic parallelism

---

[170] See Yadin, *Warfare in Biblical Lands*, 302.
[171] וְהֹבִישׁוּ. *HALOT*, 117.

rests.[172] The verse reflects a chiastic arrangement that both adds beauty to the expression and makes the Lord's statement more memorable. The chiastic arrangement in English is as follows:

A   I will strengthen
  B   the house
    C   of Judah
    C'   and Joseph's
  B'   house
A'   I will save

The name "Judah" refers to the remnant of the most prominent southern tribe named for Jacob's fourth son (Gen 29:35), and "Joseph" is the tribe named after Jacob's eleventh son (Gen 30:22–24). Unlike the frequent reference to "Judah," "Joseph" occurs rarely in such a word pair. Often the prophets referred to Israel as Ephraim, the most important of the northern tribes (Isa 7:17; Hos 5:3), but since Joseph was the father of Ephraim (Gen 41:52) "Joseph" represents the northern tribes in v. 6.

Merrill adds an interesting twist on Zechariah's inclusion of Joseph.[173] He suggests that Joseph foreshadows the exodus motif emerging in 10:8–12. Joseph encouraged his entire family to move to Egypt to escape the famine raging in his day. Merrill adds that it was because of the pharaoh "who knew not Joseph" that the Egyptian oppression began, necessitating the exodus. But even if one grants the exodus motifs in the ensuing context, the connection between Joseph and the exodus event is overstated.

The point of the encompassing prediction in v. 6 is the gathering of all of God's people whom judgment and persecution had dispersed. It might tempt some to view the reference to the northern tribes literally, understanding that all of Abraham's descendants, including all of Israel, will return. The passage contains no indication that God intends to reverse his final judgment on Israel in 722 BC. Rather, the mention of both Judah and Joseph functions as a merism in which the two stated extremes stress the certainty of the restoration that God has determined to fulfill for his remnant (cf. Isa 11:10–16; Jer 30:3; 33:7; Zech 9:10 for a similar emphasis).

"I will restore them" promises renewal for the nation, but the nature of this renewal has engendered extensive discussions for centuries. The whole question turns on the verb translated "will restore" *(wĕhôšĕbôtîm)*.[174] The problem grows out of the fact that this verbal form occurs nowhere else in the Old Testament and appears to be a conflation of two distinct, yet common, Hebrew verbs. The NIV takes the word as derived from the verb *šûb*, meaning "return"

---

[172] See Y. Avishur, *Stylistic Studies of Word-Pairs*.
[173] Merrill, *Zechariah*, 274.
[174] וְהוֹשְׁבוֹתִים. *HALOT*, 1432, 1434.

or "restore."[175] Alternatively, others follow some Hebrew manuscripts and the LXX, which suggest that the verb should be *wĕhôšabtîm* ("I will cause them to dwell").[176]

Both possibilities convey the general notion of renewed dwelling and blessing in the land of promise. Jewish interpreters have often contended that Zechariah deliberately combined the meanings of both verbal forms into a single composite verb conveying the notion, "I will bring them back and cause them to dwell."[177] Most scholarship supports the "I will restore" interpretation. This is probably the most convincing explanation, largely because the preceding section has focused on restoration as well.

God's assurance, "I will answer them" *(wĕ'e'ĕnēm)*[178] concludes v. 6. Theologically this message foretelling divine blessings rests on the theological fact that "I am the LORD their God" (Gen 17:7–8; Exod 6:7; Jer 31:33; Isa 41:17). This promise of God's grace and mercy, wholly without any merit on Judah's part, shines as brightly as any other biblical affirmation about the Lord's favor. God's compassion for his people will move him to restore the nation.

The theme of God's answering the cries of his people occurs frequently in the Old Testament.[179] For instance, after subduing the Philistines at Mizpah, Samuel made an offering and praised the Lord for answering his prayer (1 Sam 7:9). A clear biblical commentary on God's compassionate response to human need occurs in Isa 30:18–19a:

> "Yet the LORD longs to be gracious to you;
>   he rises to show you compassion.
> For the LORD is a God of justice.
>   Blessed are all who wait for him!
>
>   O people of Zion, who live in Jerusalem, you will weep no more.
>   How gracious he will be when you cry for help!"

**10:7** Returning to the theme of v. 5 in which Judah will become "mighty men" *(gibbôrîm)*, v. 7 uses the same language in stating that Ephraim will become powerful warriors as well. The scene will be so exceptional that whole families will observe and rejoice. The reference to children also signals a generational message. The divine favor will not prove to be a fleeting circumstance, but rather a lasting benefit for God's chosen people. Accordingly, successive generations will recall God's wondrous acts as a part of their worship and will praise the Lord for his goodness. For such a lowly nation—one that

---

[175] שׁוּב. See GKC § 72p.
[176] וְהוֹשַׁבְתִּים, interpreting the verbal root as יָשַׁב , "to dwell."
[177] A. Cohen, *The Twelve Prophets* (New York: Soncino, 1948), 311.
[178] וְאֶעֱנֵם. *HALOT*, 851–52.
[179] Boda, *Zechariah*, 444.

had experienced persecution and deprivation for virtually all of her history—to experience a radical reversal of fortune could only mean that the God of Abraham had shown himself strong on her behalf.

The prevailing emotional atmosphere in v. 7 is one of pure joy. The poetic word pairs "be joyful" and "rejoice" emphasize the point. The first expression translates *wĕśāmēḥû*, signifying happiness or being filled with joy.[180] The latter term, *yāgēl*, closely parallels the preceding word, although the words related to *yāgēl (gîl)* refer to exuberant shouts of exultation.[181] This second word only occurs in poetic texts in the Old Testament (for example Pss 2:11; 14:7; 118:24; Isa 25:9; Hab 3:18). Meyers and Meyers add an insightful comment: "Those who are most vulnerable are the ones to rise to heights that involve exultation, as in Isa 29:19, where . . . the same two verbs that appear in this verse, are used in reference to the response of the poor and humble . . . to the eschatological events that Isaiah sets forth."[182]

**10:8** For disconsolate Judah, living in the land of promise but still awaiting the other blessings their covenantal relationship warranted, Zechariah stressed the need for a revitalized leadership to guide the nation to a new kingdom of righteousness. Ephraim's need was different because she represented Abraham's seed who had been scattered far from the land of Israel. Israel's dispersal occurred centuries before (722 BC), and the Assyrian policy of disseminating Israel widely (2 Kgs 17:6) required divine intervention in order for any reunification to happen.

"I will signal for them" translates a more picturesque means of describing the Lord's summons for his wandering people. The verb "signal" (*'ešrĕqāh*) means "to whistle."[183] Modern readers are familiar with whistling as the way someone would summon a dog. That is not the image Zechariah intended here. Zechariah regularly adopted shepherd imagery to envision the Lord's relationship with his people. Judges 5:16 describes a similar scene in which a shepherd whistles to call his flock. Accordingly, Zechariah portrayed God as a shepherd whose sheep know him and will answer his call. John 10:27 conveys a similar point about Jesus' relationship to his flock: "My sheep listen to my voice; I know them, and they follow me." The objective of the divine call is to gather to himself the people with whom he had established a covenant.

The Lord proclaims his purpose in gathering Ephraim; he intends to "redeem them." The term *pĕdîtîm* that Zechariah employed to state the goal of redemption plays a prominent theological role in the Old Testament.[184] Only one of many important Old Testament words broadly signifying "ransom" or

---

[180] וְשָׂמֵחוּ. *HALOT*, 1334.

[181] יָגֵל. *HALOT*, 189.

[182] Meyers and Meyers, *Zechariah 9–14*, 213.

[183] אֶשְׁרְקָה. *HALOT*, 1656. The cohortative verbal form conveys God's resolve to bring this action to fruition.

[184] פְּדִיתִים. *HALOT*, 912. *TLOT*, 964–76, especially 974–75.

"redemption," Old Testament writers often used *pĕdîtîm* to describe God's redemption of many different groups. For instance, the word appears when God redeemed certain individuals, such as Abraham (Isa 29:22), Job (Job 5:20), Elihu (Job 33:28), David (Pss 26:11; 31:5 [Hb. 6]; 55:18 [Hb. 19]), Jeremiah (Jer 15:21), and the righteous one (Ps 49:16).

The Old Testament also uses *pĕdîtîm* to communicate the Lord's redemption of the nation. In Deut 7:8 redemption describes God's deliverance of Israel at the exodus when the Lord "brought you out with a mighty hand and redeemed you from the land of slavery." The strong association between redemption and the exodus is particularly appropriate in light of the Old Testament's view of the exodus as the archetypal example of salvation. Zechariah's intention to associate God's future salvation of Judah with the former act of salvation in the exodus could not be clearer, particularly in light of the imagery in v. 11 where the prophet declares that "the Nile will dry up."

In David's majestic prayer in response to the Lord's establishment of the Davidic Covenant, the king prayed, "And who is like your people Israel—the one nation on earth that God went out to redeem as a people for himself, and to make a name for himself, and to perform great and awesome wonders" (2 Sam 7:23). Biblical writers also use this word for the gathered company of believers who corporately worship the Lord: "and the ransomed of the LORD will return. They will enter Zion with singing" (Isa 35:10; see 51:11). The word refers more generally to Israel: "was my arm too short to ransom you?" (Isa 50:2); to Jacob: "the LORD will ransom Jacob" (Jer 31:11); to ransoming Ephraim from the grave (Hos 13:14); and to Judah (Neh 1:10). In Neh 1:9–10 Nehemiah binds the concepts of repentance and the regathering of God's people from their dispersal in order to provide them with their ultimate redemption in a fashion much like that in Zechariah. Nehemiah says to Judah: "if you return to me and obey my commands, then even if your exiled people are at the farthest horizon, I will gather them from there and bring them to the place I have chosen as a dwelling for my Name. They are your servants and your people, whom you redeemed by your great strength and by your mighty hand." Following a comparable perspective, Zech 10:8 proceeds in the long biblical tradition of portraying God as the redeemer of his people.

Redemption is a gift that the Lord longs to give to his people. In a moving reflection of the Lord's response to his people, Hos 7:13 quotes God as saying, "I long to redeem them [the Lord's people]." But divine redemption never comes cheaply. In 1 Pet 1:18–19 the apostle argues this point forcefully, reminding all that "perishable things" such as gold or silver can never redeem anyone from their "empty way of life." Only the blood of Christ, the lamb without blemish, can effect redemption.

Verse 8 also observes that the people "will be as numerous as before." After the decimation of the population brought by the exile, it might have been difficult for downcast Judah to contemplate a repopulation of the land to preexilic levels. Yet this is precisely what the Lord declares will happen. McComiskey reminds readers to approach prophecies about the great population of God's people to include the redeemed of all ages, including the Church. He states, "When we read promises of great repopulation we must not fail to see the church, for the promise to Abraham of great posterity includes redeemed Gentiles." McComiskey adds, "the promises of victory for God's people and subsequent promise of land not only belong to the ancient people, but to God's people today, who also inherit the promise that the Lord will be God to his people."[185]

**10:9** The translation "I scatter them" (NASB also) rests on an emendation of the Hebrew text that replaces the word for "sow" in the Masoretic Text ($wĕ'ezrā'ēm$[186]; see the HCSB) with "scatter." Baldwin contends that the reason some choose to alter the Masoretic Text is that "sow" is unexpected in the context. She observes that emending the text to "scatter" means that "the vigour of the original is lost, for sowing implies a harvest and so conveys hope."[187] The emendation to "scatter" ($wā'ăzārēm$)[188] is widely advocated and maintains that the metaphor of scattering best fits the theme of the dispersal of Ephraim in the context, while "sowing" is unexpected. Those who embrace the emendation also note that the verb "scatter" ($zārāh$) also occurs in Zech 1:19 (Hb. 2:2) and 1:21 (Hb. 2:4). A more thorough examination of the proposed alteration of the text reveals the questionable nature of the change, and two important considerations argue against adopting this emendation.

First, the more cautious approach always refrains from adopting emendations (proposed changes to the Masoretic Text that have no textual support for the alteration) unless a text simply cannot be understood otherwise. The emendation in v. 9 certainly fails this initial criterion. Even though the emendation involves the deletion of only one consonant, the proposed change relies upon no manuscript evidence to support the change. Further, the meaning "sow" makes excellent sense, whether or not a modern interpreter anticipates this concept.

Second, adopting the emendation obscures the message of God's sovereignty and provision in purposefully settling his people. Thus, the figure of sowing emphasizes that the seed was intentionally sown by the sower in the place he would choose. This seed would germinate and grow, producing verdant plants. The development of the seed also foreshadows the population growth foretold in v. 8. In other passages sowing portrays population growth (Jer 31:27; Ezek 36:9–10; Hos 2:23 [Hb. v. 25]). For Ephraim, the metaphor of sowing is more appropriate than mere scattering since God intentionally planted them where he wanted them to be. Israel was not simply thrown to the wind. In discounting

---

[185] McComiskey, "Zechariah," 1183.
[186] וְאֶזְרָעֵם. *HALOT*, 282.
[187] Baldwin, *Zechariah*, 176.
[188] וְאָזָרֵם. *HALOT*, 280.

the viability of the emendation, Meyers and Meyers also observe that sowing "is eminently appropriate to the prophet's awareness of the long duration—the rootedness—of Ephraim's exile."[189] Consequently, the emendation should be rejected in favor of the traditional reading of the verse, "I will sow them."

The result of God's sowing of Ephraim will be the people's remembrance of the Lord. Despite the long years of absence, Israel will recognize and respond from afar to her shepherd's call. The emphasis on remembering the Lord permeates the entire book of Zechariah. This act of remembering involves more than simple recall; it also conveys the idea of obeying the Lord's injunctions.[190] Even the prophet Zechariah's name means "Yahweh remembers." In light of the Lord's faithful remembrance of his covenant people, how could Judah fail to remember their God?

In returning, Ephraim will do more than move back to the ancestral land of promise. Zechariah employed the verb "return" *(šûb)*, the same term that served the prophets as the standard word for returning to the Lord spiritually, that is, repentance.[191] Consequently, for Ephraim to return implies more than reunification and renewed inhabitation of the land of Israel (see Heb 3–4). When Ephraim returns to the Lord she will come with a heart of repentance and obedience to the Lord. No wonder Zechariah states that "their children will survive." When the people return again to the Lord, not only will they receive long missed blessings, but the succeeding generations will also reap the joyous benefit of God's blessing on his obedient children (Deut 5:33; 8:1; 16:20; Rom 10:11–13).

The national resurrection of Ephraim calls Ezekiel's similar message to mind. The vision of the dry bones in Ezek 37 graphically pictured the death and utter ruin that had befallen God's people. Who can resurrect the dead but God alone? By his grace and for his glory the Lord chose to bring the nation to life again, as it were, raising her to walk in newness of life.

**10:10–11** Verses 10–11 have been linked together into a literary sub-unit by a chiasm in which one finds mention of Egypt and Assyria at the beginning of v. 10 and reference to Assyria and Egypt at the conclusion of v. 11. Each of the four geo-political references in v. 10 (Egypt, Assyria, Gilead, and Lebanon) raises important interpretative questions.

The verse commences with the Lord's resolute determination to bring his people back home. Using a causative verb based on the same verb "return" *(šûb)* found in v. 9b, Zechariah states that the Lord will cause Ephraim to return. Though the NIV renders this expression accurately, "I will bring them back," this translation does not bring out the relationship between the two important theological words meaning "return."

---

[189] Meyers and Meyers, *Zechariah 9–14*, 216.
[190] McComiskey, "Zechariah," 1184.
[191] שׁוּב. *HALOT*, 1429–30. See Holladay, *The Root Šûbh in the Old Testament*.

The first significant question is the meaning of Zechariah's reference to Egypt. Presumably, Egypt serves to remind the reader of the exodus since the Egyptian bondage represents one of the most important eras of persecution in Israel's existence. Without doubt, however, the exodus from Egyptian slavery does symbolize the greatest expression of divine salvation for the nation during Israel's long history. Numerous prophetic passages view Egypt as a metaphor—rooted in deep historical experience—for the oppressive lands out of which the Lord would gather the nation in the messianic kingdom. Isaiah 11:10–16 extensively develops this eschatological point about the homecoming of Abraham's seed. Verse 11a declares, "In that day the Lord will reach out his hand a second time to reclaim the remnant that is left of his people from Assyria, from Lower Egypt, from Upper Egypt" (cf. Ezek 39:27–29). Hosea 11:1, "out of Egypt I called my son," is quoted in Matt 2:15 as a prophecy regarding Jesus's sojourn in Egypt to escape Herod's persecution and thus stresses the same theme as Isa 11 and Zech 10:11—in Jesus the nation of Israel is being restored. In Zech 10:10 Egypt symbolizes the oppressors in the south whom the Lord will defeat and from whose grasp he will retrieve his people.

The reference to Assyria has evoked far more discussion than Zechariah's reference to Egypt. The greatest question focuses on why Zechariah mentioned an empire that had ceased to exist several generations earlier.[192] Consequently, some scholars have even redated this prophetic oracle to a preexilic epoch, to a time when Assyria held an extensive hegemony.[193] Although held by numerous scholars, this interpretation enjoys little to commend it. This view is unnecessary since Assyria clearly functions as another metaphor, despite the fact that the empire had collapsed about two centuries earlier. (Similarly, references to Babylon occur throughout the Bible, including Jeremiah and Revelation, long after the Babylon empire fell.) Assyria stands for all the nations to Israel's north and northeast, including Babylon and Persia, which have actively persecuted Israel and insulted her God. References to Assyria must have been particularly poignant since those who lived through the exile, having watched the decades go by since the Assyrian attack, certainly must have felt that any promises from God regarding resettlement in the promised land and numerous descendants seemed especially hollow. Zechariah addressed these deep doubts directly and sought to show his hearers that the Lord of Hosts would bring about that which he promised to do. McComiskey summarizes, "No longer can an oppressing power sever God's people from their spiritual inheritance."[194] Like Egypt, Assyria also symbolizes the diverse places from which the Lord

---

[192] W. W. Hallo and W. K. Simpson, *The Ancient Near East: A History* (New York: Harcourt Brace Jovanovich, 1971), 147–49; A. L. Oppenheim, *Ancient Mesopotamia: Portrait of a Dead Civilization*, revised ed. (Chicago: University of Chicago Press, 1977), 167–70.

[193] B. Otzen, *Deuterosacharja*, 42–43.

[194] McComiskey, "Zechariah," 1184.

will summon his people homeward, as well as the legions of oppressors who had long troubled Israel.

Beyond the biblical symbolism of Egypt and Assyria, historical evidence shows that God's people had not only turned to these two empires for assistance, but in many cases had actually moved there (Isa 11:11,15–16; Hos 7:11; 11:5).[195] The existence of the extensive Jewish community at Elephantine further illustrates the presence of many Israelites in Egypt. Hosea 11:11 draws this point together with the message of gathering in the land expressed in Zech 10:10:

> "They will come trembling
>   like birds from Egypt,
>   like doves from Assyria.
> I will settle them in their homes,"
>   declares the LORD.

Zechariah's inclusion of Gilead and Lebanon as places where the remnant will dwell raises numerous questions. The main questions are why Zechariah chose these two unusual geographic locales and what the two places symbolize. In one sense, Gilead and Lebanon serve as the antithesis of Egypt and Assyria. Gilead and Lebanon will receive the multitudes surrendered by Egypt and Assyria.

While some claim that Gilead and Lebanon function as a metonymy for the Northern Kingdom of Israel, no historical evidence suggests that Israel's political influence included land as far north as Lebanon or as far east as Gilead in the Transjordan region. Further, no biblical descriptions of the geographic borders of the biblical land included Gilead or Lebanon (Gen 15:18–21; Num 34:2–12; Ezek 47:15–20).

The biblical references to Gilead and Lebanon portray them as fertile places (Song 4:15; Isa 29:17; Jer 22:6; Ezek 31:16). The Old Testament describes Gilead as verdant pastureland for sheep (1 Chr 6:80; Song 4:1; Mic 7:14). Because of the connotations of Gilead and Lebanon elsewhere in the Bible, it does not appear that Zechariah wished that his readers view these two sites as an idealized representation of Israel.

The most convincing interpretation sees Gilead and Lebanon as places where the overflowing population can live, since the traditional boundaries of the land of Israel cannot contain them any longer. Isaiah 49:19–21 makes a parallel affirmation. Isaiah states, "The children born during your bereavement will yet say in your hearing, 'This place is too small for us; give us more space to live in' " (v. 20; see 54:2–3). Gilead and Lebanon metaphorically emphasize two components of God's covenant with Abraham. First, the burgeoning population that must surge into Gilead and Lebanon stresses that God's promise to Abraham that he would father a multitude (Gen 15:5) will come to full fruition.

---

[195] Meyers and Meyers, *Zechariah 9–14*, 220–21.

Second, Ephraim and Judah's possession of the promised land and its environs assures Zechariah's audience that the divine promise to the patriarch of the land (Gen 15:18) will also see total fulfillment.

Verse 11 brings the themes treated in v. 10 to conclusion and also finishes the chiasm begun in the preceding verse. Further, Zech 10:11 gives rise to a series of questions about the correct reading of the Hebrew text. A general examination of various English translations not only discloses the questions, but also reveals how differently many translations resolve the issues. The verse is quite difficult, and the years have seen a number of textual emendations proposed.

Although the first word of v. 11 in the NIV is "They," the Hebrew verb is actually singular, "He."[196] What might appear to be nothing more than a simple or even inconsequential grammatical point actually shapes one's understanding of the message of the verse significantly. It is not unusual in the Old Testament to face some uncertainty in the identification of the antecedent of a pronoun. Interpreters have long pondered who functions as the antecedent of the pronoun "He" in the sentence "He will pass." Some have concluded that the subject is Ephraim, opting to change the verb from singular to plural to refer to Ephraim's people. Others maintain that God is the subject of the singular verb.

The approach employed by numerous scholars, illustrated by diverse modern translations, rejects the Masoretic reading of a singular verb as an inferior reading and accepts the plural Septuagintal reading, "They will pass,"[197] as in the NIV. This explanation believes that Ephraim remains the subject of the verb "to pass" as in the preceding verses. Previously when functioning as the subject of a sentence, Ephraim has consistently taken plural verbs (10:7). It would also be possible to argue that Ephraim is the subject of the singular verb and retain the Masoretic Text, viewing Ephraim as a collective noun that takes a singular verb.

An alternative understanding retains the singular verb of the Masoretic Text and takes the subject of the verb to be the Lord. Many have been reluctant to accept this explanation, thinking that God does not "pass through" affliction. However, there are strong reasons for concluding that the Hebrew text is the superior text, "the Lord" is the subject of the verb, and that all who change the verb from the singular to the plural, including the NIV, have erred. To understand the problem properly, one must appreciate the rationale for altering the Hebrew text.

The first reason many scholars argue for replacing the Hebrew text is the abrupt change of person from a first person narrative in which God speaks—"I will signal for them" (v. 8), "I will redeem them" (v. 8), "I sow them" (v. 9), "I will bring them back" (v. 10), and "I will bring them" (v. 10)—to a third person

---

[196] וְעָבַר. *HALOT*, 779.
[197] διελεύσονται. For example, Mitchell, *Zechariah*, 294–95.

verb, "he will pass." Clearly, in vv. 8–10 God has spoken in the first person. Further, the pronoun "them" has referred to Ephraim. The apparent change in speaker in v. 11 troubles many. However, the prophetic literature contains an abundance of dramatic shifts in person from one to another, and back to the first again, often in the space of only a few verses. Old Testament scholarship has long recognized this rapid shift in person as one of the distinguishing literary features of Old Testament writings, particularly the prophets.

Moreover, careful scholarship must never rush to replace the Masoretic Text with another reading unless compelling evidence requires doing so. Actually, the Hebrew text reads very well as it stands. Neither the external manuscript evidence nor internal literary evidence suggests that the Septuagint preserved the original reading. Rather, it appears that the Septuagint translators misunderstood the meaning of the Hebrew text.

A second argument for replacing the singular verb with the plural is the concern some have with the notion of God passing through affliction. If one retains the singular "he will pass through the sea of affliction," God is also the subject of the next verb, the singular "he will smite." Before we can comment on the matter of God experiencing affliction, we must examine the manner in which the NIV renders the following phrase in v. 11.

The NIV reads, "the surging sea *will be subdued*." As in the first clause, the NIV has decided to translate the Hebrew verb *(wĕhikkāh)* in the second clause of v. 11 as a passive verb, though the Hebrew is a singular, active verb.[198] A more accurate rendering of the verb *wĕhikkāh* would be "and he will smite." The NIV reading rests upon no manuscript evidence that would support this variant reading.[199] The passive NIV translation of the verb obscures the agent, the one who does the action. The Hebrew text plainly expresses a causative, singular idea. Although the text does not state explicitly that God is the subject, does the passage need to do so in order for the reader to understand plainly that the Lord would effect this miracle? No one besides God can calm turbulent waters (cf. Mark 4:35–39).

Without any doubt, the Lord serves as the subject of the verb "he will smite" in v. 11.[200] Those who raise concerns about the abrupt change in person fail to acknowledge that a sharp shift definitely occurs in the second clause in v. 11. Transforming the singular Hebrew verb at the beginning of v. 11 does not soften the transition.[201] Changing the second verb in the verse, without clear evidence, does not address this problem either. Furthermore, to attribute the power to still the waters or to subdue the nations to Ephraim is very unlikely.

---

[198] וְהִכָּה. *HALOT*, 697–98.

[199] The NIV seems to follow the same emendation proposed by Hanson (*Dawn of Apocalyptic*, 327) to change the active *Hiphil* verb to the passive *Hophal*.

[200] Even in the NIV translation, the passive voice implies divine agency.

[201] Meyers and Meyers, *Zechariah 9–14*, 224.

Regarding the concern about God's passing through affliction, the problem is illusory, growing out of a failure to see the expression as a figure of speech. Zechariah portrays the Lord as the Leader who guides his people through every distress. God shields his people from the force of every breaker on the sea and from any other trouble that his people do not possess the might to overcome.[202] The Lord is the one who conquers every affliction that his people suffer.

The theme of the "sea" *(yām)* links the first two cola or phrases in v. 11, further suggesting that they should be read as a pair.[203] This water motif was well known in both the ancient Near East and in the biblical writings. The literature of the ancient world, particularly the Ugaritic material, pictured a cosmic battle in which the sea, personified as the deity Yam, fought against other gods struggling for supremacy.[204] Old Testament writers rejected such mythology but condescended to use some of the same concepts to explain to a pagan world that Yahweh was the only God worthy of veneration and obedience. Psalm 74:12–25 proclaims the Lord's incomparable power over a force as immense and uncontrollable as the sea. Verse 13a states, "It was you who split open the sea *[yām]* by your power." Isaiah 27:1 pictures the Lord conquering the sea and the creatures lurking in its depths. In Jer 51:36 the Lord dries up the sea. Numerous additional examples provide the backdrop for Zechariah's message about the Lord's absolute sovereignty over the "uncontrollable" forces of nature and over the "unstoppable" might of empires who oppressed God's people and had no use for the Lord of all creation.

"Through the sea of trouble" translates the Hebrew *bayyām ṣārāh*.[205] Some want to see an explicit reference to the exodus in this Hebrew idiom and have emended the text to read "through the sea of Egypt" *(bĕyam miṣrayim)*.[206] As with the other proposed emendations in v. 11, there is neither textual witness nor literary warrant for proposing this change. While the Old Testament does not use the phrase "sea of affliction" *(bayyām ṣārāh)* for the Red Sea, it is difficult to argue for any other reference. McComiskey represents one of the few who attempt to identify "sea of affliction" or "sea of trouble" with something other than the Red Sea and the events surrounding the exodus.[207] Since the Nile did not literally dry up at the time of the exodus as v. 11 describes, McComiskey concludes that Zechariah must have intended some other historical analogy. This reasoning is strained and fails to appreciate the figurative language the prophet adopts. While it is true that "all the depths of the Nile" never

---

[202] McComiskey, "Zechariah," 1185; Unger, *Zechariah*, 184.
[203] יָם. *HALOT*, 413–14.
[204] Cross, *Canaanite Myth and Hebrew Epic* (Cambridge, Mass: Harvard University Press, 1973), 121–44; *ANET*, 67; R. P. Gordon, *Ugaritic Textbook: Texts* (Rome: Pontifical Biblical Press, 1965), especially 49, 51, 52, 129.
[205] בְּיָם צָרָה. *HALOT*, 413–14, 1054.
[206] בְּיָם מִצְרַיִם. Mitchell, *Zechariah*, 294–95 and Elliger, *Zacharja*, 155.
[207] McComiskey, "Zechariah," 1185. Also, Unger, *Zechariah*, 184.

did literally "dry up," the Red Sea was parted so that the Israelites could then pass through on dry land (Exod 14:16,21–29; Neh 9:11). Only the Lord could effect such a supernatural event. Also, the word "sea" *(yām)*, does refer directly to the Nile in Isa 19:5.

The expression "sea of trouble" evokes the memory of the exodus and the Lord's miraculous salvation of his people. As God once saved Israel, he will do so again. But the phrase "sea of trouble" likely has a broader meaning than the exodus. The Egyptian oppression, the exodus, and the deliverance at the Red Sea all symbolize more broadly the oppression Judah had suffered at the hands of numerous oppressors. God will deliver the nation from this persecution as he had done before. Hence, Zech 10:11 reverberates the tone of 9:8b: "Never again will an oppressor overrun my people, for now I am keeping watch."

Zechariah 9:9 continues the theme of deliverance, stating that the messianic King of God's people comes to bring salvation. Through this Messiah will come the deliverance and the righteous rule for which God's people of all ages have longed. Isaiah 9 develops this glorious hope further. Verse 4 declares, "you have shattered the yoke that burdens them . . . the rod of their oppressor," and verse 7 concludes the thought:

> Of the increase of his government and peace
>   there will be no end.
> He will reign on David's throne
>   and over his kingdom,
> establishing and upholding it
>   with justice and righteousness
>   from that time on and forever.
> The zeal of the LORD Almighty
>   will accomplish this.

Such is the eschatological hope for God's people. This promise does not limit itself to Ephraim or to Judah.

Verse 11 concludes with a series of devastating judgments on the most powerful kingdoms the ancient world had ever seen, as well as on any other future kingdom with pretensions of grandeur. Just as the glory of Egypt, the Nile, will dry up, so "the pride of Assyria will be brought down" and "Egypt's scepter will pass away." Both "pride" and "scepter" serve as emblems for the might and hegemony wielded by Egypt, Assyria, and other unnamed empires who desired to thwart God's kingdom.

**10:12** The theological message of the entire passage finds its summation in the chiastically arranged message of v. 12:

A   I will strengthen them[208]
    B   in the LORD
    B′  in his name
A′  they will walk

The name of God that strengthens God's people of all ages rests on the biblical foundation of Exod 3:14–15. Never in their own might, and always in the Lord's strength, will God's people find deliverance. As Zechariah stated in 4:6, "'Not by might nor by power, but my Spirit,' says the LORD Almighty." The verbal form translated "they will walk" *(yithallākû)* indicates continual, habitual action.[209] Those returning from exile, as well as God's covenantal people from all ages, will find their strength through a closer relationship with him. The verse concludes with the solemn expression of divine authority and authenticity found often in the prophetic writings, "declares the LORD" *(neʾum YHWH).*[210] This statement occurs 21 times in the book of Zechariah, always stressing the divine source of the prophet's message.

Chapter 10 balances themes of idolatry and rebellion against God with those of the coming Messiah and the victory, peace, and righteousness that his kingdom will introduce. Zechariah 10:4 boldly portrays the Messiah as a "cornerstone," "tent peg," and "battle bow," each metaphor illumining a different facet of the Messiah's earthly work. Verses 5–6 stress that the house of Judah will be triumphant "because the LORD is with them," that he "will strengthen the house of Judah and save" them, and that he will "have compassion" on Judah "for I am the LORD their God." As he has done many times in this book, Zechariah proclaims the glories of the future kingdom.

The beloved carol "Joy to the World! The Lord is Come" has been applied in recent times to the Lord's first advent. But when Isaac Watts penned the hymn, he envisioned the Savior's glorious second advent and his eschatological reign. Watts's words picture the glorious kingdom that God will introduce through his Son, Jesus the Messiah.

> Joy to the world! the Lord is come;
> Let earth receive her King;
> Let ev'ry heart prepare Him room,
> And heav'n and nature sing,
> And heav'n and nature sing,
> And heav'n and heav'n and nature sing.

---

[208] There is no need to accept the emendation recommended in BHS, "their strength [וּגְבֻרָתָם] will be in the LORD." The Masoretic Text (וְגִבַּרְתִּים) reads clearly as it stands.

[209] יִתְהַלָּכוּ. *HALOT*, 248.

[210] נְאֻם יהוה.

No more let sins and sorrows grow;
Nor thorns infest the ground;
He comes to make His blessings flow
Far as the curse is found,
Far as the curse is found,
Far as, far as the curse is found.[211]

## 6. Judgment of the Shepherds (11:1–17)

[1] Open your doors, O Lebanon,
   so that fire may devour your cedars!
[2] Wail, O pine tree, for the cedar has fallen;
   the stately trees are ruined!
Wail, oaks of Bashan;
   the dense forest has been cut down!
[3] Listen to the wail of the shepherds;
   their rich pastures are destroyed!
Listen to the roar of the lions;
   the lush thicket of the Jordan is ruined!

[4] This is what the LORD my God says: "Pasture the flock marked for slaughter. [5] Their buyers slaughter them and go unpunished. Those who sell them say, 'Praise the LORD, I am rich!' Their own shepherds do not spare them. [6] For I will no longer have pity on the people of the land," declares the LORD. "I will hand everyone over to his neighbor and his king. They will oppress the land, and I will not rescue them from their hands."

[7] So I pastured the flock marked for slaughter, particularly the oppressed of the flock. Then I took two staffs and called one Favor and the other Union, and I pastured the flock. [8] In one month I got rid of the three shepherds.

The flock detested me, and I grew weary of them [9] and said, "I will not be your shepherd. Let the dying die, and the perishing perish. Let those who are left eat one another's flesh."

[10] Then I took my staff called Favor and broke it, revoking the covenant I had made with all the nations. [11] It was revoked on that day, and so the afflicted of the flock who were watching me knew it was the word of the LORD.

[12] I told them, "If you think it best, give me my pay; but if not, keep it." So they paid me thirty pieces of silver.

[13] And the LORD said to me, "Throw it to the potter"—the handsome price at which they priced me! So I took the thirty pieces of silver and threw them into the house of the LORD to the potter.

[14] Then I broke my second staff called Union, breaking the brotherhood between Judah and Israel.

[15] Then the LORD said to me, "Take again the equipment of a foolish shepherd. [16] For I am going to raise up a shepherd over the land who will not care for the lost,

---

[211] *The Baptist Hymnal*, # 87.

or seek the young, or heal the injured, or feed the healthy, but will eat the meat of the choice sheep, tearing off their hoofs.

> [17]"Woe to the worthless shepherd,
>     who deserts the flock!
> May the sword strike his arm and his right eye!
>     May his arm be completely withered,
>     his right eye totally blinded!"

Zechariah 11 may be the most difficult and controversial chapter of the entire book. In a famous comment, S. R. Driver took this point one step further, claiming that Zech 11:4–17 stands as the most enigmatic passage in the whole Old Testament.[212] For instance, distinguishing between figurative and non-figurative language presents significant challenges in chap. 11. Identifying the appropriate topics and points of comparison in the chapter's various metaphors, whether trees or shepherds, is also extremely difficult. In many cases, locating specific historical references to Zechariah's proclamation in chap. 11 proves exceedingly trying as well. Beyond the eschatological implications of Zech 11, historical events that were nearer to Zechariah's day come into view. For instance, many scholars conclude that v. 14, the breaking of the staff named Union that symbolized the rupture of the brotherhood between Judah and Israel, lies behind the Samaritan schism.[213]

**11:1–3** Verses 1–3 stand as a discrete poem with affinities both to 10:4–12 and 11:4–17, the oracle against the two shepherds. These three verses present an unusually large number of interpretative questions over which scholarship has long found itself divided. The first question concerns whether 11:1–3 belongs to the preceding section of Zechariah or the subsequent one. Numerous scholars argue that vv. 1–3 conclude the theme of God's judging every mighty foe at the end of chap. 10.[214] Many others view 11:1–3 as an introduction to the message about the two shepherds in 11:4–17.[215]

One can make a strong case for either position. However, in such cases where a passage seems to follow closely from its previous context and also functions as an introduction to the ensuing passage, one would do well to recognize that the passage functions as a transition, much like a hinge upon which the two texts turn. In the final analysis, though, 11:1–3 does introduce the remainder of chap. 11. In particular, the prominence of the shepherds in v. 3 links the passage closely with the other shepherds in 11:4–17. The Lord speaks throughout vv. 1–3.

The nature of the poem evokes widely different interpretations, each of which influences whether one sees the poem as concluding chap. 10 or introducing

---

[212] S. R. Driver, *The Minor Prophets* (New York: Oxford University Press, 1904), 23.
[213] A. S. van der Woude, "Die Hirtenallegorie von Sacharja XI," *JNSL* 12 (1984): 140, 147–48.
[214] See Baldwin, *Zechariah*, 177; and Rudolph, *Sacharja 9–14*, 199–200.
[215] Barker, "Zechariah," 674; McComiskey, "Zechariah," 1188.

chap. 11.[216] Various scholars see 11:1–3 as a taunt, mocking the destruction of the power and pride of the mighty nations.[217] Floyd suggests an unusual category, the "mock sentinel report," largely based on the call issued in v. 1 that Floyd attributes to a sentinel.[218] Some interpretations of 11:1–3 strive for a very literal interpretation, while others see virtually every element in these verses as metaphorical. To illustrate the vexing challenges to determining the precise approach one should employ in interpreting this brief poem, Meyers and Meyers vacillate several times about how to proceed. First they write, "we are not convinced . . . that 'cedars' here in v. 2 . . . are operating at a level other than the literal one."[219] Their next sentence acknowledges that the shepherd motif in the remainder of chap. 11 is metaphorical. A few lines later, after observing the metaphorical tree, branch, and shoot imagery in earlier portions of Zechariah, they suggest that it "would be unlikely for tree imagery to lack metaphoric value" in chap. 11.[220] In their subsequent discussion, Meyers and Meyers view the passage in a fairly literal fashion, viewing the trees as real trees that the burgeoning population will displace.[221] Each of these interpretations deserves further comment.

As these references to Meyers and Meyers's interpretation of 11:1–3 demonstrate, they struggle with the best approach to the material. This ambivalence should not reflect negatively on their work, but rather shows the complexity of the material at hand. They ultimately take what one could call a physical settlement approach, viewing the trees as literal. According to this view, Zechariah prophesied that the forests will be utterly destroyed in the effort to provide sufficient territory for the swelling population (described in chap. 10) to occupy. In other words, Meyers and Meyers see the fire and destruction of this oracle to "be a literal description of land clearing."[222] Much of their discussion focuses upon the dense forests located in Lebanon and Gilead in ancient times. Burning becomes the most effective means of clearing the land for the newly arrived settlers. They maintain that while moderns would find the slash and burn approach "repugnant," the prophetic author would hold no such concern.[223]

As already indicated, Meyers and Meyers never reach a firm conclusion about whether the trees in chap. 11 also convey a symbolic meaning over and beyond that of real trees. In the end, they hold rather tightly to a literal interpretation of the entire passage. When turning to the motifs of the shepherds, they suggest that they "represent the lowest tier of leadership, the bureaucrats

---

[216] See the helpful overview of genre issues in Floyd, *Minor Prophets*, 483–84.

[217] Hanson, *Dawn of Apocalyptic*, 335; M. Saebø, *Sacharja 9–14* (Neukirchener-Vluyn: Neukirchener, 1969), 233.

[218] Floyd, *Minor Prophets*, 484.

[219] Meyers and Meyers, *Zechariah 9–14*, 241.

[220] Ibid., 242.

[221] Ibid., 242–48, especially 246.

[222] Ibid., 239.

[223] Ibid., 240.

whose livelihood is cut off by the fall of imperial power."[224] The lions stand for real lions who roar in frustration about the loss of their habitat. The shepherds wail, according to Meyers and Meyers's view, because the deforestation has deprived them of their pasturage.

Ultimately, Meyers and Meyers fail to provide sufficient evidence from the text that their approach deserves adoption. They merit commendation for struggling with the meaning of the various elements in vv. 1–3 and their attempt to link its message with the one in chap. 10 that says "there will not be room enough for them" (v. 10). Further, sound interpretative method requires that one pursue figurative interpretations only after the text is allowed to speak in a more normal fashion. Perhaps the greatest weakness of their approach, however, is the inadequate attention to the judgmental overtones found in vv. 1–3. An overview of the more prominent themes in the passage—"devour," "fallen," and "ruined"—strongly suggest judgment, particularly when one evaluates these concepts in the context of the Old Testament. The notion of wailing certainly conveys the message of judgment.

Unger firmly contends that 11:1–3 describes judgment in very strong terms, but he also attempts to avoid a figurative interpretation: "Nothing more than a literal interpretation is needed, and there is not the slightest reason to make the trees signify either nations or men despite such references as Isaiah 10:34; Ezekiel 17:8; Jeremiah 22:6; *passim*, where trees represent nations or men."[225]

One might infer from this quote that Unger handles the whole passage in a consistently literal fashion, but he does not. He sees the address to Lebanon as an apostrophe (a rhetorical device where a speaker digresses by addressing a personified object), and he claims that the doors function as a metaphor. Unger treats the trees in hierarchical fashion, seeing the cedars as the most valuable and most unassailable trees. He suggests that if the cedars fell, no hope could be offered to the lesser trees.[226] Unger also treats the trees which "howl" in a metaphorical sense. He claims that the roaring of the lions represents the severity of God's judgment on the land.

These examples of inconsistencies of metaphorical analyses do not prove Unger is wrong in trying to view the trees literally. McComiskey also contends that the trees bear only literal meaning. He writes, "The destruction this section depicts is not against the regions of Lebanon and Bashan, but against the trees for which these regions were celebrated."[227] To support his view, McComiskey lists various passages in which the text specifically mentions trees from a locale, such as Lebanon (2 Chr 2:8; Pss 29:5; 92:12 [Hb. v. 13]; Isa 2:13; Ezek 27:6). Most of these texts do not contribute to McComiskey's argument.

---

[224] Ibid., 246.
[225] Unger, *Zechariah*, 190.
[226] Ibid., 189.
[227] McComiskey, "Zechariah," 1188.

For instance, 2 Chr 2:8 states, "Send me also cedar, pine and algum logs from Lebanon." Such an exhortation does not remotely suggest a figurative meaning. Rather, in 2 Chr 2:8, Solomon asks King Hiram for wood to construct the temple. But Isa 2:12–13 provides significant background to Zech 11:1–3:

> The LORD Almighty has a day in store
> for all the proud and lofty,
> for all that is exalted,
> (and they will be humbled),
> for all the cedars of Lebanon, tall and lofty,
> and all the oaks of Bashan.

Despite the tenuous evidence offered, one can defend the position that the trees represent nothing more than real trees of differing species, largely on the broader grounds of one's understanding of the entire passage.

However, in light of Zechariah's prolific use of figurative language in this passage and beyond, as well as the extensive examples of trees used in a figurative sense elsewhere in the Old Testament, a stronger case can be made for interpreting the trees symbolically. For example, Merrill contends that "the objects mentioned under the guise of trees and animals are the same as the shepherds."[228] He claims that the metaphor of a tree serves as second only to that of shepherd to represent leaders, both in the book of Zechariah and in the broader Old Testament context. Merrill thus views the trees as emblematic of the kings in the ancient Near East, similar to the manner in which the shepherd metaphor functions. The passages Merrill cites to support his identification of trees with kings, Isa 10:33–34 and Ezek 31:3–18, refer generally to Lebanon and Assyria respectively, not to the monarch of either realm. The sole illustration offered in which a king clearly refers to himself as a tree appears in Dan 4:20–23 where Nebuchadnezzar was a tree that God would cut down and leave as a stump. Unlike Zech 11, Dan 4:22 clearly indicates that the tree is the king: "you, O king, are that tree!" This lone example fails to demonstrate that Zechariah meant for his readers to identify the various species of trees with particular monarchs. Nevertheless, this observation does not invalidate the possibility that Zechariah used trees as metaphors in 11:1–3.

Baldwin represents a third approach to the significance of trees in this passage. She suggests that "the different types of tree represent nations large and small."[229] While this interpretation is anything but certain, it does conform well to the context. More generally, Ezek 31 offers an extended metaphor likening Assyria to a tree. Ezekiel 31:3 specifically identifies Assyria with a cedar from Lebanon. Zechariah 10 introduces Assyria and Egypt as representative of the many oppressors who had persecuted Judah for centuries. Chapter 10

---

[228] Merrill, *Zechariah*, 285.
[229] Baldwin, *Zechariah*, 178.

leaves no doubt about the future of any empire that would oppose God and his people. Verse 11b declares, "Assyria's pride will be brought down and Egypt's scepter will pass away." So the trees in Zech 11 probably refer to empires that have arrayed themselves against the Lord; the message plainly decrees their doom (cf. Ps 2).

Zechariah began this oracle with the imperative "open your doors." The word for "your doors" *(dĕlāteykā)* may also signify "gates."[230] In 1 Sam 3:15 *delet* means a door, while it refers to a gate (such as a city gate) in Deut 3:5. Zechariah admonished the region of Lebanon to open its gates. Since entire lands did not possess either walls or gates, the term must function metaphorically. To open the gate means to lower the defenses in order to allow someone or something to enter unhindered. In Ps 24:7 one reads a similar exhortation: "Lift up you heads, O you gates; be lifted up, you ancient doors, that the King of glory may come in." In this psalm the Lord enters the community, bringing grace and mercy with him. Zechariah 11:1 provides the antithesis to Ps 24:7, for the Lord will come to Lebanon with judgment and devastation. The commandment to open the doors of Lebanon suggests that God's judgment had so doomed the region that it would be futile to resist.

Prophets had long linked Lebanon with Bashan in their sermons. Several passages pair these two regions in poetic verse (Isa 2:13; Jer 22:20; Ezek 27:5–6). In the biblical epoch, Lebanon was a sparsely populated territory, but was heavily forested. The geographic term "Lebanon" refers to the entire region known by that name, not merely Mount Lebanon.[231] Even though Lebanon did not present itself as a foe of Israel in the Old Testament, the land stands for every obstacle to the fulfillment of the Lord's promises.

Bashan was situated east of the Jordan and north of Mount Gilead. In Num 21:32–35 the Israelites captured Bashan from King Og at the time of the conquest. Subsequently, Bashan was assigned to the tribe of Manasseh (Num 32:33; Josh 13:30). A fertile region, Bashan was famous in antiquity for its resplendent oaks that grew on its mountain slopes (Isa 2:13; Ezek 27:6). Bashan was also renowned for its verdant pastures (Deut 32:14; Ps 22:12; Ezek 39:18; Amos 4:1).

As already indicated, it is not entirely clear whether Zechariah viewed the trees in this passage as figurative or literal. While acknowledging the possibility of a literal interpretation, the Old Testament also frequently refers to trees as emblems of other entities. The cedar represented Judah's royal house (Ezek 17:3–4,12–22). Isaiah 2:13 considers the cedars of Lebanon, as well as the oaks of Bashan, an apt symbol of everything "proud," "lofty," and "exalted." In Isa 10:33–34 it portrays the strength and notoriety of the Assyrian military that

---

[230] דְּלָתֶיךָ. *HALOT*, 223–24.
[231] Merrill (*Zechariah*, 285) maintains that "Lebanon does not refer to the nation in any sense but to the source of the mighty cedar tree."

could be felled by a mere ax. The entirety of Ezek 31 develops the theme of the cedar in Lebanon that, although beautiful and incomparable, would be felled as an expression of the Lord's judgment. Ezekiel considered these cedars to represent Pharaoh and the remainder of his Egyptian horde. Meyers and Meyers summarize the significance of the cedar: "The use of 'cedars' to represent the supreme political power(s) of the ancient world certainly emerges naturally enough from the qualities of the cedar, which is the largest and one of the longest-lived trees in the Mediterranean world. Its wood was greatly prized for the construction of monumental buildings (such as the Jerusalem Temple)."[232]

The cedar was noted for its grandeur and strength in ancient times. It would have been unimaginable for a forest of stately cedars to burn to the ground. It appears that Zechariah viewed the different species of trees in 11:1–3 in a hierarchal fashion. That is, Zechariah portrayed the cedar as the most valuable tree, while cypress and oak trees stood for important trees, but less so than cedar. Consequently, when the "unassailable" cedars vanished, what hope remained for the lesser trees like the cypress and oak?[233]

The devouring of the grand cedars that had long been her glory will result from Lebanon opening her doors. The Hebrew word for "devour" *(wĕtōʾkal)*[234] describes the destruction brought down by the Lord. Amos 1:10 illustrates the usage well: "I will send fire upon the walls of Tyre that will consume *[wĕʾākĕlāh]* her fortresses."

In v. 2 the pine trees and the oaks "wail" for the fallen cedars. The term "wail" *(hêlēl)* typically connotes despair over judgment in the Old Testament (Isa 13:6; Jer 47:2; Amos 8:3).[235] The verb "wailing" proclaims judgment against foreign nations (Jer 25:34; Isa 23:1). The term also describes the great pathos that divine judgment would bring down upon Israel (Isa 65:13–15; Hos 7:13–15). Wailing thus describes the pathos, the sorrow, and the confusion that the devastation wrought.

Verse 3 appears to draw heavily from earlier prophetic writings. Jeremiah illustrates the combination of several images found in Zech 11:1–3. Jeremiah 25:34–36 states,

> Weep and wail, you shepherds;
>    roll in the dust, you leaders of the flock.
> For your time to be slaughtered has come;
>    you will fall and be shattered like fine pottery.
> The shepherds will have nowhere to flee,
>    the leaders of the flock no place to escape."

---

[232] Meyers and Meyers, *Zechariah 9–14*, 242.
[233] Unger, *Zechariah*, 189.
[234] וְתֹאכַל. *HALOT*, 46.
[235] הֵילֵל. *HALOT*, 413.

> Hear the cry of the shepherds,
>> the wailing of the leaders of the flock,
>> for the LORD is destroying their pasture.

As in Jer 25, the shepherds in Zech 11:3 refer to foreign kings. Both prophets delivered God's message of impending judgment, which was so severe that all will anguish over the ruin of their former glory.

Not only will the shepherds wail, but the lions in the thicket surrounding the Jordan roar their pain and displeasure over what the Lord has done to them. The figurative wailing of trees in v. 2 transforms into the wailing of real beings. Several scholars view these lions as literal beasts who have lost their habitat and no longer possess a lair. While this understanding is possible, other biblical usages of the term suggest otherwise.

For instance, Jer 50:44 pictures the king of Babylon as "a lion coming up from Jordan's thickets." Further, in Ezek 19:1–9 the princes of Israel are deemed lions. Verses 1–2a proclaims, "Take up a lament concerning the princes of Israel and say: 'What a lioness was your mother among the lions!' " Verse 5 says, "When she saw her hope unfulfilled, her expectation gone, she took another of her cubs and made him a strong lion." Further, the roaring of a lion represents the sound of an invading army (Jer 2:15) and unrighteous rulers (Ezek 22:25).

In light of the highly figurative nature of Zech 11:1–3 and the clear usage of the term "lion" in biblical material that was well known both to Zechariah and his audience, one should view Zechariah's roaring lion as a metaphor for kings whose kingdoms the Lord has despoiled. Moreover, in the parallelism of this poetic couplet, "shepherds" and "lions" serve as word pairs, giving greater credence to the figurative interpretation. With the conclusion of 11:1–3 Zechariah leaves the poetic genre he has used so extensively. The only two snippets of poetry remaining in the book occur in 11:17 and 13:7–9.

Zechariah 11:1–3 concludes with the theological theme of the Lord's imminent arrival to establish his eschatological kingdom. This messianic reign will bring great joy and satisfaction to the Lord's people, but only sorrow to his opponents. Before God can establish his kingdom, those who would oppose the inauguration of the Lord's reign must be overcome.

**11:4–17** The remainder of chap. 11 presents some of the greatest challenges in the entire book of Zechariah. A brief survey of the type of questions arising includes such matters as whether the passage should be read as a symbolic action or an allegory, the meaning of several terms in the pericope, the identity of various prominent figures such as the shepherds and the flock, the significance of the symbolism of items like the staffs, and the historical fulfillment of the prophecy. Each of these questions will receive attention subsequently.

However, in the midst of so many vexing questions, it is important for the reader to remain focused on the most important aspects of the chapter, the literary and theological emphases about which most concur. For instance, the remainder of chap. 11 addresses the question of godly leadership employing the symbolism of several shepherds, one good and the others wicked. It was imperative for Judah to grasp the corruption manifested by her leaders. Until the people recognized the wickedness among their leaders and chose to reject evil as well as the shepherds who embodied sin, the Lord refused to intervene.[236] In this context God commissioned Zechariah to act out symbolically the tragedy that unfolded daily throughout the land. Zechariah saw the nation through the eyes of a shepherd, viewing Judah as a flock in constant need of guidance and protection. Little wonder that the prophet castigated the worthless shepherd and longed to see personally the coming Shepherd-Messiah who would provide the ultimate care for God's flock. When this noble Shepherd first arrives, those who do not desire a consistent, righteous reign will despise the Shepherd's faithfulness and will strive to oppose his leadership at every juncture.

Zechariah 11:4–17 unfolds with three distinct movements. First, vv. 4–6 introduce the righteous shepherd. In this subsection, those who spurn righteousness reject the shepherd, thus invoking the wrath of God. Second, vv. 7–14 overview the flock's rejection of their shepherd and the breaking of the symbolic staffs, "Favor" and "Union," symbolizing the breach of the covenant between the Lord and his people as well as the rupture between Judah and Israel. This second section also clarifies the reason for the judgment described in 11:1–3, the people's rejection of the righteous shepherd. Finally, vv. 15–17 conclude on the somber note of a new shepherd, a worthless shepherd whose unrighteousness and lack of care for the flock results in the decimation of God's people. Before one can address the particulars of the passage, one must seek to ascertain the more general character and literary genre that the text presents.

One of the more compelling and basic questions that chap. 11 poses is how to understand the shepherd's actions. The three main understandings of Zech 11 see three completely different relationships between the shepherd Zechariah and reality. The first view concludes that Zechariah actually assumed the religious and civil role of a shepherd/king in order to fulfill his commission. The second approach views the chapter as an allegory, that is, a protracted metaphor to communicate God's displeasure with his flock. The final understanding sees Zechariah's actions as examples of an extended symbolic action whereby a biblical figure, usually a prophet, acts out the message he delivers from God. A variation on the symbolic action perspective maintains that Zechariah simply conceived many of the activities described in chap. 11 mentally. After the mental experience or vision, Zechariah then proclaimed to the nation what the

---

[236] P. L. Redditt, "The Two Shepherds in Zechariah 11:4–17," *CBQ* 55 (1993): 681.

Lord had revealed to him. To restate this important interpretative question, Did God intend for Zechariah to act out every aspect introduced in vv. 4–14?

Many interpreters offer the strongest possible affirmative answer, arguing that Zechariah actually assumed the role of shepherd for the flock of Judah as described in vv. 4–17. In other words, this view contends that the prophet truly received the mantle of civil and religious leadership, becoming either a king or assuming another leadership role such as that of high priest that held comparable responsibilities over the entire postexilic nation. McComiskey favors the interpretation that Zechariah assumed some particularly significant office in order to promote righteousness in the land.[237] He concludes that Zechariah did indeed remove three shepherds in one month (v. 8), although McComiskey makes no attempt to identify the shepherds. Like a few other interpreters, McComiskey reads chap. 11 as an autobiographical narrative for Zechariah.[238]

Such a literal view of these verses is rarely embraced today, as the figurative nature of the prophet's descriptions strongly suggests that the reader was not intended to read every feature of the narrative in a literal fashion. Even more telling, the complete absence of historical material from the epoch that supports the claim that Zechariah ever assumed such a high civil or religious leadership role renders this view most unlikely. Consequently, one should look for a preferable understanding of the shepherd's actions.

Alternatively, many understand the chapter as an allegory. Admittedly, the word *allegory* conveys a very negative connotation to many interpreters who have mistakenly understood that everything in Scripture should be interpreted literally. Of course, the entire Bible bulges with examples of figurative, nonliteral expressions.[239] These figures of speech include large numbers of metaphors, a point no one would deny. Since the time of Origen, biblical interpreters have been taught to eschew allegorical interpretations, but the main difference between a metaphor and an allegory is the duration of the figure of speech in its literary context. The metaphor presents a brief comparison whose implications continue throughout a passage without the need to repeat the metaphorical language. An apt illustration for a discussion of Zech 11 would be the renowned metaphor, "The LORD is my shepherd" (Ps 23:1). An allegory simply continues the metaphor over multiple verses.[240]

While the Bible contains far fewer examples of allegory than some in the history of interpretation have suggested, there is no doubt that allegory does exist in the biblical text. The classic example of biblical allegory occurs in

---

[237] McComiskey, *Minor Prophets*, 1191, 1194–95.

[238] D. R. Jones's attempt to view much of chaps. 9–11 autobiographically has received limited acceptance, owing primarily to a lack of corroborating evidence ("A Fresh Interpretation," 41–59; cf. Floyd, *Minor Prophets*, 490).

[239] The best English treatment of the figurative language in the Bible remains the classic work of E. W. Bullinger, *Figures of Speech Used in the Bible*, reprint ed. (Grand Rapids: Baker, 1968).

[240] Ibid., 748–49.

Gal 4 where Paul presents Hagar and Sarah allegorically, each representing a differing understanding of salvation and obedience to Christ. When Paul proclaimed, "Get rid of the slave woman" (Gal 4:30), he thereby rejected the old perspective of the old covenant based solely upon obedience to the law in favor of the new covenant that Christ mediated granting righteousness through God's grace.

Baldwin represents modern interpreters who view Zech 11 allegorically.[241] She observes that Zechariah did not actually perform the deeds mentioned in vv. 7–14. Interestingly, Merrill, a strong proponent of the symbolic action view, agrees that vv. 7–14 portray "actions" that the shepherd never actually performed.[242] Numerous additional factors contribute to this figurative interpretation. Most importantly, Zechariah never reigned over postexilic Judah in the fashion of a messianic king. Likewise, the prophet never personally attempted to mandate a righteous rule that resulted in the nation's utter disdain for him as *the* shepherd for Judah; at least no record of Zechariah's leadership activities has ever emerged. Moreover, no evidence suggests that Zechariah ever reached the point where he felt utter contempt for the people God had called him to serve. Additionally, few interpreters of any persuasion suggest that the enigmatic episode about the disdainful payment of 30 pieces of silver to the shepherd and his subsequent discarding of the money at the potter's house should be viewed as an actual event.

The allegorical interpretation is that Zechariah may not have been a participant in many of the details of the passage. Additionally, the prophet was not personally a party to the breaking of the covenant between Judah and Israel when the second staff, "Union," was broken. Similarly, no evidence indicates that the complete severance of the relationship between Zechariah and the nation ever occurred as portrayed in the breaking of the staff, "Favor." Perhaps most significantly, chap. 11 appears to convey an eschatological message, much like the previous sections of the book. God chose Zechariah to communicate numerous significant truths, many of which were unpopular and unpleasant to the nation, about the events leading to the inauguration of the coming kingdom. This kingdom will require judgment on every form of insubordination against the Lord, the institution of righteousness on earth through the messianic King, and the redemption of creation from the effects of sin that have been causing it to groan continually (Rom 8:22).

Floyd argues against reading vv. 4–17 as allegory, although he concedes that the two staffs function allegorically.[243] But these allegorical elements in the account do not make the entire passage allegorical. Zechariah informs his

---

[241] Baldwin, *Zechariah*, 179. See also L. V. Meyer, "An Allegory Concerning the Monarchy: Zech 11:4–17; 13:7–9," in *Scripture in History and Theology: Essays in Honor of J. Coert Rylaarsdam*, ed. A. L. Merrill and T. W. Overholt (Pittsburgh: Pickwick, 1977), 232–33.

[242] Merrill, *Zechariah*, 288.

[243] Floyd, *Minor Prophets*, 489.

readers that the two staffs possess double meaning. Floyd does not make a similar statement about the other features in the chapter. He sympathetically notes Hanson's view of the chapter as a "commissioning narrative,"[244] but in saying this neither Floyd nor Hanson mean anything more than that the Lord instructed one of his servants to do something. Consequently, this designation does little to aid the interpretation of chap. 11.

A third view treats chap. 11 as a symbolic action.[245] Those who accept this view conclude that the prophet performed actions in plain sight of his audience in order to communicate God's message more vividly and memorably.[246] According to this viewpoint, Zech 11 represents one of many prominent symbolic actions of which the prophets seemed so fond. For instance, Samuel tore his mantle (1 Sam 15:27–28) and Isaiah wore the clothing of a captive (20:2). Jeremiah wore a yoke (27:2–7,10–12). Ezekiel dug out an opening in the wall of his house in order to picture the imminent breach of Jerusalem's walls (12:1–16), and he inscribed the names of the tribes on wood (37:15–23). In another prominent example, God commanded Hosea to marry a harlot (Hos 1:2–3). Numerous additional symbolic actions emerge throughout the Old Testament, particularly in the prophetic writings.

Merrill articulates the symbolic action interpretation of chap. 11, simply asserting that God commanded the prophet Zechariah "to play a role."[247] This interpretation of Zechariah's role in the chapter enjoys wide support largely because the other prophets often employed symbolic actions as a communicative vehicle. However, Merrill himself immediately acknowledges a possible difficulty. After stating, "there is no reason to deny that most if not all of these dramatizations actually occurred," Merrill notes that this cannot be the case with Zech 11:7–14. Concerning these eight verses he states, "The things he is said to have done there simply could not have been done by his own hand. It is most likely that he did them internally, in his own mind, and that he then communicated to his hearers what he had done."[248]

The observation that the actions portrayed in vv. 7–14 "could not have been done by his [Zechariah's] own hand" may be correct, although even this point defies certain resolution. Zechariah 11:7–14 contains all of the essential actions that one might wish to deem "symbolic." If the "actions" in these verses did not actually occur, in what sense can one deem them actions, whether symbolic or otherwise? Further, if the actions in vv. 7–14 only existed in the mind

---

[244] Hanson, *Dawn of Apocalyptic*, 341.
[245] Boda, "Reading Between the Lines," in *Bringing out the Treasure: Inner Biblical Allusion in Zechariah 9–14*, ed. M. J. Boda and M. H. Floyd (Sheffield: Sheffield Academic Press, 2003), 280–81.
[246] Sweeney, *Twelve Prophets*, 679.
[247] Merrill, *Zechariah*, 287.
[248] Ibid., 288. Unger (*Zechariah*, 191) acknowledges the same possibility.

of Zechariah (and the Lord), one certainly should not interpret these verses in a literal sense.

In the final analysis, the symbolic action approach best handles the details of the chapter and presents the fewest difficulties. Despite persistent uncertainties about certain interpretative details, handling chap. 11 as a symbolic action actually offers a simpler and more straightforward approach to the chapter.[249] Floyd observes that one "cannot mitigate the probability that this narrative at least purports to describe something that actually happened."[250] It is impossible to determine whether Zechariah received an ironic payment of 30 pieces of silver for his services as a shepherd, or whether he cast this disdainful payment into the house of a potter, or whether vv. 12–13 are metaphorical. Now, to the details of vv. 4–17.

**11:4** Verse 4 begins with the powerful assertion, "This is what the LORD my God says." The idiom "the LORD my God" stresses Zechariah's personal, intimate relationship with the Lord. The similar idiom occurs with some frequency in Psalms (see 22:11; 31:15; 38:21). At times the expression functions to identify the Lord as the one true God, in contrast to false gods (see Balaam in Num 22:18; David in 2 Sam 24:24; and Ruth in Ruth 1:16).[251] Both nuances apply to v. 4. Zechariah describes his relationship with the Lord as very close. Plus, the prophet affirms that the Lord is indeed the one true God. Both emphases underscore the authenticity of the message the prophet will deliver. Because of his closeness to God he was uniquely positioned to communicate a message to the people from the Lord, representing the Lord as the earthly shepherd of the people.

As v. 4 begins, Zechariah spoke, quoting the Lord's statement, "Pasture the flock marked for slaughter." The Hebrew term "pasture" is *rĕ'ēh*,[252] which is probably a denominative verb built upon the noun for "shepherd." The divine mandate to "pasture" is addressed to Zechariah. Hence, God instructs the prophet to fulfill the role of a shepherd in the ensuing text, clearly inferring that Zechariah was himself the shepherd of whom the Lord spoke in vv. 4–14.

Zechariah 11:4 introduces the Lord's command to Zechariah to pasture God's flock, the nation of Judah. The phrase "flock marked for slaughter" translates the genitive construction "*flock of* slaughter" (*ṣō'n hahărēgāh*).[253] The genitive functions to delineate the destiny of the flock (see Isa 22:13).[254] Although v. 4 does not clearly state why the flock has been assigned to slaugh-

---

[249] Unger, *Zechariah*, 191. Cf. Saebø, *Sacharja 9–14*, 234.
[250] Floyd, *Minor Prophets*, 491–92.
[251] Meyers and Meyers, *Zechariah 9–14*, 249.
[252] רְעֵה. *HALOT*, 1262.
[253] צֹאן הַהֲרֵגָה. *HALOT*, 992–93, 255.
[254] S. Feigin's claim ("Some Notes on Zechariah 11 4–17," *JBL* 44 [1925]: 204) that "flock of slaughter" functioned technically to describe meat on the hoof, that is, animals on their way to slaughter, remains unsubstantiated.

ter, the ensuing context suggests the reason. The symbolism portrays the judgment God intends to send against Judah for her habitual sin against the Lord, provided that she refuses to repent. The connotation of *hahărēgāh* ("slaughter") does not necessarily imply that the entire flock will face death. The term can indicate ruin without the necessity of death for all who face God's judgment (see Eccl 3:3; Lam 4:3; Hos 9:13–15).[255]

Zechariah employed the shepherd motif with a frequency approaching that with which Isaiah used the servant theme. The Hebrew term for "shepherd" (*rō'eh*) routinely serves as a metaphor for the king or some other primary ruler in Israel.[256] The Old Testament often portrays the Lord as Israel's shepherd (Gen 48:15; Pss 23:1; 80:1; 95:7; Isa 40:11; Hos 4:16; Mic 7:14). The identification of Zechariah, a prophet, as a shepherd reflects a departure from the significance of the shepherd motif in earlier Old Testament texts.[257]

Despite the indication that the prophet received the divine mandate to "pasture the flock," some interpreters view the shepherd in purely messianic terms. Barker views the shepherd as the Messiah[258] and identifies the "my" in "my God" in v. 4a as Zechariah himself. However, Barker fails to explain how v. 4a refers to Zechariah while v. 4b refers to the Messiah. To compound the difficulty, there is no intervening transition or any other indication that the Lord addressed two different individuals in v. 4. Further, Barker contends that Zechariah was "instructed to act out the role of a good shepherd for the flock, i.e., Israel," not explaining where the prophet Zechariah ceases to appear in the text and where the Messiah emerges.[259]

Unger adopts a symbolic action understanding of the chapter: "Zechariah is divinely instructed apparently to act out a parable or similitude to enforce a prophetic truth."[260] He rejects the messianic identification of the shepherd in favor of viewing Zechariah the shepherd as prefiguring the Lord himself typologically. In light of the eschatological tone of much of the book of Zechariah, including chap. 11, Unger properly notes that Zechariah performed symbolic actions that ultimately pointed to the work the Lord himself would complete.

The identity of the flock in chap. 11 represents one of the few major questions about which little controversy exists. The flock must portray Israel, and attempts to correlate the flock with another nation or the nations do not make sense in this context. The Old Testament often employs the metaphor of the flock to describe God's covenant people. Psalm 100:3 states,

---

[255] Meyers and Meyers, *Zechariah 9–14*, 252–53.
[256] רֹעֶה. *HALOT*, 1260–61. *TLOT*, 1248.
[257] Meyers and Meyers, *Zechariah 9–14*, 250–51.
[258] Barker, "Zechariah," 675.
[259] Ibid., 676.
[260] Unger, *Zechariah*, 191.

> Know that the LORD is God.
> It is he who made us, and we are his;
> we are his people, the sheep of his pasture.

Psalm 95:7 and Ezek 34:30–31 introduce similar concepts. Thus, Zechariah's sheep represent the nation, men and women who suffer daily under the heavy oppression to which their false "shepherds" subject them. If then the flock symbolizes Israel, that is, Judah, the shepherd must be responsible for God's people, irrespective of his identity. The identity of the various shepherds introduced in chap. 11 will receive attention shortly.

**11:5** Zech 11:5 presents the reason, at least in part, that God's flock is doomed to slaughter. Somewhat cryptically, Zechariah castigated those who bought and sold the flock. The metaphor of the Lord "selling" *(mākar)* his people to foreign powers as an expression of divine judgment occurs elsewhere, particularly in the book of Judges.[261] Judges 2:14 declares, "In his anger against Israel the LORD handed them over to raiders who plundered them. He sold them to their enemies all around" (cf. 3:8; 4:2; 10:7).[262] God himself does not "sell" his people in Zech 11:5.[263] However, the metaphor in prior Old Testament texts illustrates the function of the figure of speech in chap. 11.

Despite the fact that the flock of Judah belongs to God, the Lord himself does not sell the flock. One who owns a flock possesses the freedom to sell his flock at will without accountability to anyone. Nonetheless, the shepherds should show compassion to the flock and remorse for their actions against the sheep, a flock that does not even belong to them since they are merely hirelings. This emphasizes the point that the flock did not belong to the shepherds and therefore it was not theirs to sell.[264] Nonetheless, the shepherds "do not spare them" *(lōʾ yaḥmôl)*.[265] The shepherds' brutal treatment of a flock that was not even theirs plainly showed what worthless shepherds they were.

The buyers of the flock in Zechariah's narrative represent the litany of kings past, present, and future who seek to subjugate and plunder God's people. These sellers portray the general class of oppressive reigns and do not signify a particular kingdom, whether rapacious foreigners or greedy monarchs from Judah herself. The metaphor of selling Judah like a flock of cull sheep heading for slaughter poignantly describes the manner in which Judah had suffered as a pawn among both powerful neighbors and her own sinful shepherds for generations.

"Those who sell them" may either refer to foreign kings who persecuted Judah by buying and selling her at the foreigners' whims or to fellow Judahites

---

[261] מָכַר. *HALOT*, 581–82.
[262] Merrill, *Zechariah*, 288–89.
[263] וּמֹכְרֵיהֶן.
[264] Redditt, "Two Shepherds," 681.
[265] לֹא יַחְמוֹל. *HALOT*, 328.

who sought to take advantage of their own people.[266] But the phrase "their own shepherds do not spare them" strongly suggests that the sellers are none other than the flock's own shepherds, the leaders of the postexilic community. The injustice of shepherds whom God appointed forsaking their divine mandate for personal gain paints the sinfulness of the leaders in stark colors. These shepherds manifested willful disregard for the well being of their charge, even evidencing a cavalier attitude toward the suffering their actions inflicted upon innocent people. Such sinful disregard for the well being of others surpasses understanding. However, the shepherds' blatant defiance of God manifests their actions that had resulted in truly nefarious injury to Judah. The shepherds' remark, "Praise the LORD, I am rich," drips with irony. God did not enrich these faithless shepherds—their own disregard for the needs of the people enabled them to pillage those under their care. To attribute the accumulation of wealth to God foreshadows the false teaching of prosperity preachers today (cf. Mark 10:23).

Subtly, Zechariah portrayed these sellers of their flock to be more than sinful; they were financially irresponsible, even stupid.[267] The third feminine plural pronouns "their/them" on the words "their buyers" *(qōnêhen)*[268] and "slaughter them" *(yahărĕgun)*[269] refer to a flock of ewes, the breeding stock.[270] For a real shepherd, nothing could be more foolish than to sell the ewes who hold the prospects of the future flocks of sheep. The destruction of the breeding ewes surely exhibited wanton waste.

The verse concludes with the sad commentary on the effects of the shepherds' irresponsibility against God's flock, "their own shepherds do not spare them." The Hebrew term translated "spare" *(yahmōl)* conveys the meaning of having pity or compassion for someone.[271] The word describes Pharaoh's daughter's response when she saw the infant Moses in the basket among the reeds of the Nile: she "opened it [the basket] and saw the baby. He was crying, and she felt sorry *[yahmōl]* for him" (Exod 2:6). Another use of the word that shows a lack of mercy as an expression of judgment occurs in Jer 15:5, "Who will have pity *[yahmōl]* on you, O Jerusalem?"

**11:6** At the beginning of v. 6, many interpreters understand the particle *kî* causally, translating it "because."[272] The causal view might suggest that v. 6 gives the reason for the Lord's actions, his displeasure with the people. A related question asks to what the particle *kî* refers. It is unlikely that the shepherds'

---

[266] Ibid., 288.
[267] Baldwin, *Zechariah*, 180.
[268] קֹנֵיהֶן. *HALOT*, 1112–13.
[269] יַהֲרְגֻן. *HALOT*, 255.
[270] Four of the five third plural pronominal suffixes in v. 5 are third feminine plural. The lone exception, וְרֹעֵיהֶם ("their shepherd"), refers to the people collectively, having a broader antecedent than merely the brood ewes (Unger, *Zechariah*, 192–93).
[271] יַחְמוֹל. *HALOT*, 328.
[272] כִּי. *HALOT*, 470–71.

refusal to care for their flock provides the reason for the Lord's declaration that he will not have pity on the people. This conclusion would render the unintelligible perspective that God did not intend to care for the people simply because the shepherds refused to do so. The particle *kî* more likely refers to the Lord's command to Zechariah to shepherd the flock. In this view Zechariah should assume the role of shepherd *because* God himself would refuse to do so just as Judah's shepherds had refused to care for their flock.[273]

A slightly different view of the particle and the verse it introduces claims that it means "certainly" or "indeed."[274] This use of the particle is often difficult to translate, but this interpretation sees v. 6 as the climax of the passage.[275] If even their Lord refused to show them mercy, Judah had little hope until they had satisfied the punishment that God would mete out to them shortly.

Using the same verb for "pity" in v. 5b, the Lord declared the reason the judgment would ultimately fall: he would no longer extend any pity *(lō' 'eḥmōl)* to Judah because of her sinfulness.[276] Jer 13:14 states a comparable idea using the same language: "I will smash them one against the other, fathers and sons alike, declares the LORD. I will allow no pity or mercy or compassion to keep me from destroying them."

The phrase "I will *hand* everyone *over*" *(mamṣî')* translates a Hebrew participle that here communicates imminent action.[277] Hence, the Lord intends to bring the promised judgment to finality with rapidity. This punishment on the nation does not indicate that the Lord terminated his covenant with his people or that he intended to break the promises made long ago to Abraham. Leviticus 26:44 refers to this issue definitively: "when they are in the land of their enemies, I will not reject them or abhor them so as to destroy them completely, breaking my covenant with them. I am the LORD their God."[278]

Some modern translations such as the NRSV follow a scholarly emendation to the text and reject the reading "to his *neighbor*" *(rē'ēhû)* as witnessed by the Hebrew text.[279] In its place, the proposal suggests the reading "his shepherd" *(rō'ēhû).*[280] This unnecessary alteration to the text aims to harmonize the revised reading with the shepherd motif throughout the remainder of the chapter. The meaning of "neighbor" fits the context quite well, though. The passage declares that Judah and her land will become subject to the intervention and control of the neighboring peoples and kings. This doleful promise saw its prediction validated in the ensuing centuries.

---

[273] McComiskey, "Zechariah," 1192.
[274] Joüon-Muraoka, *Grammar*, § 164b and GKC, § 160; see. *HALOT*, 470–71.
[275] Merrill, *Zechariah*, 289.
[276] לֹא אֶחְמוֹל.
[277] מַמְצִיא. *HALOT*, 620. The *futur instans* use of the Hebrew participle conveys imminent and certain action, see GKC § 115 p.
[278] See McComiskey, "Zechariah," 1192.
[279] רֵעֵהוּ. *HALOT*, 1264.
[280] רֹעֵהוּ. Meyers-Meyers, *Zechariah 9–14*, 260; *HALOT*, 1265.

Many conclude that the Roman occupation of the land of Israel fulfilled the prediction in v. 6 that oppressors would come to persecute the Lord's people without any hope of divine deliverance. Unger boldly asserts that a Roman fulfillment is "obvious."[281] Unger is not alone in concluding that the Roman persecution of the Jewish community in the first two centuries after Christ aptly fulfills Zechariah's prophecy of imminent occupation. However, the entire chapter focuses on more universal and cataclysmic events than the Roman occupation of Israel. The eschatological perspective in chap. 11 suggests that any fulfillment of Zechariah's prophecies, Roman or otherwise, merely serves as a precursor of universal end-time events.

**11:7** Verse 7 begins with the affirmation that the shepherd—none other than the prophet Zechariah—did indeed assume the role of shepherd as the Lord had instructed him, though in a symbolic fashion. As the shepherd, Zechariah may have prefigured the messianic King who would provide the consummation of the Lord's promises.

The shepherd completed his divine assignment, particularly to "the oppressed of the flock." The Hebrew is *'ănîyê haṣṣō'n*,[282] and the term for "oppressed" (*'ănîyê*) frequently portrays the needy, wretched, and miserable. The Septuagint points to a different Hebrew reading, *eis tēn chanaanitin*, "for those who trafficked (in the sheep)."[283] The NRSV translation renders the variant reading as "on behalf of the sheep merchants." The idea of sheep traders undoubtedly agrees with the theme of marketing sheep in v. 5 and receives support from many quarters.[284] But the variant requires a different division of the Hebrew words from the Masoretic Text and also necessitates removing the vowels from the received text. The external evidence for making this change is not compelling, while the internal literary evidence also fails to necessitate changing the Masoretic Text. Consequently, the reading "oppressed" should be retained. Theologically, "oppressed" underscores the message of punishment on the nation for her sins against the Lord.

The two staffs the shepherd took and named serve as one of the most powerful symbolic images in the passage. Zechariah's actions clearly echoed earlier Old Testament examples where two poles or staffs symbolized something far more profound. For example, when the nation challenged Aaron's office as priest, Moses ordered that every tribe present a staff with its tribal name written on it. When every staff was gathered and placed together in the Tent of Meeting, along with Aaron's inscribed staff, the staff belonging to Aaron budded,

---

[281] Unger, *Zechariah*, 193; also Barker, "Zechariah," 676.
[282] עֲנִיֵּי הַצֹּאן. *HALOT*, 856, 992–93.
[283] εἰς τὴν Χαναανῖτιν; implying לִכְנַעֲנֵי. *HALOT*, 486.
[284] Baldwin, *Zechariah*, 180; Smith, *Micah-Malachi*, 268; Meyers and Meyers, *Zechariah 9–14*, 261–62. See T. J. Finley, "The Sheep Merchants of Zechariah 11," *GTJ* 3 (1982): 51–65. Barthélemy, et al. (*Preliminary and Interim Report*, 5:417–18) hesitatingly supports the variant reading.

blossomed, and produced almonds, vindicating the priest's mandate from the Lord to serve as priest (Num 17:1–11). Another example is Ezekiel's adaptation of two sticks to express a divine message, which for Zechariah's audience was a comparatively recent memory. The exilic prophet wrote "Belonging to Judah and the Israelites associated with him" on one pole and "Ephraim's stick, belonging to Joseph and all the house of Israel associated with him" on the other (Ezek 37:15–18). Ezekiel's symbolism underscores the restored unity of the tribes. Zechariah's message ultimately communicated the breaching of relationships, not unity, but he used the same well known vehicle to express God's message. The ironic twist in Zechariah's message, in comparison to Ezekiel's, would have made an impression on the postexilic community.

At the Lord's command, Zechariah named both staffs. The first, commonly translated "Favor," reflects the Hebrew term $nō‘am$.[285] The word expresses "grace" or "kindness." The adjectival form of the word describes the "gracious" quality of the relationship between David and Jonathan (2 Sam 1:23). "Favor" reflects one of God's fundamental divine attributes. The concluding prayer of Ps 90:17 illumines this divine trait: "May the favor of the Lord our God rest upon us; establish the work of our hands for us—yes, establish the work of our hands."

The second staff bears the name "Union," rendering the Hebrew $hōbĕlîm$.[286] "Union" with God and harmony among God's people should result from godly leadership. The meaning "Union" or "Bond" becomes clearer in v. 14 where breaking the second staff illustrates the severance of brotherly relations between Judah and Israel.

Verse 7 concludes as it begins, "and *I pastured* the flock." The verbal form (*wā'er‘eh*) links the verb to the initial verb in the verse, "so I pastured."[287] The grammatical connection between the verbs, coupled with the thematic repetition (a literary device called an *inclusio*), emphasizes the shepherd's obedience to the Lord.

**11:8** The phrase beginning v. 8, "In one month I got rid of the three shepherds," stands as one of the most enigmatic statements in the Old Testament. The lexical and grammatical features of the phrase present few problems. The word rendered "got rid of" translates *wā'akḥid*.[288] *HALOT* defines the verb in this derived form as "to efface." BDB includes the definition "efface" and clarifies the semantic point further by adding "annihilate."[289] The point of the phrase is either the outright removal, or at the least, the limitation of the influence of the faithless shepherds whose actions harm God's people.

---

[285] נֹעַם. *HALOT*, 706.
[286] חֹבְלִים. *HALOT*, 286; *TDOT*, 4:183.
[287] וָאֶרְעֶה.
[288] וָאַכְחִד. *HALOT*, 469.
[289] BDB, 470.

The prophet's specific intention in mentioning three shepherds represents the fundamental interpretative problem in v. 8, yielding a plethora of suggestions. Which month did the author intend, and to which three shepherds did the writer refer? The older commentator Mitchell counts at least forty different attempts to answer these questions.[290] The historical and theological breadth of suggested solutions ranges from Moses, Aaron, and Miriam in the ancient past to the Pharisees, Sadducees, and Essenes in the first century after Christ's birth. The dearth of information about Jewish history during the third and fourth centuries before Christ certainly does not aid the attempt to identify the three shepherds. Redditt dryly warns against unwarranted assurance in pursuing the identity of the three shepherds: "Identification of the shepherds has spanned the OT from Moses to the Maccabees, a phenomenon that inspires no confidence in the attempt."[291] One point in the phrase emerges clearly—the good shepherd will remove every unfit leader from positions where they can abuse the flock.

Interpreters generally do not interpret the time period "one month" literally.[292] Commentators normally conclude that the phrase means either a short period of time, 30 years (with each day of a month representing a year), or an extended, undetermined amount of time.[293] In a related view, some correlate Zechariah's "one month" to the eleven-month period in which Judah's final three kings reigned, arguing that this period was a relatively brief period of time.[294] Of these views the first option, the brief duration of time, offers the best explanation. Nothing in the context or in related biblical literature supports the second view that equates each day of the month with a calendar year. Further, the third explanation, a lengthy undetermined duration of time, seems odd in light of the text's specific language, "one month." The short time frame fits the context best, stressing the Lord's intention to act swiftly. Further, the participle in v. 6, "I will hand everyone over," likewise underscores the imminent action.

Related to the identity of the three shepherds, the identity of the good shepherd faces different solutions. Otzen maintains that God is the good Shepherd in chap. 11.[295] Many conclude that the identity of the good shepherd defies resolution.[296] Despite these different conclusions, the clearest interpretation views Zechariah the prophet as the one who fulfills the role of the good shepherd as a symbolic action. Identifying the good shepherd with Zechariah does

---

[290] Mitchell, *Zechariah*, 306.
[291] Redditt, "Two Shepherds," 678.
[292] McComiskey ("Zechariah," 1195) takes it literally.
[293] Baldwin, *Zechariah*, 181.
[294] Merrill, *Zechariah*, 293–94.
[295] Otzen, *Deuterosacharja*, 156.
[296] Eissfeldt, *Introduction*, 438–39.

not preclude the possibility that the prophet prefigured a fuller, eschatological role for the Messiah.

This association of the good shepherd with Zechariah does not provide much assistance with the identification of the other three shepherds, however. One noteworthy approach identifies the three shepherds with the final three kings in Judah's history—Jehoiakim, Jehoiachin, and Zedekiah. Merrill commends this Judahite king theory because the kings represented bad shepherds and their removal did demonstrate the end of the Lord's patience with the nation. Further, Merrill argues that these kings were deposed in a relatively brief amount of time: eleven months—albeit not literally one month as Zechariah proclaimed.[297]

McComiskey argues that the three shepherds refer to several anonymous officials who ruled during Zechariah's day and whom the prophet had deposed from office.[298] McComiskey contends that Zechariah must have been so heartened by the progress that he concluded that the nation was on the cusp of a major reformation. But McComiskey's acknowledgement that "it is uncertain as to whom this refers" undermines confidence in this interpretation.[299]

More scholars conclude that Zechariah's perspective focuses on the future, not the past. One relatively popular view points to the three prominent Persian monarchs, Cyrus, Cambyses, and Darius.[300] The main support for the Persian ruler view is Isaiah's use of the word "shepherd" to describe Cyrus (44:28). Unfortunately for this interpretation, the Old Testament calls so many other figures "shepherd" that the Isaianic reference holds little weight.

Still others view the shepherds as figures from a much later day, leading many to look for leaders from the Seleucid epoch in Judea (198–140 BC). These Seleucid kings range from Antiochus III (223–187 BC) through the final king in this era, Demetrius II (147–139 BC). Mitchell defends the selection of Seleucus IV (187–175 BC), Heliodorus (175 BC), and Demetrius (175 BC) because all three reigned but a brief time.[301] Different interpreters who also favor selecting Seleucid kings as the referent for Zechariah's shepherds offer alternate kings such as Antiochus IV (175–164 BC), Antiochus V (164–161 BC), and Demetrius.

To illustrate further the diversity of approaches to the identity of the three shepherds, some claim that the shepherds in 11:8 might refer to high priests. Oesterley selects Onias III (198–174 BC) for the good shepherd and takes the bad shepherds to be Jason (174–171 BC), Menelaus (171–161 BC), and Alcimus (161–159 BC), all three of whom obtained their priestly offices through

---

[297] Merrill, *Zechariah*, 293–94.
[298] McComiskey, "Zechariah," 1194–95.
[299] Ibid., 1195.
[300] Sweeney, *Twelve Prophets*, 680.
[301] Mitchell, *Zechariah*, 307.

dishonorable means.[302] Trèves attempts to solve the interpretative puzzle with a priestly key, seeing Judas Maccabeus (167–161 BC) as the good shepherd and understanding the worthless shepherds to refer to apostate priests, possibly including Alcimus.[303]

A number of treatments simply sidestep the identity question by dismissing v. 8 as a gloss, a later addition to the text that has little value for the meaning of the passage.[304] This view claims that v. 8 was added during the Maccabean epoch—long after the remainder of chap. 11—to give some contemporary significance to the prophecy. Absolutely no evidence supports this interpretation, though, leading to the wholesale rejection of this suggestion.

Yet another approach contends that interpreters have mistakenly sought to relate Zechariah's three deposed shepherds to specific historical figures. In one of the broader understandings, some see the three shepherds as symbolizing the offices of prophet, priest, and king generally.[305] Both Baldwin and Smith suggest that "three" should not receive a literal interpretation.[306] This position takes the number three symbolically, perhaps representing all of the shepherds collectively. Baldwin clarifies her point: "Apocalyptic uses numbers symbolically. Is the number three used in that way here (*cf.* Dn. 7:8,24) to signify completion? If so, the good shepherd would be removing from power all the unworthy leaders who frustrated his work."[307] Meyers and Meyers agree that the number three is symbolic in v. 8, representing all of the shepherds over Judah. They state that the number "is deliberately vague and, thereby, inclusive."[308]

Meyers and Meyers proceed to discuss Zechariah's purpose in using the shepherd imagery. They conclude that the prophet intended to picture false prophets, since Zechariah expressed such vigorous concerns about false prophecy, particularly in chap. 13.[309] Without questioning the prophet's attack on the false prophets in a subsequent chapter, one cannot provide convincing support for this position.

After exploring such a large variety of interpretations of v. 8a, one wonders how best to proceed. With some four dozen viable approaches vying for acceptance, the absence of a prevailing perspective or strong evidence to bolster any view strongly suggests that interpreters have asked the wrong questions about the passage. Both the history of interpretation and modern scholarship have utterly failed in the quest to identify Zechariah's three shepherds with three

---

[302] W. O. E. Oesterley, *A History of Israel* (Oxford: Oxford University Press, 1932), 258–59.

[303] M. Trèves, "Conjectures Concerning the Date and Authorship of Zechariah IX–XIV," *VT* 13 (1963): 196–207.

[304] Mason, *Zechariah*, 107.

[305] Redditt, "Two Shepherds," 677.

[306] Baldwin, *Zechariah*, 183; R. L. Smith, *Micah-Malachi*, 467.

[307] Baldwin, *Zechariah*, 183.

[308] Meyers and Meyers, *Zechariah 9–14*, 265.

[309] Ibid.

distinct historical figures. Consequently, the inability of literal views to explain the passage argues that a non-literal interpretation offers the best option. Likely, the three shepherds portray the entirety of faithless shepherds whose sinful approach to their leadership responsibilities harmed the sheep and hindered God's plan for the people. One probably should not view the "one month" period literally either. Most likely this period of time suggests that the Lord's actions will transpire in a relatively brief period of time.

In v. 8 Zechariah lamented, "the flock detested me." The Hebrew term for "detested" *(bāḥălāh)* occurs only twice in the Old Testament.[310] The verb in Zech 11 involves particularly strong emotion, denoting the despising of another person. One could understand a people longing to replace a bad leader who does not have the nation's best interests at heart, but the good shepherd in chap. 11 embodies a righteous rule. If such a faithful shepherd cannot please the nation, what does the people's displeasure disclose about their own commitment to divine truth? Regarding the people's vacuous offerings, the Lord declared, "They have become a burden to me; I am weary of bearing them" (Isa 1:14). The prophet's feeling was mutual as revealed by Zechariah's own expression, "I grew weary of them." The Hebrew expression *wattiqṣar napšî bāhem* suggests the shepherd's impatience with those under his charge.[311] The same verb describes the people's impatience on the route to the Red Sea during the exodus (Num 21:4). The word also portrays Delilah's incessant nagging of Samson (Judg 16:16). The verb *wattiqṣar* conveys the idea of shortness—in this case, that little remained of the shepherd's long suffering. The shepherd's patience with the unruly people had finally come to an end. He could no longer bear the burden of the people's diffidence toward righteousness and truth. Isaiah 1:13–18 reflects a similar weariness, albeit describing the Lord's fatigue in bearing the sinfulness of Judah.

To summarize the interpretation of v. 8, a normal or literal hermeneutic fails to explain the details of the verse adequately. Bullinger's famous guideline for differentiating between literal and figurative language states, "whenever and wherever it is possible, the words of Scripture are to be understood *literally*, but when a statement appears to be contrary . . . to known fact, or revealed truth; or seems to be at variance with the general teaching of the Scriptures, then we may reasonably expect that some figure is employed."[312] With about 50 interpretations vying to relate the particulars in v. 8 to precise historical situations from the past, present, and future, it seems appropriate to contend that Zech 11:8 does not literally coincide with either revealed biblical truth or known historical facts. Even the interpretations that strive to relate Zechariah's

---

[310] בָּחֲלָה. *HALOT*, 119. A *Pual* participle from this root occurs in Prov 20:21.
[311] וַתִּקְצַר נַפְשִׁי בָּהֶם. *HALOT*, 1126–27.
[312] Bullinger, *Figures of Speech*, xv.

three shepherds to the final three kings of Judah before the fall to Babylon must resort to a non-literal interpretation of the phrase "one month."

Consequently, it is best to treat v. 8 as a symbolic action in which the three shepherds metaphorically represent the host of faithless shepherds who exploit the Lord's flock for their personal advantage. Zechariah certainly pronounced God's judgment against political leaders over Judah who did not fulfill their divine mandate righteously. However, the same principle applies to modern faithless shepherds of God's flocks, insincere pastors who use their holy office for personal advantage. As mentioned above, the phrase "three shepherds" symbolizes the totality of faithless shepherds whom the Lord will ultimately judge. The single month stresses the haste with which the Lord will exact judgment when the day of reckoning finally arrives, not a literal thirty-day period.

**11:9** Verse 9 introduces the shepherd's response to the nation's rejection of his leadership and his own fatigue with their disinterest in the Lord. When the shepherd chose to cease leading the people, he relegated them to the consequences of their actions. This, of course, does not mean that Zechariah himself actually became a wicked shepherd. Instead, the prophet served as a living portrait, which symbolized the evil leadership ruling the land. The outcome of transgression for the shepherds as well as those they misled would be devastation. As stated in Ps 1:6b, "the way of the wicked will perish."

The faithful shepherd strives to care for his flock, aiding the ill sheep with the aim of preserving life whenever possible. Zechariah's shepherd well portrays the immediate results of the withdrawal of righteous leadership, demonstrated by three painful decrees. For every sheep that is ill and dying, the shepherd expresses his own wish, "let the dying die."[313] The phrase "let the perishing perish" conveys the same determination. Without the protective care of the shepherd, the flock finds itself exposed to destruction by every ravenous enemy. Both verbs emphatically communicate the disturbing message that the shepherd withholds the protection that had restrained tragedy from visiting his flock. Ezekiel communicated a similar point when he prophesied, "He that is far away will die of the plague, and he that is near will fall by the sword, and he that survives and is spared will die of famine" (Ezek 6:12).

Few themes evoke deeper revulsion than that of cannibalism. Yet Zechariah declared that those who do not perish right away as a result of judgment will face a more grim prospect, for they will "eat one another's flesh." Jeremiah predicted something similar in an earlier day when he warned Judah about the impending judgment meted out by the Babylonians: "I will make them eat the flesh of their sons and daughters, and they will eat one another's flesh during the stress of the siege imposed on them" (Jer 19:9). Josephus reported that the

---

[313] הַמֵּתָה תָמוּת. This verbal form is a jussive, expressing wish or desire. An additional question arises because the participle is feminine, not the expected masculine form. Probably the feminine refers back to the feminine noun הַצֹּאן, "flock." The view that Zechariah was only distraught with the shepherds, not the flock, does not merit acceptance.

brutal siege of Jerusalem in AD 70 by the Romans forced the surviving inhabitants of Jerusalem to do this very thing—eating the flesh of their deceased brethren.[314] Since Judah had repeatedly faced the unspeakable tragedy of sieges that led to limited occasions of cannibalism, cannibalism does not provide adequate evidence for identifying the three shepherds with any particular ruler or epoch. Further, it remains an open question whether Zechariah intended his prophecy about cannibalism to be read literally. The horror of the experience could not be clearer, though.

One cannot ignore the brutal realities Judah faced during the Roman occupation or the fact that these events might partially fulfill Zechariah's prophecy. Nonetheless, the prophet's message extends to the coming of God's kingdom at the commencement of the eschatological age. Speaking of the nation's rejection of the shepherd, McComiskey comments, "Their rejection of him runs deep in their hearts, and in words that echo over centuries to come, he abandons the dying nation to its fate and pictures an impending situation so dire that the people will resort to cannibalism in order to exist."[315]

**11:10** Verse 10 presents the climax to Zechariah's symbolic action, the breaking of the staff "Favor" first mentioned in v. 7. Shattering the staff was emblematic of the annulment of the covenant between the shepherd and "all the nations" and foreshadowed the end of the righteous rule of the shepherd as well as the resultant blessings showered on God's people.

One of the major questions arising from this verse focuses on the nature of the broken covenant. Moses's instructions in Deut 17:14–20 to Israel for the institution of kingship may serve as a background for Zech 11:8, although the Pentateuchal instruction does not incorporate covenantal terminology. But King David made "a compact" with the elders at Hebron (2 Sam 5:3). Further, Jehoiada "made a covenant between the LORD and the king and people that they would be the LORD's people" (2 Kgs 11:17). The covenant that the shepherd in Zech 11:10 revoked resembled the covenant established between the faithful kings of Judah and their people (Ezek 34:25).

From the broad perspective of the history of interpretation, most have understood the covenant in v. 10 to represent a general covenant that protected Judah from the wiles of her neighboring nations.[316] This view does not attempt to relate "covenant" *(bĕrît)* in v. 10 with a particular biblical covenant. Rather, according to this view, the broken covenant speaks metaphorically of God's protective restraint on the nations that would be withdrawn when the shepherd broke the covenant. Several Old Testament passages employ *bĕrît* similarly to describe God's protection of his people from foreign powers and even wild beasts (Job 5:23; Hos 2:18). Ezekiel 34:25 illustrates the usage well: "I will

---

[314] Josephus, *War*, VI, 193–213.
[315] McComiskey, "Zechariah," 1195.
[316] Smith, *Zechariah*, 308; Unger, *Zechariah*, 197. Smith's alternative proposal postulating an unknown covenant between Judah and her neighbors with Egypt is pure speculation.

make a covenant of peace with them and rid the land of wild beasts so that they may live in the desert and sleep in the forests in safety."

This approach focuses on a general perspective of the word *bĕrît*.[317] The word frequently refers to an agreement or a contract between two or more parties in the Old Testament. For instance, in 2 Sam 3:12 Abner sought to establish a *bĕrît*, an agreement with David (cf. Josh 9:6; 1 Sam 18:3; 23:18).

Regarding "*my* covenant," to whom does the pronoun "my" refer? The immediate referent, the shepherd, cannot satisfy the scope of the prophecy. No shepherd or shepherds throughout Judah's history possessed sufficient might to shield the nations from the wolves that surrounded her. Ultimately, the only one with adequate power to extend or withhold protection to Judah was the Lord himself (see Zech 1:11–12,15; 2:12–13). According to this interpretation "my covenant" speaks of the general, restraining influence exerted by the Lord on the nations to protect his own flock, Judah. Without divine protection, God's people were defenseless.

Another question seeks to understand the significance of the phrase "made with all the nations." The Hebrew *kol–hā'ammîm* reflects usage found elsewhere in the book of Zechariah and in the Old Testament.[318] In Zech 8:18–23 the prophet employs the term *'ammîm* to signify the diverse peoples who in the coming kingdom will stream to Zion to receive the word of God and to embrace the Messiah's righteous rule. Similarly, Isa 2:2–4 chronicles the torrent of peoples who will come to the "mountain of the LORD's temple" in the last days to learn and to walk in the ways of God. Micah 4:15 closely parallels both the wording and the theological themes in Isaiah. In Zech 8, Isaiah 2, and Micah 4 the peoples *('ammîm)* refer to nations who do not belong to Judah but who turn to God wholeheartedly despite the absence of a heritage in their relationship with the Lord.[319] The breaking of the covenant in Zech 11:10 suggests that these nations must experience judgment for their sin before any corporate repentance and restoration can occur.

Alternatively, some maintain that the human parties to the covenant all belong to Judah, not to foreign nations.[320] For instance, Baldwin suggests that the expression refers to diverse "Jewish colonies scattered among the nations."[321] This point of view notes the absence of any mention of a specific covenant between the Lord and Gentiles in either the book of Zechariah or elsewhere in the Old Testament. The strongest evidence to undergird the Judah view occurs in v. 14 where the breaking of the second staff, "Union," symbolizes the rupture of the union between Judah and Israel. While possible, this interpretation likely misunderstands the point of v. 14. One cannot take the predicted

---

[317] בְּרִית. *HALOT*, 157.
[318] כָּל־הָעַמִּים. *HALOT*, 838.
[319] Sweeney, *Twelve Prophets*, 680–81.
[320] Redditt, "Two Shepherds," 683; Meyers and Meyers, *Zechariah 9–14*, 270–71.
[321] Baldwin, *Zechariah*, 184; cf. Merrill, *Zechariah*, 295.

separation between Judah and Israel literally since Israel had ceased to exist as a distinct national entity, let alone an identifiable people, about two centuries before Zechariah's prophecy. Consequently, the point in v. 14 about the disunity between the northern and southern nations does not lead one to infer that the entire passage focuses solely on peoples who descended directly from Abraham. Even those who embrace the view that the covenant was only with Abraham's seed acknowledge that the normal Old Testament usage of ʿammîm portrays Gentiles.[322]

**11:11** Verse 11 begins with the words, "It was revoked *on that day*." The temporal phrase links this verse to the preceding one, serving as a conclusion to the breaking of the staff Favor. On the very day that the shepherd broke the symbolic staff, the Lord broke his covenant and withdrew his protective care from the nation. With Judah vulnerable and exposed, it was only a matter of time before she faced the onslaught of surrounding nations who cared nothing about the welfare of God's people. The phrase "on that day" often has eschatological meaning in the prophets, pointing to an end-time fulfillment. The phrase signifies both immediate and eschatological perspectives. While it was the case that Zechariah broke Favor immediately, thus severing the covenant, the implications of this prophecy would extend to a much later epoch.

The phrase "the afflicted of the flock" in this verse mirrors the idiom found in v. 7. The Hebrew wording in both verses is identical.[323]

Zechariah stressed the point that the nation understood that God had spoken to them. The oppressed people, facing affliction brought on by their sinful intransigence, recognized that the Lord had delivered a message to them through Zechariah. When the crowd observed the prophet cleaving the staff "Favor," the theme from God was as clear as the symbolic actions Hosea acted out before all Israel. For example, when Hosea named his daughter "Lo-Ruhamah" he declared that God would "no longer show love to the house of Israel" (Hos 1:6). Similarly, Hosea's son, "Lo-Ammi," proclaimed to Israel that "you are not my people, and I am not your God" (Hos 1:8). When Judah saw the staff "Favor" broken, they knew that their love for disobedience would lead to devastation.

Unger contends that the oppressed people who observed Zechariah's actions responded to God's message with faith and obedience.[324] But to suggest that a movement of repentance among the people emerged that might lead the Lord to revoke his sentence of judgment would be to overstate the evidence of the text and the subsequent historical developments. Rather, those who had long treated obedience to the Lord lightly observed the broken staff lying on the ground—a mute yet powerful testimony that God had decreed judgment.

---

[322] *TDOT*, 11:163–77; *TLOT*, 896–919.
[323] עֲנִיֵּי הַצֹּאן. *HALOT*, 856, 992–93.
[324] Unger, *Zechariah*, 198.

The Lord had resolved to cease protecting his people until their wickedness could be punished and purged.

The next noteworthy invasion of the land of Israel occurred when the Roman emperor Titus completed his brutal siege of Jerusalem in AD 70. The extreme political, social, and religious instability at the time of her total national implosion harmonizes well with Josephus's portrayal of the tragic scene. With insurrection and fratricide rife throughout Israel, Josephus commented, "For barbarity and iniquity those of the same nation [the Jews] did no way differ from the Romans."[325] Sounding much like what Zechariah had prophesied earlier, the renowned Jewish historian described the famine: "When those that were most dear were perishing under their [the Romans'] hands, they were not ashamed to take from them the very last drops that might preserve their lives."[326] Though neither the people living at that time nor Zechariah would personally see the invading hordes on the horizon, the truth of God's word remained undiminished.[327]

Jesus spoke of the fulfillment of this prophecy, at least in a limited sense, when he warned that the Jewish community would face terrible days of judgment because of their refusal to pursue true righteousness and their rejection of the Good Shepherd (Matt 23:33–39).[328] Jesus told the Pharisees that "upon you will come all the righteous blood that has been shed on earth, from the blood of righteous Abel to the blood of Zechariah son of Berekiah, whom you murdered between the temple and the altar" (23:35). Numerous interpretations struggle to identify precisely which "Zechariah" the Gospel writer had in mind. Further, rabbinic tradition also affirmed the memory that "Zechariah son of Berekiah" was martyred in the temple precincts.[329] Although certainty remains elusive, apparently Matthew informed his readers that our prophet was martyred by the people he was called to serve in the holiest place in the temple.[330]

**11:12** Verse 12 overviews the final severance of the employment between the shepherd, portrayed by Zechariah, and the people he sought to lead back to God. The request for pay leads to the final transaction when terminating their relationship. The shepherd's desire for money only partially provides his motivation. Rather, the shepherd sought to underscore the finality of the broken relationship between himself and the nation, and symbolically between the Lord and Judah. The price, 30 pieces of silver, represents the lowly price a

---

[325] Flavius Josephus, *Works of the Jews*, chapter 3, part 2, in *The Complete Works of Josephus*, trans. W. Whiston (Grand Rapids: Kregel, 1981), 527.

[326] Ibid., chap. 10, part 3, 564.

[327] McComiskey, "Zechariah," 1197.

[328] Blomberg, *Matthew* (Nashville: Broadman, 1992), 348–49.

[329] Blank, "The Death of Zechariah in Rabbinic Literature," 327–46.

[330] R. H. Gundry, *The Use of the Old Testament in St. Matthew's Gospel* (Leiden: E. J. Brill, 1967), 86–88; Blomberg, *The Historical Reliability of the Gospels* (Downers Grove: InterVarsity, 1987), 193–95; cf. S. H. Blank, "'The Death of Zechariah in Rabbinic Literature," *HUCA* 12–13 (1937–38): 327–46. For further discussion, see the Introduction.

slave was worth in the earliest era in Israel's history (Exod 21:32). The money the shepherd received was tantamount to slave wages. The exchange drips with the people's disdain for their estimation of the value of the shepherd. His value to the entire nation did not even surpass the worth of one slave to a single family. The monetary value ascribed to the shepherd forcefully spoke of the trifling attitude of the nation to their shepherd and their God who had sent him.

Baldwin curiously claims that the payment reflected a great sum, basing the view on Neh 5:15 where 40 shekels represented a heavy payment of tribute to the Persian governor.[331] Nonetheless, Baldwin misunderstands the exilic context described by Nehemiah. To one who possessed virtually nothing—as was the case for the exilic community in Nehemiah's time—any tribute payment, even an amount similar to the price of a slave in patriarchal times, was burdensome and odious. But the symbolism of the 30 pieces remains: it was the paltry price of a slave.

When the shepherd cried out, "give me my pay" or "keep it," he could not contain the depths of emotion that had built over time to an unbearable level. When he said "keep it," the shepherd did not attempt to conceal his disdain for the people's cavalier attitude toward righteousness and his efforts to lead the people back to God. The translation "don't bother" would well reflect the exasperation the shepherd felt toward the people and the impossible task of shepherding them.[332]

The Hebrew word for "paid" *(wayyišqĕlû)* in the phrase "they paid me thirty pieces" means to weigh out.[333] In the era before coinage became common, precious metals were meted out by weight. Matthew 26:15 clearly alludes to Zech 11:12 when describing how the details of Jesus' betrayal completed the prior biblical themes.[334] Some early Church Fathers also highlighted how the payment of the 30 pieces of silver to the shepherd in Zech 11:12 foreshadowed the payment to Judas for his betrayal of the Good Shepherd. The Fathers' primary concern was to demonstrate that Jesus was the crucified and resurrected Messiah who fulfilled what the Old Testament had foretold. Of particular interest was the precise correspondence between the amount paid. After quoting Zech 11:12 Cyril of Jerusalem wrote, "O prophetic accuracy! A great and unerring wisdom of the Holy Spirit! For he did not say ten or twenty but thirty, exactly the right amount."[335] Subsequently, Cyril underscored the Spirit's guidance when comparing what happened to the pieces of silver in Zech 11 to that of Judas's ill-gotten money (see Matt 27:3–10; Acts 1:16–19).

---

[331] Baldwin, *Zechariah*, 184–85; cf. Sweeney, *Twelve Prophets*, 681.

[332] McComiskey, "Zechariah," 1200.

[333] וַיִּשְׁקְלוּ. *HALOT*, 1642–43.

[334] Blomberg, *Matthew*, 386–87. The Greek ἔστησαν can mean "weigh out" as in the LXX of Zech 11:12 and Jer 32:9–10 [39:9–10].

[335] Cyril of Jerusalem, *Catechesis*, 13.10 [FC 64:11–12].

**11:13** Zechariah did not inform his readers why the shepherd felt compelled to surrender the thirty pieces of silver. In light of the shepherd's noble service to the nation on behalf of God who had sent him, the issue certainly was not ill-gotten gain. He deserved what payment he received and far more.

A significant textual problem raises the question of where the shepherd relinquished the payment of silver. The Masoretic Text reads *hayyôṣēr* ("the potter").[336] The textual apparatus to *BHS* proposes an alternative reading, *hāʾôṣār* ("the treasury"), following a Syriac manuscript.[337] An apocryphal book describes the treasury associated with the temple as a repository for both private and public funds (see 2 Macc 3:4–11).[338] The picture clouds further with the realization that both readings fit the context well and that both meanings figure into the account in Matt 27:6–9.[339]

Matthew 27:6–8 says, "The chief priests picked up the coins and said, 'It is against the law to put this into the treasury, since it is blood money.' So they decided to use the money to buy the potter's field as a burial place for foreigners." Matthew 27:9 attributes this action to the fulfillment of what "Jeremiah the prophet" had prophesied. Although this question has already received attention in the Introduction, the basic conclusion found there follows the traditional understanding of the question. The Matthean reference to Jeremiah should not be understood as an inadvertent error. Rather, the Gospel writer conflated the prominent theme of Israel's rejection of their godly leaders and the resultant suffering found in both Jeremiah and Zechariah. Matthew apparently made literary allusions to both texts while attributing authorship to the more prominent of the two sources. The primary themes Matthew draws from Jer 19 include "the blood of the innocent" (v. 4), "the potter" (vv. 1,11), the renaming of the valley (v. 6), the violence associated with the site (v. 11), and the judgment and burial of leaders (v. 11). These numerous and prominent themes make Matthew's reference to Jeremiah more understandable. Matthew's mention of both the treasury and the potter's field does not settle the question of which one occurred in Zechariah.

In the final analysis, though, "the treasury" remains an inferior reading compared to the authoritative Hebrew text in several regards. Concerning external grounds, the sole Syriac manuscript represents one of the weaker extant sources of textual evidence. Moreover, the Syriac version was a daughter text to the Septuagint, that is, it was translated directly from the Septuagint. As a result, since the Septuagint and the Syriac of 11:13a differ markedly from one another, this disparity casts further doubt on the strength of the Syriac textual testimony. When assessing internal evidence, "the treasury" appears to reflect

---

[336] הַיּוֹצֵר. *HALOT*, 403, 428–29.
[337] הָאוֹצָר. *HALOT*, 23–24.
[338] Smith, *Zechariah*, 310.
[339] Sjef van Tilborg, "Matthew 27. 3–10: An Intertextual Reading," in *Intertextuality in Biblical Writings*, ed. S. Draisma (Kampen: J. H. Kok, 1989), 159–74.

a scribal attempt to smooth out the slightly more difficult reading "the potter." Consequently, the traditional reading "potter" merits final acceptance.

Accordingly, one must wrestle with the significance of the potter in v. 13. Some suggest that the phrase "throw it to the potter" represented no more than a proverbial expression, something like the modern idiom "throw it to the dogs."[340] However credible this may sound, no evidence supports this view. Another view claims that since potters were artisans, they worked within the temple confines and under the oversight of the religious authorities. Yet it is impossible to explain the precise connection between the potter and other artisans with the temple and its religious organization. Some formal arrangement may have existed. If so, the shepherd's throwing the money at the potter represented giving the money back to the religious establishment in general for which the shepherd held such total disdain. However, this interpretation is conjectural and unnecessary.

Sweeney offers an innovative, albeit unconvincing, interpretation for the reference to the potter in v. 13. He notes that the word for potter *(yōṣēr)* often refers to the Lord himself (see Gen 2:7–8; Isa 27:11; 43:1; 44:21; 45:7,9,11). Sweeney contends that the Lord "instructs the prophet to throw the money to 'the creator,' i.e., to YHWH in the Temple."[341] But this view does not harmonize with the tenor of chap. 11. While his observation about the occasional use of potter as a metaphor for the Lord is accurate, Sweeney fails to explain how his approach handles the problem of giving the money to the Lord by returning the silver to those who spurn God and his righteous ways. Doing so would have amounted to supporting the religious hierarchy whom the shepherd and Zechariah had so long opposed. Additionally, it is reasonable to conclude that the act of giving the money to a lowly potter underscored the theme of the disrespectfully low wages paid to the shepherd.[342]

More plausibly, Zechariah may have alluded to Jer 19 where the prophet went to the potter's house as a symbolic action foretelling the impending destruction of Jerusalem, much as one encounters in Zech 11. This suggestion agrees well with the overall theme of judgment that pervades chap. 11.

Reviewing the theological message of v. 13, the shepherd represented righteous leadership for a nation with no longing for faithful shepherding. The utter rejection of the shepherd and the spiteful payment of only 30 pieces of silver paint a poignant picture of the people's hatred of what is righteous and their love of what is evil. These events, coupled with the prior severing of God's covenant of protection for his people, led the people to brace themselves for the coming judgment. Each of these elements in chap. 11 foreshadows significant components of Christ's earthly ministry. As the Good Shepherd par excellence (John

---

[340] Unger, *Zechariah*, 199.
[341] Sweeney, *Twelve Prophets*, 681.
[342] McComiskey, "Zechariah," 1200.

10:11), Jesus Christ faced brutal rejection and betrayal for 30 pieces of silver at the hands of Judas (Matt 26:15; 27:3,9). The blood money was paid to the temple treasury and then went to purchase a potter's field (Matt 27:6–7). Finally, only 40 years elapsed from the utter rejection of the Savior by the Jewish community until Jerusalem suffered Roman defilement and destruction.[343]

With ancient Judah, the promised destruction would not hang over the people indefinitely, nor would it wipe out the nation and her fortunes forever. God promised that a glorious day of regathering and restoration would come in the future. In a similar vein, after the Jewish community suffered judgment at the hands of the Romans, a future hope remained for those who would only exercise faith in the Lord (Rom 9–11). Paul's words of summation promise that "all Israel will be saved" (Rom 11:26).

**11:14** The next inevitable consequence of Judah's rejection of the Lord and the shepherd he had sent would be disunity among the people. The breaking of the second staff named "Union" portrayed this final rupture in the relationship between the tribes of Israel and Judah. The Hebrew term for "brotherhood" *(hāʾahăwāh)* is a unique word in the Old Testament.[344] Related to *ʾāh* ("brother"), *hāʾahăwāh* conveys the idea of family ties. As the broken staff "Union" foreshadowed, every vestige of unity among Abraham's seed would cease. The next five or six centuries of Jewish history would indeed manifest the most bitter internecine strife ever witnessed, providing a sobering, albeit partial, fulfillment of Zechariah's prophecy.

Although v. 14b explicitly states that the broken staff "Union" symbolizes the disunity between the northern and southern tribes, some scholars have sought to relate the breaking of the staff to the Samaritan schism (c. 325 BC),[345] which occurred when the Samaritans rejected the established temple worship in order to establish their own rival temple on Mount Gerizim. The significance of this breach for the intertestamental epoch, as well as the first century AD, is beyond dispute. But it is difficult to relate Zechariah's prophecy to the Samaritans since the prophet explicitly identifies other referents and no other evidence exists to suggest that the Samaritans fulfilled the prophecy.

On the surface, the act of breaking "Union" seems straightforward, describing the end of the relationship between Israel and Judah. The prophecy does seem a bit unusual since the northern tribes constituting Israel essentially ceased to exist some two centuries before Zechariah's act of breaking the staff (722 BC). Moreover, long before Israel's demise, distrust and enmity had characterized the attitudes between Israel and Judah. More puzzling still, Zechariah mentioned Israel by name in promising future salvation for God's people (8:13; 10:6). Zechariah 9:1 states that "the eyes of men and all the tribes of

---

[343] Ibid., 1201.
[344] הָאַחֲוָה. *HALOT*, 31.
[345] Elliger, *Zacharja*, 163.

Israel are on the LORD." Prior to Zechariah, Isaiah said that the "house of Jacob," which includes both the northern and the southern tribes of Israel, would enjoy the eschatological blessings God would bestow in his coming kingdom when nations will "beat their swords into plowshares" (Isa 2:2–5). Ezekiel's symbolic precursor of Zechariah's two staffs promised a future for Judah and Israel together. Ezekiel (37:16) pictures a stick of wood with "Belonging to Judah and the Israelites" written on it. Even more emphatic, Ezek 37:21–22 predicts, "I will take the Israelites out of the nations where they have gone. I will gather them from all around and bring them back into their own land. I will make them one nation in the land, on the mountains of Israel. . . . they will never again be two nations or be divided into two kingdoms." What then did the broken staff "Union" signify regarding the revocation of the Lord's promises to Israel?

The primary common denominator among Isa 2, Ezek 37, and Zech 8, 11 is the eschatological perspective all passages share. In whatever sense the biblical authors employed the term "Israel," God's people would not experience the full revitalization of the nation until the eschatological kingdom when the Lord will recreate his world as he had originally intended. This raises the question of how Zechariah employed "Israel."

"Israel" conveys several distinct meanings throughout the Old Testament depending upon its context. The term applies to the nation as a whole (Deut 34:10); the northern tribes (Hos 1:1); and even the southern kingdom (2 Chr 11:3; Isa 5:7; Mic 3:9). Particularly after the fall of Israel in 722 BC, "Israel" no longer refers exclusively to the northern tribes. In many later texts "Israel" emphasizes the entirety of God's people (see Jer 31:27).[346]

**11:15** This verse introduces the final movement of the symbolic action of a shepherd. The Lord orders his prophet to assume the role of a shepherd, but this time the shepherd embodies corruption and diffidence both to God and the needs of his people. This latter shepherd demonstrates for the people what manner of leadership lies ahead of them. God allowed the people to receive their wish. The nation rejected the Lord's faithful shepherd and the protection God entrusted to him. In the place of the good shepherd would follow an evil shepherd whose service would culminate in Judah's doom.

The word "again" in v. 15 links this verse with v. 7 where the good shepherd assumed his mandate of leadership from God. The same person plays the role of both the good shepherd and the foolish shepherd, fulfilling the symbolic actions God ordained. But the roles he played before the watching nation could not be more different. As discussed previously (under **11:4–17**), the shepherd was presumably Zechariah himself. Many interpreters have attempted in vain to associate the "foolish shepherd" with later historical figures ranging from

---

[346] Mitchell, *Zechariah*, 310; *HALOT*, 442; *TLOT*, 581–84.

Herod to the Antichrist.[347] Each of these identifications remains purely speculative, lacking any supporting evidence. Consequently, it is best to conclude that the "foolish shepherd" does not symbolize one particular historical individual. Rather, he represents every leader of God's people from Zechariah's day to the present who seek their own evil desires, not the selfless way of the Lord's righteousness. An ancient prophet or a modern preacher may claim to represent God, but that does not prove that he does. Faithful servants, those who serve at God's bidding, will "do the work of him who sent" them (John 9:4; cf. Matt 24:45–46).

The text does not bother identifying the "equipment of a . . . shepherd" that was to be taken. Most likely these items included the necessities for the shepherd to remain close to the flock, as well as the tools for protecting and caring for the sheep. Other Old Testament texts list a staff, a sling, smooth stones, and a pouch (1 Sam 17:40); Judges 5:16 adds the pipe with which the shepherd "whistled" to summon the flock; the shepherd's equipment probably included the clothing required to brave the elements while caring for the flock—the word for "equipment" *(kĕlî)* refers to leather garments in Lev 13:49.[348] Possibly, the phrase "equipment of a shepherd" refers solely to the shepherd's clothing.

The Hebrew term for "foolish" *(ʾĕwilî)* carries great significance, particularly in the wisdom literature.[349] The word's connotation is brutally frank, suggesting a stupid, brutish person. The same word occurs in Prov 1:7 where, in contrast to the fear of the Lord, "fools despise wisdom and discipline" (cf. Prov 14:29; 24:9). In Hos 9:7 the Israelites used the same word ("foolish") to mock the prophet, the man of God delivering the inspired word of the Lord. Jeremiah described those people who refused to seek God, who possessed no understanding, and who did not know how to do good as "foolish people" (Jer 4:22). In Zech 11:15 the foolish shepherd is one who had no interest in seeking God and who could do nothing but evil. Thus, foolishness represents the very opposite of the wisdom of the Lord.

**11:16** The Lord promised to raise up a faithless shepherd to demonstrate to Judah what the sinfulness of her leaders would yield. The metaphor of a shepherd who deserted the sheep he was charged with protecting draws upon the Lord's rebuke of Judah's leaders: "you do not take care of the flock. You have not strengthened the weak or healed the sick or bound up the injured. You have not brought back the strays or searched for the lost. You have ruled them harshly and brutally" (Ezek 34:3b–4). Zechariah 11:15 also characterizes the shepherd as "a foolish shepherd." Verse 16 expounds on the adjective "foolish" with a description "marked with negligence alternating with cruelty."[350]

---

[347] Unger, *Zechariah*, 202. For a survey of suggestions, see Merrill, *Zechariah*, 303.
[348] כְּלִי. *HALOT*, 479.
[349] אֱוִילִי. *HALOT*, 21.
[350] Mitchell, *Zechariah*, 315.

Zechariah did not describe hypothetical circumstances. He portrayed actual events racking the people.

Zechariah delineated several classes of needy sheep in order to paint the complete picture of the shepherd's shameful behavior and the injury he inflicted upon Judah. The prophet arranged v. 16 in an artful poetic style designed to highlight each element of the shepherd's wicked behavior and to make each aspect more memorable for Zechariah's audience.[351] The prophet described four types of sheep, each of which the shepherd neglected in some egregious manner. The verse concludes with two types of sheep who suffer, not from passive neglect, but from his active and malicious deeds.

The first group of sheep facing abandonment are "the lost," the group the shepherd refuses to tend. The Hebrew term for "lost" *(hannikḥādôt)* has seen numerous translations.[352] The Hebrew expression refers to "those who are cut off" or who face annihilation and does not necessarily signify one who has lost his way. The term speaks of those who are perishing from some calamity, although the verse gives no indication of what kind of distress pursued the sheep to the point of death. The same verbal form, although in the singular, occurs in 11:9 ("the perishing"). To "care for" indicates protective care.[353] McComiskey argues that the verb means "to give attention to."[354] In summary, the Lord accuses the shepherd of failing to do his duty, namely, meeting the needs of his flock.

The shepherd's next failing is his refusal "to seek the young" (cf. Matt 18:12–14). The word translated "the young" *(hannaʿar)* never describes animals in any other passage of the Old Testament, just humans.[355] Some interpreters argue for an emendation of the Hebrew text to *hannaʿ* ("to wander").[356] The translation resulting from the emendation would be "seek those who wander." However smooth the emendation might sound, no evidence supports the change, and the Masoretic Text reads clearly as it stands. The use of *naʿar* makes the connection between the metaphorical lambs and the literal children more immediate. Of the six scenes Zechariah presented, this may be the most shocking. How could a shepherd turn his back on tender, defenseless lambs? How could anyone, much less a leader charged with safeguarding the well-being of all of the people, turn his back on children? What kind of national future could a leader contemplate if he willingly allowed the children, the future hope of the nation, to be lost?

---

[351] For a helpful analysis of the poetic features in v. 16, see Meyers and Meyers, *Zechariah 9–14*, 284–86.

[352] הַנִּכְחָדוֹת. *HALOT*, 469.

[353] יָפְקֹד. *HALOT*, 955–57.

[354] McComiskey, "Zechariah," 1205.

[355] הַנַּעַר. *HALOT*, 707.

[356] Mitchell, *Zechariah*, 319; Meyers and Meyers, *Zechariah 9–14*, 287.

The next two images summarize the lack of care-giving suffered by Judah. First, the shepherd ignored his responsibility "to heal the injured." The term translated "heal" *(yĕrappē')* has a rich context in the Old Testament.[357] The cognate to the word "heal" applies to God in the well loved divine name "The Lord heals," popularly pronounced "Jehovah Rapha."[358]

As a final expression of neglect, the shepherd failed to complete the most basic task expected from the shepherd—he was unwilling even to feed the healthy sheep that needed no special attention. The Hebrew word rendered "feed" *(yĕkalkēl)* is an unusual term with differing meanings.[359] The word can mean "to contain" (1 Kgs 8:27) or "to provide" (Gen 45:11). The former meaning would suggest condemning the shepherd for his failure to offer protection to the flock. The latter meaning is more likely, though, since the one example of neglect Zechariah has yet to mention is failure to provide food for the flock.[360]

Zechariah concluded the verse with two scenes that convey the violent behavior of the shepherd. The first shows the hired shepherd killing and consuming sheep belonging to his master. Not only did the shepherd steal, but he also killed and devoured sheep solely to satisfy his own selfish, rapacious desires. As Unger notes, the shepherd fed on the sheep instead of feeding them.[361]

The passage climaxes with the shepherd's senseless violence against Judah. One struggles in vain to comprehend any reason for "tearing off their hoofs." Zechariah's point is that no reason for such actions exists. Even though it was wrong for the shepherd to consume someone else's sheep, one might understand the motives of a hungry person doing such a thing, but mutilation is senseless. The metaphorical image "tearing off their hoofs" captures the unconscionable evil that the shepherd acts out against the defenseless sheep. Even if tearing of hoofs is hyperbole, the message remains clear. The evil shepherd would become notorious for the depths of his ill treatment of the flock, God's people. Meyers and Meyers comment, "The grisly image of eating raw flesh completes the six clauses that catalog intolerable behavior on the part of anyone with a responsibility toward others."[362]

Although he does not read this prophecy literally, Unger contends that this startlingly evil shepherd whom God himself had raised must signify the Antichrist.[363] He equates this evil shepherd with the little horn (Dan 7:24–26), the one who "sets up an abomination that causes desolation" (Dan 9:27; cf. Matt 24:15), "the man of lawlessness" (2 Thess 2:4–8), and the beast who arises

---

[357] יְרַפֵּא. *HALOT*, 1272–74.
[358] יהוה רֹפֵא.
[359] יְכַלְכֵּל. *HALOT*, 463–64.
[360] McComiskey, "Zechariah," 1205.
[361] Unger, *Zechariah*, 203.
[362] Meyers and Meyers, *Zechariah 9–14*, 289.
[363] Unger, *Zechariah*, 204; cf. Barker, "Zechariah," 679–80.

out of the sea (Rev 13:1–10). However, Zechariah set the context of the two shepherds in chap. 11 squarely in his own historical setting, striving to use familiar metaphors to draw Judah's attention to the inevitable results for the nation from the good shepherd's service, as well as the outcome of the evil shepherd's duplicity. Nothing in chap. 11 suggests otherwise. Further, while one might conclude that Zechariah's evil shepherd finds its fulfillment in some secondary sense, it is anything but clear that one should read the passage with the Antichrist in mind. The New Testament does not clearly indicate that one should link Zechariah's evil shepherd with the Antichrist.

Other attempts to identify the evil shepherd with historical figures fail to persuade because of a lack of supporting evidence. For example, Jewish commentators have frequently suggested that the ruthless ruler Herod the Great fulfilled Zechariah's prophecy.[364] In another unconvincing suggestion, Mitchell conjectures that the evil shepherd is Ptolemy IV who came into power in 222 BC.[365] Every effort to link the evil shepherd to a known historical figure fails to fill out the broad dimensions of the prophecy.

**11:17** Zechariah concludes his oracle about the false shepherd with a poetic expression of woe pronounced against the shepherd whose sinister behavior certainly merited condemnation. The initial word in the verse is "woe" *(hōy)*, which commonly introduces laments or pronouncements of judgments in the Old Testament[366] (cf. Amos 6:1). Figuratively the prophet proclaimed judgment on the shepherd who had abused his people through neglect and acts of violence. The final verse in chap. 11 draws again from Ezek 34, a judgment against the false shepherds in the exilic era. Verse 2b reads, "This is what the Sovereign LORD says: Woe to the shepherds of Israel who only take care of themselves! Should not shepherds take care of the flock?" Verse 10 says, "I am against the shepherds and I will hold them accountable for my flock. I will remove them from tending the flock so that the shepherds can no longer feed themselves. I will rescue my flock from their mouths, and it will no longer be food for them." One wonders why the shepherd was not killed, the judgment he surely deserved. Perhaps the walking shell of the former mighty shepherd would warn the people, and subsequent shepherds, that the Lord will not tolerate unfaithfulness.

Zechariah characterizes the prophet in v. 17 as "worthless" *(hāʾĕlîl)*, similar to his description in v. 15.[367] In Job 13:4 the expression castigates "worthless physicians" who are powerless to heal. The term often describes idols in the Old Testament, portraying them as undeserving of worship.

---

[364] Cohen, *Twelve Prophets*, 317.
[365] Mitchell, *Zechariah*, 315.
[366] הוֹי. *HALOT*, 242.
[367] הָאֱלִיל. *HALOT*, 21. See GKC § 90.3 k for an explanation of the unusual spelling of the form.

Without an arm and his right eye the shepherd becomes powerless, no longer capable of injuring the flock, or even able to retain his position.[368] The eye and the arm symbolize the shepherd's physical and mental abilities.[369] Merrill puts the point well, "Without the arm to retrieve and carry the sheep (cf. Luke 15:5) and the eye with which to search and find (cf. Matt 18:12), the shepherd truly is worthless, now not only in a moral sense but in a practical, functional sense as well."[370]

The message of chap. 11 clearly communicates the Lord's furious anger with Judah. Time and again God sent shepherds to administer justice and to promote righteousness. With equal consistency, the nation utterly rejected every shepherd and their God who had sent godly leaders. The consequence of this disregard for the Lord was increasing levels of divine judgment just as Deut 28 had promised long ago.

The only shepherd God's people esteemed in the least was the evil one who sought to subvert the Lord's word. No one stands in greater contrast to this shepherd than Jesus Christ who employed the shepherd metaphor to contrast his own righteousness and care for the flock with the faithless shepherds. Jesus said, "I am the good shepherd. The good shepherd lays down his life for the sheep" (John 10:11). The Lord continued, "I am the good shepherd; I know my sheep and my sheep know me—just as the Father knows me and I know the Father—and I lay down my life for the sheep" (John 10:14–15).

The rejection of the shepherd by the flock is woven into the warp and woof of this entire passage, echoing the rejection of the Lord's Servant in Isaiah (see chaps. 42, 49, 50, 52:13–53:12). Compounding the rejection of the shepherd by the people, the shepherd became so exasperated with the sinful intransigence of the nation that he grew weary of trying to serve them. Meyers and Meyers offer a helpful conclusion to the verse: "The idea of getting rid of shepherds . . . is part of the process of having God's will correctly known by the people so that they will comprehend the true meaning of what takes place in the world in the past, present, and future."[371]

Chapter 11 grieves for the devastation that faithless shepherds had inflicted upon God's people. In the midst of this spiritual abuse by selfish shepherds the Lord promises to come and care tenderly for his people. Zechariah certainly appreciated the prior Old Testament motif in which the Lord himself served as Judah's ultimate Shepherd (Ps 23:1; cf. Isa 40:11). The theme of the Lord Jesus Christ's faithful shepherding of his people recalls the beloved hymn "Savior,

---

[368] Sweeney notes that in Isa 45:1 the Lord declares his intention to take Cyrus's right hand, suggesting that Zech 11:17 refers to Cyrus (*Twelve Prophets*, 682–83). But Sweeney overstates the linguistic similarity between the two passages. Further, Zech 11 looks to the present and future circumstances and is not a retrospective.

[369] Meyers and Meyers, *Zechariah 9–14*, 292.

[370] Merrill, *Zechariah*, 305.

[371] Meyers and Meyers, *Zechariah 9–14*, 265.

Like a Shepherd Lead Us," which reminds us of how good the Good Shepherd really is:

> Savior, like a shepherd lead us, much we need Thy tender care;
> In Thy pleasant pastures feed us, for our use Thy folds prepare:
> Blessed Jesus, blessed Jesus, Thou has bought us, Thine we are;
> Blessed Jesus, blessed Jesus, Thou has bought us, Thine we are.
>
> We are Thine; do Thou befriend us, be the guardian of our way;
> Keep Thy flock, from sin defend us, seek us when we go astray:
> Blessed Jesus, blessed Jesus, Hear, O hear us when we pray;
> Blessed Jesus, blessed Jesus, Hear, O hear us when we pray.[372]

## 7. Israel's Battle and Victory (12:1–9)

### ¹An Oracle

**This is the word of the LORD concerning Israel. The LORD, who stretches out the heavens, who lays the foundation of the earth, and who forms the spirit of man within him, declares: ²"I am going to make Jerusalem a cup that sends all the surrounding peoples reeling. Judah will be besieged as well as Jerusalem. ³On that day, when all the nations of the earth are gathered against her, I will make Jerusalem an immovable rock for all the nations. All who try to move it will injure themselves. ⁴On that day I will strike every horse with panic and its rider with madness," declares the LORD. "I will keep a watchful eye over the house of Judah, but I will blind all the horses of the nations. ⁵Then the leaders of Judah will say in their hearts, 'The people of Jerusalem are strong, because the LORD Almighty is their God.'**

**⁶"On that day I will make the leaders of Judah like a firepot in a woodpile, like a flaming torch among sheaves. They will consume right and left all the surrounding peoples, but Jerusalem will remain intact in her place.**

**⁷"The LORD will save the dwellings of Judah first, so that the honor of the house of David and of Jerusalem's inhabitants may not be greater than that of Judah. ⁸On that day the LORD will shield those who live in Jerusalem, so that the feeblest among them will be like David, and the house of David will be like God, like the Angel of the LORD going before them. ⁹On that day I will set out to destroy all the nations that attack Jerusalem.**

Zechariah 12 commences the second and final movement in chaps. 9–14. Both sections, 9:1–11:17 and 12:1–14:21, begin with the common prophetic word *maśśāʾ*.[373] The word *maśśāʾ* may be translated either "burden" or "oracle." Zechariah 9–11 overviews themes that stress the Lord's dominion over all humanity. That first section consists of the judgment on Judah's foes, the dramatic appearance of Zion's delivering king, God's protection of Judah herself, the condemnation of the foolish shepherd, and the coming curse on God's people for their rejection of the faithful shepherd's righteous reign. The first

---

[372] *The Baptist Hymnal*, # 61.
[373] מַשָּׂא. See *HALOT*, 639–40.

of Zechariah's two oracles also incorporates a review of Judah's history, with special attention given to the failure of the nation's shepherds and the people's rejection of the Lord.

If the book concluded with Zech 11:17, serious questions about Judah's future would remain. Chapter 11 concludes on a melancholy note. For instance, what did the breaking of the staff "Favor," symbolizing God's covenant with his people, portend? After the breaking of the second staff the people sat defenseless before every marauding nation. Moreover, God's chosen people willingly suffered under the ravages of the foolish shepherd who inflicted great injury on his own family. Had God's patience finally reached its end, resulting in the ultimate rejection of Abraham's seed? Or did national Israel retain a future hope based on their place in God's plans?[374] Zechariah 12–14 answers these questions. This final oracle turns its gaze from Judah's dismal past and contemporary circumstances to the glorious and triumphant future that Judah, and indeed all nations, would experience.[375]

Zechariah 12–14 focuses on Judah, often described with the encompassing national moniker, "Israel." While chaps. 9–11 largely concern Judah's past and present circumstances, although not completely so, chaps. 12–14 look almost exclusively to a future time of eschatological deliverance. The phrase "on that day" echoes throughout the final chapters of the book of Zechariah, pointing to a coming time of restoration.

These clear differences in emphases between chaps. 9–11 and chaps. 12–14 should not suggest that the two sections share no theological similarities. Merrill surveys manifold examples of theological parallels between the two oracles.[376] For instance, Zech 9:11–17 and 12:1–9 both extend the hope of future salvation to God's people. The Lord's burning anger against false prophets and shepherds in 10:1–3 foreshadows similar judgments in 13:1–6. The messianic Savior introduced in 10:4–7 prefigures the notable messianic prophecy in 13:7–9. The Lord's triumphant victory over all of his foes in 9:1–8 anticipates the eschatological conquest in 14:1–8. The Lord's regal reign in 9:9–10 parallels the one in 14:9–10. Lastly, both 10:8–12 and 14:12–21 draw upon exodus motifs to convey the Lord's miraculous victory over enemies that Israel had insufficient might to defeat in her own strength.

**12:1** Jerusalem provides the setting for the great conflagration that the nation had never seen nor could even imagine. Hopelessly outnumbered,

---

[374] McComiskey, "Zechariah," 1209.

[375] Ibid. McComiskey allows for Judah's future hope, but he sees this promise fulfilled by the Church. While a viable interpretation, it remains preferable to view subsequent biblical references to "Israel" as applying to national Israel. Accordingly, the Church and Israel both participate in God's eschatological promises. This interpretation rejects the replacement theology in which national Israel disappears by reinterpreting clear biblical declarations to Israel figuratively in order to apply them to the Church.

[376] Merrill, *Zechariah*, 309–10.

Jerusalem and her environs find themselves surrounded by all the nations. As the battle unfolds, Jerusalem experiences victory in a reversal of circumstances that surpassed anyone's wildest expectations. The universal scope of the battle, the struggle between good and evil, the ultimate victory from the Lord's hands, and the highly figurative language all illustrate features of biblical apocalyptic literature.[377]

The second movement in the final section of Zechariah surprisingly focuses on "Israel," not the anticipated Jerusalem or Judah. Meyers and Meyers survey several different uses for the term "Israel" in the postexilic biblical books, noting that the term can refer to Judah or to the entire Southern Kingdom, including Judah and Benjamin, as it typically functions in 1 and 2 Chronicles as well. Of course, "Israel" can also refer to the Northern Kingdom as it existed prior to 722 BC (see 11:14). "Israel," however, does not focus on the northern tribes in Zech 12–14. In the postexilic books, when "Israel" refers to the Northern Kingdom, it typically occurs in contrast with Judah. Hence, "Israel" occurring alone in v. 1 speaks of the entire nation. As such, "Israel" underscores the inclusion of all of the Lord's people in the promised future blessings.[378]

With great emphasis, Zechariah introduces the Lord as Creator of heaven and earth. The reference to the Lord's creative work in chap. 12 has two points. To speak of God as Creator of all that exists stresses his power in incomparable fashion. If God holds the might to create the universe, he assuredly possesses the ability to bring his promises to Judah to fruition, however difficult they might appear from a human vantage point. Somewhat more subtly, the Old Testament also links creation with redemption and salvation. The latter sections of Isaiah and Zechariah share a similar concern with portraying the Lord as powerful enough to effect the promises of deliverance that far exceeded human capacity to achieve. Consequently, 12:1 presents the Lord as Israel's Savior, the one who will deliver her from her sin and her foes. The story of redemption is also the account of God's restoration. The Lord promises to recreate the world he had originally created to be a perfect setting for him to reign over his creatures in righteousness.

Further, the prophet discusses the Lord's work as Creator with a threefold statement. Each of Zechariah's declarations about the Creator draws upon Isaiah's previous pronouncements.[379] The first expression, "who stretches out the heavens," echoes themes found in Gen 1–2. The Hebrew term for "stretches out" *(nōṭeh)* introduces a metaphor, that of stretching out a tent.[380] Isaiah twice spoke of the Lord's creative activity with the same image, "he stretches out the heavens like a canopy, and spreads them out like a tent to live in" (40:22; cf. 42:5; 51:13).

---

[377] See Introduction for further discussion on the Apocalyptic genre.
[378] See Meyers and Meyers, *Zechariah 9–14*, 309–10; Clendenen, "Malachi," 243–44.
[379] Merrill, "Literary Genres in Isaiah 40–55," *BSac* 144 (1987): 144–56.
[380] נָטָה. *HALOT*, 692–93.

The next idiom, "who lays the foundation *[yōsēd]* of the earth," employs a different metaphor in which the Lord builds a mighty edifice as the Master Builder.[381] Zechariah echoes the creation motif in Isa 51:13. Together with the first creation reference, "heavens" coupled with "earth" express a merism, implying the totality of all creation. The modern claim that Zechariah simply repeated an ancient Near Eastern perspective that viewed the universe as bipartite ignores the sophistication of the prophet's use of figurative language.[382] Zechariah's main point was a theological one—no part of the universe exists without the Lord's active role in its formation and sustenance. Moreover, the universal aspects of God's creative endeavors intimates that the blessings Judah and Jerusalem receive will impact the world at large.

The final creation statement, "who forms *[yōṣēr]* the spirit of man within him," shifts from the broader dimensions of creation to the personal dimension of the Lord's relationship with humans.[383] Much more personal than the previous two affirmations concerning the Lord's creative activities, the participle *yōṣēr* can also mean "potter" (see Jer 18:4). In Gen 2:7, like a heavenly potter, the Lord formed mankind out of clay and blew the breath of life into him. As in the previous examples, Isaiah first employed similar creation language, illustrating the theological linkage between creation and salvation. Isaiah wrote, "But now, this is what the LORD says—he who created you, O Jacob, he who formed *[yōṣēr]* you, O Israel: 'Fear not, for I have redeemed you; I have summoned you by name; for you are mine'" (Isa 43:1).

In defending a biblical understanding of the person of God, Augustine drew upon Zech 12:1 to demonstrate that the human spirit was not the same as the Holy Spirit. Augustine fought against Manichaeism, a third-century dualistic heresy which taught that the spiritual essence of man was one in nature with God. Manichaeism also taught that the physical component of humanity was evil, created by the prince of darkness. Augustine noted that 12:1 plainly indicated that God had created "the spirit of man." Accordingly, man—and every constituent part of his being—was created by God and was not part of the person of God. Augustine observed that "pride is the mother of all the heretics, they dared to say that the soul is the nature of God." Later he added, "But there cannot be a greater sign of pride than that the human soul says that it is what God is, while it still groans under such great burdens of vice and unhappiness."[384]

**12:2–3** From this juncture on, Zechariah elevated the city of Jerusalem to a level of prominence not seen elsewhere in the book—he mentions Jerusalem 11 times in vv. 2–11. This differs somewhat from the emphasis on Judah and Israel in chaps. 9–10. Despite the prominence he gives her, Zechariah does

---

[381] יָסַד. *HALOT*, 417.
[382] Meyers and Meyers, *Zechariah 9–14*, 311.
[383] יָצַר. *HALOT*, 428–29.
[384] Ferreiro, *The Twelve Prophets*, 270.

not explain why the nations attack Jerusalem in vv. 2–3 (see 14:2). The city certainly did not possess significant amounts of wealth that would tempt envious neighbors. Neither did the land hold material resources that would appeal to other kingdoms. Perhaps the question remains unanswerable, as perplexing as the question why the Jewish community has consistently faced persecution over the millennia. However, on a glorious future day the suffering and defeat will have a different outcome than in all previous onslaughts. At that time, the Lord will come to his people bringing final deliverance and security.

The Lord's actions will transform Jerusalem into "a cup [Hb. *sap*] that sends all the surrounding peoples reeling" and into "an unmovable rock."[385] These two metaphors capture the miraculous victory God will give to Zion. The first figure of speech, the "cup of reeling," sounds particularly unusual to modern ears. The "cup" metaphor, however, occurs in numerous places in the Old Testament with differing nuances. Baldwin summarizes the "cup" metaphor as "the life experience which God purposed for man." For instance, Ps 116:13a declares, "I will lift up the cup of salvation." With an equally positive connotation, Ps 23:5b describes the abundance of the Lord's blessing on the psalmist with the image, "my cup overflows."[386]

However, the cup metaphor often conveys judgment, not blessing. Isaiah 51:17 exemplifies the cup of judgment: "Awake, awake! Rise up, O Jerusalem, you who have drunk from the hand of the LORD the cup of his wrath, you who have drained to its dregs the goblet that makes men stagger." In the same chapter Isaiah speaks of the cup of divine wrath being "taken out of your hand . . . [so that] you will never drink again" (v. 22). Jeremiah 25:15–28 develops the cup of wrath metaphor much like one reads in Isa 51. The main difference in Jer 25 is the recipient of divine judgment: Jeremiah focuses on the nations, not Jerusalem. Jeremiah recorded, "So I took the cup from the LORD's hand and made all the nations to whom he sent me drink it" (Jer 25:17). As in Jer 25, the nations surrounding Zion will be forced to drink the cup in Zech 12.

In 1 Kgs 7:50 and Jer 52:19 the *sap* serves as a temple utensil. The word *sap* (or perhaps its homonym) also serves in another temple context, referring to the door sockets of the temple (1 Kgs 14:17; 2 Chr 3:7; Isa 6:4; Jer 35:4; Amos 9:1).[387] Both usages of *sap* evoke the significance of the temple, the physical domain of the Lord's presence on earth and a powerful force that plays a role in incapacitating all who dare to oppose God.[388]

This begins the dominant theme of Zech 12–14—the prophet prophesies that Judah's marauding neighbors will face defeat at the hand of the Lord.

---

[385] סַף. *HALOT*, 762–63.

[386] Baldwin, *Zechariah*, 188.

[387] *HALOT*, 763 views this noun as סַף II, "threshold, stone under the door-frame," distinguishing it from סַף I, "bowl."

[388] Sweeney, *Twelve Prophets*, 685.

These foes must drink from a "cup of reeling," *sap–ra'al*.[389] Thus, the contents of the cup produce reeling as an intoxicated person would stagger under the influence of alcohol. The ironic picture is one of a marauder who, mad with greed, might drink down the dregs contained in a stolen goblet, only to find himself too drunk to carry away the booty.

The next phrase in the Masoretic Text presents significant difficulties. The Hebrew translates literally "and it will be against Judah also" *(wĕgam 'al–yĕhûdāh yihyēh)*.[390] The ancient versions also struggled to understand the phrase. Merrill claims that Judah will also cause the foreign intruders to fall back and reel as though they were inebriated.[391] But the text does not indicate that Judah will serve as a tool of the Lord's deliverance. Further, the preposition *'al*, frequently translated "against," functions adversatively in this verse.[392]

The NIV translators have added their understanding, rendering the phrase in question, "Judah will be besieged as well as Jerusalem." While the Masoretic Text does not explicitly state this, the phrase could indicate that somehow Judah will become embroiled in the siege against Zion. Although it is linguistically possible that Judah actively opposed Jerusalem, the notion that it confronted Zion makes no sense in this context. Rather, it appears that Judah found herself swept up in the conflagration. Apparently, the nations' siege against Jerusalem also included battle against Judah.[393]

Verse 3 begins with a verbal form *(wĕhāyāh)* that unambiguously indicates a future setting for the immediate context.[394] Following this future verb, one encounters the common prophetic temporal marker "on that day" *(bayyôm–hahû')*.[395] In chaps. 12–14 the phrase occurs 17 times, always with an eschatological gaze. Sometimes prophecies introduced with this phrase speak of divine judgment, and at other times, blessing.

Consistent with the apocalyptic teaching that focuses on God's dealings with the entire creation, 12:3 introduces the whole world arrayed together against the Lord and his people, somewhat reminiscent of Ps 2:1–2. Later in Zechariah the prophet stresses the same point. For example, 14:2 declares, "I will gather all the nations to Jerusalem to fight against it" (see also v. 16).

In 12:3 Zechariah used a second metaphor, stating that God would make Jerusalem an immovable (lit. "heavy") rock that the nations could not budge *('eben ma'ămāsāh)*.[396] The metaphor of a large, heavy stone plays a significant role in the first portion of the book of Zechariah as well (3:9; 4:7,10; 5:8),

---

[389] סַף־רַעַל. *HALOT*, 762–63, 1266.
[390] וְגַם עַל־יְהוּדָה יִהְיֶה.
[391] Merrill, *Zechariah*, 313.
[392] GKC § 119 dd.
[393] McComiskey, "Zechariah," 1209.
[394] וְהָיָה.
[395] בַּיּוֹם־הַהוּא. Somewhat incongruously, McComiskey ("Zechariah," 1209) asserts without evidence that this phrase refers to events in the past.
[396] אֶבֶן מַעֲמָסָה. *HALOT*, 7–8, 614.

although with a different point of comparison. The image Zechariah paints in chap. 12 shows looters who swarm over the city looking for items of value to steal. All of Zechariah's hearers would have appreciated the miraculous irony of this proclamation, realizing all too well their own "lightness," that is, their relative weakness and inability to defend themselves. In contrast to the overwhelming might of their opponents, God would have to perform a great miracle in her presence before Jerusalem could become "heavy." Indeed, Jerusalem will become so weighty that any foe who attempts to lift her "will injure" himself.

As a result, many of Zion's enemies will actually hurt themselves because of their own sinful opposition to God and his people. The verb translated by the NIV "injure themselves" *(yiśśārēṭû)* occurs elsewhere only in Lev 21:5 where it means "to cut oneself."[397] Just as one might cut himself trying to handle a jagged and heavy boulder, so Jerusalem's opponents will hurt themselves when they attempt to lift Jerusalem's miraculous mass.

Grudgingly, these neighbors will be forced to acknowledge the Lord's superiority and abandon additional efforts to vanquish Zion. Joel 3:9–16 expresses a comparable eschatological deliverance of Jerusalem, putting down the onslaught of the unrighteous foes of God's people. Verse 16 summarizes the passage well: "The LORD will roar from Zion and thunder from Jerusalem; the earth and the sky will tremble. But the LORD will be a refuge for his people, a stronghold for the people of Israel" (cf. Rev 16:16–21).

**12:4–5** The scene in v. 4 shifts to that of a furious cavalry charge against Judah by her foes that have surrounded the Southern Kingdom. The battlefield Zechariah sketches is truly unusual in one important respect. Judah suffers the onslaught of the horseback warriors, but there is no mention that she offers any resistance, perhaps because she is overwhelmed with fright at the horde of warriors seeking her demise. Judah's complete lack of ability to defend herself, let alone grasp victory, serves as an effective backdrop against which the Lord emerges to snatch victory from the pagan soldiers.

In a scene comparable to Judg 5:22, where the Lord struck Sisera's steeds, Zechariah reveals God's future supernatural victory on Judah's behalf. The scene in 12:4 is one of pandemonium and total chaos. The war horses bolt in terror at the Lord's mighty hand. As a result, their riders cannot carry the battle to God's people. Instead, the mighty army finds itself utterly defeated by an unseen but very real foe, the Lord himself.

A proper appreciation of the message of this passage demands an understanding of the role horses played in ancient Near Eastern warfare.[398] The war horse functioned as the elite military weapon in antiquity. Modern analogies, although inexact, might include such materiel as advanced aircraft and armory.

---

[397] יִשָּׂרֵטוּ. *HALOT*, 1355.
[398] O. Keel, *Symbolism*, 298–301.

In the ancient world, only the most prosperous nations could afford a cavalry, a luxury Judah most assuredly could not field. The overwhelming odds Judah faced and her pitiful weakness left her no hope for deliverance but in God alone. Zechariah employed horses frequently, albeit in diverse ways, throughout his prophecy to portray military might as well as the Lord's sovereignty (1:8; 6:2–3,6–7; 9:10).

Verse 4 draws from the list of curses for disobedience in Deut 28. In particular, Deut 28:28 provides the backdrop for Zech 12:4 by linking madness with blindness: "The LORD will afflict you with madness, blindness and confusion of mind." In Deut 28 madness and blindness function as two of many curses that Moses declared would befall God's people for disobeying God. In Zech 12 the Lord reverses the recipients of these curses. Instead of afflicting Judah for disobedience, God will visit these ailments on the unbelieving nations.

At the beginning of v. 4 the prophet quotes the Lord as saying, "I will strike" *(ʾakkeh)*.[399] The term possesses particular significance growing out of its prominence elsewhere in the Old Testament to describe God's military defeat of his foes. The most important examples of God's striking his foes occur when the Lord visited the Egyptians with the dramatic series of plagues intended to demonstrate his might, as well as the impotence of the Egyptians and their gods (Exod 7:25; 9:15; 12:13).

The verb "to strike" has two consequences in v. 4. First, the Lord will strike the war horses with "panic" *(timmāhôn)*.[400] The noun means "to freeze with fear" or "to be horrified." As a consequence of divine interdiction, the mighty warhorses, the greatest weapon in Zechariah's day, would prove completely useless due to their state of panic. Second, God will afflict the horses' riders with "madness" *(šiggāʿôn)*.[401] Occurring elsewhere only in 2 Kgs 9:20, this term refers to the "confusion" or "godly terror" inflicted on the riders by the Lord. As a result, these riders will cease being a military threat to Jerusalem or to Judah. Panic and its resulting disarray will render these enemies an impotent fighting force.

God promised, "I will keep a watchful eye over the house of Judah." The Hebrew expression *ʾepqaḥ ʾet-ʿênay* means "to open my eyes,"[402] underscoring God's constant attention and careful watch on behalf of someone (2 Kgs 19:16; Isa 37:17; Jer 32:19; Dan 9:18).[403] The Lord's seeing eye also prevents him from striking out indiscriminately in the tumult, and therefore his blows will land only on Judah's opponents. For the fourth time in the book, the prophet emphasized the Lord's "eye" (see 3:9; 4:10; 9:8). The Lord's eye serves as an

---

[399] אָכֶּה. *HALOT*, 697–98.
[400] תִּמָּהוֹן. *HALOT*, 1745. The noun form occurs in 14:13 as well as Deut 7:23.
[401] שִׁגָּעוֹן. *HALOT*, 1415.
[402] אֶפְקַח אֶת־עֵינַי. *HALOT*, 959.
[403] McComiskey, "Zechariah," 1210.

anthropomorphism to convey God's watchful care over his people. The nation need not fear because their God was watching over them continually.

The Lord's watchful gaze on his people serves as a counterpoint to the blindness he cast over the eyes of the horses. Verse 4 concludes with an emphatic assertion that the Lord "will blind all the horses." "I will blind" in the NIV translates the verb *'akkeh* ("I will strike") as in the beginning of the verse. The repetition of the Lord's resolve to inflict pandemonium on Judah's foes, coupled with the assertion that God will afflict "*all* the horses of the nations," underscores the totality of divine judgment.

Judah's response in v. 5 to God's deliverance is one of unqualified praise of their Lord, an infrequent event in the book. The perspective shifts from the raging battle surrounding the nation to the private thoughts and conversations of Judah's leaders. The affirmation of Judah's newly found strength as a nation and the astounding victory she had won both rest solely on her covenant relationship with the Lord. This national expression of faith contrasts sharply with the cavalier attitude toward God evidenced by the faithless shepherd who cared nothing for the welfare of his flock (9:5).

The word rendered "leaders" (*'allupê*) warrants comment.[404] Alternatively translated as "chieftain" or "leader of a clan," the word may speak of the heads of families. However, this translation is far from certain. It is much more common to translate the term as "family, clan, tribe" (Gen 36:15; 1 Chr 1:51). This understanding shifts the focus from the representatives of the families to the entire clans themselves.[405] According to this perspective, the whole nation raised its collective voice in praise and thanksgiving for their relationship to God and the salvation he had given them. The familial reference underscores the grave circumstances from which the Lord extricated Judah. Every member of every clan throughout the nation had faced terrible jeopardy, from tender little ones to the frail elderly.

**12:6** Beginning with the familiar eschatological introduction "on that day," v. 6 continues the theme of divine retribution against Judah's enemies introduced in vv. 4–5. Verse 6 incorporates the same word (*'allupê*) used in v. 5, which the NIV renders "leaders." As argued above, the word in this context likely refers to "clans, families," not just the "leaders."

The prophet employs an unusual simile to explain the role the families would play in the defeat of the people's foes. "Like a firepot in a woodpile," an incendiary device in the midst of flammable material, so would Judah's families wreak devastation on their enemies as long as "the LORD Almighty is their God" (v. 5). The word translated "firepot" (*kîyôr*) normally refers to a basin employed in the worship at the tabernacle (Exod 30:18) or for cooking

---

[404] אַלֻּפֵי. *HALOT*, 59–60.
[405] Mitchell, *Zechariah*, 323–24; Meyers and Meyers, *Zechariah 9–14*, 322. See *HALOT*, 59–60.

sacrifices (1 Sam 2:14).[406] The connection between the utensil's use in holy rites to the Lord and its use in the fiery destruction reinforce the idea that God's righteousness serves as a consuming fire (Heb 11:29).

The Old Testament often employs the fire metaphor to portray judgment. God sent fire against pagan nations: "I will send fire upon Moab that will consume the fortresses of Kerioth" (Amos 2:2). At times, prophets foretold coming fire against Israel: "But if you do not obey me to keep the Sabbath day holy by not carrying any load as you come through the gates of Jerusalem on the Sabbath day, then I will kindle an unquenchable fire in the gates of Jerusalem that will consume her fortresses" (Jer 17:27).

The resulting fire "will consume right and left all the surrounding peoples." The ravenous fire devouring all to the right and left seemingly refocuses an oracle from Isa 9:19–20:

> By the wrath of the LORD Almighty
>   the land will be scorched
> and the people will be fuel for the fire;
>   no one will spare his brother.
> On the right they will devour,
>   but still be hungry;
> on the left they will eat,
>   but not be satisfied.
> Each will feed on the flesh of his own offspring.

The metaphor of fiery judgment suggests at least two theological points. First, fire indicates cataclysmic and total destruction. Zechariah prophesies that Judah's foes will cease to exist, no longer able to disregard the Creator of heaven and earth or to thwart his people. Second, the ease with which tinder could catch fire further intimates the ease with which Judah's enemies will face defeat, all because of the intervention of the Lord Almighty.

Obviously, the geographic significance of "right and left" depends on the speaker's spatial orientation when making the statement. Zechariah's silence on this point makes it impossible to reach a definitive conclusion. Nonetheless, speakers in the Old Testament regularly oriented themselves on the East-West axis, not on the North-South axis so foundational in modern cartography.[407] Accordingly, Babylon and its political successor Persia would lay on one hand, while Egypt would fall on the other. Thus, the eschatological victory of the Lord would consign Judah's two great historical nemeses to their ultimate destiny. A slightly different interpretation takes "right and left" to be a merism, expressing the totality of all nations that opposed Judah.[408] Both views underscore the

---

[406] כִּיּוֹר. *HALOT*, 472.
[407] Merrill, *Zechariah*, 315.
[408] Meyers and Meyers, *Zechariah 9–14*, 326.

Lord's ultimate victory over powers that no force could overcome in their own strength, certainly not Judah.

The final phrase in the verse, "but Jerusalem will remain intact in her place," precludes the possibility that any dissension existed between the rural folk of Judah and the leadership in Jerusalem. More significantly, Jerusalem and the temple it contained remained unharmed by the battle swirling around it. Mitchell calls Zion "the inviolate and inviolable centre and stronghold of the Chosen People."[409]

**12:7–8** A more precise understanding of the relational problem Zechariah addressed rests on the significance of the phrase "house of David." A common expression in the Old Testament, "house of David" functions as King David's immediate family or household (2 Sam 3:1), the sitting Davidic king (Isa 7:2), and the Davidic dynasty (2 Kgs 17:21). McComiskey contends that none of these meanings fit the context, preferring the meaning "the inhabitants of Jerusalem."[410] McComiskey's arguments do not prove very convincing since they lack the evidence necessary to adopt such a non-typical use of the phrase. Among the known uses, the Davidic line interpretation fits the message of v. 7, as well as the sense of vv. 10,12 where the phrase also occurs.[411] Throughout the book of Zechariah the future fortunes of Judah rest on the messianic hope of the coming Davidic king.[412] This messianic king will fulfill the divine promise made to David that one of his descendants would sit on the throne forever (2 Sam 7:11–13).

A rivalry between the nation of Judah and the house of David in Jerusalem may have erupted. One may surmise from v. 7 that the house of David sought more honor for itself than was its due, downplaying the importance of the "common" people. At least there existed the perception that the Davidic house sought its own glory to excess. The text gives no indication of what might have precipitated this dissension, but the occasion of the tension is of no real consequence.

The real issue is twofold. On a literary level, the elevation of the prominence of Judah over the capital city of Jerusalem foreshadows the mourning of Zion and the house of David for their actions toward "the one they have pierced" (v. 10).[413] First, the disunity among God's people was something that God never condoned. A beloved text extols the Lord's desire for harmony among his people: "How good and pleasant it is when brothers live together in unity" (Ps 133:1). This theme reverberates throughout the New Testament as well (John 17:23; Rom 15:5; Eph 4:3,13; Col 3:14). Second, however prominent

---

[409] Mitchell, *Zechariah*, 324.
[410] McComiskey, "Zechariah," 1211.
[411] Mitchell, *Zechariah*, 326.
[412] Meyers and Meyers, *Zechariah 9–14*, 329.
[413] Sweeney, *Twelve Prophets*, 687.

the house of David had been earlier in the Old Testament, the kingdom would place equal value upon every member of the eschatological dominion.

The word "honor" *(tip'eret)* signifies "beauty, splendor, radiance" elsewhere in the Old Testament.[414] At times, *tip'eret* refers to the temple, a point Sweeney stresses.[415] He notes the association of the term with the temple (Isa 60:7), the ark (Ps 78:61), and the high priestly vestments (Exod 28:2). Although Sweeney associates *tip'eret* with the temple, the resulting meaning argues against the glory of the temple exceeding the honor that rural Judah would receive. Sweeney's suggestion that Zechariah's use of "honor" here downplays the prominence of the temple holds little merit.

*HALOT* surveys various meanings of *tip'eret* that have no connection to the temple or other ritual connotations. In particular, the term may speak of the fame or honor belonging to an individual or a community (see Judg 4:9; Prov 17:6). This meaning fits the context of Zech 12:7 more appropriately.

Verse 7 begins with the promise that the Lord "will save the dwellings of Judah," employing the word *'ohŏlê* ("tents").[416] The choice of this word to describe the dwellings of the common people in the environs of Judah paints an unfavorable comparison to the grandeur of Zion. The humble houses of the lower classes reveal a measure of social inferiority compared to Jerusalem.[417] The Lord's salvation of the commoners first demonstrates God's unwillingness to respect such social or economic distinctions. As resplendent as God intended for Zion to be in the future day of deliverance, v. 7 indicates that the glory of the rural areas of Judah will equal that of the capital itself. Baldwin notes: "Each needs the other and neither is to lord it over the other."[418] In the kingdom to come, no one will gain special standing before God on the basis of their social or material standing (Gal 3:26–29).

Verse 8 turns the Lord's attention from Jerusalem's environs back to the city itself. The verse begins with the fourth in the sequence of "on that day" sayings in 12:2–11. Zechariah 12:5 declares, "The people of Jerusalem are strong, because the LORD Almighty is their God." The causal clause states the obvious: the people's strength comes not from themselves but from their God with whom they enjoyed a covenant relationship. With the Lord as their shield and strength, even the weakest people in Zion would be as strong as the great warrior David and the dynasty following him. Verse 8 continues this theme, asserting the Lord's protection over all with whom he had established a covenant.

The "shield" of the Lord is a favorite Old Testament metaphor for divine protection. The earliest occurrence of the metaphor offers one of the best examples. To Abram the Lord promised, "Do not be afraid, Abram, I am your

---

[414] תִּפְאָרֶת. *HALOT*, 1772–73.
[415] Sweeney, *Twelve Prophets*, 687.
[416] אֹהֶל. *HALOT*, 19.
[417] Merrill, *Zechariah*, 316. Meyers and Meyers (*Zechariah 9–14*, 328) disagree.
[418] Baldwin, *Zechariah*, 189.

shield, your very great reward" (Gen 15:1). God's shield will safeguard even those in most desperate need of divine aid.

The three similes ("like" statements) in 12:8 offer comparisons the reader could never have anticipated. All three statements express hyperbole that the prophet employed to strengthen the theological point of God's astounding provisions for all of Judah. The first affirmation proclaims that the feeblest of the land "will be like David." Of course, David was the most important, and most powerful, king in the Old Testament. What could have been more remarkable than for the frailest ones in an already weakened nation to embody the strength and sufficiency of the greatest king in Judah's entire history? In other words, the weakest ones will become as strong as if they were the mightiest king in their ancient past.

The word translated "feeblest" in the NIV is *hannikšāl*.[419] On its simplest level, the word means "to stumble or stagger," and thus it represents the antithesis of strength (see Isa 40:30–31). Meyers and Meyers note that the same word and its derivatives occur with frequency in the book of Jeremiah.[420] Jeremiah chose this word to describe the prospects faced by those who had persecuted him for his righteousness and faithful proclamation of God's word. Jeremiah 20:11 illustrates this point: "But the LORD is with me like a mighty warrior; so my persecutors will stumble *[yikkāšĕlû]* and not prevail."[421] If Zechariah did indeed choose the word *hannikšāl* to allude to false prophets like the ones Jeremiah faced, then the postexilic prophet declares that false prophecy and those who declared falsehood would cease loving evil and would begin heeding God's word. Meyers and Meyers summarize the point: "In this sense, the comparison of such elements to David, and of David to God, is perhaps a way of proclaiming that the historical opposition to Yahweh's prophets will be utterly reversed in the future age of Davidic restoration."[422]

The second declaration affirms that "the house of David will be like God." As argued in 12:7, "house of David" refers to those descended from King David, upon whom rests the Lord's promise of a descendant perpetually sitting on the throne. Thus, this comparison shifts Zechariah's focus from the most feeble in the land to the strongest and most privileged. Zechariah does not claim that these Davidic descendants will *become* God. Rather, he asserts that these kings in waiting will become *like* God in the sense that they will manifest supernatural strength, although in their case it will be strength that comes from without. Even the house of David—with its comparative strength and advantages—is ultimately woefully weak and ill-prepared to face the overwhelming forces arrayed against them. Any strength the house of David felt that it possessed was illusory. The descendant of David needed God's strength as desperately as did

---

[419] הַנִּכְשָׁל. *HALOT*, 502–3.
[420] Meyers and Meyers, *Zechariah 9–14*, 330–31.
[421] יִכָּשְׁלוּ.
[422] Meyers and Meyers, *Zechariah 9–14*, 331.

those who could barely care for their own daily needs. The Lord's decision to share his might with all of the frail humans comprising Judah, even the mightiest, would ultimately glorify God for the deliverance he extended to them. The Lord's statement to Paul makes the point well: "My grace is sufficient for you, for my power is made perfect in weakness" (2 Cor 12:9; see Phil 4:13). The repeated references to the Davidic dynasty show that the human rule of Davidic kings will exist during the eschatological era.

Lastly, the house of David will become "like the Angel of the LORD." Almost as surprising as the comparison between the house of David and God, this final comparison affirms that the future leaders of Judah will borrow strength from God and the Angel of the Lord who was a divine emissary. The postexilic prophets presented the Angel of the Lord prominently (Hag 1:13; Zech 1:11,12; 3:1,5,6; Mal 2:7; 3:1).

Exod 14:19 reveals one of many important passages describing the activities of the Angel of the Lord: "Then the angel of God, who had been traveling in front of Israel's army, withdrew and went behind them." The twofold statement that "the house of David will be like God, like the Angel of the LORD," has received differing interpretations. Some see the reference to the Angel of the Lord as the portrayal of a being who is less than God himself. But the Old Testament frequently pictures the Angel of the Lord as equivalent to God. Consequently, it is preferable to view these two "like" statements as paralleling one another, expressing virtually identical sentiments. The restatement intensifies the comparison to divine power and ascribes greater praise to the Lord for his gracious extension of power to the powerless. This view treats the Angel of the Lord as a manifestation of God, not a lesser being.[423]

Mitchell's claim that the phrase "like the Angel of the LORD" is a gloss, a scribal addition to the text, cannot be correct.[424] Since there is no objective evidence that the phrase is a gloss, Mitchell's explanation that a scribe was uncomfortable with comparing men to God and accordingly added the phrase about the Angel of the Lord makes little sense when the commentator allows the preceding phrase ("the house of David will be like God") to remain in place. For Mitchell's understanding to fit the literary point of the verse, the hypothetical scribe would have had to excise the offending phrase before he added the Angel of the Lord expression.

**12:9** Verse 9 serves to restate the message of vv. 1–8. One must not miss the underlying prophecy about the global conflagration in which Judah finds herself. Zechariah repeatedly forewarned his hearers about the universal scope of the coming war against Judah. This would truly be a world war. In this chapter, Zechariah repeatedly referenced "the surrounding peoples" (12:2), "all the nations of the earth are gathered against her" (12:3), "all the surrounding

---

[423] Merrill, *Zechariah*, 316.
[424] Mitchell, *Zechariah*, 326.

peoples" (12:6), and "all the nations that attack Jerusalem" (12:9). Judah's God would give her a victory against the most impossible odds. God's response to the array of warring pagans would prove cataclysmic, as the word translated "destroy" *(hašmîd,* meaning "exterminate, utterly annihilate"[425]) indicates.

## 8. The Lord's Servant Pierced; Mourning and Purification (12:10–13:1)

**10"And I will pour out on the house of David and the inhabitants of Jerusalem a spirit of grace and supplication. They will look on me, the one they have pierced, and they will mourn for him as one mourns for an only child, and grieve bitterly for him as one grieves for a firstborn son. ¹¹On that day the weeping in Jerusalem will be great, like the weeping of Hadad Rimmon in the plain of Megiddo. ¹²The land will mourn, each clan by itself, with their wives by themselves: the clan of the house of David and their wives, the clan of the house of Nathan and their wives, ¹³the clan of the house of Levi and their wives, the clan of Shimei and their wives, ¹⁴and all the rest of the clans and their wives.**

**¹"On that day a fountain will be opened to the house of David and the inhabitants of Jerusalem, to cleanse them from sin and impurity.**

Zechariah 12:10–13:1 represents a complete literary and theological unit, comprising the piercing of the Lord's servant and the national mourning for their role in this piercing. These dramatic events all culminate in the purification for the sins of the nation and their spiritual restoration. One can view the current section as an answer to the implicit theological question of why the Lord would desire to save the nation from their foes (12:1–9) when the people have only given him disobedience and disdain as motivation.

The doleful tone of this section contrasts sharply with the previous paragraph in the book that rings with the praises of all the people for the Lord's unparalleled deliverance in the face of all the amassed foes seeking their defeat. All the people of Judah exulted in God's goodness in saving them (12:1–9). The present movement in the Book of Zechariah stresses sorrow (vv. 10–14), the need for a new spirit (v. 10), and cleansing from sin and impurity (13:1). The sorrow for the one Judah had a role in murdering would bring the nation to its knees. The previous section of chap. 12 focuses on physical deliverance for Judah, while the present passage concerns spiritual salvation.

**12:10** The Lord speaks dramatically in the first person in v. 10, beginning with the statement "I will pour out." Often, when God is the subject of the verb "pour out" *(wěšāpaktî),*[426] the outcome is negative, such as the outpouring of divine wrath on Israel (Hos 5:10). But in 12:10 the Lord reverses the pouring out of judgment by extending his grace. Furthermore, the term *wěšāpaktî* can describe the manifestation of God's grace in the eschatological era. In a notable

---

[425] הַשְׁמִיד. *HALOT*, 1552–53.
[426] וְשָׁפַכְתִּי. *HALOT*, 1629–30.

example, the Lord will pour out his Spirit on all mankind (Ezek 39:29; see Acts 2:16–21). In another passage, Joel 2:28–29 declares,

> And afterward, I will pour out my Spirit on all people.
> Your sons and daughters will prophesy,
> > your old men will dream dreams,
> > your young men will see visions.
> Even on my servants, both men and women,
> I will pour out my Spirit in those days.

Zechariah 12:10 begins by describing God's outpouring on "the house of David." This reference to the Davidic line assumes great prominence in this portion of the book of Zechariah. The expression occurs twice in vv. 7–8, referring to the descendants of David who inherited the divine promise of a perpetual Davidic king sitting on the throne (cf. 2 Sam 7:11–16). The Davidic rulers' attitude of repentance for their sinfulness and for their lack of trust in God contrasts with the faithless shepherds in chap. 11 who cared little about obedience to the Lord. Nothing in the passage implicates the house of David that did not apply in equal measure to all of the inhabitants of Jerusalem.[427]

Not only will the Davidic leaders benefit from the Lord's mercy, but God will pour out his grace on all of "the inhabitants of Jerusalem." The Jerusalemites function as a metonymy, signifying the entirety of God's covenant people. Thus, all will experience the Lord's grace, from the highest echelons of Judah's society to the lowest.

The Lord's outpouring will grant "a spirit of grace and supplication" to all of the inhabitants of Jerusalem. This gift of grace does not grow out of anything Judah has done to deserve the Lord's favor. Rather, the grant grows solely out of God's determination to bestow his favor on his people. Also, Zechariah emphasizes that the Lord himself is the source of the renewal.

The word for "spirit" *(rûaḥ)* has evoked extensive discussions in v. 10, Zech 13:2, and throughout the Old Testament.[428] The diversity of translations that *rûaḥ* may suggest has encouraged different interpretations of the "spirit." Some understand *rûaḥ* as a reference to the Spirit of God, that is, the Holy Spirit, the third Person of the Trinity. For example, Barker contends that this Trinitarian view is "in keeping with what appear to be parallel passages (Isa 32:15; 44:3; 59:20–21; Jer 31:31,33; Ezek 36:26–27; 39:29; Joel 2:28–29). Because of the convicting work of God's Spirit, Israel will turn to the Messiah with mourning."[429] Barker is not wrong in affirming that *rûaḥ* can refer to God in the Old Testament, but his interpretation of v. 10 is far from certain.

---

[427] Meyers and Meyers attempt to establish a historical courtly intrigue (*Zechariah 9–14*, 334–35), but this view is contradicted by the reference to all of the inhabitants of Zion.

[428] רוּחַ. *HALOT*, 1197–1201. *TWOT*, 3:1202–20; *TDOT*, 13:361–402.

[429] Barker, "Zechariah," 683; see Unger, *Zechariah*, 215–16.

McComiskey does not even acknowledge the possibility of a Trinitarian understanding of *rûaḥ*.[430] McComiskey revisits the occurrences of *rûaḥ* in previous passages in Zechariah. In the three texts where *rûaḥ* occurs, the word "spirit" has a pronominal suffix that refers the noun back to God himself. Zechariah 4:6 and 6:8 refer to "my Spirit," where the Lord does the speaking. Zechariah 7:12 contains "his Spirit," but again the clear antecedent to the pronoun is God. But no markers exist in 12:10 to indicate that the "spirit" Zechariah introduced refers to the Lord.

The "spirit" in v. 10 portrays the new heart God's people possess. When "spirit" occurs in a "spirit of" construction, the expression speaks of an emotional disposition, such as a "spirit of jealousy" (Num 5:14) and a "spirit of justice" (Isa 28:6).[431] Ezekiel 36:26 exemplifies this use of the word *rûaḥ*: "I will give you a new heart and put a new spirit in you; I will remove from you your heart of stone and give you a heart of flesh." Like that miraculous metamorphosis in Ezek 36, God's work of grace in his people will transform their hardened sinful hearts into hearts characterized by grace, faith, and repentance. This change does not rest on human resolve or effort. Instead, the heart of "grace and supplication" represents the outcome of God's gracious gift to them.

"Grace and supplication" describe the spirit that the Lord will bestow on the otherwise recalcitrant nation.[432] "Grace" *(ḥēn)* represents the mercy that God granted to an undeserving people.[433] Some commentators wrongly translate the word as "compassion" or "pity," missing the theological point of the passage.[434] Grace represents God's favor granted to those who deserved anything but divine blessing. This grace led the people to repent for the sin of piercing the one whom God had sent to deliver them. Grace also moved the nation to seek forgiveness. In turn, the forgiveness that only the Lord could extend resulted in a restored relationship between God and his people.[435] The theological message parallels that in Rom 2:4b: "God's kindness leads you toward repentance."

Coupled with "grace," Judah will also receive "supplication" *(taḥănûnîm)*.[436] *HALOT* defines the term as "pleading," a word which has far greater emotive connotations than does "supplication." The word *taḥănûnîm* communicates pleading for grace from the Lord. A clear parallel appears in Ps 143:1: "O LORD, hear my prayer, listen to my cry for mercy *[taḥănûnay]*; in your faithfulness and righteousness come to my relief."[437] Grace signifies the blessing

---

[430] McComiskey, *Zechariah*, 1214; see Merrill, *Zechariah*, 318–19.
[431] Meyers and Meyers, *Zechariah 9–14*, 335.
[432] The construct relationship, "spirit of grace and supplication," expresses an attributive idea (see GKC § 128 p)—it describes the nature of the spirit/heart that Judah will receive from God.
[433] חֵן. *HALOT*, 332; *TDOT*, 5:22–36.
[434] Hanson, *Dawn of Apocalyptic*, 356.
[435] Merrill, *Zechariah*, 319.
[436] תַּחֲנוּנִים. *HALOT*, 1718–19.
[437] תַּחֲנוּנַי.

that comes from the Lord alone; no one other than he can give the gift of grace. Supplication, or pleading for grace, represents the human side of the equation. Miraculously, the people of Judah would soon long for her relationship with their God to be restored.

This miraculous revitalization of Judah does not emerge in the book of Zechariah only. It is also the theme of Ezek 37, comprising the revitalization of the valley of dry and disheveled bones (37:1–14) as well as the prophecy regarding the pieces of wood that symbolized the eschatological establishment of Judah's new kingdom (37:15–28). In this future era "the nations will know that I the LORD make Israel holy, when my sanctuary is among them forever" (Ezek 37:28). Isaiah's prophecy regarding the coming Branch (Isa 11:1–16) and Micah's mountain of the Lord oracle (Mic 4:1–8) both foretell a similar message of God's people gathered and restored so that they may "walk in the name of the LORD our God for ever and ever" (Mic 4:5b).

After receiving God's gift of grace and a changed heart, Judah will reflect "on me, the one they have pierced." The issues arising from this phrase form the nexus of the interpretative questions in this profound passage. Questions include the proper form of the Hebrew text, the identity of "me," the significance of piercing, and the identity of the one who had been pierced.

The phrase, "they will look on me" *(wěhibbîṭû ʾēlay)* has received significant discussion over the centuries.[438] Text critical, hermeneutical, and theological issues all contribute to the interpretation. But the verb *wěhibbîṭû* offers no particular problems since it simply means "to gaze at."

The first significant question about the authentic reading of the Hebrew text concerns the prepositional phrase, *ʾēlay* (NIV "on me"). Before determining the significance of the particle, one must determine whether this form represents the correct Masoretic reading. All of the major ancient versions support the reading, but many scholars propose emending the text to *ʾēlô* ("to him").[439] At least two factors lead some to accept this alternate reading. Since God speaks in v. 10, the emendation avoids the theological tension that God himself was pierced. This concern will receive further attention subsequently in the discussion about the identity of the martyr. The reference to Zech 12:10 in both John 19:37 and Rev 1:7 read "him." Nonetheless, since New Testament authors typically "quoted" the Old Testament rather loosely, this textual evidence is marginal and does not provide adequate evidence for revising the Hebrew text of Zech 12:10.

The basic sense of the preposition *ʾel* is "towards,"[440] and *ʾel* with the first person singular pronominal suffix *(ʾēlay)* normally means "to me." The verse

---

[438] וְהִבִּיטוּ אֵלַי. *HALOT*, 661, 50–51. LXX reads ἐπιβλέψονται πρός με.
[439] אֵלוֹ. Meyers and Meyers, *Zechariah 9–14*, 336.
[440] אֶל. *HALOT*, 50–51.

stresses the Judahites turning their gaze toward the pierced one in faith (Num 21:9; Isa 45:22).[441]

Zechariah pictures the Lord's servant as "pierced" *(dāqārû)*.[442] Meyers and Meyers underscore the magnitude of understanding this verb for the proper interpretation of the prophecy, stating that the meaning of *dāqārû* "is surely one of the major interpretive cruxes in Second Zechariah, if not in all of prophecy."[443] Biblical usage of this word describes someone who has been "pierced through" by a sword or some other weapon of warfare (see Num 25:8; Judg 9:54). To be pierced generally means to be put to death (see Zech 13:3 where the NIV translates the same verb with "stab"). In a central messianic passage that parallels Zech 12:10, though with different vocabulary, Isaiah prophesied, "But he was pierced *[měḥōlāl]*[444] for our transgressions, he was crushed for our iniquities; the punishment that brought us peace was upon him, and by his wounds we are healed" (Isa 53:5). The nation's outpouring of remorse and repentance for this piercing is unparalleled in the Old Testament.

The Septuagint in Zech 12:10 offers an alternative reading to "pierced" with the Greek word *katōrchēsanto*, which means "insulted, treated spitefully."[445] One can only speculate on the origins of the Greek reading, but on text critical grounds alone, the reading must be rejected. Additionally, treating someone spitefully does not fit the theme of profound mourning and inconsolable weeping pervading the remainder of the passage.

The identity of the one who suffers piercing through at the hands of Judah stands as one of the most important questions in the entire passage. One view suggests that the Lord himself was the pierced one, albeit in a figurative sense. According to this interpretation, the piercing serves as a metaphor for the "wounding" God experienced at the sinfulness of his people. However, this view does not explain how God's symbolic wound could provide cleansing for sin (13:1), nor does it account for the sense of the same verb "pierced" *(dāqārû)* that has a literal use in 13:3.[446]

Mitchell represents the interpretive school that seeks a non-messianic identification. He argues that the one who was pierced could not be "the Messiah, whose advent, all will agree, was still future when these words were written, but some one who had at the time already suffered martyrdom."[447] This argument rests on the temporal value of the verb *dāqārû*, a perfect tense commonly rendered "pierced." However, Mitchell's evidence does not rule out a future fulfillment of the pierced martyr. In numerous other passages Zechariah em-

---

[441] Barker, "Zechariah," 683.
[442] דָּקָרוּ. *HALOT*, 230.
[443] Meyers and Meyers, *Zechariah 9–14*, 337.
[444] מְחֹלָל. *HALOT*, 320.
[445] ἀνθ᾽ ὧν κατωρχήσαντο, "against whom they mocked."
[446] For a more detailed critique, see Merrill, *Zechariah*, 320–21.
[447] Mitchell, *Zechariah*, 330.

ployed perfect tense verbs to describe future events (see 8:3; 9:11). One must appreciate that the Hebrew verbal system does not focus on the time of action but on the kind of action. The perfect tense, more aptly named "perfective," presents actions as though they were completed from the biblical author's vantage point, regardless of whether the action had occurred in the past.[448] One should note that rabbinic interpretations, certainly not favorable to Christological understandings of 12:10, frequently claimed that Zechariah's reference to "the one they have pierced" would see a future fulfillment in the person of the Messiah.[449]

Having misapplied the significance of the perfect tense *dāqārû*, Mitchell proceeds to survey the major recommendations for the identity of the pierced one. He introduces and critiques several possibilities. These strained options include Zechariah, son of Jehoiada, whom King Joash ordered murdered; Zerubbabel; Onias III, who was assassinated in 170 BC; and Simon the Maccabee, who was assassinated in 134 BC. Sweeney adds an unsupported identification with an unknown individual "somehow associated with King Josiah of Judah."[450] In a related approach, Hanson contends that this text reflects political tensions in postexilic Judah.[451]

Mitchell concedes the problems that his historical perspective engenders: "Under the circumstances any plausible suggestion is welcome. One of the more attractive is that the object of consideration in the clause quoted is not a single unfortunate individual, but a considerable number of godly persons who have perished by violence."[452]

Meyers and Meyers's approach to the question provides insight into the difficulties one faces with identifying the pierced one with a historical figure in exilic or postexilic Judah. In their 1993 commentary, they contend that Zechariah's prophecy concerning "the one they have pierced" does not allude "to a single, real event."[453] They make the point emphatically: "We eschew political specificity here despite the temptation to read it that way, as do so many commentators and critics."[454] But in a significant article published not long after their commentary, they argue at length that Zech 12:10 has its roots in the assassination of Gedaliah (2 Kgs 25:25).[455] They guess that the fast mentioned in Zech 7:5 must have commemorated Gedaliah. Their conclusion about Zech 12:10 is mere guesswork: "The disappearance of a royal figure from a position of leadership may just . . . be the result of an astute move on

---

[448] See Klein, "The Prophetic Perfect," 45–60.

[449] Cohen, *Twelve Prophets*, 321–22; cf. Roy A. Rosenberg, "The Slain Messiah in the Old Testament," *ZAW* 99 (1987): 259–61.

[450] Sweeney, *Twelve Prophets*, 689.

[451] Hanson, *Dawn of Apocalyptic*, 363–67.

[452] Mitchell, *Zechariah*, 331.

[453] Meyers and Meyers, *Zechariah 9–14*, 340.

[454] Ibid., 338.

[455] Meyers and Meyers, "Future Fortunes of the House of David," 215–19.

the part of Persian authorities to have local rule securely fixed in the hands of non-royal individuals."[456] To compound the point about Meyers and Meyers's vacillation further, in a different discussion in their commentary they suggest "that the stabbing victim may represent prophetic figures wrongfully injured or put to death by national leaders in the preexilic period."[457] In the final analysis, absolutely no biblical or other historical evidence corroborates these speculations.

The collective martyr view Mitchell mentions also has some adherents in the Jewish community. Although Cohen ultimately rejects this interpretation, he surveys the understanding that the pierced one spoke of "those Jews who fell in defence of their city as martyrs for their faith and country."[458] This interpretation is also purely conjectural.

The plausibility of the Christological interpretation rests squarely on the biblical message about the connection between the pierced Messiah and the resultant cleansing from sin and impurity in 13:1. Like the identity of the Servant in Isa 53:4–6, attempts to identify the pierced one with a group such as the nation face insurmountable difficulties. How can the nation suffer vicariously for the nation? A further problem, if the Servant and the pierced martyr in v. 10 represent the nation, what sense does the verse make if the nation mourns for the murdering of itself? Without a Christological interpretation, Zech 12:10—like Isa 53—presents a conundrum. The New Testament, then, serves to specify the One who would fulfill what had remained enigmatic in the Old Testament, since the piercing of God with its concomitant cleansing from sin lay outside the understanding of those living before the advent of Christ. With the incarnation of Jesus, the prophecies come into sharp focus, finding their fulfillment.

"Mourn" occurs five times in vv. 10–12. The Old Testament employs the verb to express public mourning rites as well as to bewail the loss of someone or a particularly calamitous event. The ancient Near Eastern world, including Judah, had well established rites of mourning. These practices included fasting, wearing sack cloth, and employing funerary singers (2 Chr 35:25). One glimpses many of these practices in passages such as 1 Sam 25:1: "Now Samuel died, and all Israel assembled and mourned for him."

To what might Zechariah compare the depths of grief and mourning the nation would suffer once they received the new spirit from the Lord? Perhaps no sorrow in human experience could compare to the depths of grief parents feel at the death of "an only child." The prophet chose the word *yāḥîd* to express the idea of "only child."[459] This same word occurs prominently in Gen 22:2,12 to emphasize Isaac's status as Abraham's only son, and to make the reader

---

[456] Ibid., 215.
[457] Meyers and Meyers, *Zechariah 9–14*, 376.
[458] Cohen, *Twelve Prophets*, 321.
[459] יָחִיד. *HALOT*, 406–7.

understand the anguish of the situation when God commanded him to sacrifice the boy. Although "only child" is a correct translation, this English idiom fails to convey the full emotive force of the term in the biblical account. The word *yāḥîd* also describes Jephthah's daughter whom he had vowed to sacrifice to the Lord (Judg 11:34). There is little doubt that Zechariah appreciated the poignancy carried by the unusual word *yāḥîd* in Gen 22 and Judg 11. Particularly in the Abraham and Isaac passage, the personal pathos of the circumstances was compounded by the fact that through Isaac the covenant promises of God to the patriarch would flow. Without the son, the promise of God could not come to fruition. The phrase "firstborn son" translates the Hebrew word *běkôr*, and reinforces the "only child" motif in the verse.[460] The only child theme underscores the intensity of grief, mourning, and guilt for the murder of the pierced martyr.

The New Testament alludes to Zech 12:10 on two separate occasions. First, John referred to v. 10 when presenting the death of Jesus as a fulfillment of Old Testament prophecy. John wrote, "as another scripture says, 'They will look on the one they have pierced'" (John 19:37; see v. 34).[461] Second, in introducing his vision on the isle of Patmos, John presented the "son of man" (Rev. 1:13) with the following doxology: "Look, he is coming with the clouds, and every eye will see him, even those who pierced him; and all the peoples of the earth will mourn because of him. So shall it be! Amen" (v. 7).[462]

The ultimate fulfillment for Israel remains in the future, in the eschatological age. Romans 11:25b–26 states, "Israel has experienced a hardening in part until the full number of the Gentiles has come in. And so all Israel will be saved, as it is written: 'The deliverer will come from Zion; he will turn godlessness away from Jacob.'" Justin Martyr spoke of Zech 12:10 when teaching about the second advent of Christ. He gave special attention to the response of the Jews when they saw the crucified Savior returning in glory. He declared, "Tribe by tribe they shall mourn, and then they shall look on him whom they have pierced; and they shall say, 'Why, O Lord, have you made us to err from your way? The glory which our fathers blessed has for us been turned into shame.'"[463]

Augustine also placed emphasis on Zech 12:10 in his writings. For instance, when speaking about Christ's literal return in human form he wrote, "'They shall see him whom they have pierced.' If they will see him whom they have pierced, they will see the same body that they thrust through with a spear."[464]

---

[460] בְּכוֹר. *HALOT*, 131.

[461] M. J. J. Menken, "The Textual Form and the Meaning of the Quotation from Zechariah 12:10 in John 19:37," *CBQ* 55 (1993): 494–511.

[462] C. M. Tuckett, "Zechariah 12:10 and the New Testament," in *The Book of Zechariah and Its Influence*, ed. C. Tuckett (Burlington: Ashgate, 2003): 111–21.

[463] *First Apology*, 52, cited by Ferreiro, *The Twelve Prophets*, 271.

[464] *Tractates on the Gospel of John* 21:3, cited by Ferreiro, *The Twelve Prophets*, 272.

In another work, Hippolytus noted the biblical emphasis on the physical return of Christ at the end of the age. He stated,

> And he will show them "the prints of the nails" in his hands and feet, and his side pierced with the spear, and his head crowned with thorns, and his honorable cross. And once for all shall the people of the Hebrews see all these things, and they shall mourn and weep, as the prophet exclaims, "They shall look on him whom they have pierced."[465]

It is possible, although not at all certain, that Zechariah viewed the martyr in a typological sense. In other words, the prophet may have signified some martyr known to his audience, but not to modern interpreters, who partially fulfilled the prophecy. Just as the ʿalmāh prophecy in Isa 7:14 had significance to Ahaz, but also found its ultimate fulfillment in Christ, so the pierced one might have limited application to a pre-Christian referent.[466] The typological approach remains conjectural, though, in the absence of either historical fulfillment or biblical support of a typological interpretation.

**12:11** Verse 11 continues the theme of deep sorrow begun in v. 10. Zechariah compares Jerusalem's inconsolable grief to "the weeping of Hadad Rimmon in the plain of Megiddo." Unfortunately, the precise point of the prophet's simile defies certainty, allowing several different views to compete for acceptance.

One approach takes Hadad Rimmon as the name of an individual person, in which case the translation might mention mourning "for" or "over" Hadad Rimmon, as in the RSV: "the mourning in Jerusalem will be as great as the mourning for Hadad-rimmon" (cf. REB "over"). As a variant of this viewpoint, some have made this Hadad Rimmon responsible for the death of Ahab (1 Kgs 22:34).[467] Ancient historical accounts leave no record of a person with this name.

A second interpretation views Hadad Rimmon as a reference to a Canaanite religious festival that mourned the ritual death of the god.[468] Hadad does occur as the name of a Canaanite storm god in the Ugaritic Texts.[469] Rimmon may be related to the Assyrian storm god Ramimu, otherwise known as Adad.[470] In a related view, Ramman may have been an Aramean deity.[471] For still another take on the question, the wailing in Hadad Rimmon may refer to weeping for the Babylonian god Tammuz (Ezek 8:14–15). In an era when biblical prophets

---

[465] *On the End of the World*, 40, cited by Ferreiro, *The Twelve Prophets*, 273.
[466] R. T. France, *Jesus and the Old Testament* (London: Tyndale, 1971), 83–86, 153.
[467] Surveyed by Baldwin, *Zechariah*, 193.
[468] Meyers and Meyers, *Zechariah 9–14*, 343–44.
[469] *UT*, § 749.
[470] W. von Soden, *Akkadisches Handwörterbuch* (Wiesbaden: Otto Harrassowitz, 1972), 2:950.
[471] J. C. Greenfield, "The Aramean God Ramman/Rimmon," *IEJ* 26 (1976): 195–98.

had long focused their efforts on attacking every vestige of paganism, it is difficult to understand why Zechariah would make such an overt parallel between a pagan mourning ritual and the appropriate sorrow felt by God's people for their role in the piercing of the Messiah.

A third interpretation treats Hadad Rimmon as a place name.[472] The suggestion makes sense in the context. Further, the qualifying phrase, "in the plain of Megiddo," may have differentiated one Hadad Rimmon from another, although this observation cannot be proven. Since King Josiah was slain in the valley of Megiddo (2 Kgs 23:28–30), a reference to the Megiddo valley might evoke powerful memories of profound national grief. The reference to mourning for the death of Josiah in 2 Chr 35:21–25 may add further significance to the mention of Megiddo, but this notion is conjectural.[473] Since no record of a place bearing this name survives, interpretative certainty remains out of reach. Nonetheless, the place name viewpoint offers the most promising solution.

**12:12–14** The introductory phrase "the land will mourn" receives magnification and clarification in vv. 12–14. The pericope stresses the totality of mourning in Judah, from the highest levels of society to the common people who comprise the majority of the population. Royalty, priests, women, and everyone else will bewail their sinfulness and unwillingness to repent beforehand.

Each clan will lament their culpability in the martyrdom of the pierced one. The phrases "their wives by themselves" and "their wives" do not indicate a cultural practice where women must mourn separately. Sweeney's suggestion to the contrary rests solely on biblical passages that simply list both male and female funerary singers without any indication that men and women mourned separately (2 Chr 35:25; see Ezek 32:16).[474] Rather, the repeated statements about the mourning women emphasize the sincerity of the grief. The lamentation thus grows out of deep grief, not an obligatory public expression of mourning as was the well known ancient Near Eastern practice.

The "house of David" refers to the entire dynastic line as it does in 12:7,8,10, but "the house of Nathan" represents one of the few questions in this section of chap. 12. The uncertainty arises from the number of individuals named Nathan in the Old Testament, numbering at least seven. Nathan the prophet offers an attractive option (2 Sam 11–12) since he would represent the prophetic tradition and their culpability for the sin against the Lord. However, nowhere in

---

[472] NJPS translates "at Hadad-rimmon." For a thorough survey of the development of this interpretation, see Mitchell, *Zechariah*, 332–33.

[473] For possible New Testament appropriation of Zech 12:11, see J. Day, "The Origin of Armageddon: Revelation 16:16 as an Interpretation of Zechariah 12:11," in *Crossing the Boundaries: Essays in Biblical Interpretation in Honour of Michael D. Goulder*, ed. S. E. Porter, P. Joyce, and D. E. Orton (Leiden: E. J. Brill, 1994), 315–26.

[474] Sweeney, *Twelve Prophets*, 691; Smith, *Micah-Malachi*, 277.

the Old Testament can one detect evidence of a prophetic dynasty.[475] Consequently, it is quite unlikely that a "house of Nathan" could signify Nathan the prophet. As a result, most conclude that Nathan in 12:12 refers to David's son (2 Sam 5:14; 1 Chr 3:5; cf. Luke 3:31).

"The house of Levi" (v. 13) represents the whole priestly clan in a similar way that "the house of David" stands for the entire royal line. Following this interpretation, the priests joined the royal house in conspiring against the martyr. The priests also served as accomplices with the king in their attack on Jeremiah (Jer 37:15; 38:4). Numbers 3:18 states that Levi had a son named Shimei, presumably the same individual mentioned here in v. 13. If "Nathan" in v. 12 speaks of David's son, then Zechariah lists two representatives of the royal line and two who stand for the priesthood in Judah.

Zechariah began his catalog of mourners with the royal line and the priests to charge these two groups with the greatest responsibility for the crime against the martyred Messiah. Yet despite the role the social leaders played in the death of the Messiah, Zechariah clearly stated that all in society bore responsibility for the deed. Unger concludes that "the sorrow will be for sin, and deep personal and national iniquity in putting to death the One who was resurrected and has the keys of hell and death."[476]

**13:1** Beginning with a promise, v. 1 extends hope to the nation for cleansing from sin. Like so many other eschatological passages in this section of the book of Zechariah, this verse begins with the phrase "on that day" *(bayyôm–hahûʾ)*. All people of the nation mourned their guilt in the crime against the pierced one and their Lord who had sent him. Verse 1 offers a miraculous cleansing from the Lord, the one against whom they had sinned. Zechariah's promise continues an earlier prophecy from Ezekiel: "I will sprinkle clean water on you, and you will be clean; I will cleanse you from all your impurities and from all your idols" (Ezek 36:25).

The prophet introduces the unmerited promise of divine cleansing by using an unusual metaphor, "a fountain" *(māqôr)*.[477] This term describes a source of water that flows unaided by human hands, more like an artesian well (Hos 13:15) than a fountain. From the beginnings of creation, rivers flowed from Eden, watering the garden. Flowing waters often symbolize the manifold blessings that the Lord showered on all of his creation.

The first occasion when God opened a fountain to cleanse sin is in Gen 7:11, although this passage differs linguistically as well as in the judgmental overtones of the passage. Various passages in the Torah mandate washing with water to accompany repentance and sacrifice for cleansing from impurity. Numbers 31:23 states, "And anything else that can withstand fire must be put

---

[475] Meyers and Meyers, *Zechariah 9–14*, 346.
[476] Unger, *Zechariah*, 219.
[477] מָקוֹר. *HALOT*, 627.

through the fire, and then it will be clean. But it must also be purified with the water of cleansing. And whatever cannot withstand fire must be put through the water" (cf. Num 8:7; 19:9–21). Later, Ezek 47:1–12 develops the theme of life-giving waters, describing a river flowing from the eschatological temple. Ezekiel's river gives life to all, including the fruit trees whose "fruit will serve for food and their leaves for healing" (Ezek 47:12b). Ezekiel's river envisions a time when God will restore the creation to its former pristine state, including the removal of the sin and concomitant impurity that stains every person.

Zechariah 13:1 does not state who "opened" the fountain, but the context suggests that the Lord himself performed this act on behalf of his people. The passive verb *niptāḥ* shifts the focus from the action of opening to the outcome of the action.[478] In other words, Zechariah emphasizes the effects of the gushing fountain in cleansing the people from their sin and washing it far from their presence.

The fountain will be opened for the benefit of the house of David and the inhabitants of Jerusalem, the recipients of Zechariah's message. Later biblical application of Zechariah's promised spring of salvation makes it clear that the cleansing spring will not only apply to Judah, but also to all who will stand in need of the Lord's gracious and miraculous offer of cleansing and spiritual restoration. Isaiah 12:2–3 looks forward to the joyous day when cleansing from sin can belong to God's people:

> "Surely God is my salvation;
>     I will trust and not be afraid.
> The LORD, the LORD, is my strength and my song;
>     he has become my salvation."
> With joy you will draw water
>     from the wells of salvation.

Zechariah's choice for a Hebrew word meaning "sin" was *ḥaṭṭaʾt*.[479] This term connotes missing the divine standard of holiness and serves as one of the most frequent words for sin or transgression in the Old Testament. This word refers to the active role that the people had in transgressing the Lord's righteousness.

The Hebrew word for "impurity" *(niddāh)* conveys a different point from *ḥaṭṭaʾt*.[480] The term *niddāh* focuses more on the outcome of sin, particularly the breach in the relationship between the sinner and the Lord (Lev 22:1–9; Num 19; Ezek 18:6; 22:10; 36:17). The word particularly focuses on the sinner's uncleanness that makes it impossible for him to approach God in worship because unholiness has rendered him unfit to sacrifice or even to come near the

---

[478] נִפְתָּח. *HALOT*,
[479] הַטָּאת. *HALOT*, 306. *TWOT*, 1:406–11 and *TDOT*, 4:309–19.
[480] נִדָּה. *HALOT*, 673.

temple. Thus, the term *niddāh* presents a complementary idea to *ḥaṭṭa't*, giving "the obverse and reverse of the same coin."[481] Unlike many Old Testament passages, the Lord decreed no punishment to accompany cleansing for sin. From the cleansing fountain flowed only grace, mercy, and forgiveness.

It was this same grace that moved the Lord to inaugurate the new covenant, an Old Testament covenant with such far reaching scope that it shaped the New Testament message. In 13:1 the cleansing from sin for God's people, along with spiritual restoration, reprises numerous themes found in Jer 31. For instance, the Lord promised forgiveness for the guilt produced by the people's rebellion against God: "For I will forgive their wickedness and will remember their sins no more" (Jer 31:34b; cf. Ezek 36:25; Zech 3:5). The shared emphasis on forgiveness via divine grace establishes a link with the new covenant. Other important new covenant themes that provide helpful background for Zech 13:1 include the knowledge of God's word and the will to obey it. Jeremiah 31:33b proclaims, "I will put my law in their minds and write it on their hearts." The similar theme occurs in Ezekiel: "I will give you a new heart and put a new spirit in you; I will remove from you your heart of stone and give you a heart of flesh" (Ezek 36:26). Another parallel includes the close fellowship between God and the people: "I will be their God, and they will be my people"; and "they will all know me, from the least of them to the greatest" (Jer 31:33b,34b).[482]

This passage concludes with the startling imagery of a fountain that cleanses from sin. It was this evocative imagery that moved William Cowper to pen "There Is a Fountain":

> There is a fountain filled with blood
> Drawn from Immanuel's veins;
> And sinners, plunged beneath that flood,
> Lose all their guilty stains.[483]

### 9. Idolatry and Judgment (13:2–6)

**²"On that day, I will banish the names of the idols from the land, and they will be remembered no more," declares the LORD Almighty. "I will remove both the prophets and the spirit of impurity from the land. ³And if anyone still prophesies, his father and mother, to whom he was born, will say to him, 'You must die, because you have told lies in the LORD's name.' When he prophesies, his own parents will stab him.**

**⁴"On that day every prophet will be ashamed of his prophetic vision. He will not put on a prophet's garment of hair in order to deceive. ⁵He will say, 'I am not a prophet. I am a farmer; the land has been my livelihood since my youth.' ⁶If**

---

[481] Merrill, *Zechariah*, 328.
[482] Barker, "Zechariah," 685.
[483] *The Baptist Hymnal*, # 142.

**someone asks him, 'What are these wounds on your body?' he will answer, 'The wounds I was given at the house of my friends.'**

A future kingdom characterized by "a spirit of grace and supplication" and cleansing "from sin and impurity" holds no place for idolatry and false prophecy. Both Jeremiah and Ezekiel devoted a significant portion of their ministries to confronting false prophecy. Jeremiah fought the prophets of Baal and those who embraced the prosperity theology of his day, the doctrine of the inviolability of Zion. The weeping prophet condemned false prophets for living hypocritically since "they commit adultery and live a lie" (Jer 23:14a). Likewise, in Ezek 13 and elsewhere the postexilic prophet attacked false prophets for misrepresenting the Lord and leading the people into a false sense of well being: "they lead my people astray, saying, 'Peace, when there is no peace.'" (v. 10a). Zechariah assumed his position alongside Jeremiah and Ezekiel in condemning the idolatry and false prophecy that persisted throughout the exilic and postexilic eras.

**13:2** In 10:2 Zechariah expressed disdain for the idols that "speak deceit," and in v. 3 he decried the unfaithful shepherds and the injuries they inflicted on the Lord's flock. In chap. 13 the prophet returns to the related topics of idolatry and false prophecy, declaring that "on that day" God will forever remove all vestiges of such falsehood from the land. This prophecy reprises Zechariah's earlier quotation from the Lord: "I will remove the sin of this land in a single day" (3:9). Although the metaphor of the cleansing fountain in 13:1 applies to the guilt staining those who killed the pierced one (12:10), the cleansing flood also washes away sin in the form of idolatry and false prophecy.

The biblical prophets gave particularly emphatic attention to the related problems of false prophecy and idolatry (Jer 23:13–14,30; 27:8–10; Ezek 13:1–14:11), rooting their divine instruction in the foundational Pentateuchal chapter denouncing both sins (see Deut 13). To any who might question the threat of false prophecy following the traumatic Babylonian exile, Neh 6:12–14 makes it clear that false prophecy remained a problem for Israel even in the postexilic era. Furthermore, the New Testament points out that false prophecy and idolatry do not belong to the Old Testament era alone, but will also serve as signs of the end of the age (Matt 24:4–5,11,23–24; 2 Thess 2:2–4; Rev 13:4–15).

"I will banish the names of the idols from the land" represents the Lord's first resolution. Like a persistent malignancy, idolatry resisted the efforts of the faithful remnant in the Old Testament to expunge it from the land. Moreover, the future kingdom of God over which the Messiah will rule righteously holds no room for false teachings about God. The first step, then, in the establishment of the righteous Messianic reign will be the removal of false teachings about the Lord. The elimination of falsehood will then pave the way for the positive institution of righteousness into God's creation, a state unknown since the time of the fall.

The Hebrew verb translated "banish" (*'akrît*) does indeed mean "to remove, banish," but the verb carries a deeper connotation obscured by the English translation.[484] The same verb also means "to cut," and functions throughout the Old Testament to express the inauguration of God's covenant with his people. The typical idiom meaning "to establish a covenant" literally translates *kārat 'et–bĕrît* ("to cut a covenant").[485] The word choice offers a not so subtle irony for Zechariah's audience. The common English expression, "the sword cuts both ways," touches the point of the irony. The "cut" that established the Lord's gracious covenant with his people would also "cut off" everyone who rejected the holiness of the God who had "cut" a covenant with Israel (Lev 7:20; Num 9:13; Isa 9:14).[486] Zechariah leaves no room for doubt concerning who will conduct this purge—the Lord himself will complete the task.

What does it mean to expunge the names of the idols? "To cut off" one's name is tantamount to utter destruction or even consigning someone to nonexistence. The destruction of Achan in Josh 7 illustrates the principle, where Achan, his whole family, and all his possessions were destroyed, so that nothing of him remained for posterity but a burial mound. The biblical text gives no quarter to polytheism or even henotheism, consistently declaring that only the Lord God, Creator of heaven and earth, is truly God. Any other so-called deity is a non-god that possesses no power whatever. Isaiah proclaimed this message as clearly as any other: "This is what the LORD says—Israel's King and Redeemer, the LORD Almighty, 'I am the first and I am the last; apart from me there is no God'" (Isa 44:6). In other words, the Old Testament does not merely affirm that the Lord is the most worthy God to worship: Scripture asserts that he is the only God who exists at all. To serve any other deity would be the height of folly.

Consequently, whatever power an idol "possesses" has been bestowed on it by a human. This artificial spiritual force allows the "idol" to exert influence over the idol worshipper, as well as on the rest of the society.[487] Further, since the name of beings, places, and things conveys meaning,[488] for an idol, the name carries claims about existence, personality, and deeds. Zechariah described the coming day when all of these vacuous projections onto mere objects will be stripped away, exposing the utter foolishness of giving obeisance to an idol.

---

[484] אַכְרִית. *HALOT*, 500–1.
[485] כָּרַת אֶת־בְּרִית. *TLOT*, 635–37.
[486] Merrill, *Zechariah*, 329.
[487] McComiskey, "Zechariah," 1220.
[488] *TLOT*, 1348–67.

The outcome of cutting off the names of idols is that "they will be remembered *[yizzākĕrû]* no more."⁴⁸⁹ The concept of remembering represents one of the most important theological motifs in the Old Testament. The command "Remember the Sabbath day" (Exod 20:8) requires that God's lordship over creation remain in the forefront of every heart and mind. Ecclesiastes 12:1 states a similar requirement more plainly: "remember your Creator." The siren songs of idols beckoning God's people to commit spiritual adultery will never be heard again. Indeed, they will not even be remembered.

Zechariah next turned his attention to the sister sin of idolatry, false prophecy. The phrase "spirit of impurity" (or "unclean spirit") occurs nowhere else in the Old Testament. The Hebrew word for "spirit" *(rûaḥ)* does not differentiate between an actual spirit, that is, a being influencing the people's improper behavior, and that of a mental outlook that led the people to listen to the lying prophets.⁴⁹⁰ Yet this spirit represents something unique, an "unclean spirit."⁴⁹¹ The Hebrew word for "uncleanness" or "impurity" *(haṭṭum'āh)* signifies one of the most pervasive theological concepts in the Old Testament.⁴⁹² The biblical understanding of uncleanness arises largely from Leviticus where the Torah delineates divine edicts concerning the manner in which God would allow his sinful creatures to approach him in worship. In Zech 13, the unclean nature of this "spirit" arises out of the theological lies and other sinful actions that the false prophets admonished their adherents to embrace. This sin surely rendered both leader and follower alike unclean before the Lord. The expression anticipates the similar idiom found frequently in the Gospels. Mark 1:23 describes the man in the synagogue with "an evil spirit" that Jesus drove out (cf. 3:11; 5:2).⁴⁹³

**13:3** The most compelling exegetical question arising in v. 3 is how false prophecy could appear in the land. After all, vv. 1–2 emphatically state that the Lord had cut off idols from the land so that they would be remembered no more. Further, God had removed the false prophets as well.⁴⁹⁴ Baldwin represents the viewpoint that the prevalence of idolatry and false prophecy throughout Israel's long history led Zechariah to contemplate its reemergence.⁴⁹⁵ Baldwin's claim is understandable in light of Israel's sordid history with idolatry, but it fails to account for Zechariah's declaration that idols "will be remembered no more" (13:2).

---

⁴⁸⁹ יִזָּכְרוּ. *HALOT*, 269–70; *TLOT*, 381–88.

⁴⁹⁰ רוּחַ. *HALOT*, 1197–1201; *TWOT*, 3:1202–20; *TDOT*, 13:361–402.

⁴⁹¹ Lange's suggestion that "the spirit of impurity" refers to an actual demon lacks supporting evidence ("Considerations Concerning the 'Spirit of Impurity' in Zech 13:2," in *Die Dämonen/ Demons*, ed. A. Laupe, H. Lichtenberger, K. F. D. Römheld [Tübingen: Mohr Siebeck, 2003], 264–65).

⁴⁹² הַטֻּמְאָה. *HALOT*, 375–76; *TDOT*, 5:330–42; *TLOT*, 495–97.

⁴⁹³ ἐν πνεύματι ἀκαθάρτῳ.

⁴⁹⁴ Meyers and Meyers, *Zechariah 9–14*, 373.

⁴⁹⁵ Baldwin, *Zechariah*, 196.

Another interpretation better fits the theme of ultimate divine banishment of idolatry and false prophecy in the future kingdom (see v. 2). Simply put, if the Lord puts an end to falsehood *(šeqer)*, then such lying and deceit will indeed cease.[496] Accordingly, the discussion in v. 3 is best understood as a hypothetical scenario that stresses the certainty, the absolute finality, and the demise of every form of theological heresy. Hosea 9:11b-12a presents a similar, contrary to fact argument: "no birth, no pregnancy, no conception. Even if they rear children, I will bereave them of every one." McComiskey explains, "Should a lying prophet arise (but none will), his parents will pierce him through. Nothing will stand in the way of the complete elimination of false prophecy—not even an emotion as strong as parental love."[497]

Public opinion in Israel rarely condemned idolatry with rigor or consistency. It was usually considered satisfactory to offer perfunctory service to the Lord, even if one also worshipped idols. Syncretism became the norm throughout much of the history of Israel, even though the Lord always strictly forbade such worship (Exod 20:1-6; see Ezek 13:7).[498] Judah evidenced an equally lax attitude toward false prophecy throughout its history. But in the coming kingdom, such accommodation to falsehood will never be tolerated. Zechariah promised that God's people will respond to sin so emphatically that even the offender's parents will both testify against their offending children and execute their offspring for idolatry.

The parents' reaction to their child's illegal prophecy will be twofold. First, the parents will testify against him (cf. Deut 21:18-21). The emphatic direct speech, "You must die because you have told lies in the LORD's name," attests to their firm resolve to obey God first.[499] Further, Zechariah's citation of the parents' testimony for the prosecution underscores the seriousness of the charge. If the parents with all of their emotional attachments to their offspring will testify for the prosecution in a capital case, surely their testimony must be true. One would assume that family members would be the last members of society to accept the guilt of their loved one.[500] If even the family acknowledges the accuracy of the evidence against their loved one, who could rebut the evidence? Additionally, testimony from the parents underscores the gravity of the charge of idolatry in the view of the society in the eschatological future.

The second parental response to false prophecy incorporates their participation in the execution itself. The involvement of the family again emphasizes both the certainty and the magnitude of the charges against the false prophet.

---

[496] שֶׁקֶר. *HALOT*, 1648-50.
[497] McComiskey, "Zechariah," 1220.
[498] Mitchell, *Zechariah*, 338.
[499] Meyers and Meyers, *Zechariah 9-14*, 374.
[500] Sweeney, *Twelve Prophets*, 693.

In v. 3 the NIV translates *dāqārû* as "stab" and thus obscures the connection to the same verb in 12:10 ("pierce").[501] This judicial action follows the general guidelines in Deut 13 where family members assist in the execution of the offender. The means of execution is different in Deut 13:10 (stoning). The difference in modes of execution is not arbitrary, for the change lays the foundation for an important theological message. The word *dāqārû* in 13:3 forms a literary relationship with the *dāqārû* of the Messiah in 12:10. The pierced one in 12:10 deserved honor but received the ultimate expression of disrespect—execution. The malefactor in 13:3 also suffered piercing, but he deserved his punishment. Thus, the eschatological perspective of 13:3 paints a profoundly different picture, one where everyone in the kingdom will place the highest value on faithfulness to the Lord. The people's violence, which was shameful when wrongly directed against the righteous Messiah, will be rightly directed against one who deserves such severe judgment. Deuteronomy 13 views false prophecy as a test of the entire society's devotion to the Lord, even that of the offender's immediate family, stating, "The LORD your God is testing you to find out whether you love him with all your heart and with all your soul. It is the LORD your God you must follow, and him you must revere" (Deut 13:3–4a; cf. 18:9–22; 21:18–21). Without a doubt, "on that day" God's people will revere the Lord their God and will value their relationship with God more than that of any other.

**13:4** This verse begins with the familiar reference to the eschatological era, "on that day" *(bayyôm–hahû᾿)*. This temporal clause does not appear again in chap. 13. The coming kingdom will see the Lord cleanse his people from sin and expunge every vestige of idolatry and false prophecy. Consigning false prophecy to its deserved end requires dealing with the false prophets themselves.

In the coming age the false prophets will be ashamed of their deeds in misrepresenting the righteous Lord and in misleading God's people. The word "ashamed" *(yēbōšû)* describes the prophets' attitude toward their earlier deeds.[502] Only Zech 13:4 and Mic 3:7 use this verb to describe despicable prophetic actions. Micah 3:7 states,

> The seers will be ashamed
> and the diviners disgraced.
> They will all cover their faces
> because there is no answer from God.

Jeremiah 22:22 expresses a similar sentiment, albeit with differing idioms.

These false prophets will be ashamed of their prior "prophetic visions." This shame reflects their deep desire that their evil actions remain hidden,[503] but the

---

[501] דְּקָרֻו. *HALOT*, 230.
[502] יֵבֹשׁוּ. *HALOT*, 116–17.
[503] Merrill, *Zechariah*, 331.

false prophets' response does not constitute a repentant attitude. Unger gives no support for his optimistic claim, "the false prophet shall be deeply convicted of his deceptive 'oracle or prophecy' " and "the false prophet shall also be abashed with guilt concerning the deception he has practiced."[504] These prophets' willingness to lie about their prior misdeeds (vv. 5–6) manifests their deepest intentions in removing their prophetic robes. Eschewing their days of glory, they exchanged their prophetic mantles that had symbolized their fame, in the hopes of fading into obscurity and thus avoiding the punishment they so deserved.

In an attempt to escape the death penalty, these frauds would cease clothing themselves with the "garment of hair" (*'adderet sēʿār*), the attire that publicly set prophets apart.[505] The term *'adderet* ("garment, mantle") can also mean "splendor" or "wealth." One encounters a non-theological usage of the term when Achan stole a valuable Babylonian mantle from Shinar (Josh 7:21,24). For the genuine prophet, the distinctive splendor of the *'adderet* would be appropriate attire in light of the prophet's exalted position as God's spokesman. In the Old Testament, the word *'adderet* is best known for its association with the prophetic ministries of Elijah and Elisha. Elijah used his mantle to part the Jordan river (2 Kgs 2:8), a deed repeated by Elisha (2:14). As an additional example of the importance of the mantle, when Elijah transferred his own prophetic office to Elisha and ascended to heaven, the young prophet clothed himself with the mantle that had belonged to his elder, symbolizing the importance of the divine office (1 Kgs 19:13,19; 2 Kgs 2:8,13–14).[506] Following in Elijah's prophetic tradition, John the Baptist clothed himself in a mantle of camel hair (Matt 3:4), though Elijah's mantle was not described as "hairy."

The only passage that contains the identical phrase *'adderet sēʿār* "garment of hair" (that is, a "fur coat") is Gen 25:25 to describe Esau's hairy body at birth. The reference to Esau's hairy body played a significant role in Jacob's deception of his blind father Isaac. This combination of motifs—the "hairy garment" and the ignominious deception by individuals holding one of the most trusted and esteemed offices in the land—links Gen 25 with Zech 13:4. Sweeney expands on this observation: "The use of this tradition in Zechariah is clearly intended to demonstrate that a trusted figure, such as a prophet, might deceive just as the patriarch Jacob deceived his father Isaac. In order to make this point, it draws upon a tradition in which even a figure like Jacob, the eponymous ancestor of Israel, can represent a figure worthy of punishment."[507]

The final clause makes the motivation of the false prophets clear beyond doubt; the seers intended to "deceive" *(kaḥēš)* Judah.[508] As employed in v. 4,

---

[504] Unger, *Zechariah*, 226.
[505] אַדֶּרֶת שֵׂעָר. *HALOT*, 17, 1344–45.
[506] Meyers and Meyers, *Zechariah 9–14*, 379.
[507] Sweeney, *Twelve Prophets*, 694; cf. Meyers and Meyers, *Zechariah 9–14*, 379.
[508] כָּחֵשׁ. *HALOT*, 469–70.

this verb means "to tell lies to someone" (see 1 Kgs 13:18). These charlatan prophets were like "wolves in sheep's clothing," willfully desiring to mislead God's people and persuading them that they were authentic men of God.

**13:5–6** Verse 4 reveals the false prophets' attempt to conceal their past actions by removing the official attire of the prophetic office. In vv. 5–6 they continue their charade with the verbal equivalent of taking off their prophetic mantles, the disavowal that they ever served in a prophetic role. Whenever it will better serve their personal interests, a common theme in Zechariah's excoriation of false prophets, they would not hesitate to lie. These evil men will seek to hide among the humblest individuals in society by pretending to be something they are not, a role they have had great experience in playing.[509]

The false prophets adopted traditional prophetic language to deny their prior activities, drawing from the language of Amos, who told Amaziah, priest at Bethel, "I was neither a prophet nor a prophet's son, but I was a shepherd, and I also took care of sycamore-fig trees" (7:14). Amos meant that when God called him he was neither already a prophet *(nābî')* nor the "son of a prophet" *(ben–nābî')*, the latter commonly understood to mean that he did not belong to a prophetic guild.[510]

Zechariah 13:5 represents the first intertextual interpretation of Amos 7:14.[511] Zechariah cited the first portion of Amos's statement precisely, "I am not a prophet," while offering a simplified job description for the false prophets in the second half of the verse. Amos associated himself with agrarian life, intending to underscore the validity of his prophetic message. In an ironic twist, the false prophet's allusion to Amos 7:14 in Zech 13:5 emphasizes "the false prophet's lack of credibility" since he cannot be trusted to speak truthfully.[512]

The rather neutral sounding phrase "I am a farmer" *('ānōkî 'îš–'ōbēd 'ǎdāmāh)* also carries significant connotations.[513] The first occurrence of this expression is Gen 2:5,15; 3:23 where *'ōbēd 'ǎdāmāh* describes the human responsibility to till the soil. More importantly, the same idiom identifies Cain's occupation (Gen 4:2). Since Cain ultimately murdered his brother Abel, Zechariah's use of the same language "reinforces the portrayal of false prophets as despicable characters worthy of punishment."[514]

Although the general meaning of v. 5b reads clearly, the precise nuance of the Hebrew text has elicited extensive discussion over the centuries. A perusal of English translations illustrates the point. The NRSV reads, "the land has been my possession," but the Masoretic Text is literally, "I was made a

---

[509] Mitchell, *Zechariah*, 338.
[510] בֶּן־נָבִיא. *HALOT*, 661–62.
[511] Å. Viberg, "Amos 7:14: A Case of Subtle Irony," *TynBul* 47 (1996): 108.
[512] Sweeney, *Twelve Prophets*, 694.
[513] אָנֹכִי אִישׁ־עֹבֵד אֲדָמָה. *HALOT*, 773–74, 15.
[514] Sweeney, *Twelve Prophets*, 695.

bondman" or "a man acquired me" *('ādām hiqnanî)*.⁵¹⁵ Meyers and Meyers confidently maintain that "the Hebrew text of this verse is corrupt."⁵¹⁶ The perceived awkwardness of the Hebrew text has led many scholars to suggest numerous emendations over the years. The most widely accepted emendation reads, *'ădāmāh qinyānî* ("the land is my possession").⁵¹⁷ A Targumic variant has attested the same reading as the emendation.⁵¹⁸ Nonetheless, the Masoretic reading makes sense, with claims of its awkwardness being exaggerated.⁵¹⁹ Accordingly, the false prophets assert that they have always worked as farmers, becoming indentured starting when they were young.⁵²⁰ The allusion to the earliest years of their working life attempts to preclude any possibility that they ever held a prophetic office, whether genuine or false.⁵²¹

Mitchell introduces the theme of v. 6 in particularly powerful fashion: "A cowering wretch has been accused by an indignant mob of being a false prophet."⁵²² Clothed with the attire of common laborers, the false prophets find it difficult to obscure their former activities. Perhaps when the charlatans stripped to work in the fields the wounds that testified to their prophetic activities condemned them. The accusatory question, "What are these wounds on your body?" sought to disclose the prophets' true identity. This question holds the potential both to reveal the imposters as false prophets and to catch them in an outright lie. The connection between physical injuries or scars and false prophets requires examination.

Zechariah's expression "wounds on your body" merits scrutiny. The word "wounds" *(hammakkôt)* is a general term for "injuries" (1 Kgs 22:35; Isa 1:6).⁵²³ Canaanite religious rites included various expressions of self mutilation. The clearest biblical example of these practices appears in the contest between Elijah and the prophets of Baal on Mount Carmel (1 Kgs 18). At the height of the religious frenzy, the Baal worshippers "shouted louder and slashed themselves with swords and spears, as was their custom, until the blood flowed" (1 Kgs 18:28). Leviticus 19:28 and Deut 14:1 explicitly forbid any such behavior by the divine rationale, "I am the LORD." The Mount Carmel episode suggests that the fervent self wounding hoped to impress the deity with the worshipper's devotion and to move the god to act as requested. The pagan background to Zech 13:6 suggests that self mutilation characterized false

---

⁵¹⁵ אָדָם הִקְנַנִי. *HALOT*, 1113.
⁵¹⁶ Meyers and Meyers, *Zechariah 9–14*, 381.
⁵¹⁷ אֲדָמָה קִנְיָנִי. Mitchell, *Zechariah*, 340.
⁵¹⁸ R. P. Gordon, "Targum Variant Agrees With Wellhausen!" *ZAW* 87 (1975): 218–19.
⁵¹⁹ Although the Septuagint ὅτι ἄνθρωπος ἐγέννησέν με ἐκ νεότητός μου apparently attempted to smooth the Masoretic reading somewhat, it does appear that the Hebrew *Vorlage* of the Greek translation read a causative verb as occurs in the MT.
⁵²⁰ Merrill, *Zechariah*, 333; McComiskey, "Zechariah," 1221; and Unger, *Zechariah*, 227.
⁵²¹ McComiskey, "Zechariah," 1220–21.
⁵²² Mitchell, *Zechariah*, 339.
⁵²³ הַמַּכּוֹת. *HALOT*, 579.

prophets. Thus, when these wounds would become visible to their neighbors, the false prophets could hide their true identity no longer.[524]

The words "on your body" *(bên yādeykā)* translate literally as "between your hands,"[525] which has also engendered significant discussion. The same expression occurs in 2 Kgs 9:24 to describe the location of the wound on Joram's body where Jehu shot him with an arrow (NIV "between the shoulders"). The equivalent idiom appears in the Ugaritic literature to describe the center of the torso, the place where the Canaanite deity Yam received a blow.[526]

The charlatans' feeble reply contends that the false prophets had received their wounds "at the house of my friends." One interpretation of the dialogue claims that the attempt to give a believable alibi might suggest that the wounds resulted from a brawl.[527] But this explanation raises the additional question about the quality of the friends the false prophets claimed. Furthermore, the Hebrew word for "friends" is *mĕ'ahăbāy*, often translated "lovers."[528] The expression sometimes refers to an adulterous relationship (Jer 22:20; Ezek 16:33; Hos 2:7), but in this passage it must mean "friends" or "companions."[529] The word *mĕ'ahăbāy* is used to refer to companions in idolatrous or false prophetic practices (Hos 2:7,10; Ezek 23:5,9),[530] but it would be incomprehensible for individuals who are attempting to persuade others that they are not false prophets to intend such a nuance.

The reply from the false prophets contains its own ironies, and offers such an unlikely explanation that it raises its own questions. The inept answer highlights the image of the false prophets as deceptive persons who cannot even lie persuasively and who will not escape the punishment their sinful deceit richly deserved.[531] On a broader theological level, the unbelievable story recounted by the false prophets reveals the inherent flaws and weaknesses in the false prophetic movement in Judah during the postexilic epoch.[532]

Unger's Messianic interpretation is profoundly different from the others and deserves examination.[533] Unger contends that v. 6 does not refer to false prophets, but to the Messiah. He argues that the entire section focuses on national cleansing for Israel, and that the antecedent of the pronoun "him" in v. 6 is "the one they have pierced" (12:10). Not surprisingly, Unger places great emphasis on the wounds in v. 6. Furthermore, he reinterprets the preposition "between"

---

[524] Petersen, *Zechariah 9–14*, 35.
[525] בֵּין יָדֶיךָ. *HALOT*, 123, 386–88.
[526] *UT*, § 68.14, 16. In this text the idiom *bn ydm* ("between the hands") parallels the plain meaning of the noun *ktp* ("shoulder").
[527] Baldwin, *Zechariah*, 197.
[528] מְאַהֲבַי. *HALOT*, 18.
[529] McComiskey, "Zechariah," 1221; see Mason, *Zechariah*, 122.
[530] Meyers and Meyers, *Zechariah 9–14*, 383; Baldwin, *Zechariah*, 197.
[531] Sweeney, *Twelve Prophets*, 695.
[532] McComiskey, "Zechariah," 1221.
[533] Unger, *Zechariah*, 227–30.

*(bēn)* to mean "in" or "on." Unger views these wounds as a prophecy about the wounds the Messiah, Jesus Christ, will bear when crucified. Citing John 20:25,27–28, Unger points to the wounds on Christ's hands.[534]

Few have accepted Unger's interpretation, even among those with strong affinities to Unger's theological positions. Although deeply influenced by Unger in innumerable ways, Barker bluntly deems Unger's arguments "weak, forced, irrelevant, or debatable."[535] Dodd notes that the New Testament never connected the crucifixion of Jesus with the prophecy in Zech 13:6, although later Christian tradition sometimes did.[536] Perhaps the most serious flaw to the Messianic interpretation is taking the antecedent to "him" in v. 6 back to the pierced one, skipping the most obvious antecedents in the nearest context in the process. Pronouns in Biblical Hebrew routinely refer to antecedents in their immediate context, not more remote nouns without clear indication to the contrary. Similarly, Unger's attempt to reinterpret the phrase "between the hands" lacks biblical evidence to corroborate his view. Consequently, the Messianic view does not merit acceptance.

Verses 2–6 present an outright assault on idolatry and false prophecy, cautioning Zechariah's contemporaries not to extend any hope to anything or anyone other than the Lord himself. One cannot reduce Zechariah's predicted judgment against false prophets merely to an attack on a supposed Jerusalem hegemony.[537] Nor does Zechariah declare that all prophecy will cease. Instead, in predicting the future demise of false prophecy, he warns the nation not to heed the words of anyone other than the Lord or his emissaries until the day when all falsehood ceases.

### 10. Shepherd Struck; Judgment, Purification, and Return to God (13:7–9)

> **⁷"Awake, O sword, against my shepherd,**
> **against the man who is close to me!"**
> **declares the Lord Almighty.**
> **"Strike the shepherd,**
> **and the sheep will be scattered,**
> **and I will turn my hand against the little ones.**
> **⁸In the whole land," declares the Lord,**
> **"two-thirds will be struck down and perish;**
> **yet one-third will be left in it.**

---

[534] See H. L. Ginsberg, "The Oldest Record of Hysteria with Physical Stigmata, Zech 13:2–6," in *Studies in the Bible and Ancient Near East*, ed. Y. Avishur and J. Blau (Jerusalem: E. Rubenstein, 1978), 23–27.

[535] Barker, "Zechariah," 686.

[536] Dodd, *According to the Scriptures*, 65.

[537] P. L. Redditt, "Israel's Shepherds: Hope and Pessimism in Zechariah 9–14." *CBQ* 51 (1989): 631–42; cf. Robert Rhea, "Attack on Prophecy, Zechariah 13, 1–6," *ZAW* 107 (1995): 292–93.

⁹"This third I will bring into the fire;
   I will refine them like silver
   and test them like gold.
They will call on my name
   and I will answer them;
I will say, 'They are my people,'
   and they will say, 'The LORD is our God.'"

Zechariah 13:7–9 presents three developing themes. Verse 7 treats the assault of the sword against the Lord's shepherd. The next verse examines the suffering the flock will experience as a consequence of the shepherd's fate. Finally, v. 9 concludes the chapter with themes of purification and restoration. The chapter closes as it began, focusing on the purification that the Lord will offer to his people.[538] These three grand prophecies will see their fulfillment in an eschatological age, like many other predictions from this section of Zechariah. In the structure of the book, this section picks up the themes of 12:10–13:1. The striking of the shepherd in v. 7 calls to mind the pierced one in 12:10, and the refining in v. 9 is similar to the cleansing in 13:1.

**13:7** This verse contains numerous difficult interpretative issues that have challenged students of the text for centuries. Perhaps no question surpasses that of the identity of the shepherd. One's view of the shepherd influences the understanding of the striking of the shepherd as well as the scattering of the sheep. Moreover, the interpretation of the shepherd shapes whether one attempts to move 13:7–8 from its present canonical setting to follow the previous shepherd oracle concluding in 11:17. Finally, the significance of turning the hand "against the little ones" also offers difficulties.

The verse begins with an apostrophe (a rhetorical device where a speaker digresses by addressing a personified object) in which the Lord addresses the sword *(ḥereb)*.[539] The sword functions as a metonymy for the death accomplished by the sword. In Ps 22:20 the sword represents a violent end to one's life. Jeremiah 47:6–7 employs the sword imagery similarly:

"'Ah, sword of the LORD,' you cry
   'how long till you rest?
Return to your scabbard;
   cease and be still.'
But how can it rest
   when the LORD has commanded it,
   when he has ordered it to attack Ashkelon and the coast?"

The Lord commands the sword to "awake" *('ûrî)*, a verb not otherwise associated with a sword in the Old Testament.[540] However, a similar use of the verb

---
[538] Merrill, *Zechariah*, 335.
[539] חֶרֶב. *HALOT*, 349–50.
[540] עוּרִי. *HALOT*, 802–3.

"awake" occurs in Isa 51:9: "Awake, awake! Clothe yourself with strength, O arm of the LORD." The employment of the sword as an offensive, not defensive, weapon is made clear by the use of the verb "strike." God himself will wield this sword of judgment. The text does not indicate that the shepherd dies, but the conclusion is inescapable.

Zechariah continued to reprise the shepherd motif, using the familiar word *rō'eh*, which frequently serves as a metaphor for the king of Israel.[541] Even though the term "shepherd" does not appear explicitly in 12:1–13:6, the matter of leadership remains in the forefront of this section of the book.[542] Since the Lord speaks throughout v. 7, the antecedent to the pronoun "my" in the phrase "my shepherd" refers to none other than God. As a result, the idiom *"my shepherd"* sets this divinely ordained monarch apart because of his special connection to God. No ordinary leader, this shepherd serves as the Lord's special representative on earth, doing God's bidding by advancing his kingdom. The title "my shepherd" *(rō'î)* also applies to Cyrus (Isa 44:28).[543] Cyrus's momentous assignment from God was to release Judah from her exile and to resettle her in the promised land with material resources and protection to rebuild Zion.

While the pronoun alone does not convey messianic significance, nonetheless Zechariah sought to set the shepherd in v. 7 apart from other shepherds in a truly unique fashion with the following phrase. The prophet further enhanced the status of the shepherd with the phrase "the man who is close to me." The Hebrew words *geber 'ămîtî* occur elsewhere in the Old Testament only in Lev 6:2; 18:20.[544] The Hebrew word for "man" *(geber)* connotes someone who is young and strong (Prov 30:19). The term translated "close to me" *('amîtî)* conveys a far more significant theological point. The expression stresses community or close association with someone. In v. 7, *'amîtî* paints a uniquely intimate relationship with the Lord himself.

Interpreters do not always agree on the theological significance of the shepherd's close association with the Lord.[545] Many suggest that the phrase means that the shepherd is the Lord's equal.[546] The word "peer" communicates the idea of closeness well in modern parlance. This understanding also elevates the importance of the question of the identity of the shepherd. The theme of God's shepherd who enjoys close association with the Lord grows out of the biblical message that the individual so chosen by God was the Lord's "son" (2 Sam 7:14; Pss 2:7; 89:26–27).[547]

---

[541] רָעָה. *HALOT*, 1260–61; *TLOT*, 1248.

[542] Barker, "Zechariah," 686.

[543] רֹעִי.

[544] גֶּבֶר עֲמִיתִי. *HALOT*, 175–76, 845.

[545] Mason's contention that Zechariah's use of עֲמִיתִי is "ironic" does not make sense in light of the positive presentation of the shepherd in chap. 13, including the shepherd's close relationship to the Lord (*Zechariah*, 111).

[546] Baldwin, *Zechariah*, 198.

[547] Sweeney, *Twelve Prophets*, 696.

Several factors also indicate that the shepherd in v. 7 is none other than the pierced one in 12:10. One of the more important points is the uniquely close association between God and the shepherd. Further, both figures in 12:10 and 13:7 serve God faithfully, and the death of both evokes mourning. The New Testament's appropriation of 13:7 also seems to ratify this identification. In Matt 26:31 and Mark 14:27 Jesus quoted Zech 13:7, clearly equating himself with the "shepherd" in Zechariah. Jesus employed Zech 13:7 to predict and to explain the scattering of his disciples when his crucifixion was drawing near.

Consequently, Barker takes "close to me" as a reference to Christ, citing John 10:30, "I and the Father are one," along with John 14:9, "Anyone who has seen me has seen the Father."[548] In the broader context of chaps. 12–13, this unity presents forgiveness and restoration as its aim. McComiskey states, "This discourse contains strong implications that the relationship between the Lord and the shepherd is one of cooperative redemption, for the restoration of God's people does not occur apart from the intervention of one who suffers the shedding of blood."[549] Unger calls this prophecy "an unmistakable Old Testament reference to the deity of the Coming One, the Lord's Shepherd."[550]

A significant question remains: How can the Lord summon the sword to execute his "equal"? Although Zechariah never explicitly identified his shepherd with Isaiah's servant, it appears quite likely that Zechariah had the Isaianic passage in mind.[551] God's judgment on the servant in Isa 53 provides insight into the question. Verse 10 says,

> Yet it was the LORD's will to crush him and cause him to suffer,
>   and though the Lord makes his life a guilt offering,
> he will see his offspring and prolong his days,
>   and the will of the LORD will prosper in his hand.

God commands the sword to "strike the shepherd." The shepherd in 13:7 should be identified with the pierced one in 12:10 as well as with the Isaianic servant.[552] Ultimately, Jesus Christ interpreted the "shepherd" in 13:7 to refer to himself (Matt 26:31). Consequently, it is difficult to view Zechariah's prophecy otherwise. The fact that Jesus was killed by crucifixion, not the sword, presents no difficulty in light of the metaphorical use of "sword."

Zechariah states, "Strike the shepherd and the sheep will be scattered."[553] Surprisingly, the attention turns away from the anticipated comment concerning

---

[548] Barker, "Zechariah," 686.
[549] McComiskey, "Zechariah," 1223.
[550] Unger, Zechariah, 231.
[551] Baldwin, Zechariah, 198.
[552] McComiskey, "Zechariah," 1223.
[553] In Zech 13:7 the imperative "strike" (הַךְ. HALOT, 697–98) is a masculine verb, although the word "sword" is feminine (the imperative "awake" is feminine). Perhaps this shift of gender occurs because the Lord wields the sword (Barker, "Zechariah," 686). But the change may reflect no more than Biblical Hebrew's inconsistency in maintaining gender agreement (GKC § 144 a).

the result of the sword's attack on the shepherd. Instead, Zechariah focused on the outcome for the sheep. This sheep metaphor found commonly in the book draws from the extended sheep and shepherd metaphor in Ezek 34, although the exilic prophet certainly drew from earlier theological uses of this metaphor also. The motif of a divinely ordained scattering goes back as far as the sobering catalog of covenant curses for disobedience to the Lord in Deut 28. Verse 26 warns, "Then the LORD will scatter you among the nations, from one end of the earth to the other."

The work of the sword will result in the scattering of the sheep (Jer 49:20; 50:45). Just as the nation found itself without effective leadership during the exile, so will the people find themselves in like circumstances in the coming day of judgment. Israel will face scattering because of her rejection of the Lord's shepherd. However, Israel's refinement promised in vv. 8–9 places the ultimate fulfillment of the prophecy in a distant eschatological epoch.

Verse 7 concludes with an enigmatic phrase: "I will turn my hand against the little ones." The words "to turn the hand to/against" *(šûb yād ʿal)* may have either positive (Isa 1:25) or negative import (Ezek 38:12).[554] Some understand this phrase as a positive assertion of the Lord's resolve to protect the defenseless in society.[555] McComiskey defends this position, arguing that if the Lord decimated the young in the flock, that is, the next generation, then God's people would have no future whatever, so it cannot mean that—rather, God will protect the young.[556] But this positive interpretation does not fit within a passage that otherwise expresses forceful judgment from the Lord.

Even if one understands God's turning his hand "against the little ones" as an expression of hostile intent, the phrase does not necessarily suggest that the Lord will annihilate the young. If the preposition ʿal functions adversatively here (meaning "against"),[557] this prophecy is negative, the declaration of unfortunate, but necessary, suffering that lies in the future.[558] But this suffering will refine the people like precious metals (v. 9).

Finally, the complex relationship between the shepherd struck by the sword and the false shepherd merits discussion. First, some scholars such as Redditt argue that the shepherds in both 11:1–17 and 13:7–9 represent evil leaders.[559] The argument Redditt offers is rather convoluted and not widely accepted in the broader scholarly community.[560] Redditt's perspective rests on complicated conjectures about the pre-history of these passages, including the as-

---

[554] שׁוּב יָד עַל. Cf. McComiskey, 1223–24.
[555] P. Lamarche, *Zacharie IX–XIV* (Paris: Librairie Lecoffre, 1961), 92.
[556] McComiskey, "Zechariah," 1224.
[557] GKC, § 119 dd. Mitchell, *Zechariah*, 317.
[558] Sweeney, *Twelve Prophets*, 696.
[559] Redditt, "Israel's Shepherds," 632, 639.
[560] S. L. Cook, "The Metamorphosis of a Shepherd: The Tradition History of Zechariah 11:17 + 13:7–9." *CBQ* 55 (1993): 453–54.

sumption of differing authors for each passage, followed by multiple layers of redactional activities in shaping the passages.

Merrill rejects Redditt's assumptions about the tradition history of Zech 13. Somewhat surprisingly, however, he comes to similar conclusions about the nature of the shepherd. Merrill sees the individual whom God deems "my shepherd" in exclusively human terms, rejecting any association with the pierced one in 12:10 or the Messiah.[561] While Merrill acknowledges the Messianic significance of 12:10, he claims that any connection between the shepherd in 13:7 and Isa 53:10 "seems wide of the mark."[562] Although he acknowledges the New Testament's use of 13:7, Merrill offers no support for positing a distinction between the shepherd and Isaiah's servant.

Contrary to Merrill's claim though, the servant in Isaiah 53 and the shepherd in Zech 13 share much in common. Both suffer because it was the Lord's will for them to do so. Both experience death wrongfully and evoke sorrow and consternation among the people for the wrong done to them. Most importantly, both figures suffer in order to effect purification for sins. The result of the suffering of the servant and the shepherd will bring great benefit to God's people. Although v. 7 states this point somewhat more obliquely than Isa 53:10, Zech 13:7 does indeed affirm purification for God's people. The text says "strike the shepherd . . . *that* the sheep will be scattered" (13:7), where the conjunction *waw* introduces a purpose clause.[563] Verse 9 clearly indicates God's purpose for the shepherd's suffering and the scattering of the sheep. The Lord states, "I will refine them like silver." Further, Merrill discounts the import of the Lord's statement that the shepherd is "close to" God, that is a "peer." The language Zechariah employed does not comport well with a mere human monarch. The close associate or peer suggests more than an unknown, unnamed human associate. Rather, the term points to the coming Messiah.

However tenuous Redditt's conclusions about the character of the shepherd in chap. 13 are, the possibility of a literary connection between the accounts of the two shepherds in chaps. 11 and 13 remain. Ever since Ewald's suggestion in 1840, numerous scholars have concluded that 13:7–9 originally followed 11:17.[564] It is not uncommon to find commentaries that propose moving 13:7–9 and provide comments on the final three verses of chap. 13 at the conclusion of the discussion on chap. 11.

Cook summarizes the arguments for moving 13:7–9, which include the following: (1) "the form of Zech 13:7–9 stands out as peculiar within Zech 12–14"; (2) "it is more poetic than are the chapters which surround it"; and (3) "the

---

[561] Merrill, *Zechariah*, 334–35, 337.
[562] Ibid., 321–22, 337.
[563] Joüon-Muraoka, *Grammar*, § 116 c; cf. *IBHS*, 39.2.2 a.
[564] Mitchell, *Zechariah*, 254–55; Rudolph, *Sacharja 9–14*, 227; Hanson, *Dawn of Apocalyptic*, 338–39.

pericope seems misplaced."[565] The subjectivity of this evidence is manifest. Cook wisely cautions against the rush to move 13:7–9. He notes that very limited evidence actually supports viewing 11:1–17 and 13:7–9 as originally constituting a unified poetic oracle. Cook further observes that the thematic differences between the two passages are far more expansive than have been acknowledged.[566] He concludes: "Since the shepherd's death in these verses, thus interpreted, appears as a tragedy to be mourned, the figure's identity as a good shepherd is indicated."[567] Thus 11:1–17 pertains to the bad shepherd while 13:7–9 refers to the Good Shepherd.

The New Testament and Jewish history in the first century AD provide important clues to the fulfillment of this prophecy. One should anticipate the close biblical connection between the shepherd in Zech 13 and Jesus' portrayal of himself as a shepherd of God's flock. After surveying a large crowd gathered to hear him teach, Jesus lamented that the people were like sheep in desperate need of a shepherd (Mark 6:34). R. T. France concludes that Zech 13:7 apparently influenced Jesus' teaching more than any other shepherd text in the Old Testament.[568] For him, John 10:1–16, where Jesus gave a fuller explanation of his role as shepherd, demonstrates the accuracy of his observation about the influential role 13:7 held. Jesus declared, "I am the good shepherd" (John 10:10,14). Unlike the faithless, worthless shepherd in 11:17, Jesus promised that he would "lay down his life for the sheep" (John 10:15).

The suffering of Jesus' family and followers also illustrates the point of scattering the sheep in 13:7 (Luke 2:35). Additionally, shortly before his arrest and crucifixion, Jesus cited the end of Zech 13:7: " 'You will all fall away,' Jesus told them, 'for it is written: "I will strike the shepherd, and the sheep will be scattered" ' " (Mark 14:27; cf. Matt 26:31).[569] In Matt 26:56 Jesus explained the desertion by his disciples with Zechariah's prophecy. In addition to the application of 13:7 in the Gospels, the destruction of Jerusalem and the ensuing Diaspora at the hands of the Roman emperor Titus in AD 70 represents a subsequent fulfillment of v. 7. Further, the pains the Church will experience in the end times (Mark 13:19,24; Rev 11:3–10) may also relate to Zech 13:7.[570]

Subsequent to the New Testament, the early Church Fathers paid close attention to Christ's fulfillment of Zech 13:7. In speaking about Christ's comments on his betrayer, Chrysostom saw this prediction as evidence of Jesus' divinity. Chrysostom wrote, "After he had foretold all these things as a sufficient

---

[565] Cook, "Metamorphosis," 454–55.
[566] Ibid., 455; cf. Merrill, *Zechariah*, 334; Meyers and Meyers, *Zechariah 9–14*, 384.
[567] Ibid., 462.
[568] France, *Jesus and the Old Testament*, 103–8.
[569] J. Muddiman, "Zechariah 13:7 and Mark's Account of the Arrest in Gethsemane," *The Book of Zechariah and Its Influence*, ed. C. Tuckett (Burlington: Ashgate, 2003), 101–9.
[570] Baldwin, *Zechariah*, 198.

proof that he possessed knowledge of what was going to happen, he went to a certain place to pray."[571]

Justin Martyr also saw Christ's prediction about the scattering of his disciples, based on Zech 13, as evidence of the Lord's divinity. In fact, Justin Martyr built an evangelistic theology on the solid foundation of Jesus' deity. Justin claimed that when the Church rests firmly on the deity of Christ, it will take its evangelistic charge seriously. He wrote, "When they [the disciples] were convinced of this [Jesus' divinity], they went out to all the world teaching these things."[572]

**13:8–9** Zechariah's reference to "the whole land" raises the question of how the prophet employed the word "land." The common Hebrew word *'ereṣ* occurs here, a term spanning broad nuances of meaning.[573] While "land" may refer to a specific "territory" (Gen 47:13), v. 8 focuses on the population, not the land under their feet. Accordingly, "land" functions as a metonymy for the people who dwell in the land. Meyers and Meyers paraphrase this concept as "the pasture of the flock."[574]

The seemingly unobtrusive phrase "declares the LORD" translates the important prophetic formula *nĕ'um YHWH*.[575] This significant expression predominates in prophetic writings to reiterate the divine origins and therefore the consummate authority of the message the prophet delivered. This occurrence of *nĕ'um YHWH* represents the final occurrence in chap. 13 (cf. vv. 2,7), an important emphasis in a chapter focusing on sweeping eschatological events.

Students of Zech 13 have long detected the similarities between v. 8 and Ezek 5:2,12. In one of his more memorable symbolic actions, Ezekiel took one third of his own shaved hair and burned it inside the city to symbolize the devastation the population would soon see. Shortly, Ezekiel expanded the message: "A third of your people will die of the plague or perish by famine inside you; a third will fall by the sword outside your walls; and a third I will scatter to the winds and pursue with drawn sword' (5:12). Ezekiel's ratio may well approximate the actual effects of the Babylonian conquest of Judah,[576] but Ezekiel did not destine his final third for destruction. The theological point in Ezek 5 and Zech 13:8 stresses the point that a remnant will survive in the midst of wide scale devastation of the populace. The surviving remnant must face further trials, the refiner's fire.

Zechariah 13 concludes much as it began, addressing the theme of purification and forming a thematic inclusion. Numbers 31:23, where Eleazar the priest required the captured goods from the Midianite battle to be purified by

---

[571] "Against the Anomoeans, Homily," cited by Ferreiro, *The Twelve Prophets*, 276.
[572] Dialogue with Trypho, 53, cited by Ferreiro, *The Twelve Prophets*, 276.
[573] אֶרֶץ. *HALOT*, 90–91.
[574] Meyers and Meyers, *Zechariah 9–14*, 390.
[575] נְאֻם יהוה. *HALOT*, 657–68; *TLOT*, 692–94.
[576] Meyers and Meyers, *Zechariah 9–14*, 391.

fire, illustrates the cleansing use of fire. The expression to pass through "the fire" *(bāʾēš)* also appears frequently in the Old Testament as a figure for affliction and judgment (Isa 43:2; cf. Isa 6:13; Zech 3:2).[577] Unger equates this fire with the tribulation (Rev 11–18).[578] Further, some identify the remnant with the 144,000 from the various tribes of Israel (Rev 7:1–8; 14:1–5).[579]

While possible, this conclusion is far from certain. Although the specific nature of the burning and the remnant remains ambiguous, God's intent in lighting the fire is not. Malachi stressed similar themes, maintaining that the Lord's people must go through the fire in order for Judah's offerings to be acceptable to the Lord as in former days. Malachi asks two rhetorical questions that anticipate the answer "no one" and then he gives the reason: "Who can endure the day of his coming? Who can stand when he appears? For he will be like a refiner's fire or a launderer's soap. He will sit as a refiner and purifier of silver; he will purify the Levites and refine them like gold and silver" (3:2–3).

Zechariah employed two verbs to develop the metallurgy metaphor to convey the process of spiritual cleansing the nation would undergo. The first verb is "refine" *(ûṣĕraptîm)*, which frequently describes the process of melting precious metals in order to purify the metal by precipitating any impurities (Ezek 22:17–22).[580] Several other prophetic texts express comparable messages (Isa 1:21–26; 48:10; Jer 6:27–30; 9:6). The promised heat from the Lord's refining fire anticipates the ultimate sorrows and victories surveyed in Zech 14.

The second verb is "test" *(ûbĕḥantîm)*, which has even broader application in the Old Testament.[581] Job 23:10 shows the verb in an illustrative context: "But he knows the way that I take; when he has tested me, I will come forth as gold." God will put the people to the test, not to punish, but to judge and to effect their purity, that is, their ability to serve in God's kingdom.[582] Thus, the Lord's purpose in putting his people through times of suffering has a positive objective for the nation and especially for the kingdom.

Through this purified remnant the Lord will continue his redemptive work on earth.[583] These spiritually renewed members of the Lord's flock will emerge from the fire as a regenerated people.[584] The statement that "they will call on my name and I will answer them" characterizes the new relationship between God and his people. The verb "call" *(yiqrāʾ)* often signifies calling on God in prayer and dependence.[585] One of the first biblical occurrences of the word is in Gen 4:26b: "At that time men began to call on the name of the LORD." This

---

[577] בָּאֵשׁ. *HALOT*, 92.
[578] Unger, *Zechariah*, 235.
[579] Barker, "Zechariah," 687.
[580] וּצְרַפְתִּים. *HALOT*, 1057.
[581] וּבְחַנְתִּים. *HALOT*, 119.
[582] Meyers and Meyers, *Zechariah 9–14*, 395.
[583] McComiskey, "Zechariah," 1224.
[584] Unger, *Zechariah*, 234.
[585] יִקְרָא. *HALOT*, 1128–30.

term also appears in Joel 2:23: "And everyone who calls on the name of the LORD will be saved; for on Mount Zion and in Jerusalem there will be deliverance, as the LORD has said, among the survivors whom the LORD calls."

God's promise to "answer" *('e'ĕneh)* employs an important Old Testament verb that often carries great theological weight (see 1 Kgs 18:24–26,36–37).[586] When God is subject of the verb *'ānāh*, it signifies that the Lord listens attentively to the needs of his people. Isaiah 30:19 portrays the idea well: "O people of Zion, who live in Jerusalem, you will weep no more. How gracious he will be when you cry for help! As soon as he hears, he will answer you" (cf. Zech 10:6). The final four lines of v. 9 reveal a chiastic interplay: "they" and "I" followed by "I" and "they." Apart from the literary observation, the interchange between the references to God and his people stress the contributions both parties must make to a relationship.[587]

The exultant affirmation of the close relationship with God, "The LORD is our God," recalls Ps 23:1, "The LORD is my shepherd" (cf. Jer 32:37–42; Ezek 37:23–28). The use of direct quotation makes Zechariah's argument more powerful. The affirmation draws from Exod 6:7: "I will take you as my own people, and I will be your God. Then you will know that I am the LORD your God, who brought you out from under the yoke of the Egyptians." The same language is used several times elsewhere (see Lev 26:12; Jer 7:23; 31:33; Ezek 36:28; Hos 2:23; Zech 3:8).

For many interpreters, the cataclysmic destruction of Jerusalem in AD 70 provides the fulfillment of 13:7–8. Despite how devastating it was, the survivors of Titus's sack of Jerusalem and the destruction of the temple did not come forth as a renewed people spiritually. Further, these remnants, with rare exception, did not evidence faith in the Messiah who had so recently suffered piercing on their behalf. Instead, these people persisted in their unbelief. Moreover, the universal scope of Zechariah's prophecies in chap. 13 look to an eschatological fulfillment.[588] Zechariah 13:8–9 gazes on a more remote period, just as Paul predicted: "And so all Israel will be saved, as it is written: 'The deliver will come from Zion; he will turn godlessness away from Jacob. And this is my covenant with them when I take away their sins'" (Rom 11:26–27).

The eschatological perspective of Zech 13 finds eloquent expression in the moving hymn written by Charles Wesley, "Lo, He Comes with Clouds Descending":

> Lo, He comes with clouds descending,
> Once for favored sinners slain;
> Thousand, thousand saints attending
> Swell the triumph of His train:

---

[586] אָנָה. *HALOT*, 851–52.
[587] Baldwin, *Zechariah*, 198.
[588] Barker, "Zechariah," 687; Unger, *Zechariah*, 234–35.

Alleluia, alleluia!
God appears on earth to reign.

Ev'ry eye shall now behold Him,
Robed in splendor's majesty;
Those who set at naught and sold Him,
Pierced and nailed Him to the tree,
Deeply wailing, deeply wailing,
Shall the true Messiah see.

Now the Savior, long expected,
See in solemn pomp appear;
All who have not Him rejected
Now shall meet him in the air:
Alleluia, alleluia!
See the day of God appear.[589]

## 11. Israel's Battle and Victory (14:1–15)

¹A day of the LORD is coming when your plunder will be divided among you.
²I will gather all the nations to Jerusalem to fight against it; the city will be captured, the houses ransacked, and the women raped. Half of the city will go into exile, but the rest of the people will not be taken from the city.
³Then the LORD will go out and fight against those nations, as he fights in the day of battle. ⁴On that day his feet will stand on the Mount of Olives, east of Jerusalem, and the Mount of Olives will be split in two from east to west, forming a great valley, with half of the mountain moving north and half moving south. ⁵You will flee by my mountain valley, for it will extend to Azel. You will flee as you fled from the earthquake in the days of Uzziah king of Judah. Then the LORD my God will come, and all the holy ones with him.
⁶On that day there will be no light, no cold or frost. ⁷It will be a unique day, without daytime or nighttime—a day known to the Lord. When evening comes, there will be light.
⁸On that day living water will flow out from Jerusalem, half to the eastern sea and half to the western sea, in summer and in winter.
⁹The Lord will be king over the whole earth. On that day there will be one Lord, and his name the only name.
¹⁰The whole land, from Geba to Rimmon, south of Jerusalem, will become like the Arabah. But Jerusalem will be raised up and remain in its place, from the Benjamin Gate to the site of the First Gate, to the Corner Gate, and from the Tower of Hananel to the royal winepresses. ¹¹It will be inhabited; never again will it be destroyed. Jerusalem will be secure.
¹²This is the plague with which the LORD will strike all the nations that fought against Jerusalem: Their flesh will rot while they are still standing on their feet, their eyes will rot in their sockets, and their tongues will rot in their mouths. ¹³On

---

[589] *The Baptist Hymnal*, # 199.

that day men will be stricken by the Lord with great panic. Each man will seize the hand of another, and they will attack each other. **¹⁴Judah too will fight at Jerusalem. The wealth of all the surrounding nations will be collected—great quantities of gold and silver and clothing. ¹⁵A similar plague will strike the horses and mules, the camels and donkeys, and all the animals in those camps.**

Zechariah 14 serves as the climax to the entire book by drawing together themes woven throughout the previous 13 chapters. These motifs include the return of fertility like that in paradise (cf. 8:12 with 14:6–8); the prosperous city of Jerusalem living securely without walls (cf. 2:9; 9:8 with 14:11); the curse going out over all of the land and the ban removed (cf. 5:3 with 14:11); God's judgment on the nations (cf. 2:1–4, 12–13; 9:1–8; 10:11; 12:4 with 14:12–15); the alteration of worship practices (cf. 8:18–23 with 14:20); and the nations coming to Jerusalem to worship (cf. 2:11; 8:20–23 with 14:16).[590] More broadly, Zech 14 makes extensive use of earlier biblical texts, applying and sometimes broadening the focus of these passages in presenting the eschatological message.[591]

Zechariah 14 opens with Jerusalem in the midst of utter defeat, bereft of her possessions and any self respect she had once enjoyed. Jerusalem had become so ignominious that all of the nations will seek to wage war against her. Half of the population of Zion will sit in its squalor at home, and half will go into an unspecified exile. After what must have seemed like unending degradation, the Lord will appear with such cataclysmic results that Zechariah drew from the earthquake metaphor to express the upheaval God's arrival will effect. Figuratively, Zion will rise to unparalleled heights, where all mankind will see the Lord ruling as King over the entire earth. Millennia of suffering for Jerusalem will transform into an eternity of blessing for Zion and for all who submit to the Lord in faith and worship. Barker summarizes this complicated chapter well: "Man is having his day now; the Lord's day is yet to come."[592]

For centuries, Zech 14 has functioned as something of a hermeneutical, historical, and theological watershed. The approaches taken to this unparalleled chapter both influence and are influenced by one's understanding of the remainder of the Bible. The difficulty of interpreting the contents of chap. 14 only heightens the interpretative significance of the material. One of the most memorable comments about the interpretive rigors of Zech 14 comes from Martin Luther, who penned two commentaries on Zechariah. The first was published in 1526 and stopped at the end of Zech 13 without explanation.[593]

---

[590] K. R. Schaefer, "Zechariah 14 and the Composition of the Book of Zechariah," *RB* 100 (1993): 375–76.

[591] Schaefer, "Zechariah 14: A Study in Allusion," 66–91. See the Introduction for further discussion.

[592] Barker, "Zechariah," 689.

[593] A. Wolters, "Zechariah 14: A Dialogue with the History of Interpretation." *Mid-America Journal of Theology* 13 (2002): 40.

Luther's second commentary on Zechariah was written one year after his first but still offers only limited comments on chap. 14. But in the second one Luther begins with the following admission: "Here, in this chapter, I give up. For I am not sure what the prophet is talking about."[594] Luther's consternation about the proper understanding of Zech 14 should caution any student of this chapter about overconfidence when working through the particular elements of the chapter.

Not surprisingly, the history of interpretation manifests significant diversity of approaches to this chapter, with substantial variations within every particular approach. Wolters concludes that there are seven distinct interpretations of Zech 14. The following represents a brief summary of Wolters's detailed analysis of these seven views.[595]

First, the oldest view comes from the Church Fathers, many of whom concluded that chap. 14 was fulfilled in the Maccabean uprising in the early second century BC. Wolters notes that the Dutchman, Hugo Grotius (1583–1645), likewise adopted a Maccabean interpretation.

Second, a more common interpretation applies Zech 14 to the entire period of history beginning with the New Testament era and culminating at the second coming of Christ. Luther is the most prominent adherent of this approach.

Third, another method sees the fulfillment of chap. 14 in Zechariah's past. Calvin exemplifies those who advocate this method of interpretation. Calvin applies the message of the chapter to postexilic Israel.

The fourth and fifth approaches both apply Zech 14 to the end times. The difference between these two interpretations is the degree of literalness with which they interpret the chapter. The fourth view takes the statements in chap. 14 figuratively, making room for significant latitude in explaining Zechariah's statements. The late Thomas McComiskey represents the fourth approach. The fifth interpretation includes but is not limited to dispensational perspectives. Representatives of this approach include Charles Feinberg, Merrill Unger, Kenneth Barker, and Eugene Merrill. Both the fourth and fifth interpretations of chap. 14 maintain that the entire chapter is prophetic; that is, its fulfillment is still in the future. Perhaps the single greatest difference between the fourth and fifth views is the way each takes the references to Israel. The fourth view affirms the eschatological perspective but claims that the Church inherits the Old Testament promises to Israel, including those in Zech 14. The fifth approach differentiates between biblical promises to Israel and those made to the Church, irrespective of where the prophecies lie in the biblical canon.

The sixth and seventh interpretations both grow out of modern critical methodologies. The sixth view takes Zech 9–14 to be preexilic, a view long since

---

[594] M. Luther, "Lectures on Zechariah. The German Text, 1527" in *Luther's Works, Vol. 20: Lectures on the Minor Prophets III: Zechariah*, ed. H. C. Oswald (Saint Louis: Concordia, 1973), 153–347, especially 337.

[595] Wolters, "Zechariah 14," 42–55.

abandoned by critical scholarship. This approach represents little more than a relic of an untenable position. Scholars such as Ewald believed that Zech 14 predicted that Jerusalem would not fall to Nebuchadnezzar in 586 BC. When Jerusalem did fall, according to the sixth view, Zechariah's prophecy was discredited.

The seventh and final view catalogued by Wolters focuses on the apocalyptic character of the chapter. But the view of apocalyptic maintained by this interpretation claims that the language of Zech 14 disallows any claim about a future fulfillment. Wolters suggests that Hanson, Meyers and Meyers, Petersen, and many other contemporary scholars reflect this view.

Wolters assesses the strengths and weaknesses of each position but declines to advocate a particular approach. He notes that each of the seven viewpoints contains multiple variations. He also emphasizes an important, but obvious, point: "There is nothing approaching a consensus among interpreters of Zech 14—not even among interpreters of the same confessional persuasion."[596] In conclusion, Wolters warns interpreters against undue dogmatism in handling Zech 14.

Although Wolters offers limited analysis of the seven hermeneutical approaches to chap. 14, a word is in order here. Despite the history of interpretation, there is no warrant for continued confidence in any hermeneutical approach that sees a historical fulfillment to the chapter. No matter how freely one might interpret the affirmations made by Zechariah, it remains hopeless to find any past events that even begin to capture the essence of Zechariah's prophecies. Likewise, the final two critical approaches fail to persuade for numerous reasons, not the least of which is their almost cynical understanding of the text.

The only satisfactory interpretation views chap. 14 as a series of momentous prophecies focusing on the future, the eschatological day that Zechariah regularly referred to with the words "on that day." The remaining issue is how literally should one read Zech 14.

One should not expect a consensus on the question of how literally to read Zechariah's oracles. Nor can the issue receive adequate discussion here. In short, it seems best to attempt to read the prophet's language as normally as makes sense in this context. The word *literal* is so burdened with negative connotations and misconceptions that it does not aid a discussion about the issue. Furthermore, even the most strident advocate of a literal hermeneutic cannot apply this approach consistently. Unger, for instance, notes with no explanation that the "Canaanite' in 14:21 is a "figure of a morally and spiritually unclean person."[597] On the other hand, if Zechariah predicts a glorious future for Jerusalem, is it appropriate to interpret the passage as though it only refers to the New Testament portrayal of "heaven," with no consideration given to national

---

[596] Ibid., 55.
[597] Unger, *Zechariah*, 270.

Israel whatsoever?[598] A preferable hermeneutic reads Zechariah's statements in a normal, straightforward fashion, unless forced to do otherwise by some compelling literary or theological factor. For example, when Zechariah declares, "never again will it [Jerusalem] be destroyed," such affirmations normally read as applying to the city of Jerusalem's security in the eschatological future. Other statements from Zech 14 may prove even more controversial.

As mentioned above, the apocalyptic language, coupled with the universal scope of the prophecies in chap. 14, render any attempt to find a past historical fulfillment to the chapter impossible. Numerous statements in chap. 14 have no equivalent in history. For instance, the following prophecies from chap. 14 demand an eschatological fulfillment: God will "gather all the nations to Jerusalem to fight against it" (v. 2); "it will be a unique day ... known to the LORD" (v. 7); "the LORD will be king over the whole earth" (v. 9); "never again will it [Jerusalem] be destroyed" (v. 11); and "the survivors from all the nations that have attacked Jerusalem will go up year after year to worship the King, the LORD Almighty" (v. 16).

The sevenfold reverberation of the eschatological formula "on that day" *(bayyôm–hahûʾ)* (vv. 4,6,8,9,13,20,21) also makes the futuristic outlook of chap. 14 certain.[599] The messianic implications of Zech 9–11 focus on events surrounding Christ's first advent. Zechariah 9:9 epitomizes this emphasis: "See, your king comes to you, righteous and having salvation, gentle and riding on a donkey." Chapters 12–14 encompass Christ's second advent when he establishes the eternal kingdom of God. The theological climax of the Messiah's arrival appears in 14:9: "The LORD will be king over the whole earth. On that day there will be one LORD, and his name the only name."

The chapter unfolds in a unified fashion, repeatedly stressing the Lord's kingship over all creation. The structure of chap. 14 is as follows:

> The recapture of Jerusalem, the City of God (vv. 1–5)
> The transformation of Jerusalem (vv. 6–11)
> The judgment of the disobedient nations (vv. 12–15)
> The temple for "the peoples of the earth" (vv. 16–21)[600]

Unlike chap. 13 where the Lord speaks, the prophet Zechariah is the speaker throughout most of chap. 14.

**14:1** Many modern translations choose to ignore the first Hebrew word of the verse *(hinnēh)*, which is often rendered "behold" in older English versions.[601] Admittedly, "behold" left the English vernacular long ago, but this Hebrew particle has important meaning and serves to intensify the immediacy of the passage.

---

[598] See McComiskey, "Zechariah," 1238.
[599] בַּיּוֹם הַהוּא. De Vries, "Futurism in the Preexilic Minor Prophets," 267–70.
[600] Mitchell, *Zechariah*, 341–53; see Meyers and Meyers, *Zech 9–14*, 493.
[601] הִנֵּה. *HALOT*, 252; Joüon-Muraoka, *Grammar*, § 105 d.

The promise of the coming "day of the LORD" foretells a threat for Zion, not deliverance (see Joel 1:15). Several features of this idiom require discussion. First, the verbal form translated "is coming" renders the Hebrew word *(bāʾ)*.[602] This form is a participle that communicates imminent action.[603] Zechariah informs his readers that the apocalyptic events of chap. 14 would occur soon. From the perspective of two millennia later, one might challenge the veracity of this claim, but Ps 90:4 gives a different view of the passing of time: "For a thousand years in your sight are like a day that has just gone by, or like a watch in the night" (cf. 2 Pet 3:8). The phrase "a day of the LORD" *(yôm laYHWH)* differs slightly from the expression "on that day" and occurs elsewhere in the book of Zechariah.[604] The expression indicates that this future day "belongs to" the Lord (Isa 22:5).

The word "plunder" *(šĕlālēk)* carries painful connotations in the Old Testament, particularly in the prophetic writings.[605] The overwhelming majority of occurrences of *šĕlālēk* refers to property acquired forcibly as a result of military action. Property taken as plunder in the Old Testament includes prisoners of war, precious metals, food, livestock, and clothing. The word sometimes holds out hope for Israel, such as Jeremiah's promise that Babylon will be "plundered" (Jer 50:10). Tragically, Judah often found herself in the role of the one being plundered by a marauding nation (Ezek 7:21; 29:19). In the same way, 14:1 tells the tragic story of the future day in which Jerusalem will become the spoil for another (see Rev 11:3–10).

Zechariah surprised his readers with the abrupt shift from statements concerning Jerusalem's future security in previous chapters to the shattering images of Zion's overthrow in chap. 14. One of the strongest affirmations of Jerusalem's well-being appears in 12:3: "I will make Jerusalem an immovable rock for the nations. All who try to move it will injure themselves." There are many similar statements, yet Scripture is clear that before Zion's ultimate exaltation comes judgment. The apocalyptic prophecy in Dan 9:24–27 overviews an eschatological scene very similar to that in Zech 14. The destruction of Jerusalem, the continual wars until the end of the age, and the desecration of true worship of the Lord all echo chap. 14.[606]

Baldwin perceptively comments that God's people typically believe themselves to be undeserving of judgment, although they always did deserve it.[607] Judgment from the Lord begins with the people of God (Ezek 9:6; 1 Pet 4:17). Even the unparalleled judgment on God's own people foretold by chap. 14 is not unique to Zechariah's teaching. Several of the most notable passages

---

[602] בָּא. *HALOT*, 112–14.
[603] GKC § 116 p.
[604] יוֹם־לַיהוה.
[605] שָׁלָל. *HALOT*, 1531–32.
[606] McComiskey, *Zechariah*, 1227.
[607] Baldwin, *Zechariah*, 200.

predicting a catastrophic judgment on Zion and environs include Isa 2:12; 4:1; Joel 2:1–2; and Mal 4:1–5. Verse 1 overviews the sad story of the nations plundering Jerusalem; v. 2 presents yet more detail.

**14:2–3** Verse 1 shifts abruptly to direct speech from the Lord. God leaves no doubt about his role in the conflagration against Jerusalem. "I will gather" represents a verbal form that conveys divine resolve that an action will occur as God decrees.[608] The poignant irony to this epic battle is the name Jerusalem, which means "city of peace"—a tragic misnomer during those days. The battle against Zion will not catch God by surprise. Neither will the Lord respond impassively to the winds of war, merely allowing sinful humans to choose war. Rather, God will participate actively in arraying Jerusalem's pagan foes against the holy city. The Lord does not give his reason for leading the battle into the heart of Zion. But this very significant theological theme could not be clearer: Zechariah emphasized the Lord's absolute and sovereign reign over history. His reign is such that even the pagan nations submit to his control.

Zechariah quoted God saying that he would gather "all the nations" *(kol–haggôyim)* to fight against his own people.[609] The scope of the prophecy recalls Ezekiel's similar prophecy regarding God (Ezek 38; cf. Joel 3:1–3; Mic 4:11–13). In the Old Testament, the word for "people" *(haggôyim)* represents those who do not possess a covenant relationship with the Lord.[610] Of course, it would be impossible for everyone from all the nations to come physically to do battle against Jerusalem. The expression "all the nations" may represent hyperbole, emphasizing the overwhelming, indeed global, enmity against Zion.[611] Zechariah may intend "contingents of the armies of the various world powers, representing them as nations."[612] To press this question, though, is to miss the thrust of Zechariah's argument.

It would seem that 14:2 emphasizes the overwhelming numerical superiority of Jerusalem's attackers. Defeat and desecration were utterly inescapable without the Lord's help. As Zechariah has already shown, the Lord intervened, but not on behalf of his people. Further, the global scope of the battle against Jerusalem appears to reflect an "ideological conflict to remove a non-cooperative element that blocked the way to an international world order" (see Rev 16:16–21).[613]

Tragically, history records innumerable examples of military conquerors devastating the general populace.[614] Biblical history contains more than its

---

[608] וְאָסַפְתִּי. *HALOT*, 74. GKC, § 48 e; Joüon-Muraoka, *Grammar*, § 114.
[609] כָּל־הַגּוֹיִם. *HALOT*, 474, 182–83.
[610] *TDOT*, 2:426–33; *TLOT*, 896–919.
[611] McComiskey, "Zechariah," 1227.
[612] Unger, *Zechariah*, 242.
[613] Baldwin, *Zechariah*, 200.
[614] F. du T. Laubscher, "Epiphany and Sun Mythology in Zechariah 14," *JNSL* 20/1 (1994):

share of conquerors who pillaged non-combatants. Israel often bore the brunt of such atrocities meted out by her more powerful neighbors. However disturbing the news of Zion's defeat might be, nothing prepares Zechariah's readers for the shocking account of the misdeeds committed in the name of the majority.

The first description of defeat speaks of the houses "ransacked" (see Zeph 1:13).[615] Warriors routinely stole from the homes of the defeated to sustain themselves in an era when armies had to acquire their own foodstuffs in the field, unlike the modern notion of armies supplied from materiel originating from the armies' homeland (Amos 7:17). Beyond meeting their basic needs, soldiers often relished the opportunity to enrich themselves personally by seizing items of value for their own satisfaction. "The houses ransacked" conveys both nuances. The eschatological armies will triumph over Jerusalem and will utterly devastate every home by stealing its food and all other contents that possess any monetary value.

The violation of the vanquished female inhabitants also follows in a line of abusive behavior that goes back millennia. The rapacity of soldiers who wield total control over the populace but exercise limited control over their behavior has often led to wide scale sexual abuse. Zechariah warned that in the final battle in the end times, the women of Zion would not escape this brutal indignity. The Hebrew word translated "raped" is *tiššāgalnāh*, also occurring in Deut 28:30; Jer 3:2.[616]

Zechariah prophesied that "half of the city will go into exile," but he did not clarify what the exile signified specifically nor where these exiles would be sent. Despite the lack of specificity, the very mention of an exile was fearful enough to the community that recalled painful memories of the Babylonian exile and recoiled at the prospect of facing another one.

Verse 2 concludes with an unexpected ray of hope. A remnant of the people will miraculously remain in the city. The biblical concept of the "remnant" rests solidly on the covenant that the Lord had established with his people. This covenant commitment was a two-edged sword. On the one hand, the people's disobedience led to the judgment in the first place; hence, a remnant would be sentenced to the punishment that their sin merited. On the other hand, from the beginning of the Old Testament record God promised the patriarchs and their descendants that he would never cut them off totally. Consequently, a remnant

---

125–38.

[615] וְנָשַׁסּוּ. *HALOT*, 1608.

[616] תִּשָּׁגַלְנָה. *HALOT*, 1415. The Masoretic scholars viewed this word as indelicate, if not obscene, and deliberately altered the text. The scribes replaced the *Kethib* word תִּשָּׁגַלְנָה with the *Qere* reading, the euphemistic word תִּשָּׁכַבְנָה ("laid with"; *HALOT*, 1487–88). Isa 13:16 presents several themes from v. 2, forewarning, "Their infants will be dashed to pieces before their eyes; their houses will be looted and their wives ravished." The *Kethib* תִּשָּׁגַלְנָה is the original reading in this verse also.

would always remain through whom the Lord would channel his promises to succeeding generations.

Zechariah 14:2 uses a different word for "remainder" *(yeter)* than the one the prophets routinely employed for "remnant."[617] Nonetheless, the thematic connection with remnant remains. No biblical book emphasizes both dimensions of remnant more than the book of Isaiah does. Isaiah stressed the theme of remnant to such an extent that he named his son "Shear-Jashub," meaning "a remnant will return" (Isa 7:3).[618] In Zech 14:2, as in Isa 7, the hope of the Lord's deliverance for the nation was still in the future.

Zechariah devoted a relatively brief amount of time to the tumultuous days when Zion faced ransacking enemies. At last, the time for the Lord's earth-shaking arrival comes. Verse 3 introduces God as a divine warrior now fighting for Jerusalem, not against her. The unfolding scene in Zech 14 anticipates the announcement made by the two men clothed in white when Jesus was taken up into heaven. " 'Men of Galilee,' they said, 'why do you stand here looking into the sky? This same Jesus, who has been taken from you into heaven, will come back in the same way you have seen him go into heaven' " (Acts 1:11).

The statement that "the LORD will . . . fight against those nations" contains a significant ambiguity that has the potential to alter the meaning of the verse dramatically. "Against those nations" translates the Hebrew *baggôyim hāhēm*.[619] The question turns on the meaning of the preposition *bĕ*. This preposition commonly means "in" or "among" (Zech 6:5). If this is the intended meaning of the preposition, it would mean that the Lord continues to fight with the nations against Jerusalem.

Alternatively, the preposition can also mean "against" (Exod 1:10; Jer 46:20). The latter adversative meaning of the preposition signifies that the Lord has ceased fighting against Zion and has allied with his people to fight their mutual foes. The evidence points strongly to the latter meaning of "against" in this context. For one thing, when this preposition occurs with the verb "to fight," as it does in v. 3 and elsewhere (see Exod 1:10), it normally carries the adversative nuance "against."[620] Furthermore, the context also calls for the adversative meaning as v. 3 introduces the new movement in chap. 14 in which the Lord goes out to fight on Jerusalem's behalf (see Mic 1:3).

The "day of battle" *(yôm qĕrāb)* refers to any time when the Lord himself interposes in events on earth (see Exod 14:13–14).[621] This Hebrew word *qĕrāb* ("battle") also appears in Ps 144:1 (translated "war" in NIV):

---

[617] יֶתֶר. *HALOT*, 452. שְׁאָר. *HALOT*, 1377–8.
[618] שְׁאָר יָשׁוּב. *HALOT*, 1379–80.
[619] בַּגּוֹיִם הָהֵם.
[620] The usage of the similar construction in 14:14 is ambiguous.
[621] יוֹם קְרָב. *HALOT*, 399–401, 1135.

> Praise be to the LORD my Rock,
> who trains my hands for war,
> my fingers for battle.

This uncommon term functions as a synonym to the more common expression *milḥāmāh*, which also means "battle."[622] With the Lord of Hosts, literally the Lord of Armies, fighting on their side, Zion's defeat turned immediately into a rout of the enemies. Verse 3 focuses exclusively on the Lord's deeds. Zechariah made no mention of anything that Jerusalem accomplished. These foes not only opposed God's people, but it is important to remember that they also resisted the Lord.

**14:4** Verse 4 begins Zechariah's overview of the cataclysmic eschatological events that will accompany the Lord's physical return to Zion in order to put an end to unrighteousness and to inaugurate his holy reign. This theme of God as warrior vanquishing his world-wide foes appears prominently in Psalms (see Pss 2; 46–48). Zechariah 13:4 portrays God anthropomorphically, describing his feet standing on Jerusalem's soil. The Lord appears as a colossus astride the mounts surrounding Jerusalem.

The precise location of the Lord's arrival will be on the Mount of Olives. Like its name suggests, the site was renowned in antiquity for its olive production.[623] The Mount of Olives is actually a ridge some two and one-half miles in length, running north and south. Besides v. 4, this toponym only occurs elsewhere in the Old Testament in 2 Sam 15:30, albeit in a slightly altered form. Additionally, Ezekiel made an oblique reference to the Mount of Olives: "Then the cherubim, with the wheels beside them, spread their wings, and the glory of the God of Israel was above them. The glory of the LORD went up from within the city and stopped above the mountain east of it" (Ezek 11:22–23). Ezekiel could have referred to no other mountain than the Mount of Olives.[624]

The fertility of the Mount of Olives allowed the growing of such a valuable crop as olives, hence the name. The fertility associated with this site foreshadows the reference to the Feast of Tabernacles, also known as Succoth. The Feast of Tabernacles was Israel's harvest festival celebrating and worshipping the Lord for his goodness in providing the bounty that the people required to live and to prosper (14:16, 18–19).[625]

The site of the Mount of Olives enjoys even greater prominence in the New Testament. Jesus went to the Mount of Olives on various occasions (Matt 21:1; 24:3; 26:30; Luke 19:37; 21:37). Baldwin suggests that the Lord will arrive on the Mount of Olives instead of Mount Zion because the latter site has been

---

[622] מִלְחָמָה. *HALOT*, 589.
[623] *ABD*, 5:13–15.
[624] K. R. Schaefer, "The Ending of the Book of Zechariah: A Commentary," *RB* 100 (1993): 181.
[625] Sweeney, *Twelve Prophets*, 699.

occupied by enemy forces.[626] Beyond being purely conjectural, it makes little sense to suggest that the triumphant Lord of all creation, sovereign of all history, would not seize whatever territory he desired. It is quite likely that the prophecy concerning Jesus' second coming in Acts 1:11–12 bases its prediction on Zech 14:4. Consequently, the prophecy in Acts 1 suggests a literal fulfillment of Zech 14:4 upon Christ's second return.

This prominent mount on the east of Jerusalem's horizon will be split in two when the Lord returns. In other words, half of the mount will move northward and the other half southward. Verse 4 emphasizes the resulting valley that the displaced mountain will produce. Zechariah added that the valley moved east and west. Meyers and Meyers observe that this emphatic reference to the four points of the compass suggests the entire world that God's awesome power will control. The Lord will fashion a new creation, reflecting differences in geography, political affairs, and most importantly, righteousness.[627] The apocalyptic language emphasizes the universal scope of God's dominion and the cataclysmic outcome of the Lord's work of recreation. The valley formed by the splitting of the Mount of Olives would provide a causeway through which God's people could escape.

This tectonic shift and its avenue for salvation recalls God's miraculous parting of the Red Sea (Exod 14–15). The dividing of the Red Sea also focuses on the dry land, the avenue God provided for the deliverance of his people. At the onset of the conquest, the Lord also caused the waters of the Jordan to be "cut off and stand up in a heap" (Josh 3:13). As a result, all Israel crossed the river on dry ground. Similarly, Isaiah spoke about God "making a way in the desert" to save his people at the end of the exile (Isa 43:19b; see 35:8–10; 43:14–21).[628] Isa 40:3–4 offers one of the most prominent examples:

> A voice of one calling:
> "In the desert prepare
>   the way for the LORD;
> make straight in the wilderness
>   a highway for our God.
> Every valley shall be raised up,
>   every mountain and hill made low;
> the rough ground shall become level,
>   the rugged places a plain."

Zechariah's imagery of the Lord's arrival employs an earthquake metaphor, a figure used often in the Old Testament to convey the dramatic nature of a theophany. One of the clearest examples is in Ezek 38:19–23, which describes the

---

[626] Baldwin, *Zechariah*, 201.
[627] Meyers and Meyers, *Zechariah 9–14*, 424.
[628] Sweeney, *Twelve Prophets*, 699.

judgment that the Lord will pour out on the nations when he comes to defeat all unrighteousness. These events include "a great earthquake," all creatures "will tremble at my [God's] presence," "the mountains will be overturned, the cliffs will crumble and every wall will fall to the ground" (38:19,20; cf. Exod 19:18; Judg 5:5; Ps 18:7; Joel 3:16; Mic 1:3–4; Nah 1:5; Rev 16:18–19). The symbolic nature of the verse harmonizes well with the character of biblical apocalyptic.

The ancient imagery should not obscure the theological theme of the verse. The Lord will protect his people and save them from annihilation. Perhaps the newly formed valley to the immediate east of Jerusalem provides ready escape for the inhabitants. McComiskey summarizes the message well: "The geological shift of the mountain northward and southward creates an awareness of awesome power, a vivid pictorial representation of the activity of the invisible God in history."[629]

**14:5** While the battle between the Lord and his earthly opponents rages, the newly created valley in v. 4 provides an avenue of escape for Zion's inhabitants. Unlike many disastrous episodes in history, on this occasion God's people can flee safely from this final episode of anti-Semitism in world history.

The Hebrew of v. 5 is more awkward than most. For instance, the first Hebrew word in v. 5 *(wěnastem)* is widely translated "you will flee" and presents difficulties that the scholarly literature on this verse has treated at length.[630] The Greek tradition suggests a different vocalization of the Hebrew that could be translated "will be stopped up" *(wěnistam)*.[631] Mitchell adopts the variant reading, guessing that a spring will be stopped up, no longer providing water for the city (Gen 26:15).[632] He does not explain why he conjectures a spring. Without explanation, Mitchell dismisses the other verbs in the verse that also say that the nation fled, yet these other verbs for "fleeing" provide one of the strongest arguments for retaining the Masoretic reading. If the valley were stopped up, where could the inhabitants of Zion flee?

The essential problem for the ancient translators, as well as many modern interpreters, is the suggestion that the same people who experienced the earthquake in Uzziah's day would also flee in the future day of tumult. This understandable concern fails to appreciate Zechariah's rhetorical device that "actualizes the past event for the contemporary audience."[633]

Zechariah predicted that the people will flee "by my mountain valley" *(gê'-hāray)*, which more literally reads, "[by] the valley of my mountains."[634] The

---

[629] McComiskey, "Zechariah," 1230.
[630] וְנַסְתֶּם. *HALOT*, 681; cf. Floyd, *Minor Prophets*, 541.
[631] וְנִסְתַּם. *HALOT*, 771.
[632] Mitchell, *Zechariah*, 343; cf. Baldwin, *Zechariah*, 201.
[633] Schaefer, "Ending of the Book of Zechariah," 185. Cf. Merrill, *Zechariah*, 349–50; Meyers and Meyers, *Zechariah 9–14*, 424.
[634] גֵּיא־הָרַי.

two mountains the phrase refers to probably signify both Mount Zion and the Mount of Olives.

The new corridor will extend from Jerusalem to Azel *('āṣal)*.[635] The precise meaning of "Azel" is unclear, complicated by the fact that this is the only occurrence of this word in the Old Testament. One interpretation revocalizes the Hebrew word as *'ēṣel*, a preposition meaning "beside."[636] This emendation of the Masoretic Text yields "'the valley of the mountain shall reach to (each) side,' i.e., each of the two halves of the Mount of Olives."[637] Apart from concerns about emending the text without external textual support, the revocalization of the text does nothing substantive to clarify the meaning of the verse.

Apparently the noun Azel represents a place name whose precise location has eluded interpreters. Thus understood, the site will be expansive enough to provide shelter for all of Zion's inhabitants. Schaefer supports a credible identification: the modern-day Wadi Jasol, a site in the Kidron Valley.[638] Another identification notes the place mentioned in Mic 1:11, "Beth Ezel." The flight from Jerusalem eastward to a place of refuge evokes memories of another dramatic pilgrimage to the east.

The earthquake in the days of King Uzziah (mid eighth century BC) must have been so frightening that it held a place of prominence in Judah's corporate memory generations later. Josephus related the cause of the earthquake in Uzziah's day to Uzziah's attempt to offer incense in the temple over the protests of the priests.[639] So dramatic was the earthquake that the book of Amos dates the prophecy in terms of this seismic event: "The words of Amos, one of the shepherds of Tekoa—what he saw concerning Israel two years before the earthquake when Uzziah was king of Judah" (1:1). The twisting of the earth in Zech 14:5 may also draw upon the imagery of the "Isaianic Apocalypse," particularly chap. 24 when "it will be on the earth and among the nations, as when an olive tree is beaten" (Isa 24:13a).

After the exodus from Zion, the Lord will finally arrive with deliverance in his hand. Curiously, the text reads "the LORD my God will come *[ûbā']*."[640] Yet vv. 3–4 present God as already present to fight on Zion's side. McComiskey suggests that the Lord will come to the refugees from Jerusalem, meeting them to battle their foes.[641] More likely, the repetition serves to emphasize the dramatic point of God's theophany.

---

[635] אָצַל. *HALOT*, 82.
[636] אֵצֶל. *HALOT*, 82.
[637] See NRSV; Sweeney, *Twelve Prophets*, 699; and Meyers and Meyers, *Zechariah 9–14*, 426.
[638] Schaefer, "Ending of the Book of Zechariah," 185.
[639] Josephus, *Antiquities*, IX, 10, 4; cf. 2 Chr 26:16–21.
[640] וּבָא. *HALOT*, 112–14.
[641] McComiskey, "Zechariah," 1231.

The Hebrew text reliably reads "the LORD my God." Some have suggested emending the text to read "your God," seeking to harmonize this pronoun with the final one in the verse, "with you" *('immāk)*.[642] The NIV does not disclose this point since it opts to translate the final prepositional phrase as "with *him*." This shift of person is not unusual in Old Testament narrative, particularly prophetic material. The change of person makes the passage more vivid (see Zech 2:8). Furthermore, v. 5 concludes the section beginning with 14:1. Verse 1 addresses Jerusalem in the second person, so it would be appropriate for the final verse in the section to do likewise.[643]

At the time of the Lord's arrival, he will be accompanied by "all the holy ones" *(kol–qĕdōšîm)*.[644] The term "holy ones" also occurs in Ps 89:5:

> The heavens praise your wonders, O LORD,
>     your faithfulness too, in the assembly of the holy ones.

The term can refer to humans (Lev 21:7; Num 16:5; 2 Chr 35:3), and it also speaks of the Lord's heavenly servants (Job 5:1; Dan 8:13; see 1 Thess 3:13). The "holy ones" correlates to the heavenly venue in which the "Angel of the LORD" primarily served (see especially Zech 3). In many passages, "holy ones" carries military connotations, stressing the Lord's awesome might (Ps 89:5,7). Moreover, the phrase also has sacral connotations, as Lev 21:7 and other passages readily illustrate.[645] Some consider these holy ones to be "angels."[646] Schaefer calls the holy ones "the heavenly beings in Yhwh's entourage."[647]

**14:6–7** When the day of the Lord finally arrives, the darkness of judgment will precede the light emanating from his righteous reign. Amos sought to dispel any naïve understanding of the day of the Lord that neglected the terror which direct human contact with the holy God would evoke. Amos 5:18 states,

> Woe to you who long
>     for the day of the LORD!
> Why do you long for the day of the LORD?
>     That day will be darkness, not light.

Zechariah 14:6 begins the narrative of the new day for Jerusalem, "the most peaceful, blissful and glorious in their history."[648]

Like many other passages in the latter chapters of Zechariah, this prophecy begins with the eschatological formula "on that day." The events in vv. 6–7 will also happen on the Day of the Lord. The first affirmation declares that the

---

[642] עִמָּךְ. *HALOT*, 839–40.
[643] Meyers and Meyers, *Zechariah 9–14*, 430–31.
[644] כָּל־קְדֹשִׁים. *HALOT*, 1076–78.
[645] Meyers and Meyers, *Zechariah 9–14*, 430.
[646] Unger, *Zechariah*, 249–50. See Matt 25:31.
[647] Schaefer, "Ending of the Book of Zechariah," 187.
[648] Mitchell, *Zechariah*, 346.

coming day will see "no light."⁶⁴⁹ As v. 7b indicates, there will be light, but the light will not appear from natural sources such as the heavenly bodies. Moreover, the whole rhythm of life divided into evening and day cycles will cease. The theological point of the verse, therefore, stresses the completely new order in creation that the Lord's arrival will bring to the land so burdened by sin.

The dramatic phenomena with signs in the heavens revisits themes found in numerous other passages, and repeated in the New Testament. For instance, "the stars of heaven . . . will not show their light" (Isa 13:10); "I looked . . . at the heavens and their light was gone" (Jer 4:23); "the sun will be turned to darkness" (Joel 2:31); "the stars will no longer shine" (Joel 3:15); "the day of the LORD . . . will be darkness, not light" (Amos 5:18); and "the sun will be darkened . . . the stars will fall from the sky, and the heavenly bodies will be shaken" (Matt 24:30). Numerous examples of the same themes occur in Revelation. One of the most noteworthy examples is Rev 6:12–14 (see Isa 34:4; cf. Rev 9:1–18; 14:14–20; 16:4–9):

> I watched as he opened the sixth seal. There was a great earthquake. The sun turned black like sackcloth made of goat hair, the whole moon turned blood red, and the stars in the sky fell to earth, as late figs drop from a fig tree when shaken by a strong wind. The sky receded like a scroll, rolling up, and every mountain and island was removed from its place.

The final phrase in Zech 14:6, "no cold or frost," translates the difficult Hebrew *yĕqārôt yĕqippā'ôn*⁶⁵⁰ (literally "the splendid ones will congeal"). The word *yĕqārôt* means "noble, splendid, precious."⁶⁵¹ Most likely, *yĕqārôt* refers to the stars that have ceased giving their light.⁶⁵² The Septuagint and other ancient versions attest a different reading, "cold and ice," from the difficult Masoretic Text. Scholarly tradition has frequently defended the Greek reading.⁶⁵³ Clearly, the NIV also rejects the Hebrew text, opting for the smoother Greek reading. The literary point of "cold and ice," according to the adherents of this reading, stresses the ending of the growing cycle and the cutting off of life.⁶⁵⁴ Accordingly, this view often reads v. 6 negatively, arguing that v. 6 emphasizes the disruption of the agricultural cycle.

---

⁶⁴⁹ אוֹר. *HALOT*, 24–25. Meyers and Meyers's replacement of אוֹר is both speculative and unnecessary (*Zechariah 9–14*, 431–32).

⁶⁵⁰ יְקָרוֹת יִקְפָּאוֹן. *HALOT*, 432, 1117. Although the feminine noun (יְקָרוֹת) does not agree with the gender of its predicate, this provides insufficient grounds for emendation, particularly in light of how frequently Zechariah did not observe noun-predicate agreement.

⁶⁵¹ For an additional proposal, see R. P. Gordon, "Targumic ʿDY (Zechariah XIV 6) and the Not So Common 'Cold,'" *VT* 29 (1989): 77–80.

⁶⁵² McComiskey, "Zechariah," 1233; Unger, *Zechariah*, 251.

⁶⁵³ ψῦχος καὶ πάγος. See Rudolph, *Sacharja 9–14*, 232; Mitchell, *Zechariah*, 346; Sweeney, *Twelve Prophets*, 700.

⁶⁵⁴ Meyers and Meyers, *Zechariah 9–14*, 432.

The precise meaning of the word *yĕqippā'ôn* is notoriously difficult to ascertain, as the diverse translations attest. The attractive alternative text in the Septuagint mentioned above appears to be a translator's attempt to smooth out the rugged Masoretic Text. In the broader context, the reading "no cold or frost" does not harmonize well with the reference in v. 8 to winter. But the Hebrew word *yĕqippā'ôn* normally means "congeal, thicken." Drawing generally from the context, specifically from the parallel "no light" in the first half of the verse, "diminish or darken" fits the context better than the Septuagint reading.[655]

While the Hebrew of v. 6 presents real challenges, the overall meaning of the verse is relatively straightforward. Verse 6 begins the catalog of cosmic changes that the Lord's arrival will effect. The Lord will reverse aspects of creation to establish the new kingdom he is predicting. The undoing of God's creative work lays the foundation for what he wants to establish. In other words, demolition precedes construction. Merrill comments, "Whereas Genesis is describing creation out of chaos, Zechariah speaks of chaos out of creation."[656]

Verse 7 continues the account of God's cataclysmic events when he comes to rescue Jerusalem from her tormentors. To emphasize the fact that these coming events will be like nothing ever seen on earth, Zechariah wrote that "it will be a unique day." The phrase "unique day" *(yôm–'eḥād)* employs the numeral "one" *('eḥād)* to signify "a singular day."[657] That future day will surpass any event in human history and will even surpass human comprehension.[658]

The statement that this unique day will know neither "daytime nor nighttime" continues the thought from v. 6 that there will no longer be any light. This absence of light, as stated above, does not necessarily suggest darkness. Rather, any light visible to the people would emanate from the Lord himself. More to the point, no longer would people mark time by the movement of the earth around various heavenly bodies. The changes in physical phenomena that have delineated days since the very beginning of time could not possibly describe the scope of the changes the Lord will accomplish in his new creation. Thus, the unique character of the day reflects a completely new order on earth. Like the statement in v. 6a, this prophecy continues the reversal of God's first action in creation, the distinction between day and night (Gen 1:3–5).[659]

The end of the cosmic order known since the original creation manifests both divine judgment and incomprehensible blessing. The absence of light—darkness—signifies judgment in several Old Testament passages (Ezek 32:8; Amos 5:18; Joel 2:2; Zeph 1:15; cf. Isa 5:30; 9:2; 13:10; 42:7; Jer 31:35). The obverse

---

[655] There is a connection in Hebrew between the notion of thickness or fixedness and that of darkness (Exod 20:21; 1 Sam 4:15).
[656] Merrill, *Zechariah*, 351; cf. Sweeney, *Twelve Prophets*, 700.
[657] יוֹם אֶחָד. *HALOT*, 399–401, 29–30.
[658] McComiskey, "Zechariah," 1233.
[659] Sweeney, *Twelve Prophets*, 700.

side of the coin exposes profound divine blessing.⁶⁶⁰ Isaiah describes how darkness on the eschatological day would provide the occasion for God's spiritual people to illumine the world. Speaking to Zion, Isaiah wrote, "Arise, shine, for your light has come, and the glory of the LORD rises upon you. . . . Nations will come to your light, and kings to the brightness of your dawn" (Isa 60:1,3). On this glorious day, "the creation itself will be liberated from its bondage to decay and brought into the glorious freedom of the children of God" (Rom 8:21–22).

Isa 60:19–20 speaks of this same day:

> "The sun will no more be your light by day,
>    nor will the brightness of the moon shine on you.
> For the LORD will be your everlasting light,
>    and your God will be your glory.
> Your sun will never set again,
>    and your moon will wane no more;
> the LORD will be your everlasting light,
>    and your days of sorrow will end."

The last chapter in the Bible makes a similar announcement: "There will be no more night. They will not need the light of a lamp or the light of the sun, for the Lord God will give them light" (Rev 22:5; see 21:25).

This new day will be "known to the LORD" (Zech 14:7). Presumably, this phrase suggests that *only* the Lord can know when this momentous day will dawn. In addition to the fact that only God knows the *time* when this day will occur, it is also true that only the Lord understands the *scope* of the great day.

**14:8** In a parched land like Judah, the prospect of abundant water flowing to the city of Jerusalem and its environs would be a momentous blessing for the nation. The gentle waters of the Siloam brook (see Isa 8:6) never yielded the volume of water the city needed to prosper. The wadis intersecting the land only ran with water when a sporadic shower dropped sufficient moisture for a runoff to occur. Except for the brief hours of flowing water, these wadis disappointed with only the unfulfilled promise of water. However, the promise of abundant water symbolizes more than sufficient water for life to prosper.

This prophecy begins with the eschatological marker "on that day," reminding the reader that the events described in the following prophecy await the great eschatological Day of the Lord. When that day arrives, "living water" will flow from the temple mount.⁶⁶¹ This unusual metaphor draws from Jer 2:13:

> My people have committed two sins:
>    They have forsaken me,
>    the spring of living water,

---

⁶⁶⁰ Unger, *Zechariah*, 252–53.
⁶⁶¹ מַיִם־חַיִּים. *HALOT*, 576–77, 308.

and have dug their own cisterns,
broken cisterns that cannot hold water.

Clearly, Jeremiah applied the "living water" imagery to God himself, the source of all life (see Jer 17:13).[662] Jeremiah mocked anyone who would forsake the true fount of all life and blessings for anyone or anything else. Jeremiah stated emphatically that only God can give life and protection for his people. The headwaters of the stream of living water in Zech 14:8 originate from Zion, the seat of God's throne on earth, reiterating Jeremiah's point that only God gives life. This God-given life encompasses both spiritual and physical dimensions, different components of life that the Old Testament does not separate. Accordingly, no one other than God deserves obedience and worship.

The life-giving water described in v. 8 will flow in equal proportions toward the east and the west continually throughout the year. The water flowing eastward will drain into the Dead Sea, while the water running westward finds its way into the Mediterranean. These two bodies of water delineated the latitudinal boundaries of the promised land (Num 34:12; Deut 11:24).[663] Reprising the promised land theme reminded Zechariah's audience that God will keep his covenant promises to grant the land to his people.

Once again, Zechariah employed prophecies first delivered by Ezekiel, often adding new meaning to the exilic teachings. Ezekiel was fond of the "abundant water" motif, using it to predict a verdant world of which desert dwellers could only dream (Ezek 17:5–8; 31:5–7). Most notably, Ezek 47:1–12 introduces the grand river flowing from the temple itself. Ezekiel's eschatological river sprung up under the temple and gushed eastward in the direction the temple faced. Ezekiel stressed the volume of water, noting that it became so deep that one must swim to ford the river. The exilic prophet developed the theme of the abundant agricultural benefits this river would provide God's people. Ezekiel sketched a picture composed of "swarms of living creatures," "large numbers of fish ... of many kinds," and "fruit trees of all kinds" (47:9–12). Joel 3:18 also speaks of a fountain that will flow out of the Lord's house. Genesis 2:10–14 offers the earliest example of a river flowing at God's command to enliven his original creation, much like Zechariah's river promises to do in the new creation. One of the most moving examples occurs in Ps 46:4 (cf. 65:9):

> There is a river whose streams make glad the city of God,
>   the holy place where the Most High dwells.
> God is within her, she will not fail;
>   God will help her at break of day.

---

[662] W. L. Holladay, *Jeremiah 1* (Philadelphia: Fortress, 1986), 92.

[663] McComiskey, "Zechariah," 1234. Meyers and Meyers disagree with designating the Dead Sea as the eastern boundary of greater Israel (*Zechariah 9–14*, 437), but the eastern boundary they suggest, the Euphrates, lies north-northeast of the land of Israel.

This sampling of passages containing river imagery demonstrates that the river motif can serve in either a physical or a spiritual sense. In 14:8 the river metaphor conveys both notions. Sweeney comments that the theme of abundant harvest proves particularly appropriate, foreshadowing the Feast of Tabernacles, a harvest festival, that Zechariah shortly addresses.[664]

Zechariah's imagery of prosperity pointed to an eschatological day of blessing from God, the only one who could bring such amazing things to pass. These illustrations of agricultural blessing were themselves only metaphors for the new spirituality and new righteousness that would characterize the new world in which God's people would find themselves in that eschatological day.

The idea of spiritual blessing influenced the New Testament's use of Zech 14:8. Jesus may have drawn from the spiritual dimensions of Zech 14:8 when he promised the people, "Whoever believes in me, as the Scripture has said, streams of living water will flow from within him" (John 7:38). In the Old Testament, living water symbolizes God and the blessings he bestows. Likewise in the New Testament, living water represents the work of Jesus that will extend blessings through the lives of those who have faith in him (See John 4:14).

Zechariah did not explain why he only mentioned two of the four seasons, summer and winter. Barker conjectures that the point may be the abundance of flowing waters will be so great that it will not even dry up during the sweltering summer months.[665] Mitchell notes that the two seasons mentioned in v. 8 portray seasonal extremes, functioning like a merism. He concludes that the point is the perennial nature of the flow of water coming out from under the temple.[666]

**14:9** Three psalms begin with the identical Hebrew words *YHWH mālak* ("The LORD reigns"; see Pss 93; 97; 99),[667] which is similar to Zechariah's "The LORD will be king." This credo had embodied Israel's faith for generations. However, in Zechariah's day the Lord had not yet begun to exercise his dominion over the earth. Throughout this painful and protracted era, sin reigned over creation, while Israel awaited the day when the Lord would reign over every nation.

Zechariah emphasized that the Lord will reign triumphantly "over the whole earth." The global scope of the Lord's reign indicates that Zechariah envisioned an eschatological age. In this unparalleled day, every person will finally acknowledge that the Lord, and none other, is indeed God.

On this coming day "there will be one LORD" *(yihyeh YHWH ʾeḥād)*.[668] This statement recalls the Shema: "Hear, O Israel: The LORD our God, the LORD is

---

[664] Sweeney, *Twelve Prophets*, 700.
[665] Barker, "Zechariah," 692.
[666] Mitchell, *Zechariah*, 347; Meyers and Meyers, *Zechariah 9–14*, 438.
[667] יהוה מָלָךְ. *HALOT*, 590–91.
[668] יִהְיֶה יהוה אֶחָד.

one" *(šĕmaʿ yiśrāʾēl YHWH ʾĕlōhênû YHWH ʾeḥād)* (Deut 6:4).[669] However, Zechariah made one significant change in the emphasis of the Shema. Instead of focusing solely on the Lord's relationship with his people Israel, Zechariah broadened this emphasis and made it universal. Every person will worship the Lord and will be able to declare, "the LORD is our God."

Many Old Testament passages reaffirm the eternal truth about the Lord's unique position as the only God, the Creator of heaven and earth. Moses commanded the Israelites: "Acknowledge and take to heart this day that the LORD is God in heaven above and on the earth below. There is no other" (Deut 4:39; see v. 35). Isaiah wrote: "I am the LORD, and there is no other; apart from me there is no God" (Isa 45:5a). The Lord's name, Yahweh, expressed his uniqueness as God over all creation as well as his covenant relationship with his people. The incomparable "I AM WHO I AM" *(ʾehyeh ʾăšer ʾehyeh*; see Exod 3:14) will finally reign over the entire cosmos as he intended from the time of creation (Exod 3:13–17).[670] In Zechariah's day, Malachi preached his moving message with similar themes: "My name will be great among the nations, from the rising to the setting of the sun" (Mal 1:11; see Zeph 3:9). The bold assertion of the Lord's absolute sovereignty over all creation, including all mankind, serves as the foundation for what will transpire as stated in vv. 10–11, which reveals that God will transform Jerusalem into a secure city as never before seen in Israel's history.

Many of Jesus' statements expand on the truth of God's coming reign. He said that the kingdom of God was near (or coming soon; Mark 1:15) and that the righteous would live in it (Matt 13:43). Another important example occurs in the Model Prayer: "Our Father in heaven, hallowed be your name, your kingdom come, your will be done on earth as it is in heaven" (Matt 6:7–10).

**14:10** Verses 10–11 overview the dramatic changes the Lord will bring to Jerusalem and her surrounding regions on that great eschatological day. Continuing themes begun in 14:8, v. 10 indicates that God will elevate the city of Jerusalem while leveling her environs. Geographically, Jerusalem sits nestled beneath the gaze of mountains on every side. The mountains offered the city limited defensive advantages, particularly in her early history. Psalm 125:2 notes the benefit of Zion's mountains: "As the mountains surround Jerusalem, so the LORD surrounds his people both now and forevermore." Since the city will no longer need any defense other than the Lord, God will remove its natural fortifications. Miraculously, the Lord will transform Zion from one of the most vulnerable locales on earth to the most secure. Thus, Zechariah addressed the security needs of the holy city, beginning with a list of sites near Jerusalem that would be brought down.

---

[669] שְׁמַע יִשְׂרָאֵל יהוה אֱלֹהֵינוּ יהוה אֶחָד.
[670] אֶהְיֶה אֲשֶׁר אֶהְיֶה.

Zechariah begins by referring to the changes coming to "the whole land" *(kol–hāʾāreṣ)*.[671] The identical phrase is translated in 14:9 as "the whole earth," which is not incorrect since the word *ʾereṣ* can be translated as "land" or "earth." While the emphasis in v. 10 is on the more limited sense, the section as a whole contains both "particular and universal" elements.[672] The first location mentioned is Geba, which was located approximately six miles north of Jerusalem near the original northern boundary of Judah (1 Sam 13:3).[673] Geba was a Levitical city within the territory of Benjamin (Josh 21:17). The proper noun "Geba" *(gebaʿ)* is related linguistically to the word for "hill" *(gibʿāh)*.[674] The similarities in both sound and meaning between these two words enhances Zechariah's literary message that the hills will be brought down.[675] In 2 Kgs 23:8 one reads that Josiah desecrated the idolatrous high places in the land from Geba in the far north to Beersheba in the south (see 1 Kgs 15:22).

The Old Testament mentions more than one location named Rimmon (sometimes called En Rimmon; see Neh 11:29). The Rimmon mentioned in v. 10 lies some 30 miles southwest of Jerusalem.[676] The references to Ain and Rimmon in Josh 15:32 most likely should be combined into a single name.[677] Together, the references to Geba and Rimmon form a merism to include all of the territory of Judah.[678]

The Lord will lower the elevation of these sites so that they would become "like the Arabah" *(kāʿărābāh)*,[679] which refers to "desert regions."[680] "Arabah" also describes the lowlands comprising the Jordan valley. With this latter nuance, "Arabah" refers to a "steppe" or "plain." The Arabah stretched from the Dead Sea to the Gulf of Aqabah. The distinguishing feature of the Arabah is its flatness. Zechariah 4:7a introduces a similar theme, "What are you, O mighty mountain? Before Zerubbabel you will become level ground."

Analogous to the lowering of the surrounding cities, the Lord promises to elevate Jerusalem. This action conforms to Isaiah's well known prophecy: "In the last days the mountain of the LORD's temple will be established as chief among the mountains; it will be raised above the hills, and all nations will stream to it" (Isa 2:2; cf. Mic 4:1–5).

The phrase "Jerusalem will . . . remain in its place" reaffirms the establishment of the holy city of God. This eschatological theme also appears in Zech

---

[671] כָּל־הָאָרֶץ. *HALOT*, 474–75, 90–91.
[672] Meyers and Meyers, *Zechariah 9–14*, 440–41.
[673] *ABD*, 2:921–22.
[674] גֶּבַע and גִּבְעָה. *HALOT*, 174.
[675] Merrill, *Zechariah*, 356.
[676] *ABD*, 5:773–74.
[677] See M. H. Woudstra, *The Book of Joshua,* NICOT (Grand Rapids: Eerdmans, 1981), 246; and R. G. Boling and G. E. Wright, *Joshua,* AB (Garden City, NY: Doubleday, 1982), 384.
[678] Sweeney, *Twelve Prophets,* 702.
[679] כָּעֲרָבָה. *HALOT*, 880.
[680] *ABD*, 1:321–24.

2:4: "Jerusalem will be a city without walls because of the great number of men and livestock in it." Likewise, Zech 12:6b says, "Jerusalem will remain intact in her place" (cf. Jer 17:24–27).[681] The repopulation of Zion will be one important result of the Lord's arrival in the end times, which is developed further in v. 11.

Zechariah delineated landmarks that surrounded Zion on every side, signifying that the entire city would be included in the Lord's miraculous works.[682] Zechariah's details and the modern understanding of the various locations render it impossible to retrace the precise lines between sites. The Benjamin Gate, the First Gate, and the Tower of Hananel all were situated on the northeastern quadrant of the city. The location of the "First Gate" is unknown, but was probably situated on the northern wall as well. The word "first" *(hāri'šôn)* can also be translated "former."[683]

Although its precise location is unknown, the Benjamin Gate opened to the territory of the tribe of Benjamin to the north of Jerusalem (Jer 37:12–13; see 17:19; 38:7).[684] It is possible that the Benjamin Gate should be identified with the Sheep Gate (Neh 12:39).[685] McComiskey correlates the "Benjamin Gate" with the "Old Gate" in Neh 3:6; 12:39, although this identification is tenuous.[686]

The Corner Gate was found on Jerusalem's western wall, close to the corner formed with the northern wall, and several passages reference this gate (see 2 Kgs 14:13; 2 Chr 26:9; Jer 31:38). The Tower of Hananel represented the northern-most portion of the wall (Neh 3:1; 12:39; Jer 31:38).[687] Apparently a well known location, the location of the Tower of Hananel has eluded precise identification. The royal winepresses were located on the southern side of the city, near the King's Garden (Neh 3:15) and the King's Pool (Neh 2:14). Apparently, all three pieces of royal property were situated in close proximity to each other.[688]

**14:11** Never a large city by modern standards, Jerusalem had seen her population exiled on numerous occasions. After the Babylonian exile, Jerusalem's census never approximated its preexilic levels. Zechariah acknowledged as much when he promised that "Jerusalem will be a city without walls because of the great number of men and livestock in it" (Zech 2:4). Later he added, "The city streets will be filled with boys and girls playing there. . . . It may seem marvelous to the remnant of the people at that time" (Zech 8:5–6a).

---

[681] Meyers and Meyers, *Zechariah 9–14*, 444.
[682] Baldwin, *Zechariah*, 204.
[683] הָרִאשׁוֹן. *HALOT*, 1168–69.
[684] *ABD*, 1:673.
[685] Mitchell, *Zechariah*, 348.
[686] McComiskey, "Zechariah," 1236.
[687] *ABD*, 3:45.
[688] Meyers and Meyers, *Zechariah 9–14*, 447.

Likewise, Neh 7:4 describes postexilic Jerusalem as spacious, but having "few people in it" (cf. 11:1–2). As difficult as it might be for the remnant to envision their beloved city bursting with inhabitants, the Lord promised that this miracle would occur "on that day."

The phrase, "never again will it be destroyed," while accurately communicating the idea of security, fails to communicate the connotations of the original idiom. The statement assures the inhabitants of Zion that in the coming Day of the Lord their city will finally enjoy the security it has always craved. The word translated "destroyed" is *ḥērem*.[689] The word is often rendered "ban" or "curse" and often refers to "the extermination that will happen to a people subjected to a *ḥērem*."[690] For instance, when preparing for the siege of Jericho, Joshua cautioned the people that "the city and all that is in it are to be devoted [*ḥērem*; 'under the ban'] to the LORD" (Josh 6:17; see v. 18). Also, in Mal 4:6 the word describes the curse placed on a city that was captured. McComiskey summarizes Zechariah's contribution: "The *ḥērem* . . . that led to Israel's demise (Isa. 43:28) cannot ever hang over the heavenly community because the curse will be no more, thus guaranteeing the city's security."[691] The apostle John revisited this theme: "No longer will there be any curse. The throne of God and of the Lamb will be in the city, and his servants will serve him" (Rev 22:3).

The final summation of v. 11 guarantees Jerusalem that she will finally be "secure" *(beṭaḥ)*.[692] Zechariah had warned the nation that her future held days of great distress. For instance, in 13:8–9 two-thirds of the populace are struck down and the remaining third face the refiner's fire. Zechariah 14:1–2 speaks of the nations successfully attacking Jerusalem, pillaging the city and ravaging the women. But 14:11 introduces the glorious hope of the incomparable victory and unassailable safety that will accompany the Lord's arrival to reign perpetually from Zion (cf. 14:3). Neither walls nor any other more modern defensive means would matter to Jerusalem. With the Lord her God and King reigning in her midst, her safety will finally be assured. Jeremiah delivered a similar prophecy: "The city will never again be uprooted or demolished" (Jer 31:40b; cf. 33:16; Ezek 34:27–31). As God himself promises in Zech 2:5, "'I myself will be a wall of fire around it [Jerusalem],' declares the LORD, 'and I will be its glory within.'" When God makes a promise, his word is sure, and complete security results from his mighty presence.

Finally, the idea of "living securely" in the land pervades the entire Old Testament, always expressing God's promise to grant security to his people as a reward for their obedience to his law. Thus, the security motif grows out of the Lord's covenant with Israel.[693] Ezekiel illustrates the theme of "living se-

---

[689] חֵרֶם. *HALOT*, 354.
[690] Meyers and Meyers, *Zechariah 9–14*, 448.
[691] McComiskey, "Zechariah," 1238.
[692] בֶּטַח. *HALOT*, 120–21.
[693] Meyers and Meyers, *Zechariah 9–14*, 449.

curely" in the land particularly well: "They [the people of Israel] will live there in safety and will build houses and plant vineyards; they will live in safety when I inflict punishment on all their neighbors who maligned them. Then they will know that I am the LORD their God" (Ezek 28:26; cf. Lev 25:18–19; 26:5; Deut 33:28; Jer 23:6; 32:37; 33:16; Ezek 34:25–28).

**14:12–13** Verse 12 turns from the miraculous restoration and security of Zion to the obverse side of the fierce judgment that the Lord will inflict on all those who had opposed Jerusalem, and thereby the Lord. The overwhelming onslaught from God recalls his judgment on Sennacherib's army during the reign of Hezekiah, as 2 Kgs 19:35 declares: "That night the angel of the LORD went out and put to death a hundred and eighty-five thousand men in the Assyrian camp. When the people got up the next morning—there were all the dead bodies!" (cf. Isa 37:36). In Zech 14:12 an unspecified wasting disease, pictured in figurative language, will decimate the enemy armies.

Verse 12 begins with the Lord's promise to strike the nations with a "plague" *(hammaggēpâ)*,[694] which refers to a pestilence or gruesome disease. The plague theme reminds Zechariah's readers of the plagues the Lord inflicted on the Egyptians (Exod 7–11). Further, the allusion to the Egyptian bondage foreshadows the introduction of the Egyptians in vv. 18–19.[695] Zech 12:4 uses a parallel term (also meaning "strike, smite") to warn those who go to war against the Lord (cf. Ps 2:2). Whether explained in Zechariah or Ps 2, the end of all evildoers is the same: God "rebukes them in his anger and terrifies them in his wrath" (Ps 2:5). Both Lev 26:14–17 and Deut 28:15–22 include plagues and wasting diseases among the curses to which those who disobey God's covenant will be sentenced.

The image of necrosis and putrefying flesh is revolting, but the scene effectively communicates the sudden and utter defeat every one of Jerusalem's enemies will taste. Zechariah does not appear concerned with explaining any physical cause for these calamities. Rather, the prophet makes it clear that the Lord causes these ailments, not some natural physiological occurrence.

Zechariah's attention devoted to the "eye" and the "tongue" of the people carries symbolic importance. The concept of "their eyes" *(ʿēnāyw)* occurs in several similar forms in the book of Zechariah (9:1,8; 12:4).[696] To have eyes that see signifies both mental and spiritual acuity.[697] Ezekiel 12:2 expresses the converse:

> Son of man, you are living among a rebellious people. They have eyes to see but do not see and ears to hear but do not hear, for they are a rebellious people.

---

[694] הַמַּגֵּפָה. *HALOT*, 546.
[695] Sweeney, *Twelve Prophets*, 703.
[696] עֵינָיו. *HALOT*, 817–19.
[697] Meyers and Meyers, *Zechariah 9–14*, 291–92, 454.

With comparable symbolism, Zechariah employs the metonymy of the "tongue" *(lĕšônô)* to convey the speech of Jerusalem's foes.[698] The Old Testament contains limited occurrences in which the "tongue" serves a noble purpose, but the prayer in Ps 51:14 is one of them:

> Save me from bloodguilt, O God,
> the God who saves me,
> and (that) my tongue will sing of your righteousness.

More frequently, the biblical text portrays individuals using their tongues to lie, deceive, slander, and blaspheme the God who gave them their tongues.

For the prophecy to dwell on the symbolism carried by the "eye" and the "tongue" fittingly encompasses the unrighteousness that Jerusalem's foes have epitomized.[699] What David confessed in Ps 51:4b, these evildoers will know in the end:

> you [the LORD] are proved right when you speak
> and justified when you judge.

Verse 13 restates the fundamental point of this passage; every affliction suffered by Jerusalem's enemies comes directly from the Lord himself. The Lord's judgment will prove to be so unbearable that panic will yield to fratricide among the troops who had once opposed Jerusalem and God. Similarly, the surprise assault by Gideon's army led the panicked Midianites "to turn on each other with their swords" (Judg 7:22; cf. 1 Sam 14:15–20). These attacks will aim to hasten the inevitable demise these armies will face against an insurmountable Foe. Zechariah 11:9 has already described similar circumstances that proved too overwhelming for those experiencing divine judgment (see 12:4). Haggai, Zechariah's contemporary, concluded his prophecy with a warning that sounds familiar: "I will overturn royal thrones and shatter the power of the foreign kingdoms. I will overthrow chariots and their drivers; horses and their riders will fall, each by the sword of his brother" (Hag 2:22).

Gerhard von Rad devoted significant attention to the concept of holy war in the Old Testament. His analysis of the topic included the theme of "the terror of God."[700] Von Rad stressed the supernatural dimensions of the battlefield chaos. He noted that the fear of God created utter confusion among Israel's enemies, resulting in "friendly fire." Robert Good added that these assaults of brother against brother ultimately reflected the violation of an oath.[701]

---

[698] לִשׁוֹנוֹ. *HALOT*, 536.
[699] Meyers and Meyers, *Zechariah 9–14*, 454–55.
[700] G. von Rad, *Holy War in Ancient Israel*, trans. M. J. Dawn (Grand Rapids: Eerdmans, 1991), 41–51, 94–114.
[701] R. M. Good, "Zechariah 14:13 and Related Texts: Brother Against Brother in War," *Maarav* 8 (1992): 44.

Finally, Schaefer outlines three common motives for the Lord's judgment of people by calamities and plagues.[702] First, God used calamity "to destroy the people who deserve the curse." Deuteronomy 28 illustrates this motive, with even God's covenant people susceptible to pestilence. Second, the Lord used calamities and pestilence to compel unrepentant peoples, including Israel, to acknowledge him as God (Lev 26:23–28; 1 Kgs 8:35–38; 1 4:6–11). Third, the Lord chose to employ calamities to remove both impurity and idolatry (2 Chr 21:10–19). The first and third motives seem to come into play here.

**14:14–15** Verse 14 represents the cosmic reversal of 14:1–2 where the nations plundered Jerusalem of everything of value. Finally, Zion will plunder the nations who had treated her so spitefully. The plunder will include vast quantities of "gold and silver and clothing." Meyers and Meyers summarize this relationship well, as they picture "the despoiled city now becoming the repository of tribute from all the nations that had perpetrated the sack of Jerusalem."[703] This ironic twist will give great hope to God's suffering people.

Perhaps the most pressing exegetical question in v. 14 focuses on the precise meaning of the phrase that the NIV translates "at Jerusalem" *(bîrûšālāyim)*.[704] Many scholars and English translations (see the RSV) render the phrase "against Jerusalem."[705] The Hebrew expression is ambiguous since the preposition *bě* can be translated either "in" or "against," although "in" or "at" represents a much more common usage.[706] The same ambiguity occurs in 14:3, but there the adversative meaning "against" better fits the context.

The translation preferred by the interpreter alters the meaning of the verse dramatically. Mitchell, for example, argues in favor of "against." He does not understand the verse to say that God's people will fight each other, but he concludes that the marauding armies will force the Jerusalemites out of the city. The rural members of Judah then align themselves with the displaced inhabitants of Jerusalem to fight to recapture the city.[707]

The NIV translation clearly opts for the opposing viewpoint, understanding the *bě* as meaning "*at* Jerusalem."[708] This perspective has its own adherents.[709] One point of connection with Mitchell's view is the mutual understanding that both the rural and urban Judahites joined together to defend the capital city.

"The wealth of all the surrounding nations" echoes the similar motif in Hag 2:7–8. In Hag 2:7, "the desired of all nations" most likely refers to the precious

---

[702] Schaefer, "Ending of the Book of Zechariah," 217–18.
[703] Meyers and Meyers, *Zechariah 9–14*, 458.
[704] בִּירוּשָׁלָיִם.
[705] Mitchell, *Zechariah*, 352.
[706] *HALOT*, 103–5.
[707] Floyd, *Minor Prophets*, 554; Mitchell, *Zechariah*, 352; Sweeney, *Twelve Prophets*, 704.
[708] GKC, § 119 b.
[709] See Baldwin, *Zechariah*, 205; Barker, "Zechariah," 694; Merrill, *Zechariah*, 359; Meyers and Meyers, *Zechariah 9–14*, 458; and Unger, *Zechariah*, 264.

silver and gold (see v. 8) that the Lord will receive as spoils from his holy war against the insolent nations.[710] The Lord's might as a warrior will see no parallel in history, as Joel 3:16 illustrates:

> The LORD will roar from Zion
>   and thunder from Jerusalem;
>   the earth and the sky will tremble.
> But the LORD will be a refuge for his people,
>   a stronghold for the people of Israel.

As Hag 2:7 indicates, the collection of the world's wealth represents an important postexilic theological contribution.[711] Zech 14:14 develops this perspective by stating that "the wealth of all the nations will be collected *(wĕ'ussap).*"[712] In addition to the most basic meaning of "gather," *wĕ'ussap* anticipates the introduction of the Feast of Tabernacles (or Succoth) in 14:19. The Feast of Tabernacles was the harvest festival for agricultural ingathering.[713]

Verse 15 picks up the theme of the plague introduced in v. 12. In addition to the gold, silver, and clothing taken from the nations, in the plague with which the Lord will devastate his enemies, even their horses and beasts of burden will be disabled. Consequently, these work animals will also belong to the Lord and are under the ban. In other words, these animals will be dedicated solely to God. Moreover, Zechariah's inclusion of these domestic animals serves to restate the message that the Lord would utterly devastate these worldwide foes. The list of the exiles who returned from Babylon includes 736 horses, 245 mules, 435 camels, and 6,720 donkeys, clearly highlighting the importance of these animals in this era (Ezra 2:66–67). Such animals would not be available to the nations for escape or for rebuilding their military and economic might (Ezek 38:20).

In contrast to the Lord's promise in 14:11 that Jerusalem would never again be destroyed, that is, be under a ban, the extent of the destruction of the enemies suggests a ban. When the Lord declared that a city was placed under the ban, everything within the city boundaries was dedicated to the Lord. For instance, when Joshua prepared to attack Jericho, the Lord cautioned the people not to take anything for themselves that belonged to God. Joshua 6:21 states, "They devoted the city to the LORD and destroyed with the sword every living thing in it—men and women, young and old, cattle, sheep and donkeys." To underscore the gravity of the Lord's decree, when Achan disregarded the ban, "all Israel stoned him" (Josh 7:24–25).

---

[710] See R. A. Taylor, "Haggai," in Taylor and Clendenen, *Haggai, Malachi,* 165.
[711] McComiskey, "Zechariah," 1240.
[712] וְאָסַף. *HALOT,* 74–75; see Schaefer, "Ending of the Book of Zechariah," 221–22.
[713] Sweeney, *Twelve Prophets,* 704–5.

## 12. Judgment and Salvation of All Nations (14:16–21)

¹⁶**Then the survivors from all the nations that have attacked Jerusalem will go up year after year to worship the King, the LORD Almighty, and to celebrate the Feast of Tabernacles. ¹⁷If any of the peoples of the earth do not go up to Jerusalem to worship the King, the LORD Almighty, they will have no rain. ¹⁸If the Egyptian people do not go up and take part, they will have no rain. The LORD will bring on them the plague he inflicts on the nations that do not go up to celebrate the Feast of Tabernacles. ¹⁹This will be the punishment of Egypt and the punishment of all the nations that do not go up to celebrate the Feast of Tabernacles.**
²⁰**On that day HOLY TO THE LORD will be inscribed on the bells of the horses, and the cooking pots in the LORD's house will be like the sacred bowls in front of the altar. ²¹Every pot in Jerusalem and Judah will be holy to the LORD Almighty, and all who come to sacrifice will take some of the pots and cook in them. And on that day there will no longer be a Canaanite in the house of the LORD Almighty.**

The final section of the book of Zechariah is 14:16–21, which shows great affinity with the final section of the first half of the book (8:20–23). In 8:20–21 the prophet says that "many peoples" will join together on a pilgrimage to Jerusalem "to seek the LORD Almighty and to entreat him." Likewise, chap. 14 concludes with "the survivors from all the nations" faithfully completing their annual trip to Zion "to worship the King, the LORD Almighty" (v. 16).[714] Both passages predict mass conversions of Gentiles who will worship the Lord righteously.

**14:16** Despite the overwhelming show of divine force against the sinful nations, survivors will remain. The preceding scene portraying the utter defeat of the nations does not give any inkling of the vast numbers who will survive in order to worship God. These survivors "from all the nations" will become followers of the Lord alone. The emphasis of v. 16 lies solely with exalting the Lord in the eyes of all humanity.[715] This eschatological worship finds further development in Isa 2:2–4 and Ezek 40–48.

Zechariah employed a distinctive term for "survivors" *(hannôtār)*.[716] The only other occasions when the prophet selected this term, he applied it to Judah (13:8; 14:2). He could have used the common word for "remnant" *(šĕʾār)*, but by selecting a word that otherwise only applied to Judah in his prophecies, Zechariah connects the remnants of "all the nations" with God's covenant people.[717]

It will be the Lord's will for these nations to worship him. In its prophecies of the sovereign restoration of Israel, Zech 14 is connected to Jeremiah's new covenant (Jer 31:31–34) and Ezekiel's declaration that the Lord will give Israel

---

[714] Baldwin, *Zechariah*, 205–6.
[715] Mitchell, *Zechariah*, 354.
[716] הַנּוֹתָר. *HALOT*, 451–52.
[717] Meyers and Meyers, *Zechariah 9–14*, 463–64.

a new heart and a new spirit (Ezek 36:22–32). Unlike Jer 31 and Ezek 36, however, Zech 14 explicitly includes Gentiles in the worship of the Lord.[718]

The verb "will go up" *(wĕʿālû)* occurs frequently in the Old Testament to describe a pilgrimage to Jerusalem to worship.[719] The term occurs in the headings of the Psalms of Ascent (Pss 120–34), generally understood to be psalms associated with the journey of the faithful to go to the temple to worship. Isaiah chose the same verb to signify the many peoples who will "go up to the mountain of the LORD, to the house of the God of Jacob" (Isa 2:3; Mic 4:2). In light of the widespread association of the verb "go up" with the worship of God in the Old Testament, Zechariah's use of this verb for non-Israelites participating in worship at the temple is particularly emphatic.[720]

Zechariah's acknowledgement that some may not worship faithfully (vv. 17–19) does not argue against the integrity of worship for those who do worship the Lord.[721] The verb "to worship" *(lĕhištaḥăwōt)* has the greatest emotive impact of all the words in this paragraph.[722] Each element in the context stresses the unparalleled response of "the survivors from all the nations" to the Lord.

The Gentile converts will come to Zion annually "to worship the King, the LORD Almighty." This combination of divine epithets occurs also in Ps 24:10 and Isa 6:5. Both passages contribute to the lofty grandeur the terms connote. The call of Isaiah in Isa 6:5 expresses the prophet's glimpse of God sitting on his throne in heaven. Isaiah lamented what he believed would be his imminent demise since as a sinful human his "eyes have seen the King, the LORD Almighty." Similarly, in a glorious Davidic hymn the psalmist asked a rhetorical question and then answered it:

> Who is he, this King of glory?
> The LORD Almighty—
> he is the King of glory (Ps 24:10).

The annual pilgrimage to Jerusalem will be for the purpose of celebrating the Feast of Tabernacles. This feast commemorated the final harvest of crops, acknowledging the Lord's goodness and sovereignty in providing for their physical needs (Lev 23:33–43; Deut 15:13–17). In Israel's annual cycle of religious feasts, only three required a pilgrimage to Jerusalem: Passover, Pentecost, and Tabernacles (Deut 16:1–17).

Zechariah did not explain why he mentioned only the Feast of Tabernacles. Several observations based on biblical accounts deserve comment. Some

---

[718] See W. Harrelson, "The Celebration of the Feast of Booths According to Zechariah XIV 16–21," in *Religions in Antiquity*, ed. J. Neusner (Leiden: E. J. Brill, 1968), 94.
[719] וְעָלוּ. *HALOT*, 828–30.
[720] Meyers and Meyers, *Zechariah 9–14*, 465.
[721] Contra Merrill, *Zechariah*, 361–62.
[722] לְהִשְׁתַּחֲוֹת. *HALOT*, 295–96; cf. *TLOT*, 398–400; *TDOT*, 4:248–56.

scholars argue that it was one of the most prominent and possibly the oldest of the feasts (Judg 21:19; 1 Sam 1:3).[723] It was also the last feast of the annual cycle and noteworthy for the joyful celebration associated with it.[724] The Feast of Tabernacles incorporated Gentiles (Deut 16:14), and the inclusion of Gentiles "implies that the fundamental distinction between Yahweh's people and all others will in effect be—like the other fundamental distinctions of the old order—effaced."[725] In celebrating the Feast of Tabernacles, the people lived in "booths" as a reminder that their forefathers lived in booths when the Lord brought them out of the Egyptian bondage (Lev 23:42–43).

In the postexilic era, the reading of the law became an essential component of the Feast of Tabernacles (Ezra 3:4; Neh 8:14–18). The reading of the law probably included the people's renewal of their commitment to the covenant with the Lord.[726] In the eschatological era, Gentiles will be included in the covenant with God. Unger offers a different argument for the inclusion of the Feast of Tabernacles. He contends that the Feast of Tabernacles was "the only one of the seven feasts of the Lord which at that time will be unfulfilled typically and the only one which will be in process of fulfillment by the kingdom itself."[727] It is also possible that the Feast of Tabernacles represents a metonymy for all of Israel's feasts.[728] However, the reference to rain in vv. 17–18 implies that the harvest aspect of the Feast of Tabernacles is the focus. The main idea Zechariah promoted is the obligation on Gentiles to observe the Feast of Tabernacles. Now these foreigners have an obligation equivalent to what Israel has had for generations.

Schaefer argues that the Feast of Tabernacles emerges in Zech 14 because the observance of this feast in the second temple period was largely eschatological in character, no longer focusing on harvest and thanksgiving elements.[729] Rubenstein concluded that no evidence exists to confirm Schaefer's thesis. Instead, Rubenstein affirms that although "the prophet drew on Sukkot imagery for the components of his vision and refracted them through an eschatological lens, the festival itself did *not* involve an eschatological experience."[730]

**14:17–18** Verse 17 describes punishment for anyone who failed to celebrate the Feast of Tabernacles as mandated. Since the Feast of Tabernacles was a harvest festival, failing to commemorate it indicated both disrespect and ingratitude to the Lord (Ps 65:9–13). God's measured response to this lack

---

[723] R. de Vaux, *Ancient Israel*, 495–502; Mitchell, *Zechariah*, 354.
[724] Barker, "Zechariah," 695.
[725] Floyd, *Minor Prophets*, 555.
[726] Baldwin, *Zechariah*, 206.
[727] Unger, *Zechariah*, 265.
[728] Meyers and Meyers, *Zechariah 9–14*, 470–71.
[729] Schaefer, "Ending of the Book of Zechariah," 165–238.
[730] J. L. Rubenstein, "Sukkot, Eschatology and Zechariah 14," *RB* 103 (1996): 161–95; see H. Fox, "The Forelife of Ideas and the Afterlife of Texts," *RB* 105 (1998): 520–25.

of thankfulness will be the withholding of rain and the resultant effect on the crops, a punishment that aptly fits the offense. In the list of curses for covenant disobedience, Deut 28:22–24 predicted divinely ordained drought as one of the punishments God's people would suffer (see Amos 4:7–8).

It is unclear whether the circumstances sketched by Zechariah in v. 17 are hypothetical or actual. McComiskey argues emphatically that any discussion about anyone not worshipping the Lord as required is purely hypothetical.[731] Barker suggests that "rain" functions figuratively for spiritual blessing.[732] Arguing a perspective similar to McComiskey, Baldwin maintains that the "rain" should not be interpreted literally.[733] In the day when "the survivors from all the nations that have attacked Jerusalem" will worship the Lord, and when God finally reigns on earth, it is difficult to imagine sin reemerging to mar God's creation with such flagrant disobedience to the Lord. Alternatively, many commentators conclude that the disobedience will be real.[734] The common denominator between both actual and figurative understandings is the absolute sovereignty that the Lord will wield over his newly established kingdom. The Lord will also demand and receive absolute allegiance from all the peoples of the earth.

Verse 17 consigns a drought to "any of the peoples of the earth" who failed to worship the Lord through the Feast of Tabernacles. However inclusive this phrase was, Zechariah focused on Egypt specifically. Zechariah had good reason for singling out Egypt for special mention. The Old Testament indicates that Egypt will come to Jerusalem to worship (Isa 19:18–22; Mic 7:12). Unlike the other nations that depended on rainfall for their agricultural yield, Egypt relied on irrigation water provided by the Nile (Deut 11:10–11; Jer 46:7–8). Consequently, "a threat to withhold rain would have been ridiculous."[735] Zechariah's inclusion of Egypt ensured that no nation would escape divine judgment for their disobedience. A further reason for emphasis on Egypt is the connection of the Feast of Tabernacles to the exodus from Egypt (Lev 23:43). In the last days, the Egyptians will join the Jews in celebrating the release of the captives. At least one additional perspective merits comment. A significant number of Israelites from various tribes lived in Egypt from the late eighth century BC onwards.[736] Several passages indicate that many Israelites inhabited Egypt (see Jer 24:8; 43:1–13). Extra-biblical data from sources such as Elephantine reiterate the same message. This final observation includes any Israelites who might live outside the promised land.

---

[731] McComiskey, "Zechariah," 1242.
[732] Barker, "Zechariah," 696.
[733] Baldwin, *Zechariah*, 206.
[734] Merrill, *Zechariah*, 363–64.
[735] Mitchell, *Zechariah*, 355.
[736] Meyers and Meyers, *Zechariah 9–14*, 475.

Repeating the same word for "plague" *(maggēpâ)* employed in 14:12, v. 18 warns that the Egyptians will once again face a plague from the Lord if they fail to worship God in Jerusalem. The association with Egypt and divinely sent plagues was firmly established at the time of Moses (Exod 7–11). But the exodus account used a synonym for "plague" *(negep).*[737] Since the word *negep* referred to the death of the firstborn in Exod 12:13, Merrill concludes that the plague in Zech 14:18 would also require punishment by death.[738] While possible, the meaning of *negep* does not always signify capital punishment. Moreover, the punishment meted out to the other nations for not commemorating the Feast of Tabernacles in v. 17 does not appear to be death.

The Hebrew text and clause structure in v. 18 is complex, and detailed discussion exceeds the parameters of this volume. Some resort to emendation in order to clarify the meaning of the verse.[739] However, the most likely solution follows the Septuagintal reading, omitting the third negative particle *wĕlōʾ*.[740] The NIV follows the KJV tradition of supplying the notion of "rain" from the previous verse (cf. NASB, HCSB).

**14:19** Here Zechariah linked the "punishment" *(ḥaṭṭaʾt)* of the nations with that of Egypt.[741] Thus, the prophet did not single out Egypt, but included both the sin and punishment of all peoples who may be guilty of failing "to go up to celebrate the Feast of Tabernacles." The repetition of the "going up" motif reiterates the paramount significance of worship in this context. The Hebrew word *ḥaṭṭaʾt* can be translated as "sin," "punishment," or "sin offering." Accordingly, *ḥaṭṭaʾt* represents the evil act and the punishment that the deed merits.

The repetition of "the nations" underscores their importance to the Lord. God wanted to incorporate foreigners in the formal worship of the Lord at the temple, but this development required dramatic changes both in the worship and in the culture.

**14:20–21** These verses conclude the final movement in 14:12–21. The overarching message of the final two verses in chap. 14 transfers the renewed holiness in the kingdom temple to the entire city of Jerusalem.[742] Then the holiness pervading Zion will spread to the whole nation of Judah in order to encompass the "peoples of the earth." As with all of chaps. 13–14, the momentous events envisioned by Zechariah will occur in the eschatological era the prophet deemed "on that day."

---

[737] נֶגֶף. *HALOT*, 669.
[738] Merrill, *Zechariah*, 364.
[739] A. S van der Woude, "Sacharja 14, 18," *ZAW* 97 (1985): 254–55.
[740] וְלֹא. Baldwin, *Zechariah*, 207; Merrill, *Zechariah*, 366–67; Mitchell, *Zechariah*, 355.
[741] חַטָּאת. *HALOT*, 306; see *TLOT*, 406–11; *TDOT*, 4:309–19.
[742] Baldwin, *Zechariah*, 207.

In the coming kingdom epoch, the phrase "HOLY TO THE LORD" *(qōdeš laY-HWH)* will be inscribed on various items from everyday life.[743] In Exod 28:36 the identical phrase was written on the turban worn by the high priest as a perpetual reminder to priest and people alike of his consecration to the Lord (cf. the inscription on the vestments worn by Joshua the high priest in Zech 3:9). Recently, archaeologists in Israel have uncovered a bowl with "holy" *(qdš)* inscribed on it, suggesting that a practice of inscribing such a message may have existed in antiquity.[744] God intended for the same measure of holiness to extend to the whole nation, however, not just the priest. In a passage meant to charter the spiritual course of the nation, Exod 19:4–6 exhorted all Israel (cf. Jer 2:2–3b),

> You yourselves have seen what I did to Egypt, and how I carried you on eagles' wings and brought you to myself. Now if you obey me fully and keep my covenant, then out of all nations you will be my treasured possession. Although the whole earth is mine, you will be for me a kingdom of priests and a holy nation.

This holiness will extend even to the animals in the land.

Holy is the primary attribute ascribed to the Lord in the Old Testament. The fundamental linguistic idea of *qōdeš* is the separateness or distinctiveness of something.[745] When speaking of the Lord, his holiness signifies his absolute uniqueness, separate from everything that he created and distinct from anything people may claim to be a god.

The "bells" on the horses will be attached to their bridles or harnesses. Bells also adorned the priestly vestments (Exod 28:33; 39:25–26). The sacred use of bells elsewhere indicates that even the horse with all of its negative spiritual connotations will reflect the inscription affirming its dedication as a holy object to the Lord.[746]

Earlier in the book, Zechariah introduced horses in contexts that represent war and judgment (see 1:7–17; 6:1–8). In the ancient world, the horse was primarily a weapon of warfare. For this reason, the Old Testament's attitude toward these animals was primarily negative, disparaging their use in royal pomp and warfare alike. The law of Moses expressly forbids the possession of large herds of horses: "the king, moreover, must not acquire great numbers of horses for himself" (Deut 17:16). Likewise, Isa 2:7 and Ezek 38:4 both denigrate horses as a symbol of that which opposes the values of the Lord's kingdom.[747]

---

[743] קֹדֶשׁ לַיהוה. *HALOT*, 1076–78.
[744] R. P. Gordon, "Inscribed Pots and Zechariah XIV 20–1," *VT* 42 (1992): 120–22; cf. G. Barklay, "A Bowl with the Hebrew Inscription *qdš*," *IEJ* 40 (1990): 124–29.
[745] *TLOT*, 1103–18.
[746] Meyers and Meyers, *Zechariah 9–14*, 481.
[747] Mitchell, *Zechariah*, 355.

The ultimate demotion of the status of the horse appears in Zech 9:9 where the Messianic King rides into Jerusalem on a donkey—not a horse—and v. 10 predicts God's ultimate removal of war horses from Jerusalem (see Mic 5:10). On yet another level, the horse was classified among the unclean animals (Lev 11:1–8).[748]

The positive reference to horses in 14:20 thus represents a surprising shift in attitude about the horse, since "as a beast of war and of human political aggression, it represents the antithesis of God's harmonious rule at the end of days."[749] But in 14:20 the prophet imbues the horse with completely new meaning. With wars brought to a final end, horses could serve as beasts of burden, including transporting worshippers to celebrate the Feast of Tabernacles (cf. Isa 66:20). The new kingdom will be so revolutionary that even an unclean animal routinely used for ignoble purposes in antiquity will become holy before the Lord. Mitchell summarizes the thought well: "The horse is holy because he brings, not a warrior, to kill and waste, but a pilgrim to worship at the temple of Yahweh."[750]

"Cooking pots" *(sîrôt)* refers to an article with a broad spectrum of uses in the Old Testament.[751] Not one of the more valued temple utensils, these "pots" held the ashes remaining from a sacrifice (Exod 27:3), so they stood at the bottom of the hierarchy of temple utensils.[752] The pots also functioned as cooking vessels. Baldwin suggests that Zechariah's pots were used to cook the meat for the fellowship offering.[753] The mandate for the fellowship offering occurs in Lev 3; 7:11–18. This offering includes a portion given to the Lord but differs from other offerings (such as the whole burnt offering) that are wholly dedicated to the Lord. The fellowship offering served as an occasion for thanksgiving to God, a theme that harmonizes well with the spirit of the Feast of Tabernacles. Much of the fellowship offering was consumed by the worshipper and his family in the temple court. Baldwin's conclusion may be correct, but it certainly cannot be demonstrated conclusively. Nonetheless, Zechariah's primary theological emphasis is clear.

These common cauldrons will become as holy as the "sacred bowls" at the perimeter of the altar. These bowls held the blood collected from the offering that was in turn sprinkled on the altar to symbolize the purification that the blood effected. Zechariah surveyed various items in v. 20. These items ranged from bells on the horses' harnesses to cooking pots conscripted for use in the temple. All of these items will be designated "HOLY TO THE LORD." Thus, no

---

[748] Merrill, *Zechariah*, 365.

[749] Meyers and Meyers, *Zechariah 9–14*, 480.

[750] Mitchell, *Zechariah*, 356.

[751] סירות. *HALOT*, 752.

[752] Meyers and Meyers, *Zechariah 9–14*, 483; Schaefer, "Ending of the Book of Zechariah," 234–35.

[753] Baldwin, *Zechariah*, 207.

longer will any distinction between secular and profane remain (see 8:3).[754] Even human tendencies toward aggression and oppression will be brought under submission to the Lord's righteousness as peace finally reigns on earth and weapons of warfare serve peaceful purposes.

Every cooking utensil will be holy, sacred for the service of the Lord God, which is the same point with which Zechariah concluded v. 20. The pots in v. 20 may refer to vessels employed in the temple, but the focus in this final verse is far broader. Thus, Zechariah stressed the inclusive nature of God's holiness, for *every* mundane pot, even those which were not used in the temple, would become "HOLY TO THE LORD."

The Hebrew word for "Canaanite" *(kĕna'ănî)* in v. 21 can also mean "merchant"[755] (see Prov 31:24). The gentilic use of *kĕna'ănî* appears frequently in the Old Testament to refer to the inhabitants of the promised land whom God commanded his people to displace (Josh 3:10).[756] Interpreters differ on which nuance of *kĕna'ănî* fits the context of Zech 14:21.

McComiskey argues that "merchant" cannot correspond to the discussion at the end of chap. 14.[757] He sees no thematic correlation between "merchants" and the "house of the LORD." Arguing a similar point, Merrill contends that the ancient memory of the Canaanites' abominations powerfully illustrated the idolatry and the reprehensible lifestyle that Zechariah foretold would be terminated forever.[758] Continuing the emphasis on holiness throughout the creation, this view refers to the Canaanites, not as a historical entity, but as a powerful literary symbol of illicit worship. Although Unger repeatedly argues for a "literal" interpretation of Zechariah's prophecies, he concedes that "Canaanite" in Zech 14:21 "is best taken as a figure of a morally and spiritually unclean person."[759] McComiskey writes, "The assurance that no Canaanite will exist in God's temple guarantees the end of every threat of impurity in the kingdom of God and further underscores the absolute rule of God over the new Jerusalem."[760]

Alternatively, the meaning of *kĕna'ănî* may refer to a "merchant," a perspective adopted by the Targum, Vulgate, and numerous modern students of this passage.[761] This view takes Zechariah's statement to mean that greed and avarice will no longer be a part of worship in the Lord's temple because those offerings will finally be offered from a pure heart (Isa 35:8; Ezek 44:9). Furthermore, no one will see the work of the Lord as a money-making enter-

---

[754] McComiskey, "Zechariah," 1244.
[755] כְּנַעֲנִי. *HALOT*, 485–86.
[756] D. J. Wiseman, ed., *Peoples of Old Testament Times* (Oxford: Clarendon, 1973), 29–52.
[757] McComiskey, "Zechariah," 1244.
[758] Merrill, *Zechariah*, 366; also Meyers and Meyers, *Zechariah 9–14*, 489–92.
[759] Unger, *Zechariah*, 270–71.
[760] McComiskey, "Zechariah," 1244.
[761] Baldwin, *Zechariah*, 207–8; Schaefer, "Ending of the Book of Zechariah," 236. See the discussion on 11:7 where an altered combination of consonants can also yield *kĕna'ănî*.

prise.⁷⁶² Thus, the "merchant" translation sees the primary message to be a continuation of the theme of holy worship in the temple.

Perhaps the wisest solution is to avoid pressing the issue for a single best answer. Zechariah's careful selection of *kĕna'ănî* allows for a double entendre in which both nuances of the term convey distinct and important theological points.⁷⁶³ The complete spiritual restoration will forever remove every vestige of sin from creation, allowing all to worship God righteously. The prophet's paramount message is that the temple of the Lord will be fully restored and will reflect a holiness never before seen on earth.

Zechariah 14 concludes with the promise that the Lord will recreate everything, including the Lord's people in Jerusalem. Everything will finally fall under God's jurisdiction.⁷⁶⁴ The Lord will not only reign in the lives of the faithful, but over all mankind, indeed all creation. Revelation 19:16 describes Christ's reign this way: "On his robe and on his thigh he has this name written: 'KING OF KINGS AND LORD OF LORDS.'" Baldwin states: "When that condition is fulfilled, everyday life will be 'holy to the Lord,' and all human problems solved."⁷⁶⁵

Zechariah's promised restoration of Jerusalem raises the fundamental interpretive question of how to interpret "Jerusalem." This issue far surpasses the scope of Zech 14. One approach treats "Jerusalem" and its companion "Israel" as the Old Testament precursor of the Church, with the Church inheriting the promises made to national Israel. McComiskey writes, "In Pauline theology, the key that unlocks the presence of the church in an Old Testament text is its allusion to elements of the Abrahamic promise."⁷⁶⁶

In contrast, Unger represents the interpretive solution to the question of the theological significance of the name "Israel" that seeks to differentiate biblical promises made to Israel from other scriptural assurances issued to the Church. This viewpoint tends to stress the spiritual *and* physical components to God's eternal kingdom. Unger emphasized the point that God made promises explicitly to national Israel. With a play on the meaning of the prophet Zechariah's name, Unger wrote, "in his very name, 'God remembers,' i.e., He remembers His covenants and promises to Israel involving their future kingdom."⁷⁶⁷

Biblical history points to the second coming of Jesus when wrongs will be made right and creation will cease groaning under the travails of sin. Charles

---

[762] Jesus drove the money changers out of the temple when they were acting as merchants (Matt 21:12–13; Mark 11:15–18; Luke 19:45–48; John 2:12–16). See P. B. Duff, "The March of the Divine Warrior and the Advent of the Greco-Roman King: Mark's Account of Jesus' Entry into Jerusalem," *JBL* 111 (1992): 55–71; and C. Roth, "The Cleansing of the Temple and Zechariah XIV 21," *NT* 4 (1960): 174–81.

[763] Sweeney, *Twelve Prophets*, 706; Floyd, *Minor Prophets*, 556.

[764] Schaefer, "Ending of the Book of Zechariah," 237–38.

[765] Baldwin, *Zechariah*, 208.

[766] McComiskey, "Zechariah," 1224.

[767] Unger, *Zechariah*, 240.

Wesley's hymn "Come, Thou Long-Expected Jesus" embodies much of what Zech 14 anticipated:

> Come, Thou long-expected Jesus,
> Born to set Thy people free;
> From our fears and sins release us;
> Let us find our rest in Thee.
> Israel's strength and consolation,
> Hope of all the earth Thou art;
> Dear desire of ev'ry nation,
> Joy of ev'ry longing heart.
>
> Born Thy people to deliver,
> Born a child, and yet a King,
> Born to reign in us forever,
> Now Thy gracious kingdom bring.
> By Thine own eternal spirit
> Rule in all our hearts alone;
> By Thine all-sufficient merit,
> Raise us to Thy glorious throne.[768]

---

[768] *The Baptist Hymnal*, # 77.

# Selected Bibliography

*Commentaries*

Achtemeier, Elizabeth. *Nahum-Malachi*. Interpretation. Atlanta: John Knox, 1986.
Amsler, Samuel. *Aggée Zacharie 1–8*. Neuchatel: Delachaux et Niestlé, 1981.
Baldwin, Joyce G. *Haggai, Zechariah, Malachi: An Introduction and Commentary*. TOTC. Downers Grove, IL: InterVarsity, 1972.
Barker, Kenneth L. "Zechariah." In *The Expositor's Bible Commentary, Vol. 7*, ed. F. E. Gaebelein, 593–697. Grand Rapids: Eerdmans, 1983.
Baron, David. *The Visions and Prophecies of Zechariah*. Reprint ed. Grand Rapids: Kregel, 1972.
Beuken, W. A. M. *Haggai-Sacharja 1–8*. Assen: Van Gorcum, 1967.
Bewer, J. A. *The Book of the Twelve Prophets*. Vol. 2. New York: Harper & Row, 1949.
Boda, Mark J. *The NIV Application Commentary: Haggai, Zechariah*. Grand Rapids: Zondervan, 2004.
Chisholm, Robert B. *Interpreting the Minor Prophets*. Grand Rapids: Zondervan, 1989.
Clark, David J. and Howard A. Hatton. *Haggai, Zechariah, and Malachi*. UBS Handbook Series. New York: United Bible Societies, 2002.
Cohen, A. *The Twelve Prophets*. New York: Soncino, 1948.
Conrad, Edgar W. *Zechariah*. Sheffield: Sheffield Academic Press, 1999.
Dentan, R. C. *Zechariah 9–14*. IB. 6. New York: Abingdon, 1956.
Dods, Marcus. *The Post-Exilian Prophets: Haggai, Zechariah, Malachi*. Edinburgh: T&T Clark, 1879.
Driver, S. R., ed. *The Minor Prophets*. New York: Oxford University Press, 1904.
Elliger, Karl. *Das Buch der zwölf kleinen Propheten II: Die Propheten Nahum, Habakuk, Zephanja, Haggai, Zacharja, Maleachi*. Göttingen: Vandenhoeck & Ruprecht, 1975.
Ewald, Heinrich. *Die Propheten des Alten Bundes*. Stuttgart: A. Krabbe, 1840.
Feinberg, Charles L. *God Remembers: A Study of the Book of Zechariah*. Portland, OR: Multnomah, 1965.
_____. *The Minor Prophets*. Chicago: Moody, 1976.
Ferreiro, Alberto, ed. *The Twelve Prophets*. Ancient Christian Commentary on Scripture. Downers Grove, IL: InterVarsity, 2003.
Floyd, Michael H. *Minor Prophets, Part 2*. FOTL. Grand Rapids: Eerdmans, 2000.
Gaebelein, A. C. *Studies in Zechariah*. New York: Our Hope Publishers, n.d.
Hanhart, Robert. *Sacharja 1–8*. Neukirchener-Vluyn: Neukirchener, 1998.
Ironside, H. A. *Notes on the Minor Prophets*. New York: Loizeaux, 1928.
Jones, Douglas R. *Haggai, Zechariah and Malachi*. London: SCM, 1962.
Keil, C. F. and F. Delitzsch. *The Minor Prophets*. Translated by J. Martin. Reprint ed. Grand Rapids: Eerdmans, 1980.
Kimchi, D. *Commentary upon the Prophecies of Zechariah*. Translated by A. M'Caul. London: James Duncan, 1837.
Kodell, Jerome. *Lamentations, Haggai, Zechariah, Second Zechariah, Malachi, Obadiah, Joel, Baruch*. Wilmington, DE: Michael Glazier, 1982.
Laetsch, Theodore. *The Minor Prophets*. St. Louis: Concordia, 1956.
Lamarche, Paul. *Zacharie IX–XIV*. Paris: Librairie Lecoffre, 1961.
Leupold, H. C. *Exposition of Zechariah*. Grand Rapids: Baker, 1965.
Lowe, W. H. *Zechariah*. HSC. London: Macmillan, 1882.
Luck, G. Coleman. *Zechariah*. Chicago: Moody, 1964.

# SELECTED BIBLIOGRAPHY

Luther, Martin. "Lectures on Zechariah. The German Text, 1527." In *Luther's Works, Vol. 20: Lectures on the Minor Prophets III: Zechariah*, ed. H. C. Oswald, 153–347. Saint Louis: Concordia, 1973.

McComiskey, Thomas. "Zechariah." In *The Minor Prophets, Vol. 3*, ed. T. E. McComiskey, 1003–1244. Grand Rapids: Baker, 1992.

Mason, Rex. *Haggai, Zechariah, and Malachi*. CBC. Cambridge: Cambridge University Press, 1977.

Meyers, Carol L. and Eric Meyers. *Haggai-Zechariah 1–8*. AB. Garden City, NY: Doubleday, 1987.

_____. *Zechariah 9–14*. AB. Garden City, NY: Doubleday, 1993.

Merrill, Eugene H. *Haggai, Zechariah, Malachi*. Chicago: Moody, 1994.

Miller, Stephen R. *Nahum, Habakkuk, Zephaniah, Haggai, Zechariah, Malachi*. Holman Old Testament Commentary. Nashville: Broadman and Holman, 2004.

Mitchell, H. G., J. M. P. Smith, and J. A. Bewer. *A Critical and Exegetical Commentary on Haggai, Zechariah, Malachi, and Jonah*. ICC. Edinburgh: T&T Clark, 1937.

O'Brien, Julia M. *Nahum, Habakkuk, Zephaniah, Haggai, Zechariah, Malachi*. Nashville: Abingdon, 2004.

Ollenberger, Ben C. "Zechariah." In *The New Interpreters Bible, vol. 7*. ed. L. Keck, 733–840. Nashville: Abingdon, 1996.

Orelli, Conrad Von. *The Twelve Minor Prophets*. Translated by J. S. Banks. Edinburgh: T&T Clark, 1893.

Otzen, Benedikt. *Studien über Deuterosacharja*. Copenhagen: Prostand Apud Munksgaard, 1964.

Petersen, David L. *Haggai and Zechariah 1–8*. OTL. Philadelphia: Westminster, 1984.

_____. *Zechariah 9–14*. OTL. Louisville: Westminster John Knox, 1995.

Petitjean, A. *Les oracles du Proto-Zacharie*. Paris: J. Gabalda, 1969.

Pusey, E. B. *The Minor Prophets*. Vol. 2. New York: Funk & Wagnalls, 1886.

_____. *The Minor Prophets: A Commentary*. 2 vols. Reprint ed. Grand Rapids: Baker, 1950.

Redditt, Paul L. *Haggai, Zechariah, Malachi*. NCBC. Grand Rapids: Eerdmans, 1995.

Robinson, George L. *The Prophecies of Zechariah*. Chicago: University of Chicago Press, 1896.

_____. *The Twelve Minor Prophets*. Grand Rapids: Baker, 1952.

Rudolph, W. *Haggai, Sacharja 1–8; Sacharja 9–14*. Gütersloh: Gerd Mohn, 1976

Saebø, Magne. *Sacharja 9–14*. Neukirchen-Vluyn: Neukirchener, 1969.

Smith, Ralph L. *Micah-Malachi*. WBC. Waco, TX: Word, 1984.

Speers, Theodore C. *Zechariah*. Nashville: Abingdon, 1956.

Stuhlmueller, Carroll C. P. *Haggai & Zechariah: Rebuilding with Hope*. ITC. Grand Rapids: Eerdmans, 1988.

Sweeney, Marvin A. *The Twelve Prophets, Vol. 2: Micah, Nahum, Habakkuk, Zephaniah, Haggai, Zechariah, Malachi*. Berit Olam. Collegeville, MN: Liturgical, 2000.

Tatford, Frederick. A. *A Prophet of the Myrtle Grove*. Eastbourne: Prophetic Witness, 1974.

Thomas, D. W. and R. C. Dentan. "The Book of Zechariah." *IB* 6. Nashville: Abingdon, 1956.

Unger, Merrill F. *Commentary on Zechariah*. Grand Rapids: Zondervan, 1962.

Watts, John D. W. "Zechariah." In *The Broadman Bible Commentary, Vol. 7*, ed. C. J. Allen, 308–65. Nashville: Broadman, 1972.

Wright, C. H. H. *Zechariah and His Prophecies*. London: Hodder & Stoughton, 1879.

## Special Studies

Ackroyd, Peter R. "The Book of Haggai and Zechariah I–VIII." *JSS* 3 (1952): 151–56.
_____. *Exile and Restoration*. OTL. Philadelphia: Westminster, 1968.
_____. "The Old Testament Historical Problems of the Early Persian Period." *JNES* 17 (1958): 14–27.
Adams, John. *The Man Among the Myrtles: A Study in Zechariah's Visions*. Edinburgh: T&T Clark, 1913.
Amsler, S. "Zacharie et l'origine d'apocalyptique." *VTSup* 22 (1972): 227–31.
Bailey, J. "The Usage of the Post Restoration Period Terms Descriptive of the Priest and High Priest." *JBL* 70 (1951): 217–25.
Barthélemy, Dominique, et al., ed. *Preliminary and Interim Report on the Hebrew Old Testament Text Project*. 5 vols. New York: United Bible Societies, 1980.
Ben Zvi, Ehud. "Twelve Prophetic Books or 'The Twelve': A Few Preliminary Considerations." In J. W. Watts and P. R. House, eds., *Forming Prophetic Literature: Essays on Isaiah and the Twelve in Honor of John D. W. Watts*, 125–56. Sheffield: Sheffield Academic Press, 1996.
Bewer, Julius A. "Two Suggestions on Prov 30:31 and Zech 9:16." *JBL* 67 (1948): 61–62.
Blank, Sheldon H. "The Death of Zechariah in Rabbinic Literature." *HUCA* 12–13 (1937–38): 327–46.
Blocher, Henri. "Zacharie 3: Josue et le Grand Jour des Expiations." *Etudes Theologiques et Religieuses* 54 (1979): 264–70.
Blomberg, Craig L. *The Historical Reliability of the Gospels*. Downers Grove: InterVarsity, 1987.
Boda, Mark J. *Bringing Out the Treasure: Inner Biblical Allusion and Zechariah 9–14*. JSOTSup 370. Edited by Mark J. Boda and Michael H. Floyd. Sheffield: Sheffield Academic Press, 2003.
_____. "From Fasts to Feasts: The Literary Function of Zechariah 7–8." *CBQ* 65 (2003): 390–407.
_____. *Haggai & Zechariah Research: A Bibliographic Survey*. Leiden: Deo, 2003.
_____. "Majoring on the Minors: Recent Research on Haggai and Zechariah." *Currents in Biblical Research* 2 (2003): 33–68.
_____. "Oil, Crowns and Thrones: Prophet, Priest and King in Zechariah 1:7–6:15," *Journal of Hebrew Scriptures* 3 (2001) [journal on-line]; accessed 29 November 2005; available from http://purl.org/jhs; Internet.
_____. "Reading Between the Lines." In M. J. Boda and M. H. Floyd, eds., *Bringing out the Treasure: Inner Biblical Allusion in Zechariah 9–14*, 277–91. Sheffield: Sheffield Academic Press, 2003.
_____. "Terrifying the Horns: Persia and Babylon in Zechariah 1:7–6:15." *CBQ* 67 (2005): 22–41.
_____. "Zechariah: Master Mason or Penitential Prophet?" In R. Albertz and B. Becking, eds., *Yahwism after the Exile: Perspectives on Israelite Religion in the Persian Era*, 49–69. Assen: Van Gorcum, 2003.
Bright, John. *A History of Israel*. 3rd ed. Philadelphia: Westminster, 1981.
Bruce, F. F. "The Book of Zechariah and the Passion Narrative." *BJRL* 43 (1961): 336–53.
_____. *New Testament Development of Old Testament Themes*. Reprint ed. Grand Rapids: Eerdmans, 1994.
Bruehler, Bart B. "Seeing through the עינים of Zechariah: Understanding Zechariah 4." *CBQ* 63 (2001): 430–43.

Butterworth, Mike. *Structure and the Book of Zechariah*. Sheffield: Sheffield Academic Press, 1992.
Chary, Théophane. *Aggée-Zacharie-Malachie*. Paris: Librairie Lecoffre, 1969.
Chernus, Ira. "'A Wall of Fire Round About': The Development of a Theme in Rabbinic Midrash." *JJS* 30 (1979): 68–84.
Clark, David. "The Case of the Vanishing Angel." *BT* 33 (1982): 213–18.
_____. "Discourse Structure in Zechariah 7.1–8.23." *BT* 36 (1985): 328–35.
_____. "Discourse Structure in Zechariah 9–14: Skeleton or Phantom?" In *Issues in Bible Translation*, ed. P. C. Stine, 64–80. New York: United Bible Societies, 1988.
Clements, R. E. "The Messianic Hope in the Old Testament." JSOT 43 (1989): 3–19.
Clifford, R. J. *The Cosmic Mountain in Canaan and the Old Testament*. Cambridge: Harvard University Press, 1972.
Collins, John J. "The Eschatology of Zechariah." In L. L. Grabbe and R. D. Haak, eds., *Knowing the End from the Beginning: The Prophetic, the Apocalyptic and Their Relationships*, 74–84. London: T&T Clark, 2003.
Collins, Terry. "The Literary Contexts of Zechariah 9:9." In C. Tuckett, ed., *The Book of Zechariah and Its Influence*, 29–40. Burlington: Ashgate, 2003.
Conrad, Edgar W. "The End of Prophecy and the Appearance of Angels/Messengers in the Book of the Twelve." JSOT 73 (1997): 65–79.
Cook, Stephen L. "The Metamorphosis of a Shepherd: The Tradition History of Zechariah 11:17 + 13:7–9." *CBQ* 55 (1993): 453–66.
Cornelius, Izak. "Paradise Motifs in the 'Eschatology' of the Minor Prophets and the Iconography of the Ancient Near East. The Concepts of Fertility, Water, Trees and 'Tierfrieden' and Gen 2–3." *JNSL* 14 (1988): 41–51.
Cross, Frank Moore, Jr. *Canaanite Myth and Hebrew Epic*. Cambridge: Harvard University Press, 1973.
Crotty, R. B. "The Suffering Moses of Deutero-Zechariah." *Colloquium* 14 (1982): 43–50.
Dahood, Mitchell. "Zacharia 9,1, *'EN 'ADAM*." *CBQ* 25 (1963): 123–24.
Day, John. "The Origin of Armageddon: Revelation 16:16 as an Interpretation of Zechariah 12:11." In *Crossing the Boundaries: Essays in Biblical Interpretation in Honour of Michael D. Goulder*, ed. S. E. Porter, P. Joyce, and D. E. Orton, 315–26. Leiden: E. J. Brill, 1994.
Day, Peggy L. *An Adversary in Heaven: Satan in the Hebrew Bible*. HSM 43. Atlanta: Scholars Press, 1988.
de Boer, P. A. H. *An Inquiry into the Meaning of the Term maśśa'*. Leiden: E. J. Brill, 1948.
de Jonge, Henk Jan. "The Cleansing of the Temple in Mark 11:15 and Zechariah 14:21." In C. Tuckett, ed., *The Book of Zechariah and Its Influence*, 87–100. Burlington: Ashgate, 2003.
de Vaux, Roland. *Ancient Israel*. New York: McGraw-Hill, 1965.
De Vries, Simon J. "Futurism in the Preexilic Minor Prophets Compared with That of the Postexilic Minor Prophets." *BZAW* 325 (2003): 252–72.
Delcor, M. "Deux passages difficiles: Zach XII 11 et XI 13." *VT* 3 (1953): 67–77.
_____. "Les allusions à Alexandre le Grand dans Zach IX 1–8." *VT* 1 (1951): 110–24.
Demsky, Aaron. "The Temple Steward Josiah ben Zephaniah." *IEJ* 31 (1981) 100–2.
Duff, Paul Brooks. "The March of the Divine Warrior and the Advent of the Greco-Roman King: Mark's Account of Jesus' Entry into Jerusalem." *JBL* 111 (1992): 55–71.

Duguid, Iain. "Messianic Themes in Zechariah 9–14." In *The Lord's Anointed: Interpretation of Old Testament Messianic Texts*, ed. P. E. Satterthwaite, R. S. Hess, and G. J. Wenham, 265–80. Grand Rapids: Baker, 1995.

Ellis, Richard. *Foundation Deposits in Ancient Mesopotamia*. New Haven: Yale University Press, 1968.

Ellul, Danielle. "Variations Sur Le Theme De La Guerre Sainte Dans Le Deutero-Zacharie." *Etudes Theologiques et Religieuses* 56 (1981): 55–71.

Evans, Craig A. "I Will Go before You into Galilee." *JTS* NS 5 (1954): 3–18.

———. "Jesus and Zechariah's Messianic Hope." In *Authenticating the Activities of Jesus*, ed. B. Chilton and C. F. Evans, 373–88. Leiden: E. J. Brill, 1999.

———. " 'The Two Sons of Oil': Early Evidence of Messianic Interpretation of Zechariah 4:14 in 4Q254 4 2." In *The Provo International Conference on the Dead Sea Scrolls*, eds., D. Perry and E. Ulrich, 566–75. Leiden: E. J. Brill, 1999.

Eybers, I. H. "The Rebuilding of the Temple according to Haggai and Zechariah." In *Studies in Old Testament Prophecy*, OTWSA, ed. W. C. van Wyk, 15–26. Potchefstroom: Pro Rege, 1975.

Feigin, Samuel. "Some Notes on Zechariah 11:4–17." *JBL* 44 (1925): 203–13.

Finley, Tom. "The Sheep Merchants of Zechariah 11." *Grace Theological Journal* 3 (1982): 51–65.

———. " 'The Apple of His Eye' in Zechariah II: 12." *VT* 38 (1988): 377–38.

Floyd, Michael H. "Deutero-Zechariah and Types of Intertextuality." In M. J. Boda and M. H. Floyd, eds., *Bringing out the Treasure: Inner Biblical Allusion in Zechariah 9–14*, 225–44. Sheffield: Sheffield Academic Press, 2003.

———. "The Evil in the Ephah: Reading Zechariah 5:5–11 in Its Literary Context." *CBQ* 58 (1996): 51–68.

———. "The משא as a Type of Prophetic Book." *JBL* 121 (2002): 401–22.

———. "Zechariah and the Changing Views of Second Temple Judaism in Recent Commentaries." *Religious Studies Review* 25 (1999): 257–63.

Foster, Paul. "The Use of Zechariah in Matthew's Gospel." In C. Tuckett, ed., *The Book of Zechariah and Its Influence*, 65–85. Burlington: Ashgate, 2003.

Fox, Harry. "The Forelife of Ideas and the Afterlife of Texts." *RB* 105 (1998): 520–25.

France, R. T. *Jesus and the Old Testament: His Application of Old Testament Passages to Himself*. London: Tyndale, 1971.

Freedman, David Noel. "The Flying Scroll in Zechariah 5:1–4." In *Studies in Near Eastern Culture and History*, ed. J. A. Bellamy, 42–48. Ann Arbor: University of Michigan Press, 1990.

Fuller, Russell. "Early Emendations of the Scribes: The *Tiqqun Sopherim* in Zechariah 2:12." In *Of Scribes and Scrolls*, ed. H. Attridge, J. J. Collins, T. H. Tobin, 21–28. Lanham, MD: University Press of America, 1990.

Gese, H. "Anfang und Ende der Apokalyptik, dargestellt am Sacharjabuch." *Theologie und Kirche* 70 (1973): 20–49.

Ginsberg, Harold L. "The Oldest Record of Hysteria with Physical Stigmata, Zech 13:2–6." In *Studies in the Bible and Ancient Near East*, ed. Y. Avishur and J. Blau, 23–27. Jerusalem: E. Rubenstein, 1978.

Glasson, T. Francis. "Theophany and Parousia." *NTS* 34 (1988): 259–70.

Good, Robert M. "Zechariah 14:13 and Related Texts: Brother Against Brother in War." *MAARAV* 8 (1982): 39–47.

———. "Zechariah's Second Night Vision (Zech 2,1–4)." *Bib* 63 (1982): 56–59.

Gordon, R. P. "Inscribed Pots and Zechariah XIV 20–1." *VT* 42 (1992): 120–23.

———. "Targum Variant Agrees With Wellhausen!" *ZAW* 87 (1975): 218–19.

_____. "Targumic ʿdy (Zechariah XIV 6) and the Not So Common 'Cold.' " *VT* 29 (1989): 77–81.
Gowan, Donald E. "Wealth and Poverty in the Old Testament." *Int* 41 (1987): 341–53.
Gundry, Robert H. *The Use of the Old Testament in St. Matthew's Gospel*. Leiden: E. J. Brill, 1967.
Halpern, Baruch. "The Ritual Background of Zechariah's Temple Song." *CBQ* 40 (1978): 167–90.
Ham, Clay Alan. *The Coming King and the Rejected Shepherd: Matthew's Reading of Zechariah's Messianic Hope*. Sheffield: Sheffield Phoenix, 2005.
Hanson, Paul D. *The Dawn of Apocalyptic*. Revised ed. Philadelphia: Fortress, 1979.
_____. "In Defiance of Death: Zechariah's Symbolic Universe." In *Love and Death in the Ancient Near East*, ed. J. Marks and R. Good, 173–79. Guilford, CN: Four Quarters, 1987.
_____. "Zechariah 9 and the Recapitulation of an Ancient Ritual Pattern." *JBL* 92 (1973): 37–59.
Harrelson, Walter. "The Celebration of the Feast of Booths According to Zechariah XIV 16–21." In *Religions in Antiquity*, ed. J. Neusner, 88–96. Leiden: E. J. Brill, 1968.
_____. "Nonroyal Motifs in the Royal Eschatology." In *Israel's Prophetic Heritage*, ed. B. W. Anderson & W. Harrelson. London: SCM, 1962.
_____. "The Trial of the High Priest Joshua: Zechariah 3." *Eretz-Israel* 16 (1982): 116–24.
_____. "Messianic Expectations at the Time of Jesus." In *Saint Luke's Journal of Theology* 32 (1988): 28–42.
Hartle, James A. "The Literary Unity of Zechariah." *JETS* 35 (1992): 145–57.
Hauge, Martin Ravndal. "Some Aspects of the Motif 'The City facing Death' of Ps 68, 21." *Scandinavian Journal of the Old Testament* 1 (1988): 1–29.
Hill, Andrew E. "Dating Second Zechariah: A Linguistic Reexamination." *HAR* 6 (1982): 105–34.
Hobbs, T. R. "The Language of Warfare in Zechariah 9–14." In J. Barton and D. J. Reimer, eds., *After the Exile: Essays in Honour of Rex Mason*, 103–28. Macon, GA: Mercer University Press, 1996.
Hoffman, Yair. "The Fasts in the Book of Zechariah and the Fashioning of National Remembrance." In O. Lipschits and J. Blenkinsopp, eds., *Judah & the Judeans in the Neo-Babylonian Period*, 169–218. Winona Lake: Eisenbrauns, 2003.
Holladay, William L. *The Root Šûbh in the Old Testament*. Leiden: E. J. Brill, 1958.
Hyatt, J. Philip. "A Neo-Babylonian Parallel to *Bethel-Sar-Eser*, Zech 7:2." *JBL* 56 (1937): 387–94.
Instone-Brewer, David. "The Two Asses of Zechariah 9:9 in Matthew 21." *TynBul* 54 (2003): 87–98.
James, Fleming. "Thoughts on Haggai and Zechariah." *JBL* 53 (1934): 229–35.
Jansma, T. "Inquiry into the Hebrew Text and the Ancient Versions of Zechariah ix–xiv." *OtSt* (1950): 1–142.
Johnson, A. R. *Sacral Kingship in Ancient Israel*. Cardiff: University of Wales Press, 1955.
Jones, Douglas R. "A Fresh Interpretation of Zech. ix–xi." *VT* 12 (1962): 241–59.
Keel, Othmar. *The Symbolism of the Biblical World*. New York: Crossroad, 1985.
Kim, Seyoon. "Jesus—The Son of God, the Stone, the Son of Man, and the Servant: The Role of Zechariah in the Self-Identification of Jesus." In *Tradition and Interpretation in the New Testament. Essays in Honor of E. Earle Ellis*, G. F. Hawthorne, ed. with O. Betz, 134–45. Grand Rapids: Eerdmans, 1987.

Klausner, Joseph. *The Messianic Idea in Israel: From Its Beginning to the Completion of the Mishnah.* London: Allen and Unwin, 1956.
Klein, George L. "The Meaning of the *Niphal* in the Hebrew Bible." Ph.D. diss., Dropsie College for Hebrew and Cognate Learning/Annenberg Research Institute, 1992.
_____. "The Prophetic Perfect." *JNSL* 16 (1990): 45–60.
Kline, Meredith G. "The Structure of the Book of Zechariah." *JETS* 34 (1991): 179–93.
Kloos, Carola J. L. "Zech. II 12: Really a Crux Interpretum." *VT* 25 (1975): 729–36.
Kraeling, E. G. H. "The Historical Situation in Zechariah 9:1–10." *AJSL* 14 (1924–25): 24–33.
Kruger, Paul A. "Grasping the Hem in Zech 8:23: The Contextual Analysis of a Gesture." In *"Feet on Level Ground:" A South African Tribute of Old Testament Essays in Honor of Gerhard Hasel*, K. Van Wyle, ed., 173–93. Berrien Center, MI: Louis Hester, 1996.
Kselman, John S. "A Note on Jer 49,20 and Ze 2,6–7." *CBQ* 32 (1970): 579–81.
Kunz, Andreas. *Ablehnung des Krieges: Untersuchungen zu Sacharja 9 und 10.* Freiburg: Herder, 1998.
Laato, Antti. "Zachariah 4,6b–10a and the Akkadian Royal Building Inscriptions." *ZAW* 106 (1994): 53–69.
Lamarche, Paul. Zacharie IX–XIV: *Structure Littéraire et Messianisme.* Paris: J. Gabalda, 1961.
Lange, Armin. "Considerations Concerning the 'Spirit of Impurity' in Zech 13:2." In A. Laupe, H. Lichtenberger, K. F. D. Römheld, eds., *Die Dämonen/Demons*, 254–68. Tübingen: Mohr Siebeck, 2003.
Larkin, K. A. *The Eschatology of Second Zechariah: A Study of the Formation of a Mantological Wisdom Anthology.* Kampen: Kok Pharos, 1994.
LaRondelle, H. K. *The Israel of God in Prophecy: Principles of Prophetic Interpretation.* Berrien Springs, MI: Andrews University Press, 1983.
Laubscher, Frans du T. "Epiphany and Sun Mythology in Zechariah 14." *JNSL* 20 (1994): 125–38.
_____. "The King's Humbleness in Zechariah 9:9. A Paradox?" *JNSL* 18 (1992): 125–34.
Le Bas, Edwin E. "Zechariah's Climax to the Career of the Corner-Stone." *PEQ* 82 (1950): 139–55.
_____. "Zechariah's Enigmatic Contribution to the Corner-Stone." *PEQ* 82 (1950): 102–22.
Leske, Adrian M. "Context and Meaning of Zechariah 9:9." *CBQ* 62 (2000): 663–78.
Lipinski, E. "Recherches sur le livre de Zacharie" *VT* 20 (1970): 25–55.
Love, Mark Cameron. *The Evasive Text: Zechariah 1–8 and the Frustrated Reader.* Sheffield: Sheffield Academic Press, 1999.
Lux, Rüdiger. "Die doppelte Konditionierung des Heils: theologische Anmerkungen zum chronologischen und literarischen Ort des Sacharjaprologs (Sach 1, 1–6)." In *Gott und Mensch im Dialog*, M. Witte, ed., 569–87. Berlin: Walter de Gruyter, 2004.
McCready, Wayne O. "The 'Day of Small Things' vs. the Latter Days: Historical Fulfillment or Eschatological Hope?" In *Israel's Apostasy and Restoration*, ed. A. Gileadi, 223–36. Grand Rapids: Baker, 1988.
McHardy, W. D. "The Horses in Zechariah." *ZAW* 103 (1968): 174–79.
MacKay, Cameron. "Zechariah in Relation to Ezekiel 40–48." *Evangelical Quarterly* 40 (1968): 197–210.

McNicol, Allan J. "The Heavenly Sanctuary in Judaism: A Model for Tracing the Origin of an Apocalypse." *Journal of Religious Studies* 13 (1987): 66–94.

Marinkovic, Peter. "What Does Zechariah 1–8 Tell Us About the Second Temple?" In *Second Temple Studies2: Temple Community in the Persian Period*, ed. T. C. Eskenazi and K. H. Richards, 88–103. Sheffield: JSOT, 1994.

Marks, Herbert. "The Twelve Prophets." In *The Literary Guide to the Bible*, 207–33. Cambridge, MA: Belknap, 1987.

Mason, Rex A. *Preaching the Tradition: Homily and Hermeneutics after the Exile.* Cambridge: Cambridge University Press, 1990.

———. "The Messiah in the Postexilic Old Testament Literature." In *King and Messiah in Israel and the Ancient Near East*, ed., J. Day, 338–64. Sheffield: Sheffield Press, 1998.

———. "The Relation of Zech. 9–14 to Proto-Zechariah." *ZAW* 88 (1976): 227–39.

———. "Some Echoes of Preaching in the Second Temple?" *ZAW* 96 (1984): 221–35.

———. "Some Examples of Inner Biblical Exegesis in Zech. IX–XIV." In *Studia Evangelica, Vol. VII*, ed. E. A. Livingstone, 343–54. Berlin: Akademie, 1982.

———. "Why is Second Zechariah so Full of Quotations?" In C. Tuckett, ed., *The Book of Zechariah and Its Influence*, 21–28. Burlington: Ashgate, 2003.

Mastin, B. A. "A Note on Zechariah VI 13." *VT* 26 (1976): 113–16.

May, H. G. "A Key to the Interpretation of Zechariah's Visions." *JBL* 57 (1938): 173–84.

Menken, Maarten J. J. "The Textual Form and the Meaning of the Quotation from Zechariah 12:10 in John 19:37." *CBQ* 55 (1993): 494–511.

Meyer, F. B. *The Prophet of Hope: Studies in Zechariah.* London: Marshall, Morgan & Scott, 1952.

Meyer, L. V. "An Allegory Concerning the Monarchy: Zech 11:4–17; 13:7–9." In *Scripture in History and Theology: Essays in Honor of J. Coert Rylaarsdam*, ed. A. L. Merrill and T. W. Overholt, 225–40. Pittsburgh: Pickwick, 1977.

Meyers, Carol L. and Eric M. Meyers. "The Future Fortunes of the House of David: The Evidence of Second Zechariah." In *Fortunate the Eyes That See: Essays in Honor of David Noel Freedman in Celebration of His Seventieth Birthday*, ed. A. B. Beck, et al., 207–22. Grand Rapids: Eerdmans, 1995.

Miller, John H. "Haggai–Zechariah: Prophets of the Now and Future." *Currents in Theology and Mission* 6 (1979): 99–104.

Moo, Douglas J. *The Old Testament in Gospel Passion Narratives.* Sheffield: Almond, 1983.

Moseman, R. David. "Reading the Two Zechariah's as One." *RevExp* 97 (2000): 487–98.

Muddiman, John. "Zechariah 13:7 and Mark's Account of the Arrest in Gethsemane." In C. Tuckett, ed., *The Book of Zechariah and Its Influence*, 101–9. Burlington: Ashgate, 2003.

North, Francis S. "Aaron's Rise in Prestige." *ZAW* 66 (1954): 191–99.

North, Robert. *Prophecy to Apocalyptic via Zechariah.* Leiden: E. J. Brill, 1972.

O'Rourke, John J. "Zecharia 9,1, 'ĒN 'ĀDĀM." *CBQ* 25 (1963): 123–28.

Otzen, B. *Studien über Deuterosacharja.* Copenhagen: Prostant Apud Munksgaard, 1964.

Parker, R. A., and W. H. Dubberstein. *Babylonian Chronology 626 BC–AD 75.* Providence: Brown University Press, 1956.

Parunak, H. Van Dyke. *Linguistic Density Plots in Zechariah.* Wooster, OH: Bible Research Associates, 1979.

Paul, Shalom M. "A Technical Expression from Archery in Zechariah IX 13a." *VT* 39 (1989): 497–98.
Person, Raymond F. *Second Zechariah and the Deuteronomic School*. Sheffield: JSOT, 1993.
Petersen, David L. "Zerubbabel and Jerusalem Temple Reconstruction." *CBQ* 36 (1974): 366–72.
_____. "Zechariah's Visions: A Theological Perspective." *VT* 34 (1984): 195–206.
_____. "Zechariah 9–14: Methodological Reflections." In M. J. Boda and M. H. Floyd, eds., *Bringing out the Treasure: Inner Biblical Allusion in Zechariah 9–14*, 210–24. Sheffield: Sheffield Academic Press, 2003.
Pierce, R. W. "Literary Connectors and a Haggai/Zechariah/Malachi Corpus." *JETS* 27 (1984): 277–89.
_____. "A Thematic Development of the Haggai/ Zechariah/ Malachi Corpus." *JETS* 27 (1984): 401–11.
Ploeger, O. *Theocracy and Eschatology*. Translated by S. Rudman. Richmond: John Knox, 1968.
Poetker, Katrina. "The Wrath of Yahweh." *Direction* 16 (1987): 55–61.
Pola, Thomas. "Form and Meaning in Zechariah 3." In R. Albertz and B. Becking, eds., *Yahwism after the Exile: Perspectives on Israelite Religion in the Persian Era*, 156–67. Assen: Van Gorcum, 2003.
Portnoy, Stephen L. and David L. Petersen. "Biblical Texts and Statistical Analysis: Zechariah and Beyond." *JBL* 103 (1984): 11–21.
Poythress, Vern Sheridan. "Divine Meaning of Scripture." *WTJ* 48 (1986): 241–79.
Raabe, Paul R. "Why Prophetic Oracles against the Nations?" In *Fortunate the Eyes That See: Essays in Honor of David Noel Freedman*, ed. A. B. Beck, et al., 236–57. Grand Rapids: Eerdmans, 1995
Radday, Yehuda T., and Dieter Wickman. "The Unity of Zechariah Examined in the Light of Statistical Linguistics." *ZAW* 87 (1975): 30–55.
Radday, Yehuda T., and Moshe A. Pollatschek. "Vocabulary Richness in Post-Exilic Prophetic Books." *ZAW* 92 (1980): 333–46.
Redditt, Paul L. "Israel's Shepherds: Hope and Pessimism in Zechariah 9–14." *CBQ* 51 (1989): 631–42.
_____. "Nehemiah's First Mission and the Date of Zechariah 9–14." *CBQ* 56 (1994): 664–78.
_____. "The Two Shepherds in Zechariah 11:4–17." *CBQ* 55 (1993): 676–86.
_____. "Zechariah 9–14, Malachi, and the Redaction of the Book of the Twelve." In J. W. Watts and P. R. House, eds., *Forming Prophetic Literature: Essays on Isaiah and the Twelve in Honor of John D. W. Watts*, 245–68. Sheffield: Sheffield Academic Press, 1996.
_____. "Zerubbabel, Joshua, and the Night Visions of Zechariah." *CBQ* 54 (1992): 249–59.
Rhea, Robert. "Attack on Prophecy: Zechariah 13, 1–6." *ZAW* 107 (1995): 288–93.
Richter, Hans-Friedemann. "Die Pferde in den Nachtgesichten des Sacharja." *ZAW* 98 (1986): 96–100.
Robinson, Donald Fay. "A Suggested Analysis of Zechariah 1–8." *ATR* 33 (1951): 65–70.
Rogers, Randolph R. "An Exegetical Analysis of John's Use of Zechariah in the Book of Revelation: The Impact and Transformation of Zechariah's Text and Themes in the Apocalypse." Ph.D. diss., Southwestern Baptist Theological Seminary, 2002.
Rose, Wolter H. "Messianic Expectations in the Early Post-Exilic Period." *TynBul* 49 (1998): 373–76.

_____. "Messianic Expectations in the Early Postexilic Period." In R. Albertz and B. Becking, eds., *Yahwism after the Exile: Perspectives on Israelite Religion in the Persian Era*, 168–85. Assen: Van Gorcum, 2003.

_____. *Zemah and Zerubbabel: Messianic Expectations in the Early Postexilic Period.* JSOTSup 304. Sheffield: Sheffield Academic Press, 2000.

Rosenberg, Roy A. "The Slain Messiah in the Old Testament." *ZAW* 99 (1987): 259–61.

Roth, Cecil. "The Cleansing of the Temple and Zechariah XIV 21." *NT* 4 (1960): 174–81.

Rubenstein, Jeffrey L. "Sukkot, Eschatology, and Zechariah 14." *RB* 103 (1996): 161–95.

Rudman, Dominic. "A Note on Zechariah 1:5." *JNSL* 29 (2003): 33–39.

_____. "The Warhorse of the Lord." *Jewish Bible Quarterly* 28 (2000): 163–68.

Ruffin, Michael Lee. "Symbolism in Zechariah: A Study in Functional Unity." Ph.D. diss., Southern Baptist Theological Seminary, 1986.

Saebø, Magne. "Vom Grossreich Zum Weltreich." *VT* 28 (1978): 83–91.

Scalise, Pamela J. "An Exegesis of Zechariah 7:4–14 in Its Canonical Context." *Faith and Mission* 3 (1986): 58–65.

Schaefer, Konrad R. "The Ending of the Book of Zechariah: A Commentary." *RB* 100 (1993): 165–238.

_____. "Zechariah 14: A Study in Allusion." *CBQ* 57 (1995): 66–91.

_____. "Zechariah 14 and the Composition of the Book of Zechariah." *RB* 100 (1993): 368–98.

Schellenberg, Angeline Falk. "One in the Bond of War: The Unity of Deutero-Zechariah." *Didaskalia* 12 (2001): 101–15.

Scott, R. B. Y. "Secondary Meanings of *'aḥar*'," *JTS* 50 (1949): 178–79.

Seybold, Klaus. *Bilder zum Tempelbau: Die Visionen des Propheten Sacharja.* Stuttgart: KBW, 1974.

Siebeneck, Robert T. "The Messianism of Aggeus and Proto-Zacharias." *CBQ* 19 (1957): 312–28.

Sinclair, Lawrence A. "Redaction of Zechariah 1–8." *BR* 20 (1975): 36–47.

Smith, Gary. *The Prophets as Preachers: An Introduction to the Hebrew Prophets.* Nashville: Broadman and Holman, 1994.

Stade, Bernhard. "Deuterozacharja," *ZAW* 1 (1881): 1–96; 2 (1882): 151–72, 275–309.

Strand, Kenneth A. "An Overlooked Old Testament Background to Revelation 11:1." *AUSS* 22 (1984): 317–25.

_____. "The Two Olive Trees of Zechariah 4 and Revelation 11." *AUSS* 20 (1982): 257–61.

Sweeney, Marvin A. "Zechariah's Debate with Isaiah." In M. A. Sweeney and E. B. Zvi, eds., *The Changing Face of Form Criticism for the Twenty-First Century*, 335–50. Grand Rapids: Eerdmans, 2003.

Sykes, Seth. "Time and Space in Haggai-Zechariah 1–8: A Bakhtinian Analysis of a Prophetic Chronicle." JSOT 76 (1997): 97–124.

Tate, Marvin E. "Satan in the Old Testament." *RevExp* 89 (1992): 461–74.

Tiemeyer, Lena-Sofia. "Compelled by Honour—A New Interpretation of Zechariah II 12A (8A)." *VT* 54 (2004): 352–72.

_____. "The Guilty Priesthood (Zech 3)." In C. Tuckett, ed., *The Book of Zechariah and Its Influence*, 1–19. Burlington: Ashgate, 2003.

Tigchelaar, Eibert J. *Prophets of Old and the Day of the End: Zechariah, the Book of Watchers and Apocalyptic.* Leiden: E. J. Brill, 1996.

Tidwell, N. L. A. "*Wā'ōmar* (Zech 3:5) and the Genre of Zechariah's Fourth Vision." *JBL* 94 (1975): 343–55.
Tollington, Janet E. *Tradition and Innovation in Haggai and Zechariah 1–8*. Sheffield: Sheffield Academic Press, 1993.
Tournay, R. "Zacharie XII–XIV et L'Histoire D'Israël." *RB* 81 (1974): 355–74.
Trèves, Marco. "Conjectures Concerning the Date and Authorship of Zechariah IX–XIV." *VT* 13 (1963): 196–207.
Tuckett, Christopher M. "Zechariah 12:10 and the New Testament." In C. Tuckett, ed., *The Book of Zechariah and Its Influence*, 111–21. Burlington: Ashgate, 2003.
VanderKam, James C. "Joshua the High Priest and the Interpretation of Zechariah 3." *CBQ* 53 (1991): 553–70.
van der Kooij, Arie. "The Septuagint of Zechariah as Witness to an Early Interpretation of the Book." In C. Tuckett, ed., *The Book of Zechariah and Its Influence*, 53–64. Burlington: Ashgate, 2003.
van der Woude, Adam S. "Die Hirtenallegorie von Sacharja XI." *Journal of Northwest Semitic Languages* 12 (1984): 139–49.
_____. "Sacharja 14,18." *ZAW* 97 (1985): 254–55.
_____. "Zion as Primeval Stone in Zechariah 3 and 4." In W. T. Claassen, ed., *Text and Context: Old Testament and Semitic Studies for F. C. Fensham*, 237–48. Sheffield: JSOT Press, 1988.
VanGemeren, Willem A. *Interpreting the Prophetic Word*. Grand Rapids: Zondervan, 1990.
van Tilborg, Sjef. "Matthew 27.3–10: An Intertextual Reading." In S. Draisma, ed., *Intertextuality in Biblical Writings*, 159–74. Kampen: J. H. Kok, 1989.
van Zijl, P. J. "A Possible Interpretation of Zech. 9:1 and the Function of 'The Eye' (*'Ayin*) in Zechariah." *JNSL* 1 (1971): 59–67.
Viberg, Åke. "Amos 7:14: A Case of Subtle Irony." *TynBul* 47 (1996): 91–114.
Visser 'T Hooft, W. A. "Triumphalism in the Gospels." *SJT* 38 (1985): 491–504.
von Rad, Gerhard. *Holy War in Ancient Israel*. Translated by M. J. Dawn. Grand Rapids: Eerdmans, 1991.
Vriezen, T. C. "Two Old Cruces." *OtSt* 5 (1948): 88–91.
Waterman, Leroy. "The Camouflaged Purge of Three Messianic Conspirators." *JNES* 13 (1954): 73–117.
Weisman, Ze'eb. "A Note on Zechariah VI 13." *VT* 26 (1976): 113–19.
Williams, Nathan E. "Looking Backward, Living Forward." *The Witness* 69 (1986): 18.
Wolters, Al. "Confessional Criticism and the Night Visions of Zechariah." In C. Bartholomew, C. Greene, K Möller, eds., *Renewing Biblical Interpretation*, 90–117. Grand Rapids: Zondervan, 2000.
_____. "Word Play in Zechariah." In S. Noegel, ed., *Puns and Pundits*, 223–30. Bethesda: CDL Press, 2000.
_____. "Zechariah 14: A Dialogue with the History of Interpretation." *Mid-America Journal of Theology* 13 (2002): 39–56.
Zolli, E. "*ʿEYN ʾĀDĀM* (Zach. IX 1)." *VT* 5 (1955): 90–92.

# Selected Subject Index

Abrahamic covenant   125, 229, 238, 247
Alexander the Great   30, 39, 40, 264, 265, 266, 269, 270, 279
allegory   319, 320
angel of the Lord   95, 96, 99, 101, 113, 162, 361
anger, God's   73, 74, 105, 106
anointing   165
apocalyptic literature   26, 27, 41, 42, 43
apple of God's eye   123
Assyria   303, 308
Augustine   86, 100, 123, 351, 369

Baal   281, 286
Babylonian exile   34
Babylonians   35, 36, 40, 80, 181, 192, 211, 212, 213
Bethel   213
blessing   129, 243
blood of the covenant   277
branch   70, 144
Branch, the   132, 143, 144, 145, 147, 151, 152, 201, 202, 203, 206, 272
bronze   186
burden   207, 254, 259, 348

Calvin, John   396
cannibalism   333, 334

chariots   184, 186, 191
children   236
church, the   115
cleansing   77, 372, 373, 374
comfort   103
compassion   223
cornerstone   293, 294
covenant   86, 244, 246
covenant, new   421
creation, new   409, 410, 411
Creator   350
crown   199, 200, 205, 283, 284
cup   352, 353
curse   171, 243
Cyrus   36, 37, 38, 40, 192, 330, 386

Damascus   261
Daniel   61
Darius   37, 38, 40, 79, 80, 211, 212
Davidic covenant   124, 300
Day of Atonement   60
Day of the Lord   73, 116, 249, 399, 407, 416
diptych   46
Divine Warrior   74, 75, 101
diviners   288
dreams   92

earthquake   404, 405, 406
entreat the Lord   215, 249

## SELECTED SUBJECT INDEX    444

eschatological kingdom   64, 67
exile, the   102, 118, 216, 240, 278
exodus, the   199, 297, 300, 303, 307
eyes   261, 262, 263, 268, 355

faithfulness, God's   75, 76, 221, 222
faithfulness, Jerusalem's   234, 235
fasting   217, 218, 245, 246
Feast of Tabernacles   422, 423, 424, 425
feasting   246
fertility   242
filthy   138
fire   117, 357, 391, 392
flying scroll   169, 170, 171
fortress   278, 286

glory   117, 120, 121, 122
gold   198, 199
grace   222, 244, 364
Greeks   30, 36, 39, 40, 279, 280
guilt   171, 172

Haggai   58–59, 241
heart   225
holy   426, 428
holy dwelling   129
horns   109
horses   274, 292, 296, 354, 355, 426, 427
Hosea   61
house, God's   268
humility   273

idolatry   288, 375, 376, 377, 378, 379
immanence   125, 129
iniquity   139
inviolability of Zion   34, 118
Isaiah   192
Israel   65, 66, 67, 342, 350, 429

jealousy   103, 104, 232, 233, 245
Jeremiah   277
Jerusalem   65, 66, 104, 107, 114, 400, 413, 414, 416, 429
Jerusalem, defeat of   400, 401, 402, 403
Joshua, the high priest   132, 133, 137, 138, 141, 142, 151
Judah   65, 66
judgment of God   73–75, 74, 129, 169
justice   220, 221, 222

King, Messianic   270, 271, 272, 273, 274, 289, 308, 309, 327, 358
Kingdom   71–73, 72, 73, 89, 274

lampstand   153, 155, 156, 166
leadership   77–78
Leviticus   60
Lord Almighty   231, 281
Lord my God   322
love   246, 247
loyalty   222, 223
Luther, Martin   395, 396

Maccabeans   31
Malachi   59–60
Matthew   62

measuring line 107, 112
menorah 155
mercy 222, 223
Messiah 69–71, 70, 71, 271, 272, 273, 274, 275, 285, 293, 294, 295, 330, 368, 383, 384, 389, 393
Mosaic covenant 171, 230, 238, 277
Mount of Olives 403
mountains 185, 186, 235
mourn 368, 369, 371, 372

nations 125, 126, 127, 205, 247, 248, 249, 256, 257, 267, 400, 425
Negev, the 219
new covenant 238, 374
New Year's festivities 94
night visions 27, 45, 95

obedience 75
oil 164, 166
olive trees 156, 157
oppression 223, 224
oracles 64, 207, 254, 259, 260, 348

peace 240, 274, 275, 282
Persians 36, 39, 40, 80, 100
Philistines 266
pierced 366, 367, 368, 369, 370, 379, 387
plague 417, 420, 425
plumb line 162
poetry 41, 258
priest 137
prophecy 43
prophecy, false 375, 377, 378, 379, 380, 381, 382, 383, 384
prophet, Biblical 84, 86, 380

prophet, secular 84
prophetic eschatology 26, 27
prose 41

rain 284, 285
redemption 299, 300
remnant 85, 237, 243, 267, 297, 391, 392, 393, 401
rest 183, 193
Revelation 63
righteousness 271, 272, 273

salvation 272, 273
Satan 134, 135, 137
scapegoat 60, 181
scrolls 170
sea 307, 308
self mutilation 382
servant 70, 145
Servant, the 144, 147
sheep, scattered 387, 388, 389, 390
shekinah glory 69
shepherd 283, 289, 290, 291, 299, 311, 312, 317, 318, 319, 320, 323, 324, 325, 326, 327, 329, 330, 331, 332, 333, 334, 335, 336, 337, 338, 339, 340, 342, 343, 344, 345, 346, 347, 348, 385, 386, 387, 388, 389, 390
shield 359, 360
silver 198, 199
sovereignty 244, 265, 355
spirit 363, 364
Spirit of the Lord 159, 363
spirits 187, 188, 192
staff 327, 328, 334, 335, 336, 341, 342
stone 70, 145, 147, 148, 149, 151, 353
supersessionism 67

supplication 364
sword 385, 386, 387, 388
symbolic action 321, 323

temple 69, 89, 90, 129, 146, 158, 160, 161, 167, 180, 201, 203, 206
theophany 280, 283, 404
transcendence 129
truth 234
Tyre 263, 264, 265, 266

uncleanness 377
universalism 126, 128, 130

visions 89, 90, 91, 92, 95

wall of fire 116
war, holy 269, 282, 295, 418
water, living 410, 412
wickedness 177, 178, 180
winds 187, 188
word of the Lord 80

wrath 73, 74
Yahweh 413

Zechariah, Book of
  authorship 22, 23, 24, 25, 27, 28, 29, 30, 31, 33, 34, 131, 254
  genre of chapters 9–14 258
  Hebrew text 49–50
  historical era 34–40, 40
  intertextuality 50–58
  linguistic features 27, 28, 29
  literary style 41, 41–44, 43, 44
  Messianic passages 61–62
  structure 44–48
  theology 63–65, 66, 67, 68, 69, 70, 71, 72, 73, 74, 75, 76, 77, 78
Zechariah, the prophet 21, 22, 83
  genealogy 20, 80, 81, 82
  lineage 20, 21, 83
  name 20, 80, 81
Zerubbabel 37, 38, 133, 145, 158, 160
ziggurats 180
Zion 65, 66, 104, 206, 233, 411, 413

# Person Index

Achtemeier, E.  82, 166
Ackroyd, P. R.  47, 204
Albright, W. F.  83
Alonso-Schökel, L.  258
Amsler, S.  158
Archer, G. L. Jr.  30
Augustine  86, 100, 123
Avishur, Y.  30, 104, 258, 297

Bailey, J.  134
Baldwin, J. G.  31, 34, 35, 39, 45, 46, 49, 50, 68, 79, 82, 87, 90, 95, 96, 101, 102, 103, 104, 109, 115, 117, 120, 124, 134, 135, 136, 138, 141, 152, 155, 156, 157, 158, 159, 160, 161, 162, 163, 165, 166, 168, 172, 174, 178, 186, 188, 190, 191, 192, 195, 200, 202, 204, 210, 212, 213, 214, 216, 220, 222, 226, 227, 231, 233, 237, 240, 241, 242, 245, 255, 261, 263, 265, 267, 268, 272, 292, 294, 301, 311, 314, 320, 325, 327, 329, 331, 335, 338, 352, 359, 370, 377, 386, 387, 390, 393, 399, 400, 403, 404, 405, 415, 419, 421, 423, 424, 425, 427, 428, 429
Barker, K. L.  40, 100, 106, 109, 113, 115, 129, 134, 147, 148, 158, 160, 163, 173, 179, 185, 190, 214, 215, 216, 232, 236, 267, 272, 273, 274, 275, 277, 278, 311, 323, 327, 345, 363, 366, 374, 384, 386, 387, 392, 393, 395, 396, 412, 419, 423, 424
Barklay, G.  426
Barthélemy, D.  49, 156, 176, 262, 268
Barton, J.  21
Bas, E. E. Le  145
Bas, Le  145
Benedikt  23
Berlin, A.  258
Beuken, W. A. M.  47, 209, 230, 232
Bewer, J. A.  31, 82, 89, 198, 211, 262
Beyerlin, W.  144
Blaising, C. A.  67, 68
Blank, S. H.  22, 337
Blenkinsopp, J.  82, 83
Block, D. I.  188
Blomberg, C. L.  22, 26, 46, 337, 338
Boda, M. J.  46, 47, 48, 50, 55, 56, 58, 71, 96, 112, 121, 183, 206, 207, 208, 209, 210, 255, 256, 279, 298, 321
Boling, R. G.  414
Bratsiotis, N. P.  128
Bright, J.  36, 37, 83, 101, 145, 184
Bronner, L.  281
Bruce, F. F.  26, 61, 62
Bruehler, B. B.  154
Bullinger, E. W.  160, 319, 332
Bush, F. W.  23
Butterworth, M.  23, 28, 29, 132, 183, 207, 208

# PERSON INDEX

Calvin, J.   175
Carson, D. A.   83
Chary, T.   120
Chernus, I.   116, 117
Childs, B. S.   30, 32, 33, 60, 61
Chisholm, R. B.   208
Claassen, W. T.   131
Clark, D. J.   96, 98, 208, 209, 231, 253, 255
Clements, R. E.   70, 143, 166
Clendenen, E. R.   260
Clifford, R. J.   160, 185
Cohen, A.   64, 121, 138, 146, 166, 175, 179, 186, 187, 198, 200, 201, 231, 298, 346, 367, 368
Collins, J. J.   44, 200
Collins, T.   269
Conrad, E. W.   20, 21, 23, 43, 123, 124, 135, 136, 145, 154, 157, 164, 169, 171, 172, 175, 178, 179, 183, 184, 187, 199, 203, 213, 224
Cook, S. L.   43, 388, 389, 390
Cooper, L. E.   167
Cross, F. M. Jr.   43, 159, 197, 307
Cryer, F. H.   288

Dahood, M.   262
Day, J.   63, 371
de Boer, P. A. H.   259, 260
Delcor, M.   264, 279
Delitzsch, F.   157
Demsky, A.   205
de Savignac, J.   186
de Vaux, R.   215, 282
Dillard, R. B.   23
Dodd, C. H.   62, 254, 384
Driver, S. R.   96, 311
Dubberstein, W. H.   79
Duff, P. B.   429
Duguid, I. M.   61, 71, 73
du T. Laubscher, F.   400

Eichrodt, W.   220, 221
Eissfeldt, O.   22, 25, 26, 59, 329
Elliger, K.   284
Ellis, R.   157, 161, 163
Erickson, M. J.   100
Evans, C. A.   61, 62, 165

Farrer, A.   63
Feigin, S.   322
Feinberg, C.   108, 115, 188
Fensham, F. C.   223
Ferreiro, A.   290, 351, 369, 370, 391
Filbeck, D.   127, 166
Finley, T. J.   122, 327
Floyd, M. H.   24, 25, 47, 50, 56, 166, 167, 171, 174, 175, 176, 181, 186, 187, 189, 199, 200, 201, 205, 213, 232, 260, 287, 312, 319, 320, 321, 322, 405, 419, 423, 429
Foster, P.   62
Fox, H.   423
France, R. T.   61, 370, 390
Freedman, D. N.   170
Fuller, R.   123

Garrett, J. L.   99
Gibson, J. C. L.   200
Ginsberg, H. L.   384
Glasson, T. F.   73
Glueck, N.   222
Good, R. M.   418
Gordon, C. H.   214
Gordon, R. P.   97, 307, 382, 426
Gowan, D. E.   224
Greenfield, J. C.   370
Grether, O.   80
Gundry, R. H.   26, 337
Hallo, W. W.   303
Halpern, B.   89, 146, 161, 170

Ham, C. A.  62
Hanhart, R.  250
Hanson, P. D.  23, 27, 43, 262, 279, 291, 306, 312, 321, 364, 367
Harrelson, W.  422
Harrison, R. K.  27, 31, 60, 136
Hatton, H. A.  231
Hengstenberg, E. W.  26, 143
Hess, R. S.  143
Hill, A. E.  29
Hobbs, T. R.  41, 274
Hoffman, Y.  215, 246
Holladay, W. L.  85, 86, 277, 411
Hubbard, D. A.  23
Hyatt, J. P.  212

Instone-Brewer, D.  274

James, F.  58
Jansma, T.  49
Johnston, J. H.  153
Jones, D. R.  254, 319
Joüon, P.  135, 389

Kaiser, W. C. Jr.  70, 73, 99, 143, 144, 224
Kane, J. H.  127, 166
Keel, O.  109, 155, 184, 185, 354
Keil, C. F.  157
Kim, S.  147
Kimchi, D.  175
Kittel, R.  41
Klausner, J.  272
Klein, G. L.  41, 107
Kline, M. G.  46, 47
Kloos, C. J. L.  120
Klouda, S.  60
Koch, K.  21, 83

Kooij, A. van der  49
Kruger, P. A.  250
Kuhrt, A.  36
Kunz, A.  51

Laato, A.  158, 160
Lamarche, P.  44, 255, 256, 388
Larkin, K. A.  53
LaRondelle, H. K.  67
LaSor, W. S.  23
Laubscher, F. Du T.  273
Leske, A. M.  51, 272
Lipinski, E.  49, 102, 150, 212, 273
Longman, T. III  23, 24, 31, 33
Love, M. C.  21, 50, 157, 177
Luther, M.  395, 396

MacKay, C.  55
Martin–Achard, R.  127
Mason, R. A.  47, 50, 51, 56, 70, 142, 177, 190, 294, 295, 331, 383, 386
Mastin, B. A.  203
Mathewson, D.  63
May, H. G.  94
Mazar, B.  197
McCarthy, D. J.  247
McComiskey, T.  67, 72, 76, 127, 134, 135, 233, 243, 259, 260, 261, 263, 265, 267, 280, 284, 301, 302, 303, 307, 311, 313, 319, 326, 329, 330, 334, 337, 338, 340, 344, 345, 349, 353, 355, 358, 364, 376, 378, 382, 383, 387, 388, 392, 396, 398, 399, 400, 405, 406, 408, 409, 411, 415, 416, 420, 424, 428, 429
McCready, W. O.  68
McHardy, W. D.  97
Menken, M. J. J.  369

Merrill, E.   30, 40, 47, 86, 89, 94, 100, 102, 105, 109, 112, 115, 116, 117, 119, 121, 125, 133, 134, 136, 145, 147, 148, 154, 155, 156, 158, 162, 163, 164, 167, 170, 175, 183, 185, 187, 189, 190, 191, 195, 199, 205, 213, 216, 240, 241, 244, 245, 246, 249, 260, 265, 267, 270, 277, 280, 282, 284, 285, 290, 295, 297, 314, 315, 320, 321, 324, 326, 329, 330, 335, 343, 347, 349, 350, 353, 357, 359, 361, 364, 366, 374, 376, 379, 382, 385, 389, 390, 396, 405, 409, 414, 419, 422, 424, 425, 427, 428

Meyer, L. V.   320

Meyers, C. L. and E.   31, 41, 47, 49, 50, 51, 58, 81, 90, 91, 95, 100, 107, 112, 121, 122, 154, 155, 157, 159, 160, 161, 163, 166, 169, 171, 172, 177, 183, 187, 189, 190, 196, 197, 200, 202, 203, 205, 220, 230, 231, 241, 242, 246, 249, 260, 261, 262, 264, 265, 267, 270, 280, 282, 291, 293, 295, 299, 302, 304, 306, 312, 313, 316, 322, 323, 326, 327, 331, 335, 344, 345, 347, 350, 351, 356, 357, 358, 359, 360, 363, 364, 365, 366, 367, 368, 370, 372, 377, 378, 380, 382, 383, 390, 391, 392, 397, 398, 404, 405, 406, 407, 408, 411, 412, 414, 415, 416, 417, 418, 419, 421, 422, 423, 424, 426, 427, 428

Miller, P. D. Jr.   84

Mitchell, H. G.   31, 33, 44, 49, 51, 82, 89, 95, 96, 101, 109, 113, 122, 129, 139, 143, 145, 147, 151, 155, 157, 163, 178, 180, 183, 184, 188, 191, 198, 200, 203, 211, 213, 218, 219, 235, 236, 240, 242, 249, 250, 262, 263, 268, 272, 277, 279, 305, 307, 329, 330, 342, 343, 344, 346, 356, 358, 361, 366, 367, 368, 371, 378, 381, 382, 388, 389, 398, 405, 407, 408, 412, 415, 419, 421, 423, 424, 425, 426, 427

Moo, D. J.   61

Moran, W. L.   247

Moseman, R. D.   23, 32, 255

Muddiman, J.   390

Muraoka, T.   135, 270, 272

Nicholson, E. W.   215

Nogalski, J. D.   47

North, C. R.   50, 143, 155-56

North, F. S.   214

O'Rourke, J. J.   262

Ollenburger, B. C.   208

Oppenheim, L.   303

Orr, A.   102

Oswalt, J. N.   43

Otzen, B.   23, 30, 31, 269

Parker, R. A.   79

Paul, S. M.   279

Perowne, T. T.   249

Person, R.   32

Petersen, D. L.   21, 28, 50, 81, 90, 92, 101, 106, 114, 116, 122, 123, 129, 137, 139, 140, 141, 143, 145, 152, 154, 155, 160, 163, 165, 166, 171, 177, 186, 211, 216, 227, 229, 231, 232, 237, 242, 244, 246, 248, 383

Petitjean, A.   104, 107, 196, 240

Pierce, R. W.   47

Pola, T.   132, 133

Pollatschek, M. A.   28

Polzin, R.   29

Porten, B.   197, 212
Pusey, E. B.   189

Raabe, P. R.   74, 256, 257
Radday, Y. T.   28, 29
Redditt, P. L.   47, 59, 318, 324, 329, 331, 335, 384, 388, 389
Richter, H.   97
Robinson, G. L.   33
Rogers, R. R.   63
Rogerson, J.   23
Rose, W. H.   132, 133, 144, 145, 164, 166, 201, 202, 204
Roth, C.   429
Rowley, H. H.   127, 166
Rubenstein, J. L.   423
Rudman, D.   51, 53, 54, 55, 56, 57, 86, 247
Rudolph, W.   82, 232, 408
Ruffin, M. L.   33

Sakenfeld, K. D.   223
Satterthwaite, P. E.   143
Sawyer, J. F. A.   84
Scalise, P. J.   208, 217
Schaefer, K.   51
Schaefer, K. R.   51, 395, 403, 405, 406, 407, 419, 420, 423, 427, 428, 429
Schellenberg, A. F.   23, 75
Scott, R. B. Y.   120
Senior, D. P.   26
Seybold, K.   89
Simpson, W. K.   303
Smith, G. V.   83
Smith, J. M. P.   31, 82, 89, 198, 211
Smith, M.   37
Smith, R. L.   31, 32, 95, 99, 103, 121, 122, 131, 149, 151, 154, 161, 171, 172, 183, 187, 190, 211, 230, 233, 239, 248, 272, 282
Speers, T. C.   236
Stade, B.   23
Stern, E.   38
Strand, K. A.   113, 156
Sweeney, M. A.   50, 81, 84, 94, 95, 96, 97, 98, 107, 114, 122, 141, 148, 150, 156, 162, 172, 175, 177, 179, 185, 190, 195, 199, 200, 206, 213, 214, 225, 287, 321, 330, 335, 338, 340, 347, 352, 358, 359, 367, 371, 378, 380, 381, 383, 386, 388, 403, 404, 406, 408, 409, 412, 414, 417, 419, 420, 429

Taeke J.   49
Tate, M. E.   134
Taylor, R. A.   260
Terrien, S.   125
Theodoret of Mopsuestia   109
Tidwell, N. L. A.   131, 136, 140
Tiemeyer, L.   120, 138
Tigchelaar, E. J.   27, 113, 154, 160, 163, 166, 175, 183, 188, 193
Tollington, J. E.   23, 123, 126, 160, 161, 199, 200, 201, 203
Tov, E.   49, 123, 175, 176
Treves, M.   23, 30, 331
Tuckett, C. M.   369

Unger, M. F.   89, 92, 96, 98, 99, 101, 106, 109, 110, 115, 120, 124, 147, 156, 158, 162, 167, 186, 187, 198, 200, 201, 202, 204, 213, 238, 242, 249, 264, 266, 267, 277, 285, 313, 316, 321, 322, 323, 325, 327, 334, 336, 340, 343, 345, 363, 372, 380, 382, 383, 384, 387, 392, 393, 396,

397, 400, 407, 408, 410, 419, 423, 428, 429

Vanderkam, J. C. 146, 150, 151
van der Toorn, K. 288
van der Woude, A. S. 131, 154, 311, 425
Van Dyke Parunak, H. 28, 244
VanGemeren, W. A. 84
van Zijl, P. J. 262
Viberg, A. 381
von Rad, G. 43, 84, 99, 183, 418
von Soden, W. 83, 370
Vriezen, T. C. 121
Waltke, B. 86
Watson, W. G. E. 258
Watts, I. 111
Webb, R. L. 42
Welch, J. W. 46
Wenham, G. J. 143

Westermann, C. 99
Whitley, C. F. 102, 222
Wickmann, D. 28, 29
Wilson, R. R. 21
Wiseman, D. J. 428
Wolff, H. W. 239, 247
Wolters, A. 64, 85, 168, 264, 291, 395, 396, 397
Woudstra, M. H. 414
Wright, D. P. 181
Wright, G. E. 414
Würthwein, E. 170, 176

Yadin, Y. 97, 282, 296
Young, E. J. 31
Youngblood, R. 43, 44

Zeitlin, S. 215

# Selected Scripture Index

**Genesis**

| | |
|---|---|
| 1:2 | 160 |
| 1:3–5 | 52, 409 |
| 1–2 | 51, 350 |
| 1–3 | 275 |
| 1–11 | 247 |
| 2:5,15 | 381 |
| 2:6,10–14 | 52 |
| 2:7 | 351 |
| 2:7–8 | 340 |
| 3 | 74, 84, 177 |
| 3:7 | 150 |
| 4:2 | 381 |
| 4:26 | 392 |
| 6 | 84 |
| 6–8 | 74 |
| 7:11 | 372 |
| 10:2 | 279 |
| 10:10 | 180 |
| 11:1–9 | 159, 180, 181, 248 |
| 12 | 125, 247 |
| 12:1 | 257 |
| 12:2–3 | 256 |
| 12:3 | 125, 243, 247, 248 |
| 14:18–20 | 70, 151, 204 |
| 15:1 | 360 |
| 15:5 | 236, 304 |
| 15:18 | 257, 275, 305 |
| 15:18–21 | 304 |
| 16:7 | 150 |
| 16:7–12 | 99 |
| 16:11,13 | 99 |
| 17:2,6 | 236 |
| 17:7–8 | 298 |
| 17:8 | 238 |
| 18:1–2,13,17 | 99 |
| 18:4 | 100, 237 |
| 19:2 | 100 |
| 20:13 | 222 |
| 21:1 | 292 |
| 22 | 369 |
| 22:2,12 | 368 |
| 22:11–12,15–18 | 99 |
| 22:18 | 236 |
| 24:12 | 222 |
| 25 | 380 |
| 25:25 | 51, 380 |
| 25:34 | 162 |
| 26:15 | 405 |
| 26:28 | 171 |
| 27:28 | 284 |
| 29:35 | 297 |
| 30:22–24 | 297 |
| 31:7 | 249 |
| 31:10–12 | 291 |
| 31:11,13 | 99 |
| 31:19 | 288 |
| 31:27 | 246 |
| 31:28 | 21, 82 |
| 31:55 | 21, 82 |
| 32:1 | 21 |
| 32:24 | 100 |
| 36:15 | 356 |
| 37:24 | 51, 278 |
| 41:52 | 297 |
| 42:28 | 225 |
| 43:14 | 223 |
| 45:11 | 345 |

47:13 . . . . . . . . . . . . . . . . . . . . . 391
48:15 . . . . . . . . . . . . . . . . . 283, 323
49. . . . . . . . . . . . . . . . . . . . . . . . 271
49:10–11 . . . . . . . . . . . . . . . 51, 271
49:11 . . . . . . . . . . . . . . . . . . . . . 274

**Exodus**

1:10 . . . . . . . . . . . . . . . . . . . . . . 402
2:6 . . . . . . . . . . . . . . . . . . . . . . . 325
3:2,4 . . . . . . . . . . . . . . . . . . . . . . 99
3:2–4:14 . . . . . . . . . . . . . . . . . . 117
3:7 . . . . . . . . . . . . . . . . . . . 269, 295
3:8,17 . . . . . . . . . . . . . . . . . . . . 226
3:13–17 . . . . . . . . . . . . . . . . . . . 413
3:14 . . . . . . . . . . . . . . . . . . 117, 413
3:14–15 . . . . . . . . . . . . . . . . . . . 309
3:15 . . . . . . . . . . . . . . . . . . . . . . . 52
3:16 . . . . . . . . . . . . . . . . . . . . . . 291
6:3 . . . . . . . . . . . . . . . . . . . . . . . . 52
6:7 . . . . . . . . . . . . . . . 238, 298, 393
7:25 . . . . . . . . . . . . . . . . . . . . . . 355
7–11 . . . . . . . . . . . . . . . . . . 417, 425
8:14 . . . . . . . . . . . . . . . . . . . . . . 264
9:15 . . . . . . . . . . . . . . . . . . . . . . 355
11:5 . . . . . . . . . . . . . . . . . . . . . . 120
12:13 . . . . . . . . . . . . . . . . . 355, 425
13:5 . . . . . . . . . . . . . . . . . . . . . . 226
13:22 . . . . . . . . . . . . . . . . . . . . . 117
14:2 . . . . . . . . . . . . . . . . . . . . . . 186
14:13–14 . . . . . . . . . . . . . . . . . . 402
14:16,21–29 . . . . . . . . . . . . . . . 308
14:19 . . . . . . . . . . . . . . . . . . . . . 361
14:20 . . . . . . . . . . . . . . . . . . . . . 117
14–15 . . . . . . . . . . . . . . . . . . . . . 404
15 . . . . . . . . . . . . . . . . . . . . . . . 269
15:8 . . . . . . . . . . . . . . . . . . . . . . 160
17:6 . . . . . . . . . . . . . . . . . . . . . . 150
18:19–23 . . . . . . . . . . . . . . . . . . 221
19:4–6 . . . . . . . . . . . . . . . . . . . . 426
19:16–19 . . . . . . . . . . . . . . . . . . 280
19:16–20 . . . . . . . . . . . . . . . . . . 280
20:1–6 . . . . . . . . . . . . . . . . . . . . 378
20:2–3 . . . . . . . . . . . . . . . . . . . . 244
20:5 . . . . . . . . . . . . . . . . . . . . . . 103
20:5–6 . . . . . . . . . . . . . . . . 232, 245
20:7,16 . . . . . . . . . . . . . . . . . . . 172
20:8 . . . . . . . . . . . . . . . . . . . 198, 377
20:15 . . . . . . . . . . . . . . . . . . . . . 172
21:32 . . . . . . . . . . . . . . . . . . . . . 338
22:22 . . . . . . . . . . . . . . . . . . . . . 223
23:5 . . . . . . . . . . . . . . . . . . . . . . 259
23:6–9 . . . . . . . . . . . . . . . . . . . . 223
24:1–8 . . . . . . . . . . . . . . . . . . . . 277
24:3 . . . . . . . . . . . . . . . . . . . . . . . 52
24:8 . . . . . . . . . . . . . . . . . . . 277, 283
24:16 . . . . . . . . . . . . . . . . . . . . . 234
24:16,17 . . . . . . . . . . . . . . . . . . 117
25:1–3 . . . . . . . . . . . . . . . . . . . . 199
25:31–40 . . . . . . . . . . . . . . . . . . 153
27:2 . . . . . . . . . . . . . . . . . . . . . . 293
27:3 . . . . . . . . . . . . . . . . . . . . . . 427
27:19 . . . . . . . . . . . . . . . . . . . . . 294
28 . . . . . . . . . . . . . . . . . 137, 149, 150
28:2 . . . . . . . . . . . . . . . . . . . . . . 359
28:9 . . . . . . . . . . . . . . . . . . . . . . 149
28:15–21 . . . . . . . . . . . . . . . . . . 149
28:17–21 . . . . . . . . . . . . . . . . . . 283
28:33 . . . . . . . . . . . . . . . . . . . . . 426
28:35 . . . . . . . . . . . . . . . . . . . . . 426
28:36 . . . . . . . . . . . . . . . . . . . . . 141
28:36–38 . . . . . . . . . . . . . . . . . . 139
28–29 . . . . . . . . . . . . . . . . . . . . . 137
29 . . . . . . . . . . . . . . . . . . . . 141, 149
29:6 . . . . . . . . . . . . . . . . . . . . . . 283
29:42–46 . . . . . . . . . . . . . . . . . . 125
29:45–46 . . . . . . . . . . . . . . . . . . 238
30:11–16 . . . . . . . . . . . . . . . . . . 199
30:18 . . . . . . . . . . . . . . . . . . . . . 356
32:11 . . . . . . . . . . . . . . . . . . . . . 215
32:11–13 . . . . . . . . . . . . . . . . . . 249
33–34 . . . . . . . . . . . . . . . . . . . . . 122
34:5–7 . . . . . . . . . . . . . . . . . . . . 221
34:6–7 . . . . . . . . . . . . . . . . 222, 223
34:7 . . . . . . . . . . . . . . . . . . . . . . . 21
34:14 . . . . . . . . . . . . . . . . . 103, 232

34:24 . . . . . . . . . . . . . . . . . . . . . . . 52
35:18 . . . . . . . . . . . . . . . . . . . . . . 294
39:25–26 . . . . . . . . . . . . . . . . . . 426
39:30 . . . . . . . . . . . . . . . . . . . . . . 141
40:34 . . . . . . . . . . . . . . . . . . . . . . 117
40:35 . . . . . . . . . . . . . . . . . . . . . . 234
43:20 . . . . . . . . . . . . . . . . . . . . . . 293

**Leviticus**

5:1 . . . . . . . . . . . . . . . . . . . . . . . . 172
5:11 . . . . . . . . . . . . . . . . . . . . . . . 174
6:2 . . . . . . . . . . . . . . . . . . . . . . . . 386
7:11–18 . . . . . . . . . . . . . . . . . . . . 427
7:20 . . . . . . . . . . . . . . . . . . . . . . . 376
8. . . . . . . . . . . . . . . . . . . . . . 141, 149
8:5–9 . . . . . . . . . . . . . . . . . . . . . . 137
8:9 . . . . . . . . . . . . . . . . . . . . . . . . 283
11:1–8 . . . . . . . . . . . . . . . . . . . . . 427
11:19 . . . . . . . . . . . . . . . . . . . . . . 179
12:3 . . . . . . . . . . . . . . . . . . . . . . . 273
13:21 . . . . . . . . . . . . . . . . . . . . . . 263
13:49 . . . . . . . . . . . . . . . . . . . . . . 343
14:2–9,33–53 . . . . . . . . . . . . . . . 181
16. . . . . . . . . 60, 113, 141, 149, 181
16:6,11 . . . . . . . . . . . . . . . . . . . . . 60
16:8,10,20–22,26 . . . . . . . . . . . . 60
16:15 . . . . . . . . . . . . . . . . . . . . . . . 60
18:12 . . . . . . . . . . . . . . . . . . . . . . 284
18:20 . . . . . . . . . . . . . . . . . . . . . . 386
19:2 . . . . . . . . . . . . . . . . . . . . . . . 221
19:15–18 . . . . . . . . . . . . . . . . . . . 223
19:18,34 . . . . . . . . . . . . . . . . . . . 246
19:36 . . . . . . . . . . . . . . . . . . . . . . 271
21:5 . . . . . . . . . . . . . . . . . . . . . . . 354
21:7 . . . . . . . . . . . . . . . . . . . . . . . 407
21:10 . . . . . . . . . . . . . . . . . . . . . . 134
22. . . . . . . . . . . . . . . . . . . . . . . . . 138
22:1–9 . . . . . . . . . . . . . . . . . . . . . 373
22:3 . . . . . . . . . . . . . . . . . . . . . . . 138
22:6–7 . . . . . . . . . . . . . . . . . . . . . 139
23:33–43 . . . . . . . . . . . . . . . . . . 422
23:42–43 . . . . . . . . . . . . . . . . . . 423

25:18–19 . . . . . . . . . . . . . . . . . . 417
26:5 . . . . . . . . . . . . . . . . . . . . . . . 417
26:12 . . . . . . . . . . . . . . . . . . . 52, 393
26:14–17 . . . . . . . . . . . . . . . . . . 417
26:23–28 . . . . . . . . . . . . . . . . . . 419
26:26 . . . . . . . . . . . . . . . . . . . . . . 249

**Numbers**

3. . . . . . . . . . . . . . . . . . . . . . . . . . 142
3:7 . . . . . . . . . . . . . . . . . . . . . . . . 142
5:11–31 . . . . . . . . . . . . . . . . . . . 172
5:14 . . . . . . . . . . . . . . . . . . . . . . . 364
5:21–28 . . . . . . . . . . . . . . . . . . . 171
7. . . . . . . . . . . . . . . . . . . . . . . . . . 199
8:7 . . . . . . . . . . . . . . . . . . . . . 52, 373
9:13 . . . . . . . . . . . . . . . . . . . . . . . 376
12:7 . . . . . . . . . . . . . . . . . . . . . . . 145
13:27 . . . . . . . . . . . . . . . . . . . . . . 226
16:5 . . . . . . . . . . . . . . . . . . . . . . . 407
17:1–11 . . . . . . . . . . . . . . . . . . . 328
19. . . . . . . . . . . . . . . . . . . . . . . . . 373
19:9–21 . . . . . . . . . . . . . . . . . . . 373
19:9–31 . . . . . . . . . . . . . . . . . . . . 52
20:8 . . . . . . . . . . . . . . . . . . . 130, 150
21:4 . . . . . . . . . . . . . . . . . . . . . . . 332
21:9 . . . . . . . . . . . . . . . . . . . 185, 366
21:32–35 . . . . . . . . . . . . . . . . . . 315
22:18 . . . . . . . . . . . . . . . . . . . . . . 322
25:8 . . . . . . . . . . . . . . . . . . . . . . . 366
27:17 . . . . . . . . . . . . . . . . . . . . . . 289
31:23 . . . . . . . . . . . . . . . . . . . . . . . 52
32:33 . . . . . . . . . . . . . . . . . . . . . . 315
34:4–12 . . . . . . . . . . . . . . . . . . . 304
34:12 . . . . . . . . . . . . . . . . . . . . . . 411
35:25,28 . . . . . . . . . . . . . . . . . . . 134

**Deuteronomy**

1:7–8 . . . . . . . . . . . . . . . . . . . . . . . 52
3:5 . . . . . . . . . . . . . . . . . . . . . . . . 315
3:23 . . . . . . . . . . . . . . . . . . . . . . . 265

| Reference | Page |
|---|---|
| 4:1–2 | 86 |
| 4:15–31 | 181 |
| 4:24 | 104, 282 |
| 4:39 | 413 |
| 5:4 | 52 |
| 5:9 | 103 |
| 5:22 | 281 |
| 5:33 | 302 |
| 6:3 | 226 |
| 6:4 | 52, 143, 413 |
| 6:5 | 246 |
| 6:25 | 271 |
| 7:8 | 300 |
| 7:13 | 165 |
| 7:23 | 52 |
| 8 | 228 |
| 8:1 | 302 |
| 8:6 | 141, 142 |
| 8:7–10 | 227 |
| 9:6 | 225 |
| 9:27 | 145 |
| 10:12–13 | 142 |
| 10:16 | 225 |
| 10:18–19 | 223 |
| 11:10–11 | 424 |
| 11:13–14 | 284 |
| 11:24 | 52, 411 |
| 12 | 68 |
| 12:2–3 | 52 |
| 12:5 | 69 |
| 12:5,11 | 52 |
| 13 | 375, 379 |
| 13:3–4 | 379 |
| 13:6–10 | 52 |
| 13:10 | 379 |
| 13:12–16 | 52 |
| 14:1 | 382 |
| 15:13–17 | 422 |
| 16:13–15 | 52 |
| 16:14 | 423 |
| 16:20 | 302 |
| 17:8–13 | 142 |
| 17:14–20 | 334 |
| 17:19 | 86 |
| 18 | 288 |
| 18:9–22 | 379 |
| 18:10–11 | 52 |
| 18:10–12 | 288 |
| 18:20–22 | 52 |
| 20:1–9 | 84 |
| 21:18–21 | 52, 378–79 |
| 24:14 | 223 |
| 25:14–15 | 174 |
| 26:15 | 129 |
| 26:17–18 | 52 |
| 27:8–10 | 86 |
| 28 | 34, 66, 118, 169, 171, 206, 243, 347, 355, 388, 419 |
| 28:1 | 206 |
| 28:1–14 | 230 |
| 28:7 | 240 |
| 28:12 | 285 |
| 28:15,45 | 85 |
| 28:15–22 | 417 |
| 28:15–68 | 230 |
| 28:17 | 178 |
| 28:21–22 | 285 |
| 28:22–24 | 424 |
| 28:28 | 52, 355 |
| 28:30 | 401 |
| 28:45–47 | 34 |
| 28:45–52 | 226 |
| 29:10–21 | 171 |
| 29:17 | 267 |
| 29:25–26 | 181 |
| 30:6 | 225 |
| 31:9–13 | 52 |
| 32:10 | 123 |
| 32:14 | 291, 315 |
| 32:16,21 | 104 |
| 33:17 | 109 |
| 33:24 | 164 |
| 33:28 | 284, 417 |
| 34:10 | 342 |

## Joshua

1:1–11 . . . . . . . . . . . . . . . . . . . . . . 84
3:10 . . . . . . . . . . . . . . . . . . . . . . . 428
3:11 . . . . . . . . . . . . . . . . . . . . . . . 264
3:13 . . . . . . . . . . . . . . . . . . . . . . . 404
5:6 . . . . . . . . . . . . . . . . . . . . . . . . 226
6:17 . . . . . . . . . . . . . . . . . . . . . . . 416
6:18 . . . . . . . . . . . . . . . . . . . . . . . 416
7. . . . . . . . . . . . . . . . . . . . . . . . . . 376
7:21,24 . . . . . . . . . . . . . . . . . . . . 380
7:24–25 . . . . . . . . . . . . . . . . . . . . 420
9:6 . . . . . . . . . . . . . . . . . . . . . . . . 335
13:5 . . . . . . . . . . . . . . . . . . . . . . . 263
13:30 . . . . . . . . . . . . . . . . . . . . . . 315
15:32 . . . . . . . . . . . . . . . . . . . . . . 414
15:45–47 . . . . . . . . . . . . . . . . . . . 267
17:16 . . . . . . . . . . . . . . . . . . . . . . . 53
20:6 . . . . . . . . . . . . . . . . . . . . . . . 134
21:17 . . . . . . . . . . . . . . . . . . . . . . 414

## Judges

1:2 . . . . . . . . . . . . . . . . . . . . . . . . 265
2:14 . . . . . . . . . . . . . . . . . . . . . . . 324
3:3 . . . . . . . . . . . . . . . . . . . . . . . . 263
3:27 . . . . . . . . . . . . . . . . . . . . . . . 281
4:9 . . . . . . . . . . . . . . . . . . . . . . . . 359
5:4–5 . . . . . . . . . . . . . . . . . . 185, 281
5:5 . . . . . . . . . . . . . . . . . . . . . . . . 405
5:10 . . . . . . . . . . . . . . . . . . . . . . . 273
5:22 . . . . . . . . . . . . . . . . . . . . . . . 354
7:11 . . . . . . . . . . . . . . . . . . . . . . . 240
7:22 . . . . . . . . . . . . . . . . . . . . . . . 418
9:9 . . . . . . . . . . . . . . . . . . . . . . . . 164
9:54 . . . . . . . . . . . . . . . . . . . . . . . 366
10:4 . . . . . . . . . . . . . . . . . . . . . . . 273
11. . . . . . . . . . . . . . . . . . . . . . . . . 369
11:34 . . . . . . . . . . . . . . . . . . . . . . 369
12:14 . . . . . . . . . . . . . . . . . . . . . . 273
16:16 . . . . . . . . . . . . . . . . . . . . . . 332
17:2 . . . . . . . . . . . . . . . . . . . . 171, 172
17:5 . . . . . . . . . . . . . . . . . . . . . . . 288
18:5 . . . . . . . . . . . . . . . . . . . . . . . 288
20:2 . . . . . . . . . . . . . . . . . . . . . . . 293
21:19 . . . . . . . . . . . . . . . . . . . . . . 423

## Ruth

1:16 . . . . . . . . . . . . . . . . . . . . . . . 322
2:17 . . . . . . . . . . . . . . . . . . . . . . . 174
2:20 . . . . . . . . . . . . . . . . . . . . . . . 222
4:1–11 . . . . . . . . . . . . . . . . . . . . . 244

## 1 Samuel

9:1–10:16 . . . . . . . . . . . . . . . . . . 199
9:9 . . . . . . . . . . . . . . . . . . . . . . . . . 95
13:3 . . . . . . . . . . . . . . . . . . . . . . . 281
14:38 . . . . . . . . . . . . . . . . . . . . . . 293
23:18 . . . . . . . . . . . . . . . . . . . . . . 335

## 2 Samuel

5:7 . . . . . . . . . . . . . . . . . . . . . . . . 105
7:13 . . . . . . . . . . . . . . . . . . . . . . . . 53
7:14 . . . . . . . . . . . . . . . . . . . . . . . 386
19:24 . . . . . . . . . . . . . . . . . . . . . . . 82

## 1 Kings

7:30–33 . . . . . . . . . . . . . . . . . . . . 184
8:1 . . . . . . . . . . . . . . . . . . . . . . . . 105
13:4 . . . . . . . . . . . . . . . . . . . . . . . . 53
19:13,19 . . . . . . . . . . . . . . . . . . . . 53
19:16 . . . . . . . . . . . . . . . . . . . . . . . 82

## 2 Kings

2:8,13,14 . . . . . . . . . . . . . . . . . . . . 53
2:8,13–14 . . . . . . . . . . . . . . . . . . 380
2:14 . . . . . . . . . . . . . . . . . . . . . . . 380
7:8 . . . . . . . . . . . . . . . . . . . . . . . . . 53
9:2,14 . . . . . . . . . . . . . . . . . . . . . . 82
9:14 . . . . . . . . . . . . . . . . . . . . . . . . 21

| | |
|---|---|
| 9:20 | 82 |
| 9:27 | 184 |
| 10:15 | 184 |
| 17:17 | 53 |
| 18:27 | 137 |
| 19:21 | 53 |
| 25:8 | 214 |
| 25:8–21 | 246 |

**1 Chronicles**

| | |
|---|---|
| 27:15 | 196 |

**2 Chronicles**

| | |
|---|---|
| 6:6 | 107 |
| 15:1–7 | 84 |
| 19:6–7 | 84 |
| 20:15–17 | 84 |
| 21:10–19 | 419 |
| 24 | 83 |
| 24:20–22 | 83 |
| 26:15 | 293 |
| 30:6–9 | 84 |
| 36:15–21 | 85 |

**Ezra**

| | |
|---|---|
| 1:1–4 | 37 |
| 1:2 | 37 |
| 1:8,11 | 37 |
| 2 | 143, 197 |
| 2:2 | 39, 133 |
| 2:28 | 213 |
| 2:36 | 197 |
| 2:60 | 196 |
| 2:66–67 | 420 |
| 2:68–69 | 198 |
| 3:1–8 | 37 |
| 3:4 | 423 |
| 3:7–13 | 240 |
| 3:8 | 39 |
| 3:8–11 | 162 |
| 3:8–13 | 37 |
| 4:1–5 | 37, 114, 240 |
| 4:1–5,24 | 37, 160 |
| 4:2 | 39 |
| 4:24 | 38 |
| 5:1 | 20, 39, 81 |
| 5:1–17 | 38 |
| 5:2 | 39 |
| 5:14 | 37 |
| 5:16 | 37, 162 |
| 6 | 204 |
| 6:1–12 | 38 |
| 6:3–5 | 37 |
| 6:5 | 198 |
| 6:11 | 173 |
| 6:14 | 20, 38, 39, 81 |
| 6:14–15 | 38 |
| 6:14–16 | 162 |
| 6:16 | 39 |
| 6:22 | 30 |
| 7:7–9 | 213 |
| 9 | 178 |
| 9:1–10:17 | 86 |
| 9:8 | 294 |
| 10:1 | 93 |
| 10:2 | 93 |

**Nehemiah**

| | |
|---|---|
| 1:6 | 93 |
| 1:9–10 | 300 |
| 1:10 | 300 |
| 2:10,19 | 197 |
| 2:14 | 415 |
| 3:1 | 415 |
| 3:6 | 415 |
| 3:15 | 415 |
| 4:10 | 159 |
| 5:15 | 338 |
| 6:12–14 | 375 |
| 7 | 143 |
| 7:4 | 416 |

7:7 . . . . . . . . . . . . . . . . . . . . . . . 133
7:39 . . . . . . . . . . . . . . . . . . . . . . 197
8:14–18 . . . . . . . . . . . . . . . . . . . 423
8:15 . . . . . . . . . . . . . . . . . . . . . . . 98
9:11 . . . . . . . . . . . . . . . . . . . . . . 308
9:20 . . . . . . . . . . . . . . . . . . . . . . 226
9:29 . . . . . . . . . . . . . . . . . . . . . . 225
9:30 . . . . . . . . . . . . . . . . . . . . . . 226
10. . . . . . . . . . . . . . . . . . . . . . . . 204
11:1–2 . . . . . . . . . . . . . . . . . . . . 115
11:10 . . . . . . . . . . . . . . . . . . . . . 197
11:29 . . . . . . . . . . . . . . . . . . . . . 414
12. . . . . . . . . . . . . . . . . . . . . . . . . 82
12:4,16 . . . . . . . . . . . . . . . . . 21, 82
12:6–7,19,21 . . . . . . . . . . . . . . . 197
12:16 . . . . . . . . . . . . . . . . . . . . . . 82
12:39 . . . . . . . . . . . . . . . . . . . . . 415

**Esther**

2:5 . . . . . . . . . . . . . . . . . . . . . . . 250
3:4 . . . . . . . . . . . . . . . . . . . . . . . 250
7:10 . . . . . . . . . . . . . . . . . . . . . . 124

**Job**

1. . . . . . . . . . . . . . . . . . . . . 133, 135
1:6–12 . . . . . . . . . . . . . . . . . . . . 135
1:7 . . . . . . . . . . . . . . . . . . . . . . . 100
1:8 . . . . . . . . . . . . . . . . . . . . . . . 145
2:1–7 . . . . . . . . . . . . . . . . . . . . . 135
5:1 . . . . . . . . . . . . . . . . . . . . . . . 407
5:20 . . . . . . . . . . . . . . . . . . . . . . 300
5:23 . . . . . . . . . . . . . . . . . . . . . . 334
11:11 . . . . . . . . . . . . . . . . . . . . . 288
13:4 . . . . . . . . . . . . . . . . . . . . . . 346
23:10 . . . . . . . . . . . . . . . . . . . . . 392
38:5 . . . . . . . . . . . . . . . . . . . . . . 107
38:6 . . . . . . . . . . . . . . . . . . . . . . 293
39:7 . . . . . . . . . . . . . . . . . . . . . . 268
39:19–25 . . . . . . . . . . . . . . . . . . . 53
42:10 . . . . . . . . . . . . . . . . . . . . . 278

**Psalms**

1:1 . . . . . . . . . . . . . . . . . . . 141, 319
1:6 . . . . . . . . . . . . . . . . . . . . . . . 333
2. . . . . . . . . . . . . 269, 296, 403, 417
2:1–2 . . . . . . . . . . . . . . . . . . . . . 353
2:2 . . . . . . . . . . . . . . . . . . . . . . . 417
2:5 . . . . . . . . . . . . . . . . . . . . . . . 417
2:7 . . . . . . . . . . . . . . . . . . . . . . . 386
2:11 . . . . . . . . . . . . . . . . . . . . . . 299
3:4 . . . . . . . . . . . . . . . . . . . . . . . . 53
4:1 . . . . . . . . . . . . . . . . . . . . . . . . 53
9. . . . . . . . . . . . . . . . . . . . . . . . 269
9:9 . . . . . . . . . . . . . . . . . . . . . . . 278
14:7 . . . . . . . . . . . . . . . . . . . . . . 299
15:2–3 . . . . . . . . . . . . . . . . . . . . 244
17:8 . . . . . . . . . . . . . . . . . . . . . . 123
18:2 . . . . . . . . . . . . . . . . . . 109, 278
18:7 . . . . . . . . . . . . . . . . . . . . . . 405
18:7–15 . . . . . . . . . . . . . . . . . . . 280
18:9 . . . . . . . . . . . . . . . . . . . . . . . 53
18:13–14 . . . . . . . . . . . . . . . . . . 280
18:28 . . . . . . . . . . . . . . . . . . . . . . 95
20:2 . . . . . . . . . . . . . . . . . . . . . . . 53
22:11 . . . . . . . . . . . . . . . . . . . . . 322
22:12 . . . . . . . . . . . . . . . . . . . . . 315
22:20 . . . . . . . . . . . . . . . . . . . . . 385
23:1 . . . . 53, 283, 289, 323, 347, 393
23:4 . . . . . . . . . . . . . . . . . . . . . . 141
23:5 . . . . . . . . . . . . . . . . . . 164, 352
24. . . . . . . . . . . . . . . . . . . . . . . . 269
24:3 . . . . . . . . . . . . . . . . . . . . . . 160
24:7 . . . . . . . . . . . . . . . . . . . 53, 315
24:10 . . . . . . . . . . . . . . . . . . 53, 422
26:8 . . . . . . . . . . . . . . . . . . . . . . 129
26:11 . . . . . . . . . . . . . . . . . . . . . 300
29. . . . . . . . . . . . . . . . . . . . 269, 280
29:3–9 . . . . . . . . . . . . . . . . . . . . 281
29:5 . . . . . . . . . . . . . . . . . . . . . . 313
29:6–8 . . . . . . . . . . . . . . . . . . . . . 53
30:5 . . . . . . . . . . . . . . . . . . . . . . . 95
31:3 . . . . . . . . . . . . . . . . . . . . . . 278
31:5 . . . . . . . . . . . . . . . . . . . . . . 300

| | | | |
|---|---|---|---|
| 31:6 | 289 | 76. | 269 |
| 31:15 | 322 | 78:61 | 359 |
| 32:4–5 | 93 | 80:1 | 53, 283, 323 |
| 33:16 | 159 | 81:3 | 281 |
| 33:20 | 159 | 84:7 | 105 |
| 34:12–14 | 224 | 86:15 | 221 |
| 34:19 | 225 | 89:5 | 407 |
| 37:13 | 265 | 89:5,7 | 407 |
| 38:21 | 322 | 89:25 | 275 |
| 41:6 | 288 | 89:26–27 | 386 |
| 44:26 | 222 | 90:4 | 399 |
| 45:4 | 204 | 90:17 | 328 |
| 45:8 | 164 | 91:2 | 278 |
| 46. | 269 | 92:12 | 313 |
| 46:4 | 411 | 93. | 412 |
| 46:5 | 95 | 94:22 | 278 |
| 46:10 | 130 | 95:7 | 283, 323, 324 |
| 46–48. | 403 | 96. | 124 |
| 47. | 248, 269 | 96:1 | 126 |
| 47:9 | 126 | 97. | 269, 412 |
| 48. | 269 | 97:1 | 126 |
| 48:1,3 | 185 | 98. | 124, 269 |
| 48:1–2 | 160 | 98:4 | 126 |
| 48:2 | 185 | 98:6 | 53 |
| 49:16 | 300 | 99. | 412 |
| 51:4 | 418 | 100:3 | 289 |
| 51:8 | 246 | 101:6 | 141 |
| 51:14 | 418 | 103:2 | 181 |
| 51:19 | 225 | 103:20 | 295 |
| 55:10 | 265 | 104. | 269 |
| 59:9,19 | 278 | 104:2 | 53 |
| 65:9 | 411 | 104:4 | 188 |
| 65:9–13 | 423 | 104:5 | 188 |
| 68. | 185, 269 | 107:8 | 222 |
| 68:17 | 184, 185 | 107:20 | 260 |
| 71:3 | 278 | 109:6 | 136 |
| 72:8 | 53, 275 | 110. | 204, 269 |
| 73:2–3,23–25 | 77 | 110:1–2 | 205 |
| 73:24 | 120 | 110:4 | 70, 151, 204 |
| 74:13–17 | 53 | 114:1 | 402 |
| 75:2 | 53 | 116:13 | 352 |
| 75:8 | 53 | 118:22 | 53, 293, 294 |
| 75:10 | 109 | 118:22–23 | 70, 147 |

| | |
|---|---|
| 118:24 | 299 |
| 119:58 | 215 |
| 120–134 | 422 |
| 121:3–4 | 128 |
| 123:1–2 | 263 |
| 127:1 | 173 |
| 132:13–14 | 185 |
| 133:1 | 53, 358 |
| 139:14 | 237 |
| 143:1 | 364 |
| 144:2 | 278 |
| 144:5 | 280 |
| 146:5–6 | 108 |
| 146:6 | 221, 234 |
| 147:10 | 274 |
| 147:15 | 173 |

**Proverbs**

| | |
|---|---|
| 1:7 | 343 |
| 1:9 | 161 |
| 1:20 | 200 |
| 1:27 | 226 |
| 5:16 | 107 |
| 5:19 | 161 |
| 6:16–19 | 244 |
| 8 | 178 |
| 13:6 | 271 |
| 13:22 | 21 |
| 14:25 | 222 |
| 14:29 | 343 |
| 17:6 | 359 |
| 17:8 | 161 |
| 20:21 | 332 |
| 23:5 | 179 |
| 24:9 | 343 |
| 29:14 | 222 |
| 30:19 | 386 |
| 31:24 | 428 |
| 31:30 | 161 |

**Ecclesiastes**

| | |
|---|---|
| 1:2,14 | 289 |
| 2:1,15,21,23,26 | 289 |
| 3:3 | 323 |
| 3:19 | 289 |
| 4:7,8,16 | 289 |
| 5:9 | 289 |
| 6:2,9,11 | 289 |
| 7:6 | 289 |
| 8:14 | 289 |
| 11:8,10 | 289 |
| 12:2 | 120 |
| 12:8 | 289 |
| 12:11 | 53 |

**Song**

| | |
|---|---|
| 4:1 | 304 |
| 4:10 | 54 |
| 4:15 | 304 |
| 7:1,6 | 54 |

**Isaiah**

| | |
|---|---|
| 1:6 | 382 |
| 1:10–17 | 217 |
| 1:11–17 | 217 |
| 1:14 | 332 |
| 1:15 | 54 |
| 1:16–17,23 | 54 |
| 1:17 | 223 |
| 1:21–26 | 392 |
| 1:25 | 388 |
| 1:26 | 149, 234, 239 |
| 2 | 335, 342 |
| 2:1–4 | 66 |
| 2:1–5 | 247 |
| 2:2 | 414 |
| 2:2–3 | 160 |
| 2:2–4 | 54, 126, 205, 335, 421 |
| 2:2–5 | 247, 342 |
| 2:2–22 | 54 |

| | |
|---|---|
| 2:3 . . . . . . . . . . . . . . . . . . . . . 54, 422 | 9:19–20 . . . . . . . . . . . . . . . . . . . . 357 |
| 2:5 . . . . . . . . . . . . . . . . . . . . . . . . . 54 | 10:5–19 . . . . . . . . . . . . . . . . . . . . 105 |
| 2:7 . . . . . . . . . . . . . . . . . . . . 274, 426 | 10:21 . . . . . . . . . . . . . . . . . . . . . . 85 |
| 2:12 . . . . . . . . . . . . . . . . . . . . . . . 400 | 10:33–34 . . . . . . . . . . . . . . . 314, 315 |
| 2:12–13 . . . . . . . . . . . . . . . . . . . . 314 | 10:34 . . . . . . . . . . . . . . . . . . . . . 313 |
| 2:13 . . . . . . . . . . . . . . . . . . . 313, 315 | 11 . . . . . . . . . . . . . . . . . . . . . 282, 303 |
| 3:13 . . . . . . . . . . . . . . . . . . . . . . . . 54 | 11:1 . . . . . . . . . . . . . . . . . . . . 70, 144 |
| 3:22 . . . . . . . . . . . . . . . . . . . . . . . 140 | 11:1–11 . . . . . . . . . . . . . . . . . . . . 238 |
| 4 . . . . . . . . . . . . . . . . . . . . . . . . . . 55 | 11:1–16 . . . . . . . . . . . . . . . . . 192, 365 |
| 4:1 . . . . . . . . . . . . . . . . . . . . . . . . 400 | 11:4 . . . . . . . . . . . . . . . . . . . . 54, 296 |
| 4:2 . . . . . . . . . . . . . . . . . . 70, 144, 284 | 11:4–6 . . . . . . . . . . . . . . . . . . . . . 271 |
| 4:2,4 . . . . . . . . . . . . . . . . . . . . . . 201 | 11:5 . . . . . . . . . . . . . . . . . . . . . . 272 |
| 4:2–3 . . . . . . . . . . . . . . . . . . . . . . . 54 | 11:6 . . . . . . . . . . . . . . . . . . . . . . 176 |
| 4:3–4 . . . . . . . . . . . . . . . . . . 139, 149 | 11:9 . . . . . . . . . . . . . . . . . . . . . . 235 |
| 5:7 . . . . . . . . . . . . . . . . . . . . . . . . 342 | 11:10–16 . . . . . . . . . . . . . . . . . . . 297 |
| 5:29 . . . . . . . . . . . . . . . . . . . . . . . 176 | 11:11,15–16 . . . . . . . . . . . . . . . . . 304 |
| 5:30 . . . . . . . . . . . . . . . . . . . . . . . 409 | 11:13 . . . . . . . . . . . . . . . . . . . . . 275 |
| 6 . . . . . . . . . . . . . . . . . . . . 84, 92, 122 | 11:15 . . . . . . . . . . . . . . . . . . . . . 123 |
| 6:3 . . . . . . . . . . . . . . . . . . . . 117, 122 | 13 . . . . . . . . . . . . . . . . . . . . . . . . 192 |
| 6:4 . . . . . . . . . . . . . . . . . . . . . 54, 352 | 13:1 . . . . . . . . . . . . . . . . . . . . . . 260 |
| 6:5 . . . . . . . . . . . . . . . . . . . . . . . . 422 | 13:1–14:23 . . . . . . . . . . . . . . . . . . 181 |
| 6:9–10 . . . . . . . . . . . . . . . . . . . . . . 54 | 13:6 . . . . . . . . . . . . . . . . . . . . . . 316 |
| 6:10 . . . . . . . . . . . . . . . . . . . . . . . 225 | 13:9,15–16 . . . . . . . . . . . . . . . . . . . 54 |
| 6:13 . . . . . . . . . . . . . . . . . . . . . . . 392 | 13:10 . . . . . . . . . . . . . . . . . . 408, 409 |
| 7 . . . . . . . . . . . . . . . . . . . . . . . . . 402 | 13:13–14 . . . . . . . . . . . . . . . . . . . . 54 |
| 7:2 . . . . . . . . . . . . . . . . . . . . . . . . 358 | 13:15–16 . . . . . . . . . . . . . . . . . . . . 54 |
| 7:3 . . . . . . . . . . . . . . . . . . . . . . . . 402 | 13:16 . . . . . . . . . . . . . . . . . . . . . 401 |
| 7:4 . . . . . . . . . . . . . . . . . . . . . . . . 137 | 13–23 . . . . . . . . . . . . . . . . . . . . . 256 |
| 7:14 . . . . . . . . . . . . . . . . . . . . . . . 370 | 14:1 . . . . . . . . . . . . . . . . . . . . . . 128 |
| 7:17 . . . . . . . . . . . . . . . . . . . . . . . 297 | 14:2 . . . . . . . . . . . . . . . . . . . . . . 124 |
| 8:2 . . . . . . . . . . . . . . . . . . . . . . 81, 83 | 14:9 . . . . . . . . . . . . . . . . . . . . . . 291 |
| 8:6 . . . . . . . . . . . . . . . . . . . . . . . . 410 | 14:28 . . . . . . . . . . . . . . . . . . . . . 260 |
| 8:13–15 . . . . . . . . . . . . . . . . . . . . 147 | 14:32 . . . . . . . . . . . . . . . . . . . . . 273 |
| 8:18 . . . . . . . . . . . . . . . . . . . . . . . 143 | 15:1 . . . . . . . . . . . . . . . . . . . . . . 260 |
| 9 . . . . . . . . . . . . . . . . . . . . . . . . . 282 | 16:1–5 . . . . . . . . . . . . . . . . . . . . . 257 |
| 9:1–7 . . . . . . . . . . . . . . . . . . . . . . 192 | 16:5 . . . . . . . . . . . . . . . . . . . . . . 271 |
| 9:2 . . . . . . . . . . . . . . . . . . . . . . . . 409 | 17:1 . . . . . . . . . . . . . . . . . . . . . . 260 |
| 9:3 . . . . . . . . . . . . . . . . . . . . . . . . 268 | 19:1 . . . . . . . . . . . . . . . . . . . . . . 260 |
| 9:4–7 . . . . . . . . . . . . . . . . . . . . . . 296 | 19:5 . . . . . . . . . . . . . . . . . . . . . . 308 |
| 9:6–7 . . . . . . . . . . . . . . . . . . . . . . 271 | 19:16 . . . . . . . . . . . . . . . . . . . . . 123 |
| 9:7 . . . . . . . . . . . . . . . . . . . . . . . . 104 | 19:16–18 . . . . . . . . . . . . . . . . . . . 258 |
| 9:8 . . . . . . . . . . . . . . . . . . . . . . . . 260 | 19:18–22 . . . . . . . . . . . . . . . . . . . 424 |
| 9:14 . . . . . . . . . . . . . . . . . . . 288, 376 | 19:22–25 . . . . . . . . . . . . . . . . . . . 128 |

| | |
|---|---|
| 20. . . . . . . . . . . . . . . . . . . . . . . 257 | 37:17 . . . . . . . . . . . . . . . . . . . . . 355 |
| 20:2 . . . . . . . . . . . . . . . . . . . . . . 321 | 37:22 . . . . . . . . . . . . . . . . . . . . . . 54 |
| 21:1,11,13 . . . . . . . . . . . . . . . . . 260 | 37:32 . . . . . . . . . . . . . . . . . . . . . 104 |
| 22:1 . . . . . . . . . . . . . . . . . . . . . . 260 | 37:35 . . . . . . . . . . . . . . . . . . . . . 282 |
| 22:5 . . . . . . . . . . . . . . . 54, 265, 399 | 37:36 . . . . . . . . . . . . . . . . . . . . . 417 |
| 22:13 . . . . . . . . . . . . . . . . . . . . . 322 | 38:6 . . . . . . . . . . . . . . . . . . . . . . 282 |
| 22:23 . . . . . . . . . . . . . . . . . . . . . . 54 | 38:8 . . . . . . . . . . . . . . . . . . . . . . 264 |
| 22:23–24 . . . . . . . . . . . . . . . . . . 294 | 40:1 . . . . . . . . . . . . . . . . . . 103, 107 |
| 22:25 . . . . . . . . . . . . . . . . . 259, 294 | 40:2 . . . . . . . . . . . . . . . . . . . . . . . 54 |
| 23:1 . . . . . . . . . . . . . . . . . . 260, 316 | 40:3–4 . . . . . . . . . . . . . . . . . . . . . 404 |
| 23:8–9 . . . . . . . . . . . . . . . . . . . . 264 | 40:4 . . . . . . . . . . . . . . . . . . . . . . 161 |
| 23:23–25 . . . . . . . . . . . . . . . . . . 247 | 40:6 . . . . . . . . . . . . . . . . . . . . . . 103 |
| 24:13 . . . . . . . . . . . . . . . . . . . . . 406 | 40:10 . . . . . . . . . . . . . . . . . . . . . 265 |
| 24:21 . . . . . . . . . . . . . . . . . . . . . 291 | 40:11 . . . . . . 54, 283, 289, 323, 347 |
| 25:6–10 . . . . . . . . . . . . . . . . . . . 126 | 40:22 . . . . . . . . . . . . . . . . . . . . . . 54 |
| 25:9 . . . . . . . . . . . . . . . . . . . . . . 299 | 40:24 . . . . . . . . . . . . . . . . . . . . . 226 |
| 26:1 . . . . . . . . . . . . . . . . . . . . . . 117 | 40:30–31 . . . . . . . . . . . . . . . . . . . 360 |
| 27:1 . . . . . . . . . . . . . . . . . . . . . . 307 | 41:8 . . . . . . . . . . . . . . . . . . 128, 145 |
| 27:11 . . . . . . . . . . . . . . . . . . . . . 340 | 41:17 . . . . . . . . . . . . . . . . . . 54, 298 |
| 27:13 . . . . . . . . . . . . . . . . . . . . . 281 | 42. . . . . . . . . . . . . . . . . . . . . . . . 347 |
| 28:6 . . . . . . . . . . . . . . . . . . . . . . 364 | 42:5 . . . . . . . . . . . . . . . . . . . . . . . 54 |
| 28:16 . . . . . . . . . . . . . 146, 147, 293 | 42:6 . . . . . . . . . . . . . . . . . . . . . . 126 |
| 29:17 . . . . . . . . . . . . . . . . . . . . . 304 | 42:7 . . . . . . . . . . . . . . . 54, 278, 409 |
| 29:19 . . . . . . . . . . . . . . . . . . . . . 299 | 42:13 . . . . . . . . . . . . . . . . . . . . . 104 |
| 29:22 . . . . . . . . . . . . . . . . . . . . . 300 | 42:16 . . . . . . . . . . . . . . . . . . . . . 161 |
| 30:18–19 . . . . . . . . . . . . . . . . . . 298 | 43:1 . . . . . . . . . . . . . . . 54, 340, 351 |
| 30:23 . . . . . . . . . . . . . . . . . . . . . 284 | 43:2 . . . . . . . . . . . . . . . . . . . . . . 392 |
| 30:25 . . . . . . . . . . . . . . . . . . . . . . 54 | 43:5–6 . . . . . . . . . . . . . . . . 119, 238 |
| 30:29 . . . . . . . . . . . . . . . . . . . . . . 55 | 43:14–21 . . . . . . . . . . . . . . . . . . . 404 |
| 30:32 . . . . . . . . . . . . . . . . . . . . . . 54 | 43:17 . . . . . . . . . . . . . . . . . . . . . . 54 |
| 31:1 . . . . . . . . . . . . . . . . . . . . . . 274 | 43:19 . . . . . . . . . . . . . . . . . . . . . 404 |
| 32:1 . . . . . . . . . . . . . . . . . . 271, 272 | 43:28 . . . . . . . . . . . . . . . . . . . . . 416 |
| 32:1–8 . . . . . . . . . . . . . . . . . . . . 149 | 44:3 . . . . . . . . . . . . . . . . . . . . . . 363 |
| 32:15 . . . . . . . . . . . . . . . . . . . . . 363 | 44:6 . . . . . . . . . . . . . . . . . . . . . . 376 |
| 32:18 . . . . . . . . . . . . . . . . . . . . . 105 | 44:21 . . . . . . . . . . . . . . . . . . . . . 340 |
| 33:13 . . . . . . . . . . . . . . . . . . . . . 176 | 44:24 . . . . . . . . . . . . . . . . . . . . . . 54 |
| 33:20 . . . . . . . . . . . . . . . . . . . . . 246 | 44:28 . . . . . . . . . . . . . . . . . . 37, 386 |
| 34:4 . . . . . . . . . . . . . . . . . . . . . . 408 | 44:28–45 . . . . . . . . . . . . . . . . . . . 192 |
| 35:8 . . . . . . . . . . . . . . . . . . . . . . 428 | 45:1 . . . . . . . . . . . . . . . . . . . . . . 347 |
| 35:8–10 . . . . . . . . . . . . . . . . . . . 404 | 45:5 . . . . . . . . . . . . . . . . . . . . . . 413 |
| 35:10 . . . . . . . . . . . . . . . . . 124, 300 | 45:8 . . . . . . . . . . . . . . . . . . . . . . 273 |
| 36:12 . . . . . . . . . . . . . . . . . . . . . 137 | 45:12 . . . . . . . . . . . . . . . . . . . . . . 54 |
| 36:17 . . . . . . . . . . . . . . . . . . . . . 284 | 45:14 . . . . . . . . . . . . . . . . . 247, 249 |

# SELECTED SCRIPTURE INDEX

| | |
|---|---|
| 45:22 . . . . . . . . . . . . . . . . . . 85, 366 | 56:6–7 . . . . . . . . . . . . . . . . 126, 205 |
| 46:3 . . . . . . . . . . . . . . . . . . . . . . . 237 | 57:13 . . . . . . . . . . . . . . . . . . . . . 289 |
| 46:13 . . . . . . . . . . . . . . . . . . . . . 273 | 58 . . . . . . . . . . . . . . . . . . . . . . . . 33 |
| 47:5–9 . . . . . . . . . . . . . . . . . . . . 105 | 58:1–7 . . . . . . . . . . . . . . . . . . . . 217 |
| 48:10 . . . . . . . . . . . . . . . . . . . . . 392 | 58:3–6 . . . . . . . . . . . . . . . . . . . . 218 |
| 48:18 . . . . . . . . . . . . . . . . . . . . . 271 | 59:4 . . . . . . . . . . . . . . . . . . . . . . 288 |
| 49 . . . . . . . . . . . . . . . . . . . . . . . 347 | 59:14 . . . . . . . . . . . . . . . . . . . . . 271 |
| 49:2 . . . . . . . . . . . . . . . . . . . . . . . 54 | 59:17 . . . . . . . . . . . . . . . . . 104, 233 |
| 49:2–3 . . . . . . . . . . . . . . . . . . . . 247 | 59:20–21 . . . . . . . . . . . . . . . . . . 363 |
| 49:6 . . . . . . . . . . . . . . . . . . . . . . 126 | 60:1,3 . . . . . . . . . . . . . . . . . . . . 410 |
| 49:8 . . . . . . . . . . . . . . . . . . . . . . . 54 | 60:1–3 . . . . . . . . . . . . . . . . . . . . 247 |
| 49:9 . . . . . . . . . . . . . . . . . . . . . . . 54 | 60:1–6 . . . . . . . . . . . . . . . . . . . . 128 |
| 49:18 . . . . . . . . . . . . . . . . . . . . . 249 | 60:1–7 . . . . . . . . . . . . . . . . . . . . 205 |
| 50 . . . . . . . . . . . . . . . . . . . . . . . 347 | 60:3 . . . . . . . . . . . . . . . . . . . . . . 128 |
| 50:2 . . . . . . . . . . . . . . . . . . . . . . 300 | 60:7 . . . . . . . . . . . . . . . . . . . . . . 359 |
| 51 . . . . . . . . . . . . . . . . . . . . . . . 352 | 60:19–20 . . . . . . . . . . . . . . . . . . 410 |
| 51:3 . . . . . . . . . . . . . . . . . . . . . . . 54 | 61:1 . . . . . . . . . . . . . . . . . . . . . . . 54 |
| 51:4–5 . . . . . . . . . . . . . . . . . . . . 273 | 61:6 . . . . . . . . . . . . . . . . . . . . . . 283 |
| 51:5 . . . . . . . . . . . . . . . . . . . . . . 271 | 61:7 . . . . . . . . . . . . . . . . . . . . . . . 54 |
| 51:9 . . . . . . . . . . . . . . . . . . . . . . 386 | 62:1–5 . . . . . . . . . . . . . . . . . . . . 128 |
| 51:11 . . . . . . . . . . . . . . . . . . . . . 300 | 62:2–3 . . . . . . . . . . . . . . . . . . . . . 54 |
| 51:13 . . . . . . . . . . . . . . . . . . . . . 351 | 62:2–4 . . . . . . . . . . . . . . . . . . . . 233 |
| 51:13,16 . . . . . . . . . . . . . . . . . . . 54 | 62:3 . . . . . . . . . . . . . . . . . . . . . . . 54 |
| 51:17 . . . . . . . . . . . . . . . . . . . . . 352 | 63:1–6 . . . . . . . . . . . . . . . . . . . . 296 |
| 51:17,22 . . . . . . . . . . . . . . . . . . . 54 | 65:4 . . . . . . . . . . . . . . . . . . . . . . 267 |
| 51:21 . . . . . . . . . . . . . . . . . . . . . 273 | 65:13–15 . . . . . . . . . . . . . . . . . . 316 |
| 52:13 . . . . . . . . . . . . . . . . . . . . . 145 | 65:20–25 . . . . . . . . . . . . . . . . . . 236 |
| 52:13–14 . . . . . . . . . . . . . . . . . . . 75 | 66:3,17 . . . . . . . . . . . . . . . . . . . 267 |
| 52:13–53:12 . . . . . . . . . . . . . . . 347 | 66:15–16 . . . . . . . . . . . . . . . . . . 184 |
| 53 . . . . . . . . . . . . . . . . . . 71, 368, 387 | 66:18 . . . . . . . . . . . . . . . . . . . . . 247 |
| 53:2 . . . . . . . . . . . . . . . . . . . . . . 203 | 66:18–24 . . . . . . . . . . . . . . . . . . 126 |
| 53:2–3 . . . . . . . . . . . . . . . . . . . . 273 | 66:19 . . . . . . . . . . . . . . . . . . . . . . 31 |
| 53:4–6 . . . . . . . . . . . . . . . . . . . . 368 | |
| 53:5 . . . . . . . . . . . . . . . . . . . 75, 366 | **Jeremiah** |
| 53:6 . . . . . . . . . . . . . . . . . . . . . . . 54 | |
| 53:10 . . . . . . . . . . . . . . . . . . 75, 389 | 1 . . . . . . . . . . . . . . . . . . . . . . . . . 84 |
| 53:11 . . . . . . . . . . . . . . . . . 145, 272 | 1:8 . . . . . . . . . . . . . . . . . . . . . . 296 |
| 53:12 . . . . . . . . . . . . . . . . . . . . . . 75 | 1:11–19 . . . . . . . . . . . . . . . . . . . . 92 |
| 54:1 . . . . . . . . . . . . . . . . . . . . . . 235 | 1:13–16 . . . . . . . . . . . . . . . . . . . 281 |
| 54:11 . . . . . . . . . . . . . . . . . . . . . 273 | 2:2–3 . . . . . . . . . . . . . . . . . . . . . 426 |
| 55:1 . . . . . . . . . . . . . . . . . . . . . . 118 | 2:13 . . . . . . . . . . . . . . . . . . . . . . 410 |
| 55:11 . . . . . . . . . . . . . . . . . . . 75, 85 | 2:15 . . . . . . . . . . . . . . . . . . . . . . 317 |
| 56:1–8 . . . . . . . . . . . . . . . . . . . . 126 | 2:30 . . . . . . . . . . . . . . . . . . . . . . 282 |

| Reference | Page(s) |
|---|---|
| 3:2 | 401 |
| 3:12 | 281 |
| 4:5–8 | 55 |
| 4:5–31 | 281 |
| 4:22 | 343 |
| 4:23 | 408 |
| 4:28 | 55, 243, 244 |
| 5:14 | 260 |
| 6:22 | 118 |
| 6:22–26 | 281 |
| 6:26 | 55 |
| 6:27–30 | 392 |
| 7:1–26 | 84 |
| 7:4 | 34 |
| 7:5–7 | 221 |
| 7:6 | 223 |
| 7:15 | 282 |
| 7:20 | 240 |
| 7:23 | 55, 393 |
| 8:13 | 55 |
| 8:19 | 289 |
| 9:6 | 392 |
| 10:12 | 55 |
| 10:14–15 | 289 |
| 10:21 | 289 |
| 10:22 | 118 |
| 11:4 | 137 |
| 11:22 | 291 |
| 12:1–16 | 321 |
| 12:7 | 267 |
| 13:14 | 326 |
| 14:14 | 55, 288 |
| 14:22 | 286 |
| 15:2 | 55 |
| 15:5 | 325 |
| 15:21 | 300 |
| 16:15 | 281 |
| 16:19 | 278 |
| 17:1 | 259 |
| 17:13 | 411 |
| 17:16 | 55 |
| 17:19 | 415 |
| 17:24–27 | 415 |
| 17:27 | 357 |
| 18:4 | 351 |
| 18:7–10 | 77 |
| 18:11 | 85 |
| 19 | 26, 339, 340 |
| 19:9 | 333 |
| 22:3 | 221 |
| 22:6 | 304, 313 |
| 22:20 | 315, 383 |
| 22:22 | 379 |
| 23:1 | 283 |
| 23:2 | 55 |
| 23:3 | 55 |
| 23:5 | 55, 70, 144, 145, 271 |
| 23:5–6 | 144, 202 |
| 23:6 | 417 |
| 23:13–14,30 | 375 |
| 23:14 | 375 |
| 23:18 | 142 |
| 23:32 | 288 |
| 23:33 | 260 |
| 24:8 | 424 |
| 24:9 | 243 |
| 25 | 317, 352 |
| 25:1–21 | 55 |
| 25:4–5 | 85 |
| 25:5 | 55 |
| 25:8–11 | 35 |
| 25:9 | 145 |
| 25:11 | 55, 102 |
| 25:11–12 | 102 |
| 25:12 | 102 |
| 25:15–31 | 55 |
| 25:17 | 352 |
| 25:18 | 243 |
| 25:20 | 55, 266 |
| 25:34 | 316 |
| 25:34–36 | 316 |
| 25:34–38 | 33 |
| 25:36 | 55 |
| 26:19 | 215 |
| 27:2–7,10–12 | 321 |
| 27:3 | 263 |

| | |
|---|---|
| 27:6 | 145 |
| 27:8–9 | 55 |
| 27:8–10 | 375 |
| 27:9–10 | 288 |
| 30 | 106 |
| 30:3 | 297 |
| 30:7–8 | 296 |
| 30:7–11 | 238 |
| 30:16 | 240 |
| 30:19–20 | 236 |
| 31 | 374, 422 |
| 31:8 | 238, 281 |
| 31:10 | 55 |
| 31:10–14 | 245 |
| 31:11 | 300 |
| 31:23 | 160 |
| 31:27 | 116, 301, 342 |
| 31:31 | 275 |
| 31:31,33 | 363 |
| 31:31–34 | 66, 421 |
| 31:33 | 55, 225, 298, 393 |
| 31:33,34 | 374 |
| 31:33–34 | 149, 206 |
| 31:34 | 374 |
| 31:35 | 409 |
| 31:38 | 415 |
| 31:39 | 107 |
| 31:40 | 416 |
| 32:19 | 355 |
| 32:37 | 417 |
| 32:37–42 | 393 |
| 32:40–41 | 243 |
| 33:2 | 55 |
| 33:3 | 55 |
| 33:7 | 297 |
| 33:15 | 70, 144 |
| 33:15–16 | 144 |
| 33:16 | 416, 417 |
| 34:9 | 250 |
| 34:26 | 284 |
| 35:4 | 352 |
| 35:15 | 85 |
| 36:37 | 283 |
| 37:12–13 | 415 |
| 37:13 | 235 |
| 37:15 | 372 |
| 37:15–23 | 321 |
| 38:4 | 372 |
| 38:6 | 278 |
| 38:7 | 214, 415 |
| 39:1 | 246 |
| 39:2 | 246 |
| 39:3 | 212 |
| 39:8 | 35 |
| 40:11 | 119 |
| 41:1–3 | 216, 246 |
| 43:1–13 | 424 |
| 43:4–7 | 119 |
| 46:7–8 | 424 |
| 46:20 | 402 |
| 46–51 | 256 |
| 47:2 | 316 |
| 47:6–7 | 101 |
| 49:12 | 55 |
| 49:20 | 186, 388 |
| 49:23 | 263 |
| 49:36 | 188 |
| 50:10 | 399 |
| 50:44 | 317 |
| 50–51 | 256 |
| 51:12 | 244 |
| 51:15 | 55 |
| 51:18 | 289 |
| 51:26 | 293 |
| 51:36 | 307 |
| 51:40 | 291 |
| 51:48 | 257 |
| 52:12–30 | 246 |
| 52:19 | 352 |
| 52:24 | 133 |
| 52:28,30 | 250 |
| 52:28–30 | 35 |

**Lamentations**

| | |
|---|---|
| 1:2 | 107 |

| | |
|---|---|
| 2:2,12,20–22 | 35 |
| 2:15 | 55 |
| 2:17 | 55 |
| 4:3 | 323 |
| 4:9–20 | 35 |
| 4:21 | 55 |
| 5:1–18 | 35 |

**Ezekiel**

| | |
|---|---|
| 1 | 84, 92 |
| 1:15–21 | 184 |
| 1:28 | 117, 122 |
| 2:2 | 189 |
| 3:8–9 | 225 |
| 3:9 | 225 |
| 5 | 391 |
| 5:2,12 | 391 |
| 5:10,12 | 56 |
| 5:12 | 56, 391 |
| 6:12 | 333 |
| 7:21 | 399 |
| 8 | 92 |
| 8:1 | 143 |
| 8:4 | 117 |
| 8:14–15 | 370 |
| 9:3 | 117 |
| 9:6 | 399 |
| 10:19 | 117 |
| 11:20 | 55 |
| 11:22 | 117 |
| 11:22–23 | 403 |
| 12:28 | 260 |
| 13 | 375 |
| 13:1–14:11 | 375 |
| 13:7 | 378 |
| 14:1 | 143 |
| 14:1–8 | 56 |
| 14:9–10 | 56 |
| 14:13 | 240 |
| 15:3 | 294 |
| 16 | 177 |
| 16:33 | 383 |
| 16:38,42 | 104 |
| 17:3–4,12–22 | 315 |
| 17:5–8 | 56, 411 |
| 17:8 | 313 |
| 17:22–24 | 70, 144 |
| 18:6 | 373 |
| 18:8 | 222 |
| 19:1–9 | 317 |
| 20:1 | 143 |
| 21:21 | 290 |
| 21:31 | 110 |
| 22:10 | 373 |
| 22:17–22 | 392 |
| 22:25 | 317 |
| 23:25 | 56 |
| 23:35 | 104 |
| 25–32 | 256 |
| 26–27 | 55 |
| 27:5–6 | 315 |
| 27:6 | 313, 315 |
| 27:8 | 263 |
| 27:13,19 | 31 |
| 28 | 265 |
| 28:11–19 | 270 |
| 28:14 | 100 |
| 28:26 | 417 |
| 29:19 | 399 |
| 31 | 314, 316 |
| 31:3–18 | 314 |
| 31:5,7 | 56 |
| 31:5–7 | 411 |
| 31:16 | 304 |
| 32:8 | 409 |
| 32:16 | 371 |
| 33:11 | 77 |
| 33:31 | 143 |
| 34 | 346, 388 |
| 34:3–4 | 343 |
| 34:6–8,10 | 289 |
| 34:8–9,23 | 56 |
| 34:23–24 | 289 |
| 34:25 | 334 |
| 34:25–28 | 417 |

SELECTED SCRIPTURE INDEX   **468**

34:27 . . . . . . . . . . . . . . . . . . . . . . . 55
34:27–31 . . . . . . . . . . . . . . . . . . . 416
34:30–31 . . . . . . . . . . . . . . . . . . . 324
36 . . . . . . . . . . . . . . . . . . . . . 364, 422
36:3–7 . . . . . . . . . . . . . . . . . 104, 232
36:9–10 . . . . . . . . . . . . . . . . . . . . 301
36:11 . . . . . . . . . . . . . . . . . . 116, 243
36:17 . . . . . . . . . . . . . . . . . . 177, 373
36:22–32 . . . . . . . . . . . . . . . . . . . 422
36:25 . . . . . . . . . . . . . . . . . . 372, 374
36:26 . . . . . . . . . . . . . . 225, 364, 374
36:26–27 . . . . . . . . . . . . . . . . . . . 363
36:28 . . . . . . . . . . . . . . . . . . . 55, 393
37 . . . . . . . . . . . . . 239, 302, 342, 365
37:1 . . . . . . . . . . . . . . . . . . . . . . . 160
37:1–14 . . . . . . . . . . . . . . . . . . . . 365
37:15–18 . . . . . . . . . . . . . . . . . . . 328
37:15–23 . . . . . . . . . . . . . . . . . . . . 56
37:15–28 . . . . . . . . . . . . . . . . . . . 365
37:16 . . . . . . . . . . . . . . . . . . . . . . 342
37:16–20 . . . . . . . . . . . . . . . . . . . 275
37:21–22 . . . . . . . . . . . . . . . . . . . 342
37:23 . . . . . . . . . . . . . . . . . . . . 55, 56
37:23–28 . . . . . . . . . . . . . . . . . . . 393
37:24 . . . . . . . . . . . . . . . . . . . . . . . 56
37:26 . . . . . . . . . . . . . . . . . . . . . . . 68
37:28 . . . . . . . . . . . . . . . . . . . . . . 365
38 . . . . . . . . . . . . . . . . . . . . . . . . 400
38:4 . . . . . . . . . . . . . . . . . . . . . . . 426
38:12 . . . . . . . . . . . . . . . . . . . . . . 388
38:12–13 . . . . . . . . . . . . . . . . . . . . 56
38:19–23 . . . . . . . . . . . 56, 104, 404
38:20 . . . . . . . . . . . . . . . . . . . . . . 420
38:21 . . . . . . . . . . . . . . . . . . . . . . . 56
38–39 . . . . . . . . . . . . . . . . . . . . . . . 44
39:10 . . . . . . . . . . . . . . . . . . . . . . 124
39:18 . . . . . . . . . . . . . . . . . . . . . . 315
39:21–29 . . . . . . . . . . . . . . . . . . . 121
39:27–29 . . . . . . . . . . . . . . . . . . . 303
39:29 . . . . . . . . . . . . . . . . . . . . . . 363
40:3 . . . . . . . . . . . . . . . . . . . . . . . 113
40–47 . . . . . . . . . . . . . . . . . . . . . . 167
40–48 . . . . . . . . . . . . . . 112, 132, 421

43 . . . . . . . . . . . . . . . . . . . . . . . . 128
43:1–5 . . . . . . . . . . . . . . . . . 106, 233
43:1–9 . . . . . . . . . . . . . . . . . . . . . 125
43:2,4,5 . . . . . . . . . . . . . . . . . . . . 117
44:4 . . . . . . . . . . . . . . . . . . . . . . . 117
44:9 . . . . . . . . . . . . . . . . . . . . . . . 428
47 . . . . . . . . . . . . . . . . . . . . . . . . 150
47:1–10 . . . . . . . . . . . . . . . . . . . . . 33
47:1–12 . . . . . . . . . . . . . 56, 373, 411
47:12 . . . . . . . . . . . . . . . . . . . . . . 373
47:13,21–22 . . . . . . . . . . . . . . . . 263
47:15–20 . . . . . . . . . . . . . . . . . . . 304
48:19,29,31 . . . . . . . . . . . . . . . . 263
48:35 . . . . . . . . . . . . . . . . . . . . . . 106

**Daniel**

2:5 . . . . . . . . . . . . . . . . . . . . . . . 173
2:31–45 . . . . . . . . . . . . . . . . . . . . 110
2:32 . . . . . . . . . . . . . . . . . . . . . . 186
2:35 . . . . . . . . . . . . . . . . . . . . . . 185
3:29 . . . . . . . . . . . . . . . . . . . . . . 173
4:20–23 . . . . . . . . . . . . . . . . . . . 314
4:22 . . . . . . . . . . . . . . . . . . . . . . 314
7 . . . . . . . . . . . . . . . . . . . . . . . . . 187
7:2–13 . . . . . . . . . . . . . . . . . . . . 110
7:13 . . . . . . . . . . . . . . . . . . . . . . . 63
7:24–26 . . . . . . . . . . . . . . . . . . . 345
8:13 . . . . . . . . . . . . . . . . . . . . . . 407
9:1–19 . . . . . . . . . . . . . . . . . . . . . 86
9:13 . . . . . . . . . . . . . . . . . . . . . . 215
9:18 . . . . . . . . . . . . . . . . . . . . . . 355
9:24 . . . . . . . . . . . . . . . . . . 149, 271
9:24–27 . . . . . . . . . . . . . . . . . . . 399
9:27 . . . . . . . . . . . . . . . . . . . . . . 345
10:6 . . . . . . . . . . . . . . . . . . . . . . 186
11:4 . . . . . . . . . . . . . . . . . . . . . . 188
11:20 . . . . . . . . . . . . . . . . . . . . . 268
11:21 . . . . . . . . . . . . . . . . . . . . . 204

## Hosea

1:1 . . . . . . . . . . . . . . . . . . . . . . . 342
1:2–3 . . . . . . . . . . . . . . . . . . . . . 321
1:6 . . . . . . . . . . . . . . . . . . . . . . . 336
1:7 . . . . . . . . . . . . . . . . . . . . . . . . 56
1:8 . . . . . . . . . . . . . . . . . . . . . . . 336
1:8–11 . . . . . . . . . . . . . . . . . . . . 239
1:9 . . . . . . . . . . . . . . . . . . . . . . . . 57
1:11 . . . . . . . . . . . . . . . . . . . . 56, 61
2:2 . . . . . . . . . . . . . . . . . . . . . . . 177
2:7 . . . . . . . . . . . . . . . . . . . 56, 383
2:8 . . . . . . . . . . . . . . . . . . . . . . . 164
2:14 . . . . . . . . . . . . . . . . . . . 56, 61
2:15 . . . . . . . . . . . . . . . . . . . . . . . 57
2:17 . . . . . . . . . . . . . . . . . . . 56, 61
2:18 . . . . . . . . . . . . . . . . . . 56, 334
2:19–20 . . . . . . . . . . . . . . . . . . 104
2:20 . . . . . . . . . . . . . . . . . . . 56, 61
2:20–23 . . . . . . . . . . . . . . . . . . . 57
2:21 . . . . . . . . . . . . . . . . . . . . . . . 56
2:21–23 . . . . . . . . . . . . . . . . 56, 61
2:22 . . . . . . . . . . . . . . . . . . . 56, 61
2:23 . . . . . . . . . 56, 57, 239, 301, 393
3:4–5 . . . . . . . . . . . . . . . . . . . . 271
4:1 . . . . . . . . . . . . . . . . . . . . . . 222
4:16 . . . . . . . . . . . . . . . . . . 283, 323
4:19 . . . . . . . . . . . . . . . . . . . . . . 226
5:3 . . . . . . . . . . . . . . . . . . . . . . . 297
5:10 . . . . . . . . . . . . . . . . . . . . . . 362
6:6 . . . . . . . . . . . . . . . . . . . . . . . 217
7:11 . . . . . . . . . . . . . . . . . . . . . . 304
7:13 . . . . . . . . . . . . . . . . . . . . . . 300
7:13–15 . . . . . . . . . . . . . . . . . . 316
8:1 . . . . . . . . . . . . . . . . . . . . . . . 267
9:6 . . . . . . . . . . . . . . . . . . . . . . . . 56
9:7 . . . . . . . . . . . . . . . . . . . . . . . 343
9:10 . . . . . . . . . . . . . . . . . . . . . . 267
9:13–15 . . . . . . . . . . . . . . . . . . 323
9:15 . . . . . . . . . . . . . . . . . . . . . . 267
11:5 . . . . . . . . . . . . . . . . . . . . . . 304
11:9 . . . . . . . . . . . . . . . . . . . . . . 139
12:6–7 . . . . . . . . . . . . . . . . . . . 223
13:14 . . . . . . . . . . . . . . . . . . . . 300
13:15 . . . . . . . . . . . . . . . . . . . . 372
14:5–8 . . . . . . . . . . . . . . . . . . . 107
14:8 . . . . . . . . . . . . . . . . . . . . . . 56

## Joel

1:15 . . . . . . . . . . . . . . . . . . . 57, 399
2:1 . . . . . . . . . . . . . . . . . . . . . . . . 57
2:1–2 . . . . . . . . . . . . . . . . . . . . 400
2:2 . . . . . . . . . . . . . . . . . . . . . . . 409
2:10 . . . . . . . . . . . . . . . . . . . . . . . 57
2:20 . . . . . . . . . . . . . . . . . . . . . . . 57
2:23 . . . . . . . . . . . . . . . . . . 285, 393
2:28 . . . . . . . . . . . . . . . . . . . . . . 285
2:28–29 . . . . . . . . . . . . . . . . . . 363
2:31 . . . . . . . . . . . . . . . . . . . . . . 408
3:1–3 . . . . . . . . . . . . . . . . . . . . 400
3:3–4 . . . . . . . . . . . . . . . . . . . . . 57
3:4 . . . . . . . . . . . . . . . . . . . . . . . 263
3:9–16 . . . . . . . . . . . . . . . . . . . 354
3:11–12 . . . . . . . . . . . . . . . . . . . 57
3:15 . . . . . . . . . . . . . . . . . . . . . . 408
3:16 . . . . . . . . . . . . . . . . . . 405, 420
3:17 . . . . . . . . . . . . . . . . . . . . . . 235
3:17,20–21 . . . . . . . . . . . . . . . . . 57
3:18 . . . . . . . . . . . . . . . . . . . 57, 411
3:18–21 . . . . . . . . . . . . . . . . . . 107
3:19 . . . . . . . . . . . . . . . . . . . . . . . 57
4:11–16 . . . . . . . . . . . . . . . . . . . 57
4:15–16 . . . . . . . . . . . . . . . . . . . 57

## Amos

1 . . . . . . . . . . . . . . . . . . . . . . . . 220
1:1 . . . . . . . . . . . . . . . . . . . . . . . . 57
1:3 . . . . . . . . . . . . . . . . . . . . . . . 261
1:3–2:3 . . . . . . . . . . . . . . . . . . . 256
1:4,7,10 . . . . . . . . . . . . . . . . . . . 57
1:6–8 . . . . . . . . . . . . . . . . . . . . 266
1:7–8 . . . . . . . . . . . . . . . . . . 57, 266
1:9–10 . . . . . . . . . . . . . . . . . . . . 33

1:10 . . . . . . . . . . . . . . . . . . . . . . . 316
1:12 . . . . . . . . . . . . . . . . . . . . . . . 186
1–2. . . . . . . . . . . . . . . . . . . . . . . . 257
2:2 . . . . . . . . . . . . . . . . . . . . . . . . 357
2:6–7 . . . . . . . . . . . . . . . . . . . . . . 223
4:1 . . . . . . . . . . . . . . . . . . . 223, 315
4:6–11 . . . . . . . . . . . . . . . . . . . . . 419
4:7–8 . . . . . . . . . . . . . . . . . . . . . . 424
4:11 . . . . . . . . . . . . . . . . . . . . 57, 137
5:8 . . . . . . . . . . . . . . . . . . . . . . . . . 57
5:11–12 . . . . . . . . . . . . . . . . . . . . 223
5:156 . . . . . . . . . . . . . . . . . . . . . . 247
5:18 . . . . . . . . . . . . . . . 407, 408, 409
5:24 . . . . . . . . . . . . . . . . . . . . . . . 221
5:27–62 . . . . . . . . . . . . . . . . . . . . . 33
6:1 . . . . . . . . . . . . . . . 105, 263, 346
7. . . . . . . . . . . . . . . . . . . . . . . . . 112
7:1–9 . . . . . . . . . . . . . . . . . . . . . . . 92
7:7–9 . . . . . . . . . . . . . . . . . . . . . . 112
7:7–9,17 . . . . . . . . . . . . . . . . . . . 112
7:14 . . . . . . . . . . . . . . . . . . . . 57, 381
7:17 . . . . . . . . . . . . . . . . . . . 112, 401
8:3 . . . . . . . . . . . . . . . . . . . . . . . . 316
8:4 . . . . . . . . . . . . . . . . . . . . . . . . 223
8:9 . . . . . . . . . . . . . . . . . . . . . . . . 265
8:10 . . . . . . . . . . . . . . . . . . . . . . . . 57
9:1 . . . . . . . . . . . . . . . . . . . . . . . . 352
9:6 . . . . . . . . . . . . . . . . . . . . . . . . . 57
9:11–12 . . . . . . . . . . . . . . . . . . . . 271
9:11–15 . . . . . . . . . . . . . . . . . . . . 107
9:13 . . . . . . . . . . . . . . . . . . . . . . . 284

**Jonah**

2:8 . . . . . . . . . . . . . . . . . . . . . . . . 289

**Micah**

1:3 . . . . . . . . . . . . . . . . . . . . . . . . 402
1:3–4 . . . . . . . . . . . . . . . . . . . . . . 405
1:11 . . . . . . . . . . . . . . . . . . . . . . . 406
2:7 . . . . . . . . . . . . . . . . . . . . . . . . 260

2:11 . . . . . . . . . . . . . . . . . . . . . . . 288
2:12 . . . . . . . . . . . . . . . . . . . . . . . 278
3:4 . . . . . . . . . . . . . . . . . . . . . . . . . 57
3:5–8 . . . . . . . . . . . . . . . . . . . . . . . 57
3:7 . . . . . . . . . . . . . . . . . . . . . . . . 379
3:9 . . . . . . . . . . . . . . . . . . . . . . . . 342
4. . . . . . . . . . . . . . . . . . . . . . . . . 335
4:1–2 . . . . . . . . . . . . . . . . . . . . . . 206
4:1–3 . . . . . . . . . . . . . . . . . . . . . . . 66
4:1–5 . . . . . . . . . . . . . . . . . . . . . . 414
4:1–8 . . . . . . . . . . . . . . . . . . . . . . 365
4:1–13 . . . . . . . . . . . . . . . . . . . . . 166
4:2 . . . . . . . . . . . . . . . . . . . 126, 422
4:2–3 . . . . . . . . . . . . . . . . . . . . 54, 57
4:2–5 . . . . . . . . . . . . . . . . . . . . . . 247
4:4 . . . . . . . . . . . . . . . . . . . . . . . . . 57
4:5 . . . . . . . . . . . . . . . . . . . . . . . . 365
4:8 . . . . . . . . . . . . . . . . . . . . . . . . . 57
4:11–13 . . . . . . . . . . . . . . . . . . . . 400
4:13 . . . . . . . . . . . . . . . . . . . . . . . 296
5:2–4 . . . . . . . . . . . . . . . . . . . . . . 272
5:4 . . . . . . . . . . . . . . . . . . . . . . . . . 57
5:10 . . . . . . . . . . . . . . . 274, 275, 427
6:6 . . . . . . . . . . . . . . . . . . . . . . . . 223
6:6–8 . . . . . . . . . . . . . . . . 76, 217, 223
6:8 . . . . . . . . . . . . . . . . . . . . 244, 247
7:10 . . . . . . . . . . . . . . . . . . . . . . . 296
7:12 . . . . . . . . . . . . . . . . . . . . . . . 424
7:14 . . . . . . . . . . . . . . . 283, 304, 323
7:19 . . . . . . . . . . . . . . . . . . . . . . . 181

**Nahum**

1:3 . . . . . . . . . . . . . . . . . . . . . . . . 281
1:5 . . . . . . . . . . . . . . . . . . . . . . . . 405
1:7 . . . . . . . . . . . . . . . . . . . . . . . . 278

**Habakkuk**

2:20 . . . . . . . . . . . . . . . . . . . . . . . 128
3. . . . . . . . . . . . . . . . . . . . . . . . . 269
3:3 . . . . . . . . . . . . . . . . . . . . . . . . 281

| | |
|---|---|
| 3:3–15 | 280 |
| 3:4 | 280 |
| 3:18 | 299 |

## Zephaniah

| | |
|---|---|
| 1:2–6,13 | 58 |
| 1:7 | 128 |
| 1:11 | 58 |
| 1:13 | 401 |
| 1:15 | 409 |
| 1:18 | 57 |
| 2:4 | 58 |
| 2:4–6 | 266 |
| 2:4–15 | 256 |
| 3:8 | 57 |
| 3:9 | 413 |
| 3:14 | 57, 58 |
| 3:14–15 | 124, 270 |

## Haggai

| | |
|---|---|
| 1:1 | 39, 47, 133 |
| 1:1,12,14 | 133 |
| 1:1–2 | 38 |
| 1:2 | 113 |
| 1:2–6,9 | 37 |
| 1:4 | 59, 210 |
| 1:6–11 | 240 |
| 1:7–11 | 240 |
| 1:8 | 233 |
| 1:10–11 | 241 |
| 1:11 | 165 |
| 1:12,14 | 237 |
| 1:13 | 96, 361 |
| 1:14 | 160 |
| 2 | 138 |
| 2:1–9 | 160 |
| 2:2 | 237 |
| 2:2,4 | 133 |
| 2:3,7,9 | 117 |
| 2:3–4 | 162 |

| | |
|---|---|
| 2:4 | 59 |
| 2:5 | 159 |
| 2:6–7 | 102 |
| 2:6–9 | 124, 257 |
| 2:8 | 198 |
| 2:7 | 126, 206, 419, 420 |
| 2:7–8 | 419 |
| 2:9 | 39 |
| 2:10–14 | 138 |
| 2:11–14 | 59 |
| 2:14 | 138 |
| 2:15–19 | 240 |
| 2:18–19 | 241 |
| 2:19 | 241 |
| 2:21–23 | 39 |
| 2:22 | 274, 296, 418 |

## Malachi

| | |
|---|---|
| 1:1 | 59, 259, 260 |
| 1:9 | 215 |
| 1:11 | 413 |
| 2:1–3 | 132 |
| 2:3 | 132 |
| 2:7 | 361 |
| 2:11 | 178 |
| 2:16 | 245 |
| 3:1 | 192, 361 |
| 3:2–3 | 392 |
| 3:5 | 288 |
| 4:1–5 | 400 |
| 4:6 | 416 |

## Matthew

| | |
|---|---|
| 1:1 | 71 |
| 1:20 | 100 |
| 2:6 | 289 |
| 2:15 | 303 |
| 3:4 | 380 |
| 3:17 | 71 |
| 5:14–15 | 166 |

# SELECTED SCRIPTURE INDEX

6:7–10 . . . . . . . . . . . . . . . . . . . . 413
9:36 . . . . . . . . . . . . . . . . . . . . . . 290
11:28–30 . . . . . . . . . . . . . . . . . . 273
12:18 . . . . . . . . . . . . . . . . . . . . . 145
17:20 . . . . . . . . . . . . . . . . . . . . . 161
18:12 . . . . . . . . . . . . . . . . . . . . . 347
18:12–14 . . . . . . . . . . . . . . . . . . 344
21:1 . . . . . . . . . . . . . . . . . . . . . . 403
21:1–11 . . . . . . . . . . . . . . . . . . . 274
21:5 . . . . . . . . . . . . . . . . . . . . . . . 62
21:5–7 . . . . . . . . . . . . . . . . . . . . 274
21:12–13 . . . . . . . . . . . . . . . . . . 429
21:21 . . . . . . . . . . . . . . . . . . . . . 161
21:42 . . . . . . . . . . . . . . . . 147, 294
22:11–13 . . . . . . . . . . . . . . . . . . 141
22:36–39 . . . . . . . . . . . . . . . . . . 224
22:39 . . . . . . . . . . . . . . . . . . . . . 246
23:33–39 . . . . . . . . . . . . . . . . . . 337
23:35 . . . . . . . . . . . . . . . . . . 22, 83
24:3 . . . . . . . . . . . . . . . . . . . . . . 403
24:4–5,11,23–24 . . . . . . . . . . . . 375
24:15 . . . . . . . . . . . . . . . . . . . . . 345
24:30 . . . . . . . . . . . . . . . . . . . . . 408
25:31 . . . . . . . . . . . . . . . . . . . . . 407
26:15 . . . . . . . . . . . . . . . . . . . . . 341
26:30 . . . . . . . . . . . . . . . . . . . . . 403
26:31 . . . . . . . . . . . . . . . 62, 387, 390
26:56 . . . . . . . . . . . . . . . . . . . . . 390
27:3,9 . . . . . . . . . . . . . . . . . . . . 341
27:3–10 . . . . . . . . . . . . . . . . . . . 338
27:6–7 . . . . . . . . . . . . . . . . . . . . 341
27:6–8 . . . . . . . . . . . . . . . . . . . . 339
27:6–9 . . . . . . . . . . . . . . . . . . . . 339
27:9 . . . . . . . . . . . . . . . . 26, 62, 339
27:9–10 . . . . . . . . . . 23, 24, 25, 62

## Mark

1:15 . . . . . . . . . . . . . . . . . . . . . . 413
1:23 . . . . . . . . . . . . . . . . . . . . . . 377
3:11 . . . . . . . . . . . . . . . . . . . . . . 377
4:35–39 . . . . . . . . . . . . . . . . . . . 306
5:2 . . . . . . . . . . . . . . . . . . . . . . . 377
6:34 . . . . . . . . . . . . . . . . . . . . . . 390
10:23 . . . . . . . . . . . . . . . . . . . . . 325
11:1–11 . . . . . . . . . . . . . . . . . . . 274
11:15–18 . . . . . . . . . . . . . . . . . . 429
12. . . . . . . . . . . . . . . . . . . . . . . 147
12:10–11 . . . . . . . . . . . . . . . . . . 294
12:31 . . . . . . . . . . . . . . . . . . . . . 246
13:19,24 . . . . . . . . . . . . . . . . . . 390
14:24 . . . . . . . . . . . . . . . . . . . . . 277
14:27 . . . . . . . . . . . . . . . 62, 387, 390
14:58 . . . . . . . . . . . . . . . . . . . . . . 69

## Luke

1:5 . . . . . . . . . . . . . . . . . . . . . . . . 20
2:35 . . . . . . . . . . . . . . . . . . . . . . 390
3:2 . . . . . . . . . . . . . . . . . . . . . . . . 20
3:31 . . . . . . . . . . . . . . . . . . . . . . 372
10:27 . . . . . . . . . . . . . . . . . . . . . 246
11:51 . . . . . . . . . . . . . . . . . . . . . . 83
15:5 . . . . . . . . . . . . . . . . . . . . . . 347
18:27 . . . . . . . . . . . . . . . . . . . . . 237
19:28–40 . . . . . . . . . . . . . . . . . . 274
19:37 . . . . . . . . . . . . . . . . . . . . . 403
19:39–44 . . . . . . . . . . . . . . . . . . 275
19:45–48 . . . . . . . . . . . . . . . . . . 429
20:17 . . . . . . . . . . . . . . . . . . . . . 294
21:24 . . . . . . . . . . . . . . . . . . . . . . 62
21:37 . . . . . . . . . . . . . . . . . . . . . 403
22:31 . . . . . . . . . . . . . . . . . . . . . 134

## John

1:14 . . . . . . . . . . . . . . . . . . . . . . 125
1:29 . . . . . . . . . . . . . . . . . . . . . . 139
1:34 . . . . . . . . . . . . . . . . . . . . . . . 71
1:48 . . . . . . . . . . . . . . . . . . . . . . 152
2:12–16 . . . . . . . . . . . . . . . . . . . 429
2:16 . . . . . . . . . . . . . . . . . . . . . . . 62
2:19 . . . . . . . . . . . . . . . . . . . . . . . 69
7:38 . . . . . . . . . . . . . . . . . . . 62, 412
8:12 . . . . . . . . . . . . . . . . . . . . . . 166

# 473 SELECTED SCRIPTURE INDEX

9:4 . . . . . . . . . . . . . . . . . . . . . . . 343
10:1–16 . . . . . . . . . . . . . . . . . . . 390
10:10,14 . . . . . . . . . . . . . . . . . . 390
10:11 . . . . . . . . . . . . . . . . . 340, 347
10:14 . . . . . . . . . . . . . . . . . . . . . 290
10:14–15 . . . . . . . . . . . . . . . . . . 347
10:15 . . . . . . . . . . . . . . . . . . . . . 390
10:27 . . . . . . . . . . . . . . . . . . . . . 299
10:30 . . . . . . . . . . . . . . . . . . . . . 387
12:12–15 . . . . . . . . . . . . . . . . . . 274
12:15 . . . . . . . . . . . . . . . . . . . . . . 62
14:9 . . . . . . . . . . . . . . . . . . . . . . 387
17:23 . . . . . . . . . . . . . . . . . . . . . 358
19:5 . . . . . . . . . . . . . . . . . . . . . . 201
19:37 . . . . . . . . . . . . . . 62, 365, 369
20:25,27–28 . . . . . . . . . . . . . . . 384

## Acts

1 . . . . . . . . . . . . . . . . . . . . . . . . 404
1:6 . . . . . . . . . . . . . . . . . . . . . . . . 89
1:11 . . . . . . . . . . . . . . . . . . . . . . 402
1:11–12 . . . . . . . . . . . . . . . . . . . 404
1:16–19 . . . . . . . . . . . . . . . . . . . 338
2:13,26 . . . . . . . . . . . . . . . . . . . 145
2:16–21 . . . . . . . . . . . . . . . . . . . 363
4:11 . . . . . . . . . . . . . . . . . . . . . . 294
4:27,30 . . . . . . . . . . . . . . . . . . . 145
8:40 . . . . . . . . . . . . . . . . . . . . . . 267

## Romans

1:18 . . . . . . . . . . . . . . . . . . . . . . . 74
2:4 . . . . . . . . . . . . . . . . . . . . . . . 364
8:21–22 . . . . . . . . . . . . . . . . . . . 410
8:22 . . . . . . . . . . . . . . . . . . . . . . 320
8:29 . . . . . . . . . . . . . . . . . . . . . . . 71
9:24 . . . . . . . . . . . . . . . . . . . . . . 239
9:24–26 . . . . . . . . . . . . . . . . . . . 239
9–11 . . . . . . . . . . . . . . . . . . . . . 341
10:1 . . . . . . . . . . . . . . . . . . . . . . 239
10:11–13 . . . . . . . . . . . . . . . . . . 302

11:26 . . . . . . . . . . . . . . . . 71, 239, 341
11:26–27 . . . . . . . . . . . . . . . 152, 393
11:29 . . . . . . . . . . . . . . . . . . . . . . 98
13:9 . . . . . . . . . . . . . . . . . . . . . . 246
14:12 . . . . . . . . . . . . . . . . . . . . . 250
15:5 . . . . . . . . . . . . . . . . . . . . . . 358
15:8 . . . . . . . . . . . . . . . . . . . . . . 145

## 1 Corinthians

3:15 . . . . . . . . . . . . . . . . . . . . . . 137
6:19 . . . . . . . . . . . . . . . . . . . . . . 125
13:2 . . . . . . . . . . . . . . . . . . . . . . 161

## 2 Corinthians

6:16 . . . . . . . . . . . . . . . . . . . . . . 125

## Galatians

2:19–22 . . . . . . . . . . . . . . . . . . . 147
3:8 . . . . . . . . . . . . . . . . . . . . . . . 248
3:26–29 . . . . . . . . . . . . . . . . . . . 359
4 . . . . . . . . . . . . . . . . . . . . . . . . 320
4:30 . . . . . . . . . . . . . . . . . . . . . . 320
5:14 . . . . . . . . . . . . . . . . . . . . . . 246
6:1 . . . . . . . . . . . . . . . . . . . . . . . 290

## Ephesians

2:20 . . . . . . . . . . . . . . . . . . . . . . 294
2:21 . . . . . . . . . . . . . . . . . . . . . . . 69
4:3,13 . . . . . . . . . . . . . . . . . . . . 358
5:8–9 . . . . . . . . . . . . . . . . . . . . . 166

## Philippians

2:5–8 . . . . . . . . . . . . . . . . . . . . . 145
2:11 . . . . . . . . . . . . . . . . . . . . . . 250
2:12–13 . . . . . . . . . . . . . . . . . . . 243
2:15 . . . . . . . . . . . . . . . . . . . . . . 166
4:6 . . . . . . . . . . . . . . . . . . . . . . . 243

## Colossians

1:15 . . . . . . . . . . . . . . . . . . . . . . . 71
3:13 . . . . . . . . . . . . . . . . . . . . . . 221
3:14 . . . . . . . . . . . . . . . . . . . . . . 358

## Titus

1 . . . . . . . . . . . . . . . . . . . . . . . . . . 78

## Hebrews

1:5 . . . . . . . . . . . . . . . . . . . . . . . . 71
1:6 . . . . . . . . . . . . . . . . . . . . . . . . 71
3:6 . . . . . . . . . . . . . . . . . . . . . . . 268
3–4 . . . . . . . . . . . . . . . . . . . . . . . 302
4:12 . . . . . . . . . . . . . . . . . . . . . . 261
4:13 . . . . . . . . . . . . . . . . . . . . . . 361
4:14–16 . . . . . . . . . . . . . . . . . . . 143
5:6 . . . . . . . . . . . . . . . . . . . . . . . 151
7 . . . . . . . . . . . . . . . . . . . . . . . . . 70
7:1–17 . . . . . . . . . . . . . . . . . . . . 151
11:6 . . . . . . . . . . . . . . . . . . . . . . 237
11:29 . . . . . . . . . . . . . . . . . . . . . 357
12:29 . . . . . . . . . . . . . . . . . . . . . 117
13:20 . . . . . . . . . . . . . . . . . . . . . 290

## James

1:22 . . . . . . . . . . . . . . . . . . . . . . 244
2:8 . . . . . . . . . . . . . . . . . . . . . . . 246
2:10 . . . . . . . . . . . . . . . . . . . . . . 172

## 2 Peter

1:21 . . . . . . . . . . . . . . . . . . . . . . 226

## Revelation

1:7 . . . . . . . . . . . . . . . . . . 62, 63, 365
1:13 . . . . . . . . . . . . . . . . . . . . . . 369
1:20 . . . . . . . . . . . . . . . . . . . . . . 166
2:10 . . . . . . . . . . . . . . . . . . . . . . . 63
3:4–5 . . . . . . . . . . . . . . . . . . . . . . 63
3:11 . . . . . . . . . . . . . . . . . . . . . . . 63
4:4 . . . . . . . . . . . . . . . . . . . . . . . . 63
6 . . . . . . . . . . . . . . . . . . . . . . 63, 187
6:1–8 . . . . . . . . . . . . . . . . . . . . . . 63
6:2 . . . . . . . . . . . . . . . . . 63, 187, 295
6:4 . . . . . . . . . . . . . . . . . . . . . . . 187
6:5–6 . . . . . . . . . . . . . . . . . . . . . 187
6:8 . . . . . . . . . . . . . . . . . . . . . . . 187
6:11 . . . . . . . . . . . . . . . . . . . . . . . 63
6:12–14 . . . . . . . . . . . . . . . . . . . 408
6:17 . . . . . . . . . . . . . . . . . . . . . . . 73
7:1–8 . . . . . . . . . . . . . . . . . . . . . 392
7:3–8:1 . . . . . . . . . . . . . . . . . . . . 63
7:9 . . . . . . . . . . . . . . . . . . . . . . . 239
7:9,13–14 . . . . . . . . . . . . . . . . . . 63
7:17 . . . . . . . . . . . . . . . . . . . . . . 290
9:1–18 . . . . . . . . . . . . . . . . . . . . 408
11 . . . . . . . . . . . . . . 63, 113, 156, 167
11:1 . . . . . . . . . . . . . . . . . . . 113, 167
11:1–2 . . . . . . . . . . . . . . . . . 63, 167
11:1–13 . . . . . . . . . . . . . . . . . . . 167
11:3–4 . . . . . . . . . . . . . . . . . . . . . 63
11:3–10 . . . . . . . . . . . . . . . . 390, 399
11:4 . . . . . . . . . . . . . . . . . . . . . . 167
11:13,15 . . . . . . . . . . . . . . . . . . . 63
11–18 . . . . . . . . . . . . . . . . . . . . 392
13:1–10 . . . . . . . . . . . . . . . . . . . 346
13:4–15 . . . . . . . . . . . . . . . . . . . 375
14:1–5 . . . . . . . . . . . . . . . . . . . . 392
14:8 . . . . . . . . . . . . . . . . . . . . . . 181
14:14 . . . . . . . . . . . . . . . . . . . . . . 63
14:14–20 . . . . . . . . . . . . . . . . . . 408
16:4–9 . . . . . . . . . . . . . . . . . . . . 408
16:14 . . . . . . . . . . . . . . . . . . . . . . 73
16:15 . . . . . . . . . . . . . . . . . . . . . . 63
16:16 . . . . . . . . . . . . . . . . . . . . . 371
16:16–21 . . . . . . . . . . . . . . . 354, 400
16:18–19 . . . . . . . . . . . . . . . . . . 405
16:19 . . . . . . . . . . . . . . . . . . . . . . 63
17:3–5 . . . . . . . . . . . . . . . . . . . . 177

| | |
|---|---|
| 18:10 . . . . . . . . . . . . . . . . . . . . . . 182 | 19:15–16 . . . . . . . . . . . . . . . . . . . 166 |
| 19. . . . . . . . . . . . . . . . . . . . . . . 63, 75 | 21:23–22:5 . . . . . . . . . . . . . . . . . . 63 |
| 19:11 . . . . . . . . . . . . . . . . . . . . . . . 98 | 21:25 . . . . . . . . . . . . . . . . . . . . . 410 |
| 19:11,14 . . . . . . . . . . . . . . . . . . . 187 | 22:3 . . . . . . . . . . . . . . . . . . . . . . 416 |
| 19:12 . . . . . . . . . . . . . . . . . . . . . . . 63 | 22:5 . . . . . . . . . . . . . . . . . . . . . . 410 |
| 19:13–15 . . . . . . . . . . . . . . . . . . . . 63 | 22:14 . . . . . . . . . . . . . . . . . . . . . . 63 |